T0233879

# Lecture Notes of the Institute for Computer Sciences, Social Informatics and Telecommunications Engineering 295

More information about this series at http://www.springer.com/series/8197

Houbing Song · Dingde Jiang (Eds.)

# Simulation Tools and Techniques

11th International Conference, SIMUtools 2019
Chengdu, China, July 8–10, 2019
Proceedings

 Springer

*Editors*
Houbing Song
Department of Electrical, Computer,
Software, and Systems Engineering
Embry-Riddle Aeronautical University
Daytona Beach, FL, USA

Dingde Jiang
School of Astronautics Aeronautics
UESTC
Chengdu, China

ISSN 1867-8211        ISSN 1867-822X   (electronic)
Lecture Notes of the Institute for Computer Sciences, Social Informatics
and Telecommunications Engineering
ISBN 978-3-030-32215-1        ISBN 978-3-030-32216-8   (eBook)
https://doi.org/10.1007/978-3-030-32216-8

This Springer imprint is published by the registered company Springer Nature Switzerland AG
The registered company address is: Gewerbestrasse 11, 6330 Cham, Switzerland

# Preface

We are delighted to introduce the proceedings of the 11th edition of the 2019 European Alliance for Innovation (EAI) International Conference on Simulation Tools and Techniques (SIMUtools). The conference focuses on a broad range of research challenges in the field of simulation, modeling, and analysis, addressing current and future trends in simulation techniques, models, practices, and software. The conference is dedicated to fostering interdisciplinary collaborative research in these areas and across a wide spectrum of application domains.

The technical program of SIMUtools 2019 consisted of 92 full papers. Coordination with the steering chair, Imrich Chlamtac, was essential for the success of the conference. We sincerely appreciate the constant support and guidance. It was also a great pleasure to work with such an excellent Organizing Committee team and we thank them for their hard work in organizing and supporting the conference. In particular, we thank the Technical Program Committee, who completed the peer-review process of technical papers and compiled a high-quality technical program. We are also grateful to the conference manager, Kristina Lappyova, for her support and all the authors who submitted their papers to the SIMUtools 2019 conference.

We strongly believe that the SIMUtools conference provides a good forum for all researchers, developers, and practitioners to discuss all scientific and technological aspects that are relevant to simulation tools and techniques. We also expect that the future SIMUtools conference will be as successful and stimulating as indicated by the contributions presented in this volume.

September 2019

Houbing Song
Yuguang Fang
Dingde Jiang

# Organization

## Steering Committee

### Chair

Imrich Chlamtac — Bruno Kessler Professor, University of Trento, Italy

## Organizing Committee

### General Co-chairs

Houbing Song — Embry-Riddle Aeronautical University, USA
Yuguang Fang — University of Florida, USA
Dingde Jiang — University of Electronic Science and Technology of China, China

### Technical Program Committee Co-chairs

Burak Kantarci — University of Ottawa, Canada
Sheng Qi — University of Electronic Science and Technology of China, China
Haijun Rong — Xi'an Jiaotong University, China

### Publicity and Social Media Co-chairs

Tao Li — Nankai University, China
Chen Qiao — University of Electronic Science and Technology of China, China

### Workshops Co-chairs

Wei Liu — Xidian University, China
Huihui Wang — Jacksonville University, USA

### Sponsorship and Exhibits Co-chairs

Jun He — Sichuan University, China
Yuqing Wang — University of Electronic Science and Technology of China, China

### Publications Co-chairs

Wenqin Wang — University of Electronic Science and Technology of China, China
Feng Wang — University of Electronic Science and Technology of China, China

**Panels Chair**

Thomas Yang                Embry-Riddle Aeronautical University, USA

**Tutorials Chair**

Qinghe Du                  Xi'an Jiaotong University, China

**Demos Chair**

Jiawei Yuan                Embry-Riddle Aeronautical University, USA

**Posters and PhD Track Co-chairs**

Yongxin Liu                Embry-Riddle Aeronautical University, USA
Bin Jiang                  Tianjin University, China

**Web Chairs**

Liuwei Hou                 University of Electronic Science and Technology of China,
                           China
Jian Wang                  Embry-Riddle Aeronautical University, USA

**Local Co-chairs**

Junyu Lai                  University of Electronic Science and Technology of China,
                           China
Yihang Zhang               University of Electronic Science and Technology of China,
                           China
Xiangnan Zhu               University of Electronic Science and Technology of China,
                           China

**Conference Manager**

Radka Pincakova            European Alliance for Innovation, China

## Technical Program Committee

Lyuchao Liao               Fujian University of Technology, China
Hui Qi                     Changchun University of Science and Technology, China
Qingshan Wang              Hefei University of Technology, China
Liuwei Hou                 University of Electronic Science and Technology of China,
                           China
Yuqing Wang                University of Electronic Science and Technology of China,
                           China
Yihang Zhang               University of Electronic Science and Technology of China,
                           China
Qi Sheng                   University of Electronic Science and Technology of China,
                           China

# Contents

xvi      Contents

# Bisecting K-Means Based Fingerprint Indoor Localization

Yuxing Chen[1(✉)], Wei Liu[1], Haojie Zhao[1], Shuling Cao[1], Shasha Fu[1],
and Dingde Jiang[2]

[1] State Key Labs of ISN, Xidian University,
Xi'an 710071, Shaanxi, People's Republic of China
{yxchen_2,hjzhao,slcao_cn,ssfu}@stu.xidian.edu.cn,
liuweixd@mail.xidian.edu.cn
[2] School of Astronautics and Aeronautic,
University of Electronic Science and Technology of China, Chengdu 611731, China
jiangdd99@sina.com

**Abstract.** This paper presents a fingerprint indoor localization system based on Bisecting k-means (BKM). Compared to k-means, BKM is a more robust clustering algorithm. Specifically, BKM based indoor localization consists of two stages: offline stage and online positioning stage. In the offline stage, BKM is used to divide all the reference points (RPs) into $k$ clusters. A series of experiments have been made to show that our system can greatly improve localization accuracy.

**Keywords:** Fingerprint · Bisecting K-means · WiFi · Indoor localization

## 1 Introduction

With the rapid development of wireless communication technologies and the Internet industry, the demand for LBS (location-based services) is also growing. LBS has developed rapidly and received extensive attention and has been widely used in social networks, advertising services, travel, shopping, public safety services, and emergency assistance [1].

In terms of its application scenario, localization can be distinguished into indoor localization and outdoor localization. GPS is a commonly used outdoor wireless positioning technology, and has been relatively mature. Owing to the fact that GPS signal becomes weak after passing through the building, the satellite positioning cannot give reliable position information [2]. Therefore, traditional outdoor positioning technology cannot be used in indoor environments [3].

The financial support of the program of Key Industry Innovation Chain of Shaanxi Province, China (2017ZDCXL-GY-04-02), of the program of Xi'an Science and Technology Plan (201805029YD7CG13(5)), Shaanxi, China, of National S&T Major Project (No. 2016ZX03001022-003), China, and of Key R&D Program - The Industry Project of Shaanxi (Grant No. 2018GY-017) are gratefully acknowledged.

H. Song et al. (Eds.): SIMUtools 2019, LNICST 295, pp. 1–12, 2019.
https://doi.org/10.1007/978-3-030-32216-8_1

Consequently, wireless indoor positioning technology emerged. The commonly used wireless indoor positioning technologies include: ultrasonic positioning technology, ultra-wideband positioning technology, Bluetooth technology, and WiFi technology. Among them, WiFi is one of the most commonly used wireless communication technologies that covers a wider area, and has the advantages of easy-to-install, low cost, and relatively stable. A variety of terminal devices such as mobile phones, computers, and pads support WiFi communication, so WiFi indoor positioning technology is portable.

Fingerprint-based localization has become one of the most attractive and promising techniques due to its performance of high accuracy and stability [4–6]. The core idea of fingerprinting positioning is to map the location information that is difficult to measure to the characteristics of the radio signal that are easy to measure [7].

In [8], a system based on database partition and Euclidean distance-weighted pearson correlation coefficient is proposed, and this system is the combination of fingerprint database and machine learning. Support Vector Machine (SVM) is also an efficient algorithm that makes a great improvement in localization [9]. A mixture Gaussian distribution model can be used to minimize the error of the measured RSSI data and neural network plays the role in excavating the relationship between RSSI data and the position [10].

In this paper, we propose an improved fingerprinting localization algorithm based on the localization method in [11]. This system consists of two stages: offline stage and online localization stage. In the offline stage, a fingerprint database or a radio map is constructed that stores the relationship between Received Signal Strength Indicator (RSSI) data and Reference Points (RPs). BKM is adopted to divide all the RPs into clusters based on the fingerprint database [12]. In the online stage, RSSI data collected at test points are matched to the database to infer the concrete position.

The rest of our paper is organized as follows. In Sect. 2, a description about the system architecture is presented. In Sect. 3, the concrete approach we adopt in our system is presented. The experiment and result are illustrated in detail in Sect. 4. Finally, we list out our conclusion and look for the future.

## 2    System Model

In the indoor localization area, multiple Access Point ($AP$) signal can be detected at each location. With a mobile terminal equipped with wireless network card, we can record the $AP$ MAC address and RSSI data. The $AP$ MAC address and corresponding RSSI data at each location constitute a fingerprint. We can represent and determine a concrete location if we collect adequate fingerprints. Fingerprint indoor localization system is composed of two stages: offline stage and online stage. Offline stage is a procedure that maps locations to fingerprint. We process the raw RSSI data collected at each RP, and build a fingerprint database. In online stage, we sample online RSSI data. Then we compare and match the online data with the fingerprint database to determine the specific location. Figure 1 shows the architecture of our system.

In indoor localization environment, we receive RSSI data at positions from different *AP*s. To make better use of existing *AP*s in the building, we do not install additional *AP*s. We pick out efficient *AP*s, and classify positions into several clusters, then we build a decision tree for each cluster in offline stage. In online positioning stage, we lump the test point with the cluster whose cluster center is nearest to the test point. And then we use decision tree to determine its concrete position.

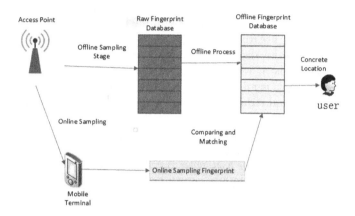

**Fig. 1.** System architecture.

## 3  BKM-Based Indoor Localization Approach

Assuming that there are $N$ RPs in the indoor environment and each RP can receive signals from part of *AP*s. The fingerprint database stores the coordinate of each location and the RSSI data from *AP*s, which can be marked as:

$$D_i = \{i, AP_j, \text{RSSI}_{ij}\} \tag{1}$$

In formula (1), $i$ represents the $i_{th}$ RP in the localization area, $(AP_j, \text{RSSI}_{ij})$ means that $AP_j$ can be detected at the $i_{th}$ location, and the RSSI data received at the $i_{th}$ position from $AP_j$. Each $D_i$ is a sampling fingerprint. Fingerprints can be stored in a database that maps RSSI data to positions.

In order to guarantee the precision of localization, we need to sample a large number of RSSI data at each location. It is clear that more data we have, the longer time it takes to fix the location. So it is necessary for us to take measures to shorten localization time. In this paper, we adopt three methods to reduce computation and space complexity: *AP* selection, clustering, and decision tree [11,13].

When row RSSI data are collected at each position, we need to select some *AP*s which will increase the localization accuracy. Then RSSI data collected from these $APs$ are stored as fingerprint database. According to the similarity between different RPs in the database, we divide the RPs into several clusters by clustering method. To guarantee the localization accuracy in a fine grain, we need to build a decision tree for each cluster. Each leaf node of a tree represents a position in the environment. Figure 2 is the offline stage process.

## 3.1  $AP$ Selection

Due to multi-path effect and signal reflection, signal may suffer from path loss, attenuation, and time delay in indoor environment. RSSI data collected from long-distance $APs$ are greatly interfered by noise. And these RSSI data may lead to the decrease in localization accuracy. Furthermore, with more $APs$, we need to handle more data, which will affect the real-time behavior. Thus, the process of selecting $APs$ is an important approach and guarantee for improving positioning accuracy, and reducing the complexity of positioning algorithms. We adopt maximum information gain to select $APs$ [11].

We take the resolution capability as the evaluation standard, and choose the $APs$ with the strongest resolution capability. That is, after the formulas below being calculated, we select $m$ $APs$ with the maximum information gains and constitute a $N$ by $m$ dimensional fingerprint information database.

For each position $G$, we can treat RSSI data from $AP_i$ as a feature. In this system, a certain position $G_j$ can be expressed as $(G_j^1, G_j^2, ...G_j^m)$ by those features. And $G_j^i$ indicates the average signal strength from $AP_i$ collected over a period of time as a feature of $G_j$. If $AP_k$ cannot be detected in $G_j$, then we set $G_j^k$ the default value $-90$ dBm.

Once we determine the localization area, we get to know the entropy of the environment. We can get the information entropy with the formula (2) [11]:

$$H(G) = -\sum_{j=1}^{n} P(G_j) \log P(G_j) \tag{2}$$

When we get the RSSI data from $AP_i$, the entropy will change into [11]:

$$H(G/AP_i)$$
$$= -\sum_{v} \sum_{j=1}^{n} P(G_j, AP_i = v) \log P(G_j/AP_i = v) \tag{3}$$

Then the variation of the information entropy, which indicates the loss of position uncertainty, or information gain is [11]:

$$\text{InfoGain}(AP_i) = H(G) - H(G/AP_i) \tag{4}$$

In the above formulas, $P(G_j)$ is the prior probability of position $G_j$. When all RPs are uniformly distributed, $P(G_j)$ is a constant $1/n$; $P(G_j, AP_i = v)$ is the joint probability under condition when RSSI data collected from $AP_i$ is $v$ at the position $G_j$, and $P(G_j/AP_i = v)$ is the conditional probability of location $G_j$ when RSSI data collected from $AP_i$ is $v$.

## 3.2  BKM Based Clustering

A cluster is the convergence of points in the test space [12]. The distance between any two points of the same cluster is less than the distance between any two points of different clusters; the cluster can be described as a space with a relatively high density. In fact, clustering is an unsupervised classification and usually does not require the use of training data for learning. We adopt BKM as the clustering method in this paper [12].

BKM can be regarded as an optimization version of k-means. The difference between BKM and k-means is that BKM reaches a global optimum, while k-means just reaches a local optimum. K-means can be greatly affected by the initial cluster centers and may lead to a nonideal division, which leads to a local optimum. Moreover, because it operates less similarity computing, BKM can accelerate the execution speed of clustering.

This algorithm first takes all the points as a cluster, and then divides all the points into two clusters. When partitioning, one point is chosen randomly as the first initial cluster center. Then the point which is farthest from the set center is selected as the second initial cluster center. The next procedure is to perform K-means algorithm to divide points into two clusters. Then one of the clusters that has the maximum value of the Sum of Squares for Error (SSE) is selected to continue the partition. The partitioning process is repeated until $k$ clusters are formed for the points.

In $n$-dimensional Euclidean space, SSE can be calculated by the formula below

$$\text{SSE} = \sum_{i=1}^{k} \sum_{p \in C_i} \text{dist}(p, c_i)^2 = \sum_{i=1}^{k} \sum_{p \in C_i} (p - c_i)^2 \qquad (5)$$

$$c_i = \frac{\sum_{p \in C_i} p}{n_{c_i}} \qquad (6)$$

In formulas above, $C_i$ is the $i_{th}$ cluster, $p$ is the point in cluster $C_i$, $n_{c_i}$ is the element number in cluster $C_i$, $\text{dist}(p, c_i)$ is the Euclidean distance between $p$ and $c_i$. The $i_{th}$ cluster center $c_i$ is updated after each iteration.

The specific implementation process of the clustering algorithm is described in Algorithm 1.

## 3.3  Decision Tree Algorithm

After constructing $k$ clusters, we can just estimate the approximate position of the user roughly. If we construct a cluster for each position, the amount of calculation will be very large and it will be very time-consuming, seriously affect the real-time positioning. So we need to use other algorithms to locate precisely. The decision tree can classify samples with a series of attributes and has the

---

**Algorithm 1.** BKM algorithm for finding k clustering

---

**Require:** The mean RSSI vectors $p$ for all RPs G;
**Require:** The number of clusters $k$;
**Ensure:** $k$ clusters: $C_1$, $C_2$,... $C_k$
    $m \leftarrow 1$
    $C_m \leftarrow G$
    **while** $m < k$ **do**
        Compute $SSE_m$
        $j^* = \arg\max_j(SSE_1, SSE_2, ...SSE_j, ...SSE_m)$
        Use k-means algorithm to split $C_j^*$ into two clusters: $C_j^*$, $C_{m+1}$
        $m \leftarrow m + 1$
    **end while**

---

advantage of high efficiency. In this paper, we use C4.5 decision tree for precise localization [11,13].

There are two steps to build a decision tree: selecting splitting attributes and choosing splitting points. We can simplify the procedure of building a decision tree for deciding which attribution to choose and how to split data at each splitting point. Different attributes are selected at different branches. We select information gain ratio as standard to choose splitting attributes. And it is necessary to decide segmentation points for each attribute. Suppose that we have dataset $D = \{D_1, D_2, ... D_n\}$, in which $D_i$ means fingerprints at position $G_i$. And $m$ APs are detectable at all $n$ positions in the cluster. We can divide D into $k$ subsets $\{T_1, T_2, ..., T_k\}$. And $T_i$ is the subset when RSSI data are collected from $AP_i$. Then we need to select splitting attributes with the maximum Ratio $(AP_i)$.

Step 1. When we have already clustered the RPs, we should make a decision tree for each cluster. For a certain cluster $\mathscr{A}$, we adopt all RSSI data collected at positions in cluster $\mathscr{A}$. We adopt information entropy Info($D$) to demonstrate the uncertainty of each position [11,13].

$$\text{Info}(D) = -\sum_{j=1}^{n} P(G_j) * \log P(G_j) \tag{7}$$

Step 2. We can learn from information gain that the information entropy decreases when we get more information. When we get the information of $M$ attributes for each position, the entropy becomes Info($D/APi$) [11,13].

$$\text{Info}(D/AP_i) = -\sum_{v}$$
$$\sum_{j=1}^{n} (P(G_j, AP_i = v) \log P(G_j/AP_i = v)) \tag{8}$$

Step 3. So we can get to know that the information gain [11,13].

$$\text{Gain}(AP_i) = \text{Info}(D) - \text{Info}(D/AP_i) \tag{9}$$

Step 4. The information entropy of attribute $AP_i$ is $H(AP_i)$ [13].

$$H(AP_i) = -\sum_{v}^{Ti} P(v) * log_2 P(v) \tag{10}$$

Step 5. The ratio of attribute $AP_i$ is Ratio($AP_i$) [13].

$$\text{Ratio}(AP_i) = \frac{\text{Gain}(AP_i)}{H(AP_i)} \tag{11}$$

In the formulas, $P(G_j)$ is the probability of $G_j$ in the environment. $P(G_j, AP_i = v)$ indicates the joint probability when RSSI value collected from $AP_i$ is $v$ at position $G_j$; $P(G_j/AP_i = v)$ is the conditional probability of $G_j$ when RSSI value collected from $AP_i$ is $v$; $v$ is the element in $T_j$, and $P(v)$ is the probability of $v$ in $T_i$.

The RSSI data are consecutive values, so we need to discretize the data first. Discretization refers to selecting some appropriate segmentation points in RSSI data and dividing them into several ranges. If some segmentation point $\mathcal{X}$ is chosen, data will be discretized into ranges (RSSI data $\leq \mathcal{X}$) and (RSSI data $\geq \mathcal{X}$). The principle of choosing segmentation points is as follows. First, we systematically arrange the RSSI data obtained at $n$ positions from $AP_i$ from small to large. And then we preselect one segmentation points ($l \leq m$, and we do not constitute segmentation points inside the same RSSI data subset). We compute the information gains corresponding to the condition of the preselected segmentation points. And the preselected segmentation point with the largest information gain is selected as the final segmentation point of $AP_i$.

## 3.4   Online Positioning Stage

In the actual online positioning process, when the user moves in the environment, the mobile terminal first detects the signals sent by the surrounding $AP$s, records RSSI data, and then traversals the fingerprint database to perform matching. Once the best match is found, the location of the user is estimated as the location of the best matching fingerprint.

The online positioning process can be regarded as the inverse process of constructing clusters and building decision trees. We first calculate the distance between the user's RSSI data and each cluster center, then select the cluster with the smallest distance as the position set the user belongs to. We use decision tree in that cluster for judgment. The feature values are compared with the corresponding split point and then compared with the left subtree and right subtree. We continue this process until it reaches the leaf node.

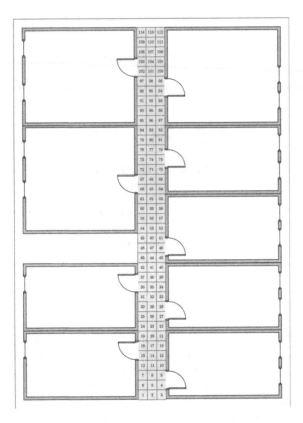

**Fig. 2.** Experimental environment

## 4   Experiment

We perform this experiment on a part of the corridor of the 4th floor of the main building. Owing to the fact that there already exist a certain number of $APs$ in the environment, we did not install any $APs$ to the environment. Figure 2 shows the schematic diagram of the corridor on the fourth floor. Each position area is 0.8 m * 0.8 m, so the interval between two measurement positions is 0.8 m. We use WirelessMon to detect $APs$ and collect RSSI data. We choose positions 1–100 to collect RSSI data. At each position, we collect 50 groups of data.

In the experiment, we first collect RSSI data at 100 positions to build a database. Then we adopt AP selection method to filter out the bad performance $APs$. We classify the RPs using clustering method with better performance $APs$. For each cluster, we build a decision tree to do precise localization. Finally, we test this algorithm with online test set.

Localization accuracy is the correct rate at a certain precision. Localization accuracy highly depends on the maximum allowed distance between actual position and the tested position ($d_{max\_allowed}$). The accuracy can be obtained with formula below:

$$\text{accuracy}(d_{max\_allowed}) = \frac{\sum_{i}^{n} 1\left\{\text{dist}(r_i, t_i) \leq d_{max\_allowed}\right\}}{n} \quad (12)$$

where we set $d_{max\_allowed}$ as 0.8 m, 1.6 m, and 2.0 m in the experiment; $r_i$ is the real location of the $i_{th}$ point, and $t_i$ is the test location of the $i_{th}$ point; dist$(r_i, t_i)$ is the Euclidean distance between $r_i$ and $t_i$; 1{} is the indicator function. With (12), we can get to know the accuracy under different precision range.

Since maximum information gain is used to select the $APs$ that are less affected by the noise in the environment, different numbers of $APs$ indicate different degrees the data in database are affected. To investigate the accuracy of AP selection method, we compare our algorithm with the one without AP selection. Furthermore, we choose different numbers of $APs$ to compare the localization accuracy. The position accuracy of different numbers of $APs$ are listed in Fig. 3. We set the number of $APs$ as $m$. In our environment, there are 17 $APs$ in total. The result shows that AP selection method improves the performance of localization accuracy, and the localization accuracy decreases once $m$ is too large or too small. In Fig. 3, the lines show the localization accuracy in 0.8 m, 1.6 m, and 2 m when we set $k$ as 5 respectively.

It can be observed that localization accuracy changes with different $AP$ numbers. And when we select 16 $APs$, we gain the best localization accuracy in 0.8 m, 1.6 m and 2 m with BKM algorithm. The result shows that the localization accuracy improves with $AP$ selection method.

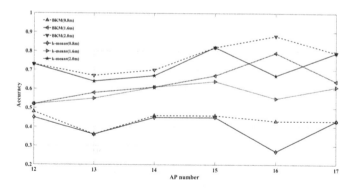

**Fig. 3.** Performance of AP selection

We adopt BKM to perform clustering in this paper. To compare the performance of BKM with k-means, we set the k-means as a comparision group. Figure 4 presents the results when we choose different $k$ in clustering algorithm. And we select 16 APs during the experiment. When $k$ is too large, the points that are Relatively relevant might be devided into different clusters. And this

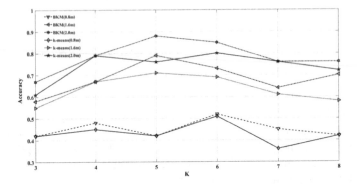

**Fig. 4.** Performance of clustering

decreases the divergence between different clusters. Furthermore, when $k$ is too small, the points that are less relevant are much more likely to be devided into a same cluster, which will decrease the resolution of a cluster. Thus, the localization accuracy decreases with $k$ being too large or too small.

Table 1 shows the comparison about localization precision between BKM and k-means. Average error is the average of localization error, which is computed using (13). Max error is the maximum localization error distance.

**Table 1.** Comparison of localization between BKM and k-means.

| Algorithm | Average error | Max error |
|---|---|---|
| BKM(m) | 1.51 | 5.60 |
| k-means(m) | 1.58 | 5.60 |

$$\text{Average error} = \sum_{i}^{n} \sum_{\text{Dist}} (\text{dist}(r_i, t_i)) \cdot P(\text{dist}(r_i, t_i)) \cdot P(r_i) \qquad (13)$$

where Dist is the set composed of all distances between real locations and test locations, and $\text{dist}(r_i, t_i) \in \text{Dist}$, $\forall$ i=1, 2..., n; $P(\text{dist}(r_i, t_i))$ is the probability of $\text{dist}(r_i, t_i)$. $P(r_i)$ is the probability of location $r_i$. The result shows that the BKM significantly reduces localization errors. It is clear that BKM outperforms k-means.

As we can see from Figs. 3 and 4, BKM almost always performs better than k-means. The result indicates that BKM can markedly improve the localization accuracy. BKM is a better performance algorithm than k-means.

# 5   Conclusion

This paper adopts an efficient indoor localization which utilizes $AP$ selection, clustering and decision tree. We adopt maximum information gain to filter out the $AP$s that do not perform well in lessening the uncertainty of localization. Clustering is presented to locate roughly. And decision tree is introduced to streamline the positioning. The result proves that our algorithm gains much better performance in improving positioning accuracy.

The future works is to utilize CSI (channel state information) in indoor localization, which is a finer-grained and more stable channel characteristic. We may also combine CSI with machine learning to improve localization accuracy.

# References

1. Liu, H., Darabi, H., Banerjee, P., et al.: Survey of wireless indoor positioning techniques and systems. IEEE Trans. Syst. Man Cybern. Part C (Appl. Rev.) **37**(6), 1067–1080 (2007)
2. Yassin, M., Rachid, E.: A survey of positioning techniques and location based services in wireless networks. In: IEEE International Conference on Signal Processing, Informatics, Communication and Energy Systems (SPICES), pp. 1–5 (2015)
3. Basri, C., Khadimi, A.E.: Survey on indoor localization system and recent advances of WiFi fingerprinting technique. In: International Conference on Multimedia Computing and Systems (ICMCS), pp. 253–259 (2016)
4. Tang, P., Huang, Z., Lei, J.: Fingerprint localization using WLAN RSS and magnetic field with landmark detection. In: International Conference on Computational Intelligence Communication Technology (CICT), pp. 1–6 (2017)
5. Zhang, G., Zhan, X., Dan, L.: Research and improvement on indoor localization based on RSSI fingerprint database and K-nearest neighbor points. In: International Conference on Communications, Circuits and Systems (ICCCAS), pp. 68–71 (2013)
6. Lemic, F., Handziski, V., Caso, G., et al.: Enriched training database for improving the WiFi RSSI-based indoor fingerprinting performance. In: IEEE Annual Consumer Communications Networking Conference (CCNC), pp. 875–881 (2016)
7. Alshamaa, D., Mourad-Chehade, F., Honeine, P.: Localization of sensors in indoor wireless networks: an observation model using WiFi RSS. In: IFIP International Conference on New Technologies, Mobility and Security (NTMS), pp. 1–5 (2018)
8. Chen, G., Liu, Q., Wei, Y., et al.: An efficient indoor location system in WLAN based on database partition and Euclidean distance-weighted Pearson correlation coefficient. In: IEEE International Conference on Computer and Communications (ICCC), pp. 1736–1741 (2016)
9. Zhou, R., Lu, S., Chen, J., et al.: An optimized space partitioning technique to support two-layer WiFi fingerprinting. In: IEEE Wireless Communications and Networking Conference (WCNC), pp. 1–6 (2017)
10. Yang, G., Gao, F., Zhang, H.: An effective calibration method for wireless indoor positioning system with mixture Gaussian distribution model. In: IEEE International Conference on Computer and Communications (ICCC), pp. 1742–1746 (2016)
11. Chen, Y., Yang, Q., Yin, J., et al.: Power-efficient access-point selection for indoor location estimation. IEEE Trans. Knowl. Data Eng. **18**, 877–888 (2006)

12. Steinbach, M., Karypis, G., Kumar, V.: A comparison of document clustering tech- niques. In: KDD Workshop on Text Mining (2000)
13. Quinlan, J.R.: Learning efficient classification procedures and their application to chess end games. In: Michalski, R.S., Carbonell, J.G., Mitchell, T.M. (eds.) Machine Learning: An Artificial Intelligence Approach. SYMBOLIC, pp. 463–482. Springer, Heidelberg (1983). https://doi.org/10.1007/978-3-662-12405-5_15

# MTAPS: Indoor Localization Algorithm Based on Multiple Times AP

Pengyu Huang[1], Haojie Zhao[1(✉)], Wei Liu[1], and Dingde Jiang[2]

[1] State Key Labs of ISN, Xidian University,
Xi'an 710071, Shaanxi, People's Republic of China
{pyhuang,liuweixd}@mail.xidian.edu.cn, hjzhao@stu.xidian.edu.cn
[2] School of Astronautics and Aeronautic,
University of Electronic Science and Technology of China,
Chengdu 611731, People's Republic of China
jiangdd@uestc.edu.cn

**Abstract.** In recent years, indoor localization base on fingerprint has become more and more common. In many fingerprint-based indoor positioning algorithms, it's very popular to use WiFi signal characteristics to represent the location fingerprint. However, with the great improvement of IEEE 802.11 protocols, WiFi has been broadly used. So there are numbers of WiFi access points (APs) have been deployed everywhere which can be used for localization purpose. The large amount of AP can greatly increase the dimension of the fingerprint and localization complexity. In this paper, we propose a novel indoor positioning algorithm MTAPS (indoor localization algorithm based on multiple times access point selection). MTAPS can effectively reduce the complexity of localization computation, and improve the performance of localization with an efficient access point selection algorithm. This indoor localization algorithm can get a better subset of APs through multiple times AP selection method. These selected APs will be more stable and can provide a better discriminative capability to reference locations. In addition, MTAPS uses k-means algorithm to cluster reference locations, and makes up a decision tree for every location cluster. After location clustering, MTAPS re-selects a suitable AP subset for every cluster. This method can further improve localization performance. Experimental results show that MTAPS has better localization performance than the indoor localization algorithm which is based on classical AP selection algorithm. And MTAPS can achieve the accuracy of over 90% within 2 m localization error.

**Keywords:** Location fingerprint · Multiple access point selections · K-means · Location clusters · Decision tree

Supported by the program of Key Industry Innovation Chain of Shaanxi Province, China (2017ZDCXL-GY-04-02), of the program of Xi'an Science and Technology Plan (201805029YD7CG13(5)), Shaanxi, China, of Key R&D Program – The Industry Project of Shaanxi (Grant No. 2018GY-017), of Key R&D Program – The Industry Project of Shaanxi (Grant No. 2017GY-191) and of Education Department of Shaanxi Province Natural Science Foundation, China (15JK1742).

H. Song et al. (Eds.): SIMUtools 2019, LNICST 295, pp. 13–24, 2019.
https://doi.org/10.1007/978-3-030-32216-8_2

# 1   Introduction

In recent years, location-based services (LBS) are more and more popular, and people have higher demands for localization and navigation. The GPS has high accuracy in open environment, but in indoor environment GPS signal can't pass through the wall. And GPS also experiences severe multipath effects, which seriously weaken the signal strength of GPS. These problems make GPS difficult to provide accurate indoor localization service. Recently, WiFi is becoming ubiquitous, and we can connect to WiFi in most common place, such as supermarkets, campuses or airports, In addition, our smart phones can easily connect WiFi and get WiFi signal RSSI (Received Signal Strength Indication). Therefore, there are a lot of indoor localization algorithms proposed based on WiFi, among which indoor localization algorithm based-fingerprint is popular.

Indoor localization algorithm based on fingerprint can be divided into two phases: offline phase and online phase. In the offline phase, the localization environment is divided into equal-sized grids, and the center of the each grid is used as a reference location. Then, collecting WiFi information in these reference locations, such as RSSI or CSI (Channel State Information). Using these WiFi information to represent fingerprint for each reference location, and make up location fingerprint database. In the online phase, fingerprint-based localization algorithm matches real-time localization data with all reference location's fingerprints in the fingerprint database. Choosing the reference location as target location, which has the highest similarity with real-time localization data.

Now WiFi is ubiquitous, when collecting WiFi data on offline phase, we can detect big numbers of WiFi access points in each reference location. If we directly use all detected access points to represent the reference location fingerprint. It means that each reference location fingerprint is a vector with big dimensions, and it also greatly increases the dimensions of the fingerprint database. Furthermore, the study in [1] found that when the number of the APs is large, the increase of AP will no longer results in any significant improvement of the location precision. Therefore, it's very important to select a suitable set of access points to represent the location fingerprint.

There are numerous AP selection algorithm proposed in recent years. Which could be divided into two main categories, as Highest Signal algorithm [2,3] and Information Gain-based AP selection [4]. In [2,3], the authors used the AP's RSSI to represent the importance of AP. The higher the signal strength, the more important the access point is. This AP selection algorithm is very easy, but WiFi RSSI changes frequently, and it is very sensitive in the indoor environment. So signal strength is not suitable to represent the importance of the AP. In [4], the author proposed an intelligent AP selection algorithm InfoGain (Information Gain-based AP selection). InfoGain algorithm uses position information entropy and conditional entropy to indicate the localization capabilities of different AP. In [5], AP selection was based on the principle of minimizing redundancy, using the correlation of APs to define redundancy. The correlation is got by computing two AP's divergence measure. Paper [6] proposed a real-time AP selection algorithm. Like [5], it was also focus on how to minimize redundancy between APs. Paper [6] proposed two algorithms to get Ideal AP subset. In [7], the AP selection algorithm combines information gain with mutual information entropy, and uses mutual information entropy to express the similarity of APs. If the mutual information entropy of two APs is big, this paper just chooses the one with higher information gain. Paper [8] proposed RBF-based location algorithm, in which the covariance matrix of RSSI is used to select AP. This paper combines RSSI covariance matrix with weight matrix, and uses scaling parameters represents the importance of AP. Then, rank APs in terms of their scaling parameters, and pick out the APs with the highest scaling parameters to form an AP set.

The statistical distribution of RSSI of APs is always been required in the above AP selection algorithm [4–8]. Because they select AP or make up the decision model based on statistical distribution of RSSI of AP. However, in the process of collecting AP data, we often can find that, some APs only could be detect for a few time. This means for some APs, we only can get a few data of them, as show in Fig. 1. Figure 1 is a histogram to show the number of APs that could be detected for different times at a reference location in our experimental environment. We sampled fifty times at this reference location, and over one hundred APs were detected. In Fig. 1, the horizontal axis is the times of AP detected during the sampling period. And the vertical axis indicates the number of APs whose detection times is within a certain range. For example, in Fig. 1, the first column represents the number of APs, who are detected one to five times during the sampling period.

From Fig. 1, we could find that nearly half of the access points are collected less than five times, and more than 70% of the access points are collected less than twenty-five times during sampling period. If an access point appears too few times during the sampling period, we get few AP data of this AP, and using those small amounts of data cannot correctly describe AP's RSSI probability distribution. However, those algorithms [4–8] all depend on the AP's RSSI probability distribution to some extent, so those algorithm is not always useful.

In this paper, we propose a novel indoor localization algorithm MTAPS. This indoor localization algorithm is based on multiple access point selection method. MTAPS can effectively solves the above problems. And MTAPS can get a reliable APs subset by multiple access point selection method, which make the signal to be more stable and to obtain higher location accuracy. At the same time, MTAPS can effectively reduce complexity of localization computation, and improve the performance of localization in the meantime. In addition, MTAPS also uses k-means algorithm to cluster reference locations, and make up a decision tree for every location cluster. After clustering reference locations, MTAPS re-selects APs subset for every cluster, obtain a suitable APs subset for every cluster. This can further improve localization performance.

The rest of the paper is organized as follows: Sect. 2 describes MTAPS in detail. Section 3 is about the experimental results and the analysis of the results. Section 4 is a conclusion of MTAPS.

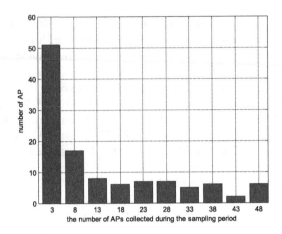

**Fig. 1.** A histogram of all APs detected at a reference location

## 2  Algorithm Description

MTAPS can be also divided into two phases: offline phase and online phase. In the offline phase, the MTAPS contains five steps, collecting AP data, AP selection, location clustering, AP re-selection and building decision tree.

### 2.1  Collecting AP Data

Collecting access point data is the basis of MTAPS. This step includes the following process: First, the localization environment is divided into equal-sized grids, and the center of the grid is used as a reference location. Then, collecting AP data for a period of time at each reference location.

**Select Pre-selected AP Set.** In this sub-step, we aim to delete access points that appear less frequently during the collecting process of AP data, and select a stable AP subset. The details of the process are as follows:

(1) Obtain the primary pre-selected AP subset.

Using $\overline{AP_i}$ represents AP set detected at reference location i, $\overline{AP_i} = \left\{AP_i^1, AP_i^2, AP_i^3, \ldots, AP_i^f\right\}$ $AP_i^j$ denotes access point $j$ detected at reference location $i$, and $f$ is AP's number detected at reference location $i$. Calculating $AP_i^j$'s number $n_i^j$ collected at reference location $i$, so we can get AP's number set $\overline{n_i}$, $\overline{n_i} = \left\{n_i^1, n_i^2, n_i^3, \ldots, n_i^f\right\}$. Such as $AP_i^j$ is collected 30 times at location $i$ during the data collecting period, so $n_i^j$ is equal to 30.

Then, we set a threshold $\boldsymbol{th1}$. If $n_i^j$ less than $\boldsymbol{th1}$, we remove $AP_i^j$ from AP set of reference location $i$. Finally, we use the rest set of AP $f$ to form primary pre-selected AP subset $PRAP$. $PRAP = \{AP_1, AP_2, AP_3, \ldots, AP_g\}$, and $g$ is the number of APs that satisfy the above-mentioned condition in localization environment.

(2) Obtain final pre-selected AP subset.

Calculating the sum times of $AP_l$ at all reference locations, marked as $N_l$. Such as, suppose $AP_l$ only appears at reference location $i$ and $j$, the number of $AP_l$ collected above 2 locations are $num_i$ and $num_j$ respectively. So $N_l$ is equal to the sum of $num_i$ and $num_j$. Therefore, we can get the set of corresponding values $\overline{N}$, $\overline{N} = \{N_1, N_2, N_3, \ldots, N_g\}$.

Then, we set another threshold $th2$. If $N_l$ is less than $th2$, we delete $AP_l$ from $PRAP$. Those remaining APs make up the final pre-selected AP subset $FPAP$, $FPAP = \{AP_1, AP_2, AP_3, \ldots, AP_h\}$, and $h$ is the size of $FPAP$.

**Obtain Final Target AP Set.** In paper [4], the author proposed InfoGain algorithm to select AP set. InfoGain algorithm uses AP's information gain to represent the AP's discriminative power to location. The more discriminative power, the more important AP is. Such as, 's Information gain is calculated as follow:

$$InfoGain\,(AP_i) = H\,(G) - H\,(G|AP_i) \tag{1}$$

where $InfoGain\,(AP_i)$ is $AP_i$'s discriminative power. $H\,(G)$ is the entropy of all reference locations without know $AP_i$'s RSSI information.

$$H\,(G) = -\sum_{i=1}^{p} P\,(G_i) \log P\,(G_i) \tag{2}$$

where $G_i$ is reference location, and $p$ is the number of reference point. $H\,(G|AP_i)$ is the conditional entropy of location given AP's RSSI information.

$$H\,(G|AP_i) = -\sum_{v} \sum_{j=1}^{p} P\,(G_j, AP_i = \mathrm{v}) \log P\,(G_j|AP_i = \mathrm{v}) \tag{3}$$

where $v$ is RSSI value of $AP_i$. $P\,(G_j, AP_i = \mathrm{v})$ and $P\,(G_j|AP_i = \mathrm{v})$ can be obtained based on collected AP data.

In this step, we calculate every AP's information gain of $FPAP$. Choosing the top $k$ APs with the largest information gain to form fingerprint AP set $FingerAP$, $FingerAP = \{AP_1, AP_2, AP_3, \ldots, AP_k\}$.

Then, we get every reference location's fingerprint based on AP data in $FingerAP$, and obtain fingerprint database formed by all reference location's fingerprint. Set $F_j$ is the location fingerprint of location $j$,

$F_j = \left\{RSSI_1^j, RSSI_2^j, RSSI_3^j, \ldots, RSSI_k^j\right\}$, where $RSSI_i^j$ is RSSI of $AP_j$ in reference location $i$.

From formulas (2) and (3), we can know that we need to know the RSSI's probability distribution of every AP, when calculating $H\,(G|AP_i)$. However, when collecting AP's data, we find some APs only are detected occasionally, so there is a few those AP's data, as Fig. 1. Therefore, for those access points detected occasionally, we cannot get reliable AP's RSSI probability distribution. Paper [1] does not consider this problem when the author proposes InfoGain algorithm. So only using information gain to select AP subset not always work well. In our algorithm, AP selection contains two step. The first step removes those APs, which are detected occasionally during AP data collecting period, and obtains pre-selected AP set. The second step gets final target AP set based on InfoGain algorithm. Those APs are stable in the pre-selected AP set, and can get their good probability distribution through their collected RSSI data. Therefore, our algorithm removes unstable APs. This method can better play the advantages of information gain algorithm.

## 2.2   Location Clustering

In the online phase, Indoor localization algorithm based on fingerprint match real-time position data with all fingerprints in the fingerprint database. Therefore, the elapsed time of real-time location is the linear relationship with the number of the reference locations in localization environment. If we divide all reference locations into some clusters, real-time positioning need just match with all fingerprints in a cluster that is most similar to it. So clustering location can effectively reduce the locating time. In our algorithm, we use a classical cluster algorithm, k-means algorithm [9], to cluster reference locations based on location fingerprint. Suppose there are $M$ reference locations in location environment, and $L$ clusters, and $C_j$ is cluster center of cluster $j$, $C_j = \left\{ c_1^j, c_2^j, c_3^j, \ldots, c_k^j \right\}$, where $k$ is cardinality of $FingerAP$.

The process of location clustering as followed:

(1) Randomly selecting L locations as clusters'center $C_j = F_j$, so $C_j = F_j = \left\{ RSSI_1^j, RSSI_2^j, RSSI_3^j, \ldots, RSSI_k^j \right\}$.

(2) Divided all reference locations into $L$ clusters base on Euclidean distance between reference locations and all cluster centers. Such as, when deciding which cluster reference locations $i$ belongs to, calculating Euclidean distance of reference location $i$ to each cluster center. Then dividing reference location $i$ to the cluster whose Euclidean distance to reference location $i$ is minimal in $L$ clusters. Euclidean distance is as followed:

$$Dis\left(F_i, C_j\right) = \sum_{h=1}^{k} \left(c_h^j - RSSI_h^i\right)^2 \qquad (4)$$

where $Dis\left(F_i, C_j\right)$ is the distance of reference location $i$ and cluster $j$.

(3) Updating the center of each cluster. When all reference locations are divided into clusters, calculating the average value of location fingerprints that the cluster contains as the new center of the cluster. Such as, cluster $j$ has $w$

reference locations, so new center can be calculated as followed:

$$C_{jnew} = \frac{1}{w} \times \left\{ \sum_{h=1}^{w} RSSI_1^h, \sum_{h=1}^{w} RSSI_2^h, \ldots, \sum_{h=1}^{w} RSSI_k^h \right\} \qquad (5)$$

(4) Determining whether to stop location cluster iteration, and updating each cluster's center with those average values. Calculating Euclidean distance between the new clusters' center and the old clusters' center. If the Euclidean distance less than a certain threshold, stopping iteration, and let $C_j$ equal to $C_{jnew}$; else let $C_j$ equal to $C_{jnew}$ and back to step (2), continuing to iteration.

## 2.3   AP Reselection and Making up Decision Tree

After clustering, our algorithm re-select APs for each cluster again. Before clustering reference location, we select $FingerAP$ based on our AP selection algorithm. MTAPS aims to obtain a good AP set, which has high discriminative power. So $FingerAP$ is a reliable AP set for the indoor localization environment. However, our localization algorithm divides all reference locations into some clusters. Each cluster has its characteristics and there are some differences between clusters. Therefore, using a same AP set cannot well represent the characteristics and differences of each cluster. For this problem, our algorithm re-select AP set for each cluster. Therefore, through our re-select algorithm, one cluster's AP set can have some differences with the other cluster's AP set. The process of APs re-select in cluster as followed:

Suppose $Cluster_i$ is the set, which is made up by reference locations that divided into cluster $i$. So $Cluster_i = \left\{ Loc_1^i, Loc_2^i, Loc_3^i, \ldots, Loc_K^i \right\}$, where $Loc_j^i$ reference location $j$, and $K$ is the number of reference locations in cluster $i$. According to those locations AP data collection in $Cluster_i$, calculating each AP's information gain in $FPAP$, and obtaining the re-selection AP set of cluster $i$, $ClusterAP_i = \left\{ AP_1^i, AP_2^i, AP_3^i, \ldots, AP_c^i \right\}$, where $c$ is the number of AP selected from $FPAP$.

After AP re-selection, we make up the decision tree for each cluster according to C4.5 algorithm [10] based on $ClusterAP$. The C4.5 algorithm is a classical algorithm for machine learning, and belongs to supervised learning algorithm. Using the C4.5 algorithm, we get the final decision tree of each cluster.

So let's do an example, as show in Fig. 2, there is a decision tree of a certain cluster. From Fig. 2, we can see that in this decision tree, the leaf nodes are the reference positions and the child nodes are APs from the $ClusterAP$. The range values on the decision tree's branches are the judgment condition to real-time data for location. For example, for the root node $AP_4$, it has three branches, and each branch has a value range. It has three branches, and each branch has a value range. If there is a test data, the value of $AP_4$ is 53, it satisfies the judgment condition on the second branch obviously. So it will go down to the second branch of the decision tree, and reach the next node $AP_5$.

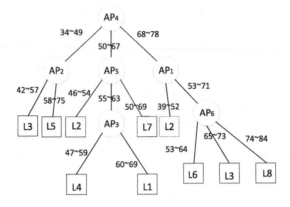

**Fig. 2.** Decision tree model

## 2.4  Online Phase

When the decision tree is established for each cluster, this means the offline phase has finished, and this localization algorithm can be used to identify the location of the user. The process of localization as followed:

Suppose the user's real-time localization data is T,

(1) Decide which cluster T belongs to. Getting localization fingerprint on the basis of *ClusterAP*, $Tfinger = \left\{ \widetilde{AP_1}, \widetilde{AP_2}, \widetilde{AP_3}, \ldots, \widetilde{AP_c} \right\}$. Calculating Euclidean distance from T to each cluster, and choosing the cluster with the smallest Euclidean distance to T as T's target cluster. The location of T can be got from target cluster.

(2) Localization based on decision tree. In the previous sub-step, we obtain the target cluster that T belongs to. Then we use the target cluster's decision tree to determine T's precise location. Suppose the target cluster is cluster i, Table 1 is a user's localization data which is obtained based on from T. Decision tree of cluster *ClusterAP* showed as Fig. 3.

From Fig. 3, we notice that the root node is $AP_4$. From Table 1, the value of $AP_4$ is 70 right between the range from 68 to 78. Obviously, next node is $AP_1$. From Table 1 the $AP_1$'s value is 63 in the range from 53 to 71, so next node is $AP_6$, and so on. As the red line shows in the Fig. 3 the target location is L6.

**Table 1.** User's localization data

| $AP_1$ | $AP_2$ | $AP_3$ |
|--------|--------|--------|
| 63 | 56 | 45 |
| $AP_4$ | $AP_5$ | $AP_6$ |
| 70 | 61 | 57 |

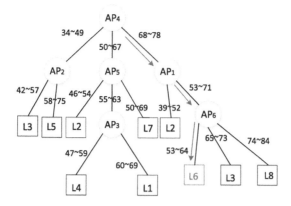

**Fig. 3.** The process of localization by using decision tree

## 3    Experimental Evaluation

In this section, we describe our experimental testbed, and assess the performance of the indoor localization algorithm based on multiple times access point selection.

Our experiment is carried out in the fourth-floor corridor of main building of Xidian University, as Fig. 4 showed. The experimental testbed include 177 reference locations, and every reference location is a 0.8 m * 0.8 m grid. In the phase of collecting AP data, we collect 50 samples at every reference location. Each sample lasts six seconds. And we can scan more than one hundred APs at every reference location in our localization environment.

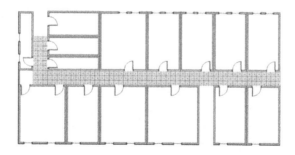

**Fig. 4.** Experimental testbed

Under the condition that the number of location clusters is 5, Fig. 5 indicates the localization accuracy of our localization algorithm changes with the number of APs within different positioning errors. From Fig. 5, we can see that our indoor localization algorithm has better localization accuracy. The algorithm in this paper can achieve the best accuracy of over ninety percent within 2 m localization error. And within 1.6 m localization error, MTAPS also almost has the best accuracy of eighty percent.

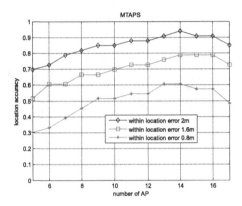

**Fig. 5.** The performance of MTAPS within different localization error under different AP number

Under the condition that the number of location clusters is 5, we compare MTAPS with InfoGain algorithm [1] within 2 m location error, as Fig. 6 shows. Figure 6 illustrates that the performance of our algorithm far exceeds that of the information gain algorithm. Therefore in the same condition, our algorithm always has better performance.

Under the condition that the number of location clusters is 5, we also did several experiments to observe the performance of InfoGain algorithm within different localization error. As Fig. 7 shows, the performance of InfoGain algorithm is very bad in our experimental environment. The main reason for this

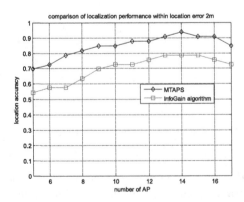

**Fig. 6.** Comparison of localization performance for MTAPS and InfaGain under different AP number

result is that in paper [1], their testbed is relatively simple, and a total of 25 access points can be detected in the environment. Duo to the number of APs is so small in their experimental environment, so there is less interference in their experimental environment. Therefore, information gain algorithm gets a good performance in their experiment.

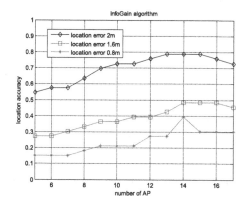

**Fig. 7.** The performance of InfoGain algorithm within different localization error under different AP number

However, today WiFi is everywhere, and we can detect hundreds of WiFi in my university or in a mall. Therefore, there is serious interference between APs, and at the same time the state of APs is more complex. Especially in the sampling process, some access points are merely detected. As a result, we can't correctly get those APs' probability distribution base on collected AP data under serious conditions of interference. But the performance of InfoGain algorithm is heavily dependent on probability distribution. So only using information gain algorithm to choose APs can't obtain satisfactory results. Our algorithm can remove unstable APs, and use reliable APs represent fingerprint. Therefore, our algorithm gets better performance.

## 4    Conclusion

In this paper, we propose an indoor localization algorithm MTAPS. This algorithm can get a reliable AP subset to represent fingerprint, and effectively remove unstable APs based on multiple access point selection method. In addition, our algorithm re-select AP subset for each location cluster, to get a special AP subset for location cluster. This localization algorithm divides all reference locations into some clusters by k-means algorithm, which can effectively decrease the cost-time of localization and improve efficiency. The results of the experiments show that our algorithm has the better performance. On the other side, we also analyze the causes of the bad performance for information gain algorithm. Our algorithm can effectively solve the defect of information gain algorithm, and obtains satisfactory positioning performance.

# References

1. Kaemarungsi, K., Krishnamurthy, P.: Modeling of indoor positioning systems based on location fingerprinting. IEEE INFOCOM **2**, 1012–1022 (2004)
2. Youssef, M.A., Agrawala, A., Shankar, A.U.: WLAN location determination via clustering and probability distributions. In: IEEE International Conference on Pervasive Computing and Communications, pp. 143–150 (2003)
3. Du, L., Bai, Y., Chen, L.: Access point selection strategy for large-scale wireless local area networks. In: IEEE Wireless Communications and Networking Conference, pp. 2161–2166 (2007)
4. Chen, Y., Yang, Q., Yin, J., et al.: Power-efficient access-point selection for indoor location estimation. IEEE Trans. Knowl. Data Eng. **18**(7), 877–888 (2006)
5. Zhao, Q., et al.: An effective preprocessing scheme for WLAN-based fingerprint positioning systems. In: IEEE International Conference on Communication Technology, pp. 592–595 (2010)
6. Kushki, A., Plataniotis, K.N., Venetsanopoulos, A.N.: Kernel-based positioning in wireless local area networks. IEEE Trans. Mob. Comput. **6**(6), 689–705 (2007)
7. Zou, G., et al.: An indoor positioning algorithm using joint information entropy based on WLAN fingerprint. In: IEEE International Conference on Computing, pp. 1–6 (2014)
8. Laoudias, C., Panayiotou, C.G., Kemppi, P.: On the RBF-based positioning using WLAN signal strength fingerprints. In: 7th Workshop on Positioning, Navigation and Communication, Dresden, pp. 93–98 (2010)
9. Duda, R.O., Hart, P.E., Stork, D.G.: Pattern Classification. Wiley, Hoboken (2012)
10. Quinlan, J.R.: C4.5: Programs for Machine Learning. Elsevier, Amsterdam (2014)

# Formalizing Model Transformations Within MDE

Zhi Zhu$^{(\boxtimes)}$(iD), Yongling Lei(iD), Qun Li(iD), and Yifan Zhu(iD)

National University of Defense Technology, Changsha 410073, China
zhuzhi@nudt.edu.cn

**Abstract.** A recent approach to tackle the ever increasing complexity of military simulation system is model-driven engineering (MDE). However, it is used mostly to produce simulation software tools, and seldom can perform formal analysis on models, resulting in a low degree of simulation model engineering. Consequently, this raises many issues such as inefficient development as well as poor qualities of product, and falls short of non-functional requirements like extensibility, maintainability, and reuse. In general, many of the success of MDE are dependent on the descriptive power of modeling languages and how conceptual models are transformed toward final implementations. Hence, this paper presents contributions in two main aspects of MDE: customizing domain specific language by metamodeling and engineering model continuity by formalizing model transformations. A military simulation application called group fire control channel system is used as a motivating example to illustrate the whole process, transforming conceptual models into other formalisms that have precise definitions of semantics until they reach final executable simulation models.

**Keywords:** MDE · Metamodeling · Model transformation · Model continuity

## 1 Introduction

Traditional military simulation models are usually represented by UML which has not precise and unambiguous semantics defined using a mixture of OCL (Object Constraint Language) and informal text, or the semantics of simulation models are left to model interpreters or simulators which are defined by general-purpose programming languages, which is clearly unacceptable for formal analysis [1]. Meanwhile, although the syntax of current domain specific modeling languages (DSML) are formally described with a lot of general metamodeling tools like UML Profile [2], EMF [3], and GME [4] etc., the semantics are left toward other less than desirable means [5]. All of these accompanying with the lack of formal model transformations contribute to difficult formal analysis at a model level. Hence, it is a real challenge to describe simulation models formally, and to improve the model continuity that exist between different models in different development stages at different levels of abstraction [6], so as to reuse existing model assets and simulation services to a great degree.

Inconsistent terminology in the model-driven engineering (MDE) context [7] means it is necessary to define basic meanings of important frequently used terms to

© ICST Institute for Computer Sciences, Social Informatics and Telecommunications Engineering 2019
Published by Springer Nature Switzerland AG 2019. All Rights Reserved
H. Song et al. (Eds.): SIMUtools 2019, LNICST 295, pp. 25–42, 2019.
https://doi.org/10.1007/978-3-030-32216-8_3

provide a common understanding. Many of these terms are used alternatively in specific contexts, but providing their definitions and/or subtle distinctions is helpful to understand the methodologies, techniques, and tools used in model-driven development. For different modeling goals, there exist three typical issues, i.e. model composability, model heterogeneity, and model continuity.

Firstly, model composability [8] concentrates on the syntactical matching and semantic relations between different simulation models. Unlike the other two issues, it is usually discussed in a MDE context and emphasizes the integration of multiple simulation models to form an effective and meaningful simulation application.

Secondly, model heterogeneity comes from the joint use of several DSMLs dedicated to particular domains or applications. In many cases, it refers to the syntactical incompatibility between different used DSMLs during the language customization process and has four sources in general [9, 10]. First, the different technical or application domains involved in a simulation system under design require different model specifications, modeling formalisms, or simulation protocols [11]. Second, the different levels of abstraction need suitable modeling techniques. Third, a simulation system is always studied from different points of view, and lastly different stages of a development cycle may use different languages for different activities.

Thirdly, Model continuity refers to the generation of an approximate morphism relation between different phases of a development process [12]. In general, model continuity is obtained if the initial and intermediate models are effectively consumed in the later steps of a development process and the modeling relation is preserved.

In a sense, model continuity is similar to the consistency between the source and target models, involving the syntactical correctness of target model, the completeness of source model consumed in model transformation, and the semantic relations preserved in target model [13]. We use $M_{com}$ to represent model composability, $M_h$ to model heterogeneity, and $M_{con}$ to model continuity, such that $M_h \cup M_{con} \subset M_{com}$ and $M_h \cap M_{con} \neq \varnothing$, as shown in Fig. 1. It means, on the one hand, if simulation models in a simulation application development satisfy the model composability, then it also satisfy the model heterogeneity and model continuity. On the other hand, model heterogeneity and model continuity may not be disjoint in some cases, which means model heterogeneity is somehow equal to the syntactical discontinuity between different development stages.

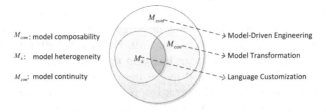

$M_{com}$: model composability
$M_h$: model heterogeneity
$M_{con}$: model continuity

$\rightarrow$ Model-Driven Engineering
$\rightarrow$ Model Transformation
$\rightarrow$ Language Customization

**Fig. 1.** Three typical issues identified in the MDE context.

This paper proposes a set of formal theories of model transformations for engineering model continuity, transforming models represented by various modeling languages into other formalisms that have precise definitions of semantics until they reach final executable simulation models [14]. A motivating example named group fire control channel system (GFCCS) [15] is used through this paper, commencing with its customization of DSML and transforming its conceptual models represented in this DSML to final executable simulation models. After that, a military simulation system in support of engineering modeling and composable simulating is capable of integrating those executable simulation models and reusing them for multiple simulation applications.

## 2  Model Transformations

### 2.1  The Basic Mode of Model Transformation

Model transformation is a process that takes a source model in a specific form as inputs and outputs another form of the target model according to a set of predefined rules. This process does not build new models from scratch, but reuse existing information when conducting a model transformation. A formal model transformation requires that the models involved in the transformation are represented clearly by well-defined modeling languages that have accurate syntax and unambiguous semantics. Furthermore, it requires that the transformation rules are written by a well-defined transformation language to ensure the transformation is conducted under a well-defined transformation template [16]. To ensure model continuity, the target model should preserve as much as possible the initial model information and modeling relations that are embedded in the source model [17].

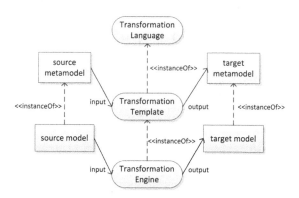

**Fig. 2.**  The basic mode of model transformation.

Figure 2 shows the basic mode of model transformation. In this mode, each node at a certain layer conforms to or is an instance of the node at a higher layer. The middle column is the transformation mechanism that inputs the left source nodes and outputs the right target nodes. For example, the transformation engine is an instance of the transformation template which is further an instance of the transformation language, which means the transformation template is written by the transformation language and prescribes the internal mechanism of the transformation engine. This engine inputs the source model which is an instance of the source metamodel and outputs the target model which is an instance of the target metamodel, and both metamodels are respectively taken as the inputs and outputs of the transformation template.

According to the concrete form of target model, model transformation has two typical categories: model to model (M2M) and model to text (M2T). In practice, M2T transformation is also called code generation when the text is in the form of source code. In general, a model-driven development process contains a sequence of M2M transformations and a final code generation. In addition, model transformation is endogenous when the source metamodel is similar to the target metamodel, and exogenous when they are different [18].

## 2.2    MDA Based Model Transformations

MDA (model-driven architecture) introduces three model development roles, and two transform mechanism types [19]. Using these MDA models, i.e. conceptual independent (CIM), platform independent (PIM), and platform specific models (PSM), developers can be classified into comparable roles, i.e. conceptual and simulation modelers, and simulation programmers, respectively, where later stages only can commence when developers for the former stages reach a consensus on an artifact. For example, once the problem owner and the conceptual modeler agree on a conceptual model, the simulation modeler can transform it into a formal model. In addition, M2M and M2T model transformation mechanisms are used as a bridge to reduce the gap between these roles. We adopt the formal MDA process as depicted in Definition 1 [12].

**Definition 1.** A MDA process is defined as

$$mda = \{n, MML, ML, MO, SL, pl, MTP, STP, MT, SM, TO\}$$

- $n = 3(CIM, PIM, PSM)$,
- $MML = \{ll_0, ll_1, ll_2\}$ is an ordered set of metamodeling languages,
- $ML = \{l_0(mm_{CIM}), l_1(mm_{PIM}), l_2(mm_{PSM})\}$ such that
  $confromTo(mm_{CIM}, ll_0)$,
  $confromTo(mm_{PIM}, ll_1)$,
  $confromTo(mm_{PSM}, ll_2)$,

This means metamodels must conform to their corresponding metamodeling languages.

- $MO = \{CIM, PIM, PSM\}$ such that $CIM$ is the initial model, $PSM$ is the final model, and

$instanceOf(CIM) = mm_{CIM},$

$instanceOf(PIM) = mm_{PIM},$

$instanceOf(PSM) = mm_{PSM},$

This means models must conform to their corresponding metamodels.

- $SL$ is a set of model transformation languages,
- $pl$ is a programming language with simulation capabilities,
- $MTP = \{p_{CIM}, p_{PIM}, p_{PSM}\}$ such that

  $p_{CIM} = \{l_0(mm_{CIM}), l_1(mm_{PIM}), r_0\},$

  $p_{PIM} = \{l_1(mm_{PIM}), l_2(mm_{PSM}), r_1\},$

  $p_{PSM} = \{l_2(mm_{PSM}), pl, r_2\},$

This represents model transformation patterns that a source language to a target language through some rules.

- $STP$ is a set of other supplementary formal model transformation patterns,
- $MT = \{$

  $transformTo(CIM, p_{CIM}) = PIM,$

  $transformTo(PIM, p_{PIM}) = PSM,$

  $transformTo(CIM, p_{PSM}) = SM$

  $\},$

This means model transformations that a source model to a target model using some patterns.

- $SM$ is the final executable simulation model,
- $TO$ is a set of tools to ease the activities.

Above definition is suitable for general model development base on the MDA principles. Given this definition, we can conclude a process for the GFCCS development as Definition 2, which will be illustrated by later sections. In the GFCCS process, we take the GFCCS DSML as the conceptual modeling language to describe CIM, P-DEVS [20] as the modeling formalism to define PIM, and JAVA as the programming language to build PSM. Hence, the GFCCS process involves the following types of metamodels and model transformations.

1. The CIM metamodel is GFCCS metamodel
2. The PIM metamodel is P-DEVS metamodel
3. The PSM metamodel is JAVA metamodel
4. The CIM-PIM transformation is GFCCS to P-DEVS transformation
5. The PIM-PSM transformation is P-DEVS to JAVA transformation
6. The PSM-SM transformation is JAVA to java code transformation.

**Definition 2.** A GFCCS simulation modeling process is defined as

$$gfccs = \{n, MML, ML, MO, SL, pl, MTP, STP, MT, SM, TO\}_{instance}$$

- $n = 3(CIM, PIM, PSM)$,
- $MML = \{Ecore, Ecore, Ecore\}$ is an ordered set of metamodeling languages,
- $ML = \{l_0(mm_{GFCCS}), l_1(mm_{DEVS}), l_2(mm_{JAVA})\}$ such that
  $confromTo(mm_{GFCCS}, Ecore)$,
  $confromTo(mm_{DEVS}, Ecore)$,
  $confromTo(mm_{JAVA}, Ecore)$,
- $MO = \{CIM, PIM, PSM\}$, and
  $instanceOf(CIM) = mm_{GFCCS}$,
  $instanceOf(PIM) = mm_{DEVS}$,
  $instanceOf(PSM) = mm_{JAVA}$,
- $SL = \{ATL, Acceleo\}$ is a set of model transformation languages,
- $pl = JAVA$ is the final programming language
- $MTP = \{p_{CIM}, p_{PIM}, p_{PSM}\}$ such that
  $p_{CIM} = \{l_0(mm_{GFCCS}), l_1(mm_{DEVS}), gfccs2devs.atl\}$,
  $p_{PIM} = \{l_1(mm_{DEVS}), l_2(mm_{JAVA}), devs2java.atl\}$,
  $p_{PSM} = \{l_2(mm_{JAVA}), JAVA, java2code.mtl\}$,
- $STP = \varnothing$ dictates there exists no other supplementary formal model transformation patterns,
- $MT = \{$
  $transformTo(CIM, p_{CIM}) = PIM$,
  $transformTo(PIM, p_{PIM}) = PSM$,
  $transformTo(CIM, p_{PSM}) = SM$
  $\}$,
- $SM$ is the final executable simulation model,
- $TO = \{ATL, Acceleo, EMF, GMF, Eclipse\_IDE\}$.

## 2.3   Criteria for Evaluating Model Continuity

Model transformation is an automated process of modifying and creating one or several target models from one or several source models. The aim of model transformation is to save effort and reduce information loss as much as possible by automating model building and modification where possible. The key to designing a successful model transformation is a set of formal transformation rules to improve model continuity. Although there is no general guidance to define a good model transformation, we can evaluate model continuity according to the following criteria.

1. Correctness. A model transformation is syntactically correct if the target model conforms to the target metamodel specification [21], and semantically correct if the target model contains information as much as possible from the source model [22].
2. Completeness. A model transformation is complete if the target model has a corresponding element for each element in the source model.
3. Uniqueness. A model transformation is unique if there are no two identical elements in the generated target model.
4. Determinism. A model transformation is determinate if it produces a uniquely defined target model output for each specific source model input.

## 3   Customizing a DSML Based on Metamodeling

### 3.1   Metamodeling Based on EMF

Metamodeling is an important mean to design DSMLs [23, 24], especially for EMF usually has close relationships with a set of OMG standards, like UML, MOF, XMI, and MDA, etc. Firstly, UML is widely used to capture various concerns of a certain system by an object-oriented method, emphasizing multi-view to describe the structure, behavior, function, and deployment, etc. While, EMF as a way of defining metamodels is only concerned with one aspect of a system, i.e. class structure. Secondly, EMF/Ecore focuses on the tool sets not the metadata warehouse management, thus avoiding some of the complex issues such as data structure, package relationships, and associations compared to MOF. Thirdly, XMI is a widely accepted serializing standard which is not only used as the format for serializing EMF models, but also suitable for serializing the metamodel, i.e. Ecore itself. This method is very different with the UML profiling mechanism because it defines metamodels from scratch without considering the UML rules [25]. Hence, it has the potential for the most direct and succinct expression of domain concepts. Furthermore, it has a collection of supporting tools (e.g. GEF and GMF) thanks to the Eclipse open source architecture. Recently, some researches also have identified the need of domain specific metamodeling to avoid the general metamodeling facilities like UML and EMF [26].

Figure 3 shows the metamodel of GFCCS. This metamodel consists of a basic diagram node named GroupFireControlSystem and two mutually related nodes named Node and Connection respectively. The Node derives a set of domain concepts such as Group, GroupNode, Weapon, Target, and Channel, which are connected by specific relationships. For example, two groups can share common information by the relation tagged as COPShare that represents common operation picture (COP) [27]. A group can have one or multiple members and zero or multiple weapons which can also be equipped by a group member. A group member may be disjoint with or affiliated by itself, and can control zero or multiple fire control channels. Each channel may be mutually exclusive with itself. It embraces two dynamic entity lists, i.e. weaponList and targetList. These two lists are used to manage weapons and targets that are alive or may be already ruined. Only one target can be assigned to one weapon for building a running fire control channel.

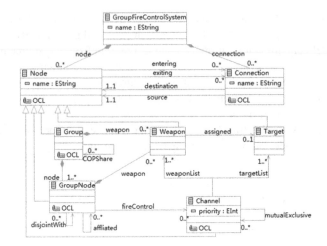

**Fig. 3.** The GFCCS metamodel.

In fact, except the abstract syntax as described above, there are other aspects need to be detailed for a well-defined metamodel [28]. Table 1 defines the static semantics of GFCCS metamodel, written by OCL [29], explaining how those elements of the abstract syntax model can be organized as a valid GFCCS metamodel.

**Table 1.** GFCCS domain specific constraints using OCL (part).

| OCL static semantics | Descriptions |
| --- | --- |
| context *Group*<br>inv: *hasNotDisjointGroupNodes*<br>self.*node->forAll(n1,n2\|n1.disjointWith-*<br>*>select(dis\|dis.name=n2.name)->isEmpty()*    *and*<br>*n2.disjointWith->select(dis\|dis.name=n1.name-*<br>*>isEmpty())* | A group can never own two disjoint members. |
| context *GroupNode*<br>inv: *hasNotDisjointChannels*<br>self.*fireControl->forAll(c1,c2\|c1.mutualExclusive-*<br>*>select(dis.name=c2.name)->isEmpty()*    *and*<br>*c2.mutualExclusive->select(dis\|dis.name=c1.name)-*<br>*>isEmpty())* | A group node can never own two mutual exclusive fire control channels. |
| context *GroupNode*<br>inv: *notDisjointWithItself*<br>self.*disjointWith->select(dis\|dis.name=self.name)-*<br>*>isEmpty()* | No group node can be disjoint with itself. |
| context *GroupNode*<br>inv: *notDisjointWithItsDownLevelNode*<br>self.*affiliated->forAll(n\|self.disjointWith-*<br>*>select(dis\|dis.name=n.name)->isEmpty())* | No group node can be disjoint with its senior node. |

## 3.2   Graphical Definitions of GFCCS Using GMF

Figure 4 shows a guidance of the definition, mapping, and generation of a graphical editor for GFCCS using GMF. According to the GMF dashboard, one can define the domain model, domain gen model, tooling model, graphical model, mapping model, and gmf gen model step by step, then generate the diagram editor.

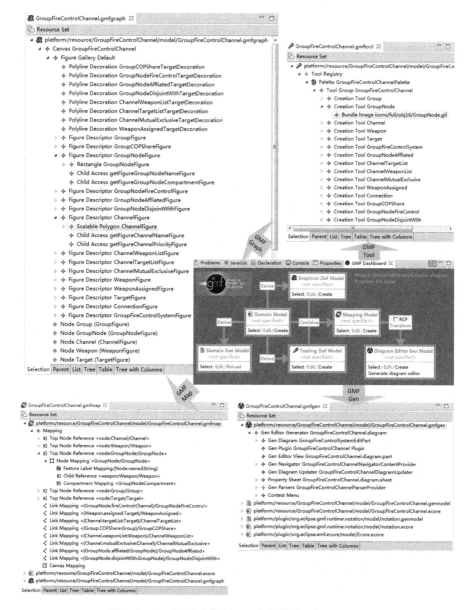

**Fig. 4.** Graphical definitions of GFCCS using GMF.

1. Tooling model. In usual, the tooling model definition provides six ways to define a tool palette of a graphical editor, including creation tool, standard tool, generic tool, tool group, palette separator, and image. In GFCCS, we created a tool for each element of the domain model except the abstract element Node, and bundled a representative image for each element.
2. Graphical model. It defines the concrete display of modeling elements that will be used in the graphical editing environment. In general, GMF provides default display based on the domain model, but one usually needs to define the figure gallery, figure descriptor, and polyline decoration in practice. In GFCCS, we set the Group and GroupNode as compartments to be able to contain other elements, for example, Group can contain GroupNode and Weapon, and GroupNode can contain Weapon. Additionally, we set the Channel as a scalable polygon, adding template points (0, 0), (40, 0), (40, 30), (30, 30), (30, 40), (40, 30), (30, 40), (0, 40).
3. Mapping model. When the domain model, tooling model, and graphical model are ready, it is necessary to map them into a whole. Usually, we need to select the corresponding tooling nodes and diagram nodes for each node mapping, and provide the correct compartment figure for each compartment node. In the properties of Channel node, for example, we select the Node Channel (Channel Figure) for the diagram node, and the Creation Tool Channel for the tooling node.
4. GMF gen model. If the mapping model is defined correctly, it can generate correct gmf gen model without much modifications. In many cases, it is possible to modify some parameters, such as the fixed background, the list layout, and the suffix of a diagram project.

### 3.3    The GFCCS DSME

Figure 5 shows a simple example of building an engagement scenario using the GFCCS DSML. On the tool palette, this domain specific modeling environment (DSME) contains a set of buttons decorated with professional denotations, including the basic language elements such as GroupFireControlSystem, Group, GroupNode, Channel, Weapon, and Target as well as various relationships. Using this environment, it is possible for domain experts to use these language elements intuitively and friendly. For example, one can draw an arrow from Channel List 1 to Enemy Fighter 1 BLUE only by ChannelTargetList, disabling the use of other relationship buttons.

In the editor, we create a scenario of many to many combat between two opposite sides RED and BLUE. The RED side consists of two defense groups, i.e. Defense System RED and Remote Surveillance System RED, which refers to the local defense system (e.g. air defense base) and the remote surveillance system (e.g. satellite). The local system is composed of a warship platform, a ground-to-air missile base, and a helicopter platform, which are armed with two surface-to-air missiles, a ground-to-air missile, and a homing torpedo, respectively. The BLUE side consists of three coming threats which are denoted by Enemy Fighter 1 BLUE, Enemy Fighter 2 BLUE, and Enemy Submarine BLUE. In addition, there exist two lists of fire control channel which are denoted by Channel List 1 and Channel List 2, respectively. The former list is managed by the warship platform and has a weapon-target pair, i.e. Surface2AirMissile1-Enemy Fighter 1 BLUE. The latter list is managed by the helicopter platform and has two weapon-target pairs.

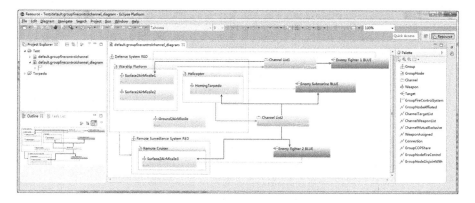

**Fig. 5.** The GFCCS DSME. (Color figure online)

## 4   Model Transformations: GFCCS Implementations

### 4.1   The Process of GFCCS Implementation

Assume we need to build the process of GFCCS implementation as illustrated in the conceptual sample of Fig. 6. Our aim is therefore to define a set of transformation rules facilitating the transformation from CIM to PIM to PSM, then to final source code. The transformation has two kinds across three levels.

In the first kind, all CIM_GFCCS model elements are expected to be transformed into specific PIM_P-DEVS model elements, and all connections are transformed into internal couplings from an output port in the source component to an input port in the target component. Ports are also generated. But in most cases, this does not apply because the connections in the source model do not always connect the elements of the same layer [30]. Therefore, it is necessary to refine such connections which cross more than one layer, and define the external input couplings (EICs) and external output couplings (EOCs) for the compartmental components. For example, while the group named Defense System RED and the group nodes named Warship Platform and Helicopter are transformed into coupled components, the weapon named Surface2AirMissile1 is transformed into an atomic component.

In the second kind, a transformation from PIM_P-DEVS to PSM_JAVA is defined according to a set of predefined transformation rules. In this transformation, all P-DEVS components are transformed into JAVA classes. Coupled components are transformed into files that include the package imports, class, constructor, port, contained component, and couplings. Atomic components are transformed into files that include package imports, class, port, and constructor.

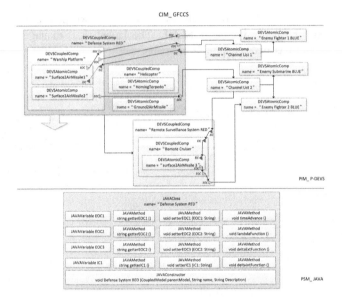

**Fig. 6.** A sample of GFCCS to P-DEVS to JAVA transformations based on MDA.

## 4.2 Detailed GFCCS to P-DEVS to JAVA Transformations

The matching rules of GFCCS to P-DEVS transformation is defined by using the GFCCS metamodel and P-DEVS metamodel, as detailed in Table 2. The basic diagram node GourpFireControlSystem matches with the DEVSModel element. The compartmental nodes like Group and GroupNode match with coupled components named DEVSCoupledComp. The connections that connect the modeling elements of the same layer are transformed into internal transitions named DEVSOutToIn_ICConnection, while those cross different layers are transformed into external transitions and output functions with a set of ports.

**Table 2.** The matching rules of GFCCS to P-DEVS transformation (part).

| GFCCS metamodel | P-DEVS metamodel |
|---|---|
| GroupFireControlSystem | DEVSModel |
| Group | DEVSCoupledComp |
| Weapon | DEVSAtomicComp |
| Target | DEVSAtomicComp |
| COPShare | DEVSOutToIn_ICConnection |
| fireControl | DEVSOutToOut_ICConnection<br>+Source.out: DEVSOutputPort<br>+Target.in: DEVSOutputPort<br>+SourceParents.EOCPorts: DEVSOutputPort |
| mutualExclusive | DEVSOutToIn_ICConnection |
| taretList | DEVSOutToIn_ICConnection |

The matching rules of P-DEVS to JAVA transformation is defined by using the P-DEVS metamodel and JAVA metamodel, as detailed in Table 3. The basic element DEVSModel matches with a JAVA package named JAVAPackage which includes javaClasses, javaConstructors, and javaExpressions. Both the coupled component DEVSCoupledComp and the atomic component DEVSAtomicComp match with JAVA classes which include JAVAVariables, javaConstructors, and javaExpressions. DEVSInputPort, DEVSOutputPort, and StateVariable are all transformed into JAVAVariables. The connections like DEVSOutToIn_ICConnection, DEVSInToIn_EICConnection, DEVSOutToOut_EOCConnection as well as Expression are transformed into JAVAExpressions. The remaining functions like DeltaIntFunction, DeltaExtFunction, LambdaFunction, TimeAdvanceFunction, DeltaConFunction are all transformed into JAVAMethods.

Such transformation rules are written in ATL, as proposed in Definition 2. ATL, the Atlas Transformation Language, is a model transformation language specified as both a metamodel and a textual concrete syntax. In the MDE field, ATL provides developers with a means to specify the way to produce a number of target models from a set of source models. An ATL transformation program is composed of rules that define how source model elements are matched and navigated to create and initialize the elements of the target models. Besides, ATL Integrated Development Environment (IDE) provides a number of standard development tools (syntax highlighting, debugger, etc.) that aim to ease the design of ATL transformations. The ATL development environment also offers a number of additional facilities dedicated to models and metamodels handling. These features include a simple textual notation dedicated to the specification of metamodels, but also a number of standard bridges between common textual syntaxes and their corresponding model representations.

**Table 3.** The matching rules of P-DEVS to JAVA transformation (part).

| P-DEVS metamodel | JAVA metamodel |
|---|---|
| DEVSModel | JAVAPackage<br>+javaClasses: JAVAClass<br>+javaConstructors: JAVAConstructor<br>+javaExpressions: JAVAExpression |
| DEVSInputPort | JAVAVariable |
| DEVSOutputPort | JAVAVariable |
| StateVariable | JAVAVariable |
| DEVSOutToIn_ICConnection | JAVAExpression |
| DEVSInToIn_EICConnection | JAVAExpression |
| DEVSOutToOut_EOCConnection | JAVAExpression |
| Expression | JAVAExpression |
| DeltaIntFunction | JAVAMethod |
| DeltaExtFunction | JAVAMethod |
| LambdaFunction | JAVAMethod |
| DeltaConFunction | JAVAMethod |

Figure 7 shows the transformations of GFCCS to P-DEVS to JAVA instances based on ATL. On the left contains two projects named GFCCS2P-DEVS and P-DEVS2JAVA, each of which includes three packages, i.e. Metamodels, Models, and TransoformationEngine. On the upper right includes three instances for the GFCCS, P-DEVS, and JAVA metamodel respectively, while the lower right is two ATL files for the GFCCS to P-DEVS and to JAVA transformations.

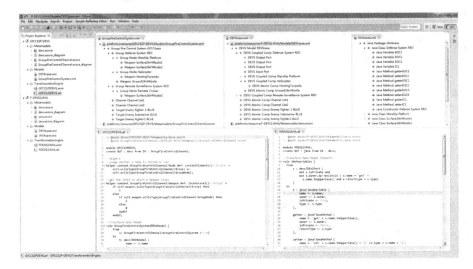

**Fig. 7.** GFCCS to P-DEVS to JAVA transformations based on ATL.

## 4.3   Source Code Generation

Figure 8 shows a screenshot of the M2T transformation model as well as its source model and the generated code framework for the node Defense_System_RED. The transformation model design should incorporate all the source model required information to satisfy completeness. The target code framework is automatically generated, but the concrete logic details must be manually implemented. In practice, not every concrete detail should be considered when designing M2T transformation models, because they may heavily burden the design phase.

Following the M2T transformation principles, the general source model is some instance models that must conform to a certain metamodel, and the target model can be text, e.g. java, C++, python, etc. Transformation model design is vital to implement the M2T transformation. This paper performed M2T transformation using Acceleo, a template based code generator incorporating a code generation editor with syntax highlighting, completion, real time error detection, and refactoring. The source model was a collection of JAVA instance models, represented by an instance file named JAVAcase.xmi, and the target model was described in Java programming text.

**Fig. 8.** JAVA xmi to code transformation based on Acceleo.

### 4.4 Model Continuity in GFCCS

The process of GFCCS implementation showed that model continuity between different development stages is obtained when applying the formal transformation definition successfully. As stated earlier, it is possible to provide model continuity in a development process when transforming the initial and intermediate models, and preserving the modeling relations during the transformations. To evaluate model continuity, we already presented the criteria for model transformations in Sect. 2.3. According to these criteria, we describe how the model continuity is obtained for the process of GFCCS implementation when the formal transformation rules are applied. In fact, except these criteria as listed, there are some other non-functional requirements such as termination and readability satisfied. Also note that maintainability, scalability, reusability, evolvability, efficiency, etc. are partially supported since these requirements need more experiments for a better evaluation.

The process of GFCCS implementation has two kinds of model transformation, with different expressions and output types. As the source input or target output of model transformations, the formal definition gives three model types: independent of computing details, independent of the computing platform, and specific to a particular computing platform, and two model transformation categories.

In the M2M category, the transformation focuses on the design of a set of formal rules to ensure model continuity when transforming CIM to PIM and to PSM. The transformation usually incorporates three steps.

1. All source concepts, relationships, and domain specific rules are transformed into particular target elements, connections, and domain specific constraints, respectively.
2. Compare all target elements, connections, and constraints to delete identical expressions.

3. Check the target model conforms to the target metamodel.

Completeness can be ensured in step (1) since all source elements are transformed, and a corresponding target element can be found for each source element. Step (2) is helpful and necessary to reduce target element redundancy, thus uniqueness is guaranteed. Syntactical correctness can be satisfied in step (3) since the target model will be expressed in a given formalism, and its semantic correctness will be evaluated in later stages of model transformation. Determinism is guaranteed implicitly in the model transformation editors, such as ATL IDE, which eases development and execution of ATL transformations [31].

In the M2T category, the transformation converts a source model into a text file, i.e. PSM to source code. If the text is in source code form, then the transformation is also called code generation, and the transformer is also called a code generator. The process of a M2T transformation is similar to that of a M2M transformation. The only difference is that step (ii) in the M2M transformation can be skipped in a M2T transformation, since uniqueness has already been checked. Therefore, the three criteria listed above are achieved according steps (i) and (iii). Similarly, determinism is satisfied because model transformation editors, such as Acceleo [32], implicitly guarantee a unique output for each particular input.

## 5   Conclusions

Abstraction is now widely admitted as an effective means to reduce the complexity of system specification. It is also generally agreed that ontology as an important form of abstraction can be employed in MDE to describe the existing world, the environment, and the domain of system. However, this consensus has not lead to a coherent research on how to enhance the semantic composability of simulation models yet. Hence, this study attempts to adopt an ontological metamodeling method for engineering the semantic composability of simulation models within MDE. We believe that the experience collected from this study can bring some new visions of simulation models development and of the state of art that relate to the semantic composability. A benefit of this study is that the formal definition of model transformation can be viewed as a referenced experience to guide other practices that have the needs of formal analysis. However, as a drawback some effort for further evaluations are required.

## References

1. Bryant, B.R., Gray, J., Mernik, M., Clarke, P.J., France, R.B., Karsal, G.: Challenges and directions in formalizing the semantics of modeling languages. ComSIS **8**(2), 225–253 (2011). Special Issue
2. Abdulah, M.S.: A UML profile for conceptual modeling of knowledge-based systems. Ph.D. thesis. University of York, York, England (2006)
3. Langer, P., Wieland, K., Wimmer, M., Cabot, J.: From UML profiles to EMF profiles and beyond. In: Bishop, J., Vallecillo, A. (eds.) TOOLS 2011. LNCS, vol. 6705, pp. 52–67. Springer, Heidelberg (2011). https://doi.org/10.1007/978-3-642-21952-8_6

4. Ledeczi, A., Maroti, M., Bakay, A., Karsai, G., et al.: The generic modeling environment. In: IEEE International Workshop on Intelligent Signal Processing, Budapest, Hungary, pp. 1–6 (2001)
5. Getir, S., Challenger, M., Kardas, G.: The formal semantics of a domain-specific modeling language for semantic web enabled multi-agent systems. Int. J. Coop. Inf. Syst. **23**(3), 1–53 (2014)
6. Meyers, B.: A multi-paradigm modeling approach to design and evolution of domain-specific modeling languages. Ph.D. thesis. University of Antwerpen, Antwerpen, Belgium (2016)
7. Schmidt, D.C.: Guest editor's introduction: model-driven engineering. IEEE Comput. **39**(2), 25–31 (2006)
8. Sarjoughian, H.S.: Model composability. In: 38th WSC Proceedings, Monterey, CA, pp. 149–158 (2006)
9. Hardebolle, C., Boulanger, F.: Exploring multi-paradigm modeling techniques. Simulation **85**(11–12), 688–708 (2009)
10. Mosterman, P.J., Vangheluwe, H.: Computer automated multi-paradigm modeling: an introduction. Simulation **80**(9), 433–450 (2004)
11. Lei, Y.L., Li, Q., Yang, F., Wang, W.P., Zhu, Y.F.: A composable modeling framework for weapon systems effectiveness simulation. Syst. Eng.-Theory Pract. **33**(11), 2954–2966 (2013)
12. Çetinkaya, D.: Model driven development of simulation models: defining and transforming conceptual models into simulation models by using metamodels and model transformations. M.S. thesis. Middle East Technical University, geboren te Konya, Turkije (2013)
13. Hu, X., Zeigler, B.P.: Model continuity in the design of dynamic distributed real-time systems. IEEE Trans. Syst. Man Cybern. - Part A: Syst. Hum. **35**(6), 867–878 (2005)
14. Balci, O.: A life cycle for modeling and simulation. Simulation **8**(7), 870–883 (2012)
15. Zhu, Z., Lei, Y.L., Zhu, N., Zhu, Y.F.: Composable modeling frameworks for networked air & missile defense systems. J. Natl. Univ. Defense Technol. **36**(5), 186–190 (2014)
16. Strembeck, M., Zdun, U.: An approach for the systematic development of domain-specific languages. Softw. Pract. Exper. **39**(15), 1253–1292 (2010)
17. Ehrig, H., Ermel, C.: Semantical correctness and completeness of model transformations using graph and rule transformation. In: Ehrig, H., Heckel, R., Rozenberg, G., Taentzer, G. (eds.) ICGT 2008. LNCS, vol. 5214, pp. 194–210. Springer, Heidelberg (2008). https://doi.org/10.1007/978-3-540-87405-8_14
18. Mens, T., Gorp, P.V.: A taxonomy of model transformation. Electron. Notes Theoret. Comput. Sci. **152**(1–2), 125–142 (2005)
19. Kleppe, A., Warmer, J., Bast, W.: MDA Explained: The Model Driven Architecture™: Practice and Promise. Addison-Wesley, Boston (2003)
20. Zeigler, B.P., Praehofer, H., Kim, T.G.: Theory of Modeling and Simulation: Integrating Discrete Event and Continuous Complex Dynamic Systems, 2nd edn. Academic Press, San Diego (2000)
21. Szabo, C., Teo, Y.M.: On syntactic composability and model reuse. In: 1st Asia International Proceedings on Modeling and Simulation, Phuket, Thailand, pp. 230–237 (2007)
22. Estanol, M., Sancho, M.R., Teniente, E.: Ensuring the semantic correctness of a BAUML artifact-centric BPM. Inf. Softw. Technol. **93**, 147–162 (2018)
23. Atkinson, C., Kuhne, T.: Model-driven development: a metamodeling foundtion. IEEE Softw. **20**(5), 36–41 (2003)
24. Nordstrom, G., Sztipanovits, J., Karsai, G., Ledeczi, A.: Metamodeling - rapid design and evolution of domain-specific modeling environments. In: IEEE Proceedings on Engineering of Computer-Based Systems, Nashville, TN, pp. 68–74 (1999)

25. Zhu, Z., Lei, Y.L., Zhu, Y.F., Sarjoughian, H.S.: Cognitive behaviors modeling using UML profile. IEEE Access **5**, 21694–21708 (2017)
26. De, L.J., Guerra, E., Cuadrado, J.S.: Model-driven engineering with domain-specific meta-modeling languages. Softw. Syst. Model **14**(1), 429–459 (2015)
27. Seo, K.M., Choi, C., Kim, T.G., Kim, J.H.: DEVS-based combat modeling for engagement-level simulation. Simulation **90**(7), 759–781 (2014)
28. Selic, B.: A systematic approach to domain-specific language design using UML. In: 10th IEEE International Proceedings on Object and Component-Oriented Real-Time Distributed Computing, Santorini Island, Greece, pp. 2–9 (2007)
29. Warmer, J., Kleppe, A.: The Object Constraint Language-Precise Modeling with UML. Addison-Wesley, Boston (1999)
30. Álvarez, J.M., Evans, A., Sammut, P.: Mapping between levels in the metamodel architecture. In: Gogolla, M., Kobryn, C. (eds.) UML 2001. LNCS, vol. 2185, pp. 34–46. Springer, Heidelberg (2001). https://doi.org/10.1007/3-540-45441-1_4
31. Jouault, F., Allilaire, F., Bezivin, J., Kurtev, I.: ATL: a model transformation tool. Sci. Comput. Program. **72**(1–2), 31–39 (2008)
32. Benouda, H., Essbai, R., Azizi, M., Moussaoui, M.: Modeling and code generation of Android applications using acceleo. Int. J. Softw. Eng. Appl. **10**(3), 83–94 (2013)

# Congestion Control for RTP Media:
# A Comparison on Simulated Environment

Songyang Zhang⬩, Weimin Lei(✉)⬩, Wei Zhang⬩, and Yunchong Guan⬩

School of Computer Science and Engineering, Northeastern University,
Shenyang, China
leiweimin@ise.neu.edu.cn

**Abstract.** The audio and video applications based on Real Time Protocol (RTP) have been exploded in recent years. To develop low latency congestion control algorithms for real time traffic to provide better quality of experience and to avoid network congestion has gained much attention. RTP Media Congestion Avoidance Techniques (RMCAT) working group was initiated for proposal draft. Currently, there are three algorithms under this group, Network Assisted Dynamic Adaptation (NADA), Google Congestion Control (GCC) and Self-Clocked Rate Adaptation for Multimedia (SCReAM). This paper integrates the three algorithms into simulated platform and their performances are compared and analyzed. Results show GCC has well fairness property and can maintain quite reasonable packet sending rate in loss link but converges a bit slowly in dynamic link, NADA stabilizes its rate quickly but suffers from "late-comer" effect, SCReAM has the lowest queue occupation but also lower link capacity utilization.

**Keywords:** Congestion control · RTP media congestion control · Real time traffic · ns3 simulation

## 1 Introduction

Pioneered by Jocobson's work [1], which later developed into TCP Reno algorithm, network congestion control has been an unfading topic in computer networks research. The control law proposed by Jocobson is to regulate TCP sending rate according to additive increase and multiplicative decrease (AIMD) rule, which developed as TCP Reno. It takes packet loss as network congestion signal. On every RTT, the sender could send one more packet into network to probe more available bandwidth and multiplicatively reduces congestion window size by half when packet loss happens to alleviate link congestion.

This work was supported by the National Key Research and Development Program of China (2018YFB1702000), the Liaoning Provincial Natural Science Foundation of China (No. 20180551007), and the National Natural Science Foundation of China (No. 61671141).

H. Song et al. (Eds.): SIMUtools 2019, LNICST 295, pp. 43–52, 2019.
https://doi.org/10.1007/978-3-030-32216-8_4

From then on, most of the research works such as Bic [2], Cubic [3], were proposed to improve TCP performance and adapted the basic AIMD control law to different network environment.

The congestion control algorithms in TCP are mainly compliant with bulk data transfer. The additive increase of TCP during its congestion avoid phase cause packet sending rate showing saw-tooth feature. If such mechanism is applied directly to real time video applications, the AIMD rate control would cause the instability of video encoder. Further, the packet lost retransmission and in order delivery in TCP would introduce further latency, which makes it unfit for time stringent traffic transmission. The real time video traffic is quite sensitive to connection latency but can suffer some packets loss to some extent. So RTP-based media is usually streamed over UDP.

In an early stage, the implementation of congestion control on UDP for video streaming is quite scarce, due to the consideration that an insufferable QoE (Quality of Experience) of connection would make the users give up video call, which can be seen as a mechanism of congestion avoidance. The network condition has changed in better direction and is used in a different manner as it was ten years ago.

If large scale video stream flows do not implement any congestion control mechanism, the bandwidth competition would lead Internet into congestion. The extra packets would be buffered in the intermediate router when the link is in congestion. Once the queue length has increased above the link queue threshold, the router would follow active queue mechanism by dropping packets and the link transmission delay will increase. Even though there were some works [4,5] making an effort to exploit congestion control for UDP streaming media before, none of these algorithms have been applied in practice.

To develop new congestion control algorithm for real time traffic has gained renewed attention in recent years, especially since the open source of Web Real-Time Communication (WebRTC) which enables real time communication between browsers. As pointed by [6], all the flows across internet should implement congestion control scheme for internet congestion avoidance and promote fair bandwidth occupation. The IETF has initiated The RTP Media Congestion Avoidance Techniques (RMCAT) Working Group to develop congestion standards for interactive real-time media. And there are mainly three congestion control drafts under this working group, namely, GCC [7], NADA [8], SCReAM [9].

In this paper, we work our way to get the three RMCAT algorithms running in ns-3[1] and make a full comparison in terms of fairness, aggressiveness, bandwidth utilization and link queue occupancy. The simulation code of NADA[2] on ns3 was already released by its author. So the work is mainly focused on the implementation of GCC, SCReAM. The simulation code of this work can be downloaded at[3].

---

[1] https://www.nsnam.org/.

[2] https://github.com/cisco/ns3-rmcat.

[3] https://github.com/SoonyangZhang/rmcat-ns3.

The main contribution of this work is the algorithms code transplantation on simulated platform and the final results can be taken for reference for interested readers.

The rest of this paper is organized as follows. Section 2 describes the principle of these algorithms involved in simulation in detail. Section 3 is the simulation results and analysis. The conclusion is in Sect. 4.

## 2  Algorithm Description

This part briefly describes the algorithms involved in our experiments. The GCC algorithm exploits one-way delay gradient as control signal. The old version of GCC has two components: a delay based congestion controller, running at the receiver side, computes a rate $A_r$ based on Kalman filter according to frame delay signal which is fed back through RTCP Receiver Estimated Maximum Bitrate (REMB) report; a loss based controller running at sender side, computes a target bitrate $A_s$ which shall not exceed $A_r$. Kalman filter is adopted at the receiver side to compute the link queue delay gradient. In newer release version of WebRTC, the congestion control logics have all been moved to the sender side. A trend line filter has been introduced for congestion inference. We refer here the old version WebRTC congestion control based on Kalman filter as REMB-GCC and the newer version based on trend-line filter is referred as TFB-GCC (transport feedback GCC). The algorithm designers have published several papers on REMB-GCC, please refer to [10] for more information. We analyze the TFB-GCC in detail considering there is no public available paper on its working principle. In GCC, the receiver will feedback packets arrival time to the sender through the RTCP extensions for transport-wide congestion control [11]. The feedback message will be sent at an adaption interval according to bandwidth. When the feedback message arrives, the sender extracts out the arriving time of a sent packet, and divides them into groups by length of five milliseconds.

The packets group is similar to the frame notation in [10] for the purpose of channel overuse detection. The time_stamp is the time sending out the first packet and complete_time is the time of last packet arriving to the destination of the same group. The $j$-th group one-way delay gradient is computed as follows:

$$
\begin{aligned}
delta\_ms_j = (G_j.complete\_time - G_{j-1}.complete\_time) \\
- (G_j.timestamp - G_{j-1}.timestamp).
\end{aligned}
\tag{1}
$$

Then compute the accumulated delay:

$$
acc\_delay_i = \sum_{j=1}^{i} delta\_ms_j.
\tag{2}
$$

And then smooth the delay signal with a coefficient alpha by default 0.9.

$$
\begin{aligned}
smoothed\_delay_i = smoothing\_coef * smoothed\_delay_{i-1} \\
+ (1 - smoothing\_coef) * acc\_delay_i
\end{aligned}
\tag{3}
$$

A linear regression was carried out in trend-line filter with input values of (x, y).

$$(x, y) \Rightarrow (G_i.complete\_time - G_1.complete\_time,$$
$$smoothed\_delay_i). \tag{4}$$

$$trendline\_slope = \frac{\sum(x_i - x_{avg})(y_i - y_{avg})}{\sum(x_i - x_{avg})^2} \tag{5}$$

The trend line slope is a reflection of link queue status. When the link queue length increases, the inter-arriving space among packets tends to increase also. The overuse detector compares the value of trend line slope with a dynamic threshold to decide if the channel is in the state of underuse or overuse. The dynamic threshold is explained by the designer [12] to tune the sensitivity of the algorithm. A small threshold will make the detector quick detect the channel state changes but with the drawback of overreacting in case of noise. A large threshold would make the algorithm robust to noise but sluggish to channel state change. And a constant threshold would make the GCC flows starvation in competing with loss based TCP flows as reported by [13]. After the overuse detector computes out the channel state, the AIMD controller adjusts the bitrate according to the equation:

$$A(t_i) = \begin{cases} A(t_{i-1}) + \overline{A} \ Increase \\ \beta R(t_{i-1}) \ Decrease, \\ A(t_i) \ Hold. \end{cases} \tag{6}$$

where $\beta = 0.85$, and $R(t_{i-1})$ is the average receiving rate estimated at the sender side based on feedback message. The value of $\overline{A}$ is depended on the rate control region. After the rate is decreased, the controller would set the rate control region in state of near-max. After the channel is detected underuse and the control region is in near-max state, the AIMD controller would additively increase rate, otherwise, the rate is multiplicatively increased.

There is a detailed description and comparison between GCC and NADA on the WebRTC codebase platform in [14]. Their experiment was conducted on real network testbed.

The NADA has experienced several updates since its original release [8]. Basically, the NADA algorithm control its packet sending rate according to an aggregated congestion signal as shown in Eq. (7). $p_{loss}$ and $p_{mark}$ are the penalty prices when a sent packet is dropped or marked by the intermediate router to indicate the link in congestion status. The mark signal has the same purpose as the explicit congestion notification in TCP to enable end to end congestion notification without dropping packets.

$$x_n(t_i) = \tilde{d}(t_i) + p_{loss} * D_{loss} + p_{mark} * D_{mark} \tag{7}$$

Here, the term $\tilde{d}(t_i)$ is computed as Eq. (8) and $QTH$ is 50 ms. $d_q$ is computed as the following. The receiver would send feedback message every 100 ms. The feedback message contains the timestamp $R_{ts}$ that a sent packet arrives the destination. The sender would record the history packets sent within 500 ms and could compute the one way delay value $d(i) = R_{ts} - S_{ts}$. Then one way delay variance is computed $owdv(i) = d(i) - d_{min}$, which is an indication of the link congestion status. $d_{min}$ is the minimal one way delay during the session. And the minimal $owdv$ during the last 500 ms is assigned to $d_q$.

$$\tilde{d}(t_i) = \begin{cases} d_q & d_q < QTH \\ QTHe^{-\lambda\frac{d_q-QTH}{QTH}} & \text{otherwise} \end{cases} \tag{8}$$

The rate control law of NADA is a piece function shown as Eq. (9). According to the link status, it would follow different control function. When the session is just established, $rmode = 0$, the sender is in accelerated ramp up state, and the sending rate is the product of the computed packet receive rate and a gain $1+\gamma$, where $\gamma = min(0.5, \frac{QTH}{rtt+\delta})$. The rate gain is exploited for available bandwidth probe purpose. The accelerated ramp up state is quite similar to TCP slow start phase. Once a packet loss event is detected during this observation period or the one way delay variance exceeds 10 ms, the sender would enter into the gradual rate update state.

$$R_n(t_k) = \begin{cases} (1+\gamma)R_n(t_{k-1}) & rmode = 0 \\ R_n(t_{k-1})(1 - K_1x_o(t_k) - K_2x_d(t_k)) & rmode = 1 \end{cases} \tag{9}$$

And $K1$, $K2$ are two constants, and $x_o$, $x_d$ are the offset value from a reference $x_{ref}$ and difference value, where $x_{ref}$ is 10 ms.

$$x_o(t_k) = x_n(t_k) - x_{ref}\frac{R_{max}}{R_n(t_k)} \tag{10}$$

$$x_d(t_k) = x_n(t_k) - x_n(t_{k-1}) \tag{11}$$

The rate control function of NADA in the gradual rate update state is similar to a PID (proportional–integral–derivative) controller. If the aggregate congestion signal has a decrease tendency ($x_d < 0$), the sender would increase its packet injecting rate according to the control function. When the current rate decreases to a small value, the component $x_o$ would control the sender to inject burst packets into network to make a quickly convergence to the available rate. When the sending rate approaches the link available rate, the action of rate increase would link queue length increase and the extra sent packet would at a high risk in lost, which would make the control term $x_o$, $x_d$ positive value, and NADA sender would actively decrease its rate to avoid congestion and self-inflicted queue delay. Such feature of NADA makes highly network bandwidth utilization, which is verified by simulation results.

SCReAM basically controls the upper limit packets in flight by sliding congestion window. The receiver will feedback the timestamp of received packet with the highest sequence number and an acknowledgement vector to indicate the reception or loss of previous packets. Its congestion control method based on queue delay signal was inspired by LEDBAT, which has claimed for the low network queue delay purpose by inferring congestion earlier. When the one-way queue delay under the target queue delay, the algorithm will increase the congestion window, otherwise decrease the window.

# 3   Simulation Comparison

The version of simulation platform is ns-3.26. A point to point link as suggested by [15] was created with link bandwidth 2 Mbps, one way delay 100 ms and buffer length (300 ms * 2 Mbps).

## 3.1   Protocol Responsiveness

Considering the popularity of mobile devices, the RTP-based media over mobile phone is quite common. The cellular access network link can present drastic change in channel bandwidth in a short time span due to noise interference and fading. The rate control algorithm for conversational video over wireless links should react quickly to network change and operates in a wide range of bandwidth. When the link bandwidth decreases, the video generator keeping the rate before would make the link queue build up and the end latency increase. When the link bandwidth increases, the sender could not make fully use of network resource if the rate do not change. The increased latency, the packet dropping event and the low video encoding rate is harmful to QoE for users.

In experiment, the link bandwidth is changed every 20 s from 500 kbps to 2 Mbps. The link is exclusively occupied by a single GCC, NADA, SCReAM. During the simulation process, the rate adjustment of the congestion control algorithm is logged and the one way delay of received packet was recorded. The one way delay is an indication of link queue occupation. When the link is in congestion status and the sent packet would be queued in router buffer, which results in high one way delay. The results in Fig. 1 have clearly shown the reaction difference of these protocols when link capacity changes. The AIMD controller in GCC for rate adjustment is the reason of its rate saw-tooth feature. When the link capacity decreases, GCC makes a quick rate adjustment to prevent link

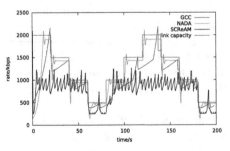

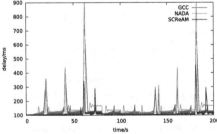

**Fig. 1.** The responsiveness of three algorithms

**Fig. 2.** Packet one way delay

from congestion. NADA can quickly respond to network change. SCReAM is sensitive to capacity decrease, but reacts sluggishly to capacity increase.

The average link bandwidth utilization is shown in Table 1. The link utilization is computed according Eq. (12), in which the term $\bar{x}$ is the average simulated encoder video packets generating rate determined by congestion algorithm and $BW$ is the link capacity during the test period. NADA has the highest channel utilization and SCReAM makes the lowest channel utilization which may cause by its rate ramp-up parameter.

$$bw\_u = \frac{\bar{x}}{BW} \tag{12}$$

**Table 1.** Average link utilization

| Utilization — Time(s) <br> Protocol | 0-20 | 20-40 | 40-60 | 60-80 | 80-100 |
|---|---|---|---|---|---|
| GCC | 56.79% | 88.10% | 89.28% | 86.19% | 71.58% |
| NADA | 80.41% | 95.54% | 95.80% | 98.69% | 92.65% |
| SCReAM | 43.41% | 61.08% | 87.54% | 62.79% | 76.76% |

From the one-way delay variation curve in Fig. 2, SCReAM reaches its claimed goal by having the lowest queue delay occupation close to one-way link transmission delay. NADA and GCC make link queue build up to some extent. All three protocols show instantaneous delay spike when faced sharp bandwidth decrease.

### 3.2   Intra Protocol Fairness

Protocol fairness is an important indication to reflect whether an end user converges to a fair bandwidth rate when sharing link with other flows. In this experiment, three flows exploiting the same congestion control protocol were initiated at different time point over a bottleneck link. The second flow was started after 40 s and the third flow was started at 80 s. The link capacity keeps to be a constant value 2 Mbps during the simulation.

In Fig. 3, the rates of all three GCC flows after 150 s are very close, indicating the GCC protocol has fine fairness property. It's worth noticing the NADA protocol suffers from "late-comer effect" in Fig. 4, the late coming flow data sending rate is higher than the flows initiated before. This result is different from the conclusion in [10]. The "late-comer effect" may be caused by that not all flows have equal aggregate congestion price in gradual rate update phase. The SCReAM protocol in Fig. 5 shows no sign that the flows converge to a fairness rate. Due to the effect of link queue building up, the rate adjustment of SCReAM shows oscillation.

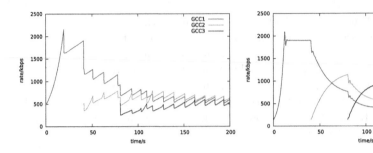

**Fig. 3.** Sending rate of GCC flows     **Fig. 4.** Sending rate of NADA flows

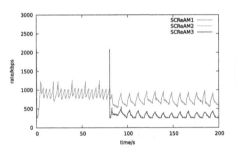
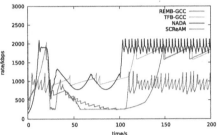

**Fig. 5.** Sending rate of SCReAM flows     **Fig. 6.** RMCAT flow sharing links with TCP

### 3.3    Inter Protocol Competition

In real network, a routing path can be shared by many flows, which may exploit different congestion control protocol. When sharing links with background traffic, the ability to make a reasonable bandwidth occupation of a protocol is quite important. For testing purpose, an experiment was designed for a RMCAT flow sharing link with a TCP Reno flow. The TCP flow was started at 20 s and stopped at 100 s. Even though the REMB-GCC was deprecated in new version of WebRTC, we test its performance here. The result is shown in Fig. 6.

When the TCP connection flows into the link, REMB-GCC flow keeps yielding its bandwidth until reaching the smallest point. TFB-GCC and NADA in Fig. 6 can maintain a reasonable sending rate. SCReAM also decreases its rate to the minimal default rate due to link delay increase caused by the loss based rate control TCP flow. When the link buffer on the merge of full, packet loss event would happen and the TCP flows would half its congestion window to relieve the link from further congestion, the queue delay decrease signal would make NADA and TFB-GCC increase its rate. This explains why the rate curves of NADA and TFB-GCC have increase tendency even in the presence of TCP flow. When TCP flow exits off the network at the time point 100, NADA can make faster increase to reach a rate near the link capacity than TFB-GCC. It should be pointed out NADA flow shows small oscillation even when the tcp flow withdraws from the link, which is caused by its piecewise rate control function. This is caused by its rate control function in gradual rate update phase for congestion avoidance.

### 3.4   Packet Loss Resistance

In wireless links, packet loss may cause by wireless link interference, channel contention and errors. A protocol takes random packet loss as congestion signal and reacts it by rate decreasing will have degenerated performance and low channel utilization. In this experiment, the link is configured with different random packet loss rate, and the link is monopolized by a single flow during the simulation.

In experiment, GCC flow is not quite affected by random packet loss. As the packet loss rate increases, NADA and SCReAM decrease bitrate quite obvious. In the case of 5% packet loss, GCC can hold 82.05% channel utilization on average, and both NADA and SCReAM have quite low link utilization shown in Table 2.

**Table 2.** Capacity utilization in lossy link

| Utilization \ loss rate <br><br> Protocol | 0.0% | 1% | 5% |
|:---:|:---:|:---:|:---:|
| GCC | 86.32% | 85.81% | 82.05% |
| NADA | 94.28% | 92.65% | 14.40% |
| SCReAM | 57.62% | 15.30% | 13.04% |

## 4   Conclusion

The main work of this paper makes a full comparison and analysis of these congestion control algorithms for RTP media in respect of protocol responsiveness, intra protocol fairness, inter protocol competence and performance in loss link.

The results from simulation are summarized here. GCC works well in intra protocol fairness but has saw tooth feature in dynamic links. NADA can quickly stabilize its rate in dynamic links and has the most efficient network capacity utilization when the link is not affected by random loss, but suffers from "late comer effect". SCReAM retains the link queue delay in a low level but has low channel utilization. GCC has better performance in loss link, which makes it particularly suitable for wireless network. To design a protocol with advantages of these algorithms should be our future work.

With the popular of video based applications, to design new congestion control algorithm for real time traffic will further draw researchers' attention. And the old tree of congestion control research areas always springs new sprouts such as TCP BBR.

# References

1. Jacobson, V.: Congestion avoidance and control. ACM SIGCOMM Comput. Commun. Rev. **18**, 314–329 (1988)
2. Xu, L., Harfoush, K., Rhee, I.: Binary increase congestion control (BIC) for fast long-distance networks. In: Twenty-Third Annual Joint Conference of the IEEE Computer and Communications Societies, INFOCOM 2004, vol. 4, pp. 2514–2524. IEEE (2004)
3. Ha, S., Rhee, I., Xu, L.: CUBIC: a new TCP-friendly high-speed TCP variant. ACM SIGOPS Oper. Syst. Rev. **42**(5), 64–74 (2008)
4. Widmer, J., Denda, R., Mauve, M.: A survey on TCP-friendly congestion control. IEEE Netw. **15**(3), 28–37 (2001)
5. Padhye, J., Kurose, J., Towsley, D., Koodli, R.: A model based TCP-friendly rate control protocol. In: Proceedings of NOSSDAV 1999 (1999)
6. Rescorla, E.: Congestion control requirements for RMCAT. https://tools.ietf.org/html/draft-ietf-rmcat-cc-requirements-09
7. Lundin, H., Holmer, S., Alvestrand, H.: A Google congestion control algorithm for real-time communication on the world wide web. https://tools.ietf.org/html/draft-ietf-rmcat-cc-requirements-09
8. Zhu, X., et al.: NADA: a unified congestion control scheme for real-time media. https://tools.ietf.org/html/draft-ietf-rmcat-nada-07
9. Johansson, I., Sarker, Z.: Self-clocked rate adaptation for multimedia, RFC 8298. https://www.rfc-editor.org/rfc/rfc8298.txt
10. Carlucci, G., De Cicco, L., Holmer, S., Mascolo, S.: Analysis and design of the Google congestion control for web real-time communication (WebRTC). In: Proceedings of the 7th International Conference on Multimedia Systems, pp. 1–13. ACM (2016)
11. Holmer, S., Flodman, M., Sprang, E.: RTP extensions for transport-wide congestion control. https://tools.ietf.org/html/draft-holmer-rmcat-transport-wide-cc-extensions-01
12. Carlucci, G., et al.: Congestion control for web real-time communication. IEEE/ACM Trans. Network. (TON) **25**(5), 2629–2642 (2017)
13. De Cicco, L., Carlucci, G., Mascolo, S.: Understanding the dynamic behaviour of the Google congestion control for RTCWeb. In: 2013 20th International Packet Video Workshop (PV), pp. 1–8. IEEE (2013)
14. Carlucci, G., De Cicco, L., Ilharco, C., Mascolo, S.: Congestion control for real-time communications: a comparison between NADA and GCC. In: 2016 24th Mediterranean Conference on Control and Automation (MED), pp. 575–580. IEEE (2016)
15. Sarker, Z., Singh, V., Zhu, X., Ramalho, M.: Test cases for evaluating RMCAT proposals. https://tools.ietf.org/html/draft-ietf-rmcat-eval-test-05

# Network Traffic Model with Multi-fractal Discrete Wavelet Transform in Power Telecommunication Access Networks

Yi Lu[1], Huan Li[2], Bin Lu[3], Yun Zhao[4], Dongdong Wang[3], Xiaoli Gong[5], and Xin Wei[6(✉)]

[1] State Grid Shenyang Electric Power Supply Company, Dalian 110006, China
[2] State Grid Liaoning Electric Power Research Institute, Shenyang 110006, China
[3] State Grid Liaoning Electric Power Company Limited, Shenyang 110006, China
[4] State Grid Dalian Electric Power Supply Company, Dalian 116011, China
[5] College of Cyber Science, Nankai University, Tianjin 300350, China
[6] College of Computer Science, Nankai University, Tianjin 300350, China
weixin@mail.nankai.edu.cn

**Abstract.** With the development of communication networks, a lot of new applications emerge in the power telecommunication access networks, which have many new features and properties of the network traffic. These features are important for modeling the network traffic in the network-level. This paper propose a new feature extraction and network traffic model method. Firstly, we analyze the features of network traffic in time-frequency domain. Then, we use discrete wavelet transform to exploit the features of network traffic in the time domain and frequency domain. We run multi-fractal discrete wavelet transform (MDWT) for network traffic to decompose them into different frequency component and train an artificial neural network to predict the low- and high-frequency components of network traffic, and use them to reconstruct the network traffic. Finally, in order to validate our network traffic model, we conduct the network traffic prediction on the actual data. Simulation results show that our approach is feasible.

**Keywords:** Network traffic · Multi-fractal · Discrete wavelet transform · Power telecommunication access networks

## 1 Introduction

With development of the communication network, there are many new applications appeared in power telecommunication access networks and the network architecture has become more complexity in the recent years, so there are more features has appeared in the telecommunication networks, which leads to a huge challenge for the network management [1, 2]. There are many researches show that flow traffic in the network has important statistical characteristics, such as correlation and self-similarity,

H. Song et al. (Eds.): SIMUtools 2019, LNICST 295, pp. 53–62, 2019.
https://doi.org/10.1007/978-3-030-32216-8_5

as well as in the power telecommunication access networks [3, 4]. The complex behavioral characteristics of network traffic are usually manifested in bursts on time domain and frequency domain.

In order to increase the performance of the network, it is important for network managements to obtain the accurately model to demonstrate the features of network traffic. Accurate traffic prediction models can influence the planning and optimization of the network. The end-to-end traffic in the network shows the data transmission in the network-level behaviors, this is very significant for the network planning, network management and service quality improvement which provided by the operators and service providers. So the end-to-end network traffic has attracted much attention of researchers and operators around the world [5]. The network traffic in the network are changed over time and there are many features for different types of applications and network devices.

Flow traffic model in the network is very hard. However, the flow traffic in the network has multi-scale features, so we can learn more information about network traffic and construct an approximate model for the end-to-end traffic in the network through feature analysis and feature extraction. The back propagation (BP) neural networks and multi-population quantum genetic algorithm are used to improve the prediction precision of network traffic. Since the neural network has a long convergence time, so the multi-population quantum genetic algorithm is proposed to adjust the initial weights and thresholds of the BP neural network to decrease the convergence time [6]. The dynamic programming (DP) based time-normalization algorithm is proposed to detect anomaly traffic in the network [7]. The spatio-temporal correlation of normal traffic and the sparse nature of anomalies are used to detect the anomalous traffic in the network with lacking of sufficient flow-level measurements [8].

The feature analysis is used to detect the anomalous traffic in the network [9]. Moreover, the model-based network event detection framework is built by analyzing and extracting the feature of network traffic [10]. The continuous wavelet transforms based on multi-scale analysis are performed to detect the anomalous in the high-speed backbone networks [11]. The combination of unsupervised feature extractor and anomaly detector to construct an anomaly detection model for high-dimensional spaces [12]. Additionally, from the network-wide traffic perspective, the anomalous of the network traffic can be correctly detected via signal transformations [13]. The manifold similarity index and manifold learning technology are used to study the spatial-temporal characteristics of highway traffic flow [14]. The time-frequency analysis of end-to-end traffic is used to localize traffic features of time-frequency properties and reconstruct network traffic in large-scale communication networks [15]. There are many methods to extract the network traffic and use them to model the network traffic, however, the prediction errors of these proposed methods are large.

This paper proposed a new scheme MDWT to accurately and effectively predict the network traffic in the network. Network traffic modeling and predicting of network traffic is very hard due to the network traffic has highly fluctuation over the time. In this paper, we analyze the features of the network traffic in the time-frequency domain. Then, we use the discrete wavelet transform to exploit the features of the network traffic in the time domain and frequency domain. Then, we run MDWT for network traffic to decompose the network traffic and train an artificial neural network to predict the low- and high-frequency component, and use them to reconstruct the network traffic. Simulation results show that our approach is effective and promising.

The architecture of this paper as follow. In Sect. 2, we describe the scheme proposed and analysis the features of the network traffic, and propose the algorithm MDWT. In Sect. 3, we do some simulations and compere the performance of different methods for modeling the network traffic. In Sect. 4, we make a conclusion about our work in this paper.

## 2 Problem Statement

Flow is also defined as a sequence of packets which are sent from origin nodes to destination nodes. We usually call the origin node and the destination node as an origin-destination (OD) pair. In the power telecommunication access networks, the flows of OD pairs have the characteristics such as correlations, self-similarity and time-varying. The traffic of flows changes over the time, therefore, it is very difficult to use mathematical models to depict the network traffic of flows in the network. The network traffic changes over time, then we represent the network traffic in the power telecommunication access network at time $t$ as $x(t)$ where $t = 1, 2, 3, \ldots$. Since the traffic in the network has the correlations on the frequency-domain and time-domain, respectively, so we characterize the time-frequent features of the network traffic. Due to the complex of the flow traffic, we extract the some features firstly from the network traffic. In the signal process domain, wavelet transform is often used to analyze the multi-scale feature of signals. Then, we use the wavelet method to process the flow traffic in the network.

Discrete wavelet transform (DWT) is a mathematical transformation of the one-dimensional discrete signal $x(t)$, it decomposes the signals into the some orthogonal one-dimensional signals. For the network traffic which has the time-frequent features, so we decompose it into two orthogonal one-dimensional signals to decompose the signals, namely time-domain and frequency-domain. In DWT, signals are usually decomposed into the smooth signal after time shifting $\phi(t)$ in the time-domain and the detail signals of the scale changing $\theta(t)$ in the frequency-domain. As we know that the network traffic at different slots have then correlations and self-similarity. Then, the smooth signals $\phi(t)$ the time-domain are low-pass signals and the detail signals at frequency-domain $\theta(t)$ are high-pass signals. So, signals can be written with the basic function as

$$\phi_{l,k}(t) = 2^{-l/2}\phi_0(2^{-l}t - k), \ k \in Z \tag{1}$$

$$\theta_{l,k}(t) = 2^{-l/2}\theta_0(2^{-l}t - k), \ k \in Z \tag{2}$$

where $\theta_0$ and $\phi_0$ are the basic function bases which are orthogonal with each other, $l$ is the scale coefficient, and $k$ is the index of basic orthogonal basis.

The network traffic $x(t)$ can be reconstructed with basic orthogonal basis as

$$x(t) = \sum_k c(k)\phi_{l,k}(t) + \sum_k \sum_{l=0}^{L} d(k)\theta_{l,k}(t) \tag{3}$$

where $l$ is the level coefficient, $c(k)$ and $d(k)$ are the scaling and translation coefficient, respectively. $k$ is the index of basic orthogonal basis. Then, we can obtain the scale coefficient and wavelet coefficient of wavelet transform with iteration method:

$$c^l(k) = 2^{-1/2}(c^{l+1}(2k) + c^{l+1}(2k+1)) \tag{4}$$

$$d^l(k) = 2^{-1/2}(c^{l+1}(2k) - c^{l+1}(2k+1)) \tag{5}$$

where $c^l(t)$ donates the scale coefficient, and $d^l(t)$ donates the wavelet coefficient. Then, from the Eq. (3), we can obtain the scale coefficient

$$c^{l+1}(2k) = 2^{-1/2}(c^l(k) + d^l(k)) \tag{6}$$

$$c^{l+1}(2k+1) = 2^{-1/2}(c^l(k) - d^l(k)) \tag{7}$$

The flow traffic from origin node $i$ to destination node $j$ can be expressed as $x_{ij}(t) = \{x_{ij}(1), x_{ij}(2), \ldots\}$, where $t$ is the measured slot. So, the network traffic can be represented as a waveform transform with limited duration and frequency

$$x_{ij}(t) = \sum_{k=-\infty}^{\infty} c_{ij}^l(k) 2^{-L/2} \phi(\frac{t}{2^L} - k) + \sum_{k=-\infty}^{\infty} \sum_{l=1}^{L} d_{ij}^l(k) 2^{-l/2} \theta(\frac{t}{2^l} - k) \tag{8}$$

where $\phi(t)$ and $\theta(t)$ are basic orthogonal basis of smooth signals and detail signals.

$$x_{ij}^{low}(t) = \sum_{k=-\infty}^{\infty} c_{ij}(k) 2^{-1/2} \phi(\frac{t}{2} - k) \tag{9}$$

$$x_{ij}^{high}(t) = \sum_{k=-\infty}^{\infty} d_{ij}(k) 2^{-1/2} \theta(\frac{t}{2} - k) \tag{10}$$

then, we use $x_{ij}^{low}(t)$ and $x_{ij}^{high}(t)$ to express the low frequency components and high frequency components, respectively.

The network traffic in the network-level can be collected by sampling the end-to-end flow, and the collected network traffic in the network-level is actually a time series signal $x_{ij}(t)$, so the multi-fractal analysis of the network traffic becomes into analyze the network traffic sampling sequence.

$$x_{ij}(t) = \{x_{ij}(1), x_{ij}(2), \ldots\} \tag{11}$$

where $x_{ij}(t)$ is the network traffic from origin node $i$ to destination node $j$ at time slot $t$. From Eq. (9), we use the Haar wavelet as the origin signals, so the $\phi(t)$ and $\theta(t)$ can be expressed as

$$\phi(t) = \begin{cases} 1, & 0 \leq t \leq 1 \\ 0, & otherwise \end{cases} \tag{12}$$

$$\theta(t) = \begin{cases} 1, & 0 \leq t \leq 1/2 \\ -1, & 1/2 \leq t \leq 1 \\ 0, & otherwise \end{cases} \tag{13}$$

The network traffic $x_{ij}(t)$ exhibits different scale features on each orthogonal basis. Then we use the Haar wavelet to execute the wavelet transform on the network traffic $x_{ij}(t)$ to find the scale coefficient $\{c^l(k)\}$ and wavelet coefficient $\{d^l(k)\}$, respectively. Then we use the network traffic $x_{ij}(t)$ as the input and use the as the $\{c^l(k)\}$ and $\{d^l(k)\}$ as the output to train an artificial neural networks to obtain the model which predict the coefficient of $x_{ij}^{low}(t)$ and $x_{ij}^{high}(t)$. Then, we reconstruct the network traffic as follow:

$$\hat{x}_{ij}(t) = x_{ij}^{low}(t) + x_{ij}^{high}(t) \tag{14}$$

With low- and high-frequency components which are predicted by artificial neural network, we con model the network traffic in the network. This model can accurately predict network traffic, and help operators to manage the network. Now we show the process of our algorithm as follows:

**Step 1:** Obtain the discrete network traffic $x(t)$ as the initial traffic data set.

**Step 2:** Based on Eqs. (3)–(7), carry the wavelet transform with Haar wavelet to obtain the scale coefficients $\{c^l(k)\}$ and wavelet coefficient $\{d^l(k)\}$.

**Step 3:** By Eqs. (11)–(13), make the scale coefficients and wavelet coefficient as the output and make the measured network traffic $\{x_{ij}(t)\}$ as input to train an artificial neural networks which used predict scale coefficients and wavelet coefficient.

**Step 4:** Use the prediction result of the scale coefficients and wavelet coefficient in step 3 to calculate the low frequency components $x_{ij}^{low}(t)$ and high frequency components $x_{ij}^{high}(t)$.

**Step 5:** According to Eq. (14), we reconstruct the network traffic $\hat{x}_{ij}(t)$.

**Step 6:** Save the results to file and exit.

## 3  Simulation Results and Analysis

In this section, we make some simulations to verify the performance of the algorithm MDWT proposed in this paper. Then, we use the actual data in the simulations to compare the performance of our algorithms. The actual data is collected from the Abilene backbone network in the United States validate MDWT. Then, we make a comparison about the performance with other methods that principal component analysis (PCA), WABR [15] which have been widely studied for the network traffic modeling. The network traffic prediction results of MDWT method has been discussed in the following. Then, we talk about the relative errors of the network traffic prediction of different methods. Finally, we discuss the prediction errors of them. In the simulation, the front 500 points data are used to train the model we proposed and the last 1500 points are used to compare the prediction errors of the network traffic for different methods.

Figure 1 curves the actual traffic and prediction results network traffic of network traffic flows 67 and 107, where the flows 67 and 107 are randomly selected from the 144 ODs in the Abilene backbone network, as well as the network traffic of other ODs has the similar trend in our simulations. Then, we make a discussion about prediction results of the OD 67 and 107 as an examples here. The end-to-end traffic of flows in the network-level can reflect the data transmission of the network. Figure 1(a) indicates that the actual network traffic has the time-varying nature, and the prediction results is similar with the actual traffic in the network, this means that the model proposed in this paper can extract the network features accurately of OD 67. Likewise the flows 107, the prediction results of flow 107 is closed with the actual network traffic and it also show our method is feasible. From Fig. 1, we very clearly know that the network traffic in each slot has the vary-time nature and the vary-time nature of network traffic of OD 67 is much larger than the network traffic of flow 107, however, our algorithms can also capture the network traffic with the high accuracy.

Then, we talk about the prediction errors of our algorithm and other methods. Since the end-to-end traffic in the network changes over time, it is very hard and meaningless to compare the absolute errors of the network traffic. Inspired by the existing researches, we compare the relative errors of different methods over the time. In order to reduce the randomness of the prediction process, we run many times to calculate the average relative errors here. The relative errors of the prediction traffic can be expressed as:

$$re_i(t) = \frac{1}{N} \sum_{n=1}^{N} \frac{|\hat{y}_i(t) - y_i(t)|}{y_i(t)} \tag{15}$$

where $N$ is the running times, we set it as 300 here, and $y_i(t)$ is the network traffic of end-to-end flow $i$ at time $t$, $\hat{y}_i(t)$ is the prediction result of network traffic of flow $i$ at time slot $t$.

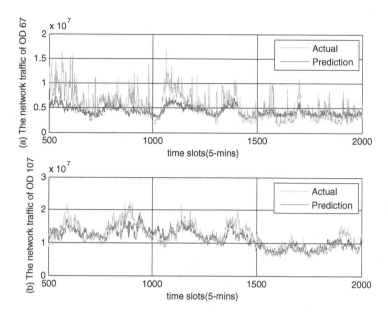

**Fig. 1.** Prediction results of network traffic of OD 67 and 107.

Figure 2 exploits the average relative errors of the network traffic prediction results of OD 67 and 107 for different methods. From Fig. 2(a), we know that the network traffic prediction results of OD 67 hold lowest relative errors for MDWT, while the relative errors basic of the prediction results for PCA is the largest of them, this shows that the traffic prediction performance of MDWT is well. Importantly, the fluctuation of the relative errors over time is more stable for the MDWT than PCA and WBAR, and the average relative errors of MDWT is the lowest of them. Thus, the MDWT can more accurately and effectively model the features of end-to-end traffic in the network. With the model MDWT, we can predict the network traffic more accurately than previous methods in the network.

In the following, we use the Root Mean Square Error (RMSE) to further compare the performance for above three algorithms. The RMSE are given as follows:

$$RMSE = \sqrt{\frac{1}{K} \sum_{k=1}^{K} (re_i(t))^2} \qquad (16)$$

where $K$ is the length of the sampling windows. $re_i(t)$ is the relative errors of the flow $i$ at time slot $t$. The RMSE can more clearly shows the accuracy and the stability of the model.

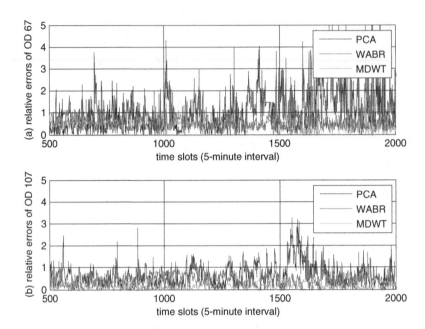

**Fig. 2.** The average relative errors for network traffic of OD 67 and 107.

Figure 3 exhibits the RMSE of relative errors of prediction results of end-to-end network traffic of OD 67 and 107 for different models. Figure 3(a) shows the RMSE of relative errors f prediction results for OD 67, when the average relative errors is about 0.5, the probability of MDWT, WABR and PCA are 95%, 30% and 5%, respectively. This shows that the relative errors of prediction results of MDWT is smallest of the three methods. The CDF curve of the MDWT is very steep, it means the network traffic prediction results of MDWT is more accurate than PCA and WABR, and the performance of network traffic prediction of the MDWT is stable. Similarly, for network traffic of OD 107, the green curve shows that MDWT can more accurately model the network-level network traffic. When the average relative errors is about 0.3, the probability of MDWT, WABR and PCA are 95%, 10% and 5%, respectively. This also shows that the relative errors of prediction results of MDWT is smallest of the three methods. Then, from Fig. 3, we know that the proposed method MDWT can accurately model the network traffic and keep better modeling performance for network traffic than the previous method PCA and WABR.

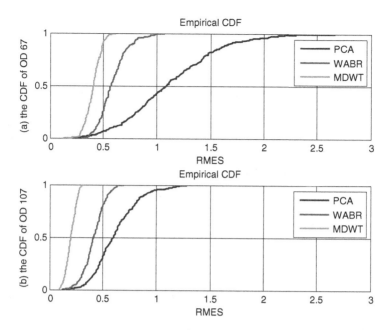

**Fig. 3.** The REMS of network traffic of OD 67 and 107. (Color figure online)

## 4 Conclusions

This paper studies the network traffic modeling and prediction in the power telecommunication access networks. Because network traffic fluctuates greatly over time, so it is very hard to model the network traffic. This paper propose a method to model and predict the network traffic. Firstly, we analyze the time-frequency features of the network traffic in the time-frequency domain. Then, we use the discrete wavelet transform to exploit the features of the network traffic in the time domain and frequency domain. Then, we run MDWT for the network traffic to decompose the network traffic and train an artificial neural network to predict the low-frequency component and high-frequency component. Finally, we do some simulations to verify our network traffic model and predict the network traffic. Simulation results show that our approach is effective and promising.

## References

1. Jiang, D., Xu, Z., Chen, Z., et al.: Joint time-frequency sparse estimation of large-scale network traffic. Comput. Netw. **55**(10), 3533–3547 (2011)
2. Jiang, D., Xu, Z., Xu, H.: A novel hybrid prediction algorithm to network traffic. Ann. Telecommun. **70**(9), 427–439 (2015)
3. Soule, A., Lakhina, A., Taft, N., et al.: Traffic matrices: balancing measurements, inference and modeling. In: Proceedings of SIGMETRICS 2005, vol. 33, no. 1, pp. 362–373 (2005)

4. Zhang, Y., Roughan, M., Duffield, N., et al.: Fast accurate computation of large-scale IP traffic matrices from link loads. In: Proceedings of SIGMETRICS 2003, vol. 31, no. 3, pp. 206–217 (2003)
5. Takeda, T., Shionoto, K.: Traffic matrix estimation in large-scale IP networks. In: Proceedings of LANMAN 2010, pp. 1–6 (2010)
6. Zhang, L., Zhang, X.: Network traffic prediction based on BP neural networks optimized by quantum genetic algorithm. Comput. Eng. Sci. **38**, 114–119 (2016)
7. Yu, Q., Gu, X.: Network traffic anomaly detection based on dynamic programming. In: Proceedings of International Conference on Computing Intelligence and Information System, pp. 62–65 (2017)
8. Morteza, M., Giannakis, G.: Estimating traffic and anomaly maps via network tomography. IEEE/ACM Trans. Network. **24**(3), 1533–1547 (2016)
9. Jiang, D., Yuan, Z., Zhang, P., et al.: A traffic anomaly detection approach in communication networks for applications of multimedia medical devices. Multimedia Tools Appl. **75**, 14281–14305 (2016)
10. Eriksson, B., Barford, P., Bowden, R., et al.: BasisDetect: a model-based network event detection framework. In: Proceedings of IMC, pp. 451–464 (2010)
11. Jiang, D., Yao, C., Xu, Z., et al.: Multi-scale anomaly detection for high-speed network traffic. Trans. Emerg. Telecommun. Technol. **26**(3), 308–317 (2015)
12. Erfani, S., Sutharshan, R., Shanika, K., et al.: High-dimensional and large-scale anomaly detection using a linear one-class SVM with deep learning. Pattern Recogn. **58**(2106), 121–134 (2016)
13. Jiang, D., Xu, Z., Zhang, P., et al.: A transform domain-based anomaly detection approach to network-wide traffic. J. Netw. Comput. Appl. **40**(2), 292–306 (2014)
14. Liu, Q., Cai, Y., Jiang, H., et al.: Traffic state spatial-temporal characteristic analysis and short-term forecasting based on manifold similarity. IEEE Access **6**, 9690–9702 (2018)
15. Jiang, D., Zhao, Z., Xu, Z., et al.: How to reconstruct end-to-end traffic based on time-frequency analysis and artificial neural network. AEU-Int. J. Electron. Commun. **68**(10), 915–925 (2014)
16. Jiang, D., Wang, W., Shi, L., Song, H.: A compressive sensing-based approach to end-to-end network traffic reconstruction. IEEE Trans. Netw. Sci. Eng. (2018). https://doi.org/10.1109/tnse.2018.2877597
17. Jiang, D., Huo, L., Song, H.: Rethinking behaviors and activities of base stations in mobile cellular networks based on big data analysis. IEEE Trans. Netw. Sci. Eng. **1**(1), 1–12 (2018)
18. Jiang, D., Huo, L., Li, Y.: Fine-granularity inference and estimations to network traffic for SDN. PLoS ONE **13**(5), 1–23 (2018)
19. Jiang, D., Huo, L., Lv, Z., et al.: A joint multi-criteria utility-based network selection approach for vehicle-to-infrastructure networking. IEEE Trans. Intell. Transp. Syst. **pp**(99), 1–15 (2018)

# Smartphone-Based Lifelogging:
# An Investigation of Data Volume Generation
# Strength of Smartphone Sensors

Inayat Khan$^{(\boxtimes)}$ ⓘ, Shaukat Ali ⓘ, and Shah Khusro ⓘ

Department of Computer Science, University of Peshawar,
Peshawar 25120, Pakistan
{inayat_khan, shoonikhan, khusro}@uop.edu.pk

**Abstract.** The lifelogging enable people to digitally record information about their daily life events for a variety of purposes including human memory augmentation. However, the lifelogging systems have several challenges regarding capturing, managing, semantic analyses, indexing, and retrieval of error-prone and noisy data produced by the sensors. The ubiquitous nature and technological developments makes smartphone as de-facto lifelogging device. The smartphone integrates a rich set of sensors, which provide unique opportunities for capturing contents and contextual information into a comprehensive lifelog archive. However, the continuous use of sensors can generate large amount of data that could raise problems for smartphone-based lifelogging systems. In addition, insight understanding of smartphone sensors data generation strength is needed for effective smartphone-based lifelogging systems development. These estimations will also help in understanding of smartphone sensors capability of fulfilling lifelogging systems objectives. To fulfill objective of this paper, an Android based application namely Sensors dAta Volume Estimator (SAVE) is developed using a proposed architecture. The SAVE utilizes smartphone sensors to capture and estimate sensors data from different real world scenarios. The results indicated that smartphone sensors can generate significant amount of data that can create storage, retrieval, and battery power issues for smartphone-based lifelogging systems.

**Keywords:** Smartphone · Sensors · Lifelogging · Personal big data · Information overload · Memory augmentation

## 1 Introduction

Acquiring and keeping of valuable information is a fundamental property of human behavior. However, unfolding users' lives could generate large volume of information resulting into information overload problem that could make storage, organization, and retrieval of information increasingly difficult [1]. Lifelogging is *"a form of pervasive computing, consisting of a unified digital record of the totality of an individual's experiences, captured multi-modally through digital sensors and stored permanently as a personal multimedia archive"* [2]. Personalized lifelogging systems are augmented memory applications, which would ease people by automatic and continuous recording

H. Song et al. (Eds.): SIMUtools 2019, LNICST 295, pp. 63–73, 2019.
https://doi.org/10.1007/978-3-030-32216-8_6

and storing of a person's life events information [3]. Lifelogging devices/systems have used sensors for capturing information about peoples and their contexts/environments, and forward the captured information to a backend server/PC for storage and retrieval. However, most of the lifelogging devices were custom-built devices or applications relying on external sensors [4].

Smartphone is the highly ubiquitous computing device that is formed by combining the features of mobile phones and personal digital assistances (PDAs). Smartphone is becoming the commonplace and its popularity can be measured from its presence in the pocket of almost every individual today [5]. It is our constant companion due to being with us all the time and has the potential to know us very well beyond our imagination [5, 6]. A smartphone integrates enormous capturing and computing capabilities in a single jacket and making it a de-facto lifelogging device [7, 8]. A smartphone integrates a rich set of built-in specialized physical, logical, and informational sensors, which extends it capability than sensors found in dedicated commercial wearable lifelogging devices (e.g., SenseCam, etc.) and the list is likely to increase in the near future [9]. The smartphone sensors can be advantageous over commercial wearable sensors and devices [9, 10]. The sensors enables smartphone to continuously and unobtrusively capture information about us and our contexts and environments, and use the captured information as contextual cues to augment our episodic memories [10]. For example, smartphone based lifelogging systems can employ different sensors such as motion sensors (i.e., accelerometer and gyroscope), positional sensor (i.e., GPS), acoustic sensor (i.e., microphone), optical sensor (i.e., camera), biomedical sensor (i.e., heart rate), etc. to capture information into a lifelog [11]. The applications of smartphone sensors for lifelogging are shown in our previous research work [9]. However, the number of sensors used depends on the types of lifelogging. A focused lifelogging (e.g., activity monitoring for self-quantified analysis) would use one or two sensors sufficiently to capture information about some aspects of a person's life experiences but extreme lifelogging would require using of a number of sensors to capture lifelog information as complete picture of life experiences as possible [12].

The storage capacity is increasing with the increasing demand of lifelogging, as indicated by the Kryder's Law [13]. The smartphone storage is also increased and smartphone with 256 GB storage is commonly available, which is enough to store images for more than 3 years if taken with a frequency of 1.65 million images per year [12]. The processing power is increased and smartphone with quad core processor are commonly available. The networking technologies are improved and massive amount of data can be received and transferred wirelessly from a smartphone. The smartphone sensors can generate tones of information (e.g., accelerometer can generate up to 21 million readings per year if operated at the lowest 1 Hz frequency) for rich lifelogging. Despite of advancements, the storage, managing, analyzing, indexing, and retrieval of stream of multimodal information from the noisy, error-prone, and gaps in continuity, etc., smartphone sensors data can poses serious challenges for smartphone-based lifelogging [14]. Furthermore, storing massive amount of unusable sensory data would be wastage of storage and resources from researchers' point of view. Therefore, researchers are interested in finding and storing patterns in continuous stream of multimodal sensory information instead, that is enough to effectively diagnose and describe user experiences in real time. However, to lay down effective criteria for recognition and selection of sensory patterns, a thorough investigation of smartphone sensors is essential to determine their strength, weaknesses, and reading speeds in real-world scenarios.

In this paper, we have investigated for detailed estimations and analysis of data volume generation strength of smartphone sensors for lifelogging. To support objective of the paper, an Android app namely Sensors dAta Volume Estimator (SAVE) is developed to automatically monitor, record, and analyze data volume generated by smartphone sensors. during daily life activities. A comprehensive test bed has been defined that is consisting of tests for estimating of sensors data volume captured during different daily life activities in different real-world scenarios. The results have indicated that smartphone sensors can generate huge personal big data (i.e., lifelog) due to their sampling frequency rates and inherent working mechanisms.

## 2 Lifelogging: History and State-of-the-Art

The history of personal lifelogging research area starts from the publication of Vannevar Bush's famous article "As We May Think" in 1945. He suggested an imaginary mechanized device called Memex (Memory Extender) [15] that will act as human memory prosthesis and will optimize humans' lives by increasing peoples' ability to record, organize, search, and exchange the massive amount of information generated during their daily lives experiences. Bush described Memex as "enlarged intimate supplement to one's memory" whose technical interpretation hints for the first lifelogging system [12]. Years later, the introduction of advanced digital technologies enabled the release of several manifestations based on the idea of recording all of a person's life time experiences in visual and audible formats by using cameras and microphones. Steve Mann (father of wearable computing) coined the idea of wearable computing and developed increasingly smaller wearable devices with innovative increasing sensing, capturing, and displaying hardware components for manipulating lifelog information and enjoyed the media status as "the world's first cyborg" [16]. To solve several of the fundamental problems in wearable lifelogging technologies, Steve Mann invented several generations of wearable camera technologies from early personal imaging to the EyeTap system [16], which could be viewed as precursor of Google Glass. Later researcher demonstrated using of high valued sensors for capturing and identifying of a complete set of contexts types (e.g., using GPS for location, etc.) to be used either as a trigger to capture pictures or as metadata for indexing and retrieval of the visually captured data [17]. A number of cheap wearable commercial products are also available in the market for monitoring certain aspects of a person's life such as SenseCam, Vicon Revue, Narrative Clip, Fit Bit One[TM], Nike FuelBand[TM], and Lark[TM]. They are composed of combination of basic sensors (i.e., accelerometer, magnetometer, gyroscope) to monitor and log activity levels (e.g., steps count, distance travelled, and caloric output) on-board and subsequently forwards the captures wirelessly to a cloud service via laptop or PC.

The ubiquitous computing devices showed their importance in lifelogging because occurrence of many significant activities and events cannot be restricted to a particular schedule or location. Smartphone allows lifelog systems by offering new opportunities to unobtrusively record nearly all aspects of a person's life to construct a digital memory [18]. Smartphone based lifelogging applications can exploit its rich sensing capabilities for determining contextual cues to effectively depict peoples' daily life activities and events such as where we go, what we do, who we interact with, what information we consume, etc. Nokia Lifeblog project [19] was the earliest smartphone based lifelogging application. Nokia Lifeblog inspired many research efforts in both industry and academia which resulted into emergence of a new breed of lifelogging applications that showed feasibility of integrating more and more sensing and logging functionalities such as Pensevie [14], MyExperience [20], UbiqLog [8]. SenseSeer [6], Digital Diary [21], and Experience Explorer [22], etc. Each of these systems have used a bunch of smartphone sensors for capturing specific contents and contextual information as per their idea and requirement. However, none of them has provided any insight to the smartphone sensors data generation strength.

## 3  Methodology

This paper focuses on presenting a methodology for gaining insight knowledge of data volume generation strength of smartphone sensors for lifelogging. An explicit architecture is proposed to effectively estimate, record, and analyze the data volume generated by each sensor explicitly and in combination with other sensors. The proposed architecture is composed of three layers: interface layer, processing layer and physical layer as shown in Fig. 1. Each layer is composed of several sub-components that exploit the capabilities of the layer below. A precise description of each of the layers is presented in the following headings.

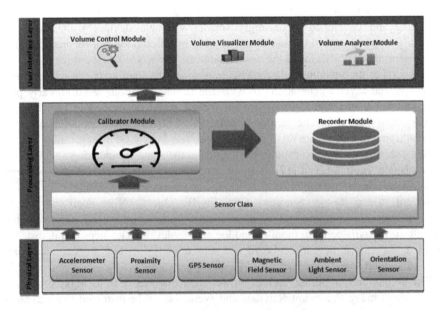

**Fig. 1.** The proposed architecture.

### 3.1   User Interface Layer

User interface is the space where users interact with the system. The user interface is easy to use, easy to understand while having lower learning curves, having professional aesthetics, and requiring minimum steps to obtain the desired results. User interface layer is composed of three modules including volume control, volume visualizer, and volume analyzer. The volume control module is responsible to adjust a sensor reading frequency and time interval between consecutive readings to minimize and maximize a sensor's data volume generation speed. The volume visualizer module displays a sensor's readings as well as maximum and minimum frequencies, maximum and minimum interval between readings, and data volume per reading. The volume analyzer module is responsible for displaying each sensor accumulative data volume with per second time stamp.

### 3.2   Processing Layer

Processing layer encompasses all of the technical operations. Processing layer is composed of three modules namely sensor, calibrator, and recorder. The sensor module accesses the physical layer for retrieving data from the sensors and processes the captured data. The calibrator module adjusts the reading rate of a sensor as per instructions from the user interface layer. The recorder module is getting sensors data from the sensor module and stores it in a local database along with reading frequency and time interval information from the calibrator module. The flow chart of calibrator module and recorder module are show in the Figs. 2 and 3 respectively.

### 3.3   Physical Layer

The physical layer encompasses Android's built-in sensors and storage capabilities and uses Android's libraries (i.e., SensorManager, etc.) to turn sensors on/off, adjust the sensors reading frequencies, and store the data generated by the sensors. SqlLite is used by the recorder module for creating database to store sensory data and associated data for analysis purposes. From SqlLite, the database can be imported to PCs for conducting more detailed and powerful analysis using applications such as MS Excel, etc.

## 4   SAVE Implementation and Sensors

Using the architecture, an Android-based application namely SAVE is developed. The SAVE is aimed running with Ice Cream Sandwich 4.0.3 or higher and is developed using Android SDK tools revision 22.6.3 with Eclipse IDE and SensorSimulator-2.0-RC1 running on a desktop machine. The target code is mainly deployed and tested on Samsung Galaxy SIII running with Android Jelly Bean 4.1.1 operating system. Figure 4 represents snapshots of SAVE user interface. The data volume generated by a sensor is calculated using formula shown in Eq. (1) where TV represents the total volume, US represents unit sample size of a sensor (e.g., accelerometer generates 12 bytes data per sample, and GPS generates 24 bytes per sample etc.), T represents the total usage time of a sensor, and S represents the number of sample taken by a sensor within the T. Reading frequency (F) of a sensor is the no of readings (N) per second (Sec) as shown in Eq. (2). Number of samples (S) of a sensor depends on the reading frequency (F) of a sensor and the time interval (TI) between consecutive samples as shown in Eq. (3). In current version of SAVE, the sensors, which are available in most of the smartphones are used to validate and execute our tests. The sensors used are:

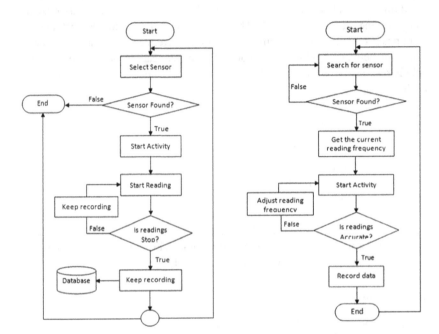

**Fig. 2.** Flowchart of calibrator module      **Fig. 3.** Flowchart of recorder module.

$$TV = US \times \sum (T \times S) \tag{1}$$

$$F = \frac{N}{Sec} \tag{2}$$

$$S = \frac{F}{TI} \tag{3}$$

## 4.1   Accelerometer Sensor

The tri-axial accelerometer sensor can have maximum reading frequency of 102 Hz and minimum reading frequency of 1 Hz or 2 Hz. The data volume generated by each accelerometer sample is 12 bytes. In case of maximum frequency (i.e., 102 Hz), accelerometer could generate data volume of 1224 bytes/sec and 105.75 MB/day. Furthermore, if accelerometer's data is collected for a year continuously, it could generate data up to 38 GB per year. However, generating such a huge volume of data raises questions related to storage and retrieval of specific patterns of data for smartphone-based lifelogging applications.

## 4.2    Orientation Sensor

The orientation sensor can have minimum reading frequency of 1 Hz and maximum reading frequency of 8 Hz. The data volume generated by each orientation sensor sample is of 12 bytes. Due to having low reading frequency, the data volume generated by a smartphone orientation sensor is much less as compared to accelerometer sensor. If orientation sensor's data is captured continuously with its maximum reading frequency, the total data volume generated could grow up to 3 GB per year.

## 4.3    Magnetic Field (MF) Sensor

The MF sensor continuously read data from its surroundings to recognize the NORTH for defining directions. Like orientation sensor, the MF sensor can have minimum reading frequency of 1 Hz and maximum reading frequency of 8 Hz. The data volume generated by each sample is 12 bytes. Therefore, like orientation sensor, the MF can generate maximum of 3 GB data, if used continuously for a year.

## 4.4    Proximity Sensor

The proximity sensor is event based sensor and captures data upon the occurrence of a target event. It has been observed that proximity sensor's reading frequency cannot be customized as per needs. The maximum reading frequency is 4 Hz and minimum reading frequency is 0 Hz and the data volume generated by a sample is 12 bytes.

## 4.5    GPS Sensor

The GPS sensor is used for users' localizations by receiving signals from satellites. The GPS sensor is event based sensor and updates location coordinates (i.e., latitude and longitude) by receiving signals from satellites accordingly. The GPS sensor reading frequency cannot be customized as per need. However, the maximum reading frequency is 1 Hz and minimum reading frequency is 0 Hz and the data volume generated by a reading sample is 24 bytes.

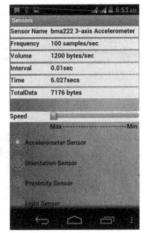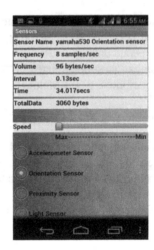

**Fig. 4.** User interfaces of SAVE.

### 4.6 Ambient Light Sensor

The ambient light sensor is event based sensor and reads data from environment with changes in the light intensity. It has been observed that ambient light sensor reading frequency cannot be customized. The maximum reading frequency is 1 Hz and minimum is 0 Hz and the data volume generated by a reading sample is 12 bytes.

## 5 Results and Discussion

For accurate estimations of data volume generated by smartphone sensors, SAVE was used in real-world scenarios. To fulfill objectives of the study, a comprehensive test program was designed to collect sensors data while performing daily life activities in different real-world scenarios (i.e., walking, driving, playing games, working in office, etc.). However, the activities and their durations were not consistent and dependent on the testing scenarios and test cases. All of the activities were performed uniformly and randomly for a period of two hours during a scenario test. To carry out tests, three participants were voluntarily selected from the junior researchers in the Department of Computer Science, University of Peshawar. All of the participants were given Samsung Galaxy SIII smartphones installed with SAVE and they were trained how to use SAVE. Furthermore, the participants were instructed to perform all of the daily life activities uniformly and randomly for a period of two hours for a week to collect maximum data out of each sensor. The sensors data collected from each sensor after performing all of the tests were analyzed and results were compiled. The details of the sensors data generated by the sensors along with their time intervals and minimum and maximum frequencies are also shown in Table 1. Analysis of the data collected from sensors showed that accelerometer, orientation and magnetic field sensors were generating huge amount of lifelog big data. Our results revealed that sensors lifelog big data volume will increase exponentially with the passage of time while recoding the daily life activities/events. This exponential increase in volume will lead to storage limitation problem because the memory size (e.g., 128 GB) would be very much less to store the data generated by a single accelerometer sensor for 5 year (i.e., 38 GB data/year). However, if we got succeeded in storing such a great amount of data by using any method, searching a specific pattern of data will be a resource intensive and cumbersome task, which could result even in completely jeopardizing the underlying smartphone platform.

**Table 1.** Data volume generated by the smartphone sensors in the testing scenarios.

| Sensor Name | Interval | | Samples/second | | Volume/sample in Bytes | Total volume/year | |
|---|---|---|---|---|---|---|---|
| | Minimum | Maximum | Minimum | Maximum | | Minimum | Maximum |
| Accelerometer | 0.01 s | 0.6 s | 1 | 102 | 12 | 373.248 MB | 38.07 GB |
| Orientation | 0.12 s | 0.6 s | 1 | 8 | 12 | 373.248 MB | 2.98 GB |
| Magnetic Field | 0.12 s | 0.6 s | 1 | 8 | 12 | 373.248 MB | 2.98 GB |
| Proximity | Not determined | Not determined | 0 | 5 | 2 | 0 | 1.86 GB |
| GPS | Not determined | Not determined | 0 | 1 | 24 | 0 | 746.49 MB |
| Ambient Light | Not determined | Not determined | 0 | 1 | 12 | 0 | 373.24 MB |

## 6  Conclusion and Future Work

The smartphone-based lifelogging systems require proper management of sensors and sensors data. The investigation of the data generation strength of smartphone sensors is provided in this paper for smartphone-based lifelogging systems. An Android-based application (i.e., SAVE) is developed using proposed architecture to accurately capture and analyze the data from the smartphone sensors. After performing the tests, the results indicated that smartphone sensors can produce huge data volume of contents and contextual information for the smartphone-based lifelogging systems. The sensors data generation strength depends on their sampling frequency rates and inherent working mechanisms. Comparatively, sensors with continuous data capturing nature are found much data prone as compared to event-based sensors. Furthermore, sensors with high reading frequencies can generate huge amount of data in a short span of time. Generating more and more sensors data is advantageous for accurate measurement and presentation of tiny changes in the measuring phenomenon and determining the states and contexts of a user. However, it would raise battery power, storage, and retrieval problems for the smartphone-based lifelogging systems. The storage of voluminous data either form a single sensor or from multiple sensors would be significant because the storage provided by the smartphone is too less even to store the data generated by a single sensor for a few years. However, if methods are investigated for storing voluminous sensors data in limited storage; other issues (e.g., indexing, searching, and retrieving specific patterns of data) would pose resource intensive and cumbersome tasks, which could jeopardize the underlying smartphone platform and quickly drain out the battery power.

In the future, we are interested in finding methods to detect users' states and dynamically adjust a sensor's reading frequency and time interval according to users' activities and contexts/environments. This would enable a smartphone-based lifelogging application to proactively control and adapt sensors' reading frequencies based on user daily life events patterns. The dynamic adjustments would not only help in reducing the sensors data volumes but would also help in solving the associated problems.

# References

1. Jones, W.: Personal information management. Ann. Rev. Inf. Sci. Technol. **41**, 453–504 (2007)
2. Dodge, M., Kitchin, R.: Outlines of a world coming into existence pervasive computing and the ethics of forgetting. Environ. Plann. B: Plann. Des. **34**, 431–445 (2007)
3. Karkkainen, T., Vaittinen, T., Vaananen-Vainio-Mattila, K.: I don't mind being logged, but want to remain in control: a field study of mobile activity and context logging. In: SIGCHI Conference on Human Factors in Computing Systems, pp. 162–173 (2010)
4. Shah, M., Mears, B., Chakrabarti, C., Spanias, A.: Lifelogging: archival and retrieval of continuously recorded audio using wearable devices. In: IEEE International Conference on Emerging Signal Processing Applications (ESPA), pp. 99–102 (2012)
5. Belimpasakis, P., Roimela, K., Yu, U.: Experience explorer: a life-logging platform based on mobile context collection. In: Third International Conference on Next Generation Mobile Applications, Services and Technologies 2009 (NGMAST 2009), pp. 77–82 (2009)
6. Albatal, R., Gurrin, C., Zhou, J., Yang, Y., Carthy, D., Li, N.: SenseSeer mobile-cloud-based lifelogging framework. In: IEEE International Symposium on Technology and Society (ISTAS), pp. 27–29 (2013)
7. Gurrin, C., Qiu, Z., Hughes, M., Caprani, N., Doherty, A.R., Hodges, S.E.: The smartphone as a platform for wearable cameras in health research. Am. J. Prev. Med. **44**(3), 308–313 (2013)
8. Rawassizadeh, R., Tomitsch, M., Wac, K., Tjoa, A.M.: UbiqLog: a generic mobile phone-based life-log framework. Pers. Ubiquitous Comput. **17**(4), 621–637 (2013)
9. Ali, S., Khusro, S., Rauf, A., Mahfooz, S.: Sensors and mobile phones: evolution and state-of-the-art. Pakistan J. Sci. **66**(4), 386–400 (2014)
10. Ali, S., Khusro, A., Khan, A.A., Hassan, L.: A survey of mobile phones context-awareness using sensing computing research. J. Eng. Appl. Sci. **33**(4), 75–93 (2014)
11. Ali, S., Khusro, S., Ullah, I., Khan, A., Khan, I.: SmartOntoSensor: ontology for semantic interpretation of smartphone sensors data for context-aware application. J. Sens. **17**(2017), 1–26 (2017)
12. Gurrin, C., Smeaton, A.F., Doherty, A.R.: LifeLogging: personal big data. Found. Trends Inf. Retr. **8**(1), 1–125 (2014)
13. Walter, C.: Kryder's law. Sci. Am. **293**(2), 32–33 (2005)
14. Aizenbud-Reshef, N., Belinsky, E., Jacovi, M., Laufer, D., Soroka, V.: Pensieve: augmenting human memory. In: CHI 2008 Extended Abstracts on Human Factors in Computing Systems, pp. 3231–3236 (2008)
15. Bush, V.: As we may think. Interactions **3**(2), 35–46 (1996)
16. Mann, S.: Wearable computing: a first step toward personal imaging. Computer **30**(2), 25–32 (1997)

17. Aizawa, K., Tancharoen, D., Kawasaki, S., Yamasaki, T.: Efficient retrieval of life log based on context and content. In: 1st ACM Workshop on Continuous Archival and Retrieval of Personal Experiences, pp. 22–31 (2004)
18. Chennuru, S., Chen, P.-W., Zhu, J., Zhang, J.Y.: Mobile lifelogger – recording, indexing, and understanding a mobile user's life. In: Gris, M., Yang, G. (eds.) MobiCASE 2010. LNICST, vol. 76, pp. 263–281. Springer, Heidelberg (2012). https://doi.org/10.1007/978-3-642-29336-8_15
19. Myka, A.: Nokia lifeblog – towards a truly personal multimedia information system. In: Mobile Data Banken and Information Systems – MDBIS 2005, pp. 21–30 (2005)
20. Froehlich, J., Chen, M.Y., Consolvo, S., Harrison, B., Landay, J.A.: MyExperience: a system for in situ tracing and capturing of user feedback on mobile phones. In: 5th International Conference on Mobile Systems, Applications and Services, pp. 57–70 (2007)
21. Memon, M.A., Bhatti, S., Mahoto, N.A.: A digital diary: remembering the past using the present context. Mehran Univ. Res. J. Eng. Technol. **35**(2), 275–286 (2016)
22. Vaittinen, T., Kärkkäinen, T., Roimela, K.: Experience explorer: a life-logging platform based on mobile context collection. In: Third International Conference on Next Generation Mobile Applications, Services and Technologies 2009 (NGMAST 2009), pp. 77–82 (2009)

# A Relay Station Deployment Algorithm for Smart Grid Based on Delay Optimization

Fanbo Meng[1]([⊠]), Baogang Zhang[2], Zhihao Zhao[2], Ang Li[2],
and Minlan Jiang[3]

[1] State Grid Liaoning Electric Power Company Limited,
Shenyang 110006, China
amengfb@163.com
[2] State Grid Dalian Electric Power Supply Company, Dalian 116011, China
[3] College of Physics and Electronic Information Engineering,
ZJNU, Jinhua, China

**Abstract.** Power line communication (PLC) technology can make full use of the existing distribution network physical network for data transmission in smart grid, with low cost, flexibility, high coverage, network reliability advantages. In order to extend the communication distance of PLC network and improve the reliability of network, it is necessary to research the networking and deployment methods of PLC network and establish a reasonable optimization model for different environments and business requirements. Therefore, in order to solve the problem of PLC relay deployment under the business scenario of power communication network, this paper proposes an algorithm of PLC network relay station deployment for time delay optimization. The graph theory is used to describe and define the reliability of the network. In order to reduce time delay, the reliability and transmission power are defined as constraints. The mathematical model of relay station deployment is proposed. The improved genetic algorithm is designed and the relay station deployment algorithm based on the improved genetic algorithm is proposed. The performance of the algorithm is verified by simulation results.

**Keywords:** Power line communication · Smart grid · Relay station

## 1 Introduction

The power distribution and utilization communication network mainly completes special-purpose user acquisition (i.e. load control system), residential user acquisition, line monitoring, distribution automation and other services [1–4]. At present, a hybrid network with a wireless public network as the main solution and a combination of optical fiber and wireless private network is generally adopted as a secondary solution [5–8]. However, the current wired optical fiber and wireless transmission methods have certain limitations, and cannot meet the "full coverage, full acquisition" requirements of the power collection service [9–13].

It is a common practice for multi-city power companies to lease GPRS wireless public network to carry out electricity distribution business. Due to the mature

H. Song et al. (Eds.): SIMUtools 2019, LNICST 295, pp. 74–83, 2019.
https://doi.org/10.1007/978-3-030-32216-8_7

development of the wireless public network, the leased public network channel has the advantages of less initial investment and short construction period, which can meet the requirements of rapid deployment and business development of the distribution service [12–15]. However, with the large-scale development of power distribution services, the commonly used GPRS wireless public network has gradually exposed many problems, such as low acquisition success rate, low controllability, reliability, and real-time performance, no priority for different power services and so on.

The fiber optic private network has a high cost and long construction period. The wireless private network has high investment, complicated deployment, and limited frequency resources, if the total number of dedicated base stations required to achieve full coverage is large [2–5]. Therefore, at present, the integration of wireless private network and wired private network is adopted in most areas to deploy power distribution services. The architecture is shown as Fig. 1.

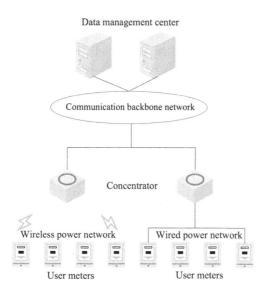

**Fig. 1.** Wireless and wired power private network architecture.

PLC technology can make full use of the physical network of the existing distribution network for data transmission, is a common communication technology in the distribution network. In this section, the PLC network networking and deployment method under the scenario of distribution power communication network is studied [8–11]. The main problem to be solved is to expand the communication range of PLC network, improve the reliability of network, and ensure that the time delay requirements of distribution power communication network are met [12–15].

In this paper, considering the characteristics of PLC relay network routing, network reliability, delay characteristics and channel characteristics of PLC and other factors, a PLC relay station deployment algorithm for delay optimization is designed. Under the scheme of selecting the relay station, the network routing selection will also be determined, and the average transmission delay, reliability, average transmission energy and other indicators will change accordingly. The relay station selection scheme is proposed as chromosome coding sequence, the performance index of the corresponding network after the relay station deployment is abstracted as multi-objective deployment model, and the optimal chromosome is selected by improved genetic algorithm to obtain the final relay station deployment scheme.

## 2 PLC Relay Station Deployment for Delay Optimization

### 2.1 PLC Network Model

The PLC power communication network model is shown as Fig. 2. PLC data relay terminals in the network need to transmit the collected data to the upper control center, which will transmit the control information to each data terminal in the network through the same path. PLC network consists of data terminal and relay station. Data terminal refers to the communication node of PLC network, which is connected with the collection terminal of smart grid to collect and transmit the information of distribution communication network. Relay stations are data terminals with relay functions. On the one hand, they assume the functions of data terminals in the covered area; on the other hand, they forward the transmitted data on the data terminals with relay connection to the control center. Answer points apply the hierarchical idea, that is, the network is divided into multiple levels, the lower data terminals communicate directly with the upper answer points, and the answer points interact with the control center for data. All data terminals and relay stations in the PLC network can be coordinated two-way data exchange, without the control of the upper control center.

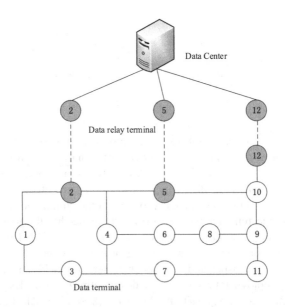

**Fig. 2.** PLC power communication network model.

## 2.2  Relay Station Deployment Model

The PLC network in this section is represented by undirected graph $G(V, L)$, where the vertices represent each communication node and the edges represent the communication links between nodes. Define the total number of all nodes in the PLC network as $N$. Set $Q$ represents the vertex set of data terminal, set $S$ represents the vertex set of relay station, and its relationship is as follows:

$$q \in Q \subseteq V, s \in S \subseteq V, Q \cup S = V \tag{1}$$

Define the set of all communication links in PLC network as $L$, and the set of routing from all data terminals to all relay stations as $L_0$. $L_{e,r}$ represents the routing set from data terminal $e$ to relay station $r$, and the following formula can be obtained:

$$L_{e,r} \subseteq L_0 \tag{2}$$

We define $L_h = \{l_1, l_2, \ldots, l_n\}$ to represent the route from data terminal $q$ to relay station $s$, and the route length is $n$, then we can get:

$$L_h \in L_{e,r} \tag{3}$$

**Reliability of PLC Network.** We define $b_{e,r}$ P as the reliability of route $L_h$, and the reliability of route is the reliability product of each link constituting the route:

$$b_{e,r} = \prod_{l \in p_h} b_l \tag{4}$$

The network consists of $N$ routes. The reliability of the network is the average of the $N$ routes. At the same time, the reliability of the data terminal link where the relay station is located is 1. The definition parameter $a_{e,r}$ represents the routing selection. When $a_{e,r} = 1$, route $L_h$ is selected. When $a_{e,r} = 0$, route $L_h$ is not selected. The number of relay stations is defined as $M$, and the proportion of network optional relay stations is determined by parameter $\alpha$, which is related to the maximum number of hops allowed by the network. From the above parameters, the reliability of PLC network is expressed as:

$$R = \frac{1}{N} \sum_{e=1}^{N} \sum_{r=1}^{M} b_{e,r} \cdot a_{e,r}, l_h \in L_{e,r} \subseteq L_0 \tag{5}$$

In order to ensure that each data terminal belongs to only one relay station and there is only one route between it and the relay station, the following constraints are proposed:

$$\sum_{r=1}^{M} a_{e,r} = 1, \forall q \in Q \tag{6}$$

**Link Quality.** We measure link quality using link maximum transmission speed. Link quality parameters describe the transmission quality of PLC network links, the higher the link quality, the smaller the transmission delay. Under the same physical parameters such as transmission frequency and bandwidth, the link quality is affected by the transmitted signal power at the sending end, and the transmitted power will affect the average transmission energy of the link and network. We define $i$ is the data terminal number of link sender and $j$ is the data terminal number of link receiver. The channel capacity of link $T_{i,j}$ is defined as:

$$C_{i,j} = \int_{B_1}^{B_2} \log_2 \left( 1 + \frac{L_{i,j}|H_{i,j}(f)|^2}{(B_2 - B_1)N(f)\Gamma} \right) df \tag{7}$$

In formula (7), $B_1$ and $B_2$ are the lowest and highest values of channel frequency band respectively. $T_{i,j}$ is the signal transmission power from node $i$ to node $j$, $N(f)$ is the channel noise, $\Gamma$ is the fixed ratio between the channel capacity and the achievable rate, which is related to the channel SNR, encoding and modulation mode. $H_{i,j}(f)$ is the frequency response of link $T_{i,j}$. In the same PLC network, the link channel has the characteristics of flat fading, and the link quality function $M_{i,j}$ of PLC is defined as the maximum channel capacity:

$$M_{i,j} = C_{i,j}(L_{i,j\max}) \tag{8}$$

Where, $L_{i,j\max}$ is the maximum signal transmitting power of link $T_{i,j}$.

**Transmission Delay.** Assuming that there are $N$ routes in the PLC network, the transmission delay $T_a$ of the average single node in the network and the energy $E_a$ of average transmission data of each node in the network are respectively expressed as:

$$T_a = \frac{1}{N}\sum_{e=1}^{N} T_{er} \quad E_a = \frac{1}{N}\sum_{e=1}^{N} E_{er} \tag{9}$$

Where $T_{er}$ is the total transmission delay and $E_{er}$ is the total transmission energy.

Based on the above conclusions, if the threshold of network average reliability is $\varphi$ and the threshold of network average transmission energy is $\psi$, the mathematical model of relay station deployment target and constraint conditions can be obtained, as shown in formula (10):

$$\min T_a = \frac{1}{N}\sum_{e=1}^{N}\sum_{r=1}^{M} T_{e,r} \cdot w_r$$

$$s.t. \begin{cases} R = \frac{1}{N} \sum_{e=1}^{N} \sum_{r=1}^{M} b_{e,r} \cdot a_{e,r} \geq \varphi \\ \sum_{r=1}^{M} a_{e,r} = 1, \forall q \in Q \\ E_a = \frac{1}{N} \sum_{e=1}^{N} E_{er} \leq \psi \\ M \leq \alpha \cdot N \end{cases} \tag{10}$$

The problem of relay station deployment belongs to NP hard problem, and heuristic algorithm is a common method to solve this kind of problem. Among heuristic algorithms, genetic algorithm is a common algorithm to solve network deployment problems because of its simple implementation and strong adaptability to multi-objective optimization problems. However, genetic algorithm is prone to fall into the local optimal solution, and the local search ability is not good after the population evolution approaches the optimal interval. In order to solve these problems, the selection, crossover and mutation operations are optimized in this section, and an improved genetic algorithm is designed, which not only improved the genetic diversity of the population at the early iteration stage, but also reduced the degree of change to the excellent genes at the later stage. The flow chart is as follows:

# 3 Simulation

In order to verify the effectiveness of relay station deployment algorithm, Matlab is used to carry out simulation experiments on PLC network with at least 20 nodes. The link reliability is randomly selected within the range of [0.9, 0.99], and the initial value of network reliability threshold $\varphi$ is set as 0.9. In the simulation, 0.01 is added to 0.99 at a time. The maximum proportion of nodes occupied by relay stations $\alpha = 0.3$. The size of a single packet is 200bit, and the data generated by the node obeys the $\lambda = 1p/s$ Poisson distribution. The transmitting power of each node's uplink is between 10 mW and 20 mW, and the average transmission energy threshold $\psi$ of the network is up to 39 mJ. Channel noise is Gaussian white noise, $\Gamma = 10$. Population size is 100 and maximum evolutionary algebra is 300, and the chromosome length is set as 20. Maximum crossover probability $L_c$ and maximum mutation probability $L_m$ are 0.6 and 0.2 respectively. Minimum crossover probability $L_{cm}$ and minimum mutation probability $L_{mm}$ are 0.2 and 0.02, respectively (Fig. 3).

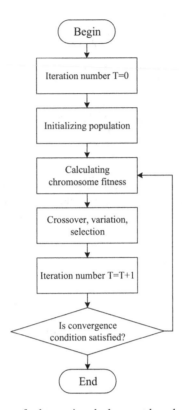

**Fig. 3.** The flow chart of relay station deployment based on genetic algorithm.

Figure 4 verifies the relationship between network reliability and the number of network relays. As known from Fig. 4, with the increase of network reliability, the number of relay stations increases significantly when the energy threshold restriction is not done. However, when the network reliability exceeds 0.97, the number of network relay stations increases slowly, which becomes obvious with the increase of network scale. Therefore, it is not necessary to deploy a large number of relay nodes in pursuit of high network reliability.

Figure 5 shows the relationship between network reliability and network transmission delay. With the increase of reliability, the transmission delay of the network decreases obviously. This is because the reliability is affected by the distribution of relay stations. The more the number of relay stations, the stronger the network reliability and the lower the network transmission delay. When the network reliability increases above 0.98, the change of transmission delay is no longer obvious, which is more obvious with the increase of network size.

Figure 6 shows the change curve of transmission delay with network transmission energy under the condition that the maximum threshold of network average transmission energy is 39 mJ and the network reliability requirement is 0.95, 0.96 and 0.97, respectively. As can be seen from Fig. 6, with the increase of transmission energy threshold, in order to reduce the average transmission delay of the network, the links

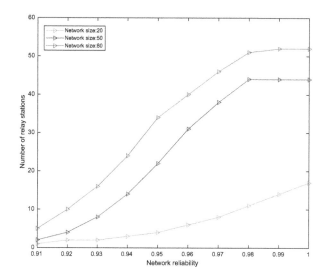

**Fig. 4.** Relay station numbers change.

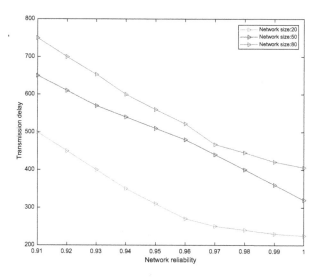

**Fig. 5.** Transmission delay change.

corresponding to the stations with high transmission power are more selected, and the link uplink node is selected as the relay station with a greater probability, thus significantly reducing the transmission delay of the network. The greater the reliability, the smaller the influence of transmission energy on the average network delay. When the transmission energy threshold is large, the improvement effect of the increase of transmission energy on the transmission delay decreases gradually. This is because when the reliability is improved to a certain extent, the quality of the relaying route

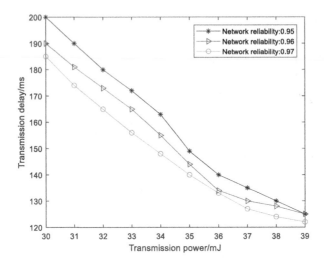

**Fig. 6.** Transmission power change.

corresponding to the link in the network is generally higher with the limitation of energy threshold, and the influence of the relay station selection result on the delay will be weakened.

Above all, simulation results show that the proposed relay station deployment results under different network environments can be obtained effectively. By deploying the relay station in a reasonable location, the network can meet the limitation of reliability and improve the network transmission delay.

## 4 Conclusion

The construction of smart grid needs to develop and optimize the deployment and scheduling methods of communication network. In this paper, the deployment and optimization methods of PLC network in smart grid are studied, and a relay station deployment algorithm based on delay optimization is proposed. Simulation results show that our algorithm can well guide the deployment of PLC network relay points and help develop a reliable, efficient, safe and friendly smart grid and its communication network.

## References

1. Jiang, D., Huo, L., Li, Y.: Fine-granularity inference and estimations to network traffic for SDN. PLoS ONE **13**(5), 1–23 (2018)
2. Artale, G.: A new low cost coupling system for power line communication on medium voltage smart grids. IEEE Trans. Smart Grid **9**(4), 3321–3329 (2018)
3. Jiang, D., Wang, W., Shi, L., Song, H.: A compressive sensing-based approach to end-to-end network traffic reconstruction. IEEE Trans. Netw. Sci. Eng. (2018). https://doi.org/10.1109/tnse.2018.2877597

4. Jiang, D., Huo, L., Song, H.: Rethinking behaviors and activities of base stations in mobile cellular networks based on big data analysis. IEEE Trans. Netw. Sci. Eng. 1(1), 1–12 (2018)
5. González, L., Mateo, C., Frías, P., et al.: Reliability analysis of PLC PRIME networks for smart metering applications. IEEE Trans. Smart Grid 9(2), 827–835 (2018)
6. Jiang, D., Nie, L., Lv, Z., et al.: Spatio-temporal Kronecker compressive sensing for traffic matrix recovery. IEEE Access 4, 3046–3053 (2016)
7. Jiang, D., Liu, J., Lv, Z., et al.: A robust energy-efficient routing algorithm to cloud computing networks for learning. J. Intell. Fuzzy Syst. 31(5), 2483–2495 (2016)
8. Jiang, D., Han, Y., Miao, L., et al.: Dynamic access approach to multiple channels in pervasive wireless multimedia communications for technology enhanced learning. J. Intell. Fuzzy Syst. 31(5), 2497–2509 (2016)
9. Garau, M., Celli, G., Ghiani, E., et al.: Evaluation of smart grid communication technologies with a co-simulation platform. IEEE Wirel. Commun. 24(2), 42–49 (2017)
10. Jiang, D., Huo, L., Lv, Z., et al.: A joint multi-criteria utility-based network selection approach for vehicle-to-infrastructure networking. IEEE Trans. Intell. Transp. Syst. 19, 1–15 (2018)
11. Jiang, D., Yuan, Z., Zhang, P., et al.: A traffic anomaly detection approach in communication networks for applications of multimedia medical devices. Multimedia Tools Appl. 75(22), 14281–14305 (2016)
12. Biagi, M., Greco, S., Lampe, L.: Geo-Routing algorithms and protocols for power line communications in smart grids. IEEE Trans. Smart Grid 9(2), 1472–1481 (2018)
13. Jiang, D., Xu, Z., Wang, W., et al.: A collaborative multi-hop routing algorithm for maximum achievable rate. J. Netw. Comput. Appl. 2015(57), 182–191 (2015)
14. Yoon, S., Kang, S., Jeong, S., et al.: Priority inversion prevention scheme for PLC vehicle-to-grid communications under the hidden station problem. IEEE Trans. Smart Grid 9(6), 5887–5896 (2018)
15. Jiang, D., Shi, L., Zhang, P., et al.: QoS constraints-based energy-efficient model in cloud computing networks for multimedia clinical issues. Multimedia Tools Appl. 75(22), 14307–14328 (2016)

# A Collection Node Planning Algorithm of Power Wireless Private Network in Smart Grid

Fanbo Meng[1(✉)], Guoqing Liu[2], Bin Lu[1], Dongdong Wang[1],
Ling Wang[2], Dongming Tang[3], and Dingde Jiang[4]

[1] State Grid Liaoning Electric Power Company Limited,
Shenyang 110006, China
amengfb@163.com
[2] State Grid Benxi Electric Power Supply Company, Benxi 117000, China
[3] School of Computer Science and Technology,
Southwest Minzu University, Chengdu, China
[4] School of Astronautics and Aeronautic, UESTC, Chengdu 611731, China

**Abstract.** The power wireless private network is a wireless broadband access system that is deeply customized for the development of smart grid terminal communication access, and is integrated with the power dedicated 230 MHz spectrum to meet the wide coverage, large capacity, strong real-time performance, high security, flexibility and easy-to-expand of the power intelligent terminal, and provide integrated wireless communication private network solutions for various services such as distribution automation, electrical information collection, and precise load control. This paper proposes a data collection node planning algorithm in wireless power private network, which can realize the data measurement of large-scale intelligent power terminals at a small cost. Simulation results show the reliability of our algorithm.

**Keywords:** Power wireless private network · Smart grid · Adaptability

## 1 Introduction

### 1.1 A Subsection Sample

The power industry is the basic industry related to people's livelihood and the country's most important infrastructure [1–4]. In the current energy transformation, in order to accelerate the realization of energy transformation, higher requirements are placed on the smart grid. The wireless private network is the foundation of the smart grid, meeting the access needs of diverse, ubiquitous, intelligent, and large-scale equipment at the end of the grid. Power wireless private network can effectively provide security guarantee for the smart grid, effectively monitoring and acquisition of power grid and the communication between the user data, such as the state of the user terminal information, equipment operation parameters, control information and other data, and make timely response to abnormal data, sends out control instructions to maintain the normal operation of power grid [5–8]. However, with the rapid increase of the number

H. Song et al. (Eds.): SIMUtools 2019, LNICST 295, pp. 84–93, 2019.
https://doi.org/10.1007/978-3-030-32216-8_8

of power users and the types of power consumption, the traditional user-by-user data collection method not only extends the time, but also tends to generate a large packet loss rate for the power consumption data with a long distance. As a result, many intelligent terminals in power distribution network deployment to convenient for data acquisition, deployment of data access nodes at the same time, it will be assigned to the corresponding data in the network, intelligent terminal access node for collection and analysis, and then transferred to the upper data processing center, such as data acquisition and monitoring control system, measurement data management system, etc. [9, 10]. By connecting the intelligent terminal with the upper data management system, the data access node can improve the real-time reliability of data acquisition in power distribution communication network. Therefore, effective planning of access nodes is the key to achieve reliable and complete information transmission between intelligent terminals and access nodes, which has a profound impact on maintaining safe and effective operation of distribution network [11–13].

At present, many researchers have begun to study the location of data access nodes in the power grid, and most of them choose the optimal location of access nodes mainly from the constraints of reliability and economy. However, in practical applications, we need to consider not only the cost and packet loss rate, but also whether the data transmission can arrive within the specified time and the network fault tolerance [11]. Therefore, this paper combines economy, reliability, real-time to select the best location of data access node, to ensure the effective operation of power wireless private network. In order to confirm the optimal location and routing table scheme of data access nodes in power distribution communication network, this paper proposes an access node planning algorithm for power wireless private network considering the economy of network construction, network delay, network reliability and network fault tolerance. Firstly, the mathematical models of network delay, network reliability and network construction cost are established respectively. Then, an access node planning algorithm based on immune algorithm is proposed. Finally, we use Matlab to verify our scheme, the experiment shows that the access nodes established by this method can maintain good network performance.

## 2 Access Node Planning Model

### 2.1 Power Wireless Private Network Introduction

The power wireless private network is mainly composed of a core network, a network management system, a base station and a wireless terminal. The specific network architecture is shown as Fig. 1.

**Core Network Equipment (EPC).** Responsible for terminal authentication, terminal IP address management, mobility management, etc., providing interfaces directly to the main service of the power service.

**Network Management Equipment (eOMC).** Responsible for remote configuration management and status monitoring of core networks, base stations, and wireless terminals.

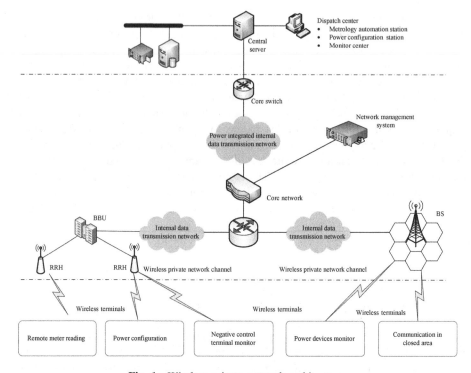

**Fig. 1.** Wireless private network architecture.

**Base Station Equipment (eNodeB).** responsible for communicating with wireless terminals through a spatial interface, and implementing functions such as resource scheduling, radio resource management, radio access control, and mobility management.

**Wireless Terminal (UE).** The wireless terminal provides wireless data collection and transmission, and can be directly embedded in a power terminal such as a power collection device and a load control.

## 2.2    The Role of Power Wireless Private Network in Smart Grid

Smart grids need to have high-speed, two-way, real-time power wireless broadband communication network support. The smart grid system has three parts, as shown in Fig. 2. One is the sensing layer, which is responsible for collecting all kinds of information of the micro grid (through various types of terminals such as smart meters, concentrators/collectors, negative controls, RFID electronic tags, voltage and current transformers, etc.) The second is the network layer, which undertakes the transmission of information (wireless private network, wireless public network, wired private network, etc.); and the third is the application layer, which analyzes, processes, controls and decides on the collected various types of power grid information to achieve grid specificity. The intelligent application and service is located at the network layer and is responsible for the collection of big data.

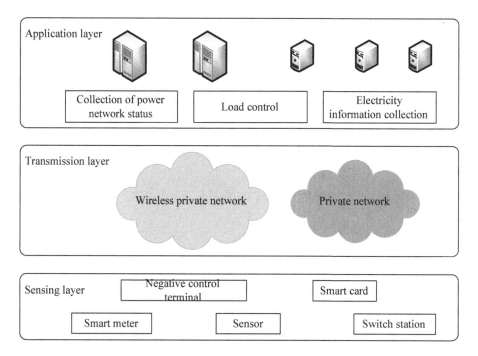

**Fig. 2.** The role of wireless private network.

## 2.3 Data Acquisition Model

Undirected graph is used to represent the network topology of the distribution communication network, where undercurrent and L represent the set of terminal nodes and link sets of the network respectively. The W in the terminal node set E is the number of terminal nodes. P represents all possible path sets from each set of terminal nodes to the location of access node, where P represents the route from terminal node I to access node j, with the number of hops n. As shown in the figure, the access node planning model diagram, where the black node is the data access node, connected with the upper data management center; the white node is an ordinary intelligent terminal node to assist in data measurement. Under this model, we consider the constraints of network construction cost, network reliability, network delay, network fault tolerance and other four aspects facing the selection of data access nodes (Fig. 3).

**Network Construction Cost.** In the planning problem of this section, it is assumed that the construction cost of network lines and common intelligent terminals is the same in different networks, and is set as $C^L$. Data acquisition location is the key to access node planning, and it needs to be protected when deployed, that is, to ensure its good

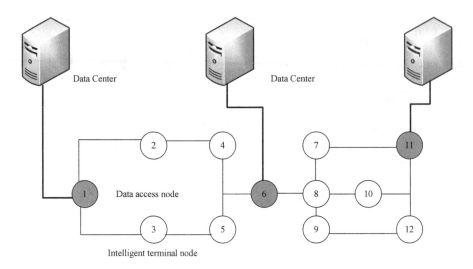

**Fig. 3.** Data acquisition model.

performance even in bad weather such as rain and snow. $c_j$ represents the construction cost required to deploy the data access node at node $j$, and the construction cost of the entire network is:

$$C = C^L + \sum_{j=1}^{M} c_j * x_j \tag{1}$$

where $x_j \in \{0, 1\}$, $x_j = 1$ means node $j$ is selected to deploy an access node; when $x_j = 0$, it means location $j$ does not need to deploy an access node; and $M$ means the number of candidate access nodes.

**Network Reliability.** $r_v$ represents the reliability of communication link $v$, and the reliability of a communication link is generally the ratio of its normal working time in a certain period of time to the total time. This section sets that the link reliability obeys uniform distribution on [0.9, 0.99]. The reliability of the route $P_{i,j}$ between terminal node $i$ and access node $j$ is the product of the reliability of all links connected by the route, which can be expressed as:

$$r_{i,j}^p = \prod_{v \in p_{i,j}} r_v \tag{2}$$

In addition, we specify an access node for each terminal and give routing information between the two nodes. Therefore, after obtaining the overall information of the routing table, the average reliability of the network can be obtained:

$$\bar{R} = \frac{1}{N} \sum_{i=1}^{M} \sum_{i=1}^{N} y_{i,j} \cdot r_{i,j}^p, p \in P \tag{3}$$

where $y_{i,j} \in \{0,1\}$, $y_{i,j} = 1$ means that the traffic of terminal node $i$ is forwarded by routing $P_{i,j}$ under the normal state of all the devices, while $y_{i,j} = 0$ means that it is not forwarded by routing $P_{i,j}$. In order to ensure that the initial terminal node can transmit information to the specified access node through only one route, the design constraints are as follows:

$$\sum_{j=1}^{M}\sum_{i=1}^{N} y_{i,j} = 1 \tag{4}$$

**Network Delay.** In the network, the end-to-end delay is to node to a message in the source system and purpose of the time required to pass between two applications, mainly including a packet through a routing table to reach the purpose of access nodes each node traversal by data processing time (including the queue time) and in each transmitted on a communications link the sum total of time consuming. Therefore, in order to simplify the calculation in this section, we only calculate one packet trans-mitting time after k jump sent to the access node, ignoring forward consume time by purpose access nodes to the upper data management system. The sum of time delay can be calculated of a packet from a terminal node transmitted to the upper data man-agement system by:

$$t_p^k = k \times t_{tra} + t_{pro} \times \sum_{p=1}^{k} l_p \tag{5}$$

Where, $t_{tra}$ refers to the transmission delay on the link, and k is the total hops of the routing table. $t_{pro}$ refers to the delay of packet in processing state, and $l_p$ refers to the queue length when packet is ready state. It is assumed that there is no difference in nodes and links. Therefore, the average delay of transmitting one packet from each terminal node to the upper data management system is:

$$\bar{t} = \frac{1}{n}\sum_{i=1}^{n}(k \times t_{tra} + t_{pro} \times \sum_{p=1}^{k} l_p) \tag{6}$$

Based on the above three constraints, the mathematical model for the optimization of access node location of distribution communication network is as follows:

$$\min C = C^L + \sum_{j=1}^{M} c_j \cdot x_j$$
$$s.t. \quad \bar{R} \geq \varphi$$
$$\sum_{j=1}^{M}\sum_{i=1}^{N} y_{i,j} = 1 \tag{7}$$
$$\bar{t} \leq \lambda$$

where, $\varphi$ and $\lambda$ refer to the reliability and the threshold of information transmission delay required by the business of a distribution communication network.

It can be seen from the formula (7) that the proposed access node location planning problem is a multi-objective optimization problem, and the heuristic algorithm can solve this problem in a limited time. Among them, the immune algorithm is not only simple and flexible in application, but also can use "vaccine" to represent the access node location strategy. Moreover, the algorithm will not fall into the local optimal solution, but can search for the global optimal solution. The steps of the access node location planning method of distribution communication network based on immune algorithm are as follows:

**Step 1:** Parameter setting. According to the network size of distribution communication network, the population size is set as 100, the number of vaccines extracted in each iterative evolution is 15, and the probability of crossover and mutation are 0.9 and 0.05, and the maximum number of iteration optimization is 300. According to the structure of distribution communication network, the coding length L, similarity parameter $\varepsilon$, reliability, and the threshold of network delay are determined.

**Step 2:** Initialization. The network data of distribution communication network are imported to randomly generate the initial antibody groups in the location planning scheme of access nodes, and the iterative evolution times are set as 0.

**Step 3:** Antibody evaluation. The affinity between the access node location planning scheme and the problem model and the affinity between different schemes are calculated for the antibody concentration and the expected reproduction probability.

**Step 4:** Make a vaccine. The affinity between the access node location planning scheme and the problem model is sorted in descending order, and the fixed gene fragments from the first $N_m$ antibodies are taken as vaccines.

**Step 5:** Form a parent subgroup. The reproductive probability of antibodies in this algorithm is sorted from high to low, and the first $N_R - N_m$ antibodies are extracted as parent subgroups.

**Step 6:** Group renewal. The new antibody group in Step 5 is mutated and updated, and the vaccine is added to form a new generation antibody group according to the affinity ratio.

**Step 7:** If $t > M$, then the optimal solution is output; Otherwise, let $t = t + 1$, go to Step 3.

## 3  Simulation

In order to verify the effectiveness of the proposed access node location algorithm based on immune algorithm, we conduct a simulation experiment on the system with 20 nodes at least, and the simulation software is Matlab. In this algorithm, the encoding length is set as 20, the similarity parameter $\varepsilon = 1$, the reliability of communication link $r \in [0.9, 1]$, the node data transmission rate is 32 Kbps, and the cost of building a data access node is assuming as 10000. The change of network construction cost with network reliability is shown in Fig. 4.

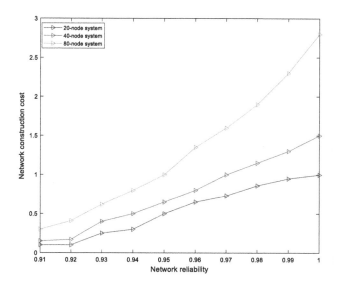

**Fig. 4.** Network construction cost changes.

As can be seen from the figure above, first of all, assuming that the network runs normally and only considering the network reliability constraints, the value of $\varphi$ is adjusted from 0.9 to 1 to calculate network construction cost. According to the figure, the construction cost and reliability are similarly proportional to each other. When the reliability requirements of the network increase, the communication quality requirements in the network become higher, so more data access nodes are needed to collect data information to prevent data loss and damage at a distance. At the same time, when the number of nodes doubles, the network cost is less than the doubling growth, it can be predicted that the average cost of large-scale network is lower than that of small-scale network.

Next, end-to-end delay is studied. As shown in Fig. 5, end-to-end delay decreases with the increase of data rate and network reliability. When the network reliability is high, it means that there are more access nodes, so the number of hops of data forwarding between terminal nodes and access nodes can be reduced, thus reducing the time of data transmission.

It can be seen from the above results, under the guide of our algorithm, with the increase of access nodes, can not only measure for more terminals, at the same time can effectively reduce the network delay, reduce the time of data transmission, when the number of nodes doubles, the network cost is less than the doubling growth, shows the good of our algorithm.

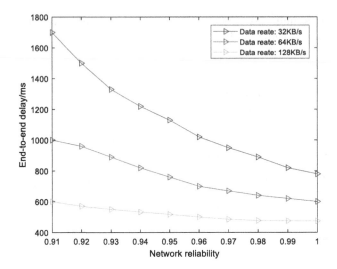

**Fig. 5.** Network construction cost changes.

## 4   Conclusion

Power wireless private network is an integrated wireless communication private network aiming at the deep customization and development of intelligent power grid terminal communication access requirements, realizing the integration of power distribution automation, power information collection, precise load control and other businesses. This paper proposes a data measurement node access planning algorithm in wireless power private network, which can realize the data measurement of large-scale intelligent power terminals at a small cost. Simulation results show the reliability of our algorithm.

## References

1. Jiang, D., Wang, W., Shi, L., Song, H.: A compressive sensing-based approach to end-to-end network traffic reconstruction. IEEE Trans. Netw. Sci. Eng. (2018). https://doi.org/10.1109/tnse.2018.2877597
2. Yang, Z., Ping, S., Aijaz, A., et al.: A global optimization-based routing protocol for cognitive-radio-enabled smart grid AMI networks. IEEE Syst. J. **12**(1), 1015–1023 (2018)
3. Jiang, D., Huo, L., Song, H.: Rethinking behaviors and activities of base stations in mobile cellular networks based on big data analysis. IEEE Trans. Netw. Sci. Eng. **1**(1), 1–12 (2018)
4. Zhang, W., Liu, W., Wang, X., et al.: Online optimal generation control based on constrained distributed gradient algorithm. IEEE Trans. Power Syst. **30**(1), 35–45 (2015)
5. Jiang, D., Huo, L., Li, Y.: Fine-granularity inference and estimations to network traffic for SDN. PLoS ONE **13**(5), 1–23 (2018)
6. Fadel, E., Gungor, V.C., Nassef, L., et al.: A survey on wireless sensor networks for smart grid. Comput. Commun. **71**, 22–33 (2015)

7. Jiang, D., Huo, L., Lv, Z., et al.: A joint multi-criteria utility-based network selection approach for vehicle-to-infrastructure networking. IEEE Trans. Intell. Transp. Syst. **19**, 1–15 (2018)
8. Jiang, D., Xu, Z., Li, W., et al.: Topology control-based collaborative multicast routing algorithm with minimum energy consumption. Int. J. Commun Syst **30**(1), 1–18 (2017)
9. Han, G.J., et al.: A grid-based joint routing and charging algorithm for industrial wireless rechargeable sensor networks. Comput. Netw. **101**(2016), 19–28 (2016)
10. Jiang, D., Li, W., Lv, H.: An energy-efficient cooperative multicast routing in multi-hop wireless networks for smart medical applications. Neurocomputing **2017**(220), 160–169 (2017)
11. Kuzlu, M., Pipattanasomporn, M., et al.: Communication network requirements for major smart grid applications in HAN, NAN and WAN. Comput. Netw. **67**, 74–88 (2014)
12. Jiang, D., Wang, Y., Han, Y., et al.: Maximum connectivity-based channel allocation algorithm in cognitive wireless networks for medical applications. Neurocomputing **2017** (220), 41–51 (2017)
13. Jiang, D., Xu, Z., Li, W., et al.: An energy-efficient multicast algorithm with maximum network throughput in multi-hop wireless networks. J. Commun. Netw. **18**(5), 713–724 (2016)

# A SDN-Based Network Traffic Estimating Algorithm in Power Telecommunication Network

Renxiang Huang[1]([⊠]), Huibin Jia[2], and Xing Huang[3]

[1] Sichuan University of Arts and Science, Dazhou 635000, China
wanddy@gmail.com
[2] School of Electrical and Electronic Engineering,
North China Electric Power University, Baoding, China
[3] State Grid Liaoning Electric Power Company, Shenyang, China

**Abstract.** Most of network management tasks in traffic engineering such as traffic scheduling, path planning, both of them are required the accurate and fine-grained network traffic. However, it is difficult to capture and estimate the volume of network traffic due to its time-varying nature. In this paper, we study the network traffic estimation scheme to estimate the fine-grained network traffic. Firstly, the network traffic is constructed as a time series and the autoregressive moving average (ARMA) method is used to characterize and model network traffic. Secondly, in order to decrease the estimation errors of the ARMA model, we use the optimization theory to adjust the estimation results. We construct an objective function with constraints. We find that objective function is an NP-hard problem, then we introduce a heuristic algorithm to find the optimization results. Finally, to evaluate the performance of our proposed scheme, we construct a simulation platform and compare our scheme with that of the other methods in an SDN simulation platform. The simulation results indicate that our approach is effective and our method can reflect the network traffic characteristics.

**Keywords:** Network traffic · Traffic estimation · Software-defined network · Optimization · ARMA

## 1 Introduction

With the rapid growth of applications in the power telecommunication network, network performance and quality of service issues are increasing. In the case of limited network resources, establishing a network traffic model, predicting network load, and timely controlling or adjusting will greatly improve network performance and service quality [1, 2]. Software defined network SDN is a new network innovation architecture which is an implementation of network virtualization [3]. SDN separates the control plane of the network device from the data plane and centralizes the control plane into the controller for centralized management. The controller is the brain of the network and has the global view of the network, and then it is flexible control the network traffic and makes the network more intelligent as a pipeline, providing a good platform for

© ICST Institute for Computer Sciences, Social Informatics and Telecommunications Engineering 2019
Published by Springer Nature Switzerland AG 2019. All Rights Reserved
H. Song et al. (Eds.): SIMUtools 2019, LNICST 295, pp. 94–103, 2019.
https://doi.org/10.1007/978-3-030-32216-8_9

innovation of core networks and applications. For time-frequency synchronization applications in (SDN), the network traffic, especially end-to-end network traffic in the network, represents the network-level behavior of users and applications. In the network, the network traffic from the origin node to the destination node is called an OD pair. There are many OD pairs in the network and the traffic for each OD pair directly affects the performance of the SDN. However, the network traffic in networks is difficult to be estimated and predicted due to their high variability over time. Therefore, network traffic estimation has become one of the hottest topics and has received increasing attention [4].

Liu et al. proposed two iterative algorithms to estimate TM between tomogravity space and gravity space, and use similar-Mahalanobis distance as a metric to control estimation errors in DCN(Data center network) [5]. Hashemi et al. presented a real-time traffic network state estimation and prediction system with built-in decision support capabilities for traffic network management [6]. Kawasaki et al. proposed a state-space model that estimates traffic states over a two-dimensional network with alternative routes available by a data assimilation technique that fuses probe vehicle data with a traffic flow model [7]. Dias et al. presented a classification module for video streaming traffic, based on machine learning, as a solution for network schemes that require adequate real-time traffic treatment [8]. Nie et al. propose a novel network traffic prediction approach based on a deep belief network [9]. Ermagun et al. studied examines the spatiotemporal dependency between traffic links and model the traffic flow of 140 traffic links in a sub-network of the Minneapolis-St [10]. Jiang et al. investigated how to estimate and recover the end-to-end network traffic matrix in fine time granularity from the sampled traffic traces which is a hard inverse problem [11]. Some of these methods had relatively large estimation errors, while others were very sensitive to prior information [6, 11]. Hence, the above models and methods are difficult to accurately capture network flow traffic, so it is still significantly necessary to find more accurate model to depict network flow traffic, to lower the complexity of algorithms, and to improve the estimation accuracy.

Different from these algorithms, this paper proposes a new estimation approach to model the network traffic in power telecommunication network. Firstly, the network traffic is described as linear-correlation random process over time and constructed as a time series. Then, we use the autoregressive moving average (ARMA) to characterize and model network traffic. Secondly, the ARMA model is trained to describe network traffic changes over time. Additionally, network traffic sample data are used to establish and determine the model parameters. In such a case, the ARMA model can be effectively and correctly capture the dynamic nature of network traffic in power telecommunication networks. We can effectively estimate network traffic in the next time. Then, we construct an objective function with constraints. We find that objective function is an NP-hard problem, then we introduce a heuristic algorithm to find the optimization results. Finally, to evaluate the performance of our proposed scheme, we construct a simulation plat-form and compare our scheme with that of the other methods in an SDN simulation platform.

The rest of this paper is organized as follows. Section 2 is a problem statement. Section 2.1 is to derive our prediction approach. Section 3 is simulation results and analysis. Finally, our work in this paper is concluded in Sect. 4.

## 2  Problem Statement

Origin-Destination (OD) traffic refers to traffic between two nodes in the network. Given the training set $D : \{X_i, t_i\}_{i=1}^{N}$ as the network traffic in power telecommunication networks, where $X_i$ is the number of training samples, $X_i$ is the vector of network traffic corresponding to time $t_i$, then the network traffic can be represented as

$$X = \{x(t_1), x(t_2), \ldots, x(t_N)\} \tag{1}$$

The flow traffic in the network is aggregated into the link on the transmitting path, then the relationship between link load and traffic can be expressed as that

$$Y = AX \tag{2}$$

where $Y$ is a column vector representing link traffic, $X$ is also a column vector representing the traffic matrix and $A$ is the routing matrix. The problem of flow calculation is an inverse problem solving of an underdetermined and ill-conditioned system.

In the network, the flow traffic in networks can be presented as a time-series model and has time correlation. The autoregressive moving average (ARMA) model is used to predict the time series; it consists of the autoregressive (AR) model and the moving average (MA) model. However, ARMA is more widely used and has lower prediction errors than AR model and MA model. The AR model presents the correlation of flow traffic in time, so the traffic sequence $x(1), x(2), \ldots, x(t)$ of a flow can be written as

$$x(t) = \sum_{i=1}^{p} \phi_i x(t - i) + Z(t) \tag{3}$$

where $x(t - i)$ is the observed value of the predicted object, $Z(t)$ is the error; $\phi_i (i = 1, 2, \ldots, p)$ are the autoregressive coefficients; $p$ is the order. As the prediction object $x(t)$ is affected by its own change. The error $Z(t)$ is the white noise, it is a random sequence. The MA model of random error can be expressed as

$$
\begin{aligned}
Z(t) &= u(t) + \theta_1 u(t - 1) + \theta_2 u(t - 2) + \cdots \theta_q u(t - q) \\
&= u(t) + \sum_{i=1}^{q} \theta_i u(t - i)
\end{aligned}
\tag{4}
$$

where $u(t)$ is the white Gaussian noise, so the mean and variance of $u(t)$ are $E(u(t)) = 0$ and $E(u(t)^2) = \sigma^2$, respectively; $q$ is the moving average order; $\theta_j (j = 1, 2, \ldots, q)$ are the moving average coefficients. Then, the ARMA($p$, $q$) model can be written as

$$x(t) = \sum_{i=1}^{p} \phi_i x(t - i) + u(t) + \sum_{i=1}^{q} \theta_i u(t - i) \tag{5}$$

The accuracy of the ARMA($p$, $q$) prediction is determined by the order $p$ and $q$. When $q = 0$, the ARMA model becomes the AR model; and when $p = 0$ the ARMA model degrades the MA model. Then, we introduce the AIC (Akaike Information Criterion) principle and BIC (Bayesian Information Criterion) principle to determine the order of the ARMA model. The AIC criterion is a weighting function of the fitting precision and the number of orders, and the model that makes the AIC function minimum is considered to be the optimal model. Define the AIC criterion function as follow:

$$AIC = N \log \hat{\sigma}^2 + 2(p + q + 1) \tag{6}$$

$$BIC = AIC + (\log(N) - 2)(p + q + 1) \tag{7}$$

where $N$ is the number of sampling points; $\hat{\sigma}^2$ is the variance of the filling residual. Then, we take the order of the best ARMA($p$, $q$) model.

In the SDN-based network, we use the pull-based scheme to collect coarse-grained network traffic statistic. We use the ARMA(p, q) model to predict the network traffic

$$\hat{x}(t) = \text{ARMA}(x(t)) \tag{8}$$

With the ARMA model, we estimate traffic with the measured time series $x(t)$. However, estimation results of flows have big errors with the actual flow traffic. In the network, the link load reflects the integrated traffic transmission in the network. So, we use the pull-based method to obtain the fine-grained link load $Y$ in networks. We try to decrease the network traffic error, the objective function can be written as

$$f = \left\| Y - A\hat{X} \right\|_2 + \left\| \hat{X} \right\|_2 \tag{9}$$

In order to decrease the deviation between the estimations and the actual traffic results, we construct an objective function to optimize the estimation results. The objective function with constraints as

$$\begin{cases} \min f \\ s.t. \\ C1 : X \geq 0 \\ C2 : Y_m \geq \sum_n a_{mn} \hat{X} \\ C3 : \sum_{i=1}^N x_{ij} = \sum_{j=1}^N x_{ji} \end{cases} \tag{10}$$

where $\hat{X}$ is estimated by the ARMA model. Constraint $C1$ shows the link load is non-negativity; constraint $C2$ is a limitation of flows on each link; constraint $C3$ represents that the traffic that input and output a switch are constants, $i$ is the source node and $j$ is the destination node. In the network, the routing matrix $A$ has $M$ rows and $N$ columns. However, the OD pairs are much larger than links, namely: $M \ll N$, then the routing matrix $A$ is an underdetermined matrix, therefore, there are infinite traffic matrices $X$.

The objective function (10) is an NP-hard problem and is difficult to solve directly. Then, we use a heuristic method to solve it.

## 2.1   Particle Swarm Optimization Algorithm

Particle swarm optimization (PSO) algorithm is one of the heuristic algorithms which utility the swarm intelligence computational model based on the natural swarm systems. The particle swarm optimization is an optimization technique based on the sociological behavior associated with birds flocking, which is a population-based stochastic optimization technique, so it is suitable to solve the non-linear optimization problem. The particle swarm optimization algorithm is a robust swarm optimization method which dynamically adjusts according to the particle movement velocity and the particle companions' status.

PSO is initialized with a population of random solutions and searches for optimal by updating particles' positions. The velocity of particles is influenced by three components namely, initial, cognitive and social components. Each particle updates its previous velocity and position vectors according to the following model.

$$v_k(t+1) = wv_k(t) + c_1 r_1 (Pbest_k(t) - x_k(t)) \\ + c_2 r_2 (Gbest(t) - x_k(t)) \tag{11}$$

$$x_k(t+1) = x_k(t) + v_k(t+1) \tag{12}$$

which $x_k(t+1)$ and $v_k(t+1)$ represent the particle position and the particle moving velocity respectively. The term $c_1$ and $c_2$ denote the personal and global learning factors respectively which are also defined as constants. $Pbest_k$ and $Gbest$ are the personal best and global best of each particle respectively. $r_1$ and $r_2$ are both random values in the range $[0, 1]$. The term $w$ is the inertia weight.

For PSO, the personal best status and the goal best statue are the two terms which should be shared among all the particles. We assume that there are K particles in the swarm, due to that there are N flows in the network, so each particle has expressed a vector with the set of flows, then each particle can be written as the vector $x_k = [x_{k1}, \ldots, x_{kn}, \ldots x_{kN}]$ for each particle position and the velocity vector can be written as $v_k = [v_{k1}, \ldots, v_{kn}, \ldots v_{kN}]$. Each particle flying based on its personal best status and the global best status during each iteration.

## 3   Simulation Result and Analysis

### 3.1   Simulation Environment

In this section, we perform some simulations to evaluate the performance of our proposed algorithm AMPSO. In order to justify the performance of our method, we construct a simple network topology with Mininet, and use Ryu as a controller. We use Iperf to generate some origin-destination (OD) pairs and measure the traffic at different nodes deployment at different places in the network. The PCA, SRSVD [12], WABR [8] are the methods studied has better performance. Here we compare AMPSO against them. The mean absolute error (MAE), mean relative error (MRE) for the network in traffic are for different methods. Finally, we discuss the performance improvement of AMPSO against PCA, SRSVD, WABR. In our simulation, we use the first 300 time slots as the training set to train the prediction model, and then we embed the prediction model into optimization module and insert them into the controller to measure the network traffic and validate the performance of all algorithms.

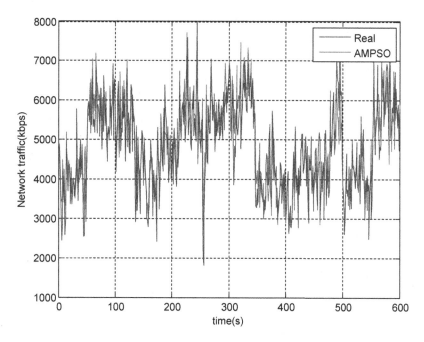

**Fig. 1.** Measurement results of network traffic.

Figure 1 shows the prediction results of network traffic flows, where network traffic flows f is selected randomly from the origin-destination (OD) pairs in the network. As our simulation tests, other OD traffic pairs holds similar results. Without loss of generality, we only discuss the network traffic flows f1 in this paper. In Fig. 1, we find that the network traffic flow is fluctuation over time as the blue line in Fig. 1. The network traffic estimation results of AMPSO can catch the trend of network traffic. Next, we will further discuss the performance of our algorithm, and compare our method against other algorithms. Although network traffic in Fig. 1 can intuitively reflect the characteristics of network traffic, it is difficult to observe the fluctuation characteristics of network traffic in detail. To further verify the performance of the proposed algorithm, we use the indicators MAE and MRE to analyze the estimation error of the network traffic. We repeated the simulation 100 runs to avoid the randomness of the simulation process.

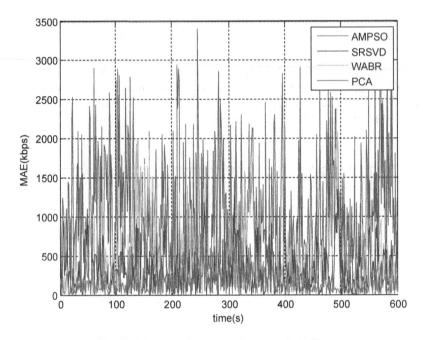

**Fig. 2.** Mean absolute errors for network traffic.

The mean absolute errors and mean relative errors over time for the network traffic are defined as:

$$\text{MAE} = \frac{1}{K}\sum\nolimits_{i=1}^{K} |\hat{x}_i(t) - x_i(t)| \tag{13}$$

$$\text{MRE} = \frac{1}{K}\sum\nolimits_{i=1}^{K} \frac{|\hat{x}_i(t) - x_i(t)|}{x_i(t)} \tag{14}$$

where $i = 1, 2, \ldots, K$, $K$ indicates the number of repetitions in the simulation process, and $\hat{x}_i(t)$ indicates the network traffic measurement, and $x_i(t)$ is the actual network traffic generate by Iperf in the network.

The mean absolute errors of the network traffic over time are shown in Fig. 2. We can find that for network traffic WABR and SRSVD exhibit lower relative errors while PCA holds the larger prediction bias. For Fig. 2, we can also see that that SRSVD holds the lowest relative errors. This shows us that in contrast to PCA, WABR and SRSVD, AMPSO holds a better performance of the network traffic prediction, while AMPSO holds the best prediction ability. We can also find that the AMPSO has the lowest fluctuation over time in terms of mean absolute errors than the other three algorithm, and has mean absolute error is smallest than the other three algorithms. AMPSO can more effectively model the network traffic with time-varying and correlation features.

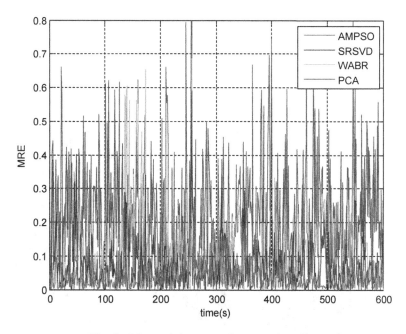

**Fig. 3.** Mean relative errors for network traffic.

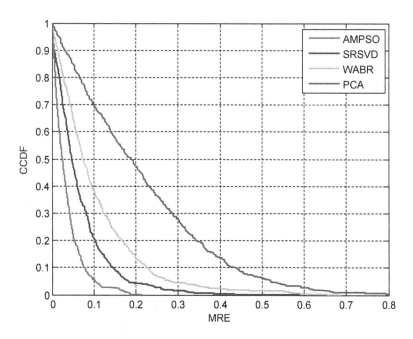

**Fig. 4.** The CCDF of the mean relative errors for network traffic.

Figure 3 depicts the mean relative errors of the network traffic. The mean relative errors reflect the ratio of estimation errors. Figure 3 shows that AMPSO has the lowest

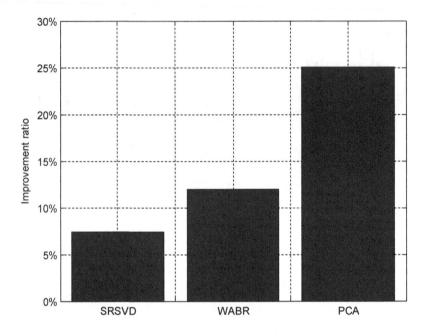

**Fig. 5.** Improvement ratio of network traffic.

mean relative errors than that of the PCA, WABR and SRSVD, and most of the mean relative errors of AMPSO is smaller than 0.1, which means that the estimation error is smaller than 10%. Then, the AMPSO is effective to estimate the network traffic in the power telecommunication networks.

Figure 4 depicts the curve of the CCDF (Complementary Cumulative Distribution Function) of mean relative errors for the different measurement methods. Mean relative errors are the standard deviation of the residuals, it shows how concentrated the data is around the line of actual flow traffic. The CCDF of the measurement Mean relative errors error in Fig. 4 reflects that 10% mean relative errors of the flow of the AMPSO, SRSVD, WABR, PCA is more than 0.078, 0.146, 0.229 and 0.435, respectively. So, the network traffic measurement scheme of AMPSO is stable and can reflect the network traffic with the mean relative error lower than 0.078.

Now, we analyze the performance improvement of AMPSO relative to the other three algorithms for the network traffic. Figure 5 exhibits the performance improvement ration of network traffic flow. In Fig. 5, AMPSO attains the performance improvement of about 7.4%, 12%, 25% against SRSVD, WABR, PCA, respectively. This clearly denotes that compared with PCA, WABR, and SRSVD, our algorithm can more accurately model the network-level network traffic. Moreover, Fig. 5 also tell us that relative to PCA and WABR, our scheme can reach larger performance improvement.

# 4 Conclusions

This paper uses the ARMA method to model network traffic in power telecommunication networks. By the ARMA model, we can capture the dynamic and time-varying features over time of the network traffic. Network traffic is converted into a time series which can be predicted by the ARMA model with some history data. Then we use the optimization theory to decrease the estimate errors. Because the objective function of the optimization process is an NP-hard problem, we propose to use a heuristic algorithm to find the solution. Then, we introduce the PSO to optimize the network traffic. Finally, we perform some simulation to verify the performance of the proposed algorithm in this paper. Simulation results show that the proposed approach in this paper is feasible.

# References

1. Jiang, D., Xu, Z., Liu, J., et al.: An optimization-based robust routing algorithm to energy-efficient networks for cloud computing. Telecommun. Syst. **63**(1), 89–98 (2016)
2. Jiang, D., Nie, L., Lv, Z., et al.: Spatio-temporal Kronecker compressive sensing for traffic matrix recovery. IEEE Access **4**, 3046–3053 (2016)
3. Guo, Y., Wang, Z., Yin, X., et al.: Traffic engineering in hybrid SDN networks with multiple traffic matrices. Comput. Netw. **126**, 187–199 (2017)
4. Jiang, D., Zhao, Z., Xu, Z., et al.: How to reconstruct end-to-end traffic based on time-frequency analysis and artificial neural network. AEU-Int. J. Electron. Commun. **68**(10), 915–925 (2014)
5. Liu, G., Guo, S., Zhao, Q., et al.: Tomogravity space based traffic matrix estimation in data center networks. Transp. Res. Part C: Emerg. Technol. **86**, 39–50 (2018)
6. Hashemi, H., Abdelghany, K.F., et al.: Real-time traffic network state estimation and prediction with decision support capabilities: application to integrated corridor management. Transp. Res. Part C: Emerg. Technol. **73**, 128–146 (2016)
7. Kawasaki, Y., Hara, Y., Kuwahara, M.: Traffic state estimation on a two-dimensional network by a state-space model. Transp. Res. Part C: Emerg. Technol. **5**, 1–17 (2019)
8. Dias, K.L., Pongelupe, M.A., Caminhas, W.M., et al.: An innovative approach for real-time network traffic classification. Comput. Netw. **158**, 143–157 (2019)
9. Jiang, D., Huo, L., Lv, Z., et al.: A joint multi-criteria utility-based network selection approach for vehicle-to-infrastructure networking. IEEE Trans. Intell. Transp. Syst. **pp**(99), 1–15 (2018)
10. Ermagun, A., Levinson, D.: Spatiotemporal short-term traffic forecasting using the network weight matrix and systematic detrending. Transp. Rese. Part C: Emerg. Technol. **104**(5), 38–52 (2019)
11. Jiang, D., Huo, L., Li, Y.: Fine-granularity inference and estimations to network traffic for SDN. PLoS One **13**(5), 1–23 (2018)
12. Roughan, M., Zhang, Y., Willinger, W., et al.: Spatio-temporal compressive sensing and internet traffic matrices. IEEE/ACM Trans. Netw. (ToN) **20**(3), 662–676 (2012)

# A Routing Algorithm Based on Weighted Graph for Power Distribution Network

Renxiang Huang[1](✉), Huibin Jia[2], and Xing Huang[3]

[1] Sichuan University of Arts and Science, Dazhou 635000, China
wanddy@gmail.com
[2] School of Electrical and Electronic Engineering,
North China Electric Power University, Baoding, China
[3] State Grid Liaoning Electric Power Company, Shenyang, China

**Abstract.** Smart power distribution network refers to the network that realizes information transmission among the power generation, transmission, transformation, consumption. With the rapid development of the power distribution network, the network topology becomes more and more complex. The scheduling of measurement, protection and control information can be realized by routing selection. However, the traditional routing algorithm cannot be applied due to its poor adaptability to the structural of the modern intelligent power system. In order to meet the requirements of low latency and high reliability in data communication of power distribution network, this paper utilize the weighted graph theory to describe the power distribution network. Then, an intelligent routing algorithm is proposed based on the analysis of the connectivity, delay, reliability and other parameters. Simulation results show that the proposed routing scheme is feasible and effective, which can also realize the load balancing of the power distribution network.

**Keywords:** Power distribution network · Routing algorithm · Weighted graph theory · Load balancing

## 1 Introduction

Power grid is one of the important part of national energy industry comprehensive transportation system [1]. Smart grid use digital information network to optimize the power grid control, including energy resources development, conversion, transmission and distribution, power supply, scheduling [2, 3]. The power distribution network is part of the grid system, which is a two-way communication network platform, using a variety of smart sensors, automation equipment, electronic devices to realize the optimization of information transmission and the reasonable use of resources [4]. The smart power distribution network belongs to the bottom of the power system, which is directly connected to the user and meets the customer demand for electricity [5]. In order to ensure the reliability of the power distribution network system, the network architecture needs to be designed in combination with the structural characteristics of the distribution network and the communication requirements of the power grid network. In intelligent power distribution network, the distribution network is composed

H. Song et al. (Eds.): SIMUtools 2019, LNICST 295, pp. 104–114, 2019.
https://doi.org/10.1007/978-3-030-32216-8_10

of a number of local communication subnets. There are a lot of sensor nodes in every communication subnet [6]. The wireless sensor nodes have formed a wireless sensor network in a local geographic area, using multiple hops links. Therefore, it is necessary to study reliable routing algorithm in smart distribution network, which can not only meet the data transmission requirements of low delay, but also realize the load balance of the whole network [7]. In recent years, more and more researchers have been starting their projects on routing design of power distribution network and there have been some important studies.

Wang et al. [8] considered the energy constraints of clustered power distribution network and proposed an improved routing protocol to achieve a global optimization in energy consumption for all cluster head nodes, which reduce the effects of hot spots in some nodes near the sink node and prevent the hot head nodes to be overloaded for data communication. But the latency of the link was not considered. The authors in [9] thought that it was a challenge to decrease the risk of different services efficiently in power distribution network. One of the method was route distribution. They proposed a routing optimization mechanism based on load balancing for power communication networks to address the abovementioned problems. Although the load balance was achieved, the reliability of the network was reduced because of the unevenly distributed network structure. The authors in [10] presents a routing algorithm to long the network lifetime oriented to the intelligent power distribution network, which can balance the energy consumption of network node, and extend the network lifetime. Similarly, the stability of this network architecture with fewer nodes was not analyzed. In order to solve the above shortcomings, this paper considers the optimal path selection problem. In particular, the transmission delay, network reliability and load balancing are analyzed in particularly.

In this paper, we study the problem of routing design for power distribution network. The rest is arranged as follows. Section 2 presents the mathematical model and proposes the routing algorithm. Section 3 displays the simulation results and analysis. We then conclude our work in Sect. 4.

## 2   Mathematical Model

In the topology of power distribution network, path stability is affected by the interference of wireless channel, path correlation, influence of geographical location, and energy efficiency of nodes, etc. In this section, the influence of node energy efficiency and path correlation on path stability is studied.

### 2.1   The Probability of Link Fracture

It is assumed that two links transmit information together and the probability of failure of each node is $p(0 \leq p \leq 1)$. Generally speaking, the routing scheme can be divided to two methods, as shown in Fig. 1. If there are no public nodes in the path, the probability of link fracture is $p_0$:

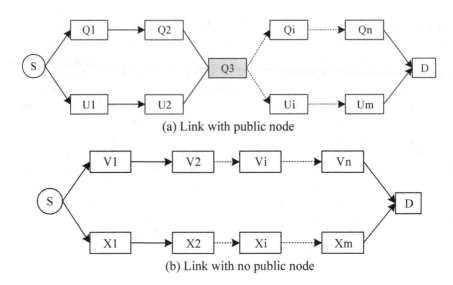

(a) Link with public node

(b) Link with no public node

**Fig. 1.** The comparison of two routing methods.

$$P_0 = P_{1-break}(V_1 V_2 \ldots V_n) P_{2-break}(X_1 X_2 \ldots X_m)$$
$$= [1 - (1-p)^n][1 - (1-p)^m] \tag{1}$$

If there is a common node in the link, the probability of link fracture is:

$$P_1 = P_{1-break}(Q_1 Q_2 \ldots Q_n) P_{2-break}(U_1 U_2 \ldots U_m)$$
$$= [1 - (1-p)^{n-1}][1 - (1-p)^{m-1}] + p \tag{2}$$

The stability comparison of these two paths is shown as $f_1(p)$:

$$
\begin{aligned}
f_1(p) &= P_1 - P_0 \\
&= \left[1 - (1-p)^{n-1}\right]\left[1 - (1-p)^{m-1}\right] + p - [1 - (1-p)^n][1 - (1-p)^m] \\
&= p - p(1-p)^{n-1} - p(1-p)^{m-1} + p(2-p)(1-p)^{n+m-2} \\
&= p\left[1 - (1-p)^{n-1} - (1-p)^{m-1} + (2-p)(1-p)^{n-1}(1-p)^{m-1}\right] \\
&\geq p\left[1 - (1-p)^{n-1} - (1-p)^{m-1} + (1-p)^{n-1}(1-p)^{m-1}\right] \\
&= p\left[1 - (1-p)^{n-1}\right]\left[1 - (1-p)^{m-1}\right] \\
&\geq 0
\end{aligned}
\tag{3}
$$

where $P_1 > P_0$. So the stability of node-independent routing is higher than that of link-independent routing when public node is 1. When comparing the link stability with k public nodes, The stability comparison of two paths is shown as $f_k(p)$:

$$f_k(p) = P_k - P_0$$
$$= \left[1 - (1-p)^{n-k}\right]\left[1 - (1-p)^{m-k}\right] + kp - \left[1 - (1-p)^{n-1}\right]\left[1 - (1-p)^{m-1}\right] - p$$
$$= p - p(1-p)^{n-k} - p(1-p)^{m-k} + [1 - (1-p)^{2k-2}](1-p)^{n-k}(1-p)^{m-k}$$
$$= p\left[1 - (1-p)^{n-k} - (1-p)^{m-k} + 2(k-2) - C_{2k-2}^2 p + C_{2k-2}^3 p^2 - \cdots - p^{2k-3}\right]$$
$$\geq p\left[1 - (1-p)^{n-k} - (1-p)^{m-k} + (1-p)^{n-k}(1-p)^{m-k}\right]$$
$$= p\left[1 - (1-p)^{n-k}\right]\left[1 - (1-p)^{m-k}\right]$$
$$\geq 0$$

$$(4)$$

where $P_k > P_1 > P_0$. It can be seen that the more nodes are public, the less stable the link is, so node-independent routing has the better stability. Therefore, the multi-path routing algorithm proposed in this section will adopt the node-independent model.

## 2.2    The Model Construction of Network Topology

In intelligent power distribution network, the distribution network is composed of a number of local communication subnets. There are a lot of sensor nodes in every communication subnet. The wireless sensor nodes have formed a wireless sensor network in a local geographic area, using multiple hops links. The multiple wireless sensor networks are connected to form the whole intelligent power distribution network. We use $V$ to express the set of nodes in intelligent distribution network communication network, $E$ to express the set of communication paths, $T$ to express the set of the delay weights in communication paths, $R$ to express the set of reliability weights in links, Thus, the whole network can be described by one connected graph $G(V,E)$, which can express the communication effectiveness between nodes as Fig. 2 shows.

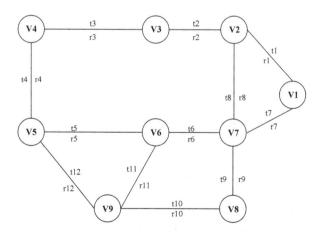

**Fig. 2.** The connected graph of intelligent power distribution network.

Meanwhile, an adjacency matrix can be denoted by $E = (e_{ij})_{N \times N}$ to express the availability between nodes, which can be formulated as:

$$e_{ij} = \begin{cases} 1 & (v_i, v_j) \in E \\ 0 & \text{otherwise} \end{cases} \tag{5}$$

where $e_{ij} = 1$ express there is a transmission link and $e_{ij} = 0$ means no available link. We define adjacency matrix $T = (t_{ij})_{N \times N}$ to express the delay weight of nodes as:

$$t_{ij} = \begin{cases} tw_{ij} & (v_i, v_j) \in E \\ \infty & \text{otherwise} \end{cases} \tag{6}$$

The reliability weights of links can be expressed as $R = (r_{ij})_{N \times N}$:

$$r_{ij} = \begin{cases} rw_{ij} & (v_i, v_j) \in E \\ 0 & \text{otherwise} \end{cases} \tag{7}$$

Considering in the power distribution network, there are strict requirements on reliability and real-time of data communication. Therefore, the analyses of alternative links for delay and reliability is necessary, so as to choose the link both satisfying the low latency and reliability for data transmission.

## 2.3   The Weight Analysis of Network Model

In the power distribution network, the communication delay between nodes mainly includes (1) path transmission delay; (2) node switching delay; (3) random jitter delay. The delay index between path nodes can be expressed as $t_{ij}$:

$$t_{ij} = \frac{A_{ij}}{c} + Bt_v + \Delta t \tag{8}$$

where $t_{ij}$ represents the communication delay between nodes $v_i$ and $v_j$, $A_{ij}$ express the communication distance, $c$ represents the data transmission rate, $B$ represents the number of nodes passed between two nodes, $t_v$ is denoted as the time consumed by node switching equipment, and $\Delta t$ represents the random jitter delay.

The path can be regarded as a combination of links and nodes, so the delay weight value of the path $T_{L_k}$ is the sum of the delay weight values of all nodes:

$$T_{L_k} = \sum_{i=1}^{n-1} \frac{l_{e_i}}{c} + nt_{v_i} + \Delta t \tag{9}$$

The link reliability $r_{ij}$ of smart distribution network can be expressed as the average of network node availability over a period of time. The value of $r_{ij}$ can be calculated from the data collected by the sensor:

$$r_{ij} = \frac{\mu}{\mu + \lambda} \tag{10}$$

where $\lambda$ represents the failure rate and $\mu$ represents the repair rate. Then, the link reliability $L_k$ of the path can be expressed as:

$$R_{L_k} = R_{v_n} \prod_{i=1}^{n-1} (R_{e_i} R_{v_i}) \tag{11}$$

where $R_{L_k}$ represents the reliability value on path $L_k$; $R_{v_n}$ represents the reliability value of the node $n$ in path $L_k$; $R_{v_i}$ represents the reliability value of the node $i$ passing through path $L_k$, and $n$ represents the number of nodes in path $L_k$. $R_{e_i}$ represents the reliability value of the link $i$ passing through the $L_k$.

## 2.4 The Path Selection Scheme

The congestion often occurs in the power communication network because of the sudden and unbalanced distribution of power services. Therefore, in order to reduce congestion, it is necessary to study routing strategies, optimize network resources and realize reasonable distribution of network traffic to ensure the performance of power communication network. Based on the analysis of the connectivity, delay, reliability and other parameters mentioned above, we can transform the path selection problem into the optimization problem, utilizing the directed connected graph theory. The objective function is $Z$:

$$Z = \min \left[ \sum_{k \in K} AT_k + B\omega \right] \tag{12}$$

where:

$$T_k = \sum_{l=1}^{L_k} \frac{S_l}{c} \eta_{ij}^{kl} + nt_v + \Delta t \tag{13}$$

$$\eta_{ij}^{kl} = \{ \begin{matrix} 1 \\ 0 \end{matrix} \tag{14}$$

$$L_k = \{ \begin{matrix} 1 \\ 2 \end{matrix} \tag{15}$$

$$n = \sum_{(i,j) \in E} \eta_{ij}^{kl} \tag{16}$$

$$\omega = \max \left[ \sum_{k=1}^{K} \sum_{l=1}^{L_k} \eta_{ij}^{kl} \lambda_k / C_{ij} \right] \tag{17}$$

The aim of the objective function is to find the minimum value of the latency and the maximum utilization of the traffic link. $K$ represents the number of business requests in the network, $T_k$ represents the sum of the delay of main path and alternative path in the $k$ flow, $S_l$ represents the length of path $l$, $n$ is the number of nodes from node $i$ to node $j$; $\omega$ represents the maximum link utilization rate, $\lambda_k$ represents the traffic of the $k$ flow, $C_{ij}$ represents the link capacity, and $A$ and $B$ are two constant coefficients. There are other constraints including:

$$\sum_{j(i,j)\in E} \eta_{ij}^k - \sum_{j(i,j)\in E} \eta_{ji}^k = \begin{cases} 1 & k \in K, l \in L_k, i = s_k \\ -1 & k \in K, l \in L_k, i = t_k \\ 0 & k \in K, l \in L_k, i \neq s_k, t_k \end{cases} \tag{18}$$

$$\sum_{k\in K} \sum_{t\in L_k} \lambda_k \eta_{ij}^{kl} \leq C_{ij}\omega \quad (i,j) \in E \quad \omega \geq 0 \tag{19}$$

$$n = \sum_{(i,j)\in E} \eta_{ij}^{kl} \leq h_k \quad k \in K \quad l \in L_k \tag{20}$$

$$\sum_{i\in S, j\notin S} \left( \eta_{ij}^{kl} + \eta_{ji}^{kl} \right) = 2 \quad \forall S \in N, S \notin \emptyset \tag{21}$$

The formula (18) represents flow conservation. Formula (19) represents the maximum link load constraint. Formula (20) represents the hop number constraint of the path $l$ of $k$ business flow. Formula (21) are reliability constraints.

It can be seen from the above mathematical model that the selection of communication path by the algorithm in this section is based on connectivity, delay, reliability and load balancing. In this paper, we use genetic algorithm to optimize the path-finding process to find the optimal path that meet the requirements.

## 3  Simulation Analysis

### 3.1  Simulation Environment and Parameters

The simulation environment of the routing algorithm are Matlab 2017a and Qualnet 2014. The 100 nodes in the network are randomly generated in the Qualnet simulator to establish the power distribution network. The transmission bandwidth of every link between two adjacent nodes is allocated 200 M. The network traffic distribution takes the normal distribution and generates randomly in the network. Then we connect the Qualnet with Matlab to obtain the dataset, where our weight-based routing (WBR) algorithm and other current main methods including minimum spanning tree algorithm (MST) and greedy algorithm (GRA) are carried out.

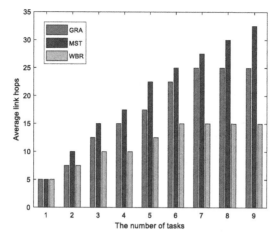

**Fig. 3.** The comparison of average link hops.

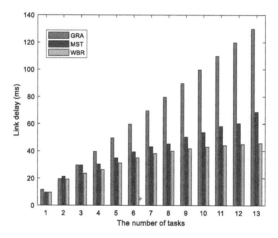

**Fig. 4.** The comparison of link delay.

The average link hops can reflect the network size and delay to some extent. Figure 3 shows the change of average link hops of three methods with the increase of the number of tasks. It can be seen that the MST As the number of tasks increases, the average link hops of the three methods also increase. The average link hop number of MST method is always the highest among the three kinds, followed by GRA. The WBR method is the least. This is because the network reliability is considered in link planning in WBR scheme. More hops will increase data packet loss rate and reduce network reliability. Therefore, the link in WBR scheme has fewer hops, which guarantees the quality of data transmission (Fig. 4).

Similarly, the link delay is measured for three methods with the increase of the number of tasks. It can be seen that the link delay is relatively low for three methods at the beginning. However, as the number of tasks increases, the link delay of GRA algorithm far exceeds the other two methods. This is because the GRA algorithm pursues the shortest path for data transmission, but does not consider the network load balancing. All data is transferred over fewer paths, overloading the node cache and causing maximum link latency.

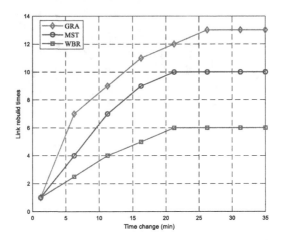

**Fig. 5.** The comparison of network availability.

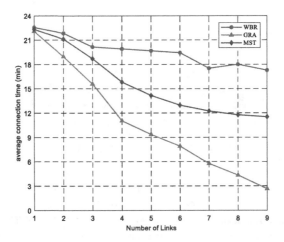

**Fig. 6.** The comparison of network robustness.

The stability of the network can be expressed by the availability and robustness of the network. Figures 5 and 6 respectively show the availability and robustness of the network. From the two figures, we can find that the link rebuild time of WBR is the smallest of three methods. This is because the reliability is served as one parameter to guide the link deployment. Meanwhile, the average connection time of WBR is the longest of the three methods, which shows a good network robustness.

From the analysis above, we can find that the proposed routing scheme has better performance in link delay and network availability and robustness, which will also realize the load balance of the whole network.

## 4 Conclusion

In this paper, a weight graph based routing scheme is proposed to improve the performance of delay and availability in smart power distribution network. The routing planning problem is changed to an optimization problem to carry out link selection. Simulation results show that compared with other methods, the proposed algorithm can effectively improve the network performance.

## References

1. Peng, W., Yuankun, L., et al.: Research on 6L0WPAN wireless sensor network and IPv6 network interconnection in power distribution system. In: Proceedings of CICED 2016, pp. 1–4 (2016)
2. Duan, Q., Ma, C., Sha, G., et al.: Research on flexible power distribution unit and its key technologies for energy Internet. In: Proceedings of ICIEA 2018, pp. 2660–2665 (2018)
3. He, S., Xie, K., Chen, W., et al.: Energy-aware routing for SWIPT in multi-hop energy-constrained wireless network. IEEE Access 6, 17996–18008 (2018)
4. Li, A., Chen, G.: Clustering routing algorithm based on energy threshold and location distribution for wireless sensor network. In: Proceedings of CCC 2018, pp. 7231–7235 (2018)
5. Abdrabou, A.: A wireless communication architecture for smart grid distribution networks. IEEE Syst. J. 10(1), 251–261 (2016)
6. Han, X.: An open energy routing network for low-voltage distribution power grid. In: Proceedings of ICEI 2017, pp. 320–325 (2017)
7. Feng, W.: Study on multi-network traffic modeling in distribution communication network access service. In: Proceedings of ICACT 2018, pp. 720–723 (2018)
8. Wang, X., Peng, Y., Huang, L.: An improved unequal cluster-based routing protocol for energy efficient wireless sensor networks. In: Proceedings of ICITBS 2019, pp. 165–169 (2019)
9. Xing, N., Xu, S., Zhang, S., et al.: Load balancing-based routing optimization mechanism for power communication networks. China Commun. 13(8), 169–176 (2016)
10. Guo, J., Yao, J., Song, T., et al.: A routing algorithm to long lifetime network for the intelligent power distribution network in smart grid. In: Proceedings of IAEAC 2019, pp. 1077–1082 (2015)
11. Wang, F., Jiang, D., Qi, S.: An adaptive routing algorithm for integrated information networks. China Commun. 7(1), 196–207 (2019)
12. Jiang, D., Wang, W., Shi, L., et al.: A compressive sensing-based approach to end-to-end network traffic reconstruction. IEEE Trans. Netw. Sci. Eng. 5(3), 1–12 (2018)
13. Jiang, D., Huo, L., Song, H.: Rethinking behaviors and activities of base stations in mobile cellular networks based on big data analysis. IEEE Trans. Netw. Sci. Eng. 1(1), 1–12 (2018)

14. Jiang, D., Huo, L., Li, Y.: Fine-granularity inference and estimations to network traffic for SDN. PLoS One **13**(5), 1–23 (2018)
15. Jiang, D., Huo, L., Lv, Z., et al.: A joint multi-criteria utility-based network selection approach for vehicle-to-infrastructure networking. IEEE Trans. Intell. Transp. Syst. **pp**(99), 1–15 (2018)

# An Adaptive Measurement Method for Flow Traffic in Software Defined Networking

Liuwei Huo[1], Dingde Jiang[2(✉)], Xiangnan Zhu[2], and Huibin Jia[3]

[1] School of Computer Science and Engineering, NEU, Shenyang 110819, China
[2] School of Astronautics and Aeronautic, UESTC, Chengdu 611731, China
jiangdd@uestc.edu.cn
[3] School of Electrical and Electronic Engineering, NCEPU, Baoding, China

**Abstract.** In Software Defined Networking (SDN), the fine-grained measurements are crucial for network management and design. However, the measurement overhead and accuracy are contradiction, how to accurately measure the network traffic with low overhead has become a hot topic. Artificial Intelligence (AI) has been used to predict the traffic in networks. Then, we propose an AI-based Lightweight Adaptive Measurement Method (ALAMM) for traffic measurement in SDN with low overhead and high measurement accuracy. Firstly, we use measurements in the front to train the AI-based traffic prediction model and utilize the model to predict traffic in SDN. Then, we obtain the sequence of sampling points by judging the change of traffic prediction and send the measurement primitive to switches to obtain coarse-grained measurements. At last, we utilize the interpolation theory to fill the coarse-grained measurement and propose an optimization function to optimize the fine-grained measurement. Simulation results show that the ALAMM is feasible, and the measurement overhead of ALAMM is low.

**Keywords:** Software Defined Networking · Adaptive network measurement · Traffic matrix · Artificial Intelligence

## 1 Introduction

Accurate traffic measurement is the foundation for network planning and management. It not only displays the current status of networks but also helps operators manage networks to detect network failure and abnormal traffic. The network traffic measurement is the basis of network monitoring and management. With the expansion of network scale and the emergence of new network applications such as cloud computing, edge computing and big data, this poses a huge challenge to the management of the network. SDN decouples the data plane and control plane of the traditional switch, and centralizes the control plane into a controller for unified management, improving network scalability and management flexibility. The network traffic measurement of SDN is different from the traditional network.

In networks, there are some direct measurement methods, such as sFlow, NetFlow, they need the support of network devices and additional software, and consume a lot of storages and computing resource in network devices. In contrast to the measurement

© ICST Institute for Computer Sciences, Social Informatics and Telecommunications Engineering 2019
Published by Springer Nature Switzerland AG 2019. All Rights Reserved
H. Song et al. (Eds.): SIMUtools 2019, LNICST 295, pp. 115–124, 2019.
https://doi.org/10.1007/978-3-030-32216-8_11

scheme of traditional networks, SDN provides flow-based measurement methods by collecting the statistics from switches, this scheme is more convenient, efficient, and flexible. The pull-based scheme is an active measurement mode and the push-based scheme is a passive measurement mode. However, when the network scale and the number of active flows are very huge in SDN, the flow-based traffic measurement will face an enormous challenge due to a large number of flow statistics from switches and increase huge overhead in the network components. So we pay attention to the pull-based mechanism with low overhead in SDN.

Artificial Intelligence (AI) has been widely used in smartphones, voice recognition and authentication, which has been changed human's behavior patterns and lifestyle. AI is a junior intelligent system that requires some knowledge and reasoning to be added to the existing applications, database, and environment to make it friendlier, smarter and more sensitive to the environment. There is a large amount of data in the communication system, which provides rich history data for training the AI model. The application of AI in communication system has attracted the interest of many researchers [1]. Javier et al. have a comprehensive survey of AI-based optical networking, from low-level devices to high-level management [2]. AI in the optimal network not only improves the utilization of the wavelength but also improve management efficiency. Proietti et al. utilize machine learning-aided Quality of Transmission (QoT) estimation for lightpath configuration of intra-inter-domain traffic and obtain high accurate Optical Signal to Noise (OSNR) prediction [3]. Hagos et al. present a robust, scalable and generic machine learning-based method which may be of interest for network operators that experimentally infers congestion window and the underlying variant of loss-based TCP algorithms within flows from passive traffic measurements collected at an intermediate node [4]. Latah et al. investigated the application of AI to SDN paradigms, such as load balancing, network security, and intelligent network applications [5]. We also have some researches about the traffic matrix prediction and estimation with the deep learning in the data center network [6]. Our previous work can be found in [11–13].

Inspired by the AI-based traffic prediction and the adaptive flow traffic measurement, we propose an adaptive lightweight measurement scheme by predicting the traffic characteristics to measure the traffic effectively and accurately. ALAMM is pull-based active flow measurement. The main contribution of this paper as follows:

(1) We propose that using the measurement data in the front in the network to train the AI-based model.
(2) We use the trained AI-based model to predict the traffic in SDN and obtain the sampling points. Then, we use the sequence of sampling points to obtain the coarse-grained measurement.
(3) We use interpolation method to fill the coarse-grained measurement and construct an optimization function which has multiple constraints to optimal the obtained fine-grained measurement.
(4) We do some simulations to verify the performance of the proposed method.

The rest of this paper is organized as follows. Section 2 describes the measurement model ALAMM and introduces the adaptive sampling frequency and fine-grained interpolation and optimization of measurements. Section 3 makes simulations to verify the performance of ALAMM and the conclusion are stated in Sect. 4.

## 2 Problem Statement

In SDN, the control plane runs in the controller which is independent of switches. So, the flow-based measurement in SDN is much easier and more flexible than traditional networks, but the overhead of the measurement is a key issue that should be considered in the measurement process. We consider a simple mesh network with a controller $\{C_0\}$ and four switches $\{S_1, S_2, S_3, S_4\}$, as shown in Fig. 1. Each switch has at least one physical link which connects with the other switches. There are two flows $\{f_1, f_2\}$ in the network, $f_1$ through switches $(S_1, S_2, S_4)$, $f_1$ through switches $(S_1, S_2, S_3, S_4)$, and there are five physical links in the network $\{L_1, L_2, L_3, L_4, L_5\}$.

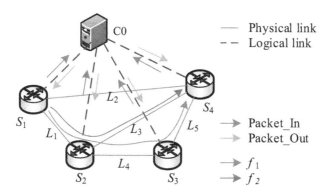

**Fig. 1.** The network topology and flows of SDN

Each switch connects into the controller directly in logical. There are two kinds of methods to deploy the controllers in SDN, in-band and out-of-band. In the In-band deployment scenario, the controllers are deployed inside the network, some switches directly connect into the controller. Control messages and data messages are exchanged between controllers and switches over the same network. In out-of-band deployment scenario, the controllers are external to the network and each switch is connected to the controller through a dedicated link. Data messages and control messages exchanged between the controllers and switches over different links. In out-of-band deployment scenario, controllers can exchange messages directly with switches. For simplicity, we consider an out-of-band scenario here.

## 2.1    Network Traffic

In this deployment scenario, each switch is directly connected to the controller, and exchange control messages through the control channel. The controller periodically sends LLDP packets to discover the links in the network, so the controller has a global view of the network topology. Flow is the traffic between each pair of the source node and the destination node, and the flow forwarding action in switches are programmed by the controller, so the controller knows all the routing information of the networks, we use $A$ to represent the routing matrix. $x$ and $y$ are the traffic of flow and link, respectively. So we can represent the traffic in the network as

$$y_j = \sum_i a_{ij} x_i \tag{1}$$

where $x_i$ is the traffic of flow $i$ and $y_i$ is the traffic on the link $j$. $a_{ij}$ is the route of flow $i$. If $a_{ij} = 1$, it means that the flow $i$ through the link $j$.

The traffic of flows and links in the network has a relationship that

$$\begin{cases} y_1 = x_1 + x_2 \\ y_3 = x_1 \\ y_4 = x_2 \\ \dots \end{cases} \tag{2}$$

From Eq. (2), we have the relationship of traffic in switch $S_2$ as

$$y_{1+} - y_{3-} - y_{4-} + y_{2+} - y_{2-} \le \theta \tag{3}$$

where $\theta$ is the error threshold of flow traffic. $y_{2+}$ and $y_{2-}$ are the traffic of $S_2$ which transmitted from $S_2$ to $S_2$. $y_{2+}$ and $y_{1+}$ are the input traffic, $y_{2-}$, $y_{3-}$ and $y_{4-}$ are the output traffic. In each switch, the traffic meets the principle of conservation. Then we represent (3) the traffic of switch $k$ as

$$\left| \sum y_{k+} - \sum y_{k-} \right| \le \theta \tag{4}$$

The traffic in the network changes over time, so we can represent the traffic of links and flows in the network as

$$\begin{cases} x_i = \{x_i(t)\} = \{x_i(1), x_i(2), x_i(3), \dots\} \\ y_j = \{y_j(t)\} = \{y_j(1), y_j(2), y_j(3), \dots\} \end{cases} \tag{5}$$

where $x_i(t)$ is the traffic of flow $i$ at time $t$, $y_j(t)$ is the traffic of flow $i$ at time $t$.

The Eq. (1) can be rewritten as

$$y_j(t) = \sum_i a_{ij} x_i(t) \tag{6}$$

In the network, measuring all the traffic of links will consume much computing and transmit resource. Su et al. proposed the CeMon method which selects the subset of switches which coverage the most active flows [7], then we can sample the flow traffic in some switches to reflect all the traffic in the network. However, the traffic measurement in switches should last a long time, so a lot of measurement overhead will be generated in this process. Then, how to find the optimal sampling sequence with high measurement accuracy and low overhead become a key issue which should be studied. There are many methods, such as unified sampling, random sampling, but both of them has high measurement overhead and not flexible. In this paper, we proposed a lightweight measurement scheme, we train an AI model to predict the network traffic feature, and sample network traffic based on the prediction. Then, the sampling method to measure the network can be written as

$$\hat{x} = \sum_i x(t)\delta(t) \tag{7}$$

where $\delta(t)$ is a sampling sequence.

## 2.2    Adaptive Sampling

Flows with the features of high density and high dynamic bring about a huge challenge for the accurate, fast, and fine-grained traffic measurement. Through short time slot sampling, we can obtain the instantaneous rate of flows and links. However, the traditional flow-based fine-grained network measurements in SDN require the controller to frequently send Read-state messages to OpenFlow-based switches and also generate a large number of report messages to the controller, which would consume much computing resource of the controller. So, we use a coarse-grained measurement method to reduce measurement overhead.

ANN is one of the most widely used methods of AI, it is a popular model for solving the multi-dimension traffic prediction issues, such as network traffic, vehicle traffic. The structure of ANN is flexible, users can change the ANN structure based on their requirement. ANN consists of one input layer and N hidden layers and one output layer, it is a stack of many neurons. In addition to the input layer, each neuron is a weighted sum of the previous layer of neurons, the neurons in the hidden and output layer are statistics variables. So the traffic prediction model of ANN can be written as

$$\begin{cases} h_m(t) = F(\sum_{n=1}^{N} w_{m-1n}h_{m-1n}(t)), m = 2, 3, \ldots, M \\ R_p(t) = F(\sum_{n=1}^{N} w_{Mn}h_{Mn}(t)) \end{cases} \tag{8}$$

where $w_{mn}$ are weighted factors between neurons in a different layer, and $h_m(t)$ are the middle results. There are $M$ hidden layers in the ANN model. $F(\cdot)$ is the activation function of neurons, $R_p(t)$ are prediction results of network traffic at time slot $t$.

The traffic prediction $R_p(t)$ has the features of the traffics, so we can use the features to adaptively adjust the sampling points, and help us to improve the measurement accuracy and decrease the measurement overhead. Then, we design an adaptive sequence of the sampling points in the following, it can be written as

$$\delta(t) = \begin{cases} 1, R_p(t) - R_p(t-1)\Delta \text{ or } R_p(t+T) - R_p(t) > \Delta \\ 0, otherwise \end{cases} \quad (9)$$

where $\delta(t)$ is a sampling point or not at time slot $t$, $R_p(t)$ is the traffic prediction at time slot $t$. If the change of flow prediction values is bigger than the threshold $\Delta$, we send a sampling primitive; otherwise, we think the flow is stable, and not send the sampling primitive; $T$ is a fixed period which is used to ensure the maximum sampling interval not exceed $T$.

## 2.3    Fine-Grained Matrix Filling and Optimization

The fine-grained measurement result of flow $j$ is $x_i$, it is obtained by filling the coarse-grained measurement with the cubic interpolation method, and the actual flow traffic of flow $j$ is $\hat{x}_i$. Due to the cubic interpolation is the smoothest possible approximations of actual flow traffic, so there is a gap between the measurement results and the actual flow traffic. In order to obtain accurate measurements, we optimize the filling data to decrease the gap between the measurement results and the actual results of flows. Then, we propose an optimal function as follows:

$$\begin{cases} \min \quad \left\| Y - A\hat{X} \right\|_2 + \lambda \|X\|_2 \\ s.t. \\ \quad C1: \quad Y_i \geq A_i\hat{X}, \quad A = (A_1, A_2, \ldots, A_M)^T \\ \quad C2: \quad x_j \geq 0, Y_i \geq 0 \\ \quad C3: \quad |\sum x_{i+} - \sum x_{i-}| \leq \theta \\ \quad C4: \quad \sum x_{i+} - \sum x_{i-} > 0 \end{cases} \quad (10)$$

where $\lambda$ is a Lagrange multiplier. Contrast to Eq. (10), the equation above can easily be solved by the following heuristic algorithm proposed in this paper.

Constraint C1 represents the constraint between link load and flow traffic; Constraint C2 denotes that the traffic in the network is non-negative. Constraint C3 and C4 means that the output traffic of node $i$ is no more than input traffic of node $i$, this is the traffic conservation principles. Under constraint C1, we know that link load and flow traffic mapping relationship matrix $A$ has $M$ rows and $N$ columns, and $M \geq N$ when multiple flows transmission through a link. Then, the routing matrix $A$ is an underdetermined matrix, there are infinite solutions for the linear constraint C1. Then, we use some heuristic method to solve it.

# 3    Simulation Result and Analysis

We evaluate the performance of the proposed measurement scheme by building a SDN test platform. In the simulation scenario, we use Ryu [8] as the controller and utilize Mininet [9] to construct the network topology. For simplicity, the network topology as

Fig. 1 shows. Iperf is used to generate TCP packets to fill each link from origin host to destination host, and all the links in the network are set as the duplex transmission mode. We analyze the traffic of flow f1 and f2, and compare the ALAMM to uniform sampling method under different intervals (Uniform60, Uniform240) and Principal Component Analysis (PCA) method, where Uniform60 and Uniform240 are the uniform sampling method with the sampling interval 60 and 240 slots, respectively. It is well known that the measured granularity is usually inversely proportional to the measurement interval. For the uniform sampling method under different sampling interval, when the sampling interval is small, we think it as the fine-grained measurement, and the sampling interval is big as the coarse-grained.

Relative Errors (RE) and Root Mean Square Error (RMSE) are mainly used parameters depict the performance of the methods [10]. For the ALAMM proposed, the sampling sequence is very important traffic measurement. Figure 2 shows the average RE of measurement under different threshold and interval of the measurement step. We find that when the interval and measurement interval are both small, the average RE of measurement is very small. When the sampling interval is larger than 150 slots, the average measurement RE trends to stable, but when the interval is larger than 200 slots, the average measurement RE becomes fluctuating. In addition, as the measurement threshold increases, the average RE also increases. When the measurement threshold is larger than 200, the average RE becomes fluctuating. Then, in the following, we use the measurement threshold and interval as 50 and 200, respectively.

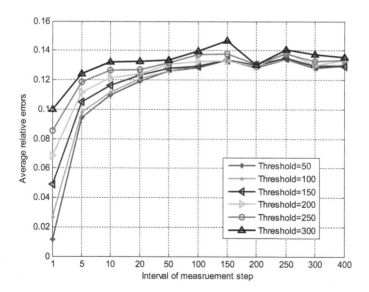

**Fig. 2.** The average RE under different threshold and interval of the measurement step

Figure 3 shows the RE cumulative distribution function (CDF) of flow f1 and f2, respectively. From Fig. 3(a), we can see that the about 80% RE of the ALAMM and Uniform sampling method are less than 0.3, while the RE is about 60% for the PCA method. Figure 3(b) has a similar trend with Fig. 3(a). However, the average RE of ALAMM is smaller than Uniform60 and larger than Uniform240 and PCA, the curves show that the ALAMM is slightly inferior to Uniform60 but better than Uniform240 and PCA. Figure 3(b) shows that the ALAMM is better than Uniform60, Uniform240, and PCA. Figure 4 curves the RMSE of different measurement methods, we note that RMSE of the ALAMM is much steeper than the other methods, this means the average measurement RE of ALAMM is much more stable than other methods. As well as, we find that the RMSE of ALAMM is close to the performance of Uniform60.

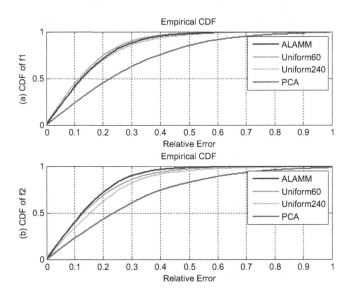

**Fig. 3.** The RE CDF of the flows f1 and f2

We compare the measurement overhead and the measurement error in Fig. 5. The bars are the measurement overhead, the left y-axis is their scale. The star on the blue line is the measurement errors of the corresponding measurement method, and the right y-axis is their scale. From Fig. 5, we note that the measurement errors of ALAMM are a little larger than the Uniform60 and smaller than the Uniform240, however, the measurement overhead of ALAMM is similar as the Uniform240 and far less than Uniform60. We know that ALAMM has lower overhead than Unifrom60, however, the average measurement errors are similar to it. For PCA, its average measurement error is about 0.35, which are larger than the ALAMM, Uniform60, and Uniform240. Although the measurement overhead of PCA is almost zero, its measurement performance is poor. Through the above analysis, we know that our ALAMM is feasible and it accurately measures the network traffic with low overhead.

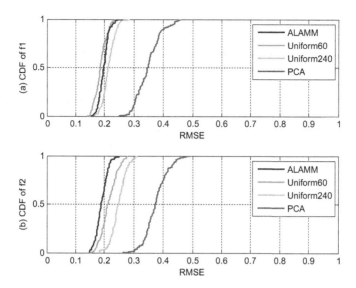

**Fig. 4.** The RMSE CDF of the flows f1 and f2

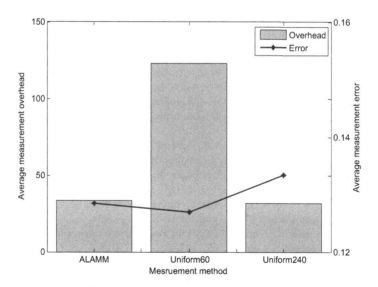

**Fig. 5.** The overhead and average error for different measurement methods

## 4  Conclusions

Accurate flow-based network measurement has a great impact on network traffic management in SDN. We propose the ALAMM for traffic measurement in SDN. In ALAMM, we use measurement results in the front to train the AI model, then use the model to predict the traffic in the network. Then, we obtain the sequence of sampling points based on prediction results and send sampling primitives to switches to obtain the coarse-grained measurement. Then, we perform the interpolation method on the coarse-grained measurement and utilize the optimization method to decrease the fine-grained measurement errors. At last, we make some simulations to verify the measurement method proposed in this paper. The simulation results show that the proposed ALAMM can accurately measure the traffic with low overhead.

**Acknowledgment.** This work was supported by the National Natural Science Foundation of China (No. 61571104), Sichuan Science and Technology Program (No. 2018JY0539), Key projects of the Sichuan Provincial Education Department (No. 18ZA0219), Fundamental Research Funds for the Central Universities (No. ZYGX2017KYQD170), and Innovation Funding (No. 2018510 007000134). The authors wish to thank the reviewers for their helpful comments.

## References

1. Li, Y., Zhang, Y., et al.: Ultra-dense HetNets meet big data: green frameworks, techniques, and approaches. IEEE Commun. Mag. **56**(6), 56–63 (2018)
2. Mata, J., de Miguel, I., Duran, R.J., et al.: Artificial intelligence (AI) methods in optical networks: a comprehensive survey. Opt. Switch. Netw. **28**, 43–57 (2018)
3. Proietti, R., Chen, X., Zhang, K., et al.: Experimental demonstration of machine-learning-aided QoT estimation in multi-domain elastic optical networks with alien wavelengths. J. Opt. Commun. Netw. **11**(1), A1–A10 (2019)
4. Hagos, D., Engelstad, P., Yazidi, A., et al.: General TCP state inference model from passive measurements using machine learning techniques. IEEE Access **6**, 28372–28387 (2018)
5. Latah, M., Toker, L.: Application of artificial intelligence to software defined networking: a survey. Indian J. Sci. Technol. **9**(44), 1–7 (2016)
6. Jiang, D., Wang, W., Shi, L., et al.: A compressive sensing-based approach to end-to-end network traffic reconstruction. IEEE Trans. Netw. Sci. Eng. **5**(3), 1–12 (2018)
7. Su, Z., Wang, T., Xia, Y., Hamdi, M.: CeMon: a cost-effective flow monitoring system in software defined networks. Comput. Netw. **92**, 101–115 (2015)
8. The Ryu Platform. https://github.com/osrg/ryu/. Accessed Dec 2017
9. The Mininet Platform. http://mininet.org/. Accessed Dec 2017
10. He, Q., Wang, X., Huang, M.: OpenFlow-based low-overhead and high-accuracy SDN measurement framework. Trans. Emerg. Telecommun. Technol. **29**(2), e3263 (2018)
11. Jiang, D., Huo, L., Song, H.: Rethinking behaviors and activities of base stations in mobile cellular networks based on big data analysis. IEEE Trans. Netw. Sci. Eng. **1**(1), 1–12 (2018)
12. Jiang, D., Huo, L., Li, Y.: Fine-granularity inference and estimations to network traffic for SDN. PLoS ONE **13**(5), 1–23 (2018)
13. Jiang, D., Huo, L., Lv, Z., et al.: A joint multi-criteria utility-based network selection approach for vehicle-to-infrastructure networking. IEEE Trans. Intell. Transp. Syst. **PP**(99), 1–15 (2018)

# A Linear Regression-Based Prediction Method to Traffic Flow for Low-Power WAN with Smart Electric Power Allocations

Bing Liu[1], Fanbo Meng[2], Yun Zhao[1], Xinge Qi[1], Bin Lu[2], Kai Yang[3], and Xiao Yan[3(✉)]

[1] State Grid Dalian Electric Power Supply Company, Dalian 116011, China
[2] State Grid Liaoning Electric Power Company Limited, Shenyang 110006, China
amengfb@163.com
[3] School of Aeronautics and Astronautics, UESTC, Chengdu 611731, China
yanxiao@uestc.edu.cn

**Abstract.** Currently power telecommunication access networks have many new requirements to meet the low-power WAN with smart electric power allocations. In such a case, network traffic in the low-power WAN has exhibited new features and there are some challenges for network managements. This paper uses the linear regression model to propose a new method to model and predict network traffic. Firstly, network traffic is modeled as a linear regression model according to the regression model theory. Then the linear regression modeling method is used to capture network traffic features. By calculating the parameters of the model, it can be decided correctly. Then, we can predict network traffic accurately. Simulation results show that our approach is effective and promising.

**Keywords:** Network traffic · Low-power WAN · Linear regression · Traffic modeling · Traffic prediction

## 1 Introduction

With current network technology development increasingly quickening and new applications quickly appearing in low-power WAN with smart electric power allocations, more and more new features have embodied in network traffic. This leads to a larger challenging for network engineering in low-power WAN [1–3]. To effectively guaranteeing electric power network performance, we need to accurately model network traffic characteristics. Low-power WAN traffic holds many properties, such as burst, self-similarity, spatio-temporal correlations and so on, which has a direct impact on network performance and management [4–7]. The low-power WAN traffic holds network-level behaviors. Hence, from a global view, network-level traffic modeling has received more and more attention from researchers, operators, and developer over the whole world [8–14]. This has become a hot research topic.

The traffic behaviors in low-power WAN for smart electric power allocations hold network-level nature, which is often used to describe kinds of network behaviors, such

H. Song et al. (Eds.): SIMUtools 2019, LNICST 295, pp. 125–134, 2019.
https://doi.org/10.1007/978-3-030-32216-8_12

as path loads, network throughput, network utilization, and so on. The statistical methods [1, 3], gravity model [4], generic evolvement [5–7], mix method [2], and compressive sensing [12] are utilized to capture the properties of the network-level traffic in low-power WAN. Although these methods attain better prediction and estimation performance for network-level traffic, they produced larger errors and often additional link load information. Hence, it is necessary to research new traffic prediction approach for low-power WAN with smart electric power allocations. The time-frequency analysis was used to describe multi-scale features of network traffic [1, 9]. Neural network models were utilized to model network-level traffic [10–15]. Moreover, network traffic prediction methods are extensively applications [16–20]. These methods still hold a larger prediction error.

In this paper, we propose a novel method to characterize and analyze network traffic accurately. Our method is based on the linear regression modeling theory. Generally, we have difficulties in modeling and describing network traffic because of their highly time-varying nature, which is difficult to be described via the analytical formulation. In this paper, we exploit the linear regression model to characterize network traffic. The linear regression theory is used to build the model parameters via the sample data about network traffic. To the end, firstly we denote a linear regression model over time. Secondly, by calculate the model parameters, we correctly create the prediction model for network traffic based on the linear regression model. Thirdly, we propose a new prediction algorithm to estimate and forecast network traffic accurately. Simulation results show that our approach is effective and promising.

The rest of this paper is organized as follows. Our method is derived in Sect. 2. Section 3 presents the simulation results and analysis. We then conclude our work in Sect. 4.

## 2  Problem Statement

The model of the time-varying network traffic for the power telecommunication access network is very hard to build. The traffic in the network is fluctuation along with the business volume and time, and the features of flow is very hard to express it directly, so it is a huge challenge to model the traffic in the power telecommunication access network. Here, we donate the traffic in network-level as $y = \{y(1), y(2), \ldots, y(t)\}$, where $y(t)$ is the traffic value of flow $y$ at the time slot $t$. We assume that the traffic value $y(t)$ in the network satisfies the independent identically distributed random process.

According to the linear regression analysis theory, linear regression model can be written as follow

$$\begin{cases} y = b_0 + b_1 x_1 + \ldots + b_m x_m + \ldots + b_n x_n + \varepsilon \\ E(\varepsilon) = 0, 0 < D(\varepsilon) = \sigma^2 < +\infty \end{cases} \tag{1}$$

where $b_0$ represents the constant variable, $\varepsilon$ represents the random error. $b_m$ (where $m = 1, 2, \ldots, n$) represents the partial regression coefficient, $x_m$ (where $m = 1, 2, \ldots, n$) represents the values of many experiments. $E(\varepsilon)$ is the mean value of the random error, and $D(\varepsilon)$ is the variance of the random error. The random errors is a normal distribution whose mean and variance are zero and $\sigma^2$, respectively. So, the distribution of the random error can be expressed as

$$p(\varepsilon) = \frac{1}{\sqrt{2\pi}}\exp(-\frac{\varepsilon^2}{2\sigma^2}) \tag{2}$$

In the network, we know that there are many users connect into the network at the same time, many flows are transmitted in the network from one node to another at the same time. The end-to-end traffic $y$ is regarded as a statistical variable which can be expressed as the Eq. (1). According to the analysis in [10–12], we know that the traffic in the access network has the correlation over time. In order to retrieve the feature of traffic in the power telecommunication access networks, we express the network traffic with the linear regression theory, so the traffic in the network can be expressed as

$$y = b_0 + \sum_{i=1}^{n} b_i x(i) + \varepsilon, \varepsilon \sim N(0, \sigma^2) \tag{3}$$

where $b_i$ (where $i = 1, 2, \ldots, n$) denotes partial regression coefficient. $\varepsilon$ represents the residual error when process network traffic. $x(i)$ is the related features of flow traffic.

As we assumed earlier, $y(t)$ (where $t = 1, 2, \ldots$) is the traffic instance at time slot $t$. From Eq. (3), we know that the statistic traffic at slot $t$ is correlation with characterizes of flows. Equation (3) shows the statistics of traffic $y(t)$ and the characterizes of flows $x(i)$ (where $i = 1, 2, \ldots, n$). $x(i)$ denotes the network traffic which can be obtain at time slot $i$. And the residual error between the estimation and the actual traffic is $\varepsilon$, so we can obtain the traffic $y(t)$ at slot $t$. Due to the residual error of the estimation is normal distribution. Based on the liner regression model, the traffic at slot $t$ can be expressed as

$$y(t) = b_0 + \sum_{i=1}^{n} b_i x_t(i) + \varepsilon, \varepsilon \sim N(0, \sigma^2) \tag{4}$$

where $b_0$ and $b_i$ (where $i = 1, 2, \ldots, n$) are the regression constant and partial regression coefficient, respectively. $x_t(i)$ is the characterizes of flow $x(i)$ at time slot $t$. So the mean of traffic satisfies that

$$E(y(t)) = E(b_0 + \sum_{i=1}^{n} b_i x_t(i)) \tag{5}$$

where $E(\cdot)$ is the expression of expectation value. If there are $k$ measurements and the characterizes $n > k$, so the linear regression can be expressed as

$$\begin{cases} y(1) = b_0 + b_1 x_1(1) + b_2 x_1(2) + \ldots + b_n x_1(n) + \varepsilon_1 \\ y(2) = b_0 + b_1 x_2(1) + b_1 x_2(2) + \ldots + b_1 x_2(n) + \varepsilon_2 \\ \ldots \\ y(k) = b_0 + b_1 x_k(1) + b_1 x_k(2) + \ldots + b_1 x_k(n) + \varepsilon_k \end{cases} \tag{6}$$

Then, we express (6) as a matrix

$$Y = XB + \Theta \tag{7}$$

where   $Y = [y(1),\ldots,y(k)]^T$,   $B = [b_0, b_1, \ldots, b_n]^T$,   $\Theta = [\varepsilon_1, \ldots, \varepsilon_k]^T$   and

$$X = \begin{bmatrix} 1 & x_1(1) & x_1(2) & \cdots & x_1(n) \\ 1 & x_2(1) & x_2(2) & \cdots & x_2(n) \\ \cdots & \cdots & \cdots & x_j(i) & \cdots \\ 1 & x_k(1) & x_k(2) & \cdots & x_k(n) \end{bmatrix}.$$

The elements $x_j(i)$ of matrix $X$ can be obtain from history data. We assume that the estimates of partial regression coefficients are $\{\hat{b}_0, \hat{b}_1, \ldots, \hat{b}_n\}$, so the Eq. (4) can be written as

$$\hat{y}(t) = \hat{b}_0 + \hat{b}_1 x_t(1) + \hat{b}_2 x_t(2) + \ldots + \hat{b}_n x_t(n) \tag{8}$$

where $\hat{y}(t)$ is the estimates of $y(t)$.

The residual error at time slot $t$ is

$$\begin{aligned} \varepsilon_t &= y(t) - \hat{y}(t) \\ &= y(t) - (\hat{b}_0 + \hat{b}_1 x_t(1) + \hat{b}_2 x_t(2) + \ldots + \hat{b}_n x_t(n)) \end{aligned} \tag{9}$$

Then, we use the ordinary least square (OLS) to estimate the residual errors. Here, we firstly make some assumptions in the following.

**Assumption 1:** the mean value of residual errors is zero.

$$E(\Theta) = E([\varepsilon_1, \ldots, \varepsilon_k]^T) = [E(\varepsilon_1), \ldots, E(\varepsilon_k)]^T = 0 \tag{10}$$

**Assumption 2:** residual errors have the same distribution.

$$Var(\varepsilon_j) = E(\varepsilon_j^2) = \sigma^2, j = 1, 2, \ldots, k \tag{11}$$

**Assumption 3:** There is no correlation between residual errors.

$$Cov(\mu_i, \mu_j) = E(\mu_i \mu_j) = 0, i, j = 1, 2, \ldots, n \tag{12}$$

**Assumption 4:** The residual error and characteristics of flow $x_t(i)$ have no relevance.

$$Cov(x_j(i), \mu_j) = E(x_j(i)\mu_j) = 0, j = 1, 2, \ldots, t, i = 1, 2, \ldots, n \tag{13}$$

Based on the least square method, we know that the regression constant and partial regression coefficients should minimize sum of squares of residual errors, so

$$RSS(\hat{b}_0, \hat{b}_1, \ldots, \hat{b}_n) = \arg\min(\sum_{k=1}^{t} \varepsilon_k^2)$$

$$= \arg\min(\sum_{k=1}^{t} (y(k) - \hat{y}(k))^2) \tag{14}$$

For an example, we make experiments that when $n = 3$ here. So, the traffic at time slot $t$ can be rewritten as

$$y(t) = b_0 + b_1 x(1) + b_2 x(2) + b_3 x(3) + \varepsilon, \varepsilon \sim N(0, \sigma^2) \tag{15}$$

and the estimates of $y(t)$ can be written as

$$\hat{y}(t) = \hat{b}_0 + \hat{b}_1 x(1) + \hat{b}_2 x(2) + \hat{b}_3 x(3) + \varepsilon, \varepsilon \sim N(0, \sigma^2) \tag{16}$$

According to Eqs. (14)–(16) and Eq. (2), we make a optimization to find the regression coefficients and the residual error.

$$\begin{cases} f(b_0, b_1, b_2, b_3, \varepsilon) \\ s.t. \ \hat{y}(k) = \hat{b}_0 + \hat{b}_1 x(1) + \hat{b}_2 x(2) + \hat{b}_3 x(3) + \varepsilon \\ p(\varepsilon) = \frac{1}{\sqrt{2\pi}} \exp(-\frac{\varepsilon^2}{2\sigma^2}) \\ RSS(\hat{b}_0, \hat{b}_1, \ldots, \hat{b}_n) = \arg\min(\sum_{k=1}^{t} (y(k) - \hat{y}(k))^2) \\ \varepsilon = y(k) - \hat{y}(k) \\ (b_0, b_1, \ldots, b_n) = (\hat{b}_0, \hat{b}_1, \ldots, \hat{b}_n) \end{cases} \tag{17}$$

Equation (17) is a multi-constraint and multi-object optimization issue. The first constraint of Eq. (17) indicates estimate $\hat{y}(k)$ of flow traffic at time slot $k$. The second one donates the distribution of residual errors, and the third one means the optimal estimates of partial regression coefficient and $y(k)$ is the measured traffic value at time slot $k$. The fourth equation in (17) calculate residual errors between the measured value of traffic and the prediction under the partial regression coefficient $(\hat{b}_0, \hat{b}_1, \ldots, \hat{b}_n)$. By training the model of (4) and adjusting the residual errors with the (2), we can obtain the prediction model and the set of parameters.

We present our prediction algorithm based on linear regression model, called Linear Regression Model Theory Traffic Modeling Algorithm (LMTMA). Based on the analysis and derivation above, the steps of algorithm LMTMA are as following.

**Step 1:** Given $t$ initial measured value of the end-to-end network traffic in the network-level $y = \{y(1), y(2), \ldots, y(t)\}$ in the front $t$ time slots.
**Step 2:** Based on the linear regression model theory and the statistical analysis methods, we initialize network traffic $y(t)$ and parameters of $\sigma^2$, respectively.
**Step 3:** Build the traffic prediction model (4) and distribution of the residual errors (2) to find the estimate of the partial regression coefficient $b_0, b_1, b_2, b_3$.

**Step 4:** In objective function (17), minimize the residual errors $\varepsilon$ and update the partial regression coefficient $b_0, b_1, b_2, b_3$.
**Step 5:** obtain the optimal parameters $b_0, b_1, b_2, b_3, \varepsilon$ from objective function (17).
**Step 6:** The traffic prediction model is constructed over, then exist the process of modeling.

## 3 Simulation Results and Analysis

Now, we conduct many tests to demonstrate our algorithm LMTMA. In order to justify the accuracy of our algorithm, we need to use real network data. Here, the real data needed in the simulation experiment is collected by the network nodes deployed at different place; we use the real data from the real Abilene backbone network in the United States to validate LMTMA. PCA [3], WABR [7], and HMPA [2] algorithms for the network traffic modeling have been reported as the better performance. Here we compare LMTMA with them. In the following, the prediction results of the network traffic are analyzed for LMTMA algorithm. The average relative errors for the network traffic are indicated for four algorithms. Finally, we discuss the performance improvement of LMTMA against PCA, WABR, and HMPA. In our simulation, the data of the first 500 time slots are used to train the models of four approaches, while other data are exploited to validate the performance of all algorithms.

Figure 1 shows the prediction results of network traffic flows 78 and 118, where network traffic flows 78 and 118 are selected randomly from the 144 end-to-end traffic flow pairs in our simulation network. Without loss of generality, we only discuss the network traffic flows 78 and 118 in this paper. The network traffic flows is also called as the Origin Destination (OD) pair. Figure 1(a) indicates that LMTMA can effectively capture the dynamic changes of the network traffic flow 78. For different time slots, the real network traffic exhibits the significant time-varying nature. From Fig. 1(a), we have seen that LMTMA can seek the trend of the network traffic flow. Likewise, the network traffic flow 118 shows the irregular and dynamic changes over the time as indicated in Fig. 1(b). From Fig. 1(b), it is very clear that although LMTMA holds the larger prediction errors for the network traffic flow 118, it can still capture its change trend. This further indicates that LMTMA can effectively predict the change of the network traffic over the time.

Next, we discuss the predict errors of four algorithms. Generally, we have difficulties in seizing the dynamic nature of the network traffic over the time via the model. To further validate our algorithm, we compare the relative prediction errors over the time for all algorithms. To avoid the randomness in the simulation process, we perform 500 runs to calculate the average relative prediction errors.

The average relative prediction errors over the time for network traffic reflect the performance of the methods for predicting network traffic, they are donated as:

$$d(t) = \frac{1}{N} \sum_{i=1}^{N} \frac{||\hat{y}_i(t) - y_i(t)||_2}{||y_i(t)||_2} \tag{18}$$

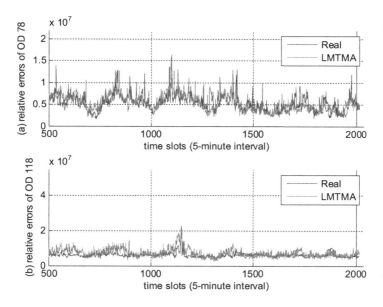

**Fig. 1.** Prediction results of network traffic flows 78 and 118.

where $i = 1, 2, \ldots, N$, $N$ is the number of runs in the simulation process, $\|\cdot\|_2$ is the norm of $L_2$, and $\hat{y}_i(t)$ indicates the traffic prediction value of run $i$ at time slot $t$.

Figure 2 shows the average relative prediction errors of four algorithm over the time for network-level traffic flows 78 and 118. We can find that for network traffic flows 78 and 118, WABR, HMPA, and LMTMA exhibit the lower relative errors while

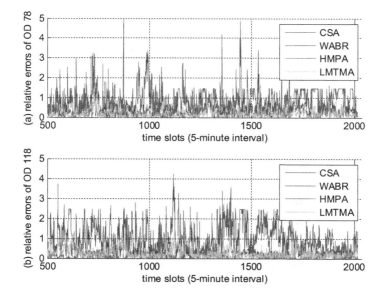

**Fig. 2.** Average relative errors for network traffic flows 78 and 118.

PCA hold the larger prediction bias. For Fig. 2, we can also see that that LMTMA holds the lowest relative errors. This tells us that in contrast to PCA, WABR, and HMPA, LMTMA holds the better prediction ability for the network traffic, while LMTMA holds the best prediction ability. More importantly, WABR, HMPA, and LMTMA indicate the lower fluctuation over the time in terms of relative errors than PCA. This shows that compared with other three algorithms, LMTMA can more effectively model the network traffic with time-varying and correlation features. Moreover, this also tell us that LMTMA can more accurately predict network-level traffic than previous methods.

Now, we analyze the performance improvement of LMTMA relative to other three algorithms for the network traffic. Figure 3 exhibits the performance improvement ration of network traffic flow 78 and 118. For network traffic flow 78, LMTMA attains the performance improvement against PCA, WABR, and HMPA, respectively. Similarly, for network traffic flow 118, LMTMA obtains the performance improvement against PCA, WABR, and HMPA, respectively. This clearly denotes that compared with PCA, WABR, and HMPA, our algorithm LMTMA can more accurately model the network-level network traffic. Moreover, Fig. 3 also tell us that relative to PCA and WABR, LMTMA can reach the larger performance improvement. Compared with HMPA, LMTMA also reaches to the better performance improvement. As mentioned in Fig. 2, this further illustrates that our algorithm LMTMA holds the better modeling capability for the network-wide network traffic. Moreover, LMTMA and HMPA hold the similar performance, while LMTMA exhibits the better performance improvement. This also shows that LMTMA can correctly model the network traffic and hold better modeling performance for network traffic.

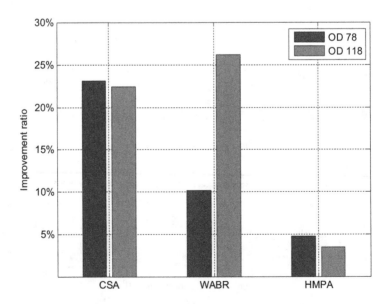

**Fig. 3.** Improvement ratio of network traffic flows 78 and 118.

# 4   Conclusions

This paper proposes a linear regression theory-based method to model and predict network traffic. Different from previous methods, the linear regression model is used to construct and determine the model parameters effectively. Firstly, the network traffic is described as an independent identically distributed exponential distribution process. Secondly, the linear regression method is exploited to capture the network-level network traffic. By calculating the parameters of the model, we build the corresponding network traffic model. Simulation results show that our approach is promising and effective.

# References

1. Jiang, D., Xu, Z., Chen, Z., et al.: Joint time-frequency sparse estimation of large-scale network traffic. Comput. Netw. **55**(10), 3533–3547 (2011)
2. Jiang, D., Xu, Z., Xu, H.: A novel hybrid prediction algorithm to network traffic. Ann. Telecommun. **70**(9), 427–439 (2015)
3. Soule, A., Lakhina, A., Taft, N., et al.: Traffic matrices: balancing measurements, inference and modeling. In: Proceedings of SIGMETRICS 2005, vol. 33, no. 1, pp. 362–373 (2005)
4. Takeda, T., Shionoto, K.: Traffic matrix estimation in large-scale IP networks. In: Proceedings of LANMAN 2010, pp. 1–6 (2010)
5. Yingxun, F.: The Research and Improvement of the Genetic Algorithm. Beijing University of Posts and Telecommunications, Beijing (2010)
6. Jiang, D., Zhao, Z., Xu, Z., et al.: How to reconstruct end-to-end traffic based on time-frequency analysis and artificial neural network. AEU-Int. J. Electron. Commun. **68**(10), 915–925 (2014)
7. Jiang, D., Yuan, Z., Zhang, P., et al.: A traffic anomaly detection approach in communication networks for applications of multimedia medical devices. Multimedia Tools Appl. **75**, 14281–14301 (2016)
8. Jiang, D., Xu, Z., Nie, L., et al.: An approximate approach to end-to-end traffic in communication networks. Chin. J. Electron. **21**(4), 705–710 (2012)
9. Vaton, S., Bedo, J.: Network traffic matrix: how can one learn the prior distributions from the link counts only. In: Proceedings of ICC 2004, pp. 2138–2142 (2004)
10. Lad, M., Oliveira, R., Massey, D., et al.: Inferring the origin of routing changes using link weights. In: Proceedings of ICNP, pp. 93–102 (2007)
11. Jiang, D., Xu, Z., Li, W., et al.: Topology control-based collaborative multicast routing algorithm with minimum energy consumption. Int. J. Commun Syst **30**(1), 1–18 (2017)
12. Jiang, D., Nie, L., Lv, Z., et al.: Spatio-temporal Kronecker compressive sensing for traffic matrix recovery. IEEE Access **4**, 3046–3053 (2016)
13. Tune, P., Veitch, D.: Sampling vs sketching: an information theoretic comparison. In: Proceedings of INFOCOM, pp. 2105–2113 (2011)
14. Jiang, D., Li, W., Lv, H.: An energy-efficient cooperative multicast routing in multi-hop wireless networks for smart medical applications. Neurocomputing **220**(2017), 160–169 (2017)
15. Zhang, Y., Roughan, M., Duffield, N., et al.: Fast accurate computation of large-scale IP traffic matrices from link loads. In: Proceedings of SIGMETRICS 2003, vol. 31, no. 3, pp. 206–217 (2003)

16. Jiang, D., Wang, Y., Han, Y., et al.: Maximum connectivity-based channel allocation algorithm in cognitive wireless networks for medical applications. Neurocomputing **2017** (220), 41–51 (2017)
17. Jiang, D., Wang, W., Shi, L., Song, H.: A compressive sensing-based approach to end-to-end network traffic reconstruction. IEEE Trans. Netw. Sci. Eng. (2018). https://doi.org/10.1109/tnse.2018.2877597
18. Jiang, D., Huo, L., Song, H.: Rethinking behaviors and activities of base stations in mobile cellular networks based on big data analysis. IEEE Trans. Netw. Sci. Eng. **1**(1), 1–12 (2018)
19. Jiang, D., Huo, L., Li, Y.: Fine-granularity inference and estimations to network traffic for SDN. PLoS ONE **13**(5), 1–23 (2018)
20. Jiang, D., Huo, L., Lv, Z., et al.: A joint multi-criteria utility-based network selection approach for vehicle-to-infrastructure networking. IEEE Trans. Intell. Transp. Syst. **99**, 1–15 (2018)

# Dynamic Computing Resource Adjustment in Edge Computing Satellite Networks

Feng Wang[1], Dingde Jiang[1(✉)], Sheng Qi[1], Chen Qiao[1],
and Jiping Xiong[2]

[1] School of Astronautics and Aeronautic, UESTC, Chengdu 611731, China
jiangdd@uestc.edu.cn
[2] College of Physics and Electronic Information Engineering,
ZJNU, Jinhua, China

**Abstract.** The LEO constellation has been a valuable network framework due to its characteristics of wide coverage and low transmission delay. Utilizing LEO satellites as edge computing nodes to provide reliable computing services for accessing terminals will be the indispensable paradigm of integrated space-air-ground network. However, the design of resource division strategy in edge computing satellite (ECS) is not easy, considering different accessing planes and resource requirements of terminals. To address these problems, we establish the resource requirements model of various terminals. Meanwhile, the advanced K-means algorithm (AKG) is provided to realize ECS resource allocation. Then, a fleet-based adjustment (FBA) scheme is proposed to realize dynamic adjustment of resource for ECSs. Simulation results show that the proposed dynamic resource adjustment scheme is feasible and effective.

**Keywords:** Edge computing · LEO satellite network · Resource adjustment · Space-air-ground network

## 1 Introduction

The Low earth orbit (LEO) constellation network is making an important role in the space-air-ground integrated communication network. Compared with about 500 ms communication delay utilizing geosynchronous earth orbit (GEO) satellites, LEO constellation has the advantages of low delay, high capacity, full coverage and manageability [1, 2]. Moreover, it can guarantee the efficient communication in the areas such as polar region, desert, oceans and air that are difficult to reach by GEO satellite or terrestrial base stations, so as to achieve global network coverage [3]. With the development of intelligent terminals, the demand for real-time data processing is impending. LEO satellite has been difficult to meet the real time data computing for terminals [4]. Therefore, the fusion of LEO constellation and the edge computing paradigm to enhance the real-time management of intelligent terminals has gradually attracted attention. As Fig. 1 shows, the edge server can be deployed in the LEO satellite, making LEO satellites become edge computing satellites (ECSs), where the data processing module for terminals are installed. Computing resources of ECS can be split into virtual machines (VMs) with different specifications to implement data

H. Song et al. (Eds.): SIMUtools 2019, LNICST 295, pp. 135–145, 2019.
https://doi.org/10.1007/978-3-030-32216-8_13

processing for various terminals [5]. However, the design of resource division strategy in edge computing satellite (ECS) is not easy, considering different accessing planes and resource requirements of terminals. Since LEO satellites are moving at a relatively high speed, its topology and coverage area in the next time slot may change, leading to the reconfiguration of the resources in ECSs. The resources and time spent on reconfiguration may affect the ability of ECS for real-time data processing. Therefore, a dynamic resource adjustment scheme is needed to help the ECS realize real-time data processing for intelligent terminals.

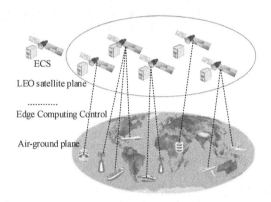

**Fig. 1.** The edge computing satellite network model.

The scheduling of resources in satellite networks is an ongoing research area and there have been some important studies. Authors in [6] considered the cooperative mechanism of relay satellites deployed in GEO and LEO and proposed a multiple access and resource allocation strategy for GEO relay in LEO satellite network. But they didn't consider the high data transmission latency of GEO satellites, about 500 ms round trip time. Sinha et al. [7] presented a multi-agent based modeling of LEO satellite network. Satellites were modeled as autonomous agents and could collaborate with other satellite agents. The allocation of tasks by the agents was modeled as a distributed constraint optimization problem. But small-scale self-organizing networks may affect other satellites, causing unnecessary link congestion. Sheng et al. [8] constructed a novel graph model to describe the evolution of multi-dimensional resources in satellite network. They proposed a resource allocation strategy to facilitate efficient cooperation among various resources. Although the performances of the LEO satellite network were improved, these studies could not provide dynamic management schemes for resources in each LEO satellite. In order to solve the above shortcomings, this paper considers the resources management in ECSs. In particular, the dynamic management strategies in ECS are provided. Traffic modeling [9], traffic estimation [10], network selection [11], energy efficiency [12] and network behaviors [13] are studied in previous work.

The rest is arranged as follows. Section 2 constructs the mathematical model of resource division in ECS and propose the dynamic resource adjustment scheme. The simulation results and analysis are shown in Sect. 3. Finally, we conclude our work in Sect. 4.

## 2 Mathematical Model

In edge computing satellite network, each ECS can connect multiple terminals by the user data links (UDLs). The ECS generates the corresponding VM to provide computing services for the terminal. Therefore, a problem need to be considered that how to allocate the computing resources of ECSs for the terminals, so as to not only meet the computing demand, but also realize reasonable resource configuration.

### 2.1 Resource Allocation in ECS

Different terminals have different data computing demands. For example, due to the relatively high-speed motion between UAVs and satellites, low delay data transmission is required to reduce signal distortion. Considering the data center has fixed location and need to receive various types of terminal data, there is a high bandwidth demand for it when accessing ECS. Frequent link switching may result in partial data loss, so for sensor nodes and ships, it is necessary to select ECS for data processing with long connection time. Therefore, intelligent terminals can be divided into three types: delay sensitivity, bandwidth sensitivity and connection time sensitivity.

**Delay Sensitivity:** Without considering the time taken by the signal transmission and reception, the time taken by transmitting the information from the terminal to the ECS is assumed as the transmission delay $d_{iE}(t)$:

$$d_{iE}(t) = \frac{\sqrt{(x_E(t) - x_i(t))^2 + (y_E(t) - y_i(t))^2 + (z_E(t) - z_i(t))^2}}{c} \tag{1}$$

where $(x_i(t), y_i(t), z_i(t))$ and $(x_E(t), y_E(t), z_E(t))$ respectively represent the three-dimensional coordinates of ECS $E$ and terminal $i$, and they are all functions of time. $c$ is the speed of light. If terminal $i$ has a fast speed it will has a large value of $d'_{iE}(t)$

$$d'_{iE}(t) = \frac{\Delta d_{iE}(t)}{\Delta t} \tag{2}$$

The value of $d'_{iE}(t)$ is denoted by $D_{iE}$ to express the delay sensitivity of terminal $i$.

**Bandwidth Sensitivity:** The data transmission rate always depends on the bandwidth provided by the ECSs' transceiver and the unit is Mbps. If the communication link is established between ECS $E$ and terminal $i$, the maximum available bandwidth $B_{Ei}$ is the smaller available bandwidth value $B$ for both nodes:

$$B_{Ei} = \min(B_E, B_i) \tag{3}$$

The value of $B_{Ei}$ can be used to describe the bandwidth sensitivity of terminal $i$.

**Connection Time Sensitivity:** Frequent link switching may result in partial data loss of terminals like sensors and ships, so these terminals have high connection time sensitivity. The link connection time starts with the establishment of transmission links and ends with the satellites lost their physical visibility. We define the critical time when link establishment as $T_0$ and when two nodes lose physical visibility as $T_{max}$, the link connection time $T_{Ei}$ can be expressed as follows:

$$T_{Ei} = T_{max} - T_0 \tag{4}$$

The three types of sensitivities of $n$ terminals can be expressed as $\{D_{1E}, D_{2E}, \ldots D_{nE}\}$, $\{B_{1E}, B_{2E}, \ldots B_{nE}\}$ and $\{T_{1E}, T_{2E}, \ldots T_{nE}\}$. For convenient comparison with the other indicators, we normalize the $D_{iE}$ as $D_{iE}^*$, $B_{iE}$ as $B_{iE}^*$ and $T_{iE}$ as $T_{iE}^*$:

$$D_{iE}^* = \frac{D_{iE} - D_{min}}{D_{max} - D_{min}} \times 100 \tag{5}$$

$$B_{iE}^* = \frac{B_{iE} - B_{min}}{B_{max} - B_{min}} \times 100 \tag{6}$$

$$T_{iE}^* = \frac{T_{iE} - T_{min}}{T_{max} - T_{min}} \times 100 \tag{7}$$

where $D_{max}$ $B_{max}$ $T_{max}$ and $D_{min}$ $B_{min}$ $T_{min}$ are the maximum and minimum values in the dataset. Finally, the terminal indicator set can be expressed as $X$:

$$X = \{x_1, x_2, \ldots x_n\} \tag{8}$$

where $x_i = (D_{iE}^*, B_{iE}^*, T_{iE}^*)$ is a three-dimension vector to represent the sensitivity characteristics of terminal $i$. In order to achieve the terminal clustering, $Dis_{ij}$ is defined as the Euclid distance between terminals of the same cluster:

$$Dis_{ij} = \sqrt{(D_{iE}^* - D_{jE}^*)^2 + (B_{iE}^* - B_{jE}^*)^2 + (T_{iE}^* - T_{jE}^*)^2} \tag{9}$$

Suppose the classified cluster is $\{C_1, C_2, \ldots C_n\}$, the average distance $\overline{Dis}$ in the same cluster can be expressed as

$$\overline{Dis_{ij}} = \frac{\sum_{i=1}^{n} \sum_{j=1, j\neq 1}^{n} Dis_{ij}}{C_n^i} \tag{10}$$

According to above equations, the standard deviation $SD_i$ of the terminals in the same cluster is:

$$SD_i = \sqrt{\frac{\sum_{i=1}^{n} \sum_{j=1, j\neq 1}^{n} (Dis_{ij} - \overline{Dis_{ij}})^2}{C_n^i}} \tag{11}$$

In the cluster $i$, the smaller the $SD_i$ value, the higher the similarity of the terminals. In the results obtained by the clustering algorithm, the minimum of the maximum standard deviation of all clusters is pursued:

$$\min\{\max SD_i\}, \ i = 1, 2, 3, \ldots \tag{12}$$

The clustering algorithm will choose k-means algorithm, which has simple and fast clustering ability. At the same time, the number of initial clusters and clustering centers can be preset to reduce the computation complexity and clustering error. The quadratic mean of each dimensional data is used to generate the initial cluster center:

$$D_{sq} = \sqrt{\frac{D_{1E}^{*2} + D_{2E}^{*2} + \cdots + D_{nE}^{*2}}{n}} \tag{13}$$

$$B_{sq} = \sqrt{\frac{B_{1E}^{*2} + B_{2E}^{*2} + \cdots + B_{nE}^{*2}}{n}} \tag{14}$$

$$T_{sq} = \sqrt{\frac{T_{1E}^{*2} + T_{2E}^{*2} + \cdots + T_{nE}^{*2}}{n}} \tag{15}$$

The initial coordinates are $(D_{sq}, 0, 0)$, $(0, B_{sq}, 0)$ and $(0, 0, T_{sq})$. In this paper, the advanced K-means algorithm (AKG) is used to cluster the terminals. The detailed steps are as follows:

**Step 1:** Select $(D_{sq}, 0, 0), (0, B_{sq}, 0)$ and $(0, 0, T_{sq})$ as the centers of three clusters;
**Step 2:** Calculate the distance from the remaining terminals $\{x_1, x_2, \ldots x_n\}$ to each cluster center and classify these terminals into the nearest cluster center;
**Step 3:** Calculate the average values $\overline{Dis}_{ij}$ of terminals in each cluster respectively and designate them as the new cluster centers.
**Step 4:** Iterate Step 2 and Step 3 until reaching the threshold or cluster centers are not changed.

Through the AKG algorithm, terminals are divided into three categories. The ECS calculates resource requirements of each type of terminals for VM resource allocation, so that each terminal can obtain appropriate computing resources.

## 2.2 Dynamic Adjustment

The above scheme help the ECS to realize the reasonable division of resources. However, the resource configuration of one ECS is different when flying over different regions. Therefore, a fleet-based adjustment (FBA) scheme is proposed to reduce the unnecessary consumption of ECSs. Actually, the ECS network can be modeled by the IM matrix like:

$$IM = (\omega_{ij})_{m \times n} = \begin{bmatrix} \omega_{11} & \omega_{12} & \cdots & \omega_{1n} \\ \omega_{21} & \omega_{22} & \cdots & \omega_{2n} \\ \vdots & \vdots & \cdots & \vdots \\ \omega_{m1} & \omega_{m2} & \cdots & \omega_{mn} \end{bmatrix} \tag{16}$$

where $\omega_{ij}$ is denoted as the weight of satellite $j$ in orbit $i$. Meanwhile, $\omega_{ij}$ is the function of parameter $D_{ij}, B_{ij}, T_{ij}, \deg_{ij}$:

$$\omega_{ij} = f(D_{ij}, B_{ij}, T_{ij}, \deg_{ij}) \tag{17}$$

where $\deg_{ij}$ is the accessing number of terminals in each ECS. The $\omega_{ij}$ can be regarded as a multi-dimensional vector. Among the parameters, $D_{ij}$ and $T_{ij}$ may not be independent for each other. So the principal component analysis (PCA) method is utilized to reduce the data dimension and improve the accurate of evaluation for each ECS. The covariance matrix of the two variables is calculated as:

$$C = \begin{pmatrix} c_{11} & c_{12} \\ c_{21} & c_{22} \end{pmatrix} \tag{18}$$

where

$$c_{11} = \text{cov}(D_{ij}, D_{ij}) = E[D_{ij} - E(D_{ij})]^2 \tag{19}$$

$$c_{12} = \text{cov}(D_{ij}, T_{ij}) = E[(D_{ij} - E[D_{ij}])(T_{ij} - E[T_{ij}])] \tag{20}$$

$$c_{21} = \text{cov}(T_{ij}, D_{ij}) = E[(T_{ij} - E[T_{ij}])(D_{ij} - E[D_{ij}])] \tag{21}$$

$$c_{22} = \text{cov}(T_{ij}, T_{ij}) = E[T_{ij} - E(T_{ij})]^2 \tag{22}$$

After that, the eigenvalues $\lambda_1$ and $\lambda_2$.of the matrix $C$ is calculated. The corresponding eigenvectors are $\alpha_1$ and $\alpha_2$. Then the eigenvector corresponding to the largest eigenvalue is selected, such as $\alpha_2$ to $\lambda_2$. Finally, the random variable $Y$ is obtained as:

$$Y = \alpha_2^T * (D_{ij}, T_{ij}) \tag{23}$$

where $Y$ is the final random variable with only one dimension:

$$Y = (y_1, y_2, \ldots, y_n) \tag{24}$$

So the function of $\omega_{ij}$ is further transferred as:

$$\omega_{ij} = f(Y_{ij}, B_{ij}, \deg_{ij}) \tag{25}$$

To compare the similarity of each ECS, firstly the values of three parameters should be converted from different dimensions into one-dimensional weight value. The weighted average method is used to calculate the final weight value of each ECS. The calculation process is as follows:

$$P_{ij} = \left( \sum_{i=1}^{l} \omega_i d_{ij} + \sum_{i=1}^{k-1} \omega_i d'_{ij} \right) / \sum_{i=1}^{k} \omega_i \tag{26}$$

where

$$d_{ij} = \frac{x_{ij} - x_i^{(s)}}{x_i^{(h)} - x_i^{(s)}}, \tag{27}$$
$$i = 1, 2, \cdots, k, \quad j = 1, 2, \cdots, n$$

$$d'_{ij} = \frac{x_i^{(h)} - x_{ij}}{x_i^{(h)} - x_i^{(s)}}, \tag{28}$$
$$i = 1, 2, \cdots, k, \quad j = 1, 2, \cdots, n$$

$P_{ij}$ is the performance evaluation of ECS $E_{ij}$. $k$ is the total number of the parameters selected. $l$ is the number of positive parameters selected. $n$ is the number of ECSs in the evaluation. $w_i$ is the weight of the parameters $i$. $x_{ij}$ is the value of the parameters $i$ in $E_{ij}$. $x_i^{(h)}$ is the optimal value of the parameters $i$. $x_i^{(s)}$ is the average value of the parameters $i$. $d_{ij}$ is the evaluation score of the parameters $i$ in $E_{ij}$. $d'_{ij}$ is the evaluation score of the inverse parameters $i$ in $E_{ij}$. The inadmissible value of a parameter is the worst value that should not appear in the evaluation. The optimal value is the best value that the parameter can achieve. The ECS network evaluation can be calculated as:

$$P_N = \left( \sum_{i=1}^{n} P_{L_i} \omega_i \right) / \sum_{i=1}^{k} \omega_i \tag{29}$$

where $P_N$ is the performance evaluation of the network. $n$ is denoted as the number of ECSs. $\omega_i$ is the performance weight of $E_{ij}$. Meanwhile, supposing that the ECS fleet is $X = (x_1, x_2, \ldots x_m)$ and the control time of $x_i$ is $t_i$:

$$x_1 = t_1, x_2 = t_2, x_3 = t_3, \ldots, x_m = t_m \tag{30}$$

Then the whole control period $Pe$ is

$$Pe = \sum_{i=1}^{m} t_i \tag{31}$$

It means satellite $x_i$ will be the ECS of the region once again after $Pe$ time. The evolution of the configuration for one certain region will be carried out after $Pe$ time. During $Pe$, ECSs with similar $\omega_{ij}$ have similar computing requirements. Configurations of ECSs can be inherited from the above ECSs in the fleet, as shown in Fig. 2. The resource for ECSs achieve dynamic management in spatio-temporal dimension.

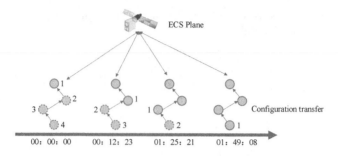

**Fig. 2.** The dynamic configuration transfer model.

## 3 Simulation Results and Analysis

The simulation is carried out in the integrated simulators where the space-air-ground network has established. A predictable LEO satellite network is constructed with the use of the Satellite Tool Kit (STK) simulator. The satellite model is established with reference to iridium constellation to guarantee the practical application. Meanwhile, we randomly created 100 UAV terminal nodes, 200 ship nodes and 200 sensor nodes in the Pacific Ocean initially using STK. Then we connect STK with MATLAB to obtain the satellites and terminal data, where the calculation and comparison of the proposed scheme and other methods are also carried out. Meanwhile, the node data is imported to the Qualnet simulator to establish the heterogeneous network for network performance evaluation. Each terminal node is assigned different values of three sensitivities according to their characteristics of resource demand.

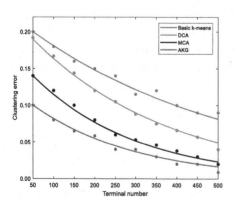

**Fig. 3.** Error comparison of two clustering algorithm.

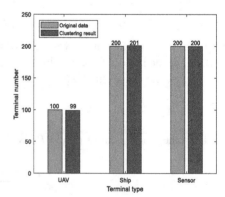

**Fig. 4.** The clustering result of AKG.

In the simulation, we first verified the classification precision of the proposed advanced k-means algorithm (AKG). As shown in Fig. 3, we compare the clustering errors of the basic k-means algorithm, meanshift clustering algorithm (MCA), density-based clustering algorithm (DCA) and the proposed AKG algorithm with the increase of terminal numbers. The trends of error change is plotted by curves. It can be seen that the clustering error of AKG is significantly lower than the other three algorithms. This is because the clustering center at the initialization of the AKG has been calculated regularly, while the basic k-means algorithm and the other two methods just randomly select the clustering center. The selection of clustering center will greatly affect the accuracy and computational complexity of the algorithm. The clustering result is expressed as Fig. 4, which shows a good terminal classification result.

The additional calculation of the ECS network for dynamic resource adjustment will be analyzed. As Fig. 5 shows, the methods of basic K-means, AKG and fleet-based adjustment (FBA) are compared. The additional calculation of method basic K-means rises rapidly with the increase of the number of involved ECSs, followed by AKG. The FBA method occupies the least amount of additional calculation. This is because the configuration of FBA is obtained from the previous ECS in the fleet, so there is no need to reuse the clustering algorithm for terminal classification. It only requires the adjustments based on the obtained configuration. Therefore, the FBA method can save more computing resources for ECSs.

The resource utilization of ECSs has a great influence on the performance of the satellite network. Next we will analyze the resource usage of ECSs under different methods to reflect the change of load balancing, total resource usage and robustness of the ECS network. In addition to the methods of AKG, DCA, MCA, Basic k-means, the TEG method in [14] is added to the comparison, which separated the computing resources and cache resources to realize efficient resource usage. Actually, the variance of resource usage of ECS nodes can reflect the load balancing of the ECS network to some extent. Figure 6 compare the variance change of different methods. It can be seen that the variance values of all five methods is increasing with ECS number increase. This is because different ECS has undertaken different amounts computing services of terminals. But the variance of the AKG method grows the slowest. Referring back to the above, the AKG method can help ECS to partition computing resources accurately, so that the uneven utilization of resources caused by allocation errors is reduced. Similarly, Fig. 7 shows the difference of total resource usage of the five methods. It can be seen that the total resource usage of AKG method is always the lowest. Therefore, accurate resource allocation can reduce resource waste and improve load balancing performance of the whole network. Meanwhile, we use the number of high capacity nodes to reflect the robustness of the ECS network in Fig. 8. The threshold of utilization of each ECS node is set to 0.7. We can see that the AKG method always has the most available ECSs with terminal number increase, which maintains the robustness of the ECS network. All the above show that the proposed scheme provides higher clustering precision and resource utilization, compared with other methods.

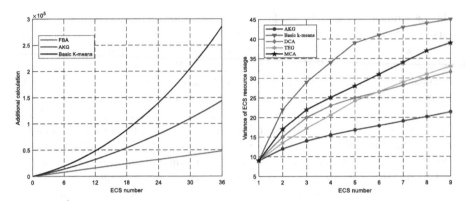

**Fig. 5.** The comparison of additional calculation.

**Fig. 6.** The comparison of load balancing.

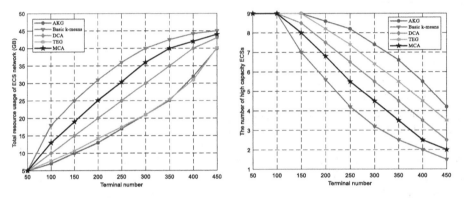

**Fig. 7.** The comparison of total resource usage.

**Fig. 8.** The comparison of robustness.

## 4    Conclusions

This paper studies the resource management in the edge computing satellite network. We jointly consider the dynamic resource division and adjustment strategies in edge computing satellite (ECS). An advanced K-means algorithm (AKG) is proposed to guide the resource division in ECS. Meanwhile, a fleet-based adjustment (FBA) scheme is designed to realize dynamic adjustment of resource for ECS. The simulation results show that the proposed dynamic resource adjustment scheme is promising.

**Acknowledgment.** This work was supported by National Natural Science Foundation of China (No. 61571104), Sichuan Science and Technology Program (No. 2018JY0539), Key projects of the Sichuan Provincial Education Department (No. 18ZA0219), Fundamental Research Funds for the Central Universities (No. ZYGX2017KYQD170), and Innovation Funding (No. 2018510007 000134). The authors wish to thank the reviewers for their helpful comments.

# References

1. Qu, Z., Zhang, G., Cao, H., et al.: LEO satellite constellation for Internet of Things. IEEE Access **5**, 18391–18401 (2017)
2. Liu, J., Shi, Y., Zhao, L., et al.: Joint placement of controllers and gateways in SDN-enabled 5G-satellite integrated network. IEEE J. Sel. Areas Commun. **36**(2), 221–232 (2018)
3. Zhang, Z., Jiang, C., et al.: Temporal centrality-balanced traffic management for space satellite networks. IEEE Trans. Veh. Technol. **67**(5), 4427–4439 (2018)
4. Tang, F., Zhang, H., Fu, L., et al.: Multipath cooperative routing with efficient acknowledgement for LEO satellite networks. IEEE Trans. Mob. Comput. **8**(1), 179–192 (2019)
5. Li, H., Ota, K., Dong, M.: Learning IoT in edge: deep learning for the internet of things with edge computing. IEEE Netw. **32**(1), 96–101 (2018)
6. Du, J., Jiang, C., Wang, J., et al.: Resource allocation in space multiaccess systems. IEEE Trans. Aerosp. Electron. Syst. **53**(2), 598–618 (2017)
7. Sinha, P.K., Dutta, A.: Multi-satellite task allocation algorithm for earth observation. In: Proceedings of TENCON 2016, pp. 403–408 (2016)
8. Sheng, M., Wang, Y., Li, J., et al.: Toward a flexible and reconfigurable broadband satellite network: resource management architecture and strategies. IEEE Wirel. Commun. **24**(4), 127–133 (2017)
9. Jiang, D., Wang, W., Shi, L., et al.: A compressive sensing-based approach to end-to-end network traffic reconstruction. IEEE Trans. Netw. Sci. Eng. **5**(3), 1–12 (2018)
10. Jiang, D., Huo, L., Li, Y.: Fine-granularity inference and estimations to network traffic for SDN. PLoS ONE **13**(5), 1–23 (2018)
11. Jiang, D., Huo, L., Lv, Z., et al.: A joint multi-criteria utility-based network selection approach for vehicle-to-infrastructure networking. IEEE Trans. Intell. Transp. Syst. **PP**(99), 1–15 (2018)
12. Jiang, D., Zhang, Y., Song, H., et al.: Intelligent optimization-based energy-efficient networking in cloud services for multimedia big data. In: Proceedings of IPCCC 2018, pp. 1–6 (2018)
13. Jiang, D., Huo, L., Song, H.: Understanding base stations' behaviors and activities with big data analysis. In: Proceedings of Globecom 2018, pp. 1–7 (2018)
14. Wang, P., Zhang, X., Zhang, S., et al.: Time-expanded graph based resource allocation over the satellite networks. IEEE Wirel. Commun. Lett. **8**(2), 360–363 (2019)

# A Security Traffic Measurement Approach in SDN-Based Internet of Things

Liuwei Huo[1], Dingde Jiang[2(✉)], and Hui Qi[3]

[1] School of Computer Science and Engineering, NEU, Shenyang 110819, China
[2] School of Astronautics and Aeronautic, UESTC, Chengdu 611731, China
jiangdd@uestc.edu.cn
[3] School of Computer Science and Technology, CUST,
Changchun 130022, China

**Abstract.** In the Internet of things (IoT), a large amount of data are exchanged through IoT networks between devices and cloud computing. However, the legacy architecture of IoT networks is not flexible and scalable for the increment of devices. Software defined networking (SDN) separates the control plane from the data plane in the legacy switches and centralizes the control plane as a logical control center, making network management more flexible and efficient. In SDN, the controller is very easy to be attacked, then, we use the Blockchain technology into the measurement framework to ensure the security and consistency of the statistics. To obtain the measurement results with low overhead and high accuracy, we collect the statistics of coarse-grained traffic of flows and fine-grained traffic of links and estimate the flow traffic with an ARIMA model. We propose an objective function to decrease the estimation errors. The objective function is an NP-hard problem, we present a heuristic algorithm to obtain the optimal solution of the fine-grained measurement. Finally, some simulations are performed to verify the validity of the proposed scheme.

**Keywords:** Internet of things · Software defined networking · Network measurement · Traffic matrix

## 1 Introduction

The Internet of things (IoT) connects many kinds of devices in urban areas, such as transportation, schools, and hospitals. A huge amount of data are integrated into cloud computing through the IoT network which is designed to provide the highest possible degree of flexibility, scalability, and security to all interconnected entities [1]. Cloud computing is a universal computing platform which has powerful computing, it supports the operation of different applications at the same time [2]. There are large amounts of data in networks should be processed and exchanged, so the network quality monitoring is very important for network maintenance.

In the legacy IoT network, its architecture is not scalable and not satisfy the requirement of the increment devices. Software Defined Networking (SDN) intends to simplify network management and improve the flexibility of the IoT. SDN separates the control plane from the underlying forwarding device and integrates the control

H. Song et al. (Eds.): SIMUtools 2019, LNICST 295, pp. 146–156, 2019.
https://doi.org/10.1007/978-3-030-32216-8_14

plane into the logically center to simplify network management and dynamically configure network rules [3]. In SDN, the controller has a global view of the networks, so the controller can program the global optimization rules for the traffic dispatching. SDN provides a novel flow-based statistical measurement method, it is very flexible and convenient to collect the traffic statistics information from switches.

SDN has one of the most important drawbacks is its increased attack surface compared to traditional networking deployments and the increased effect any successful attack will have. In distributed systems, Blockchain is a means of ensuring data security, reliability, and transparent exchange and storage, ensuring the security and consistency by having all participants share ledger. If the controller is hijacked or some nodes masquerade as controller nodes and send improper flow forwarding rules or malicious read switch information to the network, it may cause erroneous traffic or network storms in the network, causing the entire network to crash. In [4], Sharma et al. provide to use Blockchain to increase the security SDN. The information in the black chain cannot be modified unless all participants have reached a consensus to modify the ledger, this is because that all the participants share the same information in private ledger to maintain the consistency and completeness of the information. Traffic modeling [10, 11], traffic estimation [12], network selection [13], energy efficiency [14] and network behaviors [15] are studied in previous work.

According to the analysis above, we propose a pull-based and flow-based network traffic measurement in IoT network with lower measurement overhead. We measure some data of the network traffic directly and estimate the fine-grained network traffic. Then, we propose an objective optimization model to decrease the fine-grained measurement error inferred and present a heuristic algorithm to seek the optimal solution of the model. Our main contributions in this paper are as follows:

(1) We propose a framework for network traffic measurement in the IoT networks. To ensure the security and consistency of the statistics, we introduce the Blockchain technology into the measurement framework of SDN-based IoT networks. To obtain the measurement results with low overhead and high accuracy, we collect the statistics of coarse-grained traffic of flows and fine-grained traffic of links.

(2) We model the network traffic as an ARIMA model and forecast the flow of traffic with the coarse-grained flow measurement. Then, we propose an objective function to decrease the estimation errors.

(3) The objective function is an NP-hard problem, we present a heuristic algorithm to obtain the optimal solution of the fine-grained measurement. Finally, we conduct some simulations to verify the validity of the proposed measurement scheme.

The rest of this paper is organized as follows: Sect. 2 states the main security challenges of SDN networking, then we provide a fine-grained measurement scheme with Blockchain scheme, and describes the fine-grained traffic estimation and optimization in the IoT paradigm. Section 3 presents the simulation of the performance of the fine-grained measurement. Finally, Sect. 4 concludes our works in this paper.

## 2  Problem Statement

Cloud computing frequently requests the resource from cloud computing to decrease the network. Network measurements such as load balancing, path planning, and anomaly detection are required. In this section, we propose a cloud computing network measurement architecture based on SDN architecture.

### 2.1  System Model

In the IoT, a large number of devices are typically dynamically connected to the network, which requires the network to be very flexible and scalable. The flow-based measurement in SDN is much easier and more flexible than the legacy network. Network measurement is the key of the network management, then, we propose an SDN-based network measurement architecture for cloud computing networks that uses a sampling method to obtain coarse-grained measurements, then uses estimation and optimization methods to recover fine-grained measurements. In this architecture, we use Blockchain approach to ensure the security of information exchanged between the controller and switches. The measurement components are installed into the controller and are compatible with the other existing software defined measurement frameworks. The key technologies for the novel measurement architecture include coarse-grained measurements, traffic modeling and estimation, and traffic optimization. The flow-based coarse-grained measurements in SDN can be obtained by collecting the flow statistics in OpenFlow-based switches; the traffic matrix consists of link load, flow traffic, and the routing matrix, which reflects the traffic in the network, and has been widely researched in traffic engineering; estimation is a common method of data estimation; and the optimization methods are widely used to find the best solution for the complex issues.

### 2.2  Blockchain Application

In recent, most evidence preservation systems which based on a centralized repository structure have serious security issues. Centralized structures always require strong safety requirements. In SDN, the controller becomes a critical node, it will lead to serious consequences for the whole network once the controller is hijacked. For example, once a malicious application is installed in the controller or a malicious node inside the network masquerades as the controller, malicious traffic will constantly be generated in IoT networks, which takes up a large amount of bandwidth, causing link congestion and making the request of the legitimate node unresponsive, even bringing down the entire network. In order to ensure the authenticity and credibility of the network statistics collected by the controller, we propose to combine Blockchain technology with SDN in IoT networks. In SDN, all the device are accountants and update the data from the controller, and each accountant maintains a ledger. Each time data is written to the ledger, then a block is created. The header of each block contains the hash value of the previous block, blocks linked together forming a chain. Trusted timestamps can be immediately attached to newly created blocks. Most importantly, it is possible to avoid trust issues by spreading the authority of the auditor. It demonstrates the integrity, accuracy, and timeliness required for preservation.

A special number needs to be attached to the end of each block and use a hash function to generate a hash value which is difficult to decipher, as Fig. 1 shows. So, the output data is completely unpredictable unless you know the full input data and the hash function. The node who first get proof of work will broadcast the block with its proof of work, and all other nodes in the network will append this block to their own Blockchain. So if a malicious node in the network tries to tamper the information and broadcast a fake block. So, there are two different blocks will be exchanged in the network, and the Blockchain will branch in a short time. The admissibility rule for Blockchain is always to trust the longest Blockchain. However, the Blockchain branch of the malicious node is only maintained by partial nodes, while the real branch chain is maintained by most of all nodes in the network together except malicious nodes. Based on this data structure, if a malicious node attempts to modify a previous block, the hash value of that block changes. In order to make subsequent blocks connect to it, all subsequent blocks must be modified in turn, otherwise, the altered block will not be accepted by other nodes. The Blockchain technology ensures that the network statistics information collected by the controller in SDN is truly unimpeded, which greatly improves the security of the SDN network.

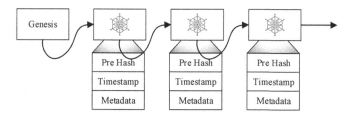

**Fig. 1.** The Blockchain model

### 2.3  Traffic Matrix and ARMA Model Construction

Origin-Destination (OD) traffic refers to traffic between any two nodes in the network and describes the distribution of network traffic between OD pairs. The flow traffic can be calculated based on the measured link traffic and the network routing matrix. The relationship can be expressed as a linear equation:

$$Y = AX \tag{1}$$

where $Y$ is a column vector representing link traffic, $X$ is also a column vector representing the traffic matrix, and $A$ is the routing matrix. The problem of flow calculation is an inverse problem-solving of an underdetermined and ill-conditioned system.

In IoT networks, the volume of large amounts of data in IoT networks is very small and require low latency, and the flow traffic fluctuates sharply, but the flow traffic in IoT networks can be represented as time series. By studying the time series and discovering changes of flows, the modeling method belongs to the field of time series analysis. The Autoregressive Integrated Moving Average Model (ARIMA) model is the most commonly used time series analysis model [5]. The ARIMA model is the extension of the ARMA model, and ARIMA model is mainly used for non-stationary time series modeling. The ARMA model can be written as

$$\begin{aligned} x(t) &= \delta + \phi_1 x(t-1) + \phi_2 x(t-2) + + \cdots + \phi_p x(t-p) \\ &+ u(t) + \theta_1 u(t-1) + \theta_2 u(t-2) + \cdots \theta_q u(t-q) \end{aligned} \tag{2}$$

In time series analysis, the Lag operator (L) on a value of a time series to produce the previous value. So the traffic with the lag operator can be written as

$$x(t-k) = L^k x(t) \tag{3}$$

where $L$ is the Lag operator, and $k$ is the lag order. So, the ARIMA($p, d, q$) model with the Lag operator can be written as

$$\begin{aligned} x(t) &= \delta + \phi_1 x(t-1) + \phi_2 x(t-2) + \cdots + \phi_p x(t-p) + u(t) \\ &+ u(t) + \theta_1 u(t-1) + \theta_2 u(t-2) + \cdots \theta_q u(t-q) \\ &= \delta + \sum_{i=1}^{p} \phi_i L^i x(t) + u(t) + \sum_{j=1}^{q} \theta_j L^j u(t) \\ &= \delta + \sum_{i=1}^{p} \phi_i L^i x(t) + (1 + \sum_{j=1}^{q} \theta_j L^j) u(t) \end{aligned} \tag{4}$$

where $x(t)$ is the predictive value; $x(t-i)(i = 1, 2, \ldots, p)$ are the actual values; $\phi_i (i = 1, 2, \ldots, p)$ and $\theta_j (j = 1, 2, \ldots, q)$ are the parameters of autoregressive coefficients and random errors coefficients, respectively; $u(t-j)(j = 0, 1, 2, \ldots, q)$ are the Gaussian white noise, their means and constant variance of 0 and $\sigma^2$, respectively; $\delta$ is a constant; $p$ and $q$ are the orders of the AR model and MA model, respectively. Then, the ARIMA model with $d$-order difference of data series can be expressed as

$$(1 - \sum_{i=1}^{p} \phi_i L^i)(1 - L)^d x(t) = \delta + (1 + \sum_{j=1}^{q} \theta_j L^j) u(t) \tag{5}$$

where $d$ is the difference order; $x(t)$, $u(t)$ are the estimation of the traffic and random errors following Gaussian distribution, respectively. $\phi$, $\theta$ are the coefficients of autoregressive and random errors, respectively; $\delta$ is a constant.

In the ARIMA model, the $d$-order difference of data series is an ARMA model, then we use ARMA model to estimate the network traffic with the time series $(1 - L)^d x(t)$ instead of the original network traffic series $x(t)$. However, estimation results of flows have big errors with the actual flow traffic. In the edge network, the link load reflects the integrated traffic transmission in the network. So, we use the pull-based method to obtain the fine-grained link load $Y$ in networks. The traffic of flows in the network can be written as

$$f = \alpha \|Y - A\hat{X}\|_2 + \beta \|\hat{X}\|_2 \tag{6}$$

where $A$ is the routing matrix, $\alpha$ and $\beta$ are the weight coefficient of the measurement results. In order to decrease the deviation between the estimations and the actual traffic results, we construct an objective function to optimize the estimation results. The objective function as the function (7) shows.

$$\begin{cases} \min \alpha \|Y - A\hat{X}\|_2 + \beta \|\hat{X}\|_2 \\ s.t. \\ \quad C1 : Y = A\hat{X} \\ \quad C2 : \hat{X} \geq 0 \\ \quad C3 : Y_m \geq \sum_n a_{mn}\hat{X} \\ \quad C4 : \sum_{i=1}^{N} x_{ij} = \sum_{j=1}^{N} x_{ji} \end{cases} \tag{7}$$

where $\hat{X}$ is estimated by ARIMA. Constraint $C1$ represents the constraint between link load and flow traffic; constraint $C2$ shows the link load is non-negativity; constraint $C3$ is the limitation of flows on each link; constraint $C4$ represents that the traffic that input and output of the switch are constant, $i$ is the source node and $j$ is the destination node. In the IoT networks, the routing matrix $A$ has $M$ rows and $N$ columns. However, the OD pairs are much larger than links, namely: $M \ll N$, then the routing matrix $A$ is an underdetermined matrix, there are infinite traffic matrices $X$ which satisfy the constraint $C1$. The objective function (7) is an NP-hard problem and is difficult to solve directly. Then, we use a heuristic method to solve it.

## 2.4   Ant Colony Algorithm

The ant colony algorithm (AC) is a probabilistic algorithm for solving the hard optimization problem [6], and it is inspired by the utilization of pheromone as a communication medium to find the optimal path in the food search process. Pheromone update is the core of AC. Ant colony algorithm process is as follows:

(a)  Initialization: Initializing the control parameters, the maximum number of iterations, and the pheromone concentration value for each candidate.
(b)  Construction of solutions: Each ant starts from its own start, and the go through each node in the network. Suppose that the pheromone concentration corresponding to the *ath* candidate traffic value of the *jth* variable is $\tau(i,j)$. When pheromone concentration is updated, the pheromone concentration value corresponding to each candidate traffic of each OD pair in the network will also be updated. The ant selects the candidate traffic according to the following equation:

$$S_i = \begin{cases} \arg(\max[\tau(i,j)]), \ q \leq q_0 \\ \dfrac{\tau(i,j)}{\sum\limits_{k=1}^{N} \tau(i,j)}, \ q > q_0 \end{cases} \tag{8}$$

(c) Pheromone concentration update: When ants pass through the solution space of traffic, change the pheromone concentration value corresponding to the candidate traffic value (s) selected by the ant in the passing traffic. The update rule of local pheromone concentration is

$$\tau(i,j) = (1-\rho)\tau(i,j) \qquad (9)$$

(d) Global pheromone concentration update: After all ants complete the pathfinding process (G), updating the pheromone concentration in the network according to the global pheromone concentration updating rule which can be expressed as

$$\tau_k(j) = (1-\alpha)\tau_k(j) + \Delta\tau_k(j) \qquad (10)$$

$$\Delta\tau_k(j) = \begin{cases} \alpha/f_{best}, & optimal \\ -\alpha'/f_{worst}, & worst \\ 0, & others \end{cases} \qquad (11)$$

(e) Analysis and calculation: The solutions constructed by ants need to be analyzed, and after all ants have constructed solutions, it is necessary to judge whether these solutions are new ones. If it is a new path, the corresponding target function value is calculated. Otherwise, the function value will be set to given default values.
(f) Looping: Performing the loop from step (b) to (e) until the termination condition is reached.

## 3  Simulation Result and Analysis

### 3.1  Simulation Environment

In order to evaluate the performance of the measurement scheme proposed, we built an SDN test platform and wrote the measurement module in python. We use Ryu [7] as the controller and simulate the switches, hosts and links by Mininet [8]. We generate the flows in the network by Iperf and set the maximum link load as 10Gbps.

To verify the performance of the measurement scheme proposed, we introduce the Relative error (RE) and Relative Error (RE). The AE reflects the deviations between the actual traffic and the measurement results. The smaller the AE, the more accurate the measurement. The RE is the ratio of measured AE to the actual value, reflecting the credibility of the measurement. Root Mean Squared Error (RMSE) is usually used to evaluate the measurement accuracy in simulations.

### 3.2  Simulation Evaluation

We use Iperf to generate packets to fill each link from origin host to destination host in the network and measure all the flow traffic with different methods. We randomly choose two flows as an example for discussion. In this paper, we combine the ARIMA model and AC model to estimate and optimize the fine-grained network traffic and use

ARIMA-AC to it. Then, we compare ARIMA-AC to Fine-grained measurement (FGM), the Principal Component Analysis (PCA) and SRSVD [9].

Figure 2 shows the flow of traffic for different estimation method. The red line is the actual traffic generated by Iperf. The blue line, pink line, and green line represent the measurement methods ARIMA-AC, SRSVD and PCA, respectively. We notice that the ARIMA-AC, SRSVD and PCA measurement methods all reflect the change of flows f2 and f3. The PCA fluctuates more sharply than that of other methods. Figures 3 and 4 show the AE and RE cumulative distribution function (CDF) of flow f2 and f3, respectively. From Fig. 3, we can see that the about 80% AE of the ARIMA-AC, SRSVD are less than 1000 Mbps in the 40 min measurement process, while the performance of PCA method is the worst. However, the average AE of the ARIMA-AC is smaller than that of SRSVD and PCA. Figure 4 is the RE of different measurement methods, and we find that about 80% AE of the ARIMA-AC, SRSVD is less than 0.2 in the 40 min measurement process, which means that the network traffic measurement is stable and effective. The performance of PCA is the worst of four measurement methods.

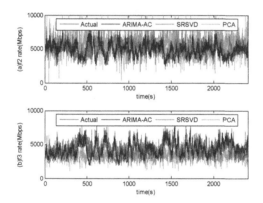

**Fig. 2.** The network traffic measurement of different methods. (Color figure online)

Figure 5 shows the curve of CCDF (Complementary Cumulative Distribution Function) of RMSE for the different measurement methods. CCDF reflects the RE RMSE of the measurement error, and it also shows that when RMSE is bigger than 0.2 of ARIMA-AC, the measurement error is very small. The performance of ARIMA-AC is better than that of ARSVD and PCA, and a little worse than that of FGM. So, when the measurement accuracy requirement is no more than 20%, the ARIMA-AC is feasible. In the measurement process, we just measure the coarse-grained flow traffic and the fine-grained link traffic, there is smaller overhead than that of FGM.

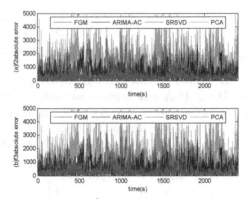

**Fig. 3.** The AE of different methods.

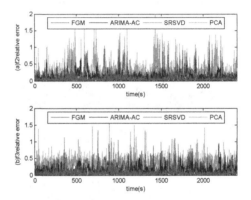

**Fig. 4.** The RE of different methods.

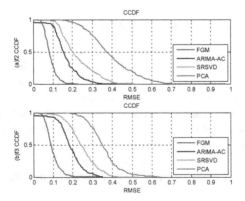

**Fig. 5.** The CCDF of RMSE of different methods.

# 4 Conclusions

In this paper, we propose a novel low-overhead measurement scheme and construct the measurement architecture of IoT network. Security is one of the most important issues in SDN, then we introduce the Blockchain to ensure the security and consistency of the statistics exchanged between the controller and switches. Then, we measure the coarse-grained traffic of flows and fine-grained traffic of links. In order to obtain the fine-grained flow traffic, we model the network traffic as an ARIMA model and forecast the network traffic, and propose an objective function to decrease the estimation errors. The objective function is a NP-hard problem, we use a heuristic algorithm to obtain the optimal solution. At last, we perform some simulations to verify the measurement architecture and scheme proposed in this paper.

**Acknowledgment.** This work was supported by National Natural Science Foundation of China (No. 61571104), Sichuan Science and Technology Program (No. 2018JY0539), Key projects of the Sichuan Provincial Education Department (No. 18ZA0219), Fundamental Research Funds for the Central Universities (No. ZYGX2017KYQD170), and Innovation Funding (No. 2018510007 000134). The authors wish to thank the reviewers for their helpful comments.

# References

1. Ray, P.P.: A survey on Internet of Things architectures. J. King Saud Univ. Comput. Inf. Sci. **30**(3), 291–319 (2018)
2. Li, S., Xu, L., Zhao, S.: 5G Internet of Things: a survey. J. Ind. Inf. Integr. **10**, 1–9 (2018)
3. Xu, H., Yu, Z., Qian, C., et al.: Minimizing flow statistics collection cost of SDN using wildcard requests. In: Proceedings OF INFOCOM 2017, pp. 1–9 (2017)
4. Sharma, P.K., Singh, S., et al.: Distblocknet: a distributed Blockchains-based secure SDN architecture for IoT networks. IEEE Commun. Mag. **55**(9), 78–85 (2017)
5. Unnikrishnan, J., Suresh, K.K.: Modelling the impact of government policies on import on domestic price of Indian gold using ARIMA intervention method. Int. J. Math. Math. Sci. **2016**, 1–6 (2016)
6. Liu, J., Yang, J., Liu, H., et al.: An improved ant colony algorithm for robot path planning. Soft. Comput. **21**(19), 5829–5839 (2017)
7. The Mininet Platform. http://mininet.org/. Accessed Dec 2018
8. The Ryu Platform. https://github.com/osrg/ryu/. Accessed Dec 2018
9. Roughan, M., Zhang, Y., et al.: Spatio-temporal compressive sensing and internet traffic matrices. IEEE/ACM Trans. Netw. **20**(3), 662–676 (2012)
10. Huo, L., Jiang, D., Zhu, X. et al.: An SDN-based fine-grained measurement and modeling approach to vehicular communication network traffic. Int. J. Commun. Syst. 1–12 (2019)
11. Jiang, D., Wang, W., Shi, L., et al.: A compressive sensing-based approach to end-to-end network traffic reconstruction. IEEE Trans. Netw. Sci. Eng. **5**(3), 1–12 (2018)
12. Jiang, D., Huo, L., Li, Y.: Fine-granularity inference and estimations to network traffic for SDN. PLoS One **13**(5), 1–23 (2018)
13. Jiang, D., Huo, L., Lv, Z., et al.: A joint multi-criteria utility-based network selection approach for vehicle-to-infrastructure networking. IEEE Trans. Intell. Transp. Syst. **PP**(99), 1–15 (2018)

14. Jiang, D., Zhang, Y., Song, H., et al.: Intelligent optimization-based energy-efficient networking in cloud services for multimedia big data. In: Proceedings of IPCCC 2018, pp. 1–6 (2018)
15. Jiang, D., Huo, L., Song, H.: Understanding base stations' behaviors and activities with big data analysis. In: Proceedings Globecom 2018, pp. 1–7 (2018)

# An Intelligent Relay Node Selection Scheme in Space-Air-Ground Integrated Networks

Feng Wang[1], Dingde Jiang[1(✉)], Jiang Zhu[2], and Zuoliang Liu[2]

[1] School of Astronautics and Aeronautic, UESTC, Chengdu 611731, China
jiangdd@uestc.edu.cn
[2] School of Communication and Information Engineering, CUPT,
Chongqing 400065, China

**Abstract.** The Space-air-ground integrated network (SAGIN) has been a valuable architecture for communication support due to its characteristics of wide coverage and low transmission delay. Both low earth orbit (LEO) satellites and UAVs can serve as relay nodes to provide reliable communication services for ground devices. However, the design of relay node selection scheme in SAGIN is not easy, considering different accessing layers and resource usage of network segments. Moreover, network topology, available resources and relative motion need to be analyzed comprehensively. To address these problems, a traffic prediction method based on autoregressive moving average (ARMA) model is utilized firstly to forecast the resource usage of SAGIN segments. After the analysis of link performance, the Adaboost algorithm is used to classify network nodes for optimal relay node selection. Simulation results show that the proposed intelligent relay node selection scheme is feasible and effective.

**Keywords:** Space-air-ground integrated network · Traffic prediction · Adaboost model · Relay node selection

## 1 Introduction

Utilizing ultramodern communication technologies and interconnecting space, air, ground network segments, the space-air-ground integrated network (SAGIN) has attracted many attentions from academia to industry [1]. LEO constellation has the advantages of low delay, high capacity, full coverage and manageability. DJI, the world leader in UAVs and aerial photography technology, has exhibited its new SkyCells communication solutions to optimize the current ground network. The UAV and LEO satellite networks can extend network coverage in highly congested city areas. The UAV and LEO satellite node will serve as the relay node to help transmit data among the ground devices. However, in the LEO satellite layer and air vehicle layer, the segments move at a high speed and the network topology is constantly changing [2]. As a result, the network performance, such as network traffic, link delay, bandwidth, and connection time, will change sequentially with the movement of segments, which causes difficulties in the selection of relay nodes [3]. Meanwhile, the ground device is always covered by multiple UAVs and LEO satellites. How to choose

H. Song et al. (Eds.): SIMUtools 2019, LNICST 295, pp. 157–167, 2019.
https://doi.org/10.1007/978-3-030-32216-8_15

the appropriate accessing node according to the communication requirements to ensure the load balance of the integrated network also needs to be considered [4].

In recent years, more and more researchers have been starting their projects on traffic prediction, network control and path planning in SAGIN. Authors in [5] tried to combine wavelet transform and autoregressive integrated moving average (ARIMA) algorithm to predict self-similar traffic in satellite-ground networks. The self-similarity of satellite network traffic is proved. In general, the SAGIN can be modeled with a directed connected graph for network analysis and control. Authors in [6] mainly considered the link planning from small satellite networks (SSNs) to ground devices. An extended time-evolving graph was exploited to characterize the network resources. The network profit was formulated as a mixed-integer linear programming model. Authors in [7] developed a new dynamic CPD algorithm while considering the time-varying property of contacts in broadband data relay satellite networks. The flow optimization problem in the time-spread graph was treated as a random optimization problem. The relay selection algorithm could improve the throughput, but the computational complexity of the proposed scheme was high, which could occupy more network resources. Most methods above did not consider the computational complexity of the scheme. A lightweight relay node scheme needs to be designed, considering the dynamic topology of SAGIN. Traffic modeling [8], traffic estimation [9], network selection [10], energy efficiency [11] and network behaviors [12] are studied in previous work.

In this paper, the network traffic is considered as an important reference because it can reflect the current load of network segments. Therefore, a network traffic prediction scheme based on ARMA model is utilized to evaluate the node performance. Furthermore, the network performance metrics such as link delay, bandwidth and connection time are all take into consideration for segment evaluation. In order to realize fast relay node selection, an Adaboost based link planning (ALP) algorithm is proposed. All relay nodes are divided into 4 levels according to their data transmission capacity (DTC). As a result, devices with different communication requirements can be assigned to the optimal relay nodes, and the load balance of the SAGIN network is also improved.

The rest of this paper is organized as follows. Section 2 constructs the mathematical model of ARMA for traffic prediction of SAGIN and then proposes the ALP algorithm. The simulation results and analysis are shown in Sect. 3. We then conclude our work in Sect. 4.

## 2   Mathematical Model

In this section, we mainly talk about network performance evaluation of space-air-ground integrated network (SAGIN). Firstly, a traffic prediction method based on autoregressive moving average (ARMA) model is utilized to forecast the resource usage of SAGIN segments. After the analysis of link performance, the Adaboost-algorithm is used to classify network nodes according to their data transmission capacity. Then, an Adaboost-based link planning (ALP) algorithm is proposed for relay node selection.

The $ARMA(p,q)$ model is a commonly used time series model to realize the optimal traffic prediction. By analyzing the structure and characteristics of time series, the minimum variance is obtained. The $ARMA(p,q)$ model is composed of the $AR(p)$ and $MA(q)$ models. The $AR(p)$ model utilizes a linear combination of present disturbance data and past observation data for traffic prediction, which can be formulated as follows:

$$X_t = \alpha_1 X_{t-1} + \alpha_2 X_{t-2} + \cdots + \alpha_p X_{t-p} + \xi_t \tag{1}$$

$X_t$ is the time series and $\alpha_i (i = 1, 2, \cdots, p)$ are the undetermined coefficients of the $AR(p)$ model. $p$ is the order of $AR(p)$, and the prediction error is denoted by $\xi_t$. The $MA(q)$ model makes use of a linear combination of present and past disturbance data to help traffic prediction. The model can be described as:

$$u_t = \varepsilon_t - \beta_1 \varepsilon_{t-1} - \beta_2 \varepsilon_{t-2} - \cdots - \beta_q \varepsilon_{t-q} \tag{2}$$

where $u_t$ is the observed value, $\varepsilon_i (i = t - q, t - q + 1, \cdots, t)$ are the prediction errors of the $X_i$, and $q$ is the order of $MA(q)$. $\beta_i (i = 1, 2, \cdots, q)$ are the undetermined coefficients. As a result, $ARMA(p,q)$ is a combination of $AR(p)$ and $MA(q)$, which can be expressed as:

$$\begin{aligned} X_t = \alpha_1 X_{t-1} + \alpha_2 X_{t-2} + \cdots + \alpha_p X_{t-p} \\ + \varepsilon_t - \beta_1 \varepsilon_{t-1} - \beta_2 \varepsilon_{t-2} - \cdots - \beta_q \varepsilon_{t-q} \end{aligned} \tag{3}$$

In order to utilize the $ARMA(p,q)$ model for traffic prediction, it is necessary to find the best fitting, that is, to determine the order $(p,q)$ and other coefficients. The order $(p,q)$ can be determined by verifying the autocorrelation function (ACF) and partial correlation function (PACF) of the time sequences $X_t$. The ACF and PACF of $X_t$ can be calculated as $\rho_k$ and $\Phi_{kk}$:

$$\rho_k = \frac{Cov(X_t, X_{t+k})}{\sigma_X^2} \tag{4}$$

$$\Phi_{kk} = \frac{\rho_k - \sum_{i=1}^{k-1} \Phi_{k-1,i} \rho_{k-i}}{1 - \sum_{i=1}^{k-1} \Phi_{k-1,i} \rho_i} \quad k = 2, 3, \ldots \tag{5}$$

Where

$$\Phi_{11} = \rho_1 \tag{6}$$

$$\Phi_{ki} = \Phi_{k-1,i} - \Phi_{kk} \Phi_{k-1,k-1} \tag{7}$$

When the PACF of $X_t$ meets $\Phi_{ki} = 0$ $(k > p)$, the value of $p$ is $k - 1$. Similarly, if the ACF of $X_t$ meets $\rho_k = 0$ $(k > q)$, the value of $q$ is $k - 1$.

The moment estimation method is used to calculate the coefficients, which has the advantages of simple calculation and high estimation accuracy. Firstly the $ARMA(p, q)$ model can be expressed as:

$$X_t = \sum_{i=1}^{p} \alpha_i X_{t-i} + \varepsilon_t + \sum_{i=1}^{q} \beta_i \varepsilon_{t-i} \tag{8}$$

where $\{\varepsilon_t\}$ is normally distributed as $N(0, \sigma^2)$. $\alpha$ and $\beta$ meet:

$$\alpha(z) = 1 - \sum_{i=1}^{p} \alpha_i z^i \tag{9}$$

$$\beta(z) = 1 + \sum_{i=1}^{q} \beta_i z^i \tag{10}$$

The $\alpha(z)$ and $\beta(z)$ are prime of each other and meets $\alpha(z)\beta(z) \neq 0$, $|z| \leq 1$. Meanwhile, $\alpha(z)$ can be calculated as:

$$\begin{bmatrix} X_{q+1} \\ X_{q+2} \\ \vdots \\ X_{p+q} \end{bmatrix} = \begin{bmatrix} X_q & X_{q-1} & \cdots & X_{q-p+1} \\ X_{q+1} & X_q & \cdots & X_{q-p+2} \\ \vdots & \vdots & & \vdots \\ X_{q+p-1} & X_{q+p-2} & \cdots & X_q \end{bmatrix} \begin{bmatrix} \alpha_1 \\ \alpha_2 \\ \vdots \\ \alpha_p \end{bmatrix} \tag{11}$$

$\hat{X}_t$ is used to represent the ACF of the time sequences $X_t$, and the moment estimate value of $\alpha$ can be calculated as follows:

$$\begin{bmatrix} \hat{\alpha}_1 \\ \hat{\alpha}_2 \\ \vdots \\ \hat{\alpha}_p \end{bmatrix} = \begin{bmatrix} \hat{X}_q & \hat{X}_{q-1} & \cdots & \hat{X}_{q-p+1} \\ \hat{X}_{q+1} & \hat{X}_q & \cdots & \hat{X}_{q-p+2} \\ \vdots & \vdots & & \vdots \\ \hat{X}_{q+p-1} & \hat{X}_{q+p-2} & \cdots & \hat{X}_q \end{bmatrix}^{-1} \begin{bmatrix} \hat{X}_{q+1} \\ \hat{X}_{q+2} \\ \vdots \\ \hat{X}_{q+p} \end{bmatrix} \tag{12}$$

The value of coefficient $\beta$ is obtained similarly. As a result, the estimate value $\hat{X}_t$ of $X_t$ at time $t$ can be acquired. Actually, $\hat{X}_t$ is utilized to predict the network traffic in the next moment, but the value cannot be directly used for relay node selection. If the total bandwidth is denoted by $B_{total}$, the normalized available bandwidth of the network can be defined as $B_a$:

$$B_a = \frac{B_{total} - \hat{X}_t}{B_{total}} \tag{13}$$

The network traffic prediction can obtain the network resource usage in the next moment. But the data transmission capacity of segments cannot be determined by one index. In order to accurately evaluate the node performance, the link delay, bandwidth and link connection time should also be comprehensively taken into consideration.

**Link Delay:** Without considering the time taken by the signal transmission and reception, the time taken by transmitting the information from the device to the relay node is assumed as the link delay $d_{iE}(t)$:

$$d_{iE}(t) = \frac{\sqrt{(x_E(t) - x_i(t))^2 + (y_E(t) - y_i(t)) + (z_E(t) - z_i(t))^2}}{c} \tag{14}$$

where $(x_i(t), y_i(t), z_i(t))$ and $(x_E(t), y_E(t), z_E(t))$ respectively represent the three-dimensional coordinates of relay node $E$ and device $i$, and they are all functions of time. $c$ is the speed of light. The value of $d_{iE}(t)$ is denoted by $D_{iE}$

**Bandwidth:** The data transmission rate always depends on the bandwidth provided by the node's transceiver and the unit is Mbps. For example, the total bandwidth $B_{Etotal}$ of relay node $E$ is 20 Mbps, and 5 Mbps has been used to forward other tasks. Meanwhile, the transceiver capacity $B_{itotal}$ of device $i$ is 18 Mbps. If the communication link is established between $E$ and $i$, the maximum available bandwidth $B_{Ei}$ is 15 Mbps, which is the smaller available $B$ value for both nodes:

$$B_{Ei} = \min(B_E, \ B_i) \tag{15}$$

where the value of $B_{Ei}$ can be used to describe the bandwidth of device $i$.

**Connection Time:** The link connection time starts with the establishment of transmission links and ends with the satellites disappeared, where the disappearance means that two nodes have lost their physical visibility. It depends on the relative position of satellites, ground targets, and the Earth. The critical time when link establishment is defined as $T_0$ and when two nodes lose physical visibility is $T_{max}$. The link connection time $T_{Ei}$ between relay node $E$ and device $i$ can be expressed as:

$$T_{Ei} = T_{max} - T_0 \tag{16}$$

For convenient comparison with the other indicators, we normalize $B_a$ as $B_a^*$, $D_{iE}$ as $D_{iE}^*$, $B_{iE}$ as $B_{iE}^*$, $T_{iE}$ as $T_{iE}^*$:

$$B_a^* = B_a \times 100 \tag{17}$$

$$D_{iE}^* = \frac{D_{iE} - D_{min}}{D_{max} - D_{min}} \times 100 \tag{18}$$

$$B_{iE}^* = \frac{B_{iE} - B_{min}}{B_{max} - B_{min}} \times 100 \tag{19}$$

$$T_{iE}^* = \frac{T_{iE} - T_{min}}{T_{max} - T_{min}} \times 100 \tag{20}$$

where $D_{max}$ and $D_{min}$, $B_{max}$ and $B_{min}$, $T_{max}$ and $T_{min}$ are the maximum and minimum values in the dataset. Finally, the dataset can be expressed as $X$:

$$X = \{x_1, x_2, \ldots, x_n\} \tag{21}$$

where $x_i$ is a 4-dimensional vector that represents the four characteristics of node $i$.

Utilizing the four parameters, the performance of the node can be evaluated. However, the calculation is too complex because the parameters are not independent of each other and require further processing. Therefore, it is necessary to find efficient and rapid evaluation methods. The Adaboost classifier is as an adaptive classifier. It trains a series of weak classifiers and combining them into a strong classifier to quickly meet the classification requirements of datasets in different dimensions, as shown in Fig. 1. Dataset $X$ is divided into $N + P$ values. The dataset $y_1, y_2, \cdots, y_N, \cdots, y_{N+P}$ are

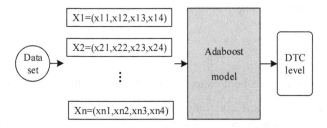

**Fig. 1.** The Adaboost model for relay node selection.

calculated as classification labels of nodes. Finally, the dataset $T$ is obtained:

$$T = \{(X_1, y_1), (X_2, y_2), \cdots, (X_{N+P}, y_{N+P})\} \tag{22}$$

where $X_i \in \chi \subseteq N^n$, $y_i \in \{1, 2, 3, 4\}$. The first $N$ sets of data are divided as the training set $T_N$, and the last $P$ sets of data are used as the testing set $T_P$. The training set $T_N$ is used to train the strong classifier as:

$$H_{final} = sign(f(x)) = sign\left(\sum_{t=1}^{T} \alpha_t H_t(x)\right) \tag{23}$$

According to the above, each node in SAGIN is classified to 1, 2, 3, 4 levels. The higher the level, the stronger the DTC. Meanwhile, the entire network topology can be described using the directed connected graph. For all nodes, there are:

$$IM = \begin{Bmatrix} E_{11}, E_{12}, \ldots, E_{1j} \\ E_{21}, E_{22}, \ldots, E_{2j} \\ \ldots \\ E_{i1}, E_{i2}, \ldots, E_{ij} \end{Bmatrix} \tag{24}$$

where the value of each $E_{ij}$ is 1, 2, 3, or 4. The value expresses the DTC of link between node $i$ and node $j$. If two nodes have no physical visibility, the value is 0. It only needs to select the nodes with the optimal level to form the data transmission links (DTL), as shown in Fig. 2. The important value of ALP is that it has low computational complexity. Further, it can promote the load balance of the whole SAGIN, so as to prevent the link congestion caused by segment overload.

## 3   Simulation Analysis

The simulation is carried out over a predictable three-layer SAGIN network with the use of the Satellite Tool Kit (STK) simulator. The LEO satellite model is established with reference to iridium constellation. 30 ground devices and 20 UAVs are deployed at Chengdu city in STK simulator. Since traffic data of SAGIN network cannot be obtained, this paper will use the dataset in [6] for traffic prediction, where the authors have proved the reasonability and self-similarity of the traffic data. Each link of the

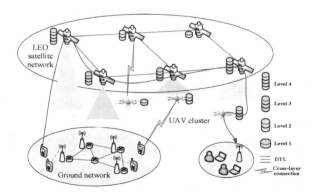

**Fig. 2.** The relay node selection according to available capacity levels.

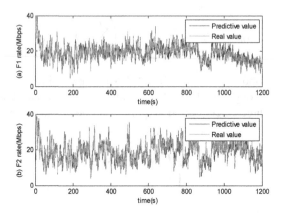

**Fig. 3.** Prediction results of network traffic flow F1 and F2.

SAGIN scenario corresponds to an origin destination (OD) flow in the dataset. Then we connect STK with MATLAB to obtain the other network data including link delay, bandwidth, and connection time. The calculation and comparison of the proposed scheme and other methods are also carried out in MATLAB. In the simulation scenario, each device is covered by multiple UAVs and LEO satellites in each time slot.

In the simulation, we first analyze the traffic prediction results. Figure 3 shows the prediction results of network traffic flows F1 and F2. In our simulation tests, other end-to-end traffic pairs holds similar results. As shown in Fig. 3(a) and (b), the real network traffic exhibits significant time-varying characteristics under different time slots. The ARMA model can capture dynamic changes of the network traffic flow F1 and F2 effectively. Although there are errors, we have seen that the ARMA model can better look for the traffic trends. These further indicates that the utilized ARMA model can effectively predict the change of the network traffic over the time.

Next we discuss the classification results of the Adaboost model. 50 data sets is selected randomly, 30 for training, 20 for testing. Figure 4(a) express the change of classification error (CE) in model training stage. It can be seen form Fig. 4(a) that the CE shows a downward trend as the weak classifier number increases, from 20% in 1 weak classifier to 0% in 18 weak classifier. The classification results of different capacity levels is expressed in Fig. 4(b). It can be seen that each set of data was classified to the correct level. This reflects that the training model is effective.

Figure 5 expresses the training results of Adaboost model with different training samples and different dataset proportions. Figure 5(a) and (b) respectively use 25 training data and 100 training data. It can be seen that Fig. 5(a) utilize 18 weak classifiers to reduce the CE to 7%, while Fig. 5(a) makes use of 20 weak classifiers to reduce the CE to 5%. It can be found that more training samples need more weak classifiers to complete feature recognition so as to achieve better classification accuracy. Particularly, the CE may fluctuate when the training samples are small. Therefore, the training sample with 50 data sets is enough to meet the requirements of Adaboost model training. Different proportions of training and test data may also affect the accuracy of the Adaboost model. Figure 5(c)–(d) represent the model training results

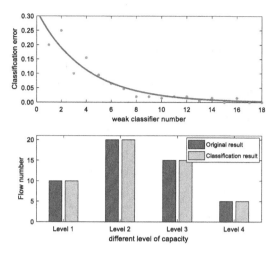

**Fig. 4.** The classification result of ALP algorithm.

under different proportions in 50 data sets. It can be found that the classification result is better when the proportion of training set is higher. But this may also produce unreliable models because of less test data. However, if the training set is reduced, the stability of the model will be challenged. Therefore, after comprehensive consideration, we select the Adaboost model with the best accuracy, including 30 training data and 20 test data. The remaining nodes in SAGIN are classified by this model.

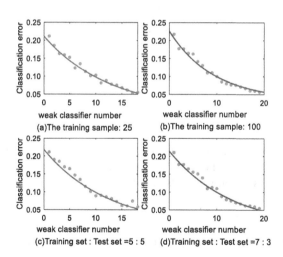

**Fig. 5.** The impact of sample size and proportion on classification error.

Next, we will evaluate the proposed ALP scheme in terms of link congestion, compared with current mainstream link construction schemes including the shortest path Dijkstra algorithm (SPDA) and the traveling salesman algorithm (TSA). We define the sum of overloads of all nodes in one link as the link congestion, and examine three schemes. Figure 6 displays the link congestion of three schemes with the increase of number of tasks. It can be seen that the SPDA method has the fastest increase in link congestion value, followed by TSA method, and ALP method has the slowest growth. This is because the node with the largest available capacity is considered first in ALP. The other two schemes put the shortest path in the first place and rarely consider the link congestion. As a result, it is easy to cause link congestion and serious packet loss, affecting the quality of data transmission. So the communications link of ALP scheme is relatively unimpeded.

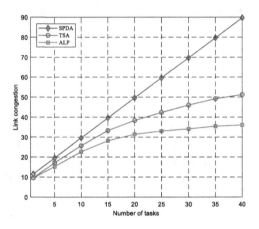

**Fig. 6.** The comparison of link congestion.

## 4   Conclusion

This paper studies the relay node selection problem in the Space-air-ground integrated network (SAGIN). In contrast to the previous studies, we jointly consider traffic prediction and segment classification in SAGIN. We utilize the autoregressive moving average (ARMA) model for traffic prediction, and the results of prediction are imported the Adaboost model with other link performances to realize the classification of involved nodes. The simulation results show that the proposed relay node selection scheme is promising.

**Acknowledgment.** This work was supported by National Natural Science Foundation of China (No. 61571104), Sichuan Science and Technology Program (No. 2018JY0539), Key projects of the Sichuan Provincial Education Department (No. 18ZA0219), Fundamental Research Funds for the Central Universities (No. ZYGX2017KYQD170), and Innovation Funding (No. 2018510 007000134). The authors wish to thank the reviewers for their helpful comments.

# References

1. Liu, J., Shi, Y., Fadlullah, Z.M., et al.: Space-air-ground integrated network: a survey. IEEE Commun. Surv. Tutor. **20**(4), 2714–2741 (2018)
2. Liu, Y., Xu, W., Tang, F., et al.: An improved multi-path routing algorithm for hybrid LEO-MEO satellite networks. In: Proceedings of ISPA 2016, pp. 1101–1105 (2016)
3. Zhang, Z., Jiang, C., Guo, S., et al.: Temporal centrality-balanced traffic management for space satellite networks. IEEE Trans. Veh. Technol. **67**(5), 4427–4439 (2018)
4. Araniti, G., Bisio, I., De Sanctis, M., et al.: Multimedia content delivery for emerging 5G-satellite networks. IEEE Trans. Broadcast. **62**(1), 10–23 (2016)
5. Han, Y., Li, D., Guo, Q.: Self-similar traffic prediction scheme based on wavelet transform for satellite internet services, In: Proceedings of MLICOM 2016, pp. 189–197 (2016)
6. Zhou, D., Sheng, M., Wang, X., et al.: Mission aware contact plan design in resource-limited small satellite networks. IEEE Trans. Commun. **65**(6), 2451–2466 (2017)
7. Wang, Y., Sheng, M., Li, J., et al.: Dynamic contact plan design in broadband satellite networks with varying contact capacity. IEEE Commun. Lett. **20**(12), 2410–2413 (2016)
8. Jiang, D., Wang, W., Shi, L., et al.: A compressive sensing-based approach to end-to-end network traffic reconstruction. IEEE Trans. Netw. Sci. Eng. **5**(3), 1–12 (2018)
9. Jiang, D., Huo, L., Li, Y.: Fine-granularity inference and estimations to network traffic for SDN. PLoS ONE **13**(5), 1–23 (2018)
10. Jiang, D., Lv, Z., Huo, L., et al.: A joint multi-criteria utility-based network selection approach for vehicle-to-infrastructure networking. IEEE Trans. Intell. Transp. Syst. **99**, 1–15 (2018). (SCI, EI)
11. Jiang, D., Zhang, Y., Song, H., et al.: Intelligent optimization-based energy-efficient networking in cloud services for multimedia big data. In: Proceedings of IPCCC 2018, pp. 1–6 (2018)
12. Jiang, D., Huo, L., Song, H.: Understanding base stations' behaviors and activities with big data analysis. In: Proceedings of Globecom 2018, pp. 1–7 (2018)

# An Semi-formal Co-verification Approach for High-Assurance CPS

Yu Zhang[1,2]($\boxtimes$) (iD), Mengxing Huang[1,3], and Wenlong Feng[1,3]

[1] State Key Laboratory of Marine Resource Utilization in South China Sea,
Hainan University, Haikou 570228, China
[2] School of Computer Science and Cyberspace Security,
Hainan University, Haikou 570228, China
yuzhang_nwpu@163.com
[3] School of Information and Communication Engineering,
Hainan University, Haikou 570228, China

**Abstract.** Cyber-Physical Systems (CPS) are often mission-critical, therefore, they must be high-assurance. High-assurance CPS require extensive formal verification. Formal verification techniques can discover subtle design errors where simulation fails. However, due to the state explosion problem, formal techniques usually cannot handle large designs. This paper introduces a semi-formal verification methodology in which formal co-verification and co-simulation are tightly coupled. We propose an online-capture offline-replay approach to improve the usefulness for formal verification. We analyze these simulation traces, find some critical states and assisted with formal verification under these circumstances. The experiment results show that our approach has major potential in verifying system level properties of complex CPS, therefore improving the high-assurance of CPS.

**Keywords:** Cyber-Physical Systems · Semi-formal · Co-simulation

## 1 Introduction

Cyber-Physical Systems(CPS) enable objects to be sensed and controlled remotely across network infrastructure, thereby creating opportunities for more direct integration of the physical world into the cyber world [2,6]. Depending on the applications, their failures could have dire consequences. Therefore, verification of correctness properties is a key step in developing high assurance CPS. Formal verification attracts great attention because of their ability to find subtle design errors where simulation fails. However, due to the state explosion problem, formal verification usually cannot handle complex system.

In this paper, we present a semi-formal cyber/physical co-verification method using co-simulation and formal co-verification to ensure the high-assurance of CPS. We analyze these simulation traces, find some critical states and assisted

H. Song et al. (Eds.): SIMUtools 2019, LNICST 295, pp. 168–179, 2019.
https://doi.org/10.1007/978-3-030-32216-8_16

with formal verification under these circumstances. This online-capture offline-replay approach combines the benefits of going deeper and expore exhaustively the state space of the system. The semi-formal verification approach can be used to overcome the drawbacks of both co-simulation and formal co-verification.

The major contributions of our approach include the semi-formal co-verification for CPS that unifies control and embedded software, and seamless integration of co-simulation and co-verification into CPS development. It has great potentials in building high-assurance CPS by enabling effective co-verification.

The rest of this paper is organized as follows. Section 2 presents the semi-formal co-verification framework. Section 3 introduce the semi-formal co-Verification execution. Section 4 presents the implementation of this approach. Section 5 elaborates on case studies we have conducted and discusses the experimental results. Section 6 reviews the related research. Section 7 concludes this paper and discusses future work.

## 2   Semi-formal Co-verification Framework for CPS

The correctness of the safety-critical scenarios plays a very important role in developing high-assurance CPS. On the one hand, due to the increasing complexity of the CPS system, formal verification has become more and more difficult. On the other hand, the simulation has been widely used in engineering practice. But simulation test can only observation incomplete system behavior in the case of a certain input operation system, and unable to test of all possible input and scenarios. Simulation test method uses concrete value to performance test scenarios and expected results, while bounded model checking uses symbolic system model to describe the expected and unexpected system behavior. Bounded model checking depends on the strict mathematical process. Simulation method is complementary to formal verification method which could be used to found unsafe events whether and under what conditions will happen in specific dynamic operation. These information can be used to improve design and the requirements. So integrated simulation and formal verification in the CPS system verification is essential, especially for complex CPS.

Therefore, Semi-Formal co-verification method which combining co-simulation and formal co-verification is proposed in this paper. On the basis of our previous work [11,12], this semi-formal co-verification approach combine simulation execution and k steps bounded model checking to verify this key scenes. As illustrated in Fig. 1, drive system starting from the initial state into a critical key state through co-simulation, and then combined with bounded model checking from the critical key state in k steps.

In the actual system, engineers will pay more attention to some key scenes or some time instead of the whole process. Such as the key point for satellite launch is whether the satellite can enter the normal orbit. If pay attention to the behavior of the system at this stage, we can first generate the simulation trace in the scenario through co-simulation, and then perform formal verification to the key scenario.

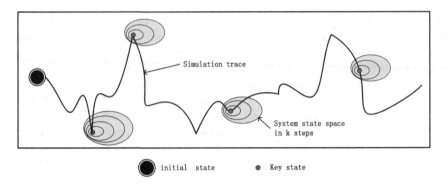

**Fig. 1.** Semi-formal co-verification for CPS.

## 3  Semi-formal Co-verification Execution

In our previous work [11,12], we define three types of primitive components in the co-verification: cyber component, physical component and cyber/physical interface component model. Cyber model is essentially a discrete event model, and its operational semantics refers to the execution sequence with a time stamp; Physical model is essentially a continuous time model, the model is formulated for differential equation. For integration of discrete event model and continuous time model, its execution sequence in the operational semantics is interaction protocols between the two heterogeneous models.

Below we characterize the dynamic of the main components in detail and discuss how their integration is handled.

**Definition 1.** A CPS model is denoted as a tuple $S = (S_{cps}, HA_{cps})$, where $S_{cps} = \bigcup_{k=1}^{n} S_{cyber} + \bigcup_{k=1}^{k} S_{interace} + \bigcup_{k=1}^{m} S_{phsical}$ is static structure of CPS model, $HA_{cps} = TA_1 \| TA_2 \| \cdots \| TA_n \| HA_1 \| HA_2 \| \cdots \| HA_m$ is a cartesian product of automata.

**Definition 2.** A state of CPS model is denoted as a tuple $S = (S_{cyber}, S_{interface}, S_{physical})$, where $S_{cyber}$ is a set of cyber model, $S_{physical}$ is a set of physical model, $S_{interface}$ is a set of interface model,

**Definition 3.** Timing parameters of a control task is denoted as a tuple $(t_k, t_i, t_o)$, where $t_k = T * k$, $T$ is the fixed sampling interval of the controller, $k$ is the number of controller iterations, $t_i$ and $t_o$ represent the A/D and D/A conversion periodical instants, respectively. Due to preemption and blocking from other tasks in the OS, the actual start of the task may be delayed for some time $L_s$. This is called the sampling latency of the controller. After some computation time and possible further preemption from other tasks, the controller will actuate the control signal. The delay of the actuation is called the input-output latency, denoted $L_{io}$.

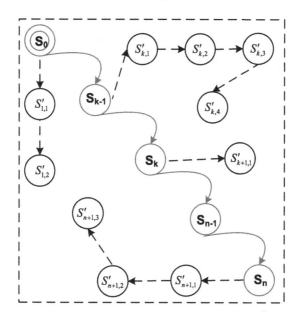

**Fig. 2.** Semi-formal co-verification for CPS.

The transaction condition of CPS is denoted as $r = \varphi \cup t$, where $\varphi$ is a set of events, $t$ is a set of clock. $r$ can be expressed either event trigger or time trigger. A trace $S_0, S_1, S_2, \cdots, S_{k-1}, S_k, \cdots, S_n$ can be denoted as $\pi = S_0 \xrightarrow{r_0} S_1 \xrightarrow{r_1} S_2 \cdots \xrightarrow{r_{k-2}} S_{k-1} \xrightarrow{r_{k-1}} S_k \cdots \xrightarrow{r_{n-1}} S_n$. From the view of the CPS system, the CPS model is consisted of a series of discrete states, and each discrete state itself may be a continuous time model.

As shown in Fig. 2, we analyze a simulation trace $\pi = S_0, S_1, S_2, \cdots, S_{k-1}$, $S_k, \cdots, S_n$. For example, take $S_{k-1}$ as a key state. Combined with the $r_{k-1}$ condition, we conduct four steps bounded model checking from start state $S_{k-1}$.

We will construct semi-formal execution by Algorithm 1. $i$ is loop iteration, $S_n$ is a simulation trace in simulation trace set $ST$, $num$ is the amount of states which need to be verified. Firstly, get the i-th state $S_i$ from simulation trace $S_n$ by the function $Get\_State(S_n, i)$. Secondly, initial the state $S_{i,0}$ by the function $Reset\_State(S_i)$. $S_{i,0}$ is the initial state in the model checking. And then perform bounded model checking within deadline until the timeout for the next state which is needed to be verified.

## 4 Semi-formal Co-verification Environment

As a proof of concept, the Semi-Formal co-verification environments are developed. Below introduces these environments. As shown in Fig. 3, the co-verification algorithm has been realized in the environment which integrates corresponding prototype tools: formal collaborative verification tools Co-VerCPS

---

**Algorithm 1.** SEMI-FORMAL_EXECUTION

---

1 Input: Simulation trace $S_n \in ST$, Deadline $Time\_Bound$;
2 Output: Verification result $Result$
3 $i \leftarrow 0$; //loop iteration;
4 $S_n \leftarrow Load\_Simulation\_Trace(ST)$;
5 $num \leftarrow number\_of\_state\_in\_checking\_states$;
6 **forall the** $i_j=num$ **do**
7     $S_i \leftarrow Get\_State(S_n, i)$;
8     $S_{i,0} \leftarrow Reset\_State(S_i)$;
9     **forall the** $t_jnum$ **do**
10        $S_{i,k+1} \leftarrow Compute\_Next\_State(S_{i,k})$;
11        $Result \leftarrow Check\_State(S_{i,k+1})$;
12        $k \leftarrow k + 1$;

---

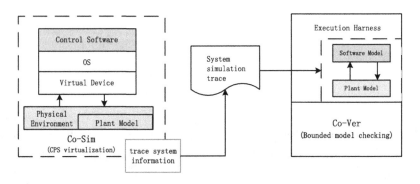

**Fig. 3.** Implementation of Semi-formal Co-verification.

and collaborative simulation tools Co-Sim [13]. Co-Ver is primarily for abstract model of C program (Labeled Pushdown System) and abstract model of a physical system (hybrid automata). Co-Sim focuses on the application, the physical simulation model (Simulink model), and virtual device platform. These models are widely used in related fields.

First, execute the test cases and record system information in the Co-Sim. Second, export simulation data into system simulation trace. Finally, execute bounded model checking and output verification results in the Co-Ver. The Execution Harness is a set which consists of system model and simulation data set (these data has been configured). Execution Harness makes a system run under different conditions, and monitor its behavior and output. It has three main parts: execution engine Co-Ver, system model and simulation state sequence set.

# 5   Evaluation

To evaluate the proposed co-verification approach, we have applied the approach
to real-world control systems. In all experiments, we want to check whether the
system meet the constrains or not with slight perturbations in the inputs and outputs to the system. All experiments were performed on a machine with 3.40 GHz
Intel(R) Core(TM) and 16 G memory. As shown in Fig. 4, a co-simulation environment is developed for TableSat. A X86 processor model is utilized to emulate
the Athena II SBC in QEMU. The embedded control program is written in
C language. The plant components are modeled mathematically according to
respective physical characteristics in Matlab/Simulink.

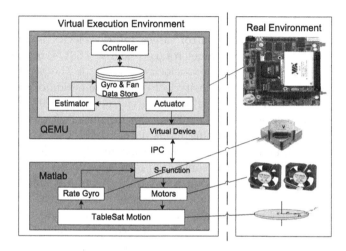

**Fig. 4.** Co-simulation environment for TableSat.

In these experiments, we select two simulation test scenarios to verify system
constrains. The first experiment is in the case of a single control target rotary
velocity, the second one is in the case of the multi control target rotary velocity.
Single control target rotary velocity means the expected target rotary velocity
value remains the same during the simulation. In each experiment, we select
a set of key state to support formal verification and certified the validity of
semi-formal verification.

## 5.1   Single Control Target Rotary Velocity

In the simulation, the initial angular velocity of TableSat is concrete value. In
a sense, the start instantaneous response of system is a key scenario. First, we
constructed the program and plant model based on the cyber/physical interface. Then we formulated the constrains of the system with LTL, and conducted bounded model checking. We chose the fixed execution time type of

cyber/physical interface in this experiment. The following initial set of parameters is used in the experiment: the sampling interval $(T=2\,\mathrm{s})$, the A/D conversion instant $(t_i=0.4\,\mathrm{s})$, and the D/A conversion instant $(t_o=1.6\,\mathrm{s})$. We specified a target rotary velocity $(TargetVelocity=30°/\mathrm{s})$ as TableSat input. We set the initial value of angular velocity $([0, 40])$ as a symbolic variable. Figure 8 summarised the results. The verification result shows that the TableSat satisfies the last six LTL constrains. For the first LTL property, bounded model checker revealed a simple bug of the controller that: If the initial value of angular velocity is $39.960621°/\mathrm{s}$, then the rotary velocity reaches $(63.649414°/\mathrm{s})$ above a threshold $(VelocityUpBound=60°/\mathrm{s})$ at $2.324336\,\mathrm{s}$. The verification run took $7015.26\,\mathrm{s}$. The running time largely depends on the backend SMT solver (Fig. 5).

## 5.2  Multi Control Target Rotary Velocity

In the period of $[0\,\mathrm{s}, 40\,\mathrm{s})$, the control target rotary velocity is $30°/\mathrm{s}$; in the period of $[40\,\mathrm{s}, 80\,\mathrm{s})$, the control target rotary velocity is $50°/\mathrm{s}$; in the period of $[80\,\mathrm{s}, 120\,\mathrm{s})$, the control target rotary velocity is $70°/\mathrm{s}$; in the period of $[120\,\mathrm{s}, 160\,\mathrm{s})$, the control target rotary velocity is $20°/\mathrm{s}$; in the period of $[160\,\mathrm{s}, 200\,\mathrm{s})$, the control target rotary velocity is $50°/\mathrm{s}$; in the period of $[200\,\mathrm{s}, 240\,\mathrm{s})$, the control target rotary velocity is $30°/\mathrm{s}$. The following initial set of parameters is used in the experiment: the sampling interval $(T=0.4\,\mathrm{s})$, the A/D conversion instant $(t_i^k \in [0, 0.1])$, and the D/A conversion instant $(t_o^k \in [0, 0.1])$. We record measurements in every $0.01\,\mathrm{s}$. The simulation result are shown in Fig. 6.

As shown in Fig. 6, the simulation result indicates that system satisfy the bounded input bounded output stability. In the simulation, the delay is generated by the random function on an interval and is actually a constant during the simulation. So the simulation test is not complete since it only observe limited system behavior. The initial state in the system is zero, there is no guaranteed that the controller can correct control plant when the sampling jitter $j_s$ and input-output jitter $J_{io}$ under uncertainty condition. Combined with the simulation data, we will verify the seven LTL constrains used in the model checking. We select eight key states on a simulation trace. The Timeout is set to $30000\,\mathrm{s}$. The experimental results showed that each key state can perform 3 step bounded model checking. The followings are two scenarios to illustrate our approach (Table 1).

**Scenario i.** Recorded the system information when the system response curve across the steady-state and reach a peak point moment for the first time. And then based on this state execute bounded model checking. According to the simulation data, at the moment $t=3.5\,\mathrm{s}$, the system response curve across the steady-state value and reach the peak point$(\omega=36.7298°/\mathrm{s})$. Set $j_s$ and $J_{io}$ as symbolic variable. As shown in Fig. 7, the verification result shows that the TableSat satisfies all LTL constrains.

**Scenario ii.** Recorded the system information when the control target rotary velocity change from $20°/\mathrm{s}$ to $50°/\mathrm{s}$. And then based on this state execute bounded model checking. According to the simulation data, at the

**Table 1.** Design constraints for TableSat

| No | LTL constraint | Result (within 4 s) |
|---|---|---|
| 1 | $\mathbf{G}(Rotary.Velocity \leq VelocityUpBound)$: The controller never accelerates the TableSat over the rotary velocity limit $VelocityUpBound$ | $\perp$ |
| 2 | $\mathbf{G}((Time \geq TimeBound) \rightarrow (Rotary.Velocity \geq VelocityDownBound))$: When running more than a threshold $TimeBound$, the controller will always accelerate the TableSat over the rotary velocity limit $VelocityDownBound$ | $\top^p$ |
| 3 | $\mathbf{G}((Rotary.Velocity < 0.4 * TargetVelocity) \rightarrow (Actuator.FanVoltage \equiv 12))$: When the rotary velocity below 0.4 times of its expected value $TargetVelocity$, the controller will set the fans to 12 V | $\top^p$ |
| 4 | $\mathbf{G}((Rotary.Velocity > 1.5 * TargetVelocity) \rightarrow (Actuator.FanVoltage \equiv 0))$: When the rotary velocity exceeds 1.5 times of its expected value $TargetVelocity$, the controller will set the fans to 0 V | $\top^p$ |
| 5 | $\mathbf{G}((Time \geq TimeBound) \rightarrow |Rotary.Velocity - TargetVelocity| \leq SteadyStateError))$: When running more than a threshold $TimeBound$, the rotary velocity must be stable at $TargetVelocity$ within the error $SteadyStateError$ | $\top^p$ |
| 6 | $\mathbf{G}((Rotary.Velocity < T) \rightarrow \mathbf{F}(Actuator.FanVoltage = full))$: after the Rotary velocity belows its bound, Actuator will set the motors to the full voltage | $\top^p$ |
| 7 | $\mathbf{G}((Rotary.Velocity > T) \rightarrow \mathbf{F}(Actuator.FanVoltage = fullNeg))$: after the Rotary velocity exceeds its bound, Actuator will set the motors to the full negative voltage | $\top^p$ |

| NO. | K. | TIME(S). | RESULT. |
|---|---|---|---|
| 1. | 1. | 14.615. | $\perp$. |
| | 2. | N/A. | N/A. |
| | 3. | N/A. | N/A. |
| | 4. | N/A. | N/A. |
| 2.<br>3.<br>4.<br>5.<br>6.<br>7. | 1. | 14.615. | $\top^p$. |
| | 2. | 164.288. | $\top^p$. |
| | 3. | 713.443. | $\top^p$. |
| | 4. | 2396.97. | $\top^p$. |

**Fig. 5.** Test results.

momentt $= 160$ s, $\omega = 25.06078°$/s), the speed of fan is 1789 RPM. Set $j_s \in [0, 0.1]$ and $J_{io} \in [0, 0.1]$ as symbolic variable. As shown in Fig. 8, the verification result shows that the TableSat satisfies all LTL constrains.

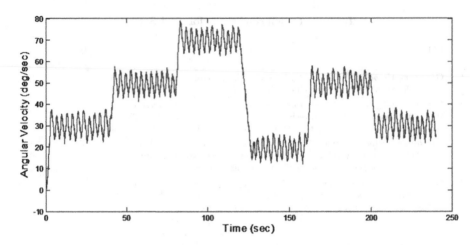

**Fig. 6.** Simulation Test results.

| NO. | $k=1$ | | $k=2$ | | $k=3$ | |
|---|---|---|---|---|---|---|
| | TIME (S) | RESULT | TIME (S) | RESULT | TIME (S) | RESULT |
| 1 | 271.57 | T | 1746.37 | T | 28422 | T |
| 2 | 271.57 | T | 1746.37 | T | 28422 | T |
| 3 | 271.57 | T | 1746.37 | T | 28422 | T |
| 4 | 271.57 | T | 1746.37 | T | 28422 | T |
| 5 | 271.57 | T | 1746.37 | T | 28422 | T |
| 6 | 271.57 | T | 1746.37 | T | 28422 | T |
| 7 | 271.57 | T | 1746.37 | T | 28422 | T |

**Fig. 7.** Test results.

The above experimental results indicate that directly using formal verification to realize the CPS has become more and more difficult. In TableSat, we can only just check three system steps form the initial state. So formal verification and simulation should effectively complement each other. The semi-formal verification method is essential to establishing the correctness of a complete system, therefore improving the high-assurance of CPS.

| NO. | $k=1$ | | $k=2$ | | $k=3$ | |
|---|---|---|---|---|---|---|
| | TIME (S) | RESULT | TIME (S) | RESULT | TIME (S) | RESULT |
| 1 | 315.027 | $T^p$ | 1841.2 | $T^p$ | 27056 | $T^p$ |
| 2 | 315.027 | $T^p$ | 1841.2 | $T^p$ | 27056 | $T^p$ |
| 3 | 315.027 | $T^p$ | 1841.2 | $T^p$ | 27056 | $T^p$ |
| 4 | 315.027 | $T^p$ | 1841.2 | $T^p$ | 27056 | $T^p$ |
| 5 | 315.027 | $T^p$ | 1841.2 | $T^p$ | 27056 | $T^p$ |
| 6 | 315.027 | $T^p$ | 1841.2 | $T^p$ | 27056 | $T^p$ |
| 7 | 315.027 | $T^p$ | 1841.2 | $T^p$ | 27056 | $T^p$ |

**Fig. 8.** Test results.

## 6 Related Work

Many scholars have did much work and gained their research results on CPS verification [7–10].

Various formal verification methods have been proposed for Cyber-Physical Systems. Well-known tools for verifying such systems include HyTech and Uppaal. In[3] and [5] they propose an approach to formally analyzing such control software using model checking of UPPAAL. In [4], they propose a delta-complete algorithm for solving satisfiability of nonlinear SMT over real numbers. This approach has a key drawback: The focus has been on control logic design on high level with simplifying assumptions. Therefor they can't handle complex systems.

Due to the scalability of formal verification is not high, simulation is a low-cost and efficient method in detecting shallow bugs. The most closely related work is presented [1], a comprehensive co-simulation platform for CPS and examples showing the capabilities of the platform were presented. The simulation platform is built on Modelica and ns-2 tools.

## 7 Conclusions

An approach has been presented to semi-formal Cyber/Physical co-verification based on the integration of co-simulation and formal co-verification. We analyze these simulation traces, find some critical states and assisted with formal verification under these circumstances. This online-capture offline-replay approach combines the benefits of going deeper and expore exhaustively the state space of the system. The semi-formal verification approach can be used to overcome the drawbacks of both co-simulation and formal co-verification. We have validated our approach by applying it to TableSat. It combines advantages of formal verification and simulation. The experiment results show that our approach has major potential in verifying system level properties of complex CPS, therefore improving the high-assurance of CPS.

**Acknowledgments.** This research received financial support from the Key R&D Project of Hainan province (Grant #: ZDYD2019020), the National Key R&D Program of China (Grant #:2018YFB1404401 and 2018YFB1404403), the National Natural Science Foundation of China (Grant #: 61662019 and 61862020), the Education Department of Hainan Province (Grant #: Hnky2019-22), the Higher Education Reform Key Project of Hainan province (Hnjg2017ZD-1) and Academician Workstation in Hainan Intelligent Healthcare Technologies.

# References

1. Al-Hammouri, A.T.: A comprehensive co-simulation platform for cyber-physical systems. Comput. Commun. **36**(1), 8–19 (2012). https://doi.org/10.1016/j.comcom.2012.01.003
2. Chen, D., Chang, G., Sun, D., Li, J., Jia, J., Wang, X.: TRM-IoT: a trust management model based on fuzzy reputation for internet of things. Comput. Sci. Inf. Syst. **8**(4), 1207–1228 (2011)
3. Herrmann, P., Blech, J.O., Han, F., Schmidt, H.: A model-based toolchain to verify spatial behavior of cyber-physical systems. Int. J. Web Serv. Res. **13**(1), 40–52 (2016)
4. Kong, S., Solar-Lezama, A., Gao, S.: Delta-decision procedures for exists-forall problems over the reals. CoRR abs/1807.08137 (2018). arxiv:1807.08137
5. Li-Jun, S., et al.: Statistical model checking of cyber-physical systems control software. J. Softw. **26**(2), 380–389 (2015)
6. Munir, A., Kansakar, P., Khan, S.U.: IFCIoT: Integrated fog cloud IoT: a novel architectural paradigm for the future internet of things. IEEE Consum. Electron. Mag. **6**(3), 74–82 (2017). https://doi.org/10.1109/MCE.2017.2684981
7. Wang, H., Maccaull, W.: An efficient explicit-time description method for timed model checking. vol. 14, pp. 77–91 (2009).https://doi.org/10.4204/EPTCS.14.6
8. Wang, X., Yang, L., Xie, X., Jin, J., Deen, M.: A cloud-edge computing framework for cyber-physical-social services. IEEE Commun. Mag. **55**, 80–85 (2017). https://doi.org/10.1109/MCOM.2017.1700360
9. Wassyng, A., et al.: Can product-specific assurance case templates be used as medical device standards? IEEE Des.Test **32**, 1–11 (2015). https://doi.org/10.1109/MDAT.2015.2462720
10. Yang, L.T., et al.: A multi-order distributed hosvd with its incremental computing for big services in cyber-physical-social systems. IEEE Trans. Big Data 1 (2018). https://doi.org/10.1109/TBDATA.2018.2824303
11. Zhang, Y., Dong, Y., Xie, F.: Bounded model checking of hybrid automata pushdown system. In: Quality Software (QSIC), 2014 14th International Conference on Quality Software, pp. 190–195. IEEE (2014)

12. Zhang, Y., Huang, M., Wang, H., Feng, W., Cheng, J., Zhou, H.: A co-verification interface design for high-assurance cps. Comput. Mater. Continua **58**, 287–306 (2019). https://doi.org/10.32604/cmc.2019.03736
13. Zhang, Y., Xie, F., Dong, Y., Yang, G., Zhou, X.: High fidelity virtualization of cyber-physical systems. Int. J. Model. Simul. Sci. Comput. **04**(02), 1340005 (2013). https://doi.org/10.1142/S1793962313400059.     http://www.worldscientific.com/doi/abs/10.1142/S1793962313400059

# Analyzing on User Behavior and User Experience of Social Network Services

Rong Bao, Lei Chen[(⊠)], and Ping Cui

Jiangsu Province Key Laboratory of Intelligent Industry Control Technology,
Xuzhou University of Technology, Xuzhou 221018, China
chenlei@xzit.edu.cn

**Abstract.** The user behavior characteristics of mobile social network services are beneficial for evaluating the user experience, and the test cases and test scenarios should be designed according to the user behavior characteristics. The current researches have been heavily addressed on the action sequence and the frequency distribution of user behavior. There is little research on the user's action triggering network flow under different scenarios. This paper analyzes the distribution character of user actions, and tests the waiting time of different user actions in different scenes. The results suggest that the complex scenarios can be consisted of some typical user behaviors.

**Keywords:** Quantify of user experience · Social network service · User behavior · Communication scenarios · Mobile internet

## 1 Introduction

With the development of 4G/5G communication technology, a large number of Social Network Services (SNS) have emerged. Mobile operators and equipment providers pay more attention to the Quality of User Experience (QoE) of such services, and improve the user experience through more intelligent scheduling strategy [1]. Some scheduling strategies adopt Deep Packet Inspection (DPI) technology to identify the specific services the packets belong to, and then use different scheduling strategies according to different services. This reflects that the communications industry has recognized that different services impact on user experience in different way. The traditional evaluation system mainly measures the service quality of large-scale business with indistinguishable general indicators. However, many test systems are still based on the data flow model [2–4], and cannot effectively trigger intelligent scheduling strategies, so it is impossible to evaluate the effectiveness of these intelligent scheduling strategies. Many communication enterprises have to use manual dial-up method to verify the new scheduling strategy, which is unable to simulate large-scale scenarios. A possible

This work is partly supported by the Natural Science Foundation of Jiangsu Province of China (No. BK20161165), the applied fundamental research Foundation of Xuzhou of China (No. KC17072), and the Open Fund of the Jiangsu Province Key Laboratory of Intelligent Industry Control Technology, Xuzhou University of Technology.

H. Song et al. (Eds.): SIMUtools 2019, LNICST 295, pp. 180–185, 2019.
https://doi.org/10.1007/978-3-030-32216-8_17

approach is to replay the real data packets captured from networks in simulation system [5]. These packets might be generated by user actions, such as login, sending message, comment, and so on. A complex test scenario should consist of these actions according to user behavior. Therefore, the new problems are how the user behavior affects the QoE, and how to reconstruct user behavior using the captured data packets.

Through the analysis of the user behavior characteristics of the main SNSs, some researchers found the concentrated distribution of common actions, action frequency and information length of users [6, 7]. Some studies suggest that the traffic model of traditional communication network can be used for reference to analyze the communication behaviors of computer network users [8]. In the model, the network user behaviors can be described by the Poisson distribution of parameter $\lambda$:

$$P_u(i,t) = \frac{(\lambda t)^i}{i!} e^{-\lambda t} \tag{1}$$

where, $i$ is the number of services during t. The amount and length of data flow of each service follow the geometric distribution of $E_f$ and $E_l$ respectively:

$$P_f(n) = \frac{1}{E_f} \left(1 - \frac{1}{E_f}\right)^{n-1} \tag{2}$$

$$P_l(k) = \frac{1}{E_l} \left(1 - \frac{1}{E_l}\right)^{k-1} \tag{3}$$

where, $n$ and $k$ are the number and length of data flows, respectively. The network traffic $n_{ij}(T)$ can thus be obtained, according to the number of users $n_{ij}(T)$, the number of data flows $f_i(T)$ and the length of data flow $n_{ij}(T)$ during (0, $T$):

$$N(T) = \sum_{i=1}^{u(T)} \sum_{j=1}^{f_i(T)} n_{ij}(T) \tag{4}$$

And the network traffic during $(t, t + \tau)$ can be written by:

$$N_t(\tau) = N(t + \tau) - N(t) \tag{5}$$

In this traffic model, the parameter $\lambda$ depends on the user density and usage habits of users in the scene, $E_f$ depends on the operation sequence and action frequency of the users, and $E_l$ is determined by the distribution of user action. If there is centralized distribution in user behaviors, a few typical action sequences can be used to simulate the entire communication scenario and form impact scenarios similar to the real scenarios.

## 2  User Behavior Analysis of SNS

According to the above model, it is possible to reconstruct the real scene with a small number of typical user behaviors, if the data length and frequency of user behaviors obey a central distribution. Related studies have found the centralized distribution of user behavior in SNS. In this paper, we analyze the online time and operation frequency of SNS users. To observe the impact of user behaviors to QoE, we also test the appreciable indicators of the end users in different scenarios with different user density and behavior.

### 2.1  Central Distribution of Online Frequency

To analyze the distribution rule of online frequency for SNS, we survey 35 college students on their usage count per day. As shown in Fig. 1(a), the result shows that the special user group has similar usage habit.

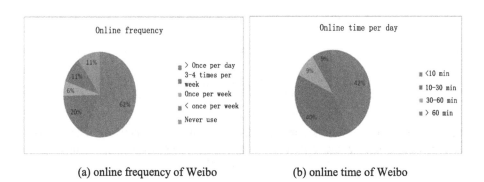

(a) online frequency of Weibo             (b) online time of Weibo

**Fig. 1.**  Online characters of Weibo

Figure 1(b) shows the distribution of users' usage time of Weibo in campus. This implies the centralized distribution of usage habit in a special communication scenario.

### 2.2  Central Distribution of User Data

We collect Weibo information of 60,000 users. We compute the average number of posts these users published per day. 90% Weibo users daily post less than 10 messages.

In addition, the length of the post is also restricted by usage habit. In this paper, the length of the 2,622 Weibo posts without links is analyzed in Fig. 2, in which the vertical coordinate is the number of blog posts and the horizontal coordinate is the length of posts. As shown in Fig. 2, the lengths of most posts are between 10 and 50 bytes. To eliminate the oscillation caused by the double-byte representation of Chinese characters in the computer system. Figure 2 retains only double-byte data. This result shows centralized distribution and heavy-tailed distribution.

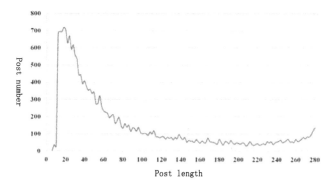

**Fig. 2.** Distribution of post length (only even bytes)

## 3 Impact of Scenario on QoE Indicators

We survey the degree to which the communication scenario affects the user experience. In this paper, the appreciable indicators of SNS are evaluated in the urban area. The cellular network access is provided by the same communication operators. Therefore, the infrastructure conditions of the tests are similar, and the performance fluctuation should be caused by the behavioral features of different user groups, such as user density, operation frequency, and other operation habits.

Figure 3 shows the delay test of QQ message sending in different scenarios. The test results show that the distribution range of delay is approximately the same. However, the number of delays with a significant deviation from the main distribution range is obviously different. In particular, Fig. 4 shows that the delay difference between different time periods in the same place is also obvious. The test results indicate that user behavior is key factor of communication scenarios, which has a certain impact on the QoE indicators.

In same area, communication capacity of communication operator is more similar. In different scenarios, the group behavior of users is different, and the usage habits are thus different. Therefore the degree to which the user behavior affects QoE indicators can be observed. In this paper, we chose to test the delay of posting Weibo comments through cellular network under different scenarios in a large research and development base. The scenarios include office area, experiment area, restaurant, lounge area, and so on. Except that the restaurant is significantly more densely populated than other areas, all other areas have similar user density. And the communication operators are known to identify data packets and adopt special scheduling strategies for SNS.

The test results in Fig. 4 also indicate that in the case of same user density and similar communication capacity user behavior causes delay fluctuation. Because the delay jitter bigger than 0.1 s is appreciable, the delay fluctuation in Fig. 4 is obvious for users.

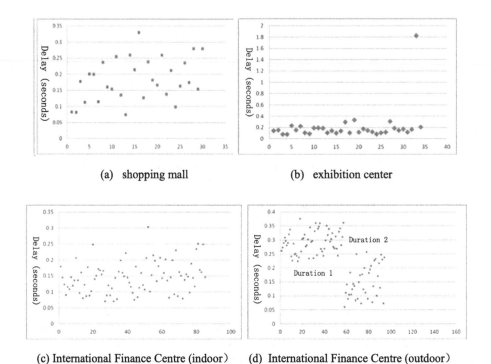

(a)  shopping mall                    (b)  exhibition center

(c) International Finance Centre (indoor）    (d)  International Finance Centre (outdoor）

**Fig. 3.**  QQ message delay in various scenairos

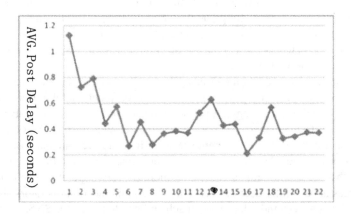

**Fig. 4.**  Average post delay in 22 test point (5 tests for each point)

## 4   Conclusions

In this paper, we mainly analyze the distribution feature of user behavior for SNS, and the degree of impact of user behavior on QoE indicators. The investigation results show the centralized distribution of user behavior. The test results in real scenarios imply that the user behavior actually affects the user experience. Therefore, we propose that a QoE test scenario can be built by the typical user behaviors. The relationship between user behavior and network load should be further studied to guide the test case design.

# References

1. Wang, Y., Li, P.L., Jiao, L., et al.: A data-driven architecture for personalized QoE management in 5G wireless networks. IEEE Wirel. Commun. 24(1), 102–110 (2017)
2. Jiang, D., Wang, W., Shi, L., Song, H.: A compressive sensing-based approach to end-to- end network traffic reconstruction. IEEE Trans. Netw. Sci. Eng. (2018). https://doi.org/10.1109/tnse.2018.2877597
3. Jiang, D., Huo, L., Song, H.: Rethinking behaviors and activities of base stations in mobile cellular networks based on big data analysis. IEEE Trans. Netw. Sci. Eng. 1(1), 1–12 (2018)
4. Jiang, D., Huo, L., Li, Y.: Fine-granularity inference and estimations to network traffic for SDN. PLoS ONE 13(5), 1–23 (2018)
5. Chen, L., Jiang, D., Song, H., et al.: A lightweight end-side user experience data collection system for quality evaluation of multimedia communications. IEEE Access 2018(6), 15408–15419 (2018)
6. Jin, Y., Duffield, N., Haffner, P., et al.: Can't see forest through the trees. In: The Proceedings of 9th Workshop on Mining and Learning with Graphs, San Diego, USA (2011)
7. Schneider, F., Feldmann, A., Krishnamurthy, B., et al.: Understanding online social network usage from a network perspective. In: Proceedings of the 9th ACM SIGCOMM Conference on Internet Measurement Conference, Chicago, USA (2009)
8. Zhang, S., Zhao, Z., Guan, H., et al.: A modified poisson distribution for smartphone background traffic in cellular networks. Int. J. Commun. Syst. 30(6) (2017). https://doi.org/10.1002/dac.3117

# ITU TWDM-PON Module
# for ns-3 Network Simulator

Yu Nakayama[1(✉)] [iD] and Ryoma Yasunaga[2]

[1] Tokyo University of Agriculture and Technology, Tokyo 184-8588, Japan
yu.nakayama@ieee.org
[2] Neko 9 Laboratories, Tokyo 140-0001, Japan

**Abstract.** Optical fiber access systems are one of the driving forces behind the success of the Internet. Time- and wavelength- division multiplexing passive optical network (TWDM-PON) is regarded as the key technology for future Internet access networks. In this paper, we propose an ITU TWDM-PON module for the ns-3 network simulator and describe its concept and design specifications. The proposed module is developed based on the XG-PON module for ns-3. It can simulate G.989 standard-compliant data packet transmission in the upstream and down- stream directions using multiple wavelength channels. It enables us to evaluate the performance issues that arise with the TWDM-PON development, including various dynamic bandwidth allocation (DBA) and dynamic wavelength allocation (DWA) algorithms. The proposed module is expected to become a good platform for studying future access networks composed of TWDM-PON and mobile networks by enabling us to simulate dynamic wavelength and bandwidth allocation (DWBA).

**Keywords:** ns-3 · TWDM-PON · Wavelength allocation ·
Bandwidth allocation

## 1 Introduction

During the last few decades, the numbers of both fixed and mobile broadband subscribers and their data consumption have increased greatly. Optical fiber access systems are one of the driving forces behind the success of the Internet. Passive optical networks (PONs) are the key technology for providing low-cost access services.

The architecture of PON based access networks is shown in Fig. 1. The optical line terminal (OLT) is usually located in a central office. The optical net- work units (ONUs) are located on the subscriber's premises. They are connected through the optical distribution network (ODN), which consists of optical fiber and power splitters located in the outside plant. As the next step in relation to optical access systems, the standardization and development of time- and wavelength- division multiplexing passive optical network (TWDM-PON) including next generation-PON2 (NG-PON2) [12], which is a 40 Gb/s capacity PON system [6, 7], are under way. TWDM-PON is expected to be a multi- service platform that includes residential, business, mobile, machine to machine (M2M), and Internet of things (IoT) services as shown in Fig. 1.

© ICST Institute for Computer Sciences, Social Informatics and Telecommunications Engineering 2019
Published by Springer Nature Switzerland AG 2019. All Rights Reserved
H. Song et al. (Eds.): SIMUtools 2019, LNICST 295, pp. 186–195, 2019.
https://doi.org/10.1007/978-3-030-32216-8_18

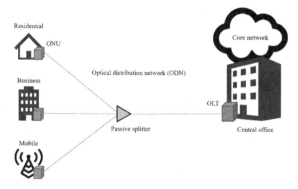

**Fig. 1.** Access network architecture.

The bandwidth and power consumption of TWDM-PON must be scalable, flexible, and efficient to provide various services. Since work on TWDM-PON is still in its early stages, a simulation of TWDM-PON would be useful and effective in terms of its development and deployment. In this paper, we present an ITU TWDM-PON module for the ns-3 [8] network simulator, which is a state of the art open source network simulator. The proposed module is expected to become a good platform for studying future access networks composed of TWDM-PON and mobile networks by enabling us to simulate dynamic wavelength and band- width allocation (DWBA).

This paper is organized as follows. Section 2 describes the background and related work. Section 3 introduces the concept of the proposed ITU TWDM-PON module. Section 4 describes the design specification of the developed module. Section 5 provides the conclusion.

## 2 Related Work

The ns-3 [8] simulator is an open source based network simulator. It has been pointed out that ns-3 uses less CPU and memory and the simulation speed is higher than other network simulators [5, 11]. For ns-3, an XG-PON module was developed, which is based on G.987 recommendations [14]. The XG-PON module focuses on the physical medium dependent (PMD) and transmission convergence (TC) layers, including frame structure, resource allocation, quality of service (QoS) management, and dynamic bandwidth allocation (DBA) algorithms. To improve the simulation speed, the ODN and the operations of physical layers are simplified. With this module, the XG-PON performance can be evaluated using existing ns-3 modules, including a realistic Internet protocol stack and various wireless networks (LTE, WiFi, WiMAX, etc.).

Several studies simulated XG-PON with this module. The need for an im- proved DBA algorithm and scheduling mechanism was revealed from the performance evaluation of three TCP variants (Reno, CUBIC, and H-TCP) [2]. The X-GIANT DBA algorithm was proposed and implemented in the XG-PON module to evaluate the delay and throughput for different classes of traffic [3]. The group-GIANT DBA algorithm was developed to assign group assured bandwidth to backhauling base stations with PON [1].

There have been some cases where a TWDM-PON simulation was performed. These include for a digital radio over fiber (DRoF) system [9], for a WDM-PON downstream physical link evaluation using an optical transmission simulator [10], and for a K-out-of-N scheduling technique for DBA with a discrete event simulation model [4]. However, there has been no simulator to evaluate packet level data transmission for TWDM-PON using various protocol stacks. The development of an ITU TWDM-PON compatible module for ns-3 is useful for studying various DBA and DWA algorithms and evaluating the integration of TWDM- PON and wireless networks. To develop the module, we need to implement WDM transmission by stacking wavelength channels based on the XG-PON module. In addition to WDM, we require ONU assignment to a wavelength and an ONU wavelength channel handover sequence, which include PLOAM message transfer and the ONU state transition. In addition, there have been limitations as regards the XG-PON module. To evaluate various DBA algorithms such as multi-thread polling and multi-cycle allocation, the DBA functions need to be redesigned. To improve the delay measurement accuracy, we need to employ differential propagation delays for the ONUs and calculate the start time of upstream traffic at each ONU should be implemented.

## 3   ITU TWDM-PON Module Concept

We describe the concept of the proposed ITU TWDM-PON module for the ns-3. The overall purpose of the module is to simulate the data packet transmission in G.989 recommendations and evaluate the throughput and delay using various DBA and DWA algorithms.

### 3.1   Overview

**Basic Idea.** We developed the ITU TWDM-PON module based on the XG-PON module [14], because the concept of the XG-PON module matches the purpose of the proposed module. Therefore, the features of the module are inherited from the XG-PON module. This module performs stand-alone and packet-level simulation. The physical layer is simplified, and the ODN is modeled as a simple channel. The optical transmission is assumed to work well, and the propagation delay and line rates are simulated. Line coding, payload encryption, cyclic redundancy check (CRC), and header error correction (HEC) are not implemented. The bandwidth overhead and the effect of forward error correction (FEC) are implemented, but the FEC procedure is not. To evaluate the performance of the TWDM-PON system during normal operation, PLOAM and OMCI channels are not fully implemented. The activation or ranging procedure in operating TWDM-PON is also not implemented.

**DWBA Simulation.** To simulate the time- and wavelength- division multiplexing (TWDM) packet transmission in the upstream and downstream directions, we decided to employ multiple PON channels, which represent individual wave- length channels between an OLT and ONUs. ONU assignment to a wavelength and ONU wavelength channel handover are performed by enabling one channel from the set of PON channels. The sequence of ONU wavelength channel handover, including the PLOAM message transfer and the ONU state transition, is implemented to evaluate and compare DWA algorithms.

For accurate measurement of the data packet transmission in each channel, the DBA functions are redesigned and the accuracy of data transmission is improved compared with the XG-PON module. We can use various DBA algorithms, including multi-thread polling and multi-cycle allocation. The delay measurement accuracy is improved by calculating the start time of the upstream traffic at an ONU, the propagation delay between an OLT and each ONU, and their frame-processing delay.

## 3.2   Channel Model

In the following, we explain the concept of major implemented functions. And, we describe the channel model. To simulate the multiple wavelength channels provided by TWDM-PON, OLT and ONU devices are connected to multiple PON channel classes. Each of the PON channel classes corresponds to a wavelength channel. ONUs are assigned and handed over using these PON channel classes.

There is one PON channel between an OLT and the ONUs in the XG-PON module. All the ONUs always use the PON channel and the bandwidth is allocated to all the ONUs by the DBA engine of the OLT. In the TWDM-PON module, there are multiple channels between an OLT and the ONUs. Each channel is connected to the OLT and all the ONUs. An ONU enables one channel and disables the other channels. We assumed that an ONU uses only one channel at a time, and the same channel is used for upstream and downstream data transmission for simplicity. The downstream frame transmission and DBA are performed at each channel considering the ONU wavelength allocation.

## 3.3   ONU Channel Handover

The implemented ONU wavelength channel handover sequence basically follows G.989 recommendations. The implemented ONU state transition is shown in Fig. 2a, which is the normal operation part of the ONU state diagram. Figure 2b shows the OLT wavelength handover states for each ONU. Simulation of the normal handover sequence does not require the implementation of inter-channel- termination protocol (ICTP) and rollback process.

The handover sequence is as follows. First, an ONU is operating in the Associated state in a specific channel. The OLT is in the *Hosting* state at a source channel termination (CT) and in the *Unaware* state at the target CT. The source OLT CT sends *Tuning Control* specifying the target ONU, target channel, and scheduled SFC. The OLT state transits to the *Redirecting* state at the source OLT CT and the *Expecting* state at the target OLT CT. After that, a PLOAMu grant is allocated to the ONU in both the source and target channels. If the ONU can start the handover, it sends *Tuning Response (ACK)* and transits to the *Pending* state. When the source OLT CT receives *Tuning Response (ACK)*, the state becomes *Seeing-off*. The ONU starts the tuning procedure at the scheduled SFC. The state transition order in the tuning is *Off-sync*,

*Profile learning*, and *US tuning state*. When the tuning is finished, the ONU sends *Tuning Response (Complete u)*. When the target OLT CT receives the message, it sends *Tuning Control (Complete d)* and downstream data. The OLT state transits to *Hosting* in the target CT and *Unaware* in the source CT. The ONU receives *Tuning Control (Complete d)* and transits to the *Associated* state.

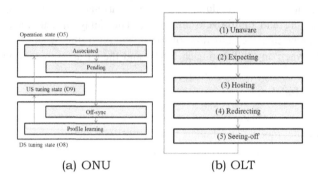

(a) ONU                    (b) OLT

**Fig. 2.** Wavelength handover state transition.

## 3.4  DBA

**DBA Procedure.** Figure 3 shows the DBA procedure assumed in this paper. An ONU sends its buffer occupancy to an OLT when it sends uplink data. We call it a request message in this paper. The OLT calls the DBA engine in order to calculate the bandwidth allocation for ONUs based on their requests. Then, the OLT sends the bandwidth allocation to each ONU, which is sent using the BW map in ITU TWDM-PON. We call it a grant message in this paper. The grant message includes the start time and the data size assigned for each ONU. The ONU sends uplink data in accordance with the grant. The DBA procedure described above enables ONUs to share the uplink bandwidth flexibly.

**Multi-cycle Allocation.** The OLT sends a grant to ONUs every 125 μs, and this is called the grant cycle in this paper. The DBA engine does not need to calculate the bandwidth allocation to all the ONUs in one grant cycle as regards the reduction in the processing time in a real machine. We call the time period between DBA calculations a DBA cycle. A DBA cycle is $k$ times a grant cycle, where $k$ is a natural number. We enabled the DBA engine to carry over its calculation result over $k-1$ grant cycles in the

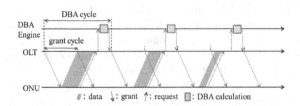

**Fig. 3.** DBA procedure.

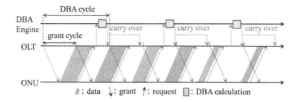

**Fig. 4.** Multi-cycle allocation.

TWDM-PON module. We call this multi-cycle allocation. Multi-cycle allocation is a natural extension of the usual DBA process (single-cycle allocation). Multi-cycle allocation can improve bandwidth utilization efficiency as shown in Fig. 4.

**Multi-thread Polling.** The sequence including a request, a DBA calculation, and a grant is called a thread in this paper. We enabled the OLT to poll multiple threads in parallel as shown in Fig. 5, which is called multi-thread polling [13]. Multi-thread polling is a natural extension of the usual DBA procedure (single- thread polling). The OLT can poll $k$ threads in parallel when the DBA cycle of a single-thread is $k$ times of the grant cycle. Multi-thread polling can reduce the time between packet arrival and the next request sent by that ONU. However, since the DBA cycle of $k$-thread polling is a $k$-th of that of single-thread polling, multi-thread polling can place a high load on a CPU in a real machine. The difference between multi-cycle allocation and multi-thread polling is the frequency of the DBA calculation.

**Start Time.** For simplicity, the XG-PON module assumes that the propagation delays of all ONUs are same, the equalization delays (EqD in Fig. 6) of all ONUs are zero, and the response time of all ONUs is zero. To improve the accuracy of the delay measurement, we implemented differential propagation delays for the ONUs and the calculation of start time of upstream traffic at each ONU. Figure 6 shows the timing relationships stated in G.989.3 [12]. The TWDM-PON module calculates the equalization delays with [12]:

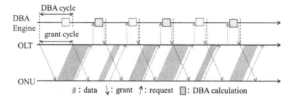

**Fig. 5.** Multi-thread polling.

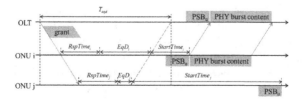

**Fig. 6.** Timing relationships.

$$EqD_i = RTD_i - T_{eqd} = RTT_i + RspTime_i - T_{eqd}. \qquad (1)$$

*EqDi* represents the equalization delay of ONU*i*, $RTD_i$ represents the round-trip delay of ONU*i*, $RTT_i$ represents the round-trip time of ONU*i*, $RspTime_i$ represents the response time of ONU*i*, and $T_{eqd}$ represents the zero-distance equalization delay. $RspTime_i$ is set at 35 µs in this module, since it is required to be 35 ± 1 µs. We can set $T_{eqd}$ based on the ODN design parameters [12].

# 4  Design Specifications

This section describes the design specifications of the ITU TWDM-PON module in detail.

## 4.1  Channel and Network Devices

An OLT and an ONU are represented as *ItutwdmponOltNetDevice* and *ItutwdmponOnuNetDevice* attached to *Node*. Four *ItutwdmponChannel* instances are attached to them, each of which represents a wavelength channel in the ODN.

*ItutwdmponOltNetDevice* sends and receives the PON frames of each *ItutwdmponChannel* using per channel *ItutwdmponOltEngines*, *ItutwdmponOltPhyAdapter*, and *ItutwdmponOltDsScheduler*. The processes related to multiple *ItutwdmponChannel*, including ONU channel handover, are managed by *ItutwdmponOltDwaEngine*.

*ItutwdmponOnuNetDevice* produces and parses PON frames with *ItutwdmponOnuEngines*. It sends and receives them through enabled *ItutwdmponChannel* using *ItutwdmponOnuPhyAdapter* of each channel. The enabling and disabling of *ItutwdmponChannel* is controlled by *ItutwdmponOnuDwaEngine*.

## 4.2  DWA Engine

*OltDwaEngine* performs the DWA procedure and manages the enabled channel of each ONU and the state transition of each channel in the OLT. The common functions for the DWA procedure are implemented in *OltDwaEngine* and DWA algorithms are implemented in subclasses. The functions of a DWA algorithm include deciding whether or not to start channel handover, and, if it decides to start the handover, selecting the target ONU and target channel. Various DWA algorithms can be easily implemented and compared with this implementation. *OnuDwaEngine* manages the enabled channel and state transition in the ONU.

*OltDwaEngine* and *OnuDwaEngine* cooperates with *OltPloamEngine* and *OnuPloamEngine* to exchange PLOAM messages. We implemented PLOAM messages, which are used for ONU wavelength channel handover signaling, namely message type ID $0 \times 15$ *Tuning Control* and message type ID $0 \times 1A$ *Tuning Response*. The generation of a PLOAM message is driven by *OltDwaEngine* and *OnuDwaEngine* in the DWA sequence. *OnuPloamEngine* processes a received PLOAMd message in 750 µs.

*OltDwaEngineFixedRroundRobin* is implemented as a default DWA algorithm. With this algorithm, when a new ONU is added, it is assigned to one of multiple wavelength channels in a round-robin manner. The wavelength assignment is static and ONUs are not handed over to another channel.

## 4.3 State Transition

Here we describe the operation of an OLT and an ONU in each state as shown in Fig. 2.

**OLT Operation.** In the *Hosting* and *Redirecting* states, downstream Tx and upstream bandwidth allocation are enabled. In the *Redirecting* and *Expecting* states, PLOAMu is always granted. Because an ONU is limited to one enabled channel in this module, the enabled channel list is updated at the end of the *Redirecting* state and waits to receive *Tuning Response* message at the target channel. As a consequence, in the *Seeing-off* state, the frame forwarding and DBA grant are disabled. Although this operation is a slight modification of the standard approach, it has little effect on the frame transaction.

**ONU Operation.** In the *Pending* state, frames are not fragmented. A connection whose amount of data exceeds the available payload length is not selected by *ItutwdmponOnuUsScheduler*. In the *Off-sync* and *Profile learning* state, Tx and Rx are disabled. When the state becomes *Us tuning*, only Tx is disabled.

## 4.4 DBA Engine

**Overview.** *ItutwdmponOltDbaEngine* and *ItutwdmponOnuDbaEngine* are responsible for the DBA procedure described in Sect. 3.4. Because their design is basically the same as that in the XG-PON module, here we focus on updates from the XG-PON module. *ItutwdmponOltDbaEngine* calculates the bandwidth allocation for T-CONTs based on the enabled channel, and the state of the ONUs, which are obtained by calling *Itutwdm-ponOltDwaEngine*. *ItutwdmponOnuDbaEngine* calculates the start time of the upstream traffic based on the equalization delay and the response time of the ONU. Because the ranging procedure is not implemented in the proposed module, the propagation delay and the equalization delay are calculated before starting the data transmission.

**Basic Algorithms.** Here we introduce the basic DBA algorithms that we employed. These subclasses will help users to understand the basic concepts of the cycle and thread of DBA.

*ItutwdmponOltDbaEngineProportional* allocates bandwidth to all T-CONTs at each DBA cycle in proportion to their request size, as shown in Fig. 3. To allot transmission opportunity fairly and reduce upstream delay, the total slot size (125 µs) is proportionally assigned in a round-robin manner. The following algorithms are developed based on *ItutwdmponOltDbaEngineProportional*.

*ItutwdmponOltDbaEngineMultiCycle* employs the multi-cycle allocation shown in Fig. 4 by keeping a grant cycle counter and a grant log. Let $k$ ($1 \leq k$) denote the initial value of the grant cycle counter, which can be set as a variable. $k$ represents that the DBA cycle length is how many times of the grant cycle length, for example, $k = 2$ in Fig. 4. Let $c$ denote the counter value, and $c$ is decremented in each grant cycle and is reset to $k$ when it reaches zero. If $c$ is equal to $k$, *Ng-pon2OltDbaEngineMultiCycle* allocates bandwidth to all T-CONTs in proportion to the latest request size in the same way as *ItutwdmponOltDbaEngineProportional*, and stores the result in the grant log. Otherwise, it copies the grant log and the bandwidth allocation is the same as the last cycle.

*ItutwdmponOltDbaEngineMultiThread* employs the multi-thread polling shown in Fig. 5. Let $K$ ($1 \leq K$) denote the maximum value of the grant cycle counters.

Let $n$ ($1 \leq n \leq K$) denote the number of threads, and $i$ ($0 \leq i \leq n-1$) denote the thread identifier. The user can set $n$ and $K$. $k_i$ denotes the initial value of the grant cycle counter of $i$-th thread. $k_i$ is set at $k_i = n - i$. Let $c_i$ denote the counter value of $i$-th thread. $c_i$ is decremented in each grant cycle and is reset to $K$ when it reaches zero. If $c_i$ is equal to $K$, *ItutwdmponOltDbaEngineMultiCycle* allocates bandwidth to all T-CONTs in proportion to the latest request size. Otherwise, it allocates no bandwidth. When $n = 1$, *ItutwdmponOltDbaEngineMultiThread* acts just like *ItutwdmponOltDbaEngineProportional*.

## 5 Conclusion

In this paper, we presented an ITU TWDM-PON module for the ns-3 network simulator and described its concept and design specifications. The proposed mod- ule is implemented based on the XG-PON module and can simulate the data packet transmission described in G.989 recommendations. TWDM packet trans- mission in the upstream and downstream directions is simulated using multiple PON channels. It enabled us to evaluate the performance issues that arise during TWDM-PON development, including various DBA and DWA algorithms. The proposed module currently implements the normal operation part of the state diagram. In the future, we will develop the activation and ranging procedure using PLOAM messages to evaluate the performance in more realistic situations.

## References

1. Alvarez, P., Marchetti, N., Payne, D., Ruffini, M.: Backhauling mobile systems with XG-PON using grouped assured bandwidth. In: 19th European Conference on Networks and Optical Communications-(NOC), pp. 91–96. IEEE (2014)
2. Arokkiam, J., Wu, X., Brown, K.N., Sreenan, C.J., et al.: Experimental evaluation of TCP performance over 10 Gb/s passive optical networks (XG-PON). In: Global Communications Conference (GLOBECOM), pp. 2223–2228. IEEE (2014)
3. Arokkiam, J.A., Brown, K.N., Sreenan, C.J.: Refining the giant dynamic bandwidth allocation mechanism for XG-PON. In: International Conference on Communications (ICC), pp. 1006–1011. IEEE (2015)
4. Das, T., Gumaste, A., Lodha, A., Mathew, A., Ghani, N.: Generalized framework and analysis for bandwidth scheduling in GPONs and NGPONs-the-out-of-approach. J. Lightwave Technol. **29**(19), 2875–2892 (2011)
5. Khan, A., Bilal, S., Othman, M.: A performance comparison of network simulators for wireless networks. In: International Conference on Control System, Computing and Engineering (ICCSCE), pp. 34–38. IEEE (2013)

6. Luo, Y., et al.: Time-and wavelength-division multiplexed passive optical network (TWDM-PON) for next-generation PON stage 2 (NG-PON2). J. Lightwave Technol. **31**(4), 587–593 (2013)

7. Nesset, D.: NG-PON2 technology and standards. J. Lightwave Technol. **33**(5), 1136–1143 (2015)

8. ns-3. http://www.nsnam.org/

9. Oliveira, R., Frances, C., Costa, J., Viana, D., Lima, M., Teixeira, A.: Analysis of the cost-effective digital radio over fiber system in the NG-PON2 context. In: 16th International Telecommunications Network Strategy and Planning Symposium (Networks), pp. 1–6. IEEE (2014)

10. Pinto, T., Farias, J.E., Reis, J.D.: Simulation and experimental results for up to 40 Gbit/s/user coherent DWDM-PON systems. In: International Workshop on Telecommunications (IWT), pp. 1–4. IEEE (2015)

11. Rampfl, S.: Network simulation and its limitations. In: Proceeding zum Seminar Future Internet (FI), Innovative Internet Technologien und Mobilkommunikation (IITM) und Autonomous Communication Networks (ACN), vol. 57 (2013)

12. Recommendations I.T.G.S.: 40-gigabit-capable passive optical networks 2 (NG-PON2)

13. Song, H., Kim, B.W., Mukherjee, B.: Multi-thread polling: a dynamic bandwidth distribution scheme in long-reach PON. J. Sel. Areas Commun. **27**(2), 134–142 (2009)

14. Wu, X., et al.: An XG-PON module for the NS-3 network simulator. In: Proceedings of the 6th International ICST Conference on Simulation Tools and Techniques, pp. 195–202 (2013)

# Research on Implementation Scheme of Power IMS Network Based on NFV Architecture

Xing Huang[✉], Fanbo Meng, Xi Li, Lei Zhang, and Xiaoyu Zhu

State Grid Liaoning Electric Power Company, Shenyang, China
staryellow@139.com

**Abstract.** At present, the State Grid Corporation switching network is evolving from a program-controlled switching network based on circuit-switched technology to a next-generation switching network based on IP technology. The virtualization of power communication core network has become the development trend of grid communication. Among them, network function virtualization (NFV) decouples the software functions and hardware functions of traditional network equipment, reduces the investment and operation costs of the network and improves the deployment efficiency of new services. This paper analyzes the benefits of NFV technology architecture and NFV to power IMS core network, proposes the implementation scheme and network evolution of power IP multimedia subsystem (IMS) network based on NFV architecture, and constructs the virtual network architecture as the architecture scheme of network function virtualization. The scheme of bearer network in the virtualized environment of power IMS core network is proposed, and the advantages and challenges of current NFV technology are summarized.

**Keywords:** Power IMS · National grid · Power communication · Virtualization

## 1 Introduction

As the core network of business control, IMS is built on the Internet standard at the beginning of design, adopts open and universal session initiation protocol (SIP) control protocol, and has good portability and easy development. The new business will not only shorten the development cycle, but also get online faster. The system is easy to upgrade and network operation and maintenance is more flexible. By introducing IMS technology, the communication network of the national grid can be upgraded to the multimedia converged communication network, and the mobile and fixed networks can be further integrated to realize support for multi-service terminals. However, despite the mature technology and strong capabilities, this architecture is different from the requirements of the State Grid Corporation's administrative and dispatch switching networks. The State Grid Corporation serves the industry. Its application population is fixed in size and demand is relatively simple. This makes the hardware equipment designed for telecom operators long-term idle and the hardware usage rate is low, which causes waste of hardware resources and energy consumption.

© ICST Institute for Computer Sciences, Social Informatics and Telecommunications Engineering 2019
Published by Springer Nature Switzerland AG 2019. All Rights Reserved
H. Song et al. (Eds.): SIMUtools 2019, LNICST 295, pp. 196–204, 2019.
https://doi.org/10.1007/978-3-030-32216-8_19

On the other hand, there is a contradiction between the centralized management of IMS and the original localized management of the State Grid Corporation. To this end, according to the characteristics of national grid demand and requirements, the implementation scheme of power IMS network based on NFV architecture is proposed, and the advantages and achievability are also analyzed.

NFV has changed the way existing network operators build networks: instead of using dedicated network equipment, information technology (IT) virtualization technology is used to implement various types of networks on standard high-performance servers, switches, and storage devices. The functionality of nodes and user front-end devices. In [1], the NFV and software defined network (SDN) technologies are introduced into the core network, and the core network is virtualized. At the same time, based on the complex stream processing platform, the long-term evolution architecture of the core network based on SDN/NFV is established. In order to study the arrangement and placement of NFV services, the NFV service orchestration mechanism and placement algorithm are proposed, and a visual NFV service orchestration and placement system is designed and implemented in [2]. In [3], NFV is used to adaptively monitor the IT infrastructure and provide data to the analytics engine to detect attacks in real time while using infrastructure to block attacks. In [4], a method based on fault injection NFV infrastructure (NFVI) reliability assessment and benchmarking is proposed. The application of this method in virtualized IMS environment is also discussed.

The above documents are all virtualized deployment of public network IMS, which is rarely involved in power. Therefore, the power IMS network is deployed for virtualization based on the characteristics of the national power grid and the virtualized deployment architecture. When deploying a power IMS network, the application of NFV can virtualize network functions, further simplify the operation and maintenance management of the underlying network facilities, and improve the management and control capabilities of the network. In order to meet the functional requirements brought by the bearer network in the deployment process of the power IMS network, the communication system resources occupied by different services are rationally allocated and dynamically adjusted through the centralized control protocol standard, and the power IMS network virtualization capability is further enhanced.

## 2   Introduction of NFV

NFV is a new type of network technology initiated by operators. It aims to carry related network functions through common hardware and virtualization technologies. Network costs are reduced and business development and deployment capabilities are improved. In the NFV architecture, all network functions are in pure software mode on the unified distribution of computing, storage and network infrastructure [5, 6]. The software functions are no longer bundled with the original dedicated hardware platform. Its architecture is shown in Fig. 1:

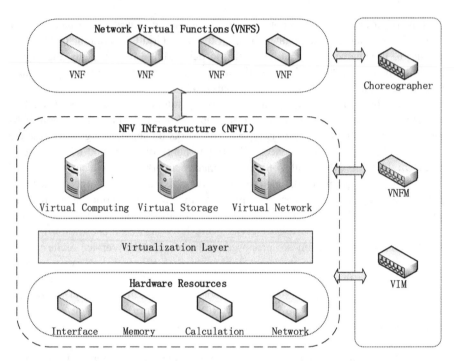

**Fig. 1.** NFV network architecture

According to this architecture, the three-part entity function of NFV is shown in Fig. 1:

(1) Virtual Network Function (VNF): Includes software that runs on the NFVI to perform specified network functions, such as Proxy/Interrogating/Serving Call Session Control Function (P/I/S-CSCF) and Home Subscriber Server (HSS) in the IMS network. The function and state of a network element node is independent of whether it is virtualized or not. A VNF can be made up of multiple internal components. In this scenario, the same VNF can be deployed on multiple virtual machines or on the same virtual machine. The former virtual machine only runs one component of the VNF.

(2) NFVI: An environment that provides deployment, management, and execution of VNFs, including hardware and software. Hardware resources include computing, storage, and networking resources that provide processing, storage, and connectivity capabilities for VNFs through the virtualization layer. The hardware resources are abstracted by the virtualization layer, and the software functions of the VNF are decoupled from the underlying hardware, so that the independence of the hardware resources from the VNFs is guaranteed.

(3) NFV management and business orchestration: including business orchestration system, VNF management system and NFVI management system. Among them, the business orchestration system is responsible for the layout and management of NFV infrastructure and software resources, and provides network services on the

NFV; the VNF management system is responsible for the management of the VNF life cycle (such as establishing, updating, expanding, and terminating); The ability of the VNF to manage and control the computing, storage, and network resources it requires is managed by the NFVI.

The introduction of NFV in the power IMS core network is to migrate power equipment from the current dedicated platform to a common device. That is to say, various network elements become independent applications, and can be flexibly deployed on a unified platform based on standards-based servers, storage, and switches, so that each application can rapidly reduce the virtual resources to achieve rapid expansion and expansion. As a result, the flexibility of the network has been greatly improved [7–9]. The key to NFV is how to decouple the traditional network functions from the proprietary network hardware, run on a common standard server while ensuring network performance, and implement NFV management and functional design.

## 3  Network Implementation Scheme of Power IMS Based on NFV

### 3.1  Power IMS Network

The public IMS network consists of a service layer, a control layer, and an access layer. Open interfaces are used between different layers. The control capability and service providing capability of the SIP-based multimedia session service are provided on the Evolved Packet Core (EPC) and other IP bearer networks. At the same time, the IMS service plane and control plane network element have the characteristics of intensive computing processing, which is consistent with the commercial off-the-shelf (COTS) server's strong computing capability and is suitable for processing the state transition and signaling interaction processes, so it is especially suitable for virtualized deployment.

Compared with the public IMS network, the power IMS network is designed according to its concept and is carried on the integrated data network. The virtual private network (VPN) is divided into other service networks. The IMS network architecture and policy control architecture features are fused in the power IMS network. In addition to the Layer 3 architecture service layer, control layer and network bearer layer of the traditional IMS network, it adds a bearer control sublayer within the control layer. And the ability of the intelligent network is called by the CSCF in the form of a third-party capability control server, which realizes the organic combination of the session control and the bearer control sub-layer, and improves the intelligence degree of the network.

### 3.2  IMS Virtualization Solution Based on NFV Architecture

According to the needs of enterprise information development, IMS technology has been identified by the State Grid Corporation as the next-generation administrative switching network technology system, and the IMS switching network is promoted in all network provinces. The network element equipment in the IMS network has a complete standard specification. After the core network element is virtualized, the NFV does not change the logical architecture of the network, and each network element function is automatically loaded or unloaded on the general hardware platform in the form of software. The interfaces of the IMS network still exist and the signaling process remains unchanged. This requires that the bearer network of the data center where the virtualized network function is located automatically supports the establishment of a virtual private network for the IMS virtualized network function. Allocate network resources and IP addresses, provide dedicated network channels with QoS guarantees, and ensure that the virtual private network can span data centers across domains.

The NFV technology was introduced by the State Grid IMS in [9, 10], enabling users to obtain the necessary protection while accessing the service on a unified hardware platform. The resource utilization rate is improved, and the equipment space occupation and energy consumption are reduced. The NFV network model implements specific application functions for general purpose hardware. Each node can implement multiple functions, and the network device type is distinguished by software on a unified hardware platform. Under normal circumstances, the unified hardware platform is relatively independent, so that the problem of tight coupling between hardware and software existing in traditional network devices is solved, and an effective fault guarantee mechanism can also be obtained.

The main structure of NFV that incorporates the characteristics of the power IMS network is shown in Fig. 2 below. Its main functional entities include: Virtualization of call control functions: P/I/S-CSCF completes session work and service control; Virtualization of network interworking functions: Media Gateway Control Function (MGCF), Border Gateway Control Function (BGCF), Media Gateway (MGW) complete analog access and interconnection of power exchange networks; Media resource control virtualization: Multimedia Resource Function Controller (MRFC) and Multimedia Resource Function Processor (MRFP) provide media resources for terminal devices; User management virtualization: the storage of information such as routing and signing of power communication services by the HSS; Virtualization of the underlying hardware resources: including intelligent access terminals such as maintenance terminals and video voice services of municipal power companies.

During this virtualization deployment process, physical network resources are virtualized through the NFV architecture to form a virtual network. The virtual network is opened to the IMS virtualized network function in a service manner, and is responsible for carrying the service flow, thereby shielding the actual physical network. The controller in the data center domain is responsible for managing physical node devices such as switches and routers in the domain, and transmits information about the physical network to the virtual infrastructure management system through the northbound application programming interface. The virtual infrastructure management system then based on the collected physical network topology information. The network topology and state of the entire virtual network are sorted out, the network resources of the virtual network are managed, and relevant information is opened to the virtual network function management system and the service orchestration system. The use of NFV technology to transform the edge network elements of the grid and virtualize the network functions can shorten the deployment cycle of new services, and the corresponding workload will be greatly reduced.

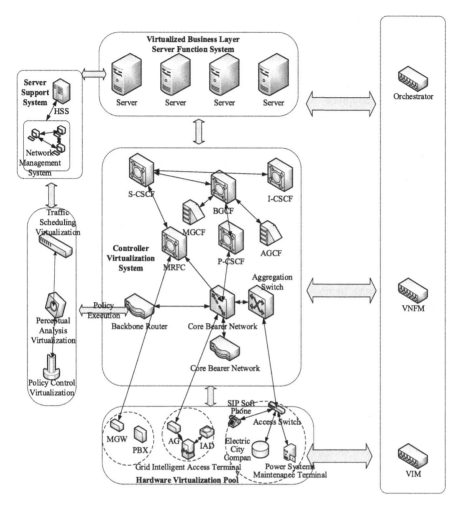

**Fig. 2.** NFV architecture model of power IMS core network

## 3.3 Application Scenario of State Gird IMS Network Virtualization Technology

After understanding the power IMS network virtualization process and its network architecture and networking solution, its application scenarios should be studied. Combined with the actual situation of the State Grid IMS network, the specific requirements of NFV technology are obtained, so that the key issues are studied in a targeted manner. The actual application environment and user scale of the State Grid IMS network and the main application environment of NFV technology are different from those of telecom operators. It is a prerequisite for the application of NFV technology to the State Grid IMS network:

(1) Application scenario 1: When the dispatching switching network fails, the basic communication capability of the dispatching switching network can be quickly restored

by using the IMS infrastructure of the administrative switching network in a very short time to maximize resource utilization.

The administrative switching IMS network is used to provide communication guarantee capability for the scheduling switching network. When the primary and backup systems of the switching network fail simultaneously, through NFV hardware and software decoupling and distributed computing, realize the resource sharing between the dispatching exchange network and the administrative switching network of the State Grid, and realize the on-demand scheduling and allocation of resources.

(2) Application scenario 2: Provide a logically independent IMS network infrastructure for different departments without increasing hardware investment.

NFV enables software from different vendors to run on a unified virtualized infrastructure. Through NFV technology, it can provide customizable communication service capabilities for different units. It will be quickly launched, flexible in configuration, and will not affect the communication security of other units and fast fault recovery.

(3) Application scenario 3: The maintenance workload is not greatly increased due to the increase of new services, and the decentralized management is developing toward cloud management.

In the use of the State Grid IMS network, in order to reduce the hardware form, the core maintenance force is put into software and service maintenance. The operation and maintenance management is developed from the traditional local equipment management to the cloud virtual resource configuration, which improves the operation and maintenance efficiency. Reduce hardware costs by decoupling hardware and software.

(4) Application scenario 4: The old and new business alternates from device update to service update, and changes from device operation and maintenance to service operation and maintenance.

With the development of computer technology, in order to comply with the trend and maintain the advantages of the State Grid Corporation in the field of information and communication, the core position of software services should be reflected in the IMS network of the State Grid, and the superior resources should be invested in the software services.

(5) Application scenario 5: The NFV network and the traditional network are mutually disaster-tolerant backups, and the NFV network has a stronger self-healing capability.

NFV provides automatic recovery of network service functions. When a running network service component (or function node) crashes, the management and orchestration (MANO) can extract corresponding mirror information (snapshot information) according to the script policy in the predefined template. Quickly implement network service components (or function nodes) to be redeployed and implement automatic recovery of network functions.

(6) Application scenario 6: Flexible configuration of system capacity, flexible and rapid deployment of new service applications, and on-demand services.

The network's more flexible capacity adjustment capabilities have been given by NFV. The operator can implement automatic elastic expansion of cloud resources when the relevant network indicators reach the threshold according to the pre-configured capacity indicators and the extended scheduling policy. Elastic expansion includes four methods: scale out/in and scale up/down. Out/in refers to the increase or decrease of the number of virtual machines in the network element. Up/down refers to the change of the size of the virtual machine of the network element.

The core of NFV is hardware and software decoupling. Applications do not rely on hardware functions. State Grid can flexibly and rapidly develop and deploy various services and applications according to requirements to meet the needs of various departments.

## 4  Advantages of Power IMS Implementation Based on NFV Architecture

The use of core network virtualization technology in the State Grid, combined with the actual needs of the State Grid for targeted research, not only meets the economic and reliability issues of power IMS network deployment, but also through the virtualization technology part of the function can be achieved.

(1) One-click completion of power IMS virtual network function deployment in [11]: According to predefined service templates and scripts, virtual network functions including all IMS network elements of P/I/S-CSCF can be automatically loaded on the cloud platform. installation.

(2) Automatic expansion of power IMS virtual network function: The virtual network function key performance indicators operation indicator is automatically monitored by the virtual network function management system. Once the monitoring of the virtual network function load has exceeded the alert value, the virtual network function management system applies computing, storage, network and other resources, and automatically installs the relevant IMS virtual on the newly added virtual machine using predefined templates and scripts. Internet function.

(3) Automatic recovery of power IMS virtual network function: Once the load of the virtual network function is detected to be lower than the minimum value, the virtual network function management system notifies the virtual network function that it is ready to be shut down. After the virtual network function shutdown preparation is completed, the virtual network function management system will reclaim the allocated resources.

(4) Automatic disaster recovery protection of the power IMS virtual network function: When the virtual machine running the virtual network function instance fails, a new identical virtual opportunity is automatically created to take over the call assumed by the failed virtual machine.

## 5  Conclusion

With the development of virtualization and cloud computing technologies, the emergence of NFV provides a good idea for solving the shortcomings of the traditional core network architecture. NFV is based on virtualization technology, a new network product environment is provided, IT and power industry convergence is promoted, operators' network deployment capabilities are enhanced, and operational capabilities are enhanced. At the same time, NFV technology is applied to the State Grid IMS network, which can solve the current difficulties faced by the switching network. In addition, the State Grid Switching Network applies network function virtualization technology to the company's private network, which can promote the development of power communication technology and provide strong support for the scientific and rational evolution of corporate switching networks including dispatching switching networks and administrative switching networks. However, after using NFV technology, the original hardware maintenance work of the State Grid provinces will be greatly reduced, and new requirements will be put forward for personnel. How to deal with new technologies and the management methods brought about by them, is also the challenge of NFV technology in the State Grid IMS network.

# References

1. Xue, M., et al.: Research on key technologies of core network evolution based on SDN/NFV. Des. Tech. Posts Telecommun. (2014)
2. Jun, L.: Research on NFV service orchestration mechanism and placement algorithm. Beijing Univ. Posts Telecommun. (2018)
3. Lioy, A., Gardikis, G., Gaston, B., et al.: NFV-based network protection: the SHIELD approach. In: IEEE Conference on Network Function Virtualization and Software Defined Networks. IEEE (2017)
4. Cotroneo, D., Simone, L.D., Iannillo, A.K., Lanzaro, A., Natella, R.: Dependability evaluation and benchmarking of Network Function Virtualization Infrastructures. In: Network Softwarization, pp. 1–9 (2015)
5. Zhao, H., Xie, Y., Shi, F.: Network virtualization and network function virtualization. ZTE Technol. J. (2014)
6. Jiang, D., Huo, L., Song, H.: Rethinking behaviors and activities of base stations in mobile cellular networks based on big data analysis. IEEE Trans. Netw. Sci. Eng. 1(1), 1–12 (2018)
7. Jiang, D., Huo, L., Li, Y.: Fine-granularity inference and estimations to network traffic for SDN. PLoS ONE 13(5), 1–23 (2018)
8. Jiang, D., et al.: A joint multi-criteria utility-based network selection approach for vehicle-to-infrastructure networking. IEEE Trans. Intell. Transp. Syst. PP(99), 1–15 (2018)
9. Jiang, D., et al.: Energy-efficient multi-constraint routing algorithm with load balancing for smart city applications. IEEE Internet Things J. PP(99), 1 (2016)
10. Rajan, D.: Common platform architecture for network function virtualization deployments. In: IEEE International Conference on Mobile Cloud Computing, Services, and Engineering, pp. 73–78. IEEE (2016)
11. Carella, G., et al.: Cloudified IP multimedia subsystem (IMS) for network function virtualization (NFV)-based architectures. In: Computers and Communication IEEE, pp. 1–6 (2014)

# A Data Fusion Algorithm and Simulation Based on TQMM

Ke Zhang[1,2(✉)], Zeyang Wang[3], and Huiling Li[4]

[1] School of Computer Science and Engineering,
University of Electronic Science and Technology of China,
Chengdu 611731, China
kezhang@uestc.edu.cn
[2] Science and Technology on Electronic Information Control Laboratory,
Chengdu 610000, China
[3] Sichuan Jiuzhou Electronic Technology Co., Ltd., Mianyang 621000, China
[4] School of Communication and Information Engineering,
University of Electronic Science and Technology of China,
Chengdu 611731, China

**Abstract.** Asynchronous data fusion is more practical than synchronous data fusion, the model of track-to-track fusion in this case has been established and the concept of Track Quality with Multiple Model (TQMM) was put forward, furthermore a data fusion algorithm is proposed, in which the TQMM is used to assign weights, to improve tracking precision in asynchronous multi-sensor data fusion system. The simulation results show that the algorithm has a better tracking performance compared with original algorithms.

**Keywords:** Data fusion · Multi-sensor · Track fusion · TQMM

## 1 Introduction

Generally, asynchronous track fusion is mainly divided into two categories. One is that different kinds of sensors have different and fixed sampling periods and the other one is the time interval of target information provided by sensors has no rule, meaning sensors have no fixed sampling interval. Due to the limitation of the sensor itself, the first category can also be divided into two parts according to the starting time of different sampling periods. In both cases, sensor information can be synchronized through track pretreatment, and then be tracked by synchronous track fusion algorithm. However, the pretreatment process will cause errors increasing and reduce the fusion data reliability. Therefore, researchers put forward a series of asynchronous track fusion algorithm [1–10]. Some asynchronous fusion algorithms introduce data registration method to the fusion algorithm for realizing the synchronization of asynchronous data before fusion, such as the least squares method, interpolation, extrapolation and so on. Besides, some algorithms deal with asynchronous data on the basis of receiving time, and select the proper fusion approach for asynchronous data fusion, such as fusion algorithm under the principle of minimum error covariance matrix trace [1, 2], asynchronous track fusion algorithm based on information matrix [3–5], distributed weighted fusion

H. Song et al. (Eds.): SIMUtools 2019, LNICST 295, pp. 205–217, 2019.
https://doi.org/10.1007/978-3-030-32216-8_20

estimators with random delays [6], time-varying bias estimation for asynchronous multi-sensor multi-target tracking systems [7] and Step by Step Prediction Fusion based on Asynchronous Multi-sensor System (SSPEA) [8, 9], etc. These algorithms also can be used in other research domain, such as traffic analysis [11, 12], big data analysis [13] and smart transportation [14, 15], etc. But, with these algorithms, the first kind of asynchronous problem could be basically solved; while, the second problem could not be solved well.

The SSPFA algorithm mainly uses the multi-sensor's measurement information in a fusion cycle to get the filtering estimation, in order to obtain the local state estimation and the corresponding error covariance of each sensor at the last moment of fusion cycle. Then after the state prediction of fusion time, the algorithm operates the order weighting of the sensor prediction information based on the obtaining order of sensor predictive values and the principle of minimum error covariance matrix. And finally, the multi-sensor asynchronous fusion is achieved. According to the filtering predictive thought of SSPFA, [9] proposes a Track - to - Track Fusion for Asynchronous Multi-sensor based on Step by Step Prediction (TFASP) algorithm. By the local state estimation of multi-sensor fusion, the algorithm predicts sampling values in the fusion cycle. Then, after the weight fusion of same sensor's predictive value at fusion moment, this algorithm regards the fusion value as sensor's equivalent observation information at fusion moment and finally achieves the global fusion of asynchronous multi-sensor by the step-by-step filter fusion. As the input value of the step-by-step filter fusion, local sensor's weight fusion decides the tracking performance of the algorithm. However, determined by the observation precision and sensors' prediction error, the weight of local sensor's weight fusion has no direct relation with the time tag between the sampling time and fusion time. Therefore, the large error of local sensor's state estimation will reduce the tracking accuracy of the whole system. Besides, there is no feedback mechanism in the entire system. These problems cause some shortcoming in TFASP algorithm. Therefore, based on Track Quality of Kalman filtering [16, 17], with the combination of the Track Quality with Multiple Model(TQMM) [18] and introduction of feedback mechanism into the system [19], this paper presents an asynchronous multi-sensor track fusion algorithm with information feedback, that is Asynchronous Fusion based on Track Quality with Multiple Model(AFTQMM) algorithm. AFTQMM feeds back the one-step prediction of global state estimation to local sensors. And then after getting TQMM of all sampling points based on this feedback, local sensors assign the weight according to TQMM of each point, which improves the accuracy of equivalent observations of local sensors at fusion moment as well as the performance of global state estimation.

## 2  Track Quality with Multiple Model and Local Tracking

### 2.1  Track Quality with Multiple Model

Assuming that the dynamic equation and measurement equation of multi-sensor system are:

$$X^l(k+1) = F^l(k)X^l(k) + w^l(k) \tag{1}$$

$$Z^l(k) = H^l(k)X^l(k) + V^l(k), \quad l=1,2,\cdots, NUM \tag{2}$$

In equations, *NUM* is the amount of the filter models, and $X^j(k+1)$ stands for the state vector of model $l$ in $k+1$ moment. $F^l(k)$ represents the one-step state transition matrix from moment $k$ to moment $k+1$ under model $l$, and the system process noise $w^l(k)$ is gaussian white noise sequence. Besides,

$$E[w^l(k)] = 0 \tag{3}$$

$$Cov(w^l(k), w^l(\tau)) = E[w^l(k)w^{l^T}(\tau)] = Q^l(k)\delta_{k\tau} \tag{4}$$

In equations, $Q^l(k)$ is nonnegative definite matrix, and $Z^l(k)$ represents the sensor's observed values of target state under model $l$. $H^l(k)$ is measurement matrix, and measurement noise $V^l(k)$ stands for gaussian white noise sequence. Besides,

$$E[v^l(k)] = 0 \tag{5}$$

$$Cov(v^l(k), v^l(\tau)) = E[v^l(k)v^{l^T}(\tau)] = R^l(k)\delta_{k\tau} \tag{6}$$

In equations, $R^l(k)$ is the positive definite matrix. System process noise and measurement noise are independent of each other, that is, to meet

$$Cov(w^l(k), v^l(\tau)) = 0 \quad \tau = 1,2,\cdots,k,\cdots \tag{7}$$

Local track quality determines the track quality of system, which means the track quality of system after fusion will not be too high [11] if local track quality is poor. Assuming that the one-step prediction and its covariance of the state of model $l$ $(l = 1, 2, \cdots, NUM)$ in time $k$ are $\hat{X}^l(k+1|k)$ and $P^l(k+1|k)$ respectively, then the state's one-step prediction and covariance of model $l$ $(l = 1, 2, \cdots, NUM)$ of sensor $i$ $(i = 1, 2, \cdots, N)$ in $k+1$ time based on $l$ $(l = 1, 2, \cdots, NUM)$ model state in $k$ time are

$$v^l(k+1) = Z(k+1) - H^l(k+1)\hat{X}^l(k+1|k) \tag{8}$$

$$S^l(k+1) = H^l(k+1)P^l(k+1|k)H^l(k+1)^T + R^l(k) \tag{9}$$

In order to describe the track quality, a standardized distance equation [12] could be defined

$$d^l(k+1) = v^l(k+1)^T S^l(k+1)^{-1} v^l(k+1) \tag{10}$$

Then, the track quality of model $l$ in time $k+1$ is

$$U^l(k+1) = \alpha U^l(k) + (1-\alpha)d^l(k+1) \tag{11}$$

The value of $U$ represents the track quality. Obviously, the smaller the $U$ is, the better the track quality is. Here, $\alpha$ is the historical power factor with the range from 0 to 1, and $\alpha = 1/5$ in the simulation. When $k+1 = 4$, the track quality of sensor $i$ in model $l$ is

$$U^l(4) = d^l(4) \tag{12}$$

Therefore, TQMM of sensor $i$ in time $k+1$ is

$$U(k+1) = \sum_{j=1}^{N} U^l(k+1)u_{k+1}(l) \tag{13}$$

## 2.2    Local Tracking

In order to adapt the target mobility and get precise local estimate information, Interacting Multiple Model (IMM) filtering algorithm is adopted for the local track of sensors. Besides, three kinds of IMM filtering algorithm are applied to reduce the computational complexity and improve the realtime performance of information processing. Among them, the system state vector is $X = [x\ \dot{x}\ \ddot{x}\ y\ \dot{y}\ \ddot{y}\ z\ \dot{z}\ \ddot{z}]^T$, and the model prior probability is $U = [1\ 0\ 0]$. The total output of IMM filters is the weighted average of multi-filters' filtering results, and the weight is the model probability. If one model plays a dominant role, then it will enjoy higher probability (between 0.9 and 1), and the others only obtain lower probabilities (between 0 and 0.1). Besides, the transition probability of Markov model is

$$P_{ij} = \begin{bmatrix} 0.95 & 0.025 & 0.025 \\ 0.025 & 0.95 & 0.025 \\ 0.025 & 0.025 & 0.95 \end{bmatrix} \tag{14}$$

# 3    Asynchronous Fusion Algorithm Based on Track Quality with Multiple Model

## 3.1    Basic Flow

The main idea of this algorithm includes: the observed filter prediction at fusion moment is gotten based on the sensors' local estimated information; then, using the weight fusion of same sensor's prediction to obtain sensors' observed information at fusion moment; finally, global fusion of asynchronous multi-sensor is achieved based on step by step filtering fusion process. The process is shown in Fig. 1.

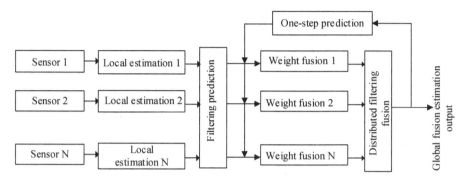

**Fig. 1.** Algorithm flow chart of step by step asynchronous track fusion based on track quality

## 3.2 Fusion Model

According to Fig. 1, assuming that the fusion period is T, and the algorithm's basic fusion model is given when the amount of sensors is $N$ in a fusion cycle, as shown in Fig. 2.

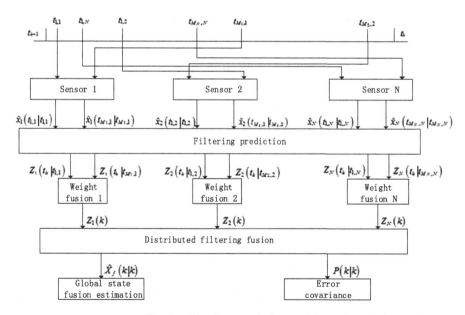

**Fig. 2.** Asynchronous fusion models

### 3.3  Steps of Algorithm

As shown in Figs. 1 and 2, the algorithm includes four parts: multi-model prediction, feedback element, local sensors' weight fusion and distributed filtering fusion. The process is shown below.

Assuming that the global state fusion estimation and the corresponding error covariance of system are $\hat{X}_f(k-1|k-1)$ and $P(k-1|k-1)$ in fusion time $t_{k-1}$. There are $N$ ($N \geq 0$) sensors with observed information in fusion period, and the observation value of sensor $i$ ($i = 1, 2, \cdots, N$) is $M_i$ ($M_i \geq 0$). The fusion model in Fig. 2 is built on the basis of each sensor with more than 2 sampling points, which means $M_i \geq 2$. However, due to the randomness of the data provided by the sensors, there are two cases in fusion period. One is $N = 0$, which means the fusion center cannot obtain the continuous target information in a certain interval. Another one is $N > 0$. In this case, based on the observation number, $M_i$ can be divided into two parts: $M_i = 1$ and $M_i \geq 2$. For different situations, different approaches are adopted to optimize the fusion process.

When $N = 0$, the state estimation of current fusion moment is achieved based on the state estimation of precious fusion moment. However, when $N = 0$ continuously exists, using this method to get information will reduce the fusion algorithm's effectiveness because of the accumulation of prediction error. With the improvement of their performance, sensors will be chosen to detect tracking object in all directions, to avoid $N = 0$ in the fusion center. When $N > 0$, if $M_i = 1$, the prediction and the step-by-step filtering fusion could be taken directly without weighted fusion process. While, if $M_i \geq 2$, the algorithm can be operated following the asynchronous fusion model in Fig. 2. Besides, if the observed information of some sensors at fusion moment exists, the information could be applied directly to participate the step-by-step filtering fusion.

Now, there are two known issue. Firstly, the number of sensors and the observed number in fusion period $(t_{k-1}, t_k]$ are $N$ and $M_i$ ($i = 1, 2, \cdots, N$). Besides, the target state estimation and the corresponding covariance error of sensor $i$ in observed time $t_{j,i}(j = 1, 2, \cdots, M_i)$ are $\hat{x}_i(t_{j,i}|t_{j,i})$ and $p_i(t_{j,i}|t_{j,i})$. The process of getting the state estimation $\hat{X}_f(k|k)$ and the covariance error $P(k|k)$ of system track in fusion center at time $t_k$ will be introduced.

### 3.3.1  Multi-model Prediction

Judge the value of N. When $N \neq 0$, search all sampling points $[t_{1,i}, t_{2,i}, \cdots, t_{M_i,i}]$ of sensor $i$ in fusion circle, and then operate one step test based on 3 models, and predict all sampling pinots to fusion moment $t_k$. The process is as follow:

$$\Delta t_{j,i} = t_k - t_{j,i}, \quad j = 1, 2, \cdots M_i \tag{15}$$

In the equation, the local state estimation and the error covariance of sensors in time $t_{j,i}$ are $\hat{x}_i(t_{j,i}|t_{j,i})$ and $p_i(t_{j,i}|t_{j,i})$. Based on time difference, the corresponding state transition matrix $F_{j,i}^l(t_{j,i})$ ($l = 1, 2, 3$) could be gotten by IMM filtering idea, and then the observation predictive value could be worked out.

$$Z_i^l(t_k|t_{j,i}) = H_i^l(k) \cdot F_{j,i}^l(t_{j,i}) \cdot \hat{x}_i(t_{j,i}|t_{j,i}), \quad l = 1, 2, 3 \tag{16}$$

In the equation, $H_i^l(k)$ is the observation matrix of sensor $i$'s model $l$. The multi-model prediction could be obtained based on the observed prediction $Z_i^l(t_k|t_{j,i})$ of model $l$

$$Z_i(t_k|t_{j,i}) = \sum_{l=1}^{3} Z_i^l(t_k|t_{j,i}) \cdot u_i^l(k) \tag{17}$$

In the equation, $u_i^l(k)$ is the probability of sensor $i$'s model $l$ at time $t_k$.

### 3.3.2  Feedback Element

Operate one step prediction for system state estimation in time $t_{k-1}$. The state vector and the covariance of that are

$$\hat{X}_f(k|k-1) = \sum_{l=1}^{3} \hat{X}_f^l(k|k-1) \cdot u^l(k) \tag{18}$$

$$P(k|k-1) = \sum_{l=1}^{3} u^l(k) \cdot \left\{ P^l(k|k-1) + \left[ \hat{X}_f^l(k|k-1) - \hat{X}_f(k|k-1) \right] \cdot \left[ \hat{X}_f^l(k|k-1) - \hat{X}_f(k|k-1) \right]' \right\} \tag{19}$$

In equations, $u_{\cdot}(k)$ is the probability of system's model at time $t_k$. $\hat{X}_f^l(k|k-1)$ and $P^l(k|k-1)$ are the one step prediction and error covariance of system track at time $t_{k-1}$ based on model $l$. The expressions are as follows.

$$\hat{X}_f^l(k|k-1) = F^l(k-1)\hat{X}_f^l(k-1|k-1) \tag{20}$$

$$P^l(k|k-1) = F^l(k-1)P^l(k-1|k-1)F^l(k-1)^T + Q^l(k-1) \tag{21}$$

$F^l(k-1)$, $\hat{X}_f^l(k-1|k-1)$ and $P^l(k-1|k-1)$ are the state transition matrix, state estimation and error covariance of system track's model $l$ at time $t_{k-1}$.

### 3.3.3  The Weight Fusion of Local Sensors

The feedback element will get one step prediction of the previous state of fusion center, and feeds back to local sensors. Then, after getting the TQMM of local sensors' states prediction, the feedback could further determine the observation state's weight and realize the weight fusion. The deterministic process of the weight factor is shown in Fig. 3.

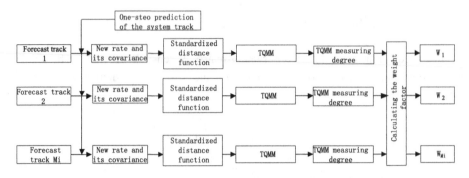

**Fig. 3.** The flow chart of the distribution of the weight factor

In fusion period $(t_{k-1}, t_k]$, the innovation and covariance of sensor $i(i = 1, 2, \cdots, N)$'s observation from time $t_{j,i}(j = 1, 2, \cdots, M_i)$ to fusion time $t_k$ are

$$v_{i,j}^l(k) = z_i(t_k|t_{j,i}) - H_i^l(k)\hat{X}_f(k|k-1) \tag{22}$$

$$S_{i,j}^l(k) = H^l(k)P(k|k-1)H_i^l(k)^T + R^l(k-1) \tag{23}$$

Based on Sect. 2.1, TQMM of the sensor $i$'s sampling point $j$ is $U_{i,j}(k)$. Then the measuring degree of TQMM of sensor $i$'s sampling point $j$ could be calculated.

$$h_i^j(k) = \exp\{-U_{i,j}(k)\} \tag{24}$$

The corresponding weight is

$$\omega_j^i(k) = h_i^j(k) / \sum_j^{M_i} h_i^j(k) \tag{25}$$

Finally, by the weight fusion, the equivalent observation data of sensor $i$ in time $t_k$ is obtained.

$$Z_i(k) = \sum_{j=1}^{M_i} w_i^j(k)Z_i(t_k|t_{j,i}) \tag{26}$$

### 3.3.4  Distributed Filtering Fusion

From steps above, we can get the observation information $Z_1(k), Z_2(k), \cdots Z_N(k)$ of $N$ sensors at fusion time $t_k$. Then, the global state fusion estimation and the corresponding error covariance at fusion moment could be worked out with the step by step fusion thought [16].

$$\begin{cases} \hat{X}_f(k|k) = \hat{X}_N(k|k) \\ P(k|k) = P_N(k|k) \end{cases} \tag{27}$$

With the known information of $\hat{X}_f(k|k-1) = F(k-1)\hat{X}_f(k-1|k-1)$ and $P(k|k-1) = F(k-1)P(k-1|k-1)F(k-1)^{\mathrm{T}} + GQG^{\mathrm{T}}$, the actual expressions of Eq. (27) are as follows. When $N = 1$, assuming $\hat{X}_1(k|k-1) = \hat{X}_f(k|k-1)$ and $P_1(k|k-1) = P(k|k-1)$, then

$$\hat{X}_1(k|k) = F(k-1)\hat{X}_f(k-1|k-1) + K_1(k)\left[Z_1(k) - H\hat{X}_1(k|k-1)\right] \tag{28}$$

$$P_1(k|k) = [I - K_1(k)H(k)]P_1(k|k-1) \tag{29}$$

When $N \geq 2$,

$$\hat{X}_N(k|k) = F(k-1)\hat{X}_f(k-1|k-1) + \sum_{i=1}^{N} \left\{K_i(k)\left[Z_i(k) - H(k)\hat{X}_i(k|k-1)\right]\right\} \tag{30}$$

$$P_N(k|k) = \left\{\prod_{i=1}^{N}[I - K_i(k)H(k)]\right\}P_1(k|k-1) \tag{31}$$

From Eq. (28) to (31), $K_i(k)$ is the filtering gain matrix of sensor $i(i = 1, 2, \cdots, N)$, and its calculating formula is shown as the following

$$K_i(k) = P_i(k|k-1)H(k)^{\mathrm{T}}\left[H(k)P_i(k|k-1)H(k)^{\mathrm{T}} + R_i(k)\right]^{-1} \tag{32}$$

When $i = 2, \cdots, N$, we can get $\hat{X}_i(k|k-1) = \hat{X}_{i-1}(k|k)$ and $P_i(k|k-1) = P_{i-1}(k|k)$.

## 4  Simulation Analysis

### 4.1  Simulation Environment

For comparative analysis, Root Mean Square Error (RMSE) and Trace of Error Covariance Matrix (TECM) are chosen as the target tracking performance index.

Assuming that six radars on the same platform observe the same target asynchronously, the sampling time of track data got by fusion center may deviate from the fixed sampling period, due to the sensor limitation and the communication time-delay from local node to fusion center. So, we should pay attention to the offset $\Delta t$ of sensor from the actual sampling period to the fixed sampling period. Besides, there is no sampling information at some sampling moments because of the target escaping from the tracking area of the corresponding radar. The tracking fusion problem in this situation is the typical second kind of asynchronous fusion problem. Each sensor correlates the observed data to form a target track and reports the track and the data to the fusion center. However, due to the disunity of measurement error and observation coordinates of each sensor, the data from each sensor needs preprocessing before fusion, generally including data space alignment, gross error rejection and so on.

The target track time is 100 s, and the monte carlo simulation will be done for 600 times ($M = 600$). Then the expression of RMSE and TECM are

$$\text{RMSE} = \sqrt{\frac{\sum_{n=1}^{M}((x-\hat{x}^n)^2 + (y-\hat{y}^n)^2 + (z-\hat{z}^n)^2)}{M}} \tag{33}$$

$$\text{TECM} = \left(\sum_{n=1}^{M} trace(P^n)\right)\Big/ M \tag{34}$$

In the equation, $\hat{x}^n$, $\hat{y}^n$, $\hat{z}^n$ are the location information of the n[th] simulation fusion track, and $P^n$ is the error covariant matrix of the n[th] simulation track.

## 4.2    Results and Analysis

The sampling periods of six radars are 0.2 s, 0.5 s, 0.8 s, 1.0 s, 1.2 s and 1.5 s. The observation precisions of radars on x, y, z directions are 50.23 m, 51.15 m, 55.57 m, 50.28 m, 57.69 m, 51.59 m and their locations are (2800 m, 0 m, 0 m), (0 m, 500 m, 0 m), (0 m, 0 m, 1800 m), (50 m, 100 m, 500 m), (50 m, 100 m, 2800 m), (100 m, 500 m, 800 m). The initial position of target is (−3000 m,1000 m,−4000 m), with the initial speed of 100 m/s. The target flies at a constant speed in 0–20 s, carry turning maneuver at a speed of 0.157 rad/s in 20–40 s, then flies at a constant speed in 40–60 s, and does turning maneuver at a speed of −0.157 m/s in 60–80 s. Finally, it flies at a constant speed in 80–120 s. The total flying time of the target is 120 s, and the flight path is shown in Fig. 4.

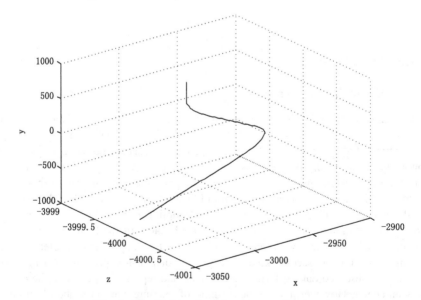

**Fig. 4.** The flight path of the maneuvering target

Systems with the number of sensors from 3 to 6 track the maneuvering target simultaneously (the fusion period of four systems is 1.0 s) to test the influence of the sensor's number on the track performance of AFTQMM (Fig. 5 and Chart 1).

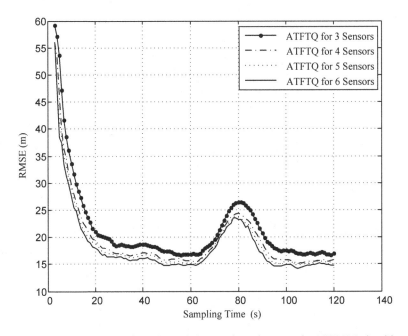

**Fig. 5.** The relationship of RMSE and the number of sensors in AFTMM algorithm

| Track method | Local track | AFTQMM (3 Sensors) | AFTQMM (4 Sensors) | AFTQMM (5 Sensors) | AFTQMM (6 Sensors) |
|---|---|---|---|---|---|
| TECM average value $(m^2)$ | 4631 | 691 | 535 | 478 | 436 |

**Chart 1.** The relationship of TECM average value and the number of sensors in AFTQMM algorithm

The figures and the charts above proves that with the increasing of the number of sensors, the RMSE and TECH curves of AFTQMM decline, and the system track performance improve gradually. However, after the number is greater than 5, the system fusion accuracy has not been significantly improved. In engineering application, based on the relationship of track performance and systematic complexity, proper number of sensors can achieve the higher tracking accuracy, real-time processing and the project cost reducing as much as possible.

**Acknowledgement.** The paper is partially supported by the National Natural Science Foundation of China (Nos. 61571104), the 6th Innovation and Entrepreneurship Leading Talents Project of Dongguan, the General Project of Scientific Research of the Education Department of Liaoning Province (No. L20150174), and the Program for New Century Excellent Talents in University (No. NCET-11-0075), and Project of Science and Technology on Electronic Information Control Laboratory.

# References

1. Liu, Q., Wang, X., Rao, N.S.V.: Information feedback for estimation and fusion in long-haul sensor networks. In: IEEE 2014 17th International Conference on Information Fusion (2014)
2. Lin, X.: One fusion-algorithm of asynchronous multi-sensor integrated navigation system. Geomat. Inf. Sci. Wuhan Univ. **37**(1), 54–57 (2012)
3. Aeberhard, M., Schlichtharle, S., Kaempchen, N., et al.: Track-to-track fusion with asynchronous sensors using information matrix fusion for surround environment perception. IEEE Trans. Intell. Transp. Syst. **PP**, 1–10 (2012)
4. Aeberhard, M., Rauch, A., Rabiega, M., et al.: Track-to-track fusion with asynchronous sensors and out-of-sequence tracks using information matrix fusion for advanced driver assistance systems. In: 2012 IEEE Intelligent Vehicles Symposium (IV), pp. 1–6 (2012)
5. Aeberhard, M., Schlichtharle, S., Kaempchen, N., et al.: Track-to-track fusion with asynchronous sensors using information matrix for surround environment perception. IEEE Trans. Intell. Transp. Syst. **PP**(99), 1–10 (2011)
6. Sun, S., Xiao, W.D.: Distributed weighted fusion estimators with random delays and packet dropping. Circ. Syst. Signal Process. **26**(4), 591–605 (2007)
7. Hu, Y., Zhou, D.: Time-varying bias estimation for asynchronous multi-sensor multi-target tracking systems using STF. Chin. J. Electron. **22**(3), 525–529 (2013)
8. Wen, C., Ge, Q.: The step by step predictive fusion of asynchronous multi-sensor system. J. Central South Univ. (Nat. Sci. Ed.) **32**(1), 652–653 (2005). (in Chinese with English Abstract)
9. Li, Q.: The research and implementation of airborne multi-sensor data fusion target's tracking technology. Mater's thesis. University of Electronic Science and Technology of China (2012). (in Chinese with English abstract)
10. Lim, S., Lee, C.: Data fusion algorithm improves travel time predictions. IET Intel. Transport Syst. **5**(4), 302–309 (2011)
11. Jiang, D., Wang, W., Shi, L., Song, H.: A compressive sensing-based approach to end-to-end network traffic reconstruction. IEEE Trans. Netw. Sci. Eng. (2018). https://doi.org/10.1109/tnse.2018.2877597
12. Jiang, D., Huo, L., Li, Y.: Fine-granularity inference and estimations to network traffic for SDN. PLoS ONE **13**(5), 1–23 (2018)
13. Jiang, D., Huo, L., Song, H.: Rethinking behaviors and activities of base stations in mobile cellular networks based on big data analysis. IEEE Trans. Netw. Sci. Eng. **1**(1), 1–12 (2018)
14. Jiang, D., Huo, L., Lv, Z., et al.: A joint multi-criteria utility-based network selection approach for vehicle-to-infrastructure networking. IEEE Trans. Intell. Transp. Syst. **PP**(99), 1–15 (2018)
15. Jiang, D., Zhang, P., Lv, Z., et al.: Energy-efficient multi-constraint routing algorithm with load balancing for smart city applications. IEEE Internet of Things J. **3**(6), 1437–1447 (2016)

16. Jeffery, T.: Track quality estimation for multiple-target tracking radars. In: IEEE Radar Conference, vol. PP, pp. 76–79 (1989)
17. Tafti, D., Sadati, N.: Novel adaptive Kalman filtering and fuzzy track fusion approach for real time applications. In: 3rd IEEE Conference on Industrial Electronics and Application, pp. 120–125 (2008)
18. Zhang, W., Wang, Z., Zhang, K.: Fusion algorithm based on multi-model track quality. Comput. Sci. **40**(2), 65–70 (2013). (in Chinese with English abstract)
19. Zhu, Y., You, Z., Li, X.R., et al.: The optimality for the distributed Kalman filtering fusion with feedback. Automatica (37), 1489–1493 (2001)

# Design of Low-Power USB Audio System Based on LPM Protocol

Hua Ren[1], Jia Cui[2], Wen Xie[3,5], Chengjun Zhou[1], and Ke Zhang[4(✉)]

[1] School of Electronic Information, Chengdu Vocational College of Agricultural Science and Technology, Chengdu 611130, China
[2] Petrochemical Research Institute, China Petroleum & Natural Gas Co., LTD., Beijing 102200, China
[3] Guangdong Electronic Information Engineering Technology Research Institute, University of Electronic Science and Technology of China, Dongguan 523000, China
[4] School of Computer Science and Engineering, University of Electronic Science and Technology of China, Chengdu 611731, China
kezhang@uestc.edu.cn
[5] Dongguan Smart Eye Co., LTD., Dongguan 523000, China

**Abstract.** Universal Serial Bus (USB) audio Devices was applied extensively in current mobile communication equipment, at the same time the low power consumption and high USB bandwidth must be satisfied, we design audio equipment based on USB2.0 High Speed (HS), adopt the latest USB Link Power Management (LPM) protocol issued by USB organization, use Field Programmable Gate Array (FPGA) as the main controller, USB2.0 HS physical layer interface (PHY) was designed externally, and then the USB audio class 3.0 equipment was realized to play music. System analysis and test results show that the system can transmit based on USB2.0 HS, and the average power consumption is lower than the USB1.1 audio equipment, has solved the demand of the high bandwidth and low power consumption of USB audio device effectively.

**Keywords:** USB LMP · Audio class 3.0 · USB2.0 HS · Intelligent energy saving · Low-powers

## 1 Introduction

USB audio devices [1] are removable external devices using USB channels and protocols for audio playback and recording. USB audio devices include many types, such as USB speakers, USB microphones, USB microphone arrays, etc. With the development of communication and networks technology [2–6], mobile communication devices are becoming increasingly slim and light. Therefore, the traditional 3.5 mm audio interface is gradually replaced by the USB interface [7], for that USB interface can be flattened, especially the USB type-c interface. There are growing types of peripherals based on USB interface, like USB audio device, one of the major categories. At the same time, the lightweight of mobile communication equipment strictly requires the endurance capability and peripheral power consumption [8]. This paper

H. Song et al. (Eds.): SIMUtools 2019, LNICST 295, pp. 218–227, 2019.
https://doi.org/10.1007/978-3-030-32216-8_21

mainly studies one USB audio device design of low power consumption and high bandwidth based on USB LPM (USB2.0 Link Power Management).

## 2 Background

USB devices to be identified on host have some same features [9], including: device enumeration, reporting configuration descriptors, reporting class descriptors, and establishing data channels for efficient data interaction. For USB host, when enumerating USB device, class descriptor is used to determine device type, and configuration descriptor is used to select suitable driver for the device. After driver installed, the data channel of USB device is established successfully. Then, application layer software can access the USB drive by calling the device driver.

Taking the identification and operation project of USB headset (with microphone) device as an example. After USB audio device connected to USB host, by enumerating, host identifies it is audio device with function of playing and recording, belongs to USB headset. Then, according to configuration descriptor, host installs driver for the USB device [10] to establish two data transmission channels of iso out (synchronous output) and iso in (synchronous input). When host playing audio, data stream will flow from iso out to USB audio device. After decoding and ADC converting, sound can be heard through the device. The working principle is as follows (Figs. 1 and 2).

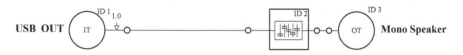

**Fig. 1.** Playing audio

When host recording audio, data stream will flow from iso in channel to host. After encoding and saving by host, the recorded file can be obtained. The working principle is as follows.

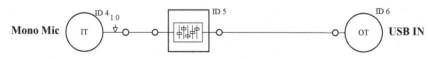

**Fig. 2.** Recording audio

Table 1. Design portfolio type of USB audio devices

| USB connection bandwidth | USB version | USB audio class version |
|---|---|---|
| USB1.1 (USB2.0 full-speed) 12 mbps | USB1.1 | Adc1.0 |
| USB2.0 high-speed 480 mbps | USB2.0 | Adc2.0 |
| USB2.0 high-speed 480 mbps | USB2.1 | Adc3.0 |

## 3  Design

Design portfolio of USB audio devices is shown below (Table 1).

Due to limitation of bandwidth and protocol version, USB1.1 cannot be applied to multi-channel and hi-fi. USB2.0 HS and ADC2.0 only satisfy bandwidth but not low power because of high consumption.

USB audio class has evolved into three versions, including ADC1.0 (audio device class 1.0), ADC2.0 and ADC3.0. Characteristics of ADC1.0 and ADC2.0 [11] are as follows.

☐ ADC 1.0:

(1)  Adopt USB2.0 full-speed, bus transmission speed is 12 mbps;
(2)  Support USB headphone devices
(3)  Support USB microphone devices
(4)  Support USB headset devices
(5)  Support mute control and volume control
(6)  Support audio streaming of pcm format

Basic USB audio devices can be implemented by ADC1.0. But with the development of audio devices and the requirement from multi-channel to multi-code and hi-fi, ADC1.0 can no longer support that. The performance of USB audio devices has been greatly improved until the advent of ADC2.0 based on USB2.0 HS.

☐ ADC2.0:

(1)  Adopt USB2.0 high-speed, bus transmission speed is 480 mbps;
(2)  Support mapping from physical channel to logical channel
(3)  Support joint descriptor of audio interface
(4)  Support sampling rate selection
(5)  Support data stream of multiple encoding formats

Utilizing 480 mbps high bandwidth of USB2.0 HS and ADC2.0 standard, complex USB audio devices could be simulated, which meets the audio requirements of multi-channel, multi-code and hi-fi. To some extent, the ADC1.0 standard is replaced. However, with the popularity of mobile communication devices and the requirement of low power consumption, disadvantages of audio devices implemented by combination of USB2.0 HS and ADC2.0 are becoming increasingly prominent. It is characterized by high power consumption of USB2.0 HS devices [12], more than four times that of USB1.1 under the same conditions, which is exactly what this design needs to solve.

## 4    Design and Implementation

After USB protocol developed to V2.1, LPM (link power management) protocol was added [13]. Its basic concept is to let USB device entering suspend state to reduce power consumption when USB device has no data transmission requirements. The suspend status of USB devices could be long or short, which is called L2 in USB specification. Table 2 shows some status of USB LPM devices.

**Table 2.**  Devices status of USB LPM

| LPM states | Description |
| --- | --- |
| L0 (on) | Port is enabled for propagation of transaction signaling traffic |
| L1 (sleep) | Similar to L2 but supports finer granularity in use |
| L2 (suspend) | Port is disabled, Enter the low-power mode |
| L3 (off) | Port is not capable of performing any data signaling |

State transition of USB devices is shown in the following figure (Fig. 3).

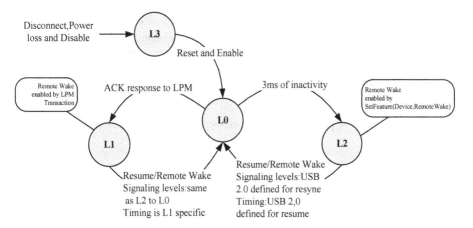

**Fig. 3.**  USB state transition

Compared with normal USB standard, USB LMP standard has the advantage of L1 (Sleep) mode. Normal USB standard only supports L0, L2, and L3 but cannot let USB devices into low power mode in real time and wake up quickly.

After USB device enters L1 (Sleep), its own state, power consumption and wakeup mode are similar to L2 (Suspend) flow of normal USB. The difference is that speed of both entering and waking up from L1 (Sleep) is faster. The following table describes the characteristics of devices in and out of L1 (Sleep)/L2 (Suspend) (Table 3).

**Table 3.** Characteristics of USB devices in and out of L1/L2

| Features | L1 (Sleep) | L2 (Suspend) |
|---|---|---|
| Entry | Explicitly entered via LPM extended transaction | Implicitly entered via 3 ms of link inactivity |
| Exit | Device or host-initiated via resume signaling; Remote-wake can be(optionally) enabled/disabled via the LPM transaction | Device or host-initiated via resume signaling; Device-initiated resumes can be (optionally) enabled/disabled by software |
| Signaling | Low and Full-speed idle | Low and Full-speed idle |
| Latencies | Entry: $\sim 10$ μs Exit: $\sim 70$ μs to 1 ms(host-specific) | Entry: $\sim 3$ ms Exit >30 ms(OS-dependent) |
| Link power consumption | $\sim 0.6$ mW(data line-pull-ups) | $\sim 0.6$ mW(data line-pull-ups) |

The table shows L1 (Sleep) is a fast mode of L2 (Suspend).

Because of 480 mbps high bandwidth of USB2.0 HS, bus idle rate is very high during audio data streams transmission. When bus is idle, with USB LPM technology, device can enter L1 (Sleep) low power state to reduce the power consumption of entire USB audio device. However, ADC1.0 and ADC2.0 don't support USB LPM.

In order to meet requirements of USB audio device in low-power applications, recently USB organization has proposed the USB ADC3.0 standard [3]. With respect to ADC2.0, the biggest difference is USB LPM technology supporting, which offers possibility of low-consumption design of audio devices based on USB2.0HS. Design of this paper is on the basis of ADC3.0.

□ Hardware implementation
System structure of low-power USB audio device in this paper is as follows (Fig. 4).

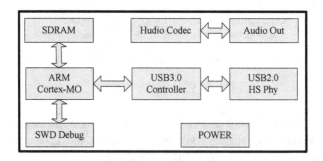

**Fig. 4.** Design of design of hardware structure

The system takes Altera Stratix III FPGA platform, low power CPU of arm-cortex-m0 with 30 MHz running frequency. Besides, it applies jtag/swd debug interface and

USB3.0 protocol analyzer to debug LPM protocol as well as using oscilloscope and high-precision multimeter to measure system function consumption (Fig. 5).

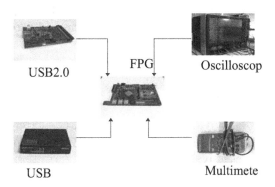

USB2.0        FPG        Oscilloscop

USB                        Multimete

**Fig. 5.** Testbed and instrument

☐ Software Implementation
Under working mode, USB host allocates the data size delivered each time according to the bandwidth requirement of current audio data stream [14]. In order to maintain synchronization with audio data rate, host sends audio data stream periodically and makes devices into L1 (sleep) state to reduce power consumption at idle time. The software implementation process is as follows (Fig. 6).

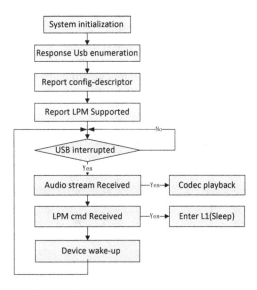

**Fig. 6.** Software implementation process

The software mainly implements two processes.

(1) Enter USB receiving audio data interrupt periodically, send audio data to decoder buffer pool to ensure the continuity of audio playback.
(2) Enter USB LPM instruction request interrupt periodically, configure system clock register and USB2.0 controller, and let the system enter L1 (sleep) state to reduce system power consumption.

## 5  Test Results and Analysis

USB 3.0 protocol analyzer [10] works as concatenation between USB audio device and host to analysis protocol. The device supports USB2.0 Link Power Management protocol package. Test result is shown below (Fig. 7).

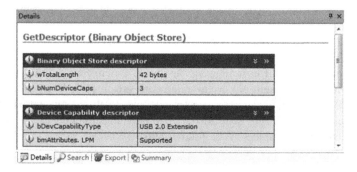

**Fig. 7.**  Test screenshot of analytical instrument for USB protocol

Host successfully identifies the audio device supporting USB LPM technology.

Data transmission of USB communication is identified by sof (Start of frame), and USB1.1 sends one sof per ms, as shown below (Fig. 8).

| Item | De... | En... | Sp... | Paylo... | Time |
|---|---|---|---|---|---|
| 在此处输入文字 | 在 | 在 | 在 | 在... | 在此处输入文字 |
| ⟳ Start of Frame | | | FS | 496 | 16.174 041 750 |
| ⊞← IN transaction | 1 | 1 | FS | No d... | 16.174 166 583 |
| ⟳ Start of Frame | | | FS | 497 | 16.175 041 817 |
| ⊞← IN transaction | 1 | 1 | FS | No d... | 16.175 164 067 |
| ⟳ Start of Frame | | | FS | 498 | 16.176 041 883 |
| ⊞← IN transaction | 1 | 1 | FS | No d... | 16.176 163 717 |
| ⟳ Start of Frame | | | FS | 499 | 16.177 041 950 |
| ⊞← IN transaction | 1 | 1 | FS | No d... | 16.177 163 867 |
| ⟳ Start of Frame | | | FS | 500 | 16.178 042 017 |

**Fig. 8.**  Sending package interval of USB1.1

USB2.0 HS sends a micro sof per 125 μs, and 8 micro sofs form one sof, as shown below (Fig. 9).

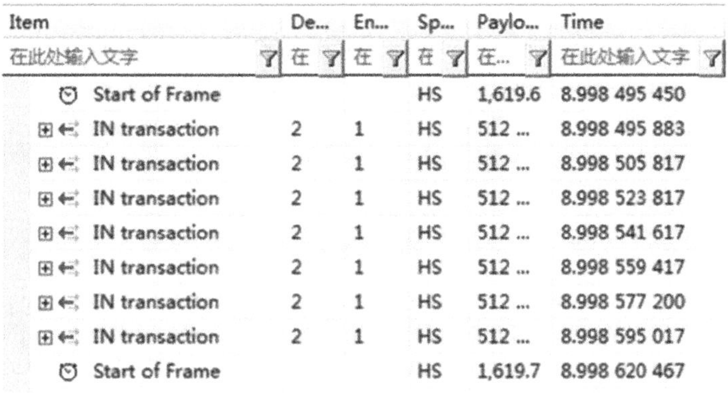

| Item | De... | En... | Sp... | Paylo... | Time |
|------|-------|-------|-------|----------|------|
| 在此处输入文字 | 在 | 在 | 在 | 在... | 在此处输入文字 |
| ⊙ Start of Frame | | | HS | 1,619.6 | 8.998 495 450 |
| ⊞ ←: IN transaction | 2 | 1 | HS | 512 ... | 8.998 495 883 |
| ⊞ ←: IN transaction | 2 | 1 | HS | 512 ... | 8.998 505 817 |
| ⊞ ←: IN transaction | 2 | 1 | HS | 512 ... | 8.998 523 817 |
| ⊞ ←: IN transaction | 2 | 1 | HS | 512 ... | 8.998 541 617 |
| ⊞ ←: IN transaction | 2 | 1 | HS | 512 ... | 8.998 559 417 |
| ⊞ ←: IN transaction | 2 | 1 | HS | 512 ... | 8.998 577 200 |
| ⊞ ←: IN transaction | 2 | 1 | HS | 512 ... | 8.998 595 017 |
| ⊙ Start of Frame | | | HS | 1,619.7 | 8.998 620 467 |

**Fig. 9.** Sending package interval of USB2.0 HS

In setting of USB2.0 HS audio driver, 521-byte data is transmitted per micro sof (microframe). With 320 kbps bitrate, there are 40k byte data per minute which needs 80 micro sofs for transmitting. Therefore, for USB2.0 HS, the time for each micro sof is 125 us. When playing music of 320 kbps rate on host, actual power consumption is calculated by measuring following parameters.

Io: Phy current during audio data transmission
Is: Phy current in L1 (sleep) state
Tp: Periodic time of audio data transmission
Ts: Periodic time in L1 (sleep)

Following table shows the average value of Io, Is, To, Ts of multimetering (Table 4).

**Table 4.** Result of actual current and packet cycle test

| Measurement | 1 | 2 | 3 | 4 | Mean |
|-------------|------|------|------|------|------|
| Io(ma) | 29.43 | 29.76 | 30.27 | 29.16 | 29.65 |
| Is(ma) | 1.84 | 1.92 | 1.87 | 1.96 | 1.89 |
| Tp(ms) | 10 | 10 | 10 | 10 | 10 |
| Ts(ms) | 990 | 990 | 990 | 990 | 990 |

$$Ia = \frac{7 * 71n\,1 * 71}{7n\,1} \text{current formula} \tag{1}$$

The following table of actual power consumption of ADC1.0/ADC2.0/ADC3.0 is got by referring actual power consumption of normal USB1.1 audio equipment and getting la = 2.16 ma with the current calculation formula (Table 5).

**Table 5.** Actual power consumption of ADC1.0/ADC2.0/ADC3.0

| USB audio class | Phy (system) average current (ma) | Audio bit rate |
| --- | --- | --- |
| Adc3.0 | 2.16 ma | 320 kbps |
| Adc2.0 | 29.65 ma | 320 kbps |
| Adc1.0 | 7.54 ma | 320 kbps |

The above test data shows the average power consumption of this design is 71% lower than that of USB1.1 audio device, which solves power consumption problem of USB audio device on mobile communication device.

## 6    Conclusion

This paper mainly analyzes USB audio class 3.0 device based on USB2.0 Link Power Management additional protocol. The device meets data flow requirement by 480 mbps high-speed bandwidth of USB2.0 HS as all as realizing lower average power consumption than USB1.1 audio devices with the advantage of USB LPM. Experimental tests and calculations show that this study meets the need of low-power peripherals in modern mobile communication devices, and the high-speed bandwidth of USB2.0 HS provides solid foundation for the development of USB audio devices.

ABC3.0 technology is the latest standard proposed by USB organization for low-power devices. Currently, audio devices supporting adc3.0 have not been officially released on the market. This design validates the possibility of low-power USB audio devices and provides a basic implementation method. But, USB host is another key for the applying of low-power devices based on USB LPM technology. Host driver must effectively allocate USB bus bandwidth to achieve the real-time and efficient USB LPM scheduling mechanism, which is the next research of author.

**Acknowledgement.** The paper is partially supported by the 6th Innovation and Entrepreneurship Leading Talents Project of Dongguan, the Industrial Upgrading Traction Engineering Project of Chengdu Technology Bureau (2016-NY02-00157-NC).

## References

1. Yue, X., Pei, D., Wang, J.: The design of high-speed data acquisition system based on the USB3.0 interface. Chin. J. Electron. Dev. **38**(01), 140–143 (2015)
2. Jiang, D., Wang, W., Shi, L., Song, H.: A compressive sensing-based approach to end-to-end network traffic reconstruction. IEEE Trans. Netw. Sci. Eng. (2018). https://doi.org/10.1109/tnse.2018.2877597

3. Jiang, D., Huo, L., Li, Y.: Fine-granularity inference and estimations to network traffic for SDN. PLoS One **13**(5), 1–23 (2018)
4. Jiang, D., Huo, L., Song, H.: Rethinking behaviors and activities of base stations in mobile cellular networks based on big data analysis. IEEE Trans. Netw. Sci. Eng. **1**(1), 1–12 (2018)
5. Jiang, D., Huo, L., Lv, Z., et al.: A joint multi-criteria utility-based network selection approach for vehicle-to-infrastructure networking. IEEE Trans. Intell. Transp. Syst. **pp**(99), 1–15 (2018)
6. Jiang, D., Zhang, P., Lv, Z., et al.: Energy-efficient multi-constraint routing algorithm with load balancing for smart city applications. IEEE Internet Things J. **3**(6), 1437–1447 (2016)
7. Kuang, P., Liu, C., Wang, Y.: Design of universal data transmission system based on FPGA and USB3.0. MicroComput. Appl. **36**(07), 26–28+34 (2017)
8. Song, Z., Pei, D., Yang, S.: Design of high-speed data transmission system based on USB3.0 interface. Mod. Electron. Tech. **40**(04), 159–162 (2017)
9. Zhang, Y., Zhang, H., Li, D.: The design and implementation of RS422 and USB transfer device. Chin. J. Electron. Dev. **39**(06), 1425–1428 (2016)
10. Li, M., Yang, L., Zhang, Y.: Design of multichannel ultrasonic testing system based on FPGA and USB. Instrum. Tech. SOR (08), 82–84+88 (2017)
11. Zhao, S., Yu, B.: Design and implementation of secure USB connection. J. Syst. Simul. **28** (06), 1400–1405 (2016)
12. Pan, Z.-K., Qin, G.-L., Luo, Y.-F.: USB wireless network card based on stream interface-driven. Comput. Syst. Appl. **25**(04), 258–262 (2016)
13. Yu, B., Li, X., Zhao, S.: USB device controller resistant eavesdropping attacks. Appl. Res. Comput. **34**(04), 1155–1158 (2017)
14. Zhang, C.-C., Chen, Y.-L., Lu, N., An, B.-W.: Design and application of a comprehensive software security module based on USB. Electron. Opt. Control **24**(03), 93–97 (2017)

# A Hybrid Virtualization Approach to Emulate Heterogeneous Network Nodes

Junyu Lai[1,2]([✉]) [iD], Jiaqi Tian[1] [iD], Dingde Jiang[1] [iD], Jiaming Sun[1] [iD],
and Ke Zhang[1] [iD]

[1] School of Aeronautics and Astronautics, University of Electronic Science
and Technologies of China, Xiyuan Avenue no. 2006, Chengdu, China
{laijy,tianjq,jiangdd,sunjm,zhangk}@uestc.edu.cn
[2] Science and Technology on Communication Networks Laboratory,
Shijiazhuang, China

**Abstract.** In the last decade, various resource virtualization technologies have
been widely applied in ICT industry, particularly the cloud computing domain.
These virtualization technologies can squeeze out hardware potential and consequently can save expenditure. Virtualization technologies are used in the
network emulation domain to emulate network nodes, which could be quite
heterogeneous in terms of hardware architecture. Currently, many network
emulators utilize x86 based virtual machines (VMs) to emulate target network
nodes of heterogeneous architectures, i.e. ARM, SPARC, PPC, etc., which may
introduce incompatibility to the original system and application software of the
target nodes, and will consequently jeopardize the emulation fidelity. This paper
focuses on alleviating the emulation incompatibility caused by node heterogeneity. Firstly, this emulation incompatibility problem is investigated and
analyzed. Then, a hybrid virtualization approach to emulate heterogeneous
nodes is elaborated and implemented in a cloud-based network emulation system. A case study of applying the proposed approach to emulate a space-ground
integrated network (SGIN) is conducted. Functional verification and performance evaluation experiments lead to the results, which show the hybrid
approach can effectively dispose of the incompatibility problem with an
affordable performance degradation.

**Keywords:** Resource virtualization · Network emulation · Heterogeneous
nodes · Incompatibility · Space-ground integrated network

## 1 Introduction

Modern networks are getting increasingly more complicated. Mathematic models can
not accurately evaluate network performance anymore. Consequently, various network
testing methods are regarded as more decent functional verification and performance
evaluation solutions for network architectures, protocols, and upper layer applications.
Computer simulation, live test-bed, and network emulation are the major three networking testing methods, among which network emulation is the focus of this work.
Network emulation is a technique for testing the real protocols and applications over a

H. Song et al. (Eds.): SIMUtools 2019, LNICST 295, pp. 228–237, 2019.
https://doi.org/10.1007/978-3-030-32216-8_22

virtual network, which varies from network simulation where abstractly mathematical models of traffic, network, channels and protocols are applied. A network emulator's major task is to emulate nodes and links with medium cost and high fidelity.

Regarding to network node emulation, physical machines are traditionally utilized to represent the target network nodes, with high cost and low scalability. As various resource virtualization technologies are booming in ICT industry, it is nature to use VMs to emulate network nodes. In real network, heterogeneous nodes, such as x86, ARM, PowerPC, Sparc, and MIPS architected, coexist. Many legacy emulator adopts x86 architected VM to emulate all the nodes, which introduces incompatibility to the original protocol and application software of the target nodes. For the sake of high fidelity emulation, it is vital to elaborate a practical approach to accurately emulate heterogeneous nodes in target networks. The contribution of this work contains the following three points.

- A hybrid virtualization approach to emulate heterogeneous network nodes;
- Practically implementing the proposed hybrid virtualization approach in a cloud-based network emulation system;
- Conduct a case study on SGIN emulation, to illustrate the effectivity of the proposed hybrid virtualization approach.

This paper proceeds as follows. Section 2 discusses the state-of-the-art, followed by the briefing of the involved cornerstone technologies in Sect. 3. The hybrid virtualization approach to emulate heterogeneous nodes is derived and implemented in Sect. 4. Then, a case study is presented in Sect. 5. Finally, Sect. 6 concludes the paper and provides the outlook.

## 2 Related Work

Resource virtualization technologies have gradually been adopted to emulate network nodes to dig up hardware potential, and to lower emulation cost. In industry, Boeing Phantom Works in 2008 [1], presented CORE (Common Open Research Emulator), a real-time network emulator that allows rapid instantiation of hybrid topologies composed of both real hardware and virtual network nodes. CORE used FreeBSD jail mechanism to form lightweight VMs. In 2015, Northrop Grumman Aerospace Systems [2], researched on the need to provide a method for studying the interaction among diverse hardware and software components and identifying potential network bottle necks in air-to-ground networks. VMware ESXi is adopted to emulate 10 virtual machines on a single physical server. In the same year, KISTI of Korea [3], presents a critical analysis on existing wired testbeds with respect to the wireless network emulation. Among the investigated testbeds, EMWIN and MobiNet utilize VM technologies to emulate real network nodes. In academia. In 2007, Maier et al. [4] from University of Stuttgart focused on scalable network emulation problems, and present a comparison of different virtual machine implementations (Xen, UML) and their virtual routing approach (NET). In 2009, Mehta et al. [5], described a virtualization technology based emulation architecture that is scalable, modular, and responds to real time changes in topology and link characteristics. In 2014, Balasubramanian et al. [6] from

Vanderbilt University, described a rapid development and testing framework for a distributed satellite system. QEMU (Quick Emulator) virtualization technology is used to launch a configurable number of instances. In 2015, Antonio et al. [7] from Universidad Galileo, presented the Dockemu tool for emulation of wired and wireless networks. The tool glues together state of the art technologies of virtualization, Linux Bridging and NS-3.

Most of the existing emulation schemes rely on x86 architected VMs or containers to emulate heterogeneous nodes, which introduces incompatibility problems to the protocol and application software running on the physical nodes.

# 3    Cornerstone Technologies

## 3.1    Virtual Machine

A VM is an emulation of a computer system, and was originally defined as an efficient, isolated duplicate of a real computer. The physical hardware running the VM is generally referred to as the host, and the VMs emulated on that machine are generally referred to as the guests. A host can emulate several guests, each of which may emulate different operating systems and hardware platforms. The software or firmware that creates VMs on the host hardware is called a hypervisor. Typically, the virtualization technologies adopted by a VM include Full virtualization and Para-virtualization.

## 3.2    KVM

KVM (Kernel-based Virtual Machine) is a full virtualization solution for Linux on x86 hardware containing virtualization extensions (Intel VT or AMD-V). It consists of a loadable kernel module, kvm.ko, that provides the core virtualization infrastructure and a processor specific module, kvm-intel.ko or kvm-amd.ko. KVM supports multiple VMs simultaneously running unmodified Linux or Windows images. By itself, KVM does not perform any emulation. Instead, it exposes the/dev/kvm interface to a userspace host. On Linux, QEMU is one such userspace host. QEMU uses KVM when available to virtualize guests at near-native speeds, but otherwise falls back to software-only emulation. Currently, KVM has been ported to S/390, PowerPC, IA-64, ARM, etc., and can support a wide variety of guest operating systems, including Linux, BSD, Solaris, Windows, OS X, Android, etc.

## 3.3    QEMU

QEMU is a free and open-source emulator that performs hardware virtualization. It emulates the machine's processor through dynamic binary translation and provides a set of different hardware and device models for the machine, enabling it to run a variety of guest operating systems. It also can be used with KVM to run virtual machines at near-native speed, by taking advantage of hardware extensions such as Intel VT. QEMU supports the emulation of various architectures, including: x86, x86-64, MIPS64, SPARC, ARM, SH4, PowerPC, RISC-V, etc. QEMU has two operating modes:

- User mode emulation. QEMU runs single programs that were compiled for a different instruction set. System calls are thunked for endianness and for 32/64 bit mismatches. Fast cross-compilation and cross-debugging are the main targets;
- Full system emulation. QEMU emulates a full computer system, including peripherals. It can be used to provide virtual hosting of several virtual computers on a single computer. QEMU can boot many guest operating systems, including Linux, Solaris, Microsoft Windows, DOS, and BSD; it supports emulating several instruction sets, including x86, MIPS, 32-bit ARMv7, ARMv8, PowerPC, SPARC, ETRAX CRIS and MicroBlaze.

### 3.4    NFV

NFV (Network functions virtualization) is a network architecture concept that uses the technologies of IT virtualization to virtualize entire classes of network node functions into building blocks that may connect, or chain together, to create communication services. A virtualized network function, or VNF, may consist of one or more virtual machines running different software and processes, on top of standard high-volume servers, switches and storage devices, or even cloud computing infrastructure. In network emulation domain, target networks nodes can be regarded as a set of VNFs, and can be emulated by means of NFV.

## 4    A Hybrid Virtualization Approach to Emulate Heterogeneous Nodes in Target Network

### 4.1    General Assumptions

Network nodes of various architectures coexist in practical networks. To emulate these heterogeneous nodes, x86 architected VMs are traditionally employed, which however may introduce incompatibility to target nodes of architectures other than x86. For example, using an x86 based VM to emulate a practical ARM node, the system and application software designed for the target node cannot be directly installed on the x86 based VM due to incompatibility. Thus, it is assumed that a target network contains two types of nodes, x86 and non-x86 architected, respectively.

### 4.2    Principle of the Hybrid Approach

In order to solve the incompatibility problem and to emulate the target network with a sufficiently high fidelity, an innovative hybrid virtualization approach is derived. More preciously, two different visualization technologies are applied simultaneously, which are QEMU-KVM technology for x86 nodes emulation and QEMU-System for non-x86 nodes emulation. Both of them work in the full system emulation mode.

QEMU-KVM is a fork of QEMU supporting using KVM acceleration when the target architecture is the same as the host architecture. Although the fork has already been merged into the QEMU upstream, the term QEMU-KVM is still adopted here to refer the technology to emulate X86 nodes. To use KVM, just pass – enable-kvm to

QEMU. QEMU-System technology implements full platform virtualization, including one or several processors and various peripherals. It runs without a host kernel driver and yet gives acceptable performance. It uses dynamic translation to native code for reasonable speed. Therefore, it can be used to emulate non-x86 nodes in the target network. For example, one can use the executable qemu-system-sparc to simulate the sparc architected machines. Figure 1 illustrates the principle of the hybrid virtualization approach.

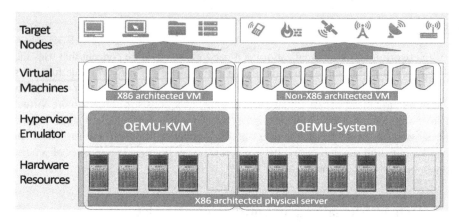

**Fig. 1.** The principle of the hybrid virtualization approach.

### 4.3   Practical Implementation

The hybrid virtualization approach is practically implemented in an innovative cloud-based network emulation system, which introduces currently prevalent cloud computing and related ICT technologies including resource virtualization, NFV, SDN, traffic control and flow steering to the network emulation domain, so to provide users Network Emulation as a Service (NEaaS). The emulation system can be deployed on either public or private cloud to satisfy diverse user needs. The network emulation principle is to utilize the VMs created and allocated by the cloud platform to imitate network nodes. Emulating network links relies on using the virtual network links in the cloud platform. To emulate network topology is to dynamically control and adjust the virtual network links between VMs in a fast enough manner to satisfy the emulation needs. The architecture of the cloud-based network emulation system is designed and presented in Fig. 2, which is divided into four layers, namely, resource virtualization, cloud computing, emulation core, and emulation interface layers. The key points to deploy the proposed hybrid virtualization approach in the aforementioned cloud-based network emulation system, is to modify the lowest two layers, namely resource virtualization layer and cloud computing layer.

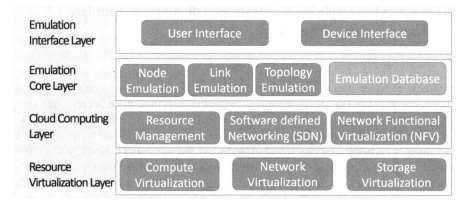

**Fig. 2.** Architecture of the cloud-based emulation platform.

In the resource virtualization layer, the xml file adopted by Libvirt to depict and to create heterogeneous VMs should be established at first. Then, for some heterogeneous architectures, OS Kernel and Initrd files should be loaded externally when creating VM instances. In the cloud computing layer, Legacy Openstack lacks the ability to manage heterogeneous VMs. Therefore, the first step of the implementation is to create heterogeneous VM images which can be recognized by Openstack. Then, front end configuration should be carried out, including updating the supported architecture list of each compute node in the MySQL database. In the meanwhile, Openstack API i.e., nova-metadata is called to configure the hardware information of heterogeneous VM images. At last, the back-end to manage the heterogeneous VMs is also implemented, with the logical demonstrated in Fig. 3, where os_kernel and os_initrd are the parameters passing addresses to the aforementioned xml files.

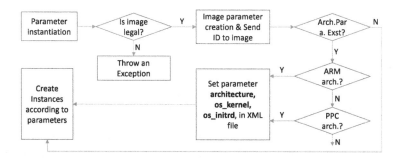

**Fig. 3.** Implementation schematic diagram.

## 5   Case Study: Applying the Hybrid Approach to Emulate a Space-Ground Integrated Network

### 5.1   Emulation Scenarios and Assumptions

A SGIN is considered as the target network to be emulated. The topology of a typical SGIN is presented in Fig. 4. As is shown, in the space section, three Sparc-architected GEO satellite nodes connected with each other forms a ring as the backbone network. Each of the GEO satellite node covers a wide area of earth surface, and connects with a large number of heterogeneous terminal nodes on the ground. To simplify the emulation scenario, this case study only concerns three ground terminal nodes (each with a different architecture) for each GEO node, namely one ARM, one PPC, and one x86 terminal node. In practice, there might be thousand or tens of thousands terminal nodes served by each single GEO satellite. Besides, a gateway station node providing access to other ground networks is connected with one of the GEO satellites; it is assumed to be x86 architecture based. The emulated SGIN network is built in the cloud-based emulation system, with applying the proposed hybrid virtualization. Particularly, the x86 nodes are emulated by QEMU-KVM technology, while the sparc nodes, ARM nodes and PPC nodes utilize QEMU-System technology.

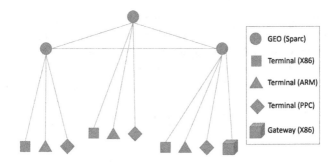

**Fig. 4.** Schematic diagram.

### 5.2   Functional Verification and Performance Evaluation

Functional verifications are carried out as fellows. Firstly, connectivity between two arbitrarily chosen nodes is tested by using ping tool. The results show no difference between scenarios with and without applying the proposed hybrid scheme. Secondly, real-time video streaming function is also verified in the emulated network. Two heterogonous nodes are randomly chosen, and on which VLC server and client are deployed, respectively. A H.264 encoded video file is streamed from the server to the client, and again, no big difference is observed between scenarios with and without using the proposed approach.

Comparative performance evaluations are carried on for the scenarios with and without using the proposed approach. The VM profiles for the two different scenarios are given in Table 1. Both computation and networking performance are considered in this case study. On one hand, for computation performance evaluation, Unix Bench is adopted. Table 2 presents the testing results. On the other hand, for the networking performance evaluation, the iperf and ping tools are utilized to measure TCP and UDP bandwidth, packet loss, transmission delay and Jitter. The results are given in Table 3.

**Table 1.** The VM profiles.

| CPU | AMD R1700X | RAM | 64 GB DDR4 2400 |
|---|---|---|---|
| Network Card | Intel 1000 Mbps * 4 | Storage | SSD 480 GB |
| QEMU | Version 2.5.0 | Libvirt | Version 1.3.1 |
| OpenStack | Mitaka | Unixbench | Version 5.1.3 |
| OS | Ubuntu 14.04 LTS | Kernel | 4.4.0-96-generic |

**Table 2.** Computational performance.

| Metric | Arch. | | | | | | | | | | | |
|---|---|---|---|---|---|---|---|---|---|---|---|---|
| | Qemu-kvm | | | | Qemu-system | | | | | | | |
| | X86 | | | | ARM | | | | PowerPC | | | |
| Ncpu | 1 | 2 | 3 | 4 | 1 | 2 | 3 | 4 | 1 | 2 | 3 | 4 |
| TCP BW (G/s) | 47.3 | 49.1 | 51.3 | 52.6 | 1.4 | 1.4 | 1.5 | 1.5 | 1.9 | 1.9 | 2.0 | 2.1 |
| UDP BW (G/s) | 0.81 | 0.81 | 0.80 | 0.81 | 0.2 | 0.2 | 0.2 | 0.2 | 0.2 | 0.1 | 0.1 | 0.1 |
| Packet loss (%) | 0.46 | 0.75 | 0.61 | 0.44 | 0 | 0 | 0 | 0 | 0 | 0 | 0 | 0 |
| Time delay (ms) | 0.36 | 0.29 | 0.38 | 0.28 | 0.7 | 0.7 | 0.7 | 0.7 | 0.8 | 0.8 | 0.9 | 0.8 |
| Jitter | 0.09 | 0.05 | 0.10 | 0.07 | 0.2 | 0.2 | 0.2 | 0.2 | 0.3 | 0.2 | 0.2 | 0.2 |

## 5.3  Results Discussion

According to the above experimental results, it is no surprised that the heterogeneous VMs emulated by the QEMU-System technology are with much lower computation and networking performance, attributed to the fact that the software-based instruction translation is much slower than the hardware-assistant virtualization. Considering the fact that only part of the target nodes will be emulated by QEMU-System technology, and the fact that QEMU-KVM starts to support virtualize more architectures, the cost of the proposed hybrid approach is still affordable.

**Table 3.** Network performance.

| Metric | Arch. | | | | | | | | | | | |
| | Qemu-kvm | | | | Qemu-system | | | | | | | |
| | X86 | | | | ARM | | | | PowerPC | | | |
| | 1 | 2 | 3 | 4 | 1 | 2 | 3 | 4 | 1 | 2 | 3 | 4 |
|---|---|---|---|---|---|---|---|---|---|---|---|---|
| Ncpu | 1 | 2 | 3 | 4 | 1 | 2 | 3 | 4 | 1 | 2 | 3 | 4 |
| String manipulation | 204.4 | 200.6 | 583.8 | 745.2 | 166.7 | 169.6 | 170.8 | 168.8 | 181.9 | 193.4 | 219.0 | 215.2 |
| Floating point processing | 31.2 | 249.2 | 221.9 | 193.1 | 55.8 | 67.1 | 73.6 | 82.4 | 24.1 | 25.1 | 23.2 | 24.8 |
| R/W | 34.8 | 34.1 | 88.6 | 110.2 | 11.5 | 13.3 | 13.9 | 14.4 | 55.9 | 56.4 | 56.8 | 56.7 |
| File replication (small) | 976.7 | 980.1 | 1567.9 | 1492.6 | 75.6 | 72.2 | 54.6 | 78.4 | 40.7 | 36.1 | 37.6 | 31.6 |
| File replication (middle) | 1601.6 | 1585.5 | 2526.1 | 2380.7 | 61.1 | 118.4 | 87.0 | 87.8 | 117.0 | 65.0 | 87.3 | 52.8 |
| File replication (large) | 3249.5 | 3229.4 | 5718.6 | 5511.6 | 169.6 | 137.6 | 172.2 | 194.5 | 151.2 | 147.5 | 143.0 | 138.3 |
| Process communication | 1049.3 | 1036.3 | 3043.2 | 3886.9 | 98.9 | 97.8 | 96.5 | 101.6 | 33.8 | 36.3 | 35.3 | 25.1 |
| Process context switching | 730.9 | 617.0 | 1889.6 | 2398.3 | 19.2 | 21.0 | 21.3 | 22.4 | 22.2 | 21.8 | 22.4 | 23.7 |
| Process creation | 137.3 | 138.3 | 342.1 | 497.1 | 56.8 | 61.9 | 68.5 | 59.7 | 57.8 | 62.4 | 64.3 | 67.8 |
| Single script operation | 93.2 | 90.1 | 240.0 | 298.6 | 33.0 | 33.2 | 33.2 | 32.4 | 100.5 | 102.1 | 113.1 | 15.2 |
| Multi script operation | 86.3 | 74.8 | 220.9 | 271.2 | 28.7 | 28.0 | 26.5 | 24.6 | 90.5 | 91.6 | 90.2 | 93.1 |
| System call | 578.1 | 569.5 | 1585.9 | 3023.5 | 255.7 | 256.9 | 252.4 | 255.4 | 31.5 | 32.3 | 23.2 | 31.8 |
| Score | 300.9 | 343.9 | 769.4 | 876.9 | 59.4 | 64.3 | 63.8 | 64.8 | 57.2 | 60.1 | 59.0 | 63.1 |

# 6 Conclusion

Network emulation is regarded as the most promising network testing method attributed to its low cost and high fidelity features. Most existing network emulators rely on x86 based VMs or containers to imitate network nodes of heterogeneous architectures, such as ARM, PowerPC, Sparc, MIPS, etc., which could bring incompatibility problems to the protocol and application software running on the real nodes. This paper focused on solving this incompatibility problem and further improving emulation fidelity. To that end, the paper designed an innovative hybrid virtualization approach to emulate the heterogeneous nodes in target networks. The proposed hybrid approach was also implemented in a practical cloud-based network emulation platform. A Case study on emulating an SGIN illustrated that the hybrid virtualization approach effectively and efficiently eliminates the incompatibility problem in practical scenarios with an affordable performance degradation.

The planned work for the next step mainly focus on the cost of VMs. Compared to the currently booming light-weighted container technologies, such as Docker, VM's cost is still too high, which promotes the authors to investigate replacement of the VMs by containers for more efficient network emulations.

**Acknowledgement.** This work is partially supported by the Science and Technology on Communication Networks Laboratory (Grant No. XX17641X011-03), the 54th Research Institute of China Electronics Technology Group Corporation, and the National Natural Science Foundation of China (Grant No. 61402085 & No. 61872051).

# References

1. Ahrenholz, J., Danilov, C., Henderson, T.R., Kim, J.H.: CORE: a real-time network emulator. In: 2008 IEEE Military Communications Conference, MILCOM 2008, San Diego, CA, USA, pp. 1–7 (2008)
2. Soles, L.R., Reichherzer, T., Snider, D.H.: Creating a cost-effective air-to-ground network simulation environment. In: SoutheastCon 2015, Fort Lauderdale, FL, USA, pp. 1–5 (2015)
3. Ramneek, T., Choi, W., Seok, W.: Wireless network mobility emulation over wired testbeds: a review. In: 2015 17th International Conference on Advanced Communication Technology (ICACT), Seoul, South Korea (2015)
4. Maier, S., Grau, A., Weinschrott, H., Rothermel, K.: Scalable network emulation: a comparison of virtual routing and virtual machines. In: 2007 12th IEEE Symposium on Computers and Communications, Las Vegas, NV, USA, pp. 395–402 (2007)
5. Mehta, D., Jaeger, J., Faden, A., Hebert, K., Yazdani, N., Yao, H.: A scalable architecture for emulating Dynamic Resource Allocation in wireless networks. In: 2009 IEEE Military Communications Conference, MILCOM 2009, Boston, MA, USA, pp. 1–7 (2009)
6. Balasubramanian, D., Dubey, A., Otte, W.R., Emfinger, W., Kumar, P.S., Karsai, G.: A rapid testing framework for a mobile cloud. In: 2014 25th IEEE International Symposium on Rapid System Prototyping, New Delhi, India, pp. 128–134 (2014)
7. To, M.A., Cano, M.: DOCKEMU – a network emulation tool. In: 2015 IEEE 29th International Conference on Advanced Information Networking and Applications Workshops, Gwanju, South Korea, pp. 593–598 (2015)

# A New MCMC Particle Filter Resampling Algorithm Based on Minimizing Sampling Variance

Juan Tian$^{(\boxtimes)}$ and Dan Li

Jiangsu Province Key Laboratory of Intelligent Industry Control Technology,
Xuzhou University of Technology, Xuzhou 221018, China
tiandidoxzit@sina.com

**Abstract.** In order to solve the problem of particle divergence caused by deviation of sample distribution before and after resampling, a new Markov Chain Monte Carlo (MCMC) resampling algorithm based on minimizing sampling variance is proposed. First, MCMC transfer in which Particle Swarm Optimization (PSO) is possessed as the transfer kernel to construct Markov Chain is applied to the impoverished sample to combat sample degeneracy as well as sample impoverishment. Second, the algorithm takes the weighted variance as the cost function to measure the difference between the weighted particle discrete distribution before and after the resampling process, and optimizes the previous MCMC resampling by the minimum sampling variance criterion. Finally Experiment result shows that the algorithm can overcome particle impoverishment and realize the identical distribution of particles before and after resampling.

**Keywords:** PF-resampling · MCMC · PSO · Minimizing sampling variance

## 1 Introduction

To combat the inevitable weight degeneracy caused by SIS [1,2], SIR [3,4]viewed as a combination between SIS and resampling procedure was proposed. The basic idea of re-sampling is to copy the large weight particles according to the size of the weight values, and replace the small weight particles with the offspring of the large weight particles. The essence is to redistribute the weights so that more particles get sampling opportunities, which is based on sacrificing the diversity

This work is partly supported by the Natural Science Foundation of Jiangsu Province of China (No. BK20161165), the applied fundamental research Foundation of Xuzhou of China (No. KC17072), Xuzhou Science and Technology Plan Project (No. KC18011), and Ministry of Housing and Urban-Rural Development Science and Technology Planning Project (NO.2016-R2-060).

H. Song et al. (Eds.): SIMUtools 2019, LNICST 295, pp. 238–247, 2019.
https://doi.org/10.1007/978-3-030-32216-8_23

of samples. This means that, after numerous times of iterations, a large number of particles in the sample are only concentrated on a few particular points in the state space. This phenomenon is called "sample impoverishment" [3,4], mainly because of the strong correlation between particles, which is not sufficient to describe the randomness of the target posterior distribution. In order to obtain the sufficient sample diversity, balance between the proposal distribution and the real target posterior distribution should be paid more attention. In another word, more particles have the chance to be resampled as they are assigned weights that cannot be ignored. The related research on maintaining diversity of samples is described explicitly in reference [5], which is not overstated here. It is worth mentioning that a new MCMC resampling strategy was employed in [5], where PSO considered as transition kernels of MCMC had been applied to each particles so that all particles, theoretically, could be adjusted to the high likelihood areas in state-space instead of merely multiplying particles with high weights. In the former case, the basic idea of MCMC resampling algorithm is, after a sufficient burn-in time, constructing a Markov Chain reaching a stationary distribution, which is approximate to target posterior distribution. However, the resampled particles can not guarantee the unbiased estimation of the real target posterior. To combat sample impoverishment, a large number of resampling strategies including PSO-MCMC mentioned above, hybird resampling [6–8], but not limited to, adopt resampling from alternative sampling sets rather than original sets. Eventually, particle filters have to suffer from side effects of these biased re-sampling strategies. This means that, SIR sample impoverishment as well as deviation of sample distribution before and after resampling will both affect the estimation accuracy of samples to real target posterior, which could eventually lead to the divergence of the filter. Therefore, it is an unavoidable problem in sample estimation to verify the deviation of samples after resampling, which is also the research content of this paper. In this paper, a new MCMC resampling strategy in terms of satisfying Minimum sampling variance (MSV) is proposed, in which the former PSO-MCMC resampling algorithm has been optimized. The MSV criterion [9] theoretically guarantee any sample subset can reach the minimum sampling variance on condition that the resampling process satisfies the optimal weight condition and the specific sample number. Identical distribution of samples after and before resampling acquired by MSV means that resampling will not drift estimation to real target posterior resulting from reducing the loss of information in the resampling process. As a tool for tracking the state of a dynamic system modeled by Bayesian Network, PF also could be employed as an estimator to predict network traffic [14,15].

## 2   Identical Distribution of Resampling and Relative Evaluation Methods

Compared with parametric filters, the advantage of PF is regarded to be complete approximation to target posterior distribution particularly in non-linear and non-gaussian state models. Therefore resampled particles are expected to approximate the original distribution as much as possible. That is to say, distribution of resampled particles should be similar to the original distribution so long as no other new observation considered, which is called identical distribution attribute of resampling. However, in fact, dissimilarity of particle distribution after and before resampling is inevitable whether in theory or in engineering practice. Accordingly, it is necessary to set up a reliable evaluation system for the deviation or even variation of posterior distribution resulted from resampling. In this system, the extent of deviation after resampling should be evaluated, that is, how much resampling is competent to keep the original distribution. Therefore, the identical distribution attribute is expected to be the basic principle of designing a resampling algorithm, and it is also required that the particles before and after resampling are suppose to meet it. Specifically, we introduce and compare several common metrics such as kullback-Leibler divergence [10] (K-L divergence), kolmogorov-smirnov statistic (K-S statistic), and MSV [9] to measure differences between two probability distributions in the same state space.

## 2.1   Kullback-Leibler Divergence

Relative entropy, also called Kullback-Leibler divergence (K-L divergence), is a measurement to describe the difference between two probability distributions such as $P(x)$ and $Q(x)$. Then the relative entropy of $P(x)$ and $Q(x)$ is as follows.

$$D(P||Q) = \sum (P(x)\log(P(x)/Q(x))) \tag{1}$$

In Eq. 1, $P(x)$ and $Q(x)$ represent the probabilistic distributions before and after resampling respectively, and $D(P||Q)$ provides a measure of the extent of distribution difference caused by resampling. The larger the K-L divergence between $P(x)$ and $Q(x)$ is, the lower the similarity is.

## 2.2   Kolmogorov-Smirnov Test

Kolmogorov-smirnov test (K-S test), also refered to kolmogorov-smirnov statistic, is a non-parametric probability distribution test that is used to measure whether a sample conforms to a certain probability distribution or to compare whether the two probability distributions are identical. In our case, the Kolmogorov-Smirnov test provides a distance between the empirical distribution functions of two samples such as $P(x)$ and $Q(x)$ that represent the posterior distribution after and before resampling respectively. The empirical distribution function $F_n$ for the observation $X_i$ is defined as Eq. 2.

$$F_x(x) = \frac{1}{n} \sum_{i-1}^{n} I_{|-\infty,x|}(X_i) \tag{2}$$

Where $I_{|-\infty,x|}(X_i)$ is the indicator function, equal to 1 if $X_i \leq x$ and equal to 0 otherwise. The K-S statistic for a given cumulative distribution function $F(x)$ is described as Eq. 3.

$$D_n = \sup_{x} |F_p(x) - F_q(x)| \tag{3}$$

where sup is the supremum of the set of distances, $F_p(x)$ and $F_q(x)$ represent empirical distribution functions of posterior distributions $P(x)$ and $Q(x)$ respectively and $D_n$ measures the discrepancy of these posterior distributions caused by resampling. According to Glivenko–Cantelli theorem, if $P(x)$ and $Q(x)$ are identical, then $D_n$ converges to 0 almost surely in the limit when $n$ goes to infinity.

### 2.3   Minimum Sampling Variance

The number of particle resampling must be an integer, that is $N_t^{(m)}$. Assuming that resampling is unbiased, the equation $E(N_t^{(m)}) = Nw_t^{(m)}$ should be satisfied. Obviously, there is a difference between the number of resampling and its expected value. Furthermore, a higher-order moment has a better ability to describe distribution difference than a first-order moment. Accordingly, we define the sampling variance is equal to the square difference mean between the number of times of the particle resampling and its definition is shown in Eq. 4.

$$SV = \frac{1}{M} \sum_{m=1}^{M} (N_t^m - Nw_t^{(m)})^2 \qquad (4)$$

SV in Eq. 4, considered as a cost function, can provide an effective measurement method for testing the discrepancy between weighted particle discrete distribution before and after resampling.

The smaller the value of SV in Eq. 4 is, the better the identical distribution attribute of the resampling algorithm is. If and only if these two distributions are exactly the same, the value of KL distance, K-S test and sampling variance are zero. Therefore, the SV, KL and K-S test are consistent in terms of describing the discrepancy of posterior distribution. Apart from that, SV has the advantages in less computation time.

## 3   A New MCMC Resampling Strategy Optimized by MSV

In order to minimize the sampling variance in Eq. 4, that is, to minimize the distribution differences to the maximum extent, the weight of the resampled particles should be set to equivalent as shown in Eq. 5.

$$\tilde{w}_t^{(n)} = \frac{1}{N} \qquad (5)$$

However, this condition, describing in Eq. 5, is only satisfied in the traditional resampling method instead of the combined resampling algorithm. In this paper, We quote the constraints of the optimal resampling algorithm as the optimal weight conditions from related reference [9]. Under this condition, the essence of resampling problem is equal to determine the sampling times of each particle.

This means that, if the optimal weight condition, defined in Eq. 5, is satisfied, Eq. 4 can provide the minimum sampling variance.

To combat the deviation of posterior distribution resulted from a certain resampling algorithm, we put forward a new resampling strategy, named MCMC(PSO)-MSV, that the MSV is employed to optimize the previous MCMC resampling strategy mentioned in [5].

The MCMC(PSO)-MSV mainly involves two processes. In the first stage, PSO considered as the transition kernel of MCMC is applied to each particle in order to move particles to the high likelihood area in state-space. Afterward, to reduce information loss prompted by the previous MCMC resampling, MSV should be adopted. For sample set $\{x_k^i\}_{i=1,\cdots,N}$, if the condition, $N_{eff} \le N_{th}$, is satisfied, then the MCMC(PSO)-MSV resampling algorithm will be applied. Specifically, the implementation of the algorithm is illustrated as follows.

**Step1:** sample set $\{x_k^i\}_{i=1,\cdots,N}$ adjusted by PSO.

- searching and determining $P_{gbest}$, the largest weight of particles, as well as $P_{gbest}^i$, the maximum of weights among its iteration history respectively,

$$P_{gbest} = F \max(\{\mu_{k,n}^i\}_{i=0,\cdots,N-M-1})$$

$$P_{gbest}^i = F \max(\{\mu_{k,n}^i\}_{n=0,\cdots,J})$$

Where $\mu_{k,n}^i$ is the weight of $X_{k,n}^i$.
- For each particle $X_{k,n}^i$, updating its moving rate $V_{k,n}^i$ and state,

$$V_{k,n+1}^i = V_{k,n}^i + \varphi_1(P_{pbest}^i - X_{k,n}^i) + \varphi_2(P_{gbest} - X_{k,n}^i)$$

$$\hat{X}_{k,n+1}^i = X_{k,n}^i + V_{k,n+1}^i$$

in which $\varphi_1$ and $\varphi_2$ are random numbers subordinating Gauss distribution, and output of this process is a new set: $\{\hat{X}_{k,n+1}^i\}_{i=0,\cdots,N-M-1}^{PSO}$.

**Step2:** Metroplis-Hastings sampling (M-H sampling).

$$\alpha = \frac{P(\hat{X}_{k,n+1}^i | z_{1:k}) q(X_{k,n}^i; \hat{X}_{k,n+1}^i)}{P(X_{k,n+1}^i | z_{1:k}) q(\hat{X}_{k,n}^i; X_{k,n+1}^i)}$$

Where we generate a random number $\rho$, $\rho \sim u(0,1)$.

if $\rho \le \min(1, \alpha)$, then accept M-H sampling $X_{k,n+1}^i = \hat{X}_{k,n+1}^i$.
Else, then refuse M-H sampling $X_{k,n+1}^i = X_{k,n}^i$.

**Step3:** Judging convergence condition.

if $P_{gbest} \le \varepsilon$, then stop MCMC (PSO) process and move to next stage.

**Step4:** Each particle is resampled $MaxInteger(Nw_t^{(m)})$ times, and the weight residuals, named $\hat{w}_t^{(m)}$, and number of particles produced in this process, named $T$, are represented respectively as follows.

$$\hat{w}_t^{(m)} = w_t^{(m)} - MaxInteger(Nw_t^{(m)})/N$$

$$T = \sum_{m=1}^{M} MaxInteger(Nw_t^{(m)})$$

Where Operator $MaxInteger(\cdot)$ provides the maximum integer.

**Step5:** For particular particles with relative larger value of $\hat{w}_t^{(m)}$ in top $N - T$ area, they will be resampled one more time. Specifically, we select $N - T$ elements with largest weight residuals from weight set $\{w\wedge_t^{(m)}\}_{m=1}^{M}$, recorded as $MaxElement_{N-T}[\{\hat{w}_t^{(m)}\}_{m=1}^{M}]$, Where Operator $MaxElement_S[S]$ returns the largest element of set $S$.

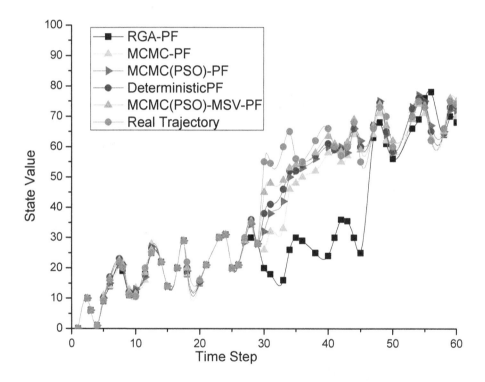

**Fig. 1.** True state VS filter estimation.

## 4  Experiment

In this paper, several resampling algorithms are numerically simulated with the classical model in [11], including an unbiased resampling, called deterministic resampling [12] (Deterministic-PF), genetic algorithm after residual resampling (RGA-PF) [13], MCMC resampling applying Metropolis-Hastings sampling (MCMC-PF), resampling with PSO as MCMC transaction kernel [5]

(MCMC(PSO)-PF), the new resampling strategy that MCMC(PSO)-PF optimized by minimum sampling variance (MCMC(PSO)-MSV-PF). Comparison will be carried out among these 5 resampling strategies in terms of estimation accuracy, sampling variance as well as RMSE. System model and observation model are presented as follows.

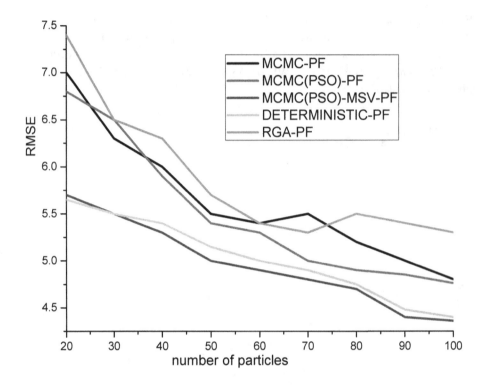

**Fig. 2.** Sampling variances of these 5 resampling strategies.

$$x_k = c_1 \cdot x_{k-1} + c_2 \cdot \frac{x_{k-1}}{1 + x_{k-1}^2} + c_3 \cdot \cos(1.2(k-1)) + \omega_k \qquad (6)$$

$$y_k = \frac{x_k^2}{20} + \upsilon_k \qquad (7)$$

in which $x_k$ and $y_k$ represent system state and observation at $t$ time respectively; $c_1 = 1$, $c_2 = 12$, $c_3 = 7$; $\omega_k$ and $\nu_k$ are state noise and observation noise from distribution $\omega_k \sim N(0, \sigma_\omega^2)$, $\nu_k \sim N(0, \sigma_v^2)$ ($\sigma_\omega = \sigma_v = 2$) respectively.

In this case the number of Monte Carlo simulation, $T$, is 60, $N_s$ means number of particles, $N_s = 200$ and $x_0$ represent initial state value, $x_0 = 0$. The state transition probability, $p(x_{t+1}|x_t)$, is applied as the proposal distribution to realize the state prediction.

In the experiment, the identical condition of sample detection is chosen as the resampling condition, that is, if $Neff \leq N_s/3$, PF enters resampling process.

Comparison of True states of targets and estimating states is shown as Fig. 1, while Fig. 2 demonstrates sampling variances of these 5 resampling strategies. SV is chosen as the unbiased evaluation strategy after resampling on account of its less expensive computing. RMSE (average mean square error) is also presented in Fig. 3 in which the number of particles has changed from 20 to 100. These figures indicate that, if the resampling algorithm satisfies the unbiased or asymptotically unbiased conditions, different resampling algorithms will obtain approximate estimation accuracy, especially when $N_0$ is greater than 90. However, the resampling algorithms with better identical distribution attributes, such as Deterministic-PF and MCMC(PSO)-MSV-PF, have obvious advantages in RMSE evaluation only when $N_0 \leq 45$. This means that whether the sample deviates from the original distribution after resampling has a greater influence on the estimation accuracy of the small sample set.

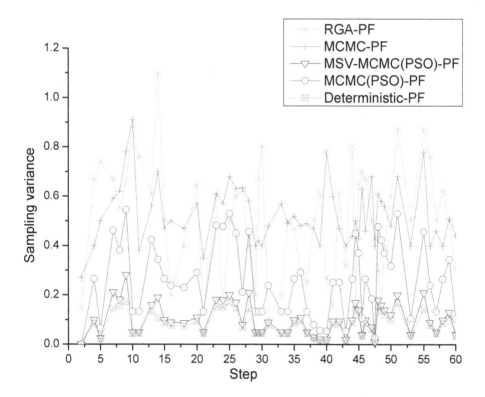

**Fig. 3.** RMSE comparison of these 5 algorithms as the number of particles changes from 20 to 100.

Besides, resampling algorithms such as MCMC-PF, RGA-PF and MCMC(PSO)-PF, are biased, which their sampling variances are shown in Fig. 2 respectively. Accordingly their RMSEs are obviously worse than that of decisive resampling and MSV-PF, as shown in the Fig. 3. This also shows the validity of sampling variance as unbiased evaluation of resampling algorithm, this means that whether the resampling algorithm is unbiased will affect the estimation accuracy. However, some resampling algorithms satisfy the unbiased condition, shown in formula 5, at the expense of sample diversity.

In Fig. 1, When the target state occurred a strong jump at $t = 30$, the Deterministic-PF diverged stemming from the loss of the diversity of samples which resulted in the filter losing ability to estimate the target posterior. While the MCMC(PSO)-MSV-PF is able to achieve a trade-off between preserving the diversity of samples and the identical distribution attributes. Consequently even coming accross the strong jump of target state, the MCMC(PSO)-MSV-PF can also estimate a posterior distribution close to the real target.

## 5    Conclusions

In order to solve the problem of particle divergence caused by particles deviation after resampling, in this paper, a new MCMC resampling strategy based on satisfying Minimum sampling variance (MSV) is proposed, in which the former PSO-MCMC resampling algorithm has been optimized. Identical distribution of samples after and before resampling acquired by MSV means that resampling will not drift estimation to real target posterior thanks to reducing the loss of information in the resampling procedure. The simulation result shows that the MCMC(PSO)-MSV-PF is superior to its counterparts in terms of preserving the diversity of samples and acquiring the identical distribution attributes before and after resampling.

## References

1. Li, T., et al.: Fighting sample degeneracy and impoverishment in particle filters: a review of intelligent approaches. Expert Syst. Appl. **41**(8), 3944–3954 (2014)
2. Punithakumar, K., Mcdonald, M., Kirubarajan, T.: Spline filter for multidimensional nonlinear/non-Gaussian Bayesian tracking. In: Spie Defense and Security Symposium International Society for Optics and Photonics (2008). https://doi.org/10.1117/12.779223
3. Duong, P.L.T., Raghavan, N.: Heuristic Kalman optimized particle filter for remaining useful life prediction of lithium-ion battery. Microelectron. Reliab. **81**, 232–243 (2018)
4. Arulampalam, M.S., Maskell, S., Gordon, N., et al.: A tutorial on particle filters for online Nonlinear/non-Gaussian Bayesian tracking. IEEE Trans. Signal Process. **50**(2), 174–188 (2002)
5. Septier, F., Peters, G.W.: Langevin and Hamiltonian based sequential MCMC for efficient Bayesian filtering in High-dimensional spaces. IEEE J. Sel. Top. Signal Process. **10**(2), 312–327 (2016)
6. Das, S.K., Mazumdar, C.: Priori-sensitive resampling particle filter for dynamic state estimation of UUVs. In: International Workshop on Systems, pp. 384–389. IEEE (2013)
7. Choe, G., Wang, T., Liu, F., et al.: Particle filter with spline resampling and global transition model. IET Comput. Vis. **9**(2), 184–197 (2014)

8. Lv, T.Z., Zhao, C.X., Zhang, H.F.: An improved FastSLAM algorithm based on revised genetic resampling and SR-UPF. Int. J. Autom. Comput. **5**, 1–10 (2014)
9. Tian-Cheng, L.I., Villarrubia, G., Sun, S.D., et al.: Resampling methods for particle filtering: identical distribution, a new method, and comparable study. Front. Inf. Technol. Electron. Eng. **16**(11), 969–984 (2015)
10. Kullback, S., Leibler, R.A.: On information and sufficiency. Ann. Math. Stat. **22**(1), 79–86 (1951)
11. Cheng, S., Zhang, J.: Fission bootstrap particle filtering. Chin. J. Electron. **36**, 500–504 (2008)
12. Li, T., Sattar, T.P., Sun, S.: Deterministic resampling: unbiased sampling to avoid sample impoverishment in particle filters. Sig. Process. **92**(7), 1637–1645 (2012)
13. Wang, W., Tan, Q.K., Chen, J., et al.: Particle filter based on improved genetic algorithm resampling. In: Guidance, Navigation and Control Conference, pp. 346–350. IEEE (2017)
14. Jiang, E., Wang, W., Shi, L., Song, H.: A compressive sensing-based approach to end-to-end network traffic reconstruction. IEEE Trans. Netw. Sci. Eng. (2018). https://doi.org/10.1109/TNSE.2018.2877597
15. Jiang, D., Huo, L., Lv, Z., et al.: A joint multi-criteria utility-based network selection approach for vehicle-to-infrastructure networking. IEEE Trans. Intell. Transp. Syst. 1–15 (2018)

# ExploreBP: A Simulation Tool for Mobile Browser Energy Optimization

Jin Zhang[1], Xin Wei[1], Zhen Liu[1], Fangxin Liu[1], Tao Li[1,3], Tingjuan Lu[2], and Xiaoli Gong[1,3(✉)]

[1] Nankai University, Tianjin, China
gongxiaoli@nankai.edu.cn
[2] IT Department, Chinese PLA 117 Hospital, Hangzhou, China
[3] State Key Laboratory of Computer Architecture,
Institute of Computing Technology, Chinese Academy of Sciences,
Beijing, China

**Abstract.** The browser is one of the most commonly used applications. Users tend to pursue a good user experience and care more about the performance of the browser, while ignoring the power consumption of the browser. This paper proposes a method to reduce the energy consumption of web browsing. In order to better quantify the user experience, this paper uses the first screen load time as the evaluation metric of user experience. First, according to the relationship between the network speed and the first screen load time, find the most suitable primary frequency at a specific network speed, and define the point as the balance point. When the primary frequency is greater than the primary frequency corresponding to the balance point, the first screen load time will almost never change. The balance points of different web pages are also different. Then adjust the CPU frequency according to the balance point of the webpage and the network speed, which can reduce the browser energy consumption and reduce the impact on the user experience. At the same time, this paper proposes a simulation tool ExploreBP, which is used to simulate the working state of the network speed and different web pages to find the optimal energy consumption configuration.

**Keywords:** Mobile web browser · Energy optimization · Web page loading · CPU frequency modulation

This work is partially supported by the National Key Research and Development Program of China (2018YFB1003405), the National Natural Science Foundation of China (61702286), the Natural Science Foundation of Tianjin, China (18JCY-BJC15600), Open Projects of State Key Laboratory of Computer Architecture, Institute of Computing Technology, Chinese Academy of Sciences (CARCH201604), and Special Funding for Excellent Enterprise Technology Correspondent of Tianjin, China (17JCTPJC49500).

H. Song et al. (Eds.): SIMUtools 2019, LNICST 295, pp. 248–257, 2019.
https://doi.org/10.1007/978-3-030-32216-8_24

# 1   Introduction

Smartphones are widely used, but energy consumption has always been a bottleneck in their development. Limited by the screen, processing power and battery life of the mobile phone [14], although the battery energy density has increased by 3 times [2] in the same period, the endurance of most smartphones has not been significantly improved.

The browser is the main application of smartphones. The survey shows that more than 73% of smartphone users frequently browse the web. Google even launched Chromium OS [5], which is an operating system that fully uses web applications. So the browser should be the goal of optimization.

The browser is a very complex application and various studies work on improve its performance. It has been proved that the main bottleneck in the performance of mobile browsers is CPU computing power rather than networking [12]. Wang et al. [15] found that the resource loading contributed the most to network latency. Nevertheless, the research on energy consumption is relatively insufficient. Bui et al. [1] proposed an application-assisted scheduling technique to reduce energy consumption. However, the scheduling technique only adjusts the thread based on the drawing speed, which doesn't fully consider the characteristics of the different processes of the browser and the load of the webpage.

The optimization of energy consumption for smart mobile devices should be combined with the user experience. The browser interacts directly with the user. We propose the first screen load time to measure the user experience. The first screen load time is the time consumed by the browser to display the first screen page. That is, the time when all the elements in the area that the user can see are loaded. As for the user experience, when the first screen area is full of content, the user can see the main content of the web page.

The first screen load time is closely related to CPU processing speed, network speed, and web content [13]. Previous studies have shown that both network and frequency may become bottlenecks. The network speed affects the download speed of the browser process, and the frequency affects the processing speed of the rendering process. Any slowdown can result in increased page load time, affecting the user experience and increasing power consumption.

This paper proposes a method for cooperative modulation of network speed and frequency. For a specific web page, we find the most suitable frequency for the current network speed and web page based on the first screen load time, which is called the balance point. Adjusting the frequency according to the balance point can reduce the energy consumption of web page loading and reduce the impact on the user experience, which can avoid the waste of resource and save energy.

In order to solve this problem, this paper proposes a simulation method. For different web pages, the optimal match of network speed and frequency is found by detecting the first screen load time under different network speeds and CPU frequencies automatically. So the goal of energy optimization can be find. According to this method, a simulation tool ExploreBP is designed to find the optimal match. And the top 50 sites in Alexa Top Sites Chinese have been tested.

The contributions of this paper are as follows: 1. We propose a method for energy optimization by adjusting the main frequency based on the network; 2. We design a simulation tool to test the network speed, main frequency and open speed; 3. The tool is implemented and experiments on 50 websites are performed.

## 2 Background

### 2.1 Chromium Browser Architecture

The architecture of Chromium browser [6] is shown in Fig. 1 [1]. Chromium includes a browser process and multiple rendering processes. The rendering process is executed on the Blink [4] rendering engine, which is parsed and executed by the JavaScript engine. The browser process maintains a network stack that receives web resources from the server and shares these web resources between all rendering processes. Every process in Chromium has multiple threads. Processes and threads are executed asynchronously. The browser process and the rendering process communicate with each other through the pipeline, and exchange data through the shared memory.

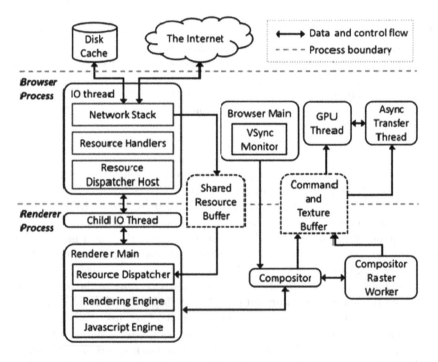

**Fig. 1.** Architecture of the Chromium browser

First, the browser process puts the received webpage resources into the shared resource buffer, and then the rendering process reads the data from the shared resource buffer to create a graphic layer corresponding to the web page. Because the render process running in the sandbox does not have the privileges of accessing to the GPU directly, the generated graphics data is loaded into the command and structure buffers through the synthesizer thread. The GPU thread processes the graphics data to produce the final web page image.

## 2.2 Webpage Loading Process

The browser loads the webpage [3] as a synchronization process that renders while parsing. As shown in Fig. 2 [3], the browser firstly parses the HTML file to build the DOM tree, and then parses the CSS file to build the rendering tree. After the rendering tree is built, the browser begins to lay out the rendering tree, which is to assign each node a geometric information that should appear on the display. The final step is to draw the nodes onto the screen.

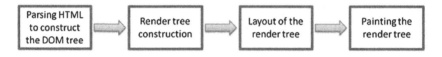

**Fig. 2.** The process of loading a webpage by a browser

## 3  Experiment

The architecture of the browser and the loading process of the webpage are very complicated. It is impossible to express the whole process of webpage loading by formula, so it is impossible to find the CPU frequency that best matches the current network speed by formula derivation. We simulate the process of loading webpage and find the CPU frequency that best suits the specific network speed and the specific website based on the experimental measured data.

In order to ensure the accuracy of the experimental results, it is necessary to eliminate the interference factors in the process of loading webpage. Network speed and caching are the two main factors. We will clear the cache and disable the cache. Since the actual network speed may be unstable at each load, we use Web Page Replay [8] store the web page locally to simulate different network speeds and CPUFreq [16] to set different CPU frequencies. Then the performance analysis tool Trace-viewer [7] is used to record the page load time and the first screen load time.

### 3.1  Experimental Tools

WPR (Web Page Replay) WPR is a tool that enables web page to playback. It is composed of the DNS server and HTTP server running locally. It generally works in two modes: Record mode [13]: WPR acts as a proxy server, sends an HTTP(s) request to the server, and then records all the responses of the server. Eventually HTTP(s) requests, responses, web content, and network delays are stored in the local HTTP Archive. Replay mode [9]: WPR starts the simulated DNS server and web server locally on the device. The communication between the browser, the DNS server and HTTP server is hijacked by WPR. The browser can only communicate with WPR.

Trace-Viewer is a data analysis tool on the Chrome browser. It records the data of the browser and visualizes the recorded data. It saves the result as a JSON file.

CPUFreq is a lightweight CPU tuning tool on Linux that can select a core and adjust the frequency. It supports multiple CPU modes and can be set manually, but the range of modulation is limited.

### 3.2  Measurement

There are many measurement for webpage loading. The most common is the page load time. In the experiment, the first screen load time is used, beacuse it better reflects the user experience.

The page load time is the time spends by the browser to initiate a request until the page is fully loaded. All web resources are added to the DOM tree, and all images, scripts, links, etc. have been loaded.

The first screen load time is defined as the time taken by the browser to display the first screen page. This means that all elements in the visible area of the user are loaded.

### 3.3  Dataset and Variable Settings

**Dataset.** The top 50 websites selected from Alexa Top Sites Chinese [10] are used as test sites.

**Network Speed Setting.** We tested the first screen load time on six network types. In order to simulate the download speed and network delay in the real scene, the network speeds and delays of these six network types are set to the values in Table 1 [11].

**Frequency Setting.** We adjust the CPU frequency to 40%, 60%, 80%, and 100% of the initial frequency.

### 3.4  Experiment Environment

Host: The CPU's single core turbo frequency is 4.0 GHz, and the full core turbo frequency is 3.8 GHz. The memory size is 8 G. Virtual machine: The system is Ubuntu17.10, quad-core processor, and the memory is 1 G.

**Table 1.** Network speed and delay for six network types.

| Network type | Download speed | Latency |
|---|---|---|
| Regular 2G | 250 Kb/s | 300 ms |
| Good 2G | 450 Kb/s | 150 ms |
| Regular 3G | 750 Kb/s | 100 ms |
| Good 3G | 1 MB/s | 40 ms |
| DSL | 3 MB/s | 2 ms |
| Regular 4G | 4 MB/s | 20 ms |

### 3.5 Experimental Procedure

Turn off all applications not related to this experiment to prevent them from affecting the results of the experiment.

- *Step 1.* Set the CPU frequency using the CPUFreq tool. During the experiment, all four cores of the processor are set to the same frequency.
- *Step 2.* Open the Chromium browser and clear your browser's cache to ensure that the experimental results are not affected by the browser cache.
- *Step 3.* Open Web Page Replay and set it to Record mode. Then one of the URLs in the dataset will be entered to the browser. Web Page Replay will receive the HTTP request from the browser and send the request to the network. After the HTTP server responses, it sends the response to the browser, and then automatically saves all the records as archive.wpr file.
- *Step 4.* Set Web Page Replay to Replay mode, sp that the browser can only communicate with Web Page Replay at this time. Web Page Replay will reply to the browser's request using the saved archive.wpr.
- *Step 5.* Use Web Page Replay to set the download speed and delay of objects on the critical path. Objects not on the critical path will not affect the first screen load time and page load time.
- *Step 6.* Enter the test URL to the browser. Web Page Replay sends saved web pages to the browser. At this time, the Trace-Viewer is opened to obtain the first screen load time and the page load time, and the test results are recorded.

## 4 Analysis of Results

Limited by space, the experimental results only show the top three websites in the 50 websites, which are Baidu, Tencent and Taobao. These websites have large traffic and different characteristics, which are very representative.

### 4.1 Relationship Between Load Time and Frequency at a Fixed Network Speed

Figures 3 and 4 show the relationship between the load time and frequency of the three websites under DSL (Digital Subscriber Line) conditions. We can see that as the CPU frequency increases, the load time of the three websites is decreasing. When the frequency increases to a certain value, the page load time and the first screen load time almost don't change. It can be speculated that as the CPU frequency increases further, the load time will keep at a certain value.

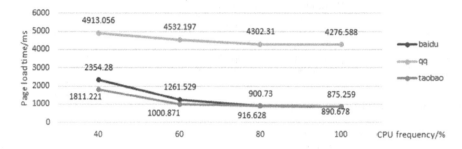

**Fig. 3.** Page load time of three websites varies with CPU frequency under DSL

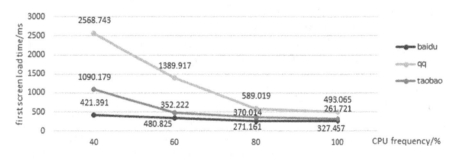

**Fig. 4.** First screen load time of three websites varies with CPU frequency under DSL

According to the architecture of the browser, the browser process firstly downloads the web resources from the network and puts it into the shared resource buffer. Then multiple rendering processes start processing the resources in the shared resource buffer. The increase of the CPU frequency means the increase of the processing speed of multiple rendering processes. So the processing speed is faster than the speed of loading the web resources into the shared resource buffer, and the resources in the shared resource buffer are rapidly reduced, causing multiple rendering processes to wait for the resource to load. From the above experimental results, we draw the following conclusions.

**Conclusion 1:** At a specific network speed, there is a threshold for CPU frequency. When the CPU frequency exceeds this threshold, the first screen load time and the page load time will not change.

## 4.2 Relationship Between Load Time and Network Speed at a Fixed Frequency

As shown in Fig. 5, we set the CPU frequency to 40% of the initial frequency, and measure the page load time of Baidu and the first screen load time of Tencent under six network speed conditions in Table 1. It can be seen that when the network speed is lower than 1MB/s, the page load time and the first screen load time change drastically with the network speed. When exceeding this value, the two load times change slowly.

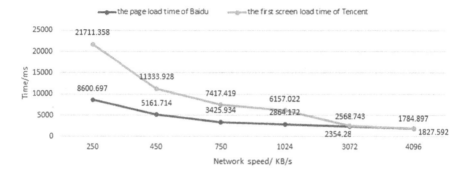

**Fig. 5.** Load time varies with network speed under 40% CPU frequency

This is due to the lower CPU frequency, which results in a lower processing speed for multiple rendering processes. When the network speed is higher than a value, the web resources loaded by the browser process into the shared buffer are always not processed in time. The shared buffer may overflow, while the browser process and the rendering process are busy. The browser may crash.

**Conclusion 2:** When the CPU frequency is low, there is also a threshold for the network speed. When the network speed exceeds this threshold, the page load time and the first screen load time decrease slowly.

## 4.3 Relationship Between Load Time and Frequency Under Three Network

From Fig. 6 we can see that whether Baidu or Taobao, with the increase of CPU frequency, the first screen load time and the page load time decrease gradually. And the faster the network speed, the greater the change in load time.

According to the browser kernel principle, when the network speed is low, the browser process downloads web resources from the network at a slow speed. So the resources placed in the shared buffer will reduce. Multiple rendering processes preempt the web resources in the buffer, and many rendering processes will be idle. From this we draw a conclusion.

**Conclusion 3:** At low network speeds, the first screen load time and the page load time are not sensitive to CPU frequency changes.

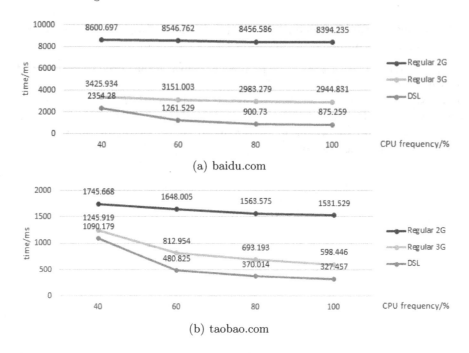

**Fig. 6.** Load time varies with CPU frequency under three network speeds

## 4.4   Network Speed and Frequency Coordinated Modulation Scheme

According to the conclusions 1, 2 and 3, we know that the page load time and the first screen load time are affected by the CPU processing speed and the network speed. The ideal state is that the high network speed corresponds to a high processor speed, and the low network speed corresponds to a low processor speed. That is, the CPU frequency matches the network speed.

According to the experimental results and the principle of browser loading webpage, we propose a browser energy optimization scheme: For a specific webpage, the most suitable frequency for the current network speed and webpage will be find based on the page load time. And this frequency is named as the balance point. The CPU frequency will be adjusted according to the balance point.

Based on this scheme, we design ExploreBP, a simulation tool for finding the balance point. We tested the top 50 sites in Alexa Top Sites Chinese and got the balance point under six network conditions. In theory, all websites will have such a balance point, and this method can be used to test more websites. When the browser loads the web page, the CPU frequency will be adjusted based on the balance point to reduce energy consumption while the browser is working.

# 5   Conclusion

This paper proposes a scheme for CPU main frequency modulation. For a specific web page, the most suitable frequency for the current network speed will be find based on the first screen load time. According to this method, a simulation tool ExploreBP for finding the optimal matching between network speed and CPU frequency is designed and experiments on the top 50 sites in Alexa Top Sites Chinese have been performed. In order to better quantify the user experience, this paper proposes using the first screen load time as an evaluation metric of the user experience.

The energy optimization scheme proposed in this paper is mainly for browsers, and in the future it can be extended from browsers to all applications that use client/server mode.

# References

1. Bui, D.H., Liu, Y., Kim, H., Shin, I., Zhao, F.: Rethinking energy-performance trade-off in mobile web page loading. In: International Conference on Mobile Computing and Networking, pp. 14–26 (2015)
2. Casas, R., Casas, O.: Battery sensing for energy-aware system design. Computer **38**(11), 48–54 (2005)
3. Garsiel, T.: How Browsers Work. http://taligarsiel.com/Projects/howbrowserswork1.htm
4. Google: Blink Rendering Engine. http://www.chromium.org/blink
5. Google: Chromium OS. https://www.chromium.org/chromium-os/
6. Google: Google Chromium. https://www.chromium.org
7. Google: Trace-Viewer. https://github.com/google/trace-viewer
8. Google: Web Page Replay. https://github.com/chromium/web-page-replay
9. Google: Webpagereplaydiagram. https://github.com/chromium/web-page-replay/blob/master/documentation/WebPageReplayDiagram.png
10. Alexa Internet Inc.: Alexa top 50 Sites in China. www.alexa.com/topsites/countries/CN2018--4
11. Kayce Basques, G.: Analyze network performance. https://developers.google.com/web/tools/chrome-devtools/network-performance/
12. Nejati, J., Balasubramanian, A.: An in-depth study of mobile browser performance. In: International Conference on World Wide Web, pp. 1305–1315 (2016)
13. Sakamoto, K.: Time to First Meaningful Paint. https://docs.google.com/document/d/1BR94tJdZLsin5poeet0XoTW60M0SjvOJQttKT-JK8HI/view?hl=zh-cn
14. Tawalbeh, M., Eardley, A., Tawalbeh, L.: Studying the energy consumption in mobile devices. Procedia Comput. Sci. **94**, 183–189 (2016)
15. Wang, Z., Lin, F.X., Zhong, L., Chishtie, M.: Why are web browsers slow on smartphones? In: Proceedings of the 12th Workshop on Mobile Computing Systems and Applications, pp. 91–96. ACM (2011)
16. Willkommen, H.: CPUFreq. https://www.brode.de/cpufreq

# Design and Simulation of a Deterministic Quantum Secure Direct Communication and Authentication Protocol Based on Three-Particle Asymmetric Entangled State

Yanyan Hou[1,2(✉)], Jian Li[2,3], Qinghui Liu[4], Hengji Li[3], Xinjie Lv[1], Xuhong Li[1,2], and Yu Zhang[5]

[1] College of Information Science and Engineering, Zaozhuang University, Zaozhuang 277160, Shandong, China
hyy@uzz.edu.cn
[2] Center for Quantum Information Research, Zaozhuang University, Zaozhuang 277160, Shandong, China
[3] School of Computer Science, Beijing University of Posts and Telecommuncations, Beijing 100876, China
[4] Network Center, Zaozhuang University, Zaozhuang 277160, Shandong, China
[5] China Mobile Group Shandong Company Limited Zaozhuang Branch, Zaozhuang 277160, China

**Abstract.** In order to improve eavesdropping detection efficiency, we propose a quantum secure direct communication and authentication protocol based on three-particle asymmetric entangled state and design an efficient quantum circuit for implementing the protocol. This protocol has two modes, in message mode, a qubit is used to transmit two bits classical information based on a Bell state, in control mode, three-particle asymmetric entangled state is inserted into the particle flow for detecting eavesdropper. Eavesdropping detection efficiency is got by calculating the relationship between the amount of information and detection probability, if eavesdroppers want to obtain all information, detection probability is 63%, the analysis results indicate that this proposal is more secure than other quantum secure direct communication protocol.

**Keywords:** Quantum secure direct communication · Three-particle asymmetric entangled state · Quantum circuit

## 1 Introduction

Quantum secure direct communication (QSDC) and authentication is a remarkable branch of quantum information. Different from the quantum key distribution (QKD) whose object is to create a common random key between two remote authorized users, the object of QSDC is to transmit a secret message directly without

This work is supported by the National Natural Science Foundation of China (Grant No. U1636106, No. 61472048).

H. Song et al. (Eds.): SIMUtools 2019, LNICST 295, pp. 258–266, 2019.
https://doi.org/10.1007/978-3-030-32216-8_25

producing quantum keys. When eavesdroppers are detected, QSDC doesn't discard the transmitted information, so communication security is more important for QSDC, some techniques are used to make eavesdroppers get only some random values instead of reading useful information.

Bostrm and Felbinger presented a famous QSDC protocol called original Ping-pong protocol (OPP) [1], in which Bell states were used to quantum secure direct communication and detecting eavesdroppers, but researchers have found many vulnerabilities of Ping-pong protocol, for example, Ping-pong protocol cannot resist the "man-in-middle" attack. Considering two qubits with four dimensional space, Gao et al. improved eavesdropping detection efficiency of Ping-pong protocol by using four Bell states which is called MPP [2], Li et al. proposed an QSDC protocol based on extended three-particle GHZ State (EPP) [3], which is with higher eavesdropping detection efficiency. Subsequently, many researchers begin to research QSDC and authentication, Quan et al. proposed a one-way quantum secure direct communication protocol based on single photon [4], Zawadzki et al. proposed that increasing the security of Ping-pong protocol by using many mutually unbiased bases [5], some researchers researched how to ensure QSDC and authentication security under the noise environment [6–8]. Recently, more and more researchers begin to study how to improve quantum direct communication efficiency [9–14], some researchers proposed using W state for QSDC and authentication [15–20], subsequently, Multi-particle entangled state were used to QSDC protocol [21–24], Zhang et al. proposed a QSDC protocol using semi quantum for improving eavesdropping detection efficiency [25], but researchers have found many vulnerabilities in Ping-pong protocol. In this paper, we not only propose a quantum security detection protocol based on three-particle asymmetric entangled state (TAPP), but also design an efficient quantum circuit for implementing the protocol. If the eavesdropper gets the full information, the detection rate of the original Ping-pong protocol is 50%, the detection rate of proposed protocol is 63%. Compared with other QSDC protocols, this protocol is with higher eavesdropping detection efficiency.

## 2   The Process of the TAPP Protocol

In original Ping-pong protocol, a Bell state was used to transmit information and detect eavesdroppers and a qubit transmitted one bit classical information, so information transmission efficiency was not high. In proposed protocol, Alice transmits information to Bob by dense coding, in which a qubit transmits two bits classical information. The steps are as follows.

(1)   Suppose that Alice wants to transmit an information sequence $x^N = (x_1, \ldots, x_N)$ to Bob, where $x_i \in \{0, 1\}, i = 1, 2, \ldots, N$. Bob prepares $N$ pairs Bell state particles $|\psi^+\rangle_{AB} = (|01\rangle_{AB} + |10\rangle_{AB})/\sqrt{2}$, all the first particles in Bell states are stored as $A$ sequence (travel particles), all the remaining particles in Bell states are transmitted to Alice as $B$ sequence (home particles).

(2)   In order to prevent Eve from eavesdropping and ensure the information communication security, this paper proposes two communication modes, message

mode and control mode. Bob prepares a large number of asymmetric three-particle entangled states $|\varphi\rangle = \frac{1}{2}|011\rangle + \frac{1}{\sqrt{2}}|100\rangle + \frac{1}{2}|101\rangle$ as detection particles, which are inserted into $A$ sequence to form $C$ sequence, only Bob knows the position of detection particles. Compared with $B$ sequence, $C$ sequence contains $3cN/(1-c)$ particles which are used to detect eavesdroppers, here, $c$ is the probability of the control mode.

(3) Bob sends $C$ sequence to Alice and notifies her the location of detection particles. If Alice receives detection particles, she switches to control mode and measures detection particles based on the three-particle unsymmetrical entanglement state. Alice sends the detection result through the public channel to Bob, if eavesdroppers are found, Alice interrupts this communication and transmits the information again, otherwise Bob notifies Alice no eavesdroppers and continues to transmit information.

(4) If Alice receives travel particles, she switches to message mode. According to transmitted information, Alice performs one of four coding operation $\{\hat{I}, \hat{\sigma}_z, \hat{\sigma}_x, i\hat{\sigma}_y\}$ on the travel particles.

$$
\begin{aligned}
\hat{I}^{(A)}|\psi^+\rangle &= |\psi^+\rangle = \frac{1}{\sqrt{2}}(|01\rangle + |10\rangle) \\
\hat{\sigma}_z^{(A)}|\psi^+\rangle &= |\psi^-\rangle = \frac{1}{\sqrt{2}}(|01\rangle - |10\rangle) \\
\hat{\sigma}_x^{(A)}|\psi^+\rangle &= |\phi^+\rangle = \frac{1}{\sqrt{2}}(|00\rangle + |11\rangle) \\
i\hat{\sigma}_y^{(A)}|\psi^+\rangle &= |\phi^-\rangle = \frac{1}{\sqrt{2}}(|00\rangle - |11\rangle)
\end{aligned}
\tag{1}
$$

The superscript $(A)$ refers to the operation of the travel particle in the Bell states. After encoding, each travel particle can indicate two bits classical information, $|\psi^+\rangle$ indicates 00, $|\psi^-\rangle$ indicates 01, $|\phi^+\rangle$ indicates 10, $|\phi^-\rangle$ indicates 11.

(5) Alice sends encoded travel particles back to Bob, Bob measures the encoded travel particles and home particles based on Bell states and gets $|\psi^+\rangle$, $|\psi^-\rangle$, $|\phi^+\rangle$ or $|\phi^-\rangle$, respectively correspond to classical bits 00, 01, 10 or 11, Bob extracts information and completes quantum secure direct communication.

## 3  Quantum Circuit Simulation of TAPP Protocol

The circuit simulation is instructive for the realization of QSDC protocol and authentication, quantum circuit is essential to the practical realization of the protocol in experiment. In this section, we construct an efficient quantum circuit for TAPP protocol simulation. Firstly, TAPP protocol is decomposed unitary transformations, secondly, the effective quantum circuit is designed through the orderly arrangement of the quantum gates. The quantum circuit implementation is shown in Fig. 1.

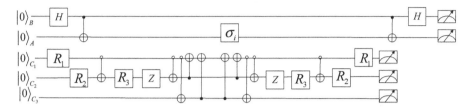

**Fig. 1.** Quantum circuit for implementation TAPP protocol

In Fig. 1, particle $A$ and $B$ are information carrier, firstly, $|0\rangle_B$ and $|0\rangle_A$ are sent to $H$ gate and Bell state $|\psi^+\rangle_{AB} = (|01\rangle_{AB} + |10\rangle_{AB})/\sqrt{2}$ is got, then the sender Alice implements quantum information coding through a unitary operation $\sigma_i \in \{\hat{I}, \hat{\sigma}_z, \hat{\sigma}_x, i\hat{\sigma}_y\}$, the receiver Bob realizes quantum measurement through $H$ gate and gets the transmitted information. Three-particle asymmetric entangled state $|\varphi\rangle = \frac{1}{2}|011\rangle + \frac{1}{\sqrt{2}}|100\rangle + \frac{1}{2}|101\rangle$ is got by making unitary transformation for $|0\rangle_{c_1}, |0\rangle_{c_2}, |0\rangle_{c_3}$, Alice measures the received three particle entangled state, so as to realize eavesdropping detection. $R_1$, $R_2$, and $R_3$ are respectively.

$$R_1 = R_y(\frac{\pi}{2}), R_2 = R_y(\frac{\pi}{4}), R_3 = R_y(-\frac{\pi}{4}) \tag{2}$$

$$R_y(\theta) = \begin{bmatrix} \cos\frac{\theta}{2} & -\sin\frac{\theta}{2} \\ \sin\frac{\theta}{2} & \cos\frac{\theta}{2} \end{bmatrix} \tag{3}$$

## 4   The Security Analysis and Simulation of TAPP

In control mode, Alice inserts asymmetric three-particle entangled state $|\varphi\rangle = \frac{1}{2}|011\rangle + \frac{1}{\sqrt{2}}|100\rangle + \frac{1}{2}|101\rangle$ into $A$ sequence for eavesdropping detection. After Eve's attack operation $\hat{E}$, the particle state $|0\rangle$ is transformed into $|\varphi_0'\rangle$, the particle state $|1\rangle$ is transformed into $|\varphi_1'\rangle$.

$$|\varphi_0'\rangle = \hat{E}|0x\rangle = \alpha|0x_0\rangle + \beta|1x_1\rangle, |\varphi_1'\rangle = \hat{E}|1y\rangle = m|0y_0\rangle + n|1y_1\rangle \tag{4}$$

$|x\rangle$ and $|y\rangle$ are determined by $\hat{E}$ uniquely, $|\alpha|^2 + |\beta|^2 = 1, |m|^2 + |m|^2 = 1$. After Eve attacks on the asymmetric three-particle entangled state, the state of the compose system is.

$$|\varphi\rangle_{Eve}= E \otimes E \otimes E[\frac{1}{2}|011\rangle + \frac{1}{\sqrt{2}}|100\rangle + \frac{1}{2}|101\rangle]$$

$$= \frac{1}{2}[\alpha|0x_0\rangle + \beta|1x_1\rangle] \otimes [m|0y_0\rangle + n|1y_1\rangle] \otimes [m|0y_0\rangle + n|1y_1\rangle]$$

$$+ \frac{1}{\sqrt{2}}[m|0y_0\rangle + n|1y_1\rangle] \otimes [\alpha|0x_0\rangle + \beta|1x_1\rangle] \otimes [\alpha|0x_0\rangle + \beta|1x_1\rangle]$$

$$+ \frac{1}{2}[m|0y_0\rangle + n|1y_1\rangle] \otimes [\alpha|0x_0\rangle + \beta|1x_1\rangle] \otimes [m|0y_0\rangle + n|1y_1\rangle]$$

$$= \frac{1}{2}[\alpha m^2|0x_00y_00y_0\rangle + \beta m^2|1x_10y_00y_0\rangle + \alpha nm|0x_01y_10y_0\rangle + \beta nm|1x_11y_10y_0\rangle \quad (5)$$

$$+ \alpha mn|0x_00y_01y_1\rangle + \beta m^2|1x_10y_01y_1\rangle + \alpha n^2|0x_01y_11y_1\rangle + \beta n^2|1x_11y_11y_1\rangle]$$

$$+ \frac{1}{\sqrt{2}}[\alpha^2 m|0y_00x_00x_0\rangle + \alpha^2 n|1y_10x_00x_0\rangle + \alpha\beta m|0y_01x_10x_0\rangle + \alpha\beta n|1y_11x_10x_0\rangle$$

$$+ \alpha\beta m|0y_00x_01x_1\rangle + \alpha\beta n|1y_10x_01x_1\rangle + \beta^2 m|0y_01x_11x_1\rangle + \beta^2 n|1y_11x_11x_1\rangle]$$

$$+ \frac{1}{2}[m^2\alpha|0y_00x_00y_0\rangle + \alpha nm|1y_10x_00y_0\rangle + m^2\beta|0y_01x_10y_0\rangle + m^2\beta|1y_11x_10y_0\rangle$$

$$+ \alpha mn|0y_00x_01y_1\rangle + \alpha^2 n|1y_10x_01y_1\rangle + mn\beta|0y_01x_11y_1\rangle + \beta^2 n|1y_11x_11x_1\rangle]$$

The probability that Alice not detect eavesdroppers is.

$$p(|\varphi\rangle) = \frac{1}{4}[|\beta m^2|^2 + |\alpha n^2|^2 + |\beta mn|^2] + \frac{1}{2}[|\alpha^2 n|^2 + $$
$$|\alpha\beta n|^2 + |\beta^2 m|^2] + \frac{1}{4}[|mn\alpha|^2 + |\alpha n^2|^2 + |\beta mn|^2] \quad (6)$$

So the lower bound of the detection probability is.

$$d_l = 1 - p(|\varphi\rangle) = 1 - \frac{1}{4}[|\beta m^2|^2 + |\alpha n^2|^2 + |\beta mn|^2]$$
$$+ \frac{1}{2}[|\alpha^2 n|^2 + |\alpha\beta n|^2 + |\beta^2 m|^2] + \frac{1}{4}[|mn\alpha|^2 + |\alpha n^2|^2 + |\beta mn|^2] \quad (7)$$

Assuming $|\alpha|^2 = a, |\beta|^2 = b, |m|^2 = s, |n|^2 = t$, $a, b, s, t$ are positive real numbers and $a + b = s + t = 1$, so $d_l$ is.

$$d_l = 1 - p(|\varphi\rangle)$$
$$= 1 - [\frac{1}{4}(1-a)(1-t) + \frac{1}{2}at^2 + \frac{1}{2}at + \frac{1}{4}t(1-t) + \frac{1}{2}(1-a)^2(1-t)] \quad (8)$$

When Alice sends $|0\rangle$ to Bob, the amount of information which be eavesdropped by Eve is.

$$I_0 = -a \log_2 a - (1 - a) \log_2 (1 - a) = H(a) \tag{9}$$

When Alice sends $|1\rangle$ to Bob, the amount of information which be eavesdropped by Eve is.

$$I_1 = -t \log_2 t - (1 - t) \log_2 (1 - t) = H(t) \tag{10}$$

Eve can eavesdrop the total amount of information is.

$$I = \frac{1}{2}(I_0 + I_1) = \frac{1}{2}(H(a) + H(t)) \tag{11}$$

Considering the equal probability of sending $|0\rangle$ and $|1\rangle$ in the general system, that is $a = t$, we can get.

$$d_l = -2a^2 + \frac{7}{4}a + \frac{1}{4} \tag{12}$$

After simple mathematical calculation, we can get $a$.

$$a = \frac{7}{16} + \frac{1}{16}\sqrt{81 - 128d_l} \tag{13}$$

Under the condition $d_l \leq 0.63$, the relationship between the information function $I$ and detection probability $d_l$ is as follows.

$$I(d_l) = H(\frac{7}{16} + \frac{1}{16}\sqrt{81 - 128d_l}) \tag{14}$$

Under the condition $d_l > 0.63$, eavesdropped information is too large to meet the requirements of quantum secure communication, the situation can be ignored. In order to realize the security detection analysis, TAPP is compared with OPP, MPP and EPP protocol, Fig. 2 shows the relationship between the information function $I$ and detection probability $d_l$ for OPP, MPP, EPP and TAPP protocol.

Comparing with OPP, MPP and EPP, we can see that if Eve eavesdrops the same amount of information ($I$), he must face greater eavesdropping detection probability in TAPP, this also shows that TAPP is more secure than OPP, MPP and EPP.

In order to get this advantage in TAPP, Alice needs to send $2cN/(1 - c)$ particles more than OPP, $cN/(1 - c)$ particles more than MPP, in other words, Bob gets better security at the cost of sending more particles. If Eve wants to get all information ($I = 1$) of Alice, $d_l$ is 0.63 in TAPP, $d_l$ is 0.5 in OPP and MPP, $d_l$ is 0.58 in EPP, so detection probability of TAPP is higher than that of OPP, MPP and EPP.

When the probability of control mode is $c$, the probability of message mode is $r = 1 - c$. Assuming Bob sends the first particle in message mode, the probability of successful eavesdropping is $1 - c$; assuming Bob sends the first particle in control

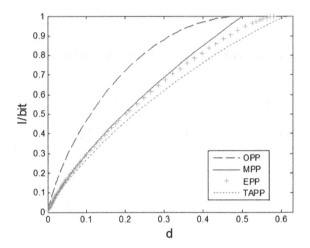

**Fig. 2.** The comparison of the three detection results

mode and the second particle in message mode, the probability of successful eaves-dropping is $c\,(1 - d)\,(1 - c)$. Similarly, the probability of successful eavesdropping by Eve can be obtained in each case. If Eve is not detected, the probability of successful eavesdropping is.

$$
\begin{aligned}
s(c,d) &= (1 - c) + c(1 - d)(1 - c) + c^2(1 - d)^2(1 - c) + \ldots \\
&= (1 - c)/[1 - c(1 - d)]
\end{aligned}
\tag{15}
$$

After $n$ successful eavesdropping, Eve can get $2nI(d)$ bits information, this probability is $s^n$, the probability for successful eavesdropping $I = 2nI(d)$ bit information is.

$$
s(I,c,d) = s(c,d)^{I/2I(d)} = ((1 - c)/(1 - c(1 - d)))^{I/2I(d)}
\tag{16}
$$

When $c = 0.5$ and $I(d) = H(\frac{7}{16} + \frac{1}{16}\sqrt{81 - 128d})$, we get eavesdropping success probability $s$ as a function of the information $I$. Figure 3 shows eavesdropping success probability as a function of the maximal eavesdropped information $I$ for different detection probabilities $d$.

In Fig. 3, When $I \to \infty$, $s \to 0$ is got, Eve only gets part of right information but does not even know which part, so the TAPP protocol can be thought as asymptotically secure. If desired, the security can arbitrarily be improved by increasing the control parameter $c$ at the cost of decreasing information transmission rate.

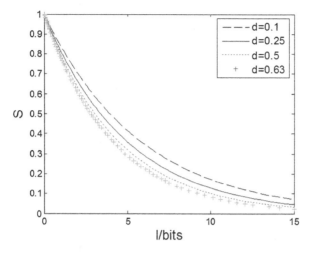

**Fig. 3.** Eavesdropping success probability as a function of the maximal eavesdropped information $I$, plotted for different detection probabilities $d$

## 5  Conclusions and Future Work

In this paper, a new quantum security direct communication protocol TAPP is proposed based on Ping-pong protocol. Two bits classical information can be transmitted by the Bell state and the three-particle asymmetric entangled state is used to realize quantum secure direct communication. By calculating the relationship between the eavesdropped information and detection probability, we find that the TAPP protocol is with higher eavesdropping detection efficiency compared with the OPP, MPP and EPP. The detection efficiency of TAPP can meet the security requirements of quantum direct communication, but the improvement of detection efficiency is at the cost of decreasing information transmission rate. This protocol is mainly theoretical research and not considering noise and Dos attack, besides, the practical application needs considering the quantum state storage, which needs to be researched in the future work.

## References

1. Bostrom, K., Felbinger, T.: Deterministic secure direct communication using entanglement. Phys. Rev. Lett **89**(18), 187902 (2002)
2. Gao, F., Guo, F.Z., Wen, Q.Y., et al.: Comparing the efficiencies of different detect strategies in the ping-pong protocol. Sci. China **51**(12), 1853–1860 (2008)
3. Li, J., Guo, X.J., Song, D.J., et al.: Improved quantum "Ping-Pong" protocol based on extended three-particle GHz state. China Commun. **9**(1), 111–116 (2012)
4. Quan, D.X., Pei, C.X., Liu, D., et al.: One-way deterministic secure quantum communication protocol based on single photons. Acta Physica Sinica **59**(4), 2493–2497 (2010)
5. Zawadzki, P., Puchała, Z., Miszczak, J.A.: Increasing the security of the ping-pong protocol by using many mutually unbiased bases. Quantum Inf. Process. **12**(1), 569–576 (2013)

6. Huang, W., Wen, Q.-Y., Jia, H.-Y., et al.: Fault tolerant quantum secure direct communication with quantum encryption against collective noise. Chin. Phys. B **21**(10), 101–109 (2012)

7. Hu, J.Y., Yu, B., Jing, M.Y., et al.: Experimental quantum secure direct communication with single photons. Light Sci. Appl. **5**(9), e16144 (2016)

8. He, Y.F., Ma, W.P.: Three-party quantum secure direct communication against collective noise. Quantum Inf. Process. **16**(10), 252 (2017)

9. Yang, C.W., Hwang, T.: Improved QSDC Protocol over a collective-dephasing noise channel. Int. J. Theor. Phys. **51**(12), 3941–3950 (2012)

10. Aravinda, S., Banerjee, A., Pathak, A., Srikanth, R., et al.: Orthogonal-state-based cryptography in quantum mechanics and local post-quantum theories. Int. J. Quantum Inf. **12**(07n08), 175–179 (2014)

11. Xu, S.J., Chen, X.B., Wang, L.H., et al.: Two quantum direct communication protocols based on quantum search algorithm. Int. J. Theor. Phys. **54**(7), 2436–2445 (2015)

12. Feng, Z.F., Yang, O.Y., Zhou, L., et al.: Entanglement assisted single-photon W state amplification. Opt. Commun. **340**, 80–85 (2015)

13. Wu, F.Z., Yang, G.J., Wang, H.B., et al.: High-capacity quantum secure direct communication with two-photon six-qubit hyperentangled states. Sci. China (Phys. Mech. Astron.) **60**(12), 120313 (2017)

14. Li, J., Li, N., Li, L.L., Wang, T.: One step quantum key distribution based on EPR entanglement. Sci. Rep. **6**, 28767 (2016)

15. Chang, S.K.: Improved protocols of secure quantum communication using W states. Int. J. Theor. Phys. **52**(6), 1914–1924 (2013)

16. Chia-Wei, T., Tzonelih, H.: Deterministic quantum communication using the symmetric W state. Sci. China (Phys. Mech. Astron.) **56**(10), 1903–1908 (2013)

17. Shukla, C.: Design and analysis of quantum communication protocols. Chem. Res. Toxicol. **15**(7), 972–978 (2015)

18. Toshinai, K., Mondal, M.S., Nakazato, M., et al.: On optimising quantum communication in verifiable quantum computing. J. Bacteriol. **165**(1), 321–323 (2015)

19. Wu, Y., Zhou, J., Gong, X., et al.: Continuous-variable measurement-device-independent multipartite quantum communication. J. Phys. Soc. Jpn. **86**(2), 2325 (2016)

20. Nie, Y.Y., Li, Y.H., Liu, J.C., et al.: Quantum state sharing of an arbitrary three-qubit state by using four sets of W-class states. Opt. Commun. **284**(5), 1457–1460 (2011)

21. Wang, M., Ma, W., Shen, D., et al.: A new controlled quantum secure direct communication protocol based on a four-qubit cluster state. Mod. Phys. Lett. B **28**(24), 1450194 (2014)

22. Li, Y.B., Song, T.T., Huang, W., et al.: Fault-tolerant quantum secure direct communication protocol based on decoherence-free states. Int. J. Theor. Phys. **54**(2), 589–597 (2015)

23. Chang, Y., Zhang, S.B., Yan, L.L.: A bidirectional quantum secure direct communication protocol based on five-particle cluster state. China Phys. Lett. **30**(9), 090301 (2013)

24. Liu, Z., Chen, H., Liu, W.: Cryptanalysis of controlled quantum secure direct communication and authentication protocol based on five-particle cluster state and quantum one-time pad. Int. J. Theor. Phys. **55**(10), 4564–4576 (2016)

25. Zhang, M.H., Li, H.F., Xia, Z.Q., et al.: Semiquantum secure direct communication using EPR pairs. Quantum Inf. Process. **16**(5), 117 (2017)

# A Multi-objective Artificial Flora Optimization Algorithm

Xuehan Wu, Huaizong Shao$^{(\boxtimes)}$, Shafei Wang, and Wenqin Wang

School of Information and Communication Engineering, University of Electronic
Science and Technology of China, Chengdu, People's Republic of China
hzshao@uestc.edu.cn

**Abstract.** Most of the practical problems need to consider many aspects at the
same time, multi-objective optimization can be used to deal with this kind of
problems. Swarm intelligence optimization algorithm can use a simple evolutionary step to find the optimal solution. Due to the advantages of swarm
intelligence optimization algorithm, many researchers focus on multi-objective
swarm intelligence optimization algorithms. Artificial flora (AF) optimization
algorithm is a recently proposed swarm intelligence optimization algorithm.
This paper proposes a multi-objective artificial flora (MOAF) optimization
algorithm based on the standard artificial flora (AF) optimization algorithm. The
algorithm uses the four basic elements and three main behavior patterns of the
migration process and adds external document to find the Pareto optimal
solution set. Simulation results show that the proposed algorithm can cover the
true Pareto front with satisfactory convergence compared with the NSGA-II.

**Keywords:** Swarm intelligence · Artificial flora (AF) optimization algorithm ·
Multi-objective optimization

## 1 Introduction

In real life, there are many complex problems that various aspects should be considered
for modeling and programming, such as urban traffic, allocation of resources, capital
budget and so on [1, 2]. To find an optimal solution set for a multi-objective problem
called multi-objective optimization [3]. There are two main methods to deal with multi-
objective optimization problem. One is to weight multiple targets to make it into a
single objective problem. This method is influenced by subjective factors. The other
method is to use Pareto dominance relation to obtain a set of optimal solution, this
method is the more widespread one [4].

Researchers mainly focus on heuristic algorithm in multi-objective optimization
problem at present [5]. The basic theory of swarm intelligence optimization algorithm
is to simulate the communication and cooperation between individuals in the actual
biological group [6]. Artificial flora (AF) optimization algorithm is a recently proposed

This work was supported by National Natural Science Foundation of China under grant 61871092
and 61471103, Sichuan Science and Technology Program under grant 2017JY0262 and
2018JY0546.

H. Song et al. (Eds.): SIMUtools 2019, LNICST 295, pp. 267–277, 2019.
https://doi.org/10.1007/978-3-030-32216-8_26

intelligent optimization algorithm [7]. AF optimization algorithm using the character-istics of the plants migration to update the solutions.

This paper proposes a multi-objective artificial flora (MOAF) optimization algo-rithm based on standard artificial flora optimization algorithm. Algorithm using four basic elements, namely original plant, offspring plant, plant location and propagation distance, and an external document to find the optimal solution set. The external document is used to store non-dominated solution of each iteration. Grid is used in the external document to produce uniform-distributed Pareto fronts and maintain the diversity of solution set [8]. The rest of this paper is organized as follows. Section 2 introduces the multi-objective optimization problem and the related work. MOAF is introduced in Sect. 3. Section 4 uses multi-objective functions to test the efficiency of MOAF algorithm and compare it with NSGA-II. The conclusion is presented in Sect. 5.

## 2   Multi-objective Optimization

Most practical problems require to satisfy multiple objectives which are conflicting with each other at the same time when certain conditions are met. Suppose there are m objective functions, the dimensions of searching space is D. Multi-objective opti-mization problem can be expressed as finding decision variables $\vec{x}^* = [x_1^*, x_2^*, \ldots, x_D^*]^T$ to minimize the function y:

$$
\begin{aligned}
\min \quad & \vec{f}(\vec{x}) = [f_1(\vec{x}), f_2(\vec{x}), \ldots, f_m(\vec{x})]^T \\
s.t. \quad & g_j(\vec{x}) \geq 0 (j = 1, 2, \ldots, p) \\
& h_j(\vec{x}) = 0 (j = 1, 2, \ldots, q)
\end{aligned}
\tag{1}
$$

Where decision variable $x_i (i = 1, 2, \ldots, D)$ satisfy $X_i^{\min} \leq x_i \leq X_i^{\max}$, $\vec{X}^{\min} = [X_1^{\min}, X_2^{\min}, \ldots, X_D^{\min}]^T$ and $\vec{X}^{\max} = [X_1^{\max}, X_2^{\max}, \ldots, X_D^{\max}]^T$ are the lower limit and the upper limit of decision variables respectively. $g_j(\vec{x}) \geq 0 (j = 1, 2, \ldots, p)$ and $h_j(\vec{x}) = 0 (j = 1, 2, \ldots, q)$ are p inequality constraints and q equality constraints. The multi-objective optimization is to find an optimal solution set rather than a unique solution, this paper uses the Pareto dominance relations to find a set of optimal solution, called Pareto optimal set [9]. If and only if component of $\vec{u}$ less than $\vec{v}$:

$$
\forall i \in (1, 2, \ldots, k), u_i \leq v_i \wedge \exists i \in (1, 2, \ldots, k), u_i < v_i
\tag{2}
$$

vector $\vec{u} = (u_1, u_2, \ldots, u_k)$ dominate $\vec{v} = (v_1, v_2, \ldots, v_k)$, recorded as $\vec{u} \prec \vec{v}$. For a certain multi-objective optimization problem, Pareto optimal set $(P^*)$ is defined as follow:

$$
P^* := \{x \in \Omega | \neg \exists x' \in \Omega \text{ and } \vec{f}(x') \prec \vec{f}(x)\}
\tag{3}
$$

Therefore, a Pareto front $(PF^*)$ can be defined as follow:

$$PF^* := \{\vec{u} = \vec{f} = (f_1(x), \ldots, f_m(x)) | x \in P^*\} \tag{4}$$

More and more multi-objective swarm intelligence optimization algorithms have been proposed. In [10], the authors present a non-dominated sorting based multi-objective evolutionary algorithm, called NSGA-II. A dynamic sub-swarms multi-objective particle swarm optimization algorithm is proposed in [11]. In [12], a multi-objective optimization method based on the artificial bee colony, called the MOABC, is presented.

# 3 A Multi-objective Artificial Flora Optimization Algorithm

MOAF optimization algorithm is based on the standard artificial flora (AF) optimization algorithm. The process of finding the optimal survival position is used in this algorithm to find the optimal solution set of problems. original plant, offspring plant, plant location and propagation distance are the four basic elements in MOAF. Evolution behavior, spreading behavior and select behavior are three main behavioral patterns. Every plant location represents to a solution, and fitness of the locations is used to denote the quality of the solution. Firstly, algorithm generate the original plants randomly. Then spread seeds to the positions within the spreading scope randomly, the spreading scope is decided by the propagation distance. Next the fitness of a seed in the position is calculated according to the objective functions, the fitness represents to the solution quality. Finally, roulette is used to decide survival seeds. survival seeds become new original plants. Repeated iteration until termination condition is satisfied. Algorithm adding external documents to store the optimal solutions.

## 3.1 Initialization

All the decision variables of test functions worked in this paper have upper limit $\vec{X}^{\max} = [X_1^{\max}, X_2^{\max}, \ldots, X_D^{\max}]^T$ and lower limit $\vec{X}^{\min} = [X_1^{\min}, X_2^{\min}, \ldots, X_D^{\min}]^T$. At the beginning, algorithm generates N original plants according to the upper and lower limits of the decision variables randomly. Algorithm use i rows and j columns matrix $P_{i,j}$ to represent the locations of original plants, where $i = 1, 2, \ldots, D$ represents dimensionality, $j = 1, 2, \ldots, N$ represents the number of original plants:

$$P_{i,j} = rand(0,1) \cdot (X_i^{\max} - X_i^{\min}) + X_i^{\min} \tag{5}$$

Where $rand(0,1)$ represents the uniformly distributed number in [0, 1].

## 3.2 Evolution Behavior

Original plants spread their offspring within a certain scope with a radius which is propagation distance, new propagation distance imitate the propagation distance of the parent plant and grandparent plant:

$$d_j = d_{1j} \cdot rand(0,1) \cdot c_1 + d_{2j} \cdot rand(0,1) \cdot c_2 \qquad (6)$$

where $c_1$ and $c_2$ denote the learning coefficient, $d_{1j}$ and $d_{2j}$ represent the propagation distance of grandparent plant and parent plant respectively, and rand(0, 1) is the uniformly distributed number in [0, 1]. The parent propagation distance become the new grandparent propagation distance:

$$d'_{1j} = d_{2j} \qquad (7)$$

The standard AF optimization algorithm use the standard deviation between the positions of the original plants and offspring plants as new parent propagation distance:

$$d'_{2j} = \sqrt{\sum_{i=1}^{N} (P_{i,j} - P'_{i,j})^2 / N} \qquad (8)$$

In order to retain the information of the optimal solutions found so far, MOAF optimization algorithm use the plants in the external document. The new parent propagation distance is the difference between the positions of plants in external document $P^*_{i,j}$ and the offspring plants $P'_{i,j}$:

$$d'_{2j} = P^*_{i,j} - P'_{i,j} \qquad (9)$$

### 3.3  Spreading Behavior

Algorithm generates offspring plants according to the original plant locations and the new propagation distance:

$$P'_{i,j \cdot b} = G_{i,j \cdot b} + P_{i,j} \qquad (10)$$

where $b = 1, 2, \ldots, B$, $B$ represents the amount of offspring plants that one original plant can propagate, $P'_{i,j \cdot b}$ denotes the position of offspring plant, $P_{i,j}$ denotes the position of the original plant, $G_{i,j \cdot b}$ represents a random number with the Gaussian distribution with mean 0 and variance $j$. Generate new original plants according to Eq. (5) if there is no offspring plant survives.

### 3.4  Select Behavior

In standard AF algorithm, the survival probability determines whether the offspring plant survived. the survival probability is as follow:

$$p = \left| \sqrt{F(P'_{i,j \cdot b}) / F_{max}} \right| \cdot Q_x^{(j \cdot b - 1)} \qquad (11)$$

Where $Q_x$ is selecting probability ranging between 0 and 1. $F_{max}$ is the fitness of the offspring plant with the highest fitness. $F(P'_{i,j \cdot b})$ is the fitness of $(j \cdot b)$th solution. Calculation formulas of fitness are the functions of the objective problem. In MOAF algorithm, the Pareto dominance relations have been used. the survival probability is defined as follow:

$$p = 0.9 \cdot \frac{\text{domi}(j \cdot b)}{B} + 0.1 \tag{12}$$

Where $\text{domi}(j \cdot b)$ represents the amount of the solutions that dominated by solution $(j \cdot b)$.$B$ represents the amount of offspring plants that one original plant can propagate.

### 3.5 External Document

MOAF adds an external document to store the optimal solutions in the iterations. At the beginning, the external document is empty, any non-dominated solution should be accepted by the external document. Then the new solution generated in the iterations and the solutions in external document were compared one by one. If the solution is dominated by the one in external document, the solution in external document will be deleted from the external document, and the new solution will be added into the external document. If the new solution dominates the one in external document, whether to delete the new one will be decided by roulette selection method. In the iterations, if dominated solution exists in the external document, delete the solution. When the number of solutions in external document is more than a preset document size, the grid is used to delete the external solutions. The number of grid is set artificially at the start of MOAF. Grid must cover all the solutions, if new solutions go beyond the scope of the grid, the grid should be redrawn. Algorithm always deletes the solution in the grid with highest density to guarantee the uniformity of the Pareto front.

## 4   A Multi-objective Artificial Flora Optimization Algorithm

Some simulation results are presented in this section to show the performance of MOAF algorithm. We use 6 benchmark functions to text the convergence of MOAF algorithm, the functions and their bounds are shown in Table 1.

We use convergence and spacing to measure performance. The convergence can use generational distance (GD) to express [13]. GD shows the distance between the elements in the set of approximate solutions found by algorithm and the elements in the Pareto optimal set. GD can be defined as follow:

$$GD = \sqrt{\sum_{i=1}^{n} E_i^2 / n} \tag{13}$$

Where n is the number of elements included in the found approximate solutions set. is the Euclidean distance between the $i$th element in the found approximate solutions set and the nearest element in the Pareto optimal set. The smaller the GD, the closer the

**Table 1.** Benchmark functions

| Functions | Expression formula | Bounds |
|---|---|---|
| ZDT1 | $f_1(x) = x_1$ <br> $f_2(x) = g(x)h(f_1(x), g(x))$ <br> $g(x) = 1 + (9/29) \cdot \sum_{i=2}^{30} x_i$ <br> $h(f_1(x), g(x)) = 1 - \sqrt{f_1(x)/g(x)}$ | $0 \le x_i \le 1$ <br> $1 \le i \le 30$ |
| ZDT2 | $f_1(x) = x_1$ <br> $f_2(x) = g(x)h(f_1(x), g(x))$ <br> $g(x) = 1 + (9/29) \cdot \sum_{i=2}^{30} x_i$ <br> $h(f_1(x), g(x)) = 1 - (f_1(x)/g(x))^2$ | $0 \le x_i \le 1$ <br> $1 \le i \le 30$ |
| ZDT3 | $f_1(x) = x_1$ <br> $f_2(x) = g(x)h(f_1(x), g(x))$ <br> $g(x) = 1 + (9/29) \cdot \sum_{i=2}^{30} x_i$ <br> $h(f_1(x), g(x)) = 1 - \sqrt{\dfrac{f_1(x)}{g(x)}} - (\dfrac{f_1(x)}{g(x)}) \sin(10\pi f_1(x))$ | $0 \le x_i \le 1$ <br> $1 \le i \le 30$ |
| Deb1 | $f_1(x) = x_1$ <br> $f_2(x) = g(x) \cdot h(x)$ <br> $g(x) = 1 + x_2^2$ <br> $h(x) = \begin{cases} 1 - (f_1(x)/g(x))^2, & \textit{if } f_1 \le g \\ 0, & \textit{otherwise} \end{cases}$ | $0 \le x_i \le 1$ <br> $i = 1, 2$ |
| Deb2 | $f_1(x) = x_1$ <br> $f_2(x) = g(x) \cdot h(x)$ <br> $g(x) = 1 + 10 \cdot x_2$ <br> $h(x) = 1 - (f_1(x)/g(x))^2 - (f_1(x)/g(x)) \cdot \sin(12\pi f_1(x))$ | $0 \le x_i \le 1$ <br> $i = 1, 2$ |
| Deb3 | $f_1(x) = 1 - e^{(-4 \cdot x_1)} \cdot \sin^4(10 \cdot \pi \cdot x_1)$ <br> $f_2(x) = g(x) \cdot h(x)$ <br> $g(x) = 1 + x_2^2$ <br> $h(x) = \begin{cases} 1 - (f_1(x)/g(x))^{10}, & \textit{if } f_1 \le g \\ 0, & \textit{otherwise} \end{cases}$ | $0 \le x_i \le 1$ <br> $i = 1, 2$ |

found solutions get to the optimal solutions. $GD = 0$ means that all the found solutions are in the Pareto optimal set.

The distance variance of neighboring elements is used to measure the spacing (SP), it can be defined as [14]:

$$SP = \sqrt{\sum_{i=1}^{n} (\overline{d} - d_i)^2 / (n - 1)} \tag{14}$$

Where $d_i = \min_j(|f_1^i(\overrightarrow{x}) - f_1^j(\overrightarrow{x})| + |f_2^i(\overrightarrow{x}) - f_2^j(\overrightarrow{x})|)$, $i, j = 1, 2, \ldots, n$, $\overline{d}$ is the mean of $d_i$, n is the number of elements included in the found approximate solutions set. $SP = 0$ means that all the elements in approximate Pareto front are equidistantly distribute.

NSGA-II is an effective algorithm and widely applied [15]. We compare the proposed algorithm with NSGA-II algorithm. The simulation results are obtained through 50 runs and both algorithms are iterated 300 times. The default parameters are shown in Table 2.

Table 2. The default parameters in NSGA-II and MOAF algorithm

| Algorithm | Parameter values |
|-----------|------------------|
| NSGA-II | N = 200 |
| MOAF | N = 200, B = 10, c1 = 1, c2 = 2 |

Table 3 shows the generational distance. According to the results in Table 3, MOAF can find a set of Pareto optimal solutions with better convergence compare with NSGA-II. For function ZDT1 and ZDT3, average generational distance of MOAF is 10 times less than the generational distance of NSGA-II. Average generational distance of MOAF reduces two orders of magnitude compared with NSGA-II for function ZDT2. For function Deb1-3, average generational distance of MOAF is smaller than NSGA-II. Table 4 shows the spacing results. For the spacing results, NSGA-II is better than MOAF.

Table 3. Comparison of GD results obtained by NSGA-II and MOAF.

| Functions | Algorithm | Best | Worst | Mean |
|-----------|-----------|------|-------|------|
| ZDT1 | NSGA-II | 0.031441 | 0.090971 | 0.067403 |
|  | MOAF | 0.001348 | 0.002232 | 0.001816 |
| ZDT2 | NSGA-II | 0.045386 | 0.160601 | 0.098721 |
|  | MOAF | 0.000550 | 0.001163 | 0.000817 |
| ZDT3 | NSGA-II | 0.021018 | 0.073688 | 0.041069 |
|  | MOAF | 0.001068 | 0.002386 | 0.001485 |
| Deb1 | NSGA-II | 0.000193 | 0.000268 | 0.000218 |
|  | MOAF | 0.000062 | 0.000173 | 0.000097 |
| Deb2 | NSGA-II | 0.001629 | 0.002109 | 0.001887 |
|  | MOAF | 0.000202 | 0.000574 | 0.000399 |
| Deb3 | NSGA-II | 0.000470 | 0.000704 | 0.000594 |
|  | MOAF | 0.000250 | 0.000525 | 0.000351 |

**Table 4.** Comparison of SP results obtained by NSGA-II and MOAF.

| Functions | Algorithm | Best | Worst | Mean |
|---|---|---|---|---|
| ZDT1 | NSGA-II | 0.002638 | 0.004918 | 0.003348 |
|  | MOAF | 0.021058 | 0.056519 | 0.033130 |
| ZDT2 | NSGA-II | 0.000008 | 0.011005 | 0.003769 |
|  | MOAF | 0.022346 | 0.045818 | 0.031371 |
| ZDT3 | NSGA-II | 0.002333 | 0.008480 | 0.003705 |
|  | MOAF | 0.011716 | 0.034163 | 0.020015 |
| Deb1 | NSGA-II | 0.003066 | 0.004088 | 0.003559 |
|  | MOAF | 0.224659 | 0.526650 | 0.321211 |
| Deb2 | NSGA-II | 0.002988 | 0.004265 | 0.003566 |
|  | MOAF | 0.031875 | 0.077694 | 0.048413 |
| Deb3 | NSGA-II | 0.002715 | 0.003754 | 0.003191 |
|  | MOAF | 0.367159 | 1.428707 | 0.646577 |

Figures 1, 2, 3, 4, 5 and 6 show the approximate Pareto front found by NSGA-II and MOAF, and the true Pareto front is shown in every figure. From Figs. 1, 2 and 3, it can be seen that NSGA-II cannot cover the true Pareto front for ZDT1-ZDT3, but MOAF can cover the true Pareto front. Although the spacing results of NSGA-II is smaller than MOAF in Table 3, it has no meaning for the approximated Pareto front cannot cover the true Pareto front. From Figs. 4, 5 and 6, the approximated Pareto front found by MOAF and NSGA-II is close to the true Pareto front for Deb1-Deb3, but it can be seen from Table 3 that the generational distance of MOAF is smaller than NSGA-II. It is easy to know that MOAF can find a set of Pareto optimal solutions with better convergence compare with NSGA-II.

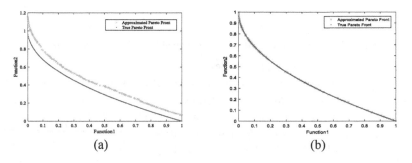

(a)                                    (b)

**Fig. 1.** Pareto fronts of ZDT1 produced by (a) NSGA-II (b) MOAF

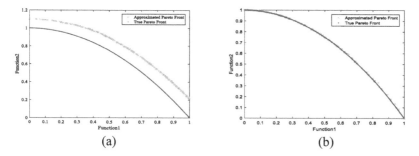

**Fig. 2.** Pareto fronts of ZDT2 produced by (a) NSGA-II (b) MOAF

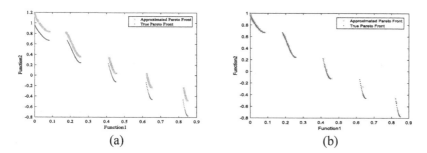

**Fig. 3.** Pareto fronts of ZDT3 produced by (a) NSGA-II (b) MOAF

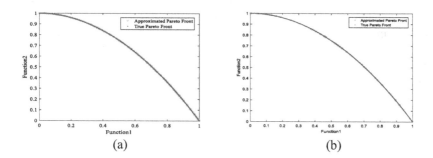

**Fig. 4.** Pareto fronts of Deb1 produced by (a) NSGA-II (b) MOAF

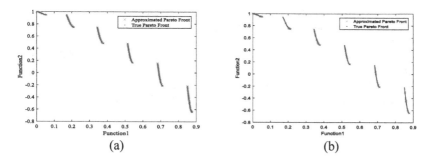

**Fig. 5.** Pareto fronts of Deb2 produced by (a) NSGA-II (b) MOAF

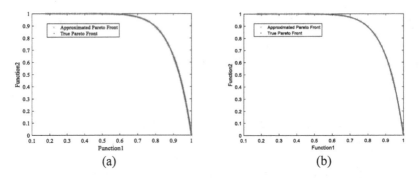

**Fig. 6.** Pareto fronts of Deb3 produced by (a) NSGA-II (b) MOAF

## 5 Conclusion

When dealing with practical problems in the real world, it is inadequate to consider only a single objective optimization, this kind of problems ask people to optimize multiple objectives equally at the same time. Multi-objective swarm intelligence optimization algorithm is an important way to solve the multi-objective problems. AF optimization algorithm is a recently proposed swarm intelligence optimization algorithm, the process of plant breeding and migration is used to find the optimal solution. Based on the standard AF optimization algorithm, this paper proposes a new multi-objective swarm intelligence optimization algorithm, called multi-objective artificial flora optimization algorithm. Algorithm uses the four basic elements and three main behavior patterns in the process of plant breeding and migration and adds external document to apply standard AF optimization algorithm to multi-objective optimization problems. The simulation results show that the approximated Pareto front found by MOAF algorithm can cover the true Pareto front and the solutions are more satisfactory than the solutions found by NSGA-II algorithm.

## References

1. Sun, Y., Ng, D., Zhu, J.: Multi-objective optimization for robust power efficient and secure full-duplex wireless communication systems. IEEE Trans. Wireless Commun. **15**(8), 5511–5526 (2016)
2. Delgarm, N., Sajadi, B., Kowsary, F.: Multi-objective optimization of the building energy performance: a simulation-based approach by means of particle swarm optimization (PSO). Appl. Energy **170**, 293–303 (2016)
3. Coello, C.A.: Evolutionary multi-objective optimization: a historical view of the field. IEEE Comput. Intell. Mag. **1**(1), 28–36 (2006)
4. Asrari, A., Lotfifard, S., Payam, M.S.: Pareto dominance-based multiobjective optimization method for distribution network reconfiguration. IEEE Trans. Smart Grid **7**(3), 1401–1410 (2016)

5. Zanchetta, P.: Heuristic multi-objective optimization for cost function weights selection in finite states model predictive control. In: Predictive Control of Electrical Drives and Power Electronics, pp. 70–75. IEEE (2011)
6. Pandit, D., Zhang, L., Chottopadhyay, S.: A scattering and repulsive swarm intelligence algorithm for solving global optimization problems. Knowl.-Based Syst. **156**, 12–42 (2018)
7. Long, C., Xuehan, W., Yan, W.: Artificial Flora (AF) optimization algorithm. Appl. Sci. **8**(3), 329 (2018)
8. Coello, C.A., Pulido, G.T., Lechuga, M.S.: Handling multiple objectives with particle swarm optimization. IEEE Trans. Evol. Comput. **8**(3), 256–279 (2004)
9. Ojha, M., Singh, K.P., Chakraborty, P.: An empirical study of aggregation operators with Pareto dominance in multiobjective genetic algorithm. IETE J. Res. **63**(4), 1–11 (2017)
10. Deb, K., Agrawal, S., Pratap, A., Meyarivan, T.: A fast elitist non-dominated sorting genetic algorithm for multi-objective optimization: NSGA-II. In: Schoenauer, M., et al. (eds.) PPSN 2000. LNCS, vol. 1917, pp. 849–858. Springer, Heidelberg (2000). https://doi.org/10.1007/3-540-45356-3_83
11. Zhang, Q., Xue, S.: An improved multi-objective particle swarm optimization algorithm. Eng. J. Wuhan Univ. **186**(3), 33–36 (2010)
12. Akbari, R., Hedayatzadeh, R., Ziarati, K., Hassanizadeh, B.: A multi-objective artificial bee colony algorithm. Swarm Evol. Comput. **2**(1), 39–52 (2012)
13. Zeng, G.Q., Chen, J., Li, L.M., Chen, M.R., Wu, L.: An improved multi-objective population-based extremal optimization algorithm with polynomial mutation. Inf. Sci. **330**(C), 49–73 (2016)
14. Tan, K.C., Goh, C.K., Yang, Y.J.: Evolving better population distribution and exploration in evolutionary multi-objective optimization. Eur. J. Oper. Res. **171**(2), 463–495 (2006)
15. Kannan, S., Baskar, S., Mccalley, J.D., Murugan, P.: Application of NSGA-II algorithm to generation expansion planning. IEEE Trans. Power Syst. **24**(1), 454–461 (2009)

# Design and Simulation of a Quantum Key Distribution Protocol Based on Single-Particle and EPR Entanglement

Leilei Li[1], Jian Li[1(✉)], Hengji Li[1], Chaoyang Li[1], Yan Zheng[1],
and Yuguang Yang[2]

[1] School of Computer Science, Beijing University of Posts and Telecommunications,
Beijing 100876, China
buptlijian@126.com

[2] College of Computer Science and Technology, Beijing University of Technology,
Beijing 100124, China

**Abstract.** Based the idea of original "Ping-pong" protocol, an improved "Ping-pong" protocol based on single-particle and Einstein-Podolsky-Rosen (EPR) entanglement is presented. The EPR entanglement is used to detect the eavesdropping and the single particle is used to transmit the information. During the protocol, the sender Alice transmits an EPR entanglement pairs and a single particle to the receiver Bob at the same time. The bit error is caused by the random position of the single particle. In our security analysis, an eavesdropping will cause at least a bit error rate of 16.7%, and the probability of detecting eavesdropping with bit error rate is 50.0%. We also give a simulation which is based on law of large numbers and Monte Carlo method. In our simulation, we use mean square error (the value is $1.8115 \times 10^{-5}$) to indicate that the simulation data is approach to the theoretical value. Compared with the original "Ping-pong" protocol, the presented protocol doesn't need the control mode, and it doesn't need to store the quantum state.

**Keywords:** Single-particle · EPR entanglement ·
The "Ping-pong" protocol · Security analysis · Monte Carlo method

## 1 Introduction

Cryptography is the basis of information security, the task of cryptography is to ensure that only legitimate users like Alice and Bob can read a secret message in a secure communication, while unauthorized users like Eve cannot. To accomplish this task, the communication protocol must ensure that only the key can encrypt and decrypt the secret message. In 1949, Shannon proved the one-time pad (OTP) [19] is perfectly secure with equal length of the key and secret message

This work is supported by the National Natural Science Foundation of China (Grant No. U1636106, No. 61472048, No. 61572053).

© ICST Institute for Computer Sciences, Social Informatics and Telecommunications Engineering 2019
Published by Springer Nature Switzerland AG 2019. All Rights Reserved
H. Song et al. (Eds.): SIMUtools 2019, LNICST 295, pp. 278–287, 2019.
https://doi.org/10.1007/978-3-030-32216-8_27

[17], that means the key can protect the secret message during transmission, but how to protect the key during distribution is still a tricky problem. [13, 23, 27].

Different from the classical communication, quantum communication and quantum cryptography is based on the theory of quantum physics and quantum entanglement which have attracted the interest of researchers in past decade, especially Quantum key distribution (QKD) [1, 14, 16, 18] and quantum secure direct communication (QSDC) [9, 21, 22, 25]. In QKD, the quantum particles is used to transmit the key while the classical bit is used to transmit the secret message. The key is determined until the end of the transmission, and the incompleteness of the quantum bits can be tolerated [4, 5, 11, 20]. In QSDC, not only the key but also the secret message is transmitted in quantum channel, that means every qubits is useful, and QSDC cannot tolerate the incompleteness of the qubits [7, 24].

In 2002, Long et al. proposed the first QSDC protocol with EPR entanglement [15]. In this protocol, the method of quantum data block transmission for security based on bit error rate analysis is introduced, before transmitting the secret message, the protocol sends a block of quantum data to make sure whether the quantum channel is security. It's an excellent method of QSDC, but it cannot detect the eavesdropping after starting transmit the secret message.

At the same year, Bostrom and Felbinger presented an excellent two-step deterministic QKD protocol which called the "Ping-pong" protocol [2]. This protocol contains two modes: the message mode is used to transmit the security message while the control mode is used to detect eavesdropper's (Eve) eavesdropping. During the protocol, the sender Alice randomly chooses the control mode or the message mode, means this protocol can detect the eavesdropping during the whole transmission process. But the "Ping-pong" protocol cannot transmit the security message in control mode, that means the more effective of detecting eavesdropping, the less effective of transmitting security message.

Based the idea of the original "Ping-pong" protocol (OPP) [2, 10, 11], we present an improved "Ping-pong" protocol based on a single-particle and an EPR entanglement which is called TPP. The receiver Bob randomly puts the single-particle in the first, second or third position of the three-particle group, that means only Bob knows the position of the single-particle, but the sender Bob and the eavesdropper Eve not. Eve can only randomly chooses the particle as the single-particle, that means the Eve will caused a bit error rate.

In 2016, we presented a QKD protocol based the idea of the BB84 protocol, which is called MEQKD [10]. In MEQKD, Alice sends two EPR entanglement pairs to Bob at one time, Bob randomly chooses the position of EPR pairs, if there is no eavesdropping, the bit error rate only caused by Bob's incorrect choice, which is the same as the BB84 protocol. But the MEQKD protocol has a higher efficiency of detecting eavesdropping. Compared with MEQKD, TPP only sends three particles at one time, which is one particle less than MEQKD, in other words, TPP is easier to application.

Compared with the OPP, TPP sends one single-particle and one EPR Entanglement every time, in other words, it sends totally three qubits once, which is more than OPP. The security analysis of TPP is also given, an eavesdropper's eavesdropping will caused at least a bit error rate of 50%. In order to achieve the same detection effect, the TPP needs 30 quantum key bits as the detection sequence, while the MEQKD needs 33 qubits and the BB84 protocol needs 72 qubits [10]. Compared with OPP, TPP can transmit the secret message and detect the eavesdropper at the same time, and TPP also doesn't need to store the quantum states.

We also give a simulation which is based on the law of large numbers and Monte Carlo method, In our simulation, the simulation data (the probability proportion of measurement result) $\hat{p}$ is approach to the theoretical probability proportion $p$, and mean square error is used to measure the similarity between $\hat{p}$ and $p$, and its value is $1.8115 \times 10^{-5}$. In another word, our theoretical security analysis is correct, TPP can detect eavesdropping effectively.

## 2    The TPP Protocol

### 2.1    The Relationship Between the Classical Bits and Quantum Bits

At the beginning of the paper, let's introduce the relationship between the classical bits and quantum bits.

The TPP only uses the $Z$-basis: $B_Z = \{|0\rangle, |1\rangle\}$ and a single-particle $|0\rangle$ and $|1\rangle$. $|+\rangle$ and $|-\rangle$ are unnecessary. Beside, the TPP protocol also uses one of the four Bell states as follows:

$$|\Phi^+\rangle = \frac{1}{\sqrt{2}}(|00\rangle + |11\rangle), |\Phi^-\rangle = \frac{1}{\sqrt{2}}(|00\rangle - |11\rangle)$$
$$|\Psi^+\rangle = \frac{1}{\sqrt{2}}(|01\rangle + |10\rangle), |\Psi^-\rangle = \frac{1}{\sqrt{2}}(|01\rangle - |10\rangle)$$

(1)

Alice and Bob agree on that there is two unitary operations as follows, just as OPP, when Bob takes a $I$ operation, Alice knows that Bob wants to send the classical bit 0, and when Bob takes a $\sigma_x$ operation, that means Bob wants to send the classical bit 1.

$$I = \begin{pmatrix} 1 & 0 \\ 0 & 1 \end{pmatrix}, \quad \sigma_x = \begin{pmatrix} 0 & 1 \\ 1 & 0 \end{pmatrix}$$

(2)

As we know, Eve usually takes an intercept-resend attack between Alice and Bob, according to the Heisenberg's uncertainty principe and no-clone theory [3], Eve needs to re-prepare the qubit particles with her measurement result and resend them to Bob. But the position of the Bell state is only known to Alice, that means Eve can only choose the position randomly, which will cause a bit error rate $\epsilon$. If there is no eavesdropping, $\epsilon$ should be 0 [18, 26], In the next section, we will analysis the bit error rate $\epsilon$ caused by Eve's eavesdropping and we will also proved that the Eve's eavesdropping will always be detected as long as the quantum sequence is long enough.

## 2.2    A Brief Introduction of TPP

Now, let's introduce the process of TPP and how TPP detects an eavesdropping. A complete process of the TPP protocol can be described as the following 9 steps.

1. Alice wants to send a message to Bob, this message can be the key or the secret message, she firstly encode the message with classical binary and get the classical bit sequence N in order.
2. Bob prepares an EPR pairs and a single-particle to form a three-particle groups and remembers their position as $(1, 2, 3)$, if all the classical bits of N have taken out, then goto the step 9, or goto the step 3.
3. For every three-particle quantum group, the single-particle can be put in the 1st, 2nd or 3rd position. For example, Bob prepares a group $\{|\Phi_{12}^+\rangle|\Phi_{12}^+\rangle||1\rangle\}$ and sends them to Alice, $|\Phi_{ij}^+\rangle$ means the $i^{th}$ and the $j^{th}$ qubits in a group make up a Bell state $|\Phi^+\rangle$. Bob records the location information and sends the qubits sequence $S$ to Alice.
4. After Alice received the group, if she wants to send a classical bit 0 to Bob, she takes a $I$ unitary operation on these three qubits. If Alice wants to sends a classical bit 1 to Bob, she can take a $\sigma_x$ unitary operation.
5. After taking an unitary operation, Alice resends the three qubits group back to Bob.
6. Bob receives the qubits from Alice, he know the position of the EPR pairs. And he takes $B_Z$ measurement on the single-particle, and a Bell measurement on the EPR pairs. If there is no bit error, the bell state's measurement should be always the same when sends $|\Phi^+\rangle = \frac{1}{\sqrt{2}}(|00\rangle + |11\rangle)$ and $|\Phi^-\rangle = \frac{1}{\sqrt{2}}(|00\rangle - |11\rangle)$, the bell state's measurement should be always different when Bob sends $|\Psi^+\rangle = \frac{1}{\sqrt{2}}(|01\rangle + |10\rangle)$ and $|\Psi^-\rangle = \frac{1}{\sqrt{2}}(|01\rangle - |10\rangle)$. If the single particle has been changed, Bob know that Alice sends a classical bit 1; If the single particle has not been changed, means Alice sends a classical bit 0.
7. Only Bob knows which Bell state he sends, so the Bell state can be used to detect the eavesdropping while the single-particle is used to transmit the classical bit.
8. If there is a wrong Bell state measurement result, Bob know there's an eavesdropping, Alice and Bob will intercept this communication and restart a new one.
9. Alice and Bob have confirmed that the channel is safety, they will transmit the remaining keys to obtain the finally key.

Table 1 gives an example that Alice sends a classical bit 0 to Bob without eavesdropper.

If there is no eavesdropping, the measurement result of the EPR pairs should always be the same when Bob sends $|\Phi^+\rangle$ or $|\Phi^-\rangle$, and the result should always be different when Bob sends $|\Psi^+\rangle$ or $|\Psi^-\rangle$.

If there is no eavesdropping, the bit error rate $\epsilon$ should be 0. In another words, if there is a bit error rate in ideal environment, means there is an eavesdropper, Alice and Bob should intercept the communication and restart a new one.

**Table 1.** Alice successfully transmits a classical bit 0

| Number of the position | 1 | 2 | 3 |
|---|---|---|---|
| EPR pairs that Bob prepares | $\|\Phi_{12}^+\rangle$ | $\|\Phi_{12}^+\rangle$ | $\|1\rangle$ |
| Unitary operation that Alice chooses | $I$ | | |
| The state after unitary operation | $\|\Phi_{12}^+\rangle$ | $\|\Phi_{12}^+\rangle$ | $\|1\rangle$ |
| The particle that Alice resends | $\|\Phi_{12}^+\rangle$ | $\|\Phi_{12}^+\rangle$ | $\|1\rangle$ |
| The measurement result (2 situations) | $\|0\rangle$ | $\|0\rangle$ | $\|1\rangle$ |
| | $\|1\rangle$ | $\|1\rangle$ | $\|1\rangle$ |
| Detecting eavesdropping | **not exist** | | |
| The classical bits Alice sends | **0** | | |

# 3  The Security Analysis and Simulation of TPP with an Eavesdropper

## 3.1  The Probability of Detecting Eavesdropper

Now let's analysis the probability of detecting the Eve's eavesdropping, Table 2 shows that Eve gets the right and wrong position.

**Table 2.** Eve gets the right or wrong position of EPR pairs

| Number of the position | Right | | | Wrong | | |
|---|---|---|---|---|---|---|
| | 1 | 2 | 3 | 1 | 2 | 3 |
| EPR pairs that Bob prepares | $\|\Phi_{12}^+\rangle$ | $\|\Phi_{12}^+\rangle$ | $\|1\rangle$ | $\|\Phi_{12}^+\rangle$ | $\|\Phi_{12}^+\rangle$ | $\|1\rangle$ |
| The position Eve chooses | $\checkmark$ | $\checkmark$ | | $\checkmark$ | | $\checkmark$ |
| The qubits group Eve resends | $\|\Phi_{12}^-\rangle$ | $\|\Phi_{12}^-\rangle$ | $\|1\rangle$ | $\|\Psi_{13}^-\rangle$ | $\|0\rangle$ | $\|\Psi_{13}^-\rangle$ |
| Unitary operation that Alice chooses | $\sigma_x$ | | | $\sigma_x$ | | |
| The state after unitary operation | $\|\Phi_{12}^+\rangle$ | $\|\Phi_{12}^+\rangle$ | $\|0\rangle$ | $\|\Psi_{13}^+\rangle$ | $\|1\rangle$ | $\|\Psi_{13}^+\rangle$ |
| The particle that Alice resends | $\|\Phi_{12}^+\rangle$ | $\|\Phi_{12}^+\rangle$ | $\|0\rangle$ | $\|\Psi_{13}^+\rangle$ | $\|1\rangle$ | $\|\Psi_{13}^+\rangle$ |
| The measurement result (2 situations) | $\|0\rangle$ | $\|0\rangle$ | $\|0\rangle$ | $\|0\rangle$ | $\|1\rangle$ | $\|1\rangle$ |
| | $\|1\rangle$ | $\|1\rangle$ | $\|0\rangle$ | $\|1\rangle$ | $\|0\rangle$ | $\|0\rangle$ |
| Detecting eavesdropping | **not exist** | | | **exist** | | |
| The classical bits Alice sends | **1** | | | **not sure** | | |

Eve randomly chooses the position of the EPR pairs, that means she has the probability of $p_1 = 2/3$ to choose a wrong position.

When Eve chooses the wrong position to take the Bell measurement, she will randomly gets one of the four Bell state: $\|\Phi^+\rangle$, $\|\Phi^-\rangle$, $\|\Psi^+\rangle$ and $\|\Psi^-\rangle$. She has the probability of $1/2$ to correct the bit error rate caused by wrongly choice of the position. So the probability that Bob gets a wrong EPR pairs is: $p_2 = 1 - 1/2 = 1/2 = 0.5$.

When Bob gets a wrong EPR pairs, the Bell measurement will change, and Eve's eavesdropping will be detected. The probability will be easy calculated [8]: $p_d = p_1 \times p_2 = 1/3 = 0.333$.

## 3.2 The Bit Error Rate Caused by Eavesdropping

When Eve chooses a wrong position of EPR pairs, the single particle will changed or unchanged with a probability of 50%. That's means when Eve's eavesdropping has been detected, Alice will also has the probability of 1/2 to receive the right particle. So the bit error rate is: $\epsilon = p_d \times (1/2) = 1/6 \approx 0.167$

If Eve's eavesdropping has been detected when the EPR pair isn't entangled or the bit error was found when the single particle is different from the expected result, Alice and Bob know that the quantum channel has been unsafe, the probability of this situation can be easily calculated because the detections in single particle and EPR pair are separated.

$$P = p_d + \epsilon = \frac{1}{2} = 50\% \tag{3}$$

If Alice wants to send the length of n classical bits to Bob, the probability of detecting the eavesdropper is:

$$P_d = 1 - (1 - P)^n = 1 - (\frac{1}{2})^n \tag{4}$$

To detect an eavesdropper with the probability of $P_d = 0.999999999$, Alice and Bob need to compare n = 30 qubits in TPP while 33 key bits in MEQKD and 72 key bits in BB84 protocol [10].

TPP costs more qubits in detecting eavesdropping, but it can detect the eavesdropper in every transmission [12]. In another words, TPP can not only used as a QKD protocol, but also as a QSDC protocol. To get the information, Eve will at the risk of the probability 0.5 to be detected.

## 3.3 The Information that Eve Obtains

When there is an eavesdropper, the probability of detecting eavesdropping is 1/2. That's to say, Bob has the probability of $P_r = 1 - 1/2 = 1/2$ to get a classical message and the probability of $P_w = 1 - P_r = 1/2$ to get a another classical message. So is Eve.

According to the theory of Shannon information entropy, we can calculate the mutual information that Eve gets [6,15]:

$$I(A, E) = 2 - \left(-\sum_{i=0}^{1} P_i \log_2 P_i\right) = 1 \tag{5}$$

Eve can still gets $(1/2) = 0.5$ of the mutual information which doesn't meet the mutual information relations of privacy amplification. If TPP is used as a QKD protocol, Eve can only gets part of the key, and she cannot read the secret message.

## 3.4    Simulation Based on Monte Carlo Method

Based on Chebyshev's law of large numbers and Monte Carlo method, we can simulate the proportion of Bob's receive measurement result.

Supposed Bob sends $|0\rangle|\Phi_{23}^+\rangle|\Phi_{23}^+\rangle$ to Alice, Alice takes an $I$ operation and resends the quantum pairs to Bob, Bob knows the single particle is the first place and he takes an $B_Z$ measurement on the first place, he also takes a Bell measurement on the second and third place. If there is no eavesdropping, the measurement will be 000 or 011 equiprobability. If there is an eavesdropping, the measurement should be one of the measurement result set:

$$S = \{000, 001, 010, 011, 100, 101, 110, 111\} \tag{6}$$

In our prior security analysis, all the measurement result should be equip probability. So, we can get the theoretical value of the result proportion.

$$p_{000} = p_{011} = \frac{1-P}{n_r} = \frac{0.5}{2} = 0.25$$

$$p_{001} = p_{010} = p_{100} = p_{101} = p_{110} = p_{111} = \frac{P}{n_w} = \frac{0.5}{6} = 0.0833 \tag{7}$$

In our simulation, the right results' probability distribution should approach to 0.25 when the wrong results' probability distribution should approach to 0.0833.

We used Python to simulate this protocol. The Table 3 shows the simulation result of TPP, in this table, the sum of each column is approached to 1.0, the value of each line is approached to the theoretical value $p_s, s \in S$. The Fig. 1 shows the proportion of the simulate results.

**Table 3.** Simulation Result, times means the simulate times, result means the simulate result

| Result/times | 100 | 250 | 500 | 1000 | 2000 | 3000 | 4000 | 5000 |
|---|---|---|---|---|---|---|---|---|
| 000 | 0.1782 | 0.2470 | 0.2555 | 0.2476 | 0.2574 | 0.2463 | 0.2467 | 0.2476 |
| 001 | 0.0792 | 0.0797 | 0.0858 | 0.0879 | 0.0920 | 0.0890 | 0.0897 | 0.0882 |
| 010 | 0.1485 | 0.1076 | 0.0938 | 0.0859 | 0.0790 | 0.0793 | 0.0792 | 0.0788 |
| 011 | 0.2178 | 0.2191 | 0.2176 | 0.2398 | 0.2429 | 0.2456 | 0.2499 | 0.2539 |
| 100 | 0.0891 | 0.0797 | 0.0938 | 0.0879 | 0.0900 | 0.0903 | 0.0910 | 0.0870 |
| 101 | 0.0891 | 0.0966 | 0.0898 | 0.0849 | 0.0825 | 0.0833 | 0.0825 | 0.0802 |
| 110 | 0.0990 | 0.0916 | 0.0758 | 0.0789 | 0.0715 | 0.0776 | 0.0752 | 0.0766 |
| 111 | 0.0990 | 0.0757 | 0.0878 | 0.0869 | 0.0850 | 0.0886 | 0.0857 | 0.0880 |

From Table 3 and Fig. 1 after 5000 times of simulation, The probability distribution of all the results $\hat{p}_s, s \in S$ is close to stability. The probability that Alice receives the right result $\hat{P}_r$ and the probability that Bob find eavesdropping $\hat{P}_w$ can be concluded:

$$\hat{P}_r = \hat{p}_{000} + \hat{p}_{011} \rightarrow 0.5000$$
$$\hat{P}_w = \sum_{s \in \mathcal{S}} p_s - \hat{P}_r \rightarrow 0.5000 \tag{8}$$

In a word, the theoretical value $p_s, s \in \mathcal{S}$ is approach to the simulate value $\hat{p}_s, s \in \mathcal{S}$. The probability of detecting eavesdropping $\hat{P}_r$ is also approach to $P = 0.5$. We use mean square error $MSE$ to determine the degree of similarity between the simulate value and theoretical value, and set a threshold $\theta = 10^{-3}$. If $MSE \leq \theta$, means the simulation results are very close to the actual results.

$$MSE(\hat{p}) = \frac{1}{n} \sum_{s \in \mathcal{S}} (\hat{p}_s - p_s)^2 = 1.8115 \times 10^{-5} \ll \theta \tag{9}$$

From formula 9, $MSE \ll \theta$, we can conclude that our simulation is close to the actual. In other word, our security analysis is right and TPP is a safe protocol.

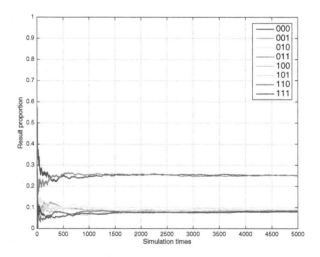

**Fig. 1.** Two lines above are $\hat{p}_{000}$ and $\hat{p}_{011}$, which is approaching to 0.25; six lines below are the rest of the measurement results, all of them approaching to 0.0833

## 4   Conclusion

In this paper, we presented an improved "Ping-pong" protocol based on single-particle and EPR pairs which is called TPP. During the transmission, TPP sends one single particle and a pair of EPR. The TPP protocol not only can use as a

QKD protocol, but also a QSDC protocol. Compared with the BB84 protocol, TPP only needs to prepare two kinds of single-particles $|0\rangle$ and $|1\rangle$, but TPP has to prepare another EPR pair.

Compared with the original "Ping-pong" protocol (OPP), TPP doesn't need the control mode, which makes TPP is easier to conduct. What's more, the TPP protocol doesn't need to store the quantum state, making it easy to application.

The security of the TPP protocol is also analyzed. If there is no eavesdropper, the bit error rate $\epsilon_0$ should be 0. The bit error rate will be $\epsilon_1 = 0.167$ if Eve intercepts and resends the quantum bits, and Eve's eavesdropping will also be detected through the EPR pairs with the probability of $p_d = 0.333$. That's to say, there is two ways to detect the eavesdropping, the total probability of detecting eavesdropper is $P = 1/2 = 0.5$.

The information that Eve can get is also analyzed, Eve can at most get $1/2 = 50\%$ information without being detected but she doesn't know which parts she has gotten.

We also give a simulation based on Monte Carlo method and use mean square error ($MSE$) to estimate the similarity between $\hat{p}$ and $p$. In our simulation, the simulate value $\hat{p}$ is approach to the theoretical value $p$ and $MSE = 1.8115 \times 10^{-5}$, so we can concluded that we have proved the security of TPP both in theory and simulation.

The TPP protocol is only discussed in ideal environment theory, When come to application, we must face to a difficult problem: how to maintain the entanglement state of quantum. And we should also take the environmental noise into account in the future.

# References

1. Bennett, C.H., Brassard, G.: An update on quantum cryptography. In: Blakley, G.R., Chaum, D. (eds.) CRYPTO 1984. LNCS, vol. 196, pp. 475–480. Springer, Heidelberg (1985). https://doi.org/10.1007/3-540-39568-7_39
2. BostroM, K., Felbinger, T.: Secure direct communication using entanglement. Phys. Rev. Lett. **89**(18), 187902 (2002)
3. Busch, P., Heinonen, T., Lahti, P.: Heisenberg's uncertainty principle. Phys. Rep. **452**(6), 155–176 (2006)
4. Chang, Y., Zhang, S.B., Zhu, J.M.: Comment on "flexible protocol for quantum private query based on B92 protocol". Quantum Inf. Process. **16**(3), 86 (2017)
5. Chong, S.K., Hwang, T.: Quantum key agreement protocol based on BB84. Opt. Commun. **283**(6), 1192–1195 (2010)
6. Deng, F.G., Gui, L.L., Liu, X.S.: Two-step quantum direct communication protocol using the Einstein-Podolsky-Rosen pair block. Phys. Rev. A **68**(4), 113–114 (2003)
7. Gao, F., Qin, S.J., Wen, Q.Y., Zhu, F.C.: Three-party quantum secure direct communication based on GHZ states. Phys. Lett. A **372**(18), 3333–3336 (2008)
8. Howard, R.A.: Dynamic programming and Markov process. Math. Gaz. **3**(358), 120 (1960)
9. Hwang, T., Luo, Y.P., Yang, C.W., Lin, T.H.: Quantum authencryption: one-step authenticated quantum secure direct communications for off-line communicants. Quantum Inf. Process. **13**(4), 925–933 (2014)

10. Jian, L., Na, L., Li, L.L., Tao, W.: One step quantum key distribution based on EPR entanglement. Sci. Rep. **6**, 28767 (2016)

11. Jian, L., Yang, Y.G., Chen, X.B., Zhou, Y.H., Shi, W.M.: Practical quantum private database queries based on passive round-robin differential phase-shift quantum key distribution. Sci. Rep. **6**, 31738 (2016)

12. Li, J., Pan, Z., Zheng, J., Sun, F., Xinxin, Y.E., Yuan, K.: The security analysis of quantum SAGR04 protocol in collective-rotation noise channel. Chin. J. Electron. **24**(4), 689–693 (2015)

13. Liao, S.K., et al.: Satellite-to-ground quantum key distribution. Nature **549**(7670), 43–47 (2017)

14. Lo, H.K., Chau, H.F.: Unconditional security of quantum key distribution over arbitrarily long distances. Science **283**(5410), 2050–2056 (1999)

15. Long, G.L., Liu, X.S.: Theoretically efficient high-capacity quantum-key-distribution scheme. Phys. Rev. A **65**(3) (2002)

16. Padmavathi, V., Vardhan, B.V., Krishna, A.: Provably secure quantum key distribution by applying quantum gate. Int. J. Netw. Secur. **20**(1), 88–94 (2018)

17. Shannon, C.E.: Communication theory of secrecy systems. M.D. Comput. Comput. Med. Pract. **15**(1), 57 (1998)

18. Shor, P.W., Preskill, J.: Simple proof of security of the BB84 quantum key distribution protocol. Phys. Rev. Lett. **85**(2), 441–444 (2000)

19. Vernam, G.S.: Cipher printing telegraph systems for secret wire and radio telegraphic communications. Trans. Am. Inst. Electr. Eng. **XLV**(2), 295–301 (2009)

20. Wan, L., Huang, Y., Huang, C.: Quantum noise theory for phonon transport through nanostructures. Phys. B **510**, 22–28 (2017)

21. Wang, C., Deng, F.G., Li, Y.S., Liu, X.S., Long, G.L.: Quantum secure direct communication with high-dimension quantum superdense coding. Phys. Rev. A **71**(4), 44305 (2005)

22. Wang, C., Deng, F.G., Long, G.L.: Multi-step quantum secure direct communication using multi-particle Green-Horne-Zeilinger state. Opt. Commun. **253**(1), 15–20 (2006)

23. Wiener, M.J.: Cryptanalysis of short RSA secret exponents. IEEE Trans. Inf. Theory **36**(3), 553–558 (1989)

24. Yang, C.W., Hwang, T., Lin, T.H.: Modification attack on QSDC with authentication and the improvement. Int. J. Theor. Phys. **52**(7), 2230–2234 (2013)

25. Yang, Y.G., Teng, Y.W., Chai, H.P., Wen, Q.Y.: Revisiting the security of secure direct communication based on ping-pong protocol [quantum inf. process. 8, 347 (2009)]. Quantum Inf. Process. **10**(3), 317–323 (2011)

26. Zhao, N.P.: Quantum key distribution secure threshold based on BB84 protocol. Acta Phys. Sin. **60**(9), 1358–1364 (2011)

27. Zhou, X.Y., Zhang, C.H., Zhang, C.M., Wang, Q.: Obtaining better performance in the measurement-device-independent quantum key distribution with heralded single-photon sources. Phys. Rev. A **96**(5), 052337 (2017)

# A Quantum Key Distribution Protocol Based on the EPR Pairs and Its Simulation

Jian Li[1,2], Hengji Li[2(✉)], Chaoyang Li[2], Leilei Li[2], Yanyan Hou[1,2], Xiubo Chen[3], and Yuguang Yang[4]

[1] Center for Quantum Information Research,
ZaoZhuang University, ZaoZhuang 277160, Shandong, China
[2] School of Computer Science,
Beijing University of Posts Telecommunications,
Beijing 100876, China
lihj@bupt.edu.cn
[3] Information Security Center,
State Key Laboratory Networking and Switching Technology,
Beijing University of Posts Telecommunications, Beijing 100876, China
[4] Faculty of Information Technology,
Beijing University of Technology, Beijing 100124, China

**Abstract.** A novel quantum key distribution protocol based on entanglement and dense coding is proposed, which does not need to store the qubits. Every four particles is divided into a group, of which $\{(1,2),(3,4)\}$ or $\{(1,3),(2,4)\}$ are in entanglement. Some of the groups are used to transfer the message, and the others are used to check the eavesdropping. In the message mode, the authorized party needn't to know the location information of the group, he only needs to make the unitary operation to the first and the forth of the group. Also, the trade-off between information and disturbance is calculated under the intercept-measure-resend attack and entanglement-measure attack, which tells that the protocol is asymptotically secure. Moreover, the quantum circuit simulation of the protocol is shown.

**Keywords:** Quantum key distribution · Entanglement · Quantum circuit simulation

With the rapid development of information technology and quantum physics [1], the quantum cryptography has become one of the rapidly developing applications of the quantum information theory. It employs quantum laws such as uncertainty principle and no-cloning theorem to solve the important problem of telecommunication channels protection from eavesdropping by the unauthorized users like Eve. It is provably secure against eavesdropping attack, in that, as a

Supported by the National Natural Science Foundation of China (Grant No. U1636106, No.61472048, No. 61671087, No. 61572053).

© ICST Institute for Computer Sciences, Social Informatics and Telecommunications Engineering 2019
Published by Springer Nature Switzerland AG 2019. All Rights Reserved
H. Song et al. (Eds.): SIMUtools 2019, LNICST 295, pp. 288–301, 2019.
https://doi.org/10.1007/978-3-030-32216-8_28

matter of fundamental principle, the secret data can not be comprised unknowingly to the illegitimate users of the channel.

In the last decade, researchers has made dramatic progress in the field of quantum cryptography. One of the quantum cryptography direction is the quantum key distribution (QKD), whose object is to create a common random key between two remote authorized users. Since Bennnett and Brassard presented the pioneer QKD protocol (BB84 protocol) [2] in 1984, a lot of attention has been focused on the protocol. In 1989, IBM and Montreal university first completed the experiment of quantum cryptography [3], which verified the feasibility of BB84 protocol. In ref [4], the researchers gave the proof of security of the BB84 protocol. Besides the BB84 protocol, there are some other typical schemes, such as Ekert 1991 protocol (Ekert91) [5], Bennett-Brassard-Mermin 1992 protocol (BBM92) [6], six-state protocol [7] and so on. In recent years, there are some new protocols proposed and developments of QKD, such as Refs [8–18].

Different from QKD, quantum secure direct communication (QSDC) protocol is designed for providing unidirectional communication in which information content is specified by the sender. Long et al. proposed the first QSDC protocol [19]. Later, Boström and Felbinger put forward a famous QSDC protocol based on EPR pairs, which is called "Ping-pong" protocol [20]. Since then, researchers have published many enhancements and modification of the ping-pong protocol, including superdense coding [21], usage of GHZ states for two [22] and multiparty [23] communication and so on. Many QSDC protocols were presented, including the protocols without using entanglement [24–28], the protocols using entanglement [29–32] and two-way QSDC protocols [33–38].

In above QSDC protocols, the transmitted message is the secret instead of random key bits. That is to say, the security requirements in the QSDC schemes are more stricter than the QKD protocol, because the message transmitted can never leaked out regardless of whether the eavesdropping would be detected or not. For example, researchers have found many security problems [39, 40] in the ping-pong protocol when it is used as QSDC.

One of the technical difficulties that have been unable to overcome is the ultrashort storage time of quantum state. At present, the world record of quantum state storage time is only 3 ms at Heifei National Laboratory for Physical Sciences at Microscale and Department of Modern Physics. All protocols that need to store quantum states in process have some limitations on the operability, like the ping-pong protocol, in which, the storage of one photon is necessary for a duration corresponding to twice the distance between Alice and Bob.

Considering the storage time limitation, in this paper, a new protocol for QKD based on entanglement and dense coding is proposed, which does not need to store quantum states in process. We emphasize that here, we restrict our protocol as just a QKD process instead of QSDC to have a more perfect secure communication. Then the securities of the protocol is analyzed. Moreover, the efficient quantum circuit simulation of the protocol is presented, which will be necessary to implement this protocol in experiment.

# 1  New QKD Protocol

For simplicity, this protocol is represented as GEQKD.

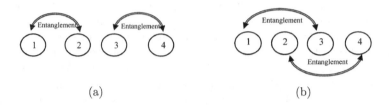

**Fig. 1.** The entanglement of two types of location

Firstly, every four bits of all classical bits is divided into a group in the GEQKD protocol and two EPR pairs are prepared for every group according to the entanglement. Then Bob transfers the two EPR states to Alice through the quantum channel. Secondly, After Alice receiving the EPR pairs, he only performs the unitary transformation on the first and fourth particle of each group and then transmit the group particles to Bob by the quantum channel. Lastly, Bob performs the correct Bell basis measurement based on the position information that he records previously, and compares the results with the EPR pairs that he previously sent. Then Bob can get the unitary operation performed by Alice and decodes the classical bits that Alice sends.

Now let us give an explicit process for GEQKD.

(p.1) Bob and Alice agree on that each of the four Bell states can carry two-quit classical information and encode $|\Phi^+\rangle$, $|\Phi^-\rangle$, $|\Psi^+\rangle$ and $|\Psi^-\rangle$ as 00, 01, 10 and 11, respectively.

(p.2) Bob prepares a large enough number of classical bits N in sequence and every four bits is divided into a group in order, which is called as $C_i$. Here the subscript indicates the group order in the sequence.

(p.3) Bob picks up one group in order, and numbers the four bits into $\{1, 2, 3, 4\}$. If all groups are took out, then go to p.7; otherwise then go to p.4.

(p.4) Bob prepares two EPR pairs based on the order of four bits of current group and dense coding mechanism, which is called the particles $S_i$ (see Fig. 1). Meanwhile, Bob remembers the entanglement and the location information of the particles $S_i$ and then transfers it to Alice by quantum channel.

(p.5) Alice receives the particles $S_i$. With probability $c_1$, she switches to control mode and proceeds with c.1, else he proceeds with m.1.

(c.1) Alice randomly chooses one location information $\{(1, 2), (3, 4)\}$ or $\{(1, 3), (2, 4)\}$ to extract every EPR pair and then makes the Bell basis measurement accordingly. Then Alice tells Bob which location he has chosen for each group and the outcomes $C_i'$ of his measurements by classical channel.

(c.2) Bob receives the location information and the outcomes $C_i'$ of her measurements. If she chooses incorrectly, discard the particles $S_i$ and go to p.3. If she chooses correctly, Bob compare $C_i'$ with the initial classical bits $C_i$. $C_i' \neq C_i$: Eve is detected. Abort transmission. $C_i' = C_i$: go to p.3.

(m.1) Alice makes one of the four unitary operations $\{I, X, Y, Z\}$ only to the first and the forth of the particles $S_i$. Table 1 shows the Bell states before and after the unitary operations. Then Alice sends the unitary particles $S_i'$ back to Bob through quantum channel.

(m.2) Bob receives the particles $S_i'$ and performs the correct Bell basis measurement based on the position information that he records previously. Then he compares his measurement results with the initial Bell states sent by himself and decodes the classical bits that Alice sends (see Table 1).

(p.6) Alice confirms that Bob receives the particles $S_i'$. With probability $c_2$, she switches to control mode and proceeds with c.3, otherwise then go to p.3.

(c.3) Alice tells Bob the classical bits she transmits by classical channel.

(c.4) After Bob receiving the classical bits $M_i$, he compares $M_i$ with the bits $M_i'$ he decodes. ($M_i' \neq M_i$): Eve is detected. Abort transmission. ($M_i' = M_i$): go to p.3.

(p.7) confirming the safety of channel, Bob and Alice negotiate about the remaining raw key and perform the correction and privacy amplification, then obtain the final keys.

**Table 1.** The Bell states before and after the unitary operation

| The initial | The end | | | |
|---|---|---|---|---|
| | $|\Phi^+\rangle$ | $|\Phi^-\rangle$ | $|\Psi^+\rangle$ | $|\Psi^-\rangle$ |
| $|\Phi^+\rangle$ | $I(00)$ | $Z(01)$ | $X(10)$ | $Y(11)$ |
| $|\Phi^-\rangle$ | $Z(01)$ | $I(00)$ | $Y(11)$ | $X(10)$ |
| $|\Psi^+\rangle$ | $X(10)$ | $Y(11)$ | $I(00)$ | $Z(01)$ |
| $|\Psi^-\rangle$ | $Y(11)$ | $X(10)$ | $Z(01)$ | $Y(11)$ |

Table 2 shows the process that every group classical bits is transmitted to Bob after Alice performs the unitary transformation. Compared with MEQKD protocol proposed in the paper [8], GEQKD protocol makes full use of every group quantum bits while transmitting the message, instead of discarding half of the groups. Meanwhile, it can be found that the implementation of the GEQKD protocol is similar to the "Ping-pong" protocol, however, there are some fundamental differences. One is GEQKD protocol needs not to store the quit. Two is that only one particle of the EPR pair is sent in the ping-pong protocol, while two particles of the EPR pair are sent in the GEQKD protocol. Thus the eavesdropper Eve can perform the Bell basis measurement on the EPR pair to obtain the information.

**Table 2.** The example of the process that every group is transferred to Bob

| Number of classical bits | 1 | 2 | 3 | 4 |
|---|---|---|---|---|
| Bobs random bit | 1 | 0 | 1 | 1 |
| Bob sending Bell states | $\|\Psi_{13}^-\rangle$ | $\|\Phi_{24}^-\rangle$ | $\|\Psi_{13}^-\rangle$ | $\|\Phi_{24}^-\rangle$ |
| Alices random bit | 0 | 1 | 1 | 0 |
| Bell states Alice measures and sends | $Z$ | / | / | $X$ |
| Bell states Bob measures | $\|\Psi_{13}^+\rangle$ | $\|\Psi_{24}^-\rangle$ | $\|\Psi_{13}^+\rangle$ | $\|\Psi_{24}^-\rangle$ |
| The message Bob decodes | 0 | 1 | 1 | 0 |

## 2    Security of GEQKD Protocol

### 2.1    Intercept-Measure-Resend (IR) Attack

The family of individual attacks describes the most constrained attacks that have been studied. An important subfamily of individual attacks is the intercept-measure-resend (IR) attack, which Eve intercepts the quantum signal flying, performs the measurement on it, and conditioned on the result she obtains, she prepares a new quantum signal to the legitimate receiver. In the GEQKD protocol, in order to gain information about Alice's operation, Eve need to perform twice IR attacks. The first attack is in the quantum channel from Bob to Alice(B-A); the second attack is in the quantum channel from Alice to Bob(A-B).

Eve has no knowledge of EPR location information $\{(1,2),(3,4)\}$ or $\{(1,3), (2,4)\}$ sent by Bob, she can only guess which quit pairs to measure in. If she chooses correctly, she measures the correct Bell states as sent by Bob, and resends the correct Bell states to Alice. After Alice performs her coding operation, to decode the message that Alice encodes, Eve measures the Bell states again with the same location as the first IR attack. It should be noted that the Bell states does not collapse due to the correct location choice, thus Eve will not be detected. Table 3 gives an example of the process that Eve eavesdrops when she chooses correctly.

However, if she chooses incorrectly, the two quits are not entangled and the states sent to Alice cannot be the same as the states sent by Bob, which will make Eve detected with a certain probability in the control mode. It is worth noting that due to the existence of entanglement swapping, the new two bits will be entangled when she chooses incorrectly. Furthermore, when entering the control mode, the detection probability is $\frac{3}{4}$ in both B-A (Considering the case A chooses correctly, or the detection fails) and A-B quantum channel. Next, we will take the initial state $|\Psi_{13}^-\rangle|\Phi_{24}^-\rangle$ as an example to explain it.

Assuming that the initial state is $|\Psi_{13}^-\rangle|\Phi_{24}^-\rangle$, after Eve's measurement in the wrong location, it will become

$$|\Psi_{13}^-\rangle|\Phi_{24}^-\rangle = \frac{1}{2}(|\Psi_{12}^-\rangle|\Phi_{34}^-\rangle + |\Phi_{12}^+\rangle|\Psi_{34}^+\rangle - |\Phi_{12}^-\rangle|\Psi_{34}^-\rangle - |\Psi_{12}^+\rangle|\Phi_{34}^+\rangle), \qquad (1)$$

**Table 3.** The example of the process that Eve eavesdrops (the right location choice)

| Number of classical bits | 1 | 2 | 3 | 4 |
|---|---|---|---|---|
| Bobs random bit | 1 | 0 | 1 | 1 |
| Bob sending Bell states | $\lvert\Psi_{13}^-\rangle$ | $\lvert\Phi_{24}^-\rangle$ | $\lvert\Psi_{13}^-\rangle$ | $\lvert\Phi_{24}^-\rangle$ |
| Bell states Eve measures and sends | $\lvert\Psi_{13}^-\rangle$ | $\lvert\Phi_{24}^-\rangle$ | $\lvert\Psi_{13}^-\rangle$ | $\lvert\Phi_{24}^-\rangle$ |
| Alices random bit | 0 | 1 | 1 | 0 |
| Bell states Alice measures and sends | $Z$ | / | / | $X$ |
| Bell states Eve measures again | $\lvert\Psi_{13}^+\rangle$ | $\lvert\Psi_{24}^-\rangle$ | $\lvert\Psi_{13}^+\rangle$ | $\lvert\Psi_{24}^-\rangle$ |
| The message Eve decodes | 0 | 1 | 1 | 0 |
| Bell states Bob measures | $\lvert\Psi_{13}^+\rangle$ | $\lvert\Psi_{24}^-\rangle$ | $\lvert\Psi_{13}^+\rangle$ | $\lvert\Psi_{24}^-\rangle$ |
| The message Bob decodes | 0 | 1 | 1 | 0 |

Suppose that Eve's measurement yields $\lvert\Phi_{12}^+\rangle\lvert\Psi_{34}^+\rangle$ with the probability $\frac{1}{4}$, which can be expanded as

$$\lvert\Phi_{12}^+\rangle\lvert\Psi_{34}^+\rangle = \frac{1}{2}(\lvert\Phi_{13}^+\rangle\lvert\Psi_{24}^+\rangle + \lvert\Phi_{13}^-\rangle\lvert\Psi_{24}^-\rangle + \lvert\Psi_{13}^+\rangle\lvert\Phi_{24}^+\rangle + \lvert\Psi_{13}^-\rangle\lvert\Phi_{24}^-\rangle), \qquad (2)$$

then Alice performing a measurement using a correct sequence after Eve's measurement using an incorrect sequence will yield $\lvert\Psi_{13}^-\rangle\lvert\Phi_{24}^-\rangle$ with the probability of $\frac{1}{4}$, that is to say, Eve is not be detected. Similarly, the other three possible outcomes of Eve's measurement will yield $\lvert\Psi_{13}^-\rangle\lvert\Phi_{24}^-\rangle$ with the probability of $\frac{1}{4}$ after Alice performing a measurement. Therefore, the detection probability is $p_1 = 1 - 4*\frac{1}{4}*\frac{1}{4} = \frac{3}{4}$ in B-A quantum channel.

In A-B quantum channel, Alice performs the unitary operations $Z$ and $X$ on the first and the forth of the particles, respectively, which will make the state $\lvert\Phi_{12}^+\rangle\lvert\Psi_{34}^+\rangle$ as a result of Eve's measurement using an incorrect sequence become $\lvert\Psi_{12}^+\rangle\lvert\Psi_{34}^-\rangle$. Then Eve measures the Bell states again with the same location as the first IR attack. At this time, the Bell states will not collapse because of Eve's measurement using an correct sequence and Eve can obtain the message Alice encodes by comparing the result $\lvert\Psi_{12}^+\rangle\lvert\Psi_{34}^-\rangle$ with the result $\lvert\Phi_{12}^+\rangle\lvert\Psi_{34}^+\rangle$ of the first eavesdropping. Then, Eve transfers the state $\lvert\Psi_{12}^+\rangle\lvert\Psi_{34}^-\rangle$ to Bob through quantum channel. After Bob receiving it, he performs the Bell basis measurement according to the location information he records previously. Due to entanglement swapping, the state $\lvert\Psi_{12}^+\rangle\lvert\Psi_{34}^-\rangle$ will yield one of the following four possible results with equal probability:

$$\lvert\Phi_{13}^-\rangle\lvert\Phi_{24}^+\rangle, \lvert\Phi_{13}^+\rangle\lvert\Phi_{24}^-\rangle, \lvert\Psi_{13}^+\rangle\lvert\Psi_{24}^-\rangle, \lvert\Psi_{13}^-\rangle\lvert\Psi_{24}^+\rangle, \qquad (3)$$

The initial state $\lvert\Psi_{13}^-\rangle\lvert\Phi_{24}^-\rangle$ sent to Alice should become $\lvert\Psi_{13}^+\rangle\lvert\Psi_{24}^-\rangle$ after Alice's unitary operations $(Z,X)$, which indicates that Eve is not detected with the probability of $\frac{1}{4}$ in A-B quantum channel. Similarly, the other three possible outcomes of Eve's measurement will yield $\lvert\Psi_{12}^+\rangle\lvert\Psi_{34}^-\rangle$ with the probability of $\frac{1}{4}$ after Bob performing a measurement on the intercepted Bell states. Therefore, the detection probability is $p_2 = 1 - 4 * \frac{1}{4} * \frac{1}{4} = \frac{3}{4}$ in B-A quantum channel. Table 4 shows the examples of the process that Eve eavesdrops while choosing the wrong location. Group 1 and Group 2 stand for the cases that Eve is detected and not detected, respectively.

The probability Eve chooses the incorrect EPR location is 50% (assuming Alice chooses randomly), therefore, the detection probability in B-A quantum channel and A-B quantum channel is $d_1 = \frac{1}{2} * \frac{1}{2} * p_1 = \frac{3}{16}$ (the probability that Alice chooses correctly is $\frac{1}{2}$) and $d_2 = \frac{1}{2} * p_2 = \frac{3}{8}$, respectively.

If Alice randomly selects n groups of bits to announces the message she encodes by public channel, then Bob compares $n$ corresponding groups of key bits with the initial random bits (thus discarding them as key bits, as they are no longer secret), the probability he find disagreement and identify the presence of Eve is $P_d = 1 - (\frac{5}{8})^n$. In order to detect an eavesdropper with the probability of 0.99999999, Alice and Bob need to compare $n = 40$ key bits, while Alice and Bob need to compare $n = 72$ key bits.

**Table 4.** The example of the process that Eve eavesdrops (the wrong location choice)

| | Group 1 (detected) | | | | Group 2 (not detected) | | | |
|---|---|---|---|---|---|---|---|---|
| Number of classical bits | 1 | 2 | 3 | 4 | 1 | 2 | 3 | 4 |
| Bobs random bit | 1 | 0 | 1 | 1 | 1 | 0 | 1 | 1 |
| Bob sending Bell states | $\lvert\Psi_{13}^-\rangle$ | $\lvert\Phi_{24}^-\rangle$ | $\lvert\Psi_{13}^-\rangle$ | $\lvert\Phi_{24}^-\rangle$ | $\lvert\Psi_{13}^-\rangle$ | $\lvert\Phi_{24}^-\rangle$ | $\lvert\Psi_{13}^-\rangle$ | $\lvert\Phi_{24}^-\rangle$ |
| Bell states Eve measures and sends | $\lvert\Psi_{13}^-\rangle$ | $\lvert\Phi_{24}^-\rangle$ | $\lvert\Psi_{13}^-\rangle$ | $\lvert\Phi_{24}^-\rangle$ | $\lvert\Psi_{13}^-\rangle$ | $\lvert\Phi_{24}^-\rangle$ | $\lvert\Psi_{13}^-\rangle$ | $\lvert\Phi_{24}^-\rangle$ |
| Alices random bit | 0 | 1 | 1 | 0 | 0 | 1 | 1 | 0 |
| Bell states Alice measures and sends | Z | / | / | X | Z | / | / | X |
| Bell states Eve measures again | $\lvert\Psi_{13}^+\rangle$ | $\lvert\Psi_{24}^-\rangle$ | $\lvert\Psi_{13}^+\rangle$ | $\lvert\Psi_{24}^-\rangle$ | $\lvert\Psi_{13}^+\rangle$ | $\lvert\Psi_{24}^-\rangle$ | $\lvert\Psi_{13}^+\rangle$ | $\lvert\Psi_{24}^-\rangle$ |
| The message Eve decodes | 0 | 1 | 1 | 0 | 0 | 1 | 1 | 0 |
| Bell states Bob measures | $\lvert\Phi_{13}^-\rangle$ | $\lvert\Phi_{24}^+\rangle$ | $\lvert\Phi_{13}^-\rangle$ | $\lvert\Phi_{24}^+\rangle$ | $\lvert\Psi_{13}^-\rangle$ | $\lvert\Psi_{24}^+\rangle$ | $\lvert\Psi_{13}^-\rangle$ | $\lvert\Psi_{24}^+\rangle$ |
| The message Bob decodes | 1 | 0 | 0 | 1 | 0 | 1 | 1 | 0 |

Taking the probability $c_1$ and $c_2$ of the decoy mode into account, the effective transmission rate, i.e. the number of message bits per protocol run, is $(1-c_1)(1-c_2)$, which is equal to the probability for a message transfer. Therefore, if Eve wants to eavesdrop one message transfer without being detected, the probability for this event reads

$$
\begin{aligned}
s(c_1, c_2, d_1, d_2) &= (1 - c_1)(1 - c_2) + [c_1(1 - d_1) + (1 - c_1)c_2 \\
&\quad (1 - d_2)](1 - c_1)(1 - c_2) + [c_1(1 - d_1) + (1 - c_1)c_2(1 - d_2)]^2 \\
&\quad (1 - c_1)(1 - c_2) + \cdots = \frac{(1 - c_1)(1 - c_2)}{1 - [c_1(1 - d_1) + (1 - c_1)c_2(1 - d_2)]}
\end{aligned}
\tag{4}
$$

Then the probability of successful eavesdropping $I = 4n$ bits is

$$
s(I, c_1, c_2, d_1, d_2) = \left( \frac{(1 - c_1)(1 - c_2)}{1 - [c_1(1 - d_1) + (1 - c_1)c_2(1 - d_2)]} \right)^{1/4}
\tag{5}
$$

In the limit $I \to \infty$ (a message or key of infinite length) we have $s \to 0$, so the GEQKD protocol is asymptotically secure. For example, a convenient choice of the control parameter is $c_1 = \frac{1}{2}, c_2 = \frac{1}{2}$, where on the average every four bit is a control bit. The probability that Eve successfully eavesdrops 8 group of key bits is as low as $s \approx 0.011$. In Fig. 2, the eavesdropping success probability as a function of the information gain $I$ is plotted for $c_1 = \frac{1}{2}, c_2 = \frac{1}{2}$.

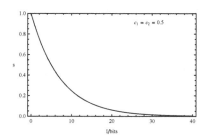

**Fig. 2.** Eavesdropping success probability as a function of the maximal eavesdropping information.

## 2.2 The Entanglement-Measure Attack

Since Alice makes the unitary operations only to the first and the forth of the particles $S_i$, Eve only needs to perform the entanglement-measure attack on the first and the forth of the particles $S_i$ (If Eve eavesdrop all the bits of the particles $S_i$, the detection probability will become larger [41]). After performing the attack operation $\hat{E}$, the states $|0\rangle$ and $|1\rangle$ become

$$\hat{E} \otimes |0, \chi\rangle = \alpha|0, \chi_{00}\rangle + \beta|1, \chi_{01}\rangle, \hat{E} \otimes |1, \chi\rangle = \beta'|0, \chi_{10}\rangle + \alpha'|1, \chi_{11}\rangle, \quad (6)$$

where $|\chi_{00}\rangle, |\chi_{01}\rangle, |\chi_{10}\rangle$ and $|\chi_{11}\rangle$ are the pure ancillary states uniquely determined by $\hat{E}$.

Firstly, let us calculate the detection probability in the B-A channel. Consider one certain checking pair, it is in the state $|\Phi^+\rangle$ at the beginning. After Eve's attack operation with exchanging the position of the second and the third qubit, it is changed to

$$|\Phi^+\rangle_{Eve} = \frac{1}{\sqrt{2}}(\alpha|0, 0, \chi_{00}\rangle + \beta|1, 0, \chi_{01}\rangle + \beta'|0, 1, \chi_{10}\rangle + \alpha'|1, 1, \chi_{11}\rangle) \quad (7)$$

When Alice performs a Bell measurement on the EPR pair in the control mode, the detection probability is

$$d = p(|\Phi^-\rangle) + p(|\Psi^+\rangle) + p(|\Psi^-\rangle) = 1 - p(|\Phi^+\rangle), \quad (8)$$

Where $p$ denotes probability. As a result, a lower bound of $d$ is obtained:

$$d_l = p(|\Psi^+\rangle) + p(|\Psi^-\rangle) = |\beta|^2 \le d. \tag{9}$$

As for Eve, one qubit of the EPR pair is indistinguishable from the complete mixture, so these qubits are considered in either of the states $|0\rangle$ or $|1\rangle$ with equal probability 0.5. Let us at first consider the case where Bob sends $|0\rangle$.

After Eve's attack operation and Alice encoding of the unitary operations $I, X, Y$ and $Z$ with the probabilities $p_0, p_1, p_2$ and $p_3$, respectively, the state can be written in the orthogonal basis $|0, \chi_{00}\rangle, |0, \chi_{01}\rangle, |1, \chi_{10}\rangle, |1, \chi_{11}\rangle$

$$\rho = \begin{pmatrix} (p_0+p_3)|\alpha|^2 & (p_0-p_3)\alpha\beta^* & 0 & 0 \\ (p_0-p_3)\alpha^*\beta & (p_0+p_3)|\beta|^2 & 0 & 0 \\ 0 & 0 & (p_1+p_2)|\alpha|^2 & (p_1-p_2)\alpha\beta^* \\ 0 & 0 & (p_1-p_2)\alpha^*\beta & (p_0+p_3)|\beta|^2 \end{pmatrix} \tag{10}$$

where $p_0 + p_1 + p_2 + p_3 = 1$. The maximal information $I_0$ that Eve can eavesdrop is $I_0 = \sum_{i=0}^{3} -\lambda_i \log_2 \lambda_i$, where $\lambda_i (i = 0, 1, 2, 3)$ are the eigenvalues of $\rho$.

In the case of $p_0 = p_1 = p_2 = p_3 = \frac{1}{4}$, the maximal information $I_0$ Eve can obtain is simplified as

$$I_0(d_l) = 1 - d_l \log_2 d_l - (1 - d_l) \log_2(1 - d_l), \tag{11}$$

Then assume that Bob sends $|1\rangle$ rather than $|0\rangle$. The above security analysis can be done in full analogy, resulting in the same relations. And the information $I_1(d)$ Eve can get is $I_1(d_l) = I_0(d_l)$. Therefore, the maximal information that Eve can obtain is

$$I(d_l) = \frac{I_0(d_l) + I_1(d_l)}{2} = 1 - d_l \log_2 d_l - (1 - d_l) \log_2(1 - d_l). \tag{12}$$

If Eve wants to obtain the full information (2 bits), the detection probability is $d_l = 0.5$, however, Eve can get 1 bit of information from each EPR pair with the error rate $d_l = 0$. In the A-B Channel, we still take the detection as $d_l$. Therefore, if Eve wants to eavesdrop one message transfer without being detected, the probability for this event reads

$$s(c_1, c_2, d_l) = (1 - c_1)(1 - c_2) + \{\frac{c_1}{2}[1 + (1 - d_l)^2] + (1 - c_1)c_2(1 - d_l)^2\}(1 - c_1)(1 - c_2)$$

$$+ \{\frac{c_1}{2}[1 + (1 - d_l)^2] + (1 - c_1)c_2(1 - d_l)^2\}^2(1 - c_1)(1 - c_2) + \cdots$$

$$= \frac{(1 - c_1)(1 - c_2)}{1 - \{\frac{c_1}{2}[1 + (1 - d_l)^2] + (1 - c_1)c_2(1 - d_l)^2\}} \tag{13}$$

Then the probability of successful eavesdropping $I = nI(d_l)$ bits is

$$s(I, c_1, c_2, d_l) = \left( \frac{(1 - c_1)(1 - c_2)}{1 - \{\frac{c_1}{2}[1 + (1 - d_l)^2] + (1 - c_1)c_2(1 - d_l)^2\}} \right)^{I/I(d_l)} \tag{14}$$

In the limit $I \to \infty$ (a message or key of infinite length) we have $s \to 0$, so the GEQKD protocol is asymptotically secure. For example, a convenient choice of the control parameter is $c_1 = \frac{1}{2}, c_2 = \frac{1}{2}$, where on the average every four bit is a control bit. The probability that Eve successfully eavesdrops 8 group of key bits is as low as $s \approx 0.0006$. In Fig. 3, the eavesdropping success probability as a function of the information gain $I$ is plotted for $c_1 = \frac{1}{2}, c_2 = \frac{1}{2}$ and for different detection probabilities d which Eve can choose. Note that for $d_l < 0.5$, Eve can only gets one part of the message right and does not even know which part she has obtained.

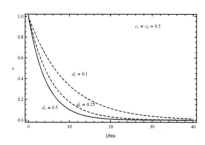

**Fig. 3.** Eavesdropping success probability as a function of the maximal eavesdropping information, plotted for a different detection probabilities $d$.

## 3  Quantum Circuit Simulation of GEQKD Protocol

At present, QKD has been studied widely in theory, however, only some important basic protocols, such as BB84 protocol [2], are implemented experimentally. Quantum circuit is essential to the practical realization of the protocol in experiment. It is well-known that any operation in quantum mechanics can be represented by a unitary evolution together with a measurement. Also, any unitary evolution can be accomplished by universal quantum logic gates [42]. Next, we will show the quantum circuit for implementing the proposed protocol.

Initially, Bob prepares four photons for each group, which are in the horizontal polarization state $|0\rangle$ or the vertical polarization state $|1\rangle$ randomly. Then he can choose the location information $\{(1, 2), (3, 4)\}$ or $\{(1, 3), (2, 4)\}$ to produce the EPR pairs. In order to achieve this goal, Bob need to perform Hadamard ($H$) and Controlled-Not (CNOT) gate based on the location information. After Alice obtains the photons, she applies the unitary operation on the first and the forth photon. After Bob receives the photons again, he makes the Bell state measurement (applying CNOT and $H$ gate and then measuring with the basis $\{|0\rangle, |1\rangle\}$) based on the location information. Without loss of generality, we will take the location $\{(1, 2), (3, 4)\}$ as an example to present the quantum circuit.

Figure 4 gives the quantum circuit for implementing the proposed protocol under Eve's attack while Eve chooses correctly. Figure 5 shows the quantum

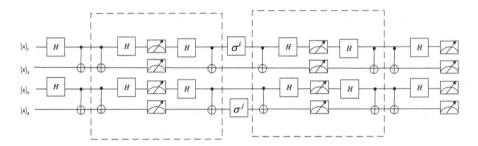

**Fig. 4.** Quantum circuit for implementing GEQKD protocol under Eve's attack while Eve chooses correctly. Where, $|x\rangle_i (i = 1, 2, 3, 4)$ represents the polarization state of the $i$th photon, which can be chosen as $|0\rangle$ or $|1\rangle$ randomly. In the dashed rectangle, Eve performs the Bell state measurement and re-prepare the new Bell state. $\sigma^i$ and $\sigma^j (i, j = I, X, Y, Z)$ is the unitary operation performed by Alice to encode the classical bits.

circuit for implementing GEQKD protocol while Eve chooses incorrectly. In this case, due to the existence of entanglement swapping, the new two photons will be entangled, which means the first and third photon, the second and forth photon will be the Bell state, respectively.

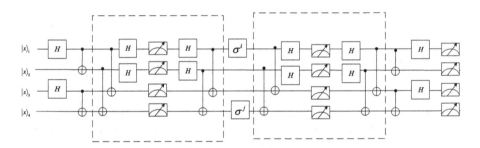

**Fig. 5.** Quantum circuit implementing GEQKD protocol under Eve's attack while Eve chooses incorrectly. Compared with Fig. 4, the difference takes places in the dashed rectangle. Eve chooses $\{(1, 3), (2, 4)\}$ to perform the Bell state and produce the new Bell state according to the location information $\{(1, 3), (2, 4)\}$.

## 4    Conclusion

In this paper, a novel QKD protocol is proposed and the security of this protocol is analyzed, which tells that the protocol is quasi-secure. Also, the efficient circuit simulation for implementing the proposed protocol is also constructed.

Compared with "Ping-pong" protocol, the proposed protocol needn't to store the qubit, which improves the maneuverability. What's more, the authorized party can make full use of the quantum bits without causing the waste of quantum bits while transmitting the messages.

Note that in this paper the proposed protocol is used as QKD instead of QSDC. Equivalently, the bits obtained in this protocol constitute the random key (i.e. the raw key but not the secert message), which generates the final key after some later operations such as error correction and privacy amplification.

One of the localizations is that the preparation of Bell state used in the protocol is more difficult than the preparation of the single photon, while we believe that the problem will be solved with the advancement of technology.

The scheme is only a theoretical model and we don't consider about the non-ideal conditions such as imperfect devices and noisy situations. In the further work, the experiment of this protocol will be made in Heifei National Laboratory for Physics Sciences at Microscale and Department of Modern Physics.

# References

1. Diffie, W., Hellman, M.: New directions in cryptography. IEEE Trans. Inf. Theory **22**(6), 644–654 (1976)
2. Bennett, C.H., Brassard, G.: Quantum cryptography: public key distribution and coin tossing. Theor. Comput. Sci. **560**(P1), 7–11 (2014)
3. Bennett, C.H., Bessette, F., Brassard, G., Salvail, L., Smolin, J.: Experimental quantum cryptography. J. Cryptol. **5**(1), 3–28 (1992)
4. Shor, P.W., Preskill, J.: Simple proof of security of the BB84 quantum key distribution protocol. Phys. Rev. Lett. **85**(2), 441 (2000)
5. Ekert, A.K.: Quantum cryptography based on bells theorem. Phys. Rev. Lett. **67**(6), 661 (1991)
6. Bennett, C.H., Brassard, G., Mermin, N.D.: Quantum cryptography without bells theorem. Phys. Rev. Lett. **68**(5), 557 (1992)
7. Bruß, D.: Optimal eavesdropping in quantum cryptography with six states. Phys. Rev. Lett. **81**(14), 3018 (1998)
8. Li, J., Li, N., Li, L.L., Wang, T.: One step quantum key distribution based on EPR entanglement. Sci. Rep. **6**, 28767 (2016)
9. Wang, Q., Zhang, C.H., Luo, S., Guo, G.C.: An enhanced proposal on decoy-state measurement device-independent quantum key distribution. Quantum Inf. Process. **15**(9), 3785–3797 (2016)
10. Máttar, A., Acín, A.: Implementations for device-independent quantum key distribution. Phys. Scr. **91**(4), 043003 (2016)
11. Kawakami, S., Sasaki, T., Koashi, M.: Security of the differential-quadrature-phase-shift quantum key distribution. Phys. Rev. A **94**(2), 022332 (2016)
12. Fröhlich, B., et al.: Long-distance quantum key distribution secure against coherent attacks. Optica **4**(1), 163–167 (2017)
13. Hatakeyama, Y., Mizutani, A., Kato, G., Imoto, N., Tamaki, K.: Differential-phase-shift quantum-key-distribution protocol with a small number of random delays. Phys. Rev. A **95**(4), 042301 (2017)
14. Hwang, W.Y., Su, H.Y., Bae, J.: Improved measurement-device-independent quantum key distribution with uncharacterized qubits. Phys. Rev. A **95**(6), 062313 (2017)

15. Lizama-Pérez, L.A., López, J.M., De Carlos López, E.: Quantum key distribution in the presence of the intercept-resend with faked states attack. Entropy **19**(1), 4 (2016)

16. Lai, H., Luo, M.X., Zhan, C., Pieprzyk, J., Orgun, M.A.: An improved coding method of quantum key distribution protocols based on fibonacci-valued oam entangled states. Phys. Lett. A **381**(35), 2922–2926 (2017)

17. Pastorello, D.: A quantum key distribution scheme based on tripartite entanglement and violation of CHSH inequality. Int. J. Quantum Inf. **15**(05), 1750040 (2017)

18. Wang, Y., Bao, W.S., Bao, H.Z., Zhou, C., Jiang, M.S., Li, H.W.: High-dimensional quantum key distribution with the entangled single-photon-added coherent state. Phys. Lett. A **381**(16), 1393–1397 (2017)

19. Long, G.L., Liu, X.S.: Theoretically efficient high-capacity quantum-key-distribution scheme. Phys. Rev. A **65**(3), 032302 (2002)

20. Boström, K., Felbinger, T.: Deterministic secure direct communication using entanglement. Phys. Rev. Lett. **89**(18), 187902 (2002)

21. Cai, Q.Y., Li, B.W.: Improving the capacity of the boström-felbinger protocol. Phys. Rev. A **69**(5), 054301 (2004)

22. Gao, T., Yan, F.L., Wang, Z.X.: Deterministic secure direct communication using GHZ states and swapping quantum entanglement. J. Phys. A: Math. Gen. **38**(25), 5761 (2005)

23. Chamoli, A., Bhandari, C.: Secure direct communication based on ping-pong protocol. Quantum Inf. Process. **8**(4), 347–356 (2009)

24. Deng, F.G., Long, G.L.: Secure direct communication with a quantum one-time pad. Phys. Rev. A **69**(5), 052319 (2004)

25. Qing-Yu, C., Bai-Wen, L.: Deterministic secure communication without using entanglement. Chin. Phys. Lett. **21**(4), 601 (2004)

26. Lucamarini, M., Mancini, S.: Secure deterministic communication without entanglement. Phys. Rev. Lett. **94**(14), 140501 (2005)

27. Jiang, D., Chen, Y., Gu, X., Xie, L., Chen, L.: Deterministic secure quantum communication using a single d-level system. Sci. Rep. **7**, 44934 (2017)

28. Guerra, A.G.A.H., Rios, F.F.S., Ramos, R.V.: Quantum secure direct communication of digital and analog signals using continuum coherent states. Quantum Inf. Process. **15**(11), 4747–4758 (2016)

29. Wang, C., Deng, F.G., Li, Y.S., Liu, X.S., Long, G.L.: Quantum secure direct communication with high-dimension quantum superdense coding. Phys. Rev. A **71**(4), 044305 (2005)

30. Li, J., Song, D., Li, R., Lu, X.: A quantum secure direct communication protocol based on four-qubit cluster state. Secur. Commun. Netw. **8**(1), 36–42 (2015)

31. Li, J., Pan, Z., Sun, F., Chen, Y., Wang, Z., Shi, Z.: Quantum secure direct communication based on dense coding and detecting eavesdropping with four-particle genuine entangled state. Entropy **17**(10), 6743–6752 (2015)

32. Zhao, X.L., Li, J.L., Niu, P.H., Ma, H.Y., Ruan, D.: Two-step quantum secure direct communication scheme with frequency coding. Chin. Phys. B **26**(3), 030302 (2017)

33. Nguyen, B.A.: Quantum dialogue. Phys. Lett. A **328**(1), 6–10 (2004)

34. Wang, H., Zhang, Y.Q., Liu, X.F., Hu, Y.P.: Efficient quantum dialogue using entangled states and entanglement swapping without information leakage. Quantum Inf. Process. **15**(6), 2593–2603 (2016)

35. Zarmehi, F., Houshmand, M.: Controlled bidirectional quantum secure direct communication network using classical XOR operation and quantum entanglement. IEEE Commun. Lett. **20**(10), 2071–2074 (2016)
36. Kao, S.H., Hwang, T.: Controlled quantum dialogue robust against conspiring users. Quantum Inf. Process. **15**(10), 4313–4324 (2016)
37. Zhou, N.R., Li, J.F., Yu, Z.B., Gong, L.H., Farouk, A.: New quantum dialogue protocol based on continuous-variable two-mode squeezed vacuum states. Quantum Inf. Process. **16**(1), 4 (2017)
38. Liu, Z.H., Chen, H.W.: Cryptanalysis and improvement of efficient quantum dialogue using entangled states and entanglement swapping without information leakage. Quantum Inf. Process. **16**(9), 229 (2017)
39. Wójcik, A.: Eavesdropping on the ping-pong quantum communication protocol. Phys. Rev. Lett. **90**(15), 157901 (2003)
40. Fu-Guo, D., Xi-Han, L., Chun-Yan, L., Ping, Z., Hong-Yu, Z.: Eavesdropping on theping-pong'quantum communication protocol freely in a noise channel. Chin. Phys. **16**(2), 277 (2007)
41. Gao, F., Guo, F.Z., Wen, Q.Y., Zhu, F.: Comparing the efficiency of different detection strategies of the ping-pong protocol. Sci. China Ser. G-Phys. Mech. Astron. **39**(2), 161–166 (2009)
42. Barenco, A., Bennett, C.H., Cleve, R., et al.: Elementary gates for quantum computation. Phys. Rev. A **52**, 3457 (2017)

# An Adaptive Threshold Algorithm for Offline Uyghur Handwritten Text Line Segmentation

Eliyas Suleyman[1], Palidan Tuerxun[1], Kamil Moydin[2], and Askar Hamdulla[2(✉)]

[1] School of Software, Xinjiang University, Urumqi 830046, People's Republic of China
[2] Institute of Information Science and Engineering, Xinjiang University, Urumqi 830046, People's Republic of China
askar@xju.edu.cn

**Abstract.** This paper presents an effective text-line segmentation algorithm and evaluates its performance on Uyghur handwritten text document images. Projection based adaptive threshold selection mechanism is implemented to detect and segment the text lines with different valued thresholds. The robustness of the proposed algorithm is admirable that experiments on 210 Uyghur handwritten document image including 2570 text lines got correct segmentation by 97.70% precision and 99.01% recall rate and outperformed the compared classic text-line segmentation algorithm on same evaluation set.

**Keywords:** Text line segmentation · Adaptive thresholding · Offline Uyghur handwritten documents

## 1 Introduction

Text line segmentation is significant stage of offline handwritten document recognition and analysis. Correctness of segmented text lines would influence the process and result of subsequent stages directly [1]. Text-line segmentation on document images of printed texts is easily handled by using simple projection method and a statistically estimated threshold. However, it is not a promising way to segment handwritten document images [2]. Unlike machine printed documents, due to high diversity in writing habits of different writers, distances within text lines are irregular and existence of touching and overlapping text lines makes this work challenging.

Modern Uyghur script is an alphabetic script which has 32 basic characters, written from right to left [3]. Almost each letter has several special ascenders or descenders which distinguish them from similar letter forms. Due to the cursive nature of Uyghur script, the special symbol may appear connected, overlapped not only in a word and text-line, but also between neighboring text-lines, as well. This makes text line segmentation more difficult than printed texts or other scripts of isolated styles.

Traditional projection-based text-line segmentation method uses a confirmed constant threshold to separate different and neighboring text lines [10]. It is suitable for machine printed text images due to equal or regular spatial distance between neighboring text lines. Yet, its effectiveness is not acceptable for handwritten documents.

H. Song et al. (Eds.): SIMUtools 2019, LNICST 295, pp. 302–312, 2019.
https://doi.org/10.1007/978-3-030-32216-8_29

In this paper, we propose a novel approach for text line segmentation based on projection and adaptive thresholding mechanism. The proposed method has proven its effectiveness and robustness during the experiments on handwritten text images of text-lines with different styles, lengths, skewing and touching degrees. Rest of the paper is organized as follows: some previous works are recalled in Sect. 2. In Sect. 3, the proposed method is described in detail. Discussion on the conducted experiments and evaluation methods are given in Sect. 4. Section 5 draws brief conclusion then.

## 2   Related Work

In 2006, Li et al. proposed an approach based on smearing [4]. They first convert a binary image to gray scale image using a Gaussian window. Then, text lines are extracted by evolving an initial estimate using level set method [1]. The algorithm correctly detected 85.6% of 2691 ground-truth text lines. The segmentation error caused by adjacent text lines and over-lapping text line makes this algorithm less compatible.

In 2009, Papavassiliou et al. proposed an algorithm based on the piece-wise projection [6]. The algorithm tested on the benchmarking datasets of IDCAR07 handwriting segmentation contest, correct rate of the segmentation reached 95.67%. Although the segmentation is mostly correct, over-segmentation is occurred.

In 2016, Bal et al. proposed a text line segmentation algorithm based on projection [7]. All Rising section in the projection is measured and the average value of rising section is treated as threshold. The algorithm is tested on the IAM database which contains more than 550 text images. This approach correctly segmented 95.65% text lines. Due to the chosen threshold is constant, it is not adaptable for various handwritten document.

In 2017, Ptak et al. proposes an algorithm based on projection with a variable threshold [9]. This method can segment handwritten text lines which text lines are in similar length. However, performance of segmentation declines when text lines are short or touched. The author tested the algorithm on their own collected Polish document images, which contains similar length text lines document and random length text lines. The testing result shows that the algorithm is not able to detect and segment the touched and short text lines in the Polish document.

In this paper, a projection based adaptive threshold estimation algorithm is proposed.

## 3   Methodology

### 3.1   Framework

The first-hand collected Uyghur handwritten text samples are preprocessed using common preprocessing techniques including turning the original image to the gray scale image, dilation, binarization and noise removal. After preprocessing the document image, horizontal projection of preprocessed image is calculated, and thresholding is performed according to projection peaks. After measuring threshold, each text line is segmented according to each previously determined threshold and the line separators are drawn at the valley point of each neighbor text lines in the original image. The major steps of proposed algorithm are shown in Fig. 1.

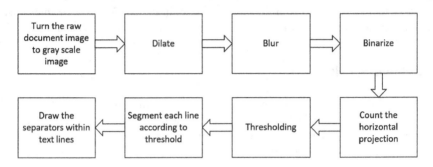

**Fig. 1.** Major steps of proposed algorithm

### 3.2   Preprocessing

Preprocessing aims to eliminate harmful or insignificant content and enhance useful features in document image. Thus, it improves generality of sample representation and performance of subsequent works [5]. Before the proposed text-line segmentation algorithm is applied, preprocessing is performed using the basic image processing technique which includes gray scaling, dilation, smoothing that contains noise removal and binarization which is utilized twice in proposed work. Firstly, weighted gray scaling method is used to turn the raw document image to gray image and binarized it afterward. Next, dilation is performed to thickening the text in document image. Then smoothing is applied to dilated image to eliminate insignificant stain points and smooth the document image in order to minimize local extrema in projection profile. Secondary binarization is conducted to at final step. Figure 2 shows the contrast of initial image and processed image.

(a). Initial image                    (b). Processed image

**Fig. 2.** Before and after processing the initial image

**Noise Removal and Smoothing**

Noise removal is important to any kind of image processing task [8], especially for handwritten document images. Since binarized image is dilated, consequently, noisy points are also becoming bigger that could affect subsequent processing. Filtering is a prevalent way to minimize or remove the noise in images. Each filter commonly contains a corresponding window. With the expansion of window size, result of filter would be vaguer. This means window size must be chosen adequately; otherwise, filtering will lose important information in image. In this paper, we use mean filtering to perform the noises removing. Mean filtering is a simple, intuitive and easy to implement method of smoothing images i.e. reducing the amount of intensity variation between one pixel and the next. For every pixel in image, the filter would calculate average value of corresponding window and replace the original value to the calculated one.

$$p_i = \frac{1}{m^2} \sum_{m=1}^{m^2} p_m \tag{1}$$

Where $p_i$ is the center of kernel, $p_m$ refers to the m-th visited pixel in a blurring kernel and $m$ indicates the size of kernel. Besides, we also used mean filter to minimize the local extrema (minima and maxima points) in projection profile. Some different blurring parameters are tested to observe their blurring effects, setting window size to 30 by 30 pixels gave the best blurring effect and is selected as blurring parameter in later experiments.

**Binarization**

Otsu thresholding method is used for image binarization [11].

$$\sigma_\omega^2(t) = \omega_0(t)\sigma_0^2(t) + \omega_1(t)\sigma_1^2(t) \tag{2}$$

Weights $\omega_0$ and $\omega_1$ are probabilities of two classes, which refers text lines and the background, separated by a threshold $t$, and $\sigma_0^2$ and $\sigma_1^2$ is variance of these two classes. In this work, binarization also enhances the generality of the text lines in our document image. The projection after binarization on each differently blurred images are shown in Fig. 3. The black straight line indicates the mean value of the projection.

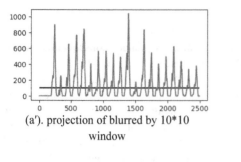

(a'). projection of blurred by 10*10 window

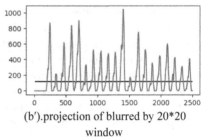

(b').projection of blurred by 20*20 window

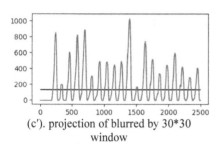

(c'). projection of blurred by 30*30 window

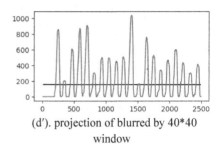

(d'). projection of blurred by 40*40 window

**Fig. 3.** Projections after binarization

### 3.3   Text Line Segmentation

Widely acknowledged text line segmentation method based on projection calculates the average gap between successive text lines, then define a constant threshold to separate these text lines [9]. However, when threshold is constant, touched or near text lines might be omitted. Therefore, the process of defining threshold must be adaptive to different gaps between each neighbor text line couples.

In this work, after calculating horizontal projection profile $H$ from the preprocessed image, significant peaks' location which might represent each potential text lines are extracted to set $P$. Next, thresholding is performed as follows: visit each location $P(i)$ in set $P$; for given $P(i)$, the algorithm would take the half of current peak's value as threshold $T$ [9].

$$T_p = \frac{P(i)}{2} \tag{3}$$

Since each threshold is differently measured form peaks of horizontal projection values, the threshold will have different values for each neighbor text lines. After measuring each threshold, the projection values are visited reversely from the current peak location. If the currently visited projection value is lesser than threshold, then the location of this projection value is assumed as starting point and added to set $S$ and break the traverse loop. Then, the ending points are determined same way using forward visiting of projection values and the estimated ending point is added to set $E$.

The pre-estimated text-line intervals and tip points (starting, ending) are checked to confirm their validity and correctness by the following algorithm. First, traverse each element in set $S$ and set $E$, then get start point $S(i)$ and end point $E(i)$, to calculate midpoint $M_i$ of each interval using equation below;

$$M_i = \frac{S(i) + E(i)}{2} \qquad (4)$$

Second, get next interval's start point $S(i+1)$, if it is greater or equal to $M_i$, then accept it as a true interval, otherwise it is omitted (5). This process makes the performance of interval selection more acceptable.

$$\begin{cases} S(i+1) \geq M_i \ true \\ S(i+1) < M_i \ false \end{cases} \qquad (5)$$

After modifying set $S$ and $E$, straight lines are drawn to separate the text-lines in the document image. The separator lines are drawn horizontally at valley points between two adjacent estimated text-line positions which is between the current interval's ending point and next interval's starting point.

### 3.4 Algorithm

**Step 1:** Read a handwritten document image as a multi-dimensional array.
**Step 2:** Convert the raw image to gray scale image as G[][].
**Step 3:** Dilate the gray scale image G[][] and store it into matrix D[][].
**Step 4:** Blur the dilated matrix D[][] and store it into matrix P[][].
**Step 5:** Binarize the blurred matrix P[][] and store it into matrix B[][].
**Step 6:** Calculate the horizontal projection profile of binarized matrix B[][] and store the projection vector into HPP[].
**Step 7:** The peaks', which is above the mean value of projection, location is added to set P.
**Step 8:** For element in set P, calculate the threshold by multiplying 0.5 to peak value. Visit the elements of the HPP[] vector from current location forwardly and reversely to determine ending point and starting point, respectively. Where projection value is lesser than threshold is measured as starting point or ending point and add to set S and set E.
**Step 9:** Check the intervals whether it is overlapped by observing the starting point of interval whether it is greater than the next interval's midpoint. If it is greater, then accept it. If it is not delete the starting point and ending point from set S and set E.
**Step 10:** Draw a straight line at the valley point between two adjacent intervals' valley point.
**Step 11:** End.

# 4  Experimental Result

## 4.1  Database

To verify the proposed algorithm, we collected 210 Uyghur handwritten document image including 2570 text lines. The collected handwritten documents are written by different writers that each document varies in length and handwriting styles. The handwriting styles in the established database are broadly categorized into three types: (1) neatly written text-lines with random lengths; (2) similar length of text-lines in casual style that contain many overlapping and ligatures; (3) skewed normal handwriting. Figure 4 shows some typical examples of the mentioned handwriting styles in the database. Each document image is separately stored in TIF format. The pixel intensity of the samples also varies between 1477 × 944 to 2175 × 2277.

**Fig. 4.**  Three samples of database

## 4.2  Evaluation Method

In this paper, we calculated precision, recall and the F-measure to evaluate the performance of proposed algorithm [12]. Precision is based on manually counting the total segmented text lines and correctly segmented text lines, recall is based on counting the total text lines and the correctly segmented text lines. Then, the F-measure is calculated according to precision and recall.

$$P = \frac{L_c}{L_s} \tag{6}$$

$$R = \frac{L_c}{L_t} \tag{7}$$

$$F = \frac{2PR}{P+R} \tag{8}$$

Where $L_c$ and $L_s$ denotes the correctly segmented text lines and total segmented text lines, respectively. $L_t$ refers the total lines in document image.

### 4.3 Result and Analysis

There are three parameters is taken in to the participant algorithm which is the input image, windows size of filter and the relative threshold. The optimum values of parameters are given that the window size takes 9 and the relative threshold takes 0.5. The experiment results of text-line segmentation on our dataset are shown in Fig. 5 and Table 1. For comparison, we evaluated the participant algorithm on our database.

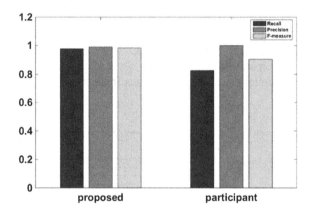

**Fig. 5.** Comparison of algorithms

**Table 1.** Result of experiments

|          | Proposed | Participant |
| -------- | -------- | ----------- |
| Recall    | 97.70%   | 82.75%      |
| Precision | 99.01%   | 99.99%      |
| F-measure | 98.35%   | 90.56%      |

In the participant algorithm [9], the Polish document image is preprocessed including turning the original image to gray scale image, binarization and noise reduction. Then count the projection profile of preprocessed image and sort it with descending order. Then visit each value of sorted projection to determine the threshold. Each time the algorithm chooses a threshold, text lines would be segmented afterward. If the text lines are already segmented, the algorithm would continue to the next iteration. The algorithm stops when the current value of projection is lesser than 1/10 of maximum value of projection.

In contrast, our algorithm's preprocessing stage has one more step which is dilation. This guarantees the important features of text in document image not to be removed by the noise reduction. In the respect of threshold measuring, we extract each location corresponding to the significant peaks to determine the threshold rather than sorting the entire projection profile. In text line extraction, our algorithm starts visiting from the location of a significant peak, terminates when algorithm find a starting point or an ending point of one interval, rather than visiting all values of projection. For checking the extracted text lines whether it is correctly segmented, we conducted checking mechanism that is totally different from the participant algorithm. The participant algorithm simply just omits if the currently segmented text lines overlaps the intervals which is segmented previously, even it is not severely overlapped. In our checking mechanism, we consider each two adjacent intervals and observe the letter intervals start point whether it is greater than the former's midpoint.

According to results of the two segmentation algorithms in Table 1, the proposed algorithm outperformed the participant algorithm in recall and F-measure. Although the precision of the participant algorithm is higher than the proposed algorithm, its recall rate is much lower than proposed algorithm. This means the participant algorithm is not as strong as the proposed algorithm in text-line detection perspective. The segmentation precision of the participant algorithm is high for neatly styled text-lines, but it is observed not strong enough to detect sufficient text lines. Some text-line segmentation

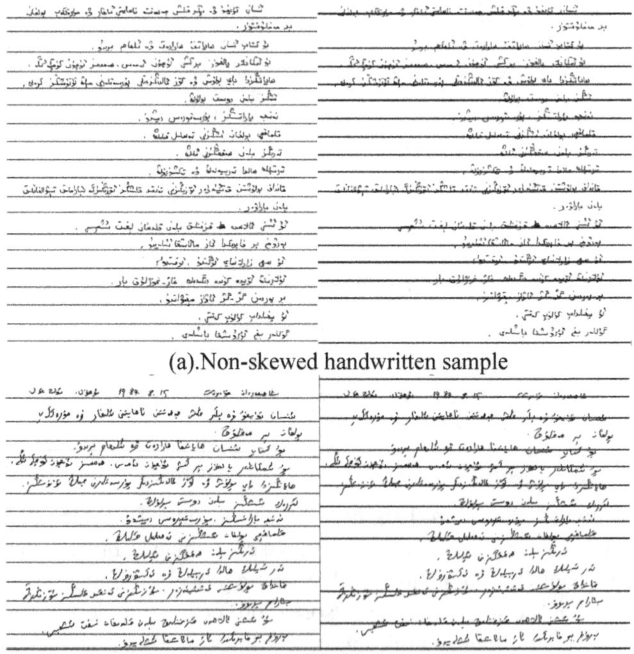

(a).Non-skewed handwritten sample

(b).Skewed handwritten sample

**Fig. 6.** Result of two different algorithms

effects of the compared algorithm are illustrated in Fig. 6. In sample (a), which is neatly written handwriting sample, the participant algorithm is unable to detect and segment short text lines. Although the text lines in sample (b) is mostly similar in the respect of length, the casual writing style and skewed text lines affected the participant algorithm's accuracy. Even the participant algorithm detected one of the skewed text lines, the segmentation is incorrect. But our algorithm segments the all text lines in both sample properly.

## 5   Conclusion

This paper proposed a novel approach for off-line Uyghur handwritten text line segmentation using projection based adaptive threshold selection. The proposed algorithm is verified on 210 different Uyghur handwritten document images. The experimental results show robustness of the proposed algorithm. Recall rate of the proposed text-line segmentation algorithm is observed as 97.70% which is much higher than 82.35% recall of the compared algorithm. However, there are some disadvantages in proposed algorithm due to its simple projection-based mechanism. If the written direction of document is severely skewed, the performance of the proposed algorithm would decline or even unable to segment skewing styled text lines. Another factor that makes the performance of the algorithm decline is incorrect peak extraction from calculated projection profile. To develop more comprehensive and general text-line segmentation algorithm is the main content of our next work.

**Acknowledgments.** This work has been supported by the National Natural Science Foundation of China (under grant of 61462080) and Ph.D. Scientific Research Startup Project of Xinjiang University.

## References

1. Razak, Z., et al.: Off-line handwriting text line segmentation: a review. Int. J. Comput. Sci. Netw. Secur. **7**, 12–20 (2008)
2. Yanikoglu, B., Sandon, P.A.: Segmentation of off-line cursive handwriting using linear programming. Pattern Recogn. **31**(12), 1825–1833 (1998)
3. Abliz, A., Simayi, W., Moydin, K., Hamdulla, A.: A survey on methods for basic unit segmentation in off-line handwritten text recognition. Int. J. Future Gener. Commun. Netw. **9**, 137–152 (2016)
4. Li, Y., Zheng, Y., Doermann, D., et al.: A new algorithm for detecting text line in handwritten documents. Proc. IWFHR La Baule **2**, 35–40 (2006)
5. Nie, L., Jiang, D., Guo, L.: A compressive sensing-based approach to end-to-end network traffic reconstruction utilising partial measured origin-destination flows. Trans. Emerg. Telecommun. Technol. **26**, 1108–1117 (2015)
6. Papavassiliou, V., et al.: Handwritten document image segmentation into text lines and words. Pattern Recogn. **43**(1), 369–377 (2010)

7. Bal, A., Saha, R.: An improved method for handwritten document analysis using segmentation, baseline recognition and writing pressure detection. Proc. Comput. Sci. **93**, 403–415 (2016)
8. Jiang, D., Huo, L., Song, H.: Rethinking behaviors and activities of base stations in mobile cellular networks based on big data analysis. IEEE Trans. Netw. Sci. Eng. **1**(1), 1–12 (2018)
9. Ptak, R., Żygadło, B., Unold, O.: Projection-based text line segmentation with a variable threshold. Int. J. Appl. Math. Comput. Sci. **27**(1), 195–206 (2017)
10. Al-Dmour, A., Zitar, R.A.: Word extraction from arabic handwritten documents based on statistical measures. Int. Rev. Comput. Softw. **11**(5), 436–444 (2016)
11. Ohtsu, N.: A threshold selection method from gray-level histograms. IEEE Trans. Syst. Man Cybern. **9**(1), 62–66 (1979)
12. Jiang, D., Huo, L., Li, Y.: Fine-granularity inference and estimations to network traffic for SDN. PLoS One **13**(5), 1–23 (2018)

# Channel Equalization Secret Communication Method Based on Time Reversal

Zhu Jiang[1,2] and Ding Qiang[1,2(✉)]

[1] School of Communication and Information Engineering, Chongqing
University of Posts and Telecommunications, Chongqing 400065, China
1325242@qq.com, 676068591@qq.com
[2] Chongqing Key Lab of Mobile Communications Technology,
Chongqing 400065, China

**Abstract.** For the eavesdropping channel problem in physical layer security research. A wireless channel equalization and secretive transmission method based on time reversal is proposed, which is called equalized time reversal (ETR) technology. The method is applicable to rayleigh fading channel, and reduces the inter-symbol interference (ISI) component of the traditional time reversal (TR) by equalizing the indoor wireless channel to improve the secrecy performance.

**Keywords:** Channel equalization · Time reversal · Secrecy performance

## 1 Introduction

In communication system, the upper network layer of protocol stack uses private key and public key cryptosystem to manage the problems related to authentication privacy. With the enhancement of modern computer functions, the encryption and decryption algorithms have been broken, and the upper-level specific security protocols ignore the most basic layer in wireless communication [1, 2]. The communication of the wireless device is transmitted by the message through the wireless channel through encoding and information data modulation. Wireless channels lack physical boundaries, and any nearby receivers may listen for transmission signals or may block transmissions. It is important to design a wireless transmission system that guarantees low probability of interception and does not rely on the upper layer encryption and key.

The wireless communication has the characteristic of openness, the information transmission of terminals is easy to be overheard by the illegal users, and the security of wireless communication system has become the hotspot of research. The wireless channel has the characteristics of frequency domain, spatial domain and time-domain diversity, and provides the space for the wireless communication security to be studied. Wyner first put forward the interception channel model, which consists of three nodes of sender (Alice), legal receiver (Bob) and illegal receiver (Eve) [3]. The study of physical layer security has obtained good results in the fields of secure coding, key extraction [4], coordinated jamming [5], random weighting of antenna array [6], artificial noise [7], and so on [8].

H. Song et al. (Eds.): SIMUtools 2019, LNICST 295, pp. 313–325, 2019.
https://doi.org/10.1007/978-3-030-32216-8_30

Time reversal (TR) is a signal processing technology, which not only has the function of focusing signal, but also simplifies the complexity of receiver, and is used for multiple input multiple output (MIMO) ultra-wideband (UWB) Communication and beyond the diffraction limit of the super resolution and other characteristics. TR can play its greatest role in a rich scattering environment. The enclosed or semi-closed interior has a rich scattering scene, the environment is relatively complex, the channel is usually slow to change, and the channel state information does not need to be updated quickly. Therefore, the use of TR in indoor communication is a good choice. TR is also widely used in indoor position [9], cancer detection [10], underwater communications [11] and many other fields. In a TR process, the time reversal mirror (TRM) which is located near the target point, receives the detection signal from the target point, TRM each unit will receive the signal after the reversal of the timeline to launch again, at the target point will receive a higher main peak amplitude signal, And the signal in the time domain has the compression phenomenon, which is called the time reversal spatial focusing characteristic and the time focusing characteristic. Because time reversal has the characteristics of space-time focusing, it gets a lot of attention in the physical layer secure transmission.

In [12], Tan presents a MIMO-UWB TR model combining MIMO-UWB systems with TR technology. The physical layer confidentiality of the MIMO-UWB system with TR was studied and compared with the system without the TR technique. It is verified that the TR technology can improve the confidentiality of the system, and also analyzes the influence of the number of the legitimate receiver antenna and the number of the interception antenna, and the multipath number on the system secrecy capacity in the TR-MIMO system. In [13], El-Sallabi presents the characterization of the secrecy capability of the time reversal technique based on physical layer security, and studies the secrecy ability of the time inversion technique of the dense diffuse scattering radio channel. For diffuse wireless channels, the signal-to-noise ratio (SNR) saturation threshold varies with the number of multipath components in the mirror channel. In [14, 15], Han proposed a time-reversed multiple access scheme for multi-path multi-user downlink networks. This scheme takes advantage of the nature of the multipath channel. Due to the spatial focusing effect of the TR structure, energy can be collected at a predetermined receiving location, reducing interference between users. Under the Rayleigh fading channel model, the proposed scheme can increase the signal to interference and noise ratio (SINR) and the reachable confidentiality rate. In [16], the concept of an average effective secret SINR is proposed by Tran, which is used to show the security of the time inversion transmission system. The authors consider two correlations, namely the correlation of channel between transmission antennas and the channel correlation between legitimate users and eavesdroppers. Based on this, the analytic formula of the average effective SINR is deduced. The numerical simulation shows that the analytic expression can measure the security of physical layer transport in the correlated multipath channel environment well. The spatial focus of TR is that all the multipath components are added in the position of the receiver, and they are incoherent in other positions in the space. This is allowed by the spatial signature contained in the channel impulse response (CIR). The in-phase increase of the multi-path component occurs at a specific sampling time. This effect is due to the matching filter behavior of the TR-Filter and the partial equalization characteristic, which reduces the Inter symbol Interference (ISI) [17]. The main advantage of TR technology relative to the traditional multicarrier system is that it decreases the complexity of receiving computation significantly in the receiver [18, 19].

From the above analysis, some researchers have analyzed the theory of TR technology in physical layer and the confidentiality of interception channel model in the context of low complexity communication, less on how to further improve the traditional TR confidentiality can further research. Based on the above background, this paper puts forward a new equalization time reversal (ETR) technique to improve the secrecy performance. This technique is used to configure the equalizer and TRM at the sending end, and to balance the wireless channel to improve the system confidentiality.

## 2   System Model

In this paper, the Wyner eavesdropping model is improved. The transmitter uses the equalizer and TRM cascade configuration. The specific system model is shown in Fig. 1.

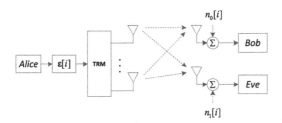

**Fig. 1.** System model

The system is mainly composed of the sender (Alice), the legal receiver (Bob), and the eavesdropping user. (Eve) constitutes. The eavesdropping user is passive eavesdropping, and no active attack is issued. The number of transmitting antennas is M, and both the legal receiver and the eavesdropping user are received by a single antenna. For convenience, 0 indicates the legal receiver Bob, and 1 indicates the eavesdropping user Eve. The CIR of the sender Alice and the receiver n (0, 1) can be expressed as

$$h_{mn}(i) = \sum_{l=0}^{L-1} \sigma_{mn,l}\delta(i - \tau_{mn,l}) \tag{1}$$

Where $L$ is the number of resolvable multi-paths of the wireless channel. $\sigma_{mn,l}$ and $\tau_{mn,l}$ respectively represent the amplitude and delay of the $l$ path. And satisfied with $E[h_{mn}(i)] = 0$, $E[|h_{mn}(i)|^2] = \sigma_{mn,i}^2$. In the TRM module, record $g_{m0}(i) \ni C^{L\times 1}$ as the information transmission pre-filtering vector and satisfy

$$g_{m0}[i] = \frac{\sqrt{\rho} h_{m0}^*[L-1-i]}{\sqrt{\sum_{m=1}^{M} E[||h_{m0}||^2]}}$$

$$= \frac{\sqrt{\rho} h_{m0}^*[L-1-i]}{\sqrt{P_0}} \qquad (2)$$

$\rho$ is the total average transmission power, $h_{m0}^*$ represents the conjugate of $h_{m0}$, $||\cdot||$ represents the Frobenius norm, defined as $||x(t)||^2 = \int_{-\infty}^{+\infty} |x(t)|^2 dt$. $P_0$ is the power normalization factor denoted as $P_0 = \sum_{m=1}^{M} E[||h_{m0}||^2]$, and the equivalent channel after time inversion is

$$h_{mn}^{eq}[i] = g_{m0}[i] \otimes h_{mn}[i]$$

$$= \frac{1}{\sqrt{P_0}} \sum_{l=0}^{L-1} h_{mn}[l] h_{m0}^*[L-1-i+l] \qquad (3)$$

where $i \in (0 \ldots 2L-2)$.

## 2.1 Equalizer Design

Traditional TR technology has a large number of ISI components at the receiving end. Depending on the specific channel implementation, ISI can represent a significant percentage of the overall received power, affecting detection. The usual solution is to use RAKE receiver or equalization technology at the receiver. However, this will increase the computational complexity. To reduce the reception complexity, this paper considers adding a single equalizer to all the transmitting antennas at the sender. The equalizer and TRM are cascaded to minimize the ISI component of the receiver through wireless channel equalization. Therefore, an equalization vector $\varepsilon[i]$ of length $L_E = 2L_\varepsilon + 1$ is designed. The equivalent power normalization factor is $P_\varepsilon$ after the equalizer and the time reversal mirror are cascaded.

$$P_\varepsilon = \sum_{m=1}^{M} \sum_{i=0}^{L+2L_E-1} |h_{m0}^*[L-1-i] \otimes \varepsilon[i]|^2 \qquad (4)$$

Then, the sender transmitting antenna m sends a signal $s[i]$ after being processed.

$$x_m[i] = \sqrt{\rho} s[i] \otimes \frac{h_{m0}^*[L-1-i \otimes \varepsilon[i]]}{\sqrt{P_\varepsilon}} \qquad (5)$$

After adopting the equalization combined with the TR scheme, the receiver receives the signal as

$$y_0[i] = \frac{\sqrt{\rho}}{\sqrt{P_\varepsilon}} x[i] \otimes \varepsilon[i] \otimes \sum_{m=1}^{M} h_{m0}^{eq}[i] + n_0[i] \qquad (6)$$

The equalizer is designed to reduce the ISI power, and its specific design satisfies the following formula.

$$\varepsilon[i] \otimes \sum_{m=1}^{M} h_{m0}^{eq}[i] = \delta[i - i_0] \tag{7}$$

where $i_0 \in (0 \dots 2L + L_E - 3)$, Eq. (8) with $L_E$ unknowns and $2L + L_E - 2$ overdetermined linear equations can be expressed as a matrix

$$\begin{pmatrix} \sum_{m=1}^{M} h_{m0}^{eq}[0] & & \\ \vdots & \ddots & \\ \sum_{m=1}^{M} h_{m0}^{eq}[2L-2] & & \ddots \\ 0 & & \\ \vdots & & \ddots \end{pmatrix} \begin{pmatrix} \varepsilon[0] \\ \vdots \\ \varepsilon[L_E - 1] \end{pmatrix} = \begin{pmatrix} 0 \\ \vdots \\ 1 \\ \vdots \\ 0 \end{pmatrix} \tag{8}$$

The first matrix $\mathbf{H} \in C^{(2L+L_E-2) \times L_E}$ in the formula is the Topliz matrix, so the vector $\boldsymbol{\varepsilon}$ has a unique solution $\boldsymbol{\varepsilon} = (\mathbf{H}^H \mathbf{H})^{-1} \mathbf{H}^H \boldsymbol{\delta}_{n0}$ [20]. When $L_E \to \infty$, the ISI is completely eliminated. $\varphi$ and $H_{m0}^{eq}$ are the DFT of $\varepsilon[i]$ and $h_{m0}^{eq}[i]$, respectively, so it can be expressed in the frequency domain

$$\varphi[k] = \frac{\exp(-j\frac{2\pi(n_0 - L + 1)}{2L + 2L_E - 1}k)}{\sum_{i=1}^{M} |H_{m0}^{eq}[k]|^2} \tag{9}$$

After the traditional TR channel is subjected to the above equalization processing, the equivalent channel is re-recorded as

$$h_{eq} \approx \frac{\sqrt{\rho}}{\sqrt{P_\varepsilon}} \varepsilon[i] \otimes \sum_{m=1}^{M} h_{m0}^{eq}[i] \tag{10}$$

It can be seen from Eqs. (3) and (4) that the equivalent channel is related to the equalizer length and the number of channel resolvable multi-paths. As $L_E$ increases, the normalization factor increases. Then according to Eq. (6), normalization is known. The increase of the factor causes the peak amplitude of the channel to decrease.

Figure 2 is an equivalent channel simulation diagram with 4 antennas at the sender and single antennas at the receiver. It can be seen from the figure that the main peak amplitude of the TR equivalent channel is high, and the sub-peaks of the main peak are also prominent. The main peak amplitude of the equivalent channel after ETR is slightly lower than TR, and the sub-peaks on both sides of the main peak have been greatly reduced, so that the ISI is alleviated. The equalized power peak amplitude of the channel after equalization decreases. The above analysis inferred consistency, thus verifying the correctness of the inference.

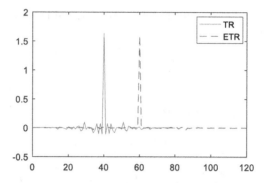

**Fig. 2.** Equivalent channel contrast diagram

## 2.2   Received Signal Component

After the equalization is used, it can be seen from the above analysis that the legal receiver can theoretically completely eliminate the ISI. In fact, it can only be greatly reduced and cannot be completely eliminated. This is because the receiver's performance limit, the receiver can determine the number of multipath. The design of the equalizer, the length of the equalization vector will also be affected.

Due to the focusing characteristics of TR, the desired signal takes a sample at the center tap of the receiver, while the other tap signal samples are the main factor of inter-symbol interference. Therefore, the Eq. (6) in Sect. 2.1 is split, and the signal received by the legal receiver is re-recorded as

$$
\begin{aligned}
y_0[i] \;=\; & \sqrt{\frac{\rho}{P_g}}\left(\boldsymbol{\varepsilon} \otimes \sum_{m=1}^{M} \mathbf{h}_{m0}^{eq}\right)x[i-L-1+L_E] + \\
& \sqrt{\frac{\rho}{P_g}}\sum_{l=0,l\neq L-1+L_E}^{2L+2L_E-2}\left(\boldsymbol{\varepsilon} \otimes \sum_{m=1}^{M} \mathbf{h}_{m0}^{eq}\right)x[i-l] + n_0[i]
\end{aligned}
\tag{11}
$$

The received signal consists of three parts: expected signal, ISI and additive white Gaussian noise.

## 3   Secrecy Performance Analysis

In this section, the secrecy performance of the system will be analyzed, starting from the secrecy SINR, the secrecy capacity and the bit error rate (BER). The theoretical analysis and derivation will be used to obtain the analytical formula, and finally the conclusion will be drawn.

### 3.1   Signal-to-Interference-Plus Noise Ratio

Consider a digital multiple input single output (MISO) baseband wireless communication system with M transmit antennas and single antennas for receiving legitimate users and eavesdropping users. According to Eq. (10), the expected signal power and symbol interference power of the legitimate users in the ETR scheme are respectively

$$P_{Sig}^0 = \frac{\rho}{P_g} |(\varepsilon \otimes \sum_{m=1}^{M} \mathbf{h}_{m0}^{eq})[L-1+L_E]| \tag{12}$$

$$P_{ISI}^0 = \frac{\rho}{P_g} \sum_{l=0, l \neq L-1+L_E}^{2L+2L_E-2} |(\varepsilon \otimes \sum_{m=1}^{M} \mathbf{h}_{m0}^{eq})[l]|^2 \tag{13}$$

It is known from Eqs. (7) and (8) that the design of the equalizer greatly reduces the ISI component of the legal receiver, so the ISI will be very small. The SNR of the legitimate user under the ETR scheme for

$$\gamma_0 = \frac{P_{Sig}^0}{P_{ISI}^0 + \sigma_0^2} \tag{14}$$

The reduction of $P_{ISI}^0$ will theoretically increase the SINR of the legal receiver. Similarly, the SINR of the eavesdropping end can be expressed as

$$\gamma_1 = \frac{P_{Sig}^1}{P_{ISI}^1 + \sigma_1^2} \tag{15}$$

The system's secret SINR is defined as

$$\gamma = \frac{\gamma_0 - \gamma_1}{1 + \gamma_1} \tag{16}$$

From the above analysis, the expectation of confidential SINR can be expressed as

$$\bar{\gamma} = E[\gamma] = E\left[\frac{\gamma_0 - \gamma_1}{1 + \gamma_1}\right] \tag{17}$$

known by the literature [10]

$$E\left[\frac{\gamma_0 - \gamma_1}{1 + \gamma_1}\right] = \frac{E[\gamma_0 - \gamma_1]}{E[1 + \gamma_1]} + \eta \tag{18}$$

where $\eta$ is a very small number, which can be ignored, and re-record the Eq. (18) as

$$E[\gamma] = E\left[\frac{\gamma_0 - \gamma_1}{1 + \gamma_1}\right] = \frac{E[\gamma_0 - \gamma_1]}{E[1 + \gamma_1]} \tag{19}$$

This will give you the expectation of secrecy SINR.

In the traditional TR scheme, the secrecy SINR of the legal receiver has a large amount of ISI, which makes the secrecy SINR greatly affected by ISI. Using the ETR scheme greatly reduces the ISI, so that the secrecy SINR is improved and the secret SINR is also improved.

## 3.2  Capacity of System

Generally, the secret capacity is inferred from the secret SINR in the eavesdropping channel. The secret capacity is defined as the difference between the legal user channel capacity and the eavesdropping user channel capacity. According to the Shannon formula, the formula for the secret capacity is defined as

$$
\begin{aligned}
C &= \log_2(1 + \gamma_0) - \log_2(1 + \gamma_1) \\
&= \log(1 + \tfrac{\gamma_0 - \gamma_1}{1 + \gamma_1})
\end{aligned}
\tag{20}
$$

From Sect. 3.1, $\frac{\gamma_0 - \gamma_1}{1 + \gamma_1}$ is the confidential SINR of the whole system, which is expressed by $\gamma$.

$$
\gamma = \max\left(\tfrac{\gamma_0 - \gamma_1}{1 + \gamma_1}, 0\right)
\tag{21}
$$

For any eavesdropping to achieve absolute secure communication, it is necessary to satisfy $0 < C_1 \leq C$ and $C_1$ as the information transmission rate of secure communication. By analyzing the secret signal to noise ratio of Sect. 3.1 to ETR, the Eqs. (14) and (15) are brought into Eq. (20). After the equalization, the system's confidential capacity $C$ is

$$
\begin{aligned}
C &= \log\left[1 + \left[\frac{E[\gamma_0 - \gamma_1]}{E[1 + \gamma_1]}\right]\right] \\
&= \log\left[1 + \left[\frac{E\left[\frac{P^0_{Sig}}{P^0_{ISI} + \sigma^2_0}\right] - E\left[\frac{P^1_{Sig}}{P^1_{ISI} + \sigma^2_1}\right]}{1 + E\left[\frac{P^1_{Sig}}{P^1_{ISI} + \sigma^2_1}\right]}\right]\right]
\end{aligned}
\tag{22}
$$

The secrecy capacity of the system is proportional to the expected signal power of the legitimate user, and inversely proportional to the power of the ISI signal.

## 3.3  Bit Error Rate Analysis

The transmitting end adopts QPSK modulation, and the expression of expected signal power, ISI signal power and noise signal power of the ETR legal receiving end has been given in the equation of Sect. 3.1. The BER can be expressed according to the literature [21].

$$
P \approx Q\left(\sqrt{\frac{P^0_{Sig}}{P^0_{ISI} + \sigma^2_0}}\right)
\tag{23}
$$

Where $Q(\cdot)$ is the complementary cumulative distribution function of the standard Gaussian random variable.

### 3.4    Complexity Analysis

In this paper, the number of transmit antennas is not considered, and the complexity of TR and ETR is analyzed and compared. The following figure compares the detection time of TR and ETR in time domain. The effect of TRM pre-filtering in traditional TR leads to the focus of the received signal at the legal receiver. The peak energy is collected at the center tap L. In ETR, the channel equalization of the TRM and the equalizer causes the focus peak energy to shift backward in the time domain. The specific time delay is extended by the length of the equalization vector and the delay of the actual detection environment determined (Fig. 3).

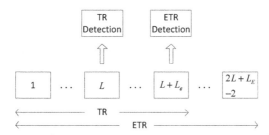

**Fig. 3.**  Comparison of TR and ETR detection maps

It can be known from Eq. (3) that the computational complexity of TR is $O(L^2)$. After adding the equalizer, it is equivalent to the TR equivalent channel convolutional equalization vector $\varepsilon[i]$. Equalizing the TR equivalent channel will perform a matrix multiplication operation on the original channel matrix. According to Eq. (8), the computational complexity of ETR is $O(L^2 \times L_E)$.

From the above analysis, the ETR calculation complexity is greater than TR. The advantage of ETR security performance is that it is exchanged for the computational complexity.

## 4    Numerical Results

From the previous theoretical analysis, the secrecy SINR of the legal receiver, the system's secrecy capacity, and the BER are closely related to the expected signal power, ISI power, and noise power at the receiver. The computer simulation experiment will be used to further analyze the secrecy performance of the indoor secure communication system. The parameter settings involved in the simulation are shown in Table 1:

The paper uses the single cluster frequency selective fading statistical channel model in [22] to carry out simulation experiments. According to the simulations of Eqs. (12), (13) and (14), the following Fig. 4 is obtained, which shows the relationship between the transmitted SNR and the system-secured SINR, and also compares the secrecy SINR of ETR and TR. It can be seen from the figure that the increase in the

**Table 1.** Simulation parameter settings

| Parameters | Values |
|------------|--------|
| $T_S$      | 2 ns   |
| $B$        | 500 MHz |
| $L_E$      | 41     |
| $L$        | 41     |
| $\theta_T$ | 80 ns  |
| $K$        | 10000  |

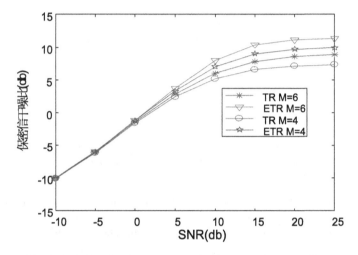

**Fig. 4.** Relationship between transmitted SNR and secrecy SINR

number of antennas also leads to an increase in the secrecy SINR. When the transmitted SNR is greater than 4 db, the secrecy SINR is significantly better than TR, which is consistent with the analysis in Sect. 3.1.

Figure 5 shows the confidential capacity map of ETR and TR. It can be seen from the figure that the transmission rate of ETR to achieve absolute secure communication is greater than TR. When the transmit SNR is greater than 25 db, the confidential capacity of TR is close to convergence, and the secrecy capacity of ETR is still improving, which also proves the advantage of ETR. The increase in transmit SNR and the increase in the number of transmit antennas increase the system's secrecy capacity.

Figure 6 is a simulation of the BER of the legal receiver. The simulation is performed when the number of antennas is 2, 4, and 6 at the sender. The BER of ETR and TR is compared. It can be seen from the curve that the BER of the two schemes is related to the number of antennas at the sender. We can see from the picture that the more antennas, the lower the BER. The simulation results are completely consistent with the analysis in Sect. 3.3, which verifies the correctness of the analysis.

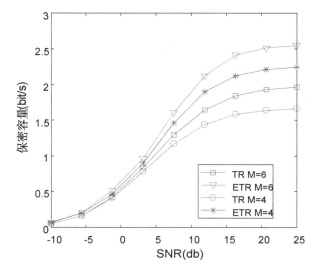

**Fig. 5.** The relationship between sending SNR and secrecy capacity

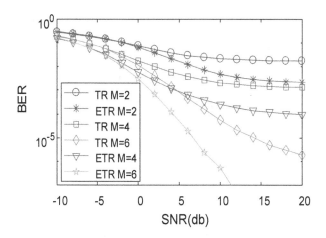

**Fig. 6.** Relation graph of sending SNR and BER

## 5 Conclusion

In order to improve the secrecy performance of TR under the eavesdropping model, this paper proposes an ETR solution. In this scheme, a forced zero equalizer is added between the source and the TRM, and the channel equalization is processed to enhance the system confidentiality. In this paper, The equalizer is designed, and the secrecy SINR, the system secrecy capacity, and the BER expression of the legal receiver are deduced. The simulation results show that the ETR technology can greatly reduce the equivalent channel sub-peak energy, but has little effect on the main peak energy.

The secrecy SINR and system secrecy capacity of the legal receiver are significantly improved, and the error performance is also improved. The main channel peak amplitude of the equivalent channel has a slight decrease compared with the traditional TR, and the effect on the focusing ability of TR is weak. The improvement of secretive performance is at the expense of the peak energy and computational complexity of the equivalent channel, and it is worth considering from the perspective of security. In the future work, the secretive performance of the richer channel model will be further studied.

# References

1. Jiang, D., Wang, Y., Han, Y., et al.: Maximum connectivity-based channel allocation algorithm in cognitive wireless networks for medical applications. Neurocomputing **220**, 41–51 (2017). (SCI, EI)
2. Jiang, D., Xu, Z., Li, W., et al.: An energy-efficient multicast algorithm with maximum network throughput in multi-hop wireless networks. J. Commun. Netw. **18**(5), 713–724 (2016). (SCI, EI)
3. Shannon, E.: Communication theory of secrecy systems. Bell Syst. Tech. J. **29**, 656–715 (1949)
4. Maurer, U.M.: Secret key agreement by public discussion from common information. IEEE Trans. Inf. Theory **39**(3), 733–742 (1993)
5. Dong, L., Han, Z., Petropulu, A.P., et al.: Improving wireless physical layer security via cooperating relays. IEEE Trans. Sig. Process. **58**(3), 1875–1888 (2010)
6. Li, X.-H., Hwu, J.: Using antenna array redundancy and channel diversity for secure wireless transmissions. J. Commun. **2**(3), 24–32 (2007)
7. Goel, S., Negi, R.: Guaranteeing secrecy using artificial noise. IEEE Trans. Wirel. Commun. **7**(6), 2180–2189 (2008)
8. Wu, D., Si, S., Wu, S., Wang, R.: Dynamic trust relationships aware data privacy protection in mobile crowd-sensing. IEEE Internet Things J. https://doi.org/10.1109/jiot.2017.2768073
9. Gao, X., Li, J., Ma, J., Shi, F.F., Wang, W., Wang, C.H.: Weighting technique for detection and location of targets by time reversal-reverse time migration mixed method. In: 2017 Symposium on Piezoelectricity, Acoustic Waves, and Device Applications (SPAWDA), Chengdu, China, pp. 393–396 (2017)
10. Tao, Y., Mu, T., Song, Y.: Time reversal microwave imaging method based on SF-ESPRIT for breast cancer detection. In: 2017 3rd IEEE International Conference on Computer and Communications (ICCC), Chengdu, pp. 2094–2098 (2017)
11. Li, C., Shen, X., Jiang, Z., Wang, X.: Mobile underwater acoustic communication based on passive time reversal. In: 2017 IEEE International Conference on Signal Processing, Communications and Computing (ICSPCC), Xiamen, pp. 1–5 (2017)
12. Tan, V.T., Ha, D.B., Tran, D.D.: Evaluation of physical layer secrecy in MIMO ultra-wideband system using time-reversal techniques. In: 2014 International Conference on Computing, Management and Telecommunications (ComManTel), Da Nang, pp. 70–74 (2014)
13. El-Sallabi, H., Aldosari, A.: Characterization of secrecy capacity of time reversal technique for wireless physical layer security. In: 2016 19th International Symposium on Wireless Personal Multimedia Communications (WPMC), Shenzhen, pp. 194–198 (2016)

14. Han, F., Yang, Y.H., Wang, B., Wu, Y., Liu, K.J.R.: Time-reversal division multiple access in multi-path channels. In: 2011 IEEE Global Telecommunications Conference - GLOBECOM 2011, Houston, TX, USA, pp. 1–5 (2011)
15. Han, F., Yang, Y.H., Wang, B., Wu, Y., Liu, K.J.R.: Time-reversal division multiple access over multi-path channels. IEEE Trans. Commun. **60**(7), 1953–1965 (2012)
16. Tran, H.V., Tran, H., Kaddoum, G., Tran, D.D., Ha, D.B.: Effective secrecy-SINR analysis of time reversal-employed systems over correlated multi-path channel. In: 2015 IEEE 11th International Conference on Wireless and Mobile Computing, Networking and Communications (WiMob), Abu Dhabi, pp. 527–532 (2015)
17. Kyritsi, P., Papanicolaou, G., Eggers, P., Oprea, A.: MISO time reversal and delay-spread compression for FWA channels at 5 GHz. IEEE Antennas Wirel. Propag. Lett. **3**, 96–99 (2004)
18. Chen, Y., Yang, Y.H., Han, F., Liu, K.J.R.: Time-reversal wideband communications. IEEE Sig. Process. Lett. **20**(12), 1219–1222 (2013)
19. Cardoso, F.D., Correia, L.M., Petersson, S., Boldi, M.: Beamforming strategies for energy efficient transmission in LTE. In: 2013 IEEE 77th Vehicular Technology Conference (VTC Spring), Dresden, pp. 1–5 (2013)
20. Viteri-Mera, C.A., Teixeira, F.L.: Equalized time reversal beamforming for frequency-selective indoor miso channels. IEEE Access **5**, 3944–3957 (2017)
21. Proakis, J., Salehi, M.: Digital Communications. McGraw-Hill, New York (2008)
22. Saleh, A.A.M., Valenzuela, R.A.: A statistical model for indoor multi-path propagation. IEEEJ. Sel. Areas Commun. **5**(2), 128–137 (1987)

# Research on Energy Efficiency in Wireless Powered Communication Network with User Cooperative Relay

Gang Feng$^{(\boxtimes)}$, Xizhong Qin, Zhenhong Jia, and Yongming Li

College of Information Science and Engineering, Xinjiang University,
Urumqi 830046, China
fenggang555@126.com, qmqqxz@163.com

**Abstract.** A user collaborative relay wireless powered communication network (UCR-WPCN) is studied in this paper, where users can harvest energy from the dedicated power device, named hybrid access point (HAP), and then transmit the information to HAP. Our goal is to study the total energy efficiency (EE) maximization of users in UCR-WPCN via joint time allocation and power control while meeting minimum rate requirements. However, because this problem is a non-convex, it is difficult for us to solve it. Then, we can use fractional programming principle theory and variable substitution to convert it into a standard convex optimization problem. Finally, we proposed an efficient optimization iterative algorithm in order to find the optimal solution. The simulation results show that the UCR plan can improve the user's information transmission rate and significantly improve the user's total energy efficiency in the system, compared with the non-cooperative relay transmission scheme.

**Keywords:** Wireless powered communication network · Energy efficiency · Harvesting energy · Optimization iterative algorithm

## 1 Introduction

With the rapid development of wireless communication, 5G, as the next generation of communication systems, will provide ubiquitous connectivity services for unprecedented devices. It is predicted that by 2020, there will be more than 50 billion connected devices [1], and the installed capacity of global Internet of Things (IoT) devices will reach 28.1 billion. The emergence of 5G networks has revolutionized the development of the IoT. The IoT will achieve ultra-low latency, efficient connectivity, low cost, low power consumption, high reliability, and full geographical coverage, which will completely reshape and change the world. Traditionally, energy constrained wireless networks (such as sensor networks) are powered by fixed sources such as batteries. However, due to the limitation of power, the operation time of the network is limited. Although the battery can be replaced or recharged to extend the life of the network, frequent battery charging is not only waste of resources, but also inconvenient (such as environmental monitoring, forest fire prevention, etc.), expensive, dangerous (such as in the toxic environment), even impossible [2] (such as sensor implanted in the

© ICST Institute for Computer Sciences, Social Informatics and Telecommunications Engineering 2019
Published by Springer Nature Switzerland AG 2019. All Rights Reserved
H. Song et al. (Eds.): SIMUtools 2019, LNICST 295, pp. 326–338, 2019.
https://doi.org/10.1007/978-3-030-32216-8_31

human body). However, as an emerging green communication technology, energy harvesting can harvest energy from the surrounding environment to extend the service life of energy-limited communication networks [3]. Traditional natural renewable resources (such as solar and wind energy) can provide a green and renewable energy supply for wireless communication systems. However, those resources are indirect and uncontrollable, which makes the wireless devices not collect energy efficiently. Compared with the traditional natural renewable resources, radio frequency (RF) energy harvesting technology will be more stable and controllable. According to reports, using the Powercast RF energy harvester at 915 MHz is possible to acquire 3.5 mW and 1 μW of wireless power from 0.6 m and 11 m RF signals respectively [4]. Wireless devices can harvest energy from RF signals generated by special equipment, which is also known as wireless energy transfer [5, 6].

There are two different research lines about WET. One is simultaneous wireless information and power transfer (SWIPT). The information received by the wireless device is divided into two parts. One is for information decoding and the other for harvesting energy [7–9]. In [7, 8], it is assumed that an ideal SWIPT receiver can acquire energy and receive information from the same signal. In order to make SWIPT feasible, several practical receiver architectures have been proposed in [9]. SWIPT has been extensively studied in various wireless systems [10–12]. The other is wireless powered communication networks (WPCN). This system is divided into two phases, wireless energy transfer (WET) and wireless information transfer (WIT), where the wireless devices are first powered in WET and then use the harvested energy to transmit data signals in WIT [13–17]. The maximum weighted rate summation problem in the relay system is studied in [13] and [14]. The rate of the relay node is treated as an optimization target in [15]. [16] investigates the maximum system rate problem in cognitive radio environment. And the authors in [17] study the maximum system rates problem by optimizing time allocation. However, the purpose of all those work focus on the maximization of the system rate and ignores the system's energy consumption. However, in the next generation communication network (5G), the energy consumption of communication system is a very critical problem. Energy efficiency (EE), measured in bit/s per joule, has been gradually becoming an important metric for future communication system design under the rapid growth of energy consumption and significant carbon emission in the existing system [18]. In addition, the attenuation of the signal is related to the transmission distance. Therefore, the problem of "doubly near-far" is studied in [17], i.e. compared the users who are close to the special base station that can transmit wireless energy and receive information, the users that are far away the special base station can not only collect less energy in the WET stage and consume more power in order to ensure reliable transmission of information in the WIT phase, which results in unfairness between users. And this problem is improved by maximizing the constraint rate with increasing the same rate constraint for all users. Based on [17, 19] adopts the separation form of base stations (i.e., the special base station that combines the dual functions of the energy transmission and the signal reception is separated into two base stations with single functions, and assume that the two base stations are distributed in both sides of the user), which can avoid the "doubly near-far" problem by the way of distance balancing (i.e., if a user is close to the signal receiving base station, it will far away from the wireless energy harvesting base station, and the reverse is also true) and studies the maximization of the system energy efficiency. But compared to [17], the system model does not have a breakthrough improvement.

The main contributions of this paper are summarized as follows.

In order to solve the problem of "doubly-near-far", we propose a plan, named user cooperative relay (UCR). Based on UCR plan, we formulate the energy efficiency maximization problem of users in WPCN system by jointly optimizing time and power allocation while taking into the account the minimum rate requirements of each user. Meanwhile, the system model takes into account the circuit energy consumption of the user terminals, which is more realistic.

The optimization problem is a fractional structure, which is a non-convex problem. Hence, it is difficult to solve this problem. Thus, we can use fractional programming principle theory and variable substitution to convert it into a standard convex optimization problem.

Using the optimal structure of time allocation and power control, an optimization iterative algorithm is proposed to solve the optimization problem. And the simulation results are compared with the benchmark scheme, i.e. no cooperative relay system.

The rest of this paper is organized as follows. The system model is described in Sect. 2. The Sect. 3 presents the problem formulation and transformation. The Sect. 4 shows the simulation results. Finally, the Sect. 5 concludes the paper.

## 2    System Model

### 2.1    System Rate Model

As is shown in Fig. 1, we formulate a user collaborative relay WPCN system (UCR-WPCN), which consists of one hybrid access point (HAP) and two users denoted by $U_1$ and $U_2$. In this model, HAP has a stable power supply. In order to simplify the model,

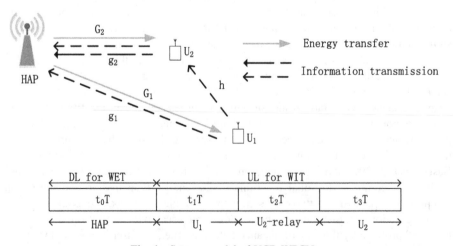

**Fig. 1.** System model of UCR-WPCN.

it is assumed that HAP and all users have a single antenna in the UCR-WPCN. Meanwhile, Time Division Multiple Access (TDMA) technology is also used in the same frequency band. Similar to [17], the "harvest and then transmit" protocol is adopted in UCR-WPCN. That is to say, the entire communication process is divided into two parts: wireless energy transmission (WET) and wireless information transmission (WIT). In the WET stage, all users collect energy from the radio frequency signals broadcast by HAP, and convert the collected electromagnetic energy into electricity and storage using the conversion circuit. In the WIT stage, all users use the energy collected during the WET phase to transmit its information to HAP. This phase is divided into three separate parts. First, $U_1$ broadcasts information to HAP and $U_2$. Secondly, $U_2$ decodes $U_1$ information, amplifies and forwards the HAP. Finally, $U_2$ transmits his own information to HAP. Thus, the total time can be limited as

$$\sum_{k=0}^{3} t_k \leq T, \quad k = 0, 1, 2, 3. \tag{1}$$

In the WET and WIT phases, we assume all channels are quasi-static block fading channels. In WET, the channel power gain between the users of U1 and U2 and HAP is expressed as $G_1$ and $G_2$, respectively. In WIT, the channel gain factor between the users of $U_1$ and $U_2$ and HAP is expressed as $g_1$ and $g_2$ respectively. And the channel gain factor of $U_1$ and $U_2$ can be expressed as h. All the channel gain factors represent the characteristics of channel path loss, shadow effect and multipath fading. It is assumed that Channel State Information (CSI) is known by UCR-WPCN and the total time T is limited to 1 s.

In the WET stage, HAP broadcast radio frequency signals for a time duration $t_0$ at transmit power $P_{HAP}$. Due to the noise power is far less than the power of received signal, and the transmission power of the users is less than the transmission power of HAP, therefore, we assume that the energy can be collected by users from the channel noise and each other can be negligible [19].

Therefore, the energy collected by the users in the WET stage can be expressed as

$$E_k^h = \eta_k t_0 T G_k^2 P_{HAP}, \quad k = 1, 2. \tag{2}$$

Where $\eta_k \in (0, 1]$ is the energy conversion efficiency of $U_i$. Without loss of generality, we assume that $\eta_1 = \eta_2 = \eta$.

At WIT stage, each user independently transmits information for a time duration $t_k$ at transmit power $P_k$ with the TDMA technology.

The information received by HAP from $U_1$ is expressed as

$$y_1 = \sqrt{P_1} g_1 x_1 + n_1 \tag{3}$$

The information received by HAP from $U_1$ is expressed as

$$y_2 = \sqrt{P_1} h x_1 + n_2 \tag{4}$$

The information received by HAP from $U_2$ forwarding $U_1$ is expressed as

$$y_3 = \sqrt{P_2^1} g_2 \overline{x_1} + n_3 \tag{5}$$

The information received by HAP from $U_2$ is expressed as

$$y_4 = \sqrt{P_2^2} g_2 x_2 + n_4 \tag{6}$$

Wherein, $x_1$, $\overline{x_1}$, $x_2$ are the information signal sent by $U_1$, the signal of $U_2$ relay $U_1$ and the signal sent by $U_2$ to transmit its own information. $P_1, P_2^1$ and $P_2^2$ are the transmission power of $U_1$, the signal power of $U_2$ forwarding $U_1$, and the power of $U_2$ to transmit its own information signal. $n_1 \sim n_4$ represent the Additive white Gaussian noise at the end of HAP and $U_2$, without loss of generality, here we assume $n_i \sim CN(0, N_0), i = 1, \ldots, 4$

Therefore, the achievable rate of U1 end-to-end is expressed as [20]

$$R_1 = \min\{R_{\text{direct}}, R_{\text{realy}}\} \tag{7}$$

$R_{\text{direct}}$ represents the total information rate of $U_1$ to HAP and $U_2$ forwarding $U_1$ information to HAP, which can be expressed as

$$R_{\text{direct}} = t_1 \log_2(1 + \frac{P_1 \|g_1\|^2}{\sigma_1^2}) + t_2 \log_2(1 + \frac{P_2^1 \|g_2\|^2}{\sigma_3^2}) \tag{8}$$

$R_{\text{relay}}$ represents the information rate from $U_1$ to $U_2$

$$R_{\text{relay}} = t_1 \log_2(1 + \frac{P_1 \|h\|^2}{\sigma_2^2}) \tag{9}$$

The achievable rate of $U_2$ end-to-end is expressed as

$$R_2 = t_3 \log_2(1 + \frac{P_2^2 \|g_2\|^2}{\sigma_4^2}) \tag{10}$$

Therefore, the total throughput of the UCR-WPCN is expressed as

$$R = R_1 + R_2 \tag{11}$$

## 2.2   Power Consumption Model of Users

The main concern about wireless sensor networks and the Internet is low power devices. Therefore, this section focuses on the total energy consumption of users in the UCR-WPCN.

The user's energy consumption is divided into two parts, transmission power consumption and circuit consumption during hardware processing.

At WIT stage, each user independently transmits information for a time duration $t_k$ at transmit power $P_k$. Therefore, the energy consumption of $U_1$ and $U_2$ can be respective modeled as

$$E_1 = (P_1 + P_{1c})t_1 \tag{12}$$

$$E_2 = (P_2^1 + P_{2c})t_2 + (P_2^2 + P_{2c})t_3 \tag{13}$$

Wherein, $P_{1c}$ and $P_{2c}$ are the circuit consumption of $U_1$ and $U_2$, respectively. According to the law of conservation of energy, we can obtain

$$E_k \leq E_k^h, \quad k = 1, 2. \tag{14}$$

Thus, the total energy consumption of the whole users system can be model as

$$E = E_1 + E_2 \tag{15}$$

# 3   The EE Model of the UCR-WPCN

## 3.1   The Optimization Model

The goal of this section is to maximize the EE of users. EE can be defined as the ratio of the total throughput to the total energy consumption of UCR-WPCN, i.e.EE = R/E. In order to maximize the EE, the time distribution and power control are jointly optimized. The EE model is defined as

$$
\begin{aligned}
&\max_{t,P} : \frac{R}{E} \\
&\text{S.t. } c1: t_0 + t_1 + t_2 + t_3 \leq T \\
&\quad\quad c2: (P_1 + P_{1c})t_1 \leq E_1 \\
&\quad\quad c3: (P_2^1 + P_{2c})t_2 + (P_2^2 + P_{2c})t_3 \leq E_2 \\
&\quad\quad c4: \{R_1, R_2\} \geq R_{min} \\
&\quad\quad c5: t_0, t_1, t_2, t_3, P_1, P_2^1, P_2^2 \geq 0
\end{aligned} \tag{16}
$$

Wherein, $t = [t_0, t_1, t_2, t_3]$, $P = [P_1, P_2^1, P_2^2]$.

In problem (16), c1 means the transmission time limit. c2, c3 ensures that energy consumption of users in the WIT phase does not exceed the harvested energy in the

WET phase respectively. c4 meets the minimum rate constraint of users. And c5 represents the non-negative constraints of time allocation and power control.

Note that problem (16) is neither convex nor quasi-convex, because the objective function is the fractional form and the coupled optimization variables is contained in c2, c3 and c4. In order to solve this problem effectively and quickly, in the following section, the principle of fractional programming and variable substitution is used to transform it into a standard convex problem.

### 3.2    The Transformation of the Objective Function

According to the principle of nonlinear fractional programming [21], the objective function of the problem (16) can be expressed as

$$q^* = \max \frac{R}{E} \tag{17}$$

The equivalent form of the objective function is as follows

$$F(q^*) = \max\{R - q^*E\} = 0 \tag{18}$$

Compared with the problem (16), the equivalent form of the objective function (18) is more handleable. But, it is still a non-convex problem, because there still contain the coupled optimization variables.

In order to solve the optimization problem (16), we introduce the auxiliary variables, which represents users' power consumption, i.e. $\gamma_1 = P_1 t_1$, $\gamma_2 = P_2^1 t_2, \gamma_3 = P_2^2 t_2$.

Therefore, (8) is further translated into

$$R'_{\text{driect}} = t_1 \log_2 \left(1 + \frac{\gamma_1 \|g_1\|^2}{t_1 \sigma_1^2}\right) + t_2 \log_2 \left(1 + \frac{\gamma_2 \|g_2\|^2}{t_2 \sigma_3^2}\right) \tag{19}$$

(9) can further translate into

$$R'_{\text{relay}} = t_1 \log_2 \left(1 + \frac{\gamma_1 \|h\|^2}{t_1 \sigma_2^2}\right) \tag{20}$$

(7) can be rewritten as

$$R'_1 = \min\left\{R'_{\text{direct}}, R'_{\text{realy}}\right\} \tag{21}$$

(10) changes into

$$R'_2 = t_3 \log_2 \left(1 + \frac{\gamma_3 \|g_2\|^2}{t_3 \sigma_4^2}\right) \tag{22}$$

(11) transforms into

$$R^{'} = R_1^{'} + R_2^{'} \tag{23}$$

Therefore, problem (16) can be reformulated as

$$
\begin{aligned}
\max_{t,\gamma} : \ & R^{'} - q(\gamma_1 + P_{1c}t_1 + \gamma_2 + P_{2c}t_2 + \gamma_3 + P_{2c}t_3) \\
\text{S.t. } & c1: t_0 + t_1 + t_2 + t_3 \leq T \\
& c2: \gamma_1 + P_{1c}t_1 \leq E_1 \\
& c3: \gamma_2 + P_{2c}t_2 + \gamma_3 + P_{2c}t_3 \leq E_2 \\
& c4: \{R_1^{'}, R_2^{'}\} \geq R_{\min} \\
& c5: t_0, \ t_1, \ t_2, t_3, \gamma_1, \gamma_2, \gamma_3 \geq 0
\end{aligned}
\tag{24}
$$

It is not difficult to find the problem (24) is a standard convex optimization problem.

Proof: Firstly, we can define a function like $f(x) = \log_2(1+x), x \geq 0$

We can find $g(x,y) = yf(x/y), y > 0$ is the perspective functions of the concave function. According to the convexity of the convex function, the optimization objective function in question (24) is also a concave function.

Furthermore, c1, c2, c3 are linear function. Therefore, problem (24) is a standard convex optimization problem [22].

### 3.3 Optimization Iterative Algorithm

In order to solve the problem (24) quickly and effectively, we propose an optimization iterative algorithm in this section. The algorithm is summarized in Table 1.

**Table 1.** Optimization iterative algorithm for UCR-WPCN.

| Algorithm |
| --- |
| 1: initialize $q$ , $t$ , $\gamma$ and the maximum tolerance $\varepsilon$ ; |
| 2: obtain $t*$ , $\gamma*$ from (24) |
| 3: obtain $F(q*)$ from (18) |
| 4: compare $F(q*)$ with $\varepsilon$ |
|    if $F(q*) \leq \varepsilon$ |
|       obtain $q*$ from (17) |
|       jump to 6; |
|    elseif |
|       jump to 5; |
|    end |
| 5: obtain and update $q$ from (17), then, jump to 2; |
| 6: break and output $q*$ ; |

## 4 Simulation Results

In this section, we present simulation results by a series of numerical experiments to validate our theoretical findings, and to demonstrate the system EE of UCR-WPCN. The distance between $U_1$, $U_2$ and HAP is 15 m and 10 m respectively, and the distance between $U_1$ and $U_2$ is 6 m. All channels obey the Rayleigh distribution $CN(0, 10^{-2}d_{x,y}^{-\alpha})$, $\alpha$ is the channel fading coefficient and is set to 3, $d_{x,y}$ represents the distance between nodes x, y. According to the mutuality of the channels, $G_1 = g_1$ and $G_2 = g_2$ can be obtained. The HAP transmission power is set to 40 W. The conversion efficiency is set to 0.9, the maximum tolerance is set to 0.01. The circuit energy consumption of HAP, $U_1$ and $U_2$ are set to 0.05 W, 0.5 mW and 0.5 mW respectively, and the minimum rate per unit bandwidth is 0.2bits/Hz.

Figure 2 reflects the relationship between the number of iteration steps of the proposed Algorithm 1 and the total EE of the user in the case of satisfying different minimum rate constraints of the user in the UCR-WPCN. It can be observed from the figure, on average at most three iterations are needed to reach the optimal solution, which reflects the fast convergence of the proposed algorithm.

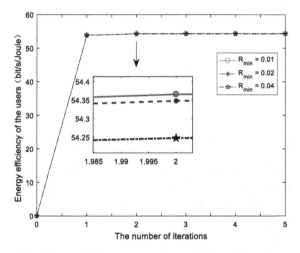

**Fig. 2.** EE of the users versus the number of iteration

It can be clearly seen from Fig. 3 that the energy harvesting time $t_0$ required by the users is decreasing with the HAP transmission power increases. Therefore, users can enjoy more information transmission time, which proves the correctness of the mode built in this paper.

As is shown in Fig. 4, under the same rate constraint conditions, the total rates in the relay system is greater than in the non-relay system. When the HAP is set to 40 W, the total rate of users in the relay system is approximately 3.5 times bigger than the total rate of the non-relay system users. Under different rate constraints, as the

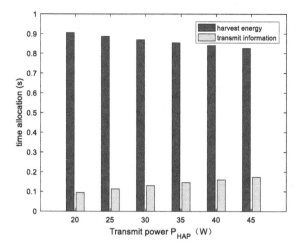

**Fig. 3.** The relationship between HAP and time allocation

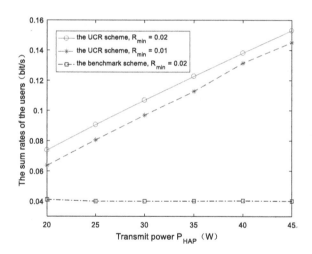

**Fig. 4.** The relationship between the sum rates of the users and HAP

minimum rate requirement of the users increases, the total rate of users in the relay system also increases accordingly. When the HAP is set to 40 W and the minimum rate doubled, the total rate of users under the relay system becomes about 1.07 times than the original.

It can be observed from Fig. 5 that the total energy efficiency of the users increase with the increase of the HAP transmission power. Because the HAP transmission power increase, the time required for the users to collect energy will decrease and the time for users to transmit information will increase, so that the information rate of the users will increase. In addition, under the same HAP transmission power, the EE of the users under the relay wireless energy communication network is always more than

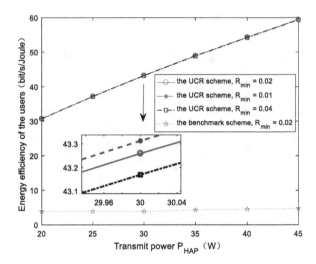

**Fig. 5.** The relationship between EE of the users and HAP

the non-relay system. When the HAP is set to 40 W and the minimum rate is set to 0.02 bit/s, the EE of users in the relay system is about 10.08 times bigger than without the relay system.

In combination with Figs. 4 and 5, it can be obtained that the form of user cooperative relay in the wireless energy communication network can not only significantly improve the total information rate of the users, but also the total energy efficiency of the users.

Figure 6 shows the relationship between EE of the users and channel fading coefficients in relay system. It can be observed from the figure that the energy efficiency

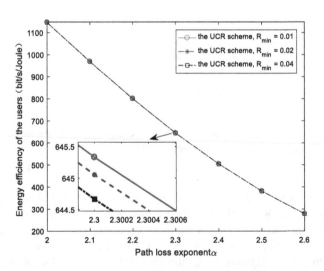

**Fig. 6.** The relationship between EE of the users and path loss exponent

of the users decreases as the channel fading coefficient increases. Because as the channel fading coefficient increases, more energy is consumed in the signal propagation, and the energy harvesting by the users will be reduced accordingly. In order to provide sufficient energy for the user to supply, the energy harvesting time in the WET stage will increase accordingly, resulting in a reduction in the time for users to use information communication, thereby reducing the information rate. In addition, it can also be observed from the figure that is in the case of the same channel fading coefficient, the EE also exhibits a decreasing condition as the minimum rate requirement increases.

## 5 Conclusion

Aiming at the "doubly-near-far" problem in WPCN, we propose an efficient user cooperative relay transmission scheme called UCR transmission scheme. In the WIT phase, the scheme can ensure the user closer to the HAP as the relay to cooperate and forward the information of the relatively distant user to the HAP in order to improve the communication quality of the remote users. Based on this scheme, the user energy efficiency maximization problem with joint optimization time allocation and power control resources is modeled under the condition of satisfying the minimum rate constraint of the user. And an effective optimization iterative algorithm is proposed to solve this problem. The simulation results show that the UCR scheme proposed in this paper improves not only the total information rate of users in the system, but also the total energy efficiency of users, compared with the non-cooperative transmission scheme. This enjoys important application value and significance in future communication systems, especially Internet of Things and wireless sensor networks.

**Acknowledgment.** This study was supported by Natural science foundation of xinjiang uygur autonomous region (2018D01C047).

## References

1. Buzzi, S., Chih-Lin, I., Klein, T.E., et al.: A survey of energy-efficient techniques for 5G networks and challenges ahead. IEEE J. Sel. Areas Commun. **34**(4), 697–709 (2016)
2. Bi, S., Ho, C.K., Zhang, R.: Wireless powered communication: opportunities and challenges. IEEE Commun. Mag. **53**(4), 117–125 (2014)
3. Alsaba, Y., Rahim, S.K.A., Leow, C.Y.: Beamforming in wireless energy harvesting communications systems: a survey. IEEE Commun. Surv. Tutor. **PP**(99), 1 (2018)
4. Zungeru, A.M., Ang, L.M., Prabaharan, S.R.S., et al.: Radio frequency energy harvesting and management for wireless sensor networks. Eprint Arxiv (2012)
5. Krikidis, I., Timotheou, S., Nikolaou, S., et al.: Simultaneous wireless information and power transfer in modern communication systems. IEEE Commun. Mag. **52**(11), 104–110 (2014)
6. Lu, X., Wang, P., Niyato, D., et al.: Wireless networks with RF energy harvesting: a contemporary survey. IEEE Commun. Surv. Tutor. **17**(2), 757–789 (2017)

7. Xu, J., Liu, L., Zhang, R.: Multiuser MISO beamforming for simultaneous wireless information and power transfer. IEEE Trans. Sig. Process. **62**(18), 4798–4810 (2014)
8. Zhao, L., Wang, X., Zheng, K.: Downlink hybrid information and energy transfer with massive MIMO. IEEE Trans. Wirel. Commun. **15**(2), 1309–1322 (2016)
9. Ghazanfari, A., Tabassum, H., Hossain, E.: Ambient RF energy harvesting in ultra-dense small cell networks: performance and trade-offs. IEEE Press (2016)
10. Zhang, R., Ho, C.K.: MIMO broadcasting for simultaneous wireless information and power transfer. IEEE Trans. Wirel. Commun. **12**(5), 1989–2001 (2011)
11. Zhou, X., Zhang, R., Ho, C.K.: Wireless information and power transfer in multiuser OFDM systems. IEEE Trans. Wirel. Commun. **13**(4), 2282–2294 (2014)
12. Ng, D.W.K., Lo, E.S., Schober, R.: Robust beamforming for secure communication in systems with wireless information and power transfer. IEEE Trans. Wirel. Commun. **13**(8), 4599–4615 (2014)
13. Chu, Z., Zhou, F., Zhu, Z., et al.: Energy beamforming design and user cooperation for wireless powered communication networks. IEEE Wirel. Commun. Lett. **PP**(99), 1 (2017)
14. Di, X., Xiong, K., Fan, P., et al.: Optimal resource allocation in wireless powered communication networks with user cooperation. IEEE Trans. Wirel. Commun. **PP**(99), 1 (2017)
15. Chen, H., Xiao, L., Yang, D., et al.: User cooperation in wireless powered communication networks with a pricing mechanism. IEEE Access **PP**(99), 1 (2017)
16. Kim, J., Lee, H., Song, C., et al.: Sum throughput maximization for multi-user MIMO cognitive wireless powered communication networks. IEEE Trans. Wirel. Commun. **PP**(99), 1 (2017)
17. Ju, H., Zhang, R.: Throughput maximization in wireless powered communication networks. IEEE Trans. Wirel. Commun. **13**(1), 418–428 (2014)
18. Wu, J., Rangan, S., Zhang, H.: Green Communications: Theoretical Fundamentals, Algorithms, and Applications. CRC Press, Boca Raton (2016)
19. Wu, Q., Tao, M., Ng, D.W.K., et al.: Energy-efficient resource allocation for wireless powered communication networks. IEEE Trans. Wirel. Commun. **15**(3), 2312–2327 (2016)
20. Liang, Y., Veeravalli, V.V.: Gaussian orthogonal relay channels: optimal resource allocation and capacity. IEEE Trans. Inf. Theory **51**(9), 3284–3289 (2005)
21. Dinkelbach, W.: On nonlinear fractional programming. Manag. Sci. **13**(7), 492–498 (1967)
22. Boyd, S., Vandenberghe, L.: Convex Optimization. Cambridge University Press, Cambridge (2004)

# Video Monitoring System Application to Urban Traffic Intersection

Jin-ping Sun, Lei Chen$^{(\boxtimes)}$, Rong Bao, Dan Li, and Dai-hong Jiang

Key Laboratory of Intelligent Industrial Control Technology of Jiangsu Province,
Xuzhou University of Technology, Xuzhou 221000, Jiangsu, China
`chenlei@xzit.edu.cn`

**Abstract.** Intelligent video surveillance technology can reduce the burden of workers and improve the efficiency of surveillance. A project of the video monitoring system with moving target detection function has been realized and applied to the urban traffic system. The background will have weak or obvious changes as time goes on, such as, the illumination change, the environmental effect, the movement of the background, and so on. If we always use the original background model, it will cause large error. Fixed threshold is not suitable for illumination change in the environment. An improved adaptive on-line Gauss mixture model is used to acquire the background model, and the background subtraction method is used to match the moving objects. Then, the motion detection function was realized in a specific region. If there are abnormal moving targets in a specific area, the linkage alarm function will be activated and handled by manual intervention. This algorithm can effectively reduce the error probability of target recognition caused by environmental changes, and provide strong technical support for real-time monitoring of traffic abnormalities.

**Keywords:** Video monitoring · Urban traffic · Gauss mixture model · Background subtraction method · Motion detection

## 1  Introduction

With the development and popularization of the computer and network, the urban traffic intersection monitoring system on the base of digital degree can be justified now. The modern solution project can make the roadway more high-speed, much safer and more efficient. ITS (Intelligent Transportation System) is a uniform information system. The design of the data information's net must be synchronous with the construct of the urban traffic system. With the construct of ITS's WLAN [1, 2], the data can be collected and the relative data of the accidental and road condition's can be statistical. The urban traffic intersection monitoring system [3, 4] is also a part of this integrated system. The basic principle is which called "Everything over IP". In the whole system, every device has been digital processed. When given the appointed address, the authorized user can visit all the data information freely [5]. All the data files, including the transmission of the vehicle's image files can be transmitted through the IP network. So, it can be concluded that the network is the basis of the whole system.

© ICST Institute for Computer Sciences, Social Informatics and Telecommunications Engineering 2019
Published by Springer Nature Switzerland AG 2019. All Rights Reserved
H. Song et al. (Eds.): SIMUtools 2019, LNICST 295, pp. 339–345, 2019.
https://doi.org/10.1007/978-3-030-32216-8_32

The paper develops a wireless video-monitoring project, which is based on the Web, and adopts the newest imbedded network camera. The video signals will be collected by the camera and then be coded, and the wireless network [6] will transmit the video data. First, the paper simply analyzes the virtue of multicast communication in a Local Area Network (LAN) [7]; expound the technical concept, the characteristic and the principle of the IP network multicast. Then, an improved adaptive on-line Gauss mixture model is used to acquire the background model, and the background subtraction method is used to match the moving objects. The motion detection function was realized in a specific region. Finally, experiments show that the target detection algorithm is effective. If there are abnormal moving targets in a specific area, the linkage alarm function will be activated and handled by manual intervention.

## 2  Realization of the System

We deploy one set of network camera at each roadway of the traffic intersection, using it to monitor the whole scale of the orientation of this roadway at the traffic intersection. We deploy one set of video server for each camera. The video server connects with the camera and the network. Its duty is to code and then to transmit the video signals collected by the camera through the network. In the monitoring center's client server of the urban traffic monitoring system, the job of monitoring and query can be done. We adopt the way of video recording when the vehicles arrive, and make it work 24 h a day to shoot all the vehicles that pass by, then give the digital video pictures to the computer to deal with directly.

After the set up of the hardware in the whole network, we also need a set of management system to make them work in phase. We can adopt a set of digital monitoring system to achieve these complicated works. The diagram of Fig. 1 can show the process.

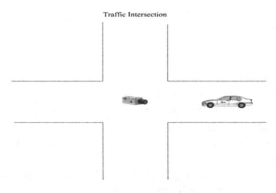

**Fig. 1.** Theory's diagram

The paper expounds the traffic intersection vehicles monitoring system's principles as follows:

## 2.1  System of the Traffic Intersection

Firstly we use a camera to video record all the vehicles passing by the toll station. Each one just records three to five seconds of these vehicles, so the quantity of the data will not be too large. Then we use the video server to connect the camera and the net to realize the digital code and transmission. Finally a main application server should be installed and a client server should be installed in the computer to check the pictures of the vehicles.

## 2.2  Function of the System

Firstly according to the need of the monitoring system, we can monitor any one, four, nine or sixteen pictures of these cameras installed and the main screen picture can be designed according to the need of the manager. Each application server should store all the vehicles' video files recorded by all these thirty-two cameras. The video record should be circular and all the video files should be stored of the latest one month. Different people should be given different permissions and doing their own business according to this. So using this technique, the system can be safe and reliable. All the servers can form an Intranet and communicate by "TCP/IP" and they can also link to the available network. The users can set their own names and passwords to monitor all sorts of information at anytime anywhere.

# 3  Realization of Alarm Linkage

## 3.1  Background Modeling

In actual environment, the background will have weak or obvious changes as time goes on, such as, the illumination change, the environmental effect, the movement of the background, and so on. If we always use the original background model, it will cause large error. So it needs update the background in time. Fixed threshold is not suitable for illumination change in the environment. The system uses an improved adaptive online Gauss mixture model to detect moving targets.

For a location point on the image plane, the historical data of I are recorded as $\{X_1, X_2, \cdots X_{t-1}\}$. The characteristics of pixels are described by L Gauss distribution. The background gradient is represented by online updating. $L = 8$ is selected for modeling in the program. The estimated probability distribution of t time observations is as follows.

$$P(X_t) = \sum_{i=1}^{L} \omega_{i,t-1,l} \times \eta_l(\chi_{i,t}, \mu_{i,t-1,l}, \sum_{i,t,l}) \tag{1}$$

$\omega_{i,t-1,l}$ is the weights of l Gauss distributions at T-1 time, $\mu_{i,t-1,l}$ is the mean vector of Gauss distribution, $\eta_l$ is the probability density function of l Gauss distributions and $\sum_{i,t,l}$ is a covariance matrix. The L models are queued according to the probability from large to small. The front of Gauss model represents the background and back of

Gauss model represents the foreground image. In the next frame, the brightness values of the pixels in this position are matched with L models respectively, so as to determine whether they belong to the foreground or background, and the updating model is based on the maximum matching degree.

## 3.2  Object Detection

In the system, video images which had been collected and compressed would be transmitted to the background server. The background server is responsible for distinguishing the moving regions, and extracts several moving regions from each image. Local region matching extracts the foreground motion region by adaptive Gauss background modeling, removes the unconcerned background region and reduces the matching range. In the same scene, there may be multiple moving targets, so matching requires matching between different targets. The two regions with the highest matching degree are matching targets. In this paper, background subtraction is used to match moving targets only.

Figure 2(a) and (b) are video thirty-second, thirty-third frame images. (c) is the foreground area detected, but it is extremely sensitive to external dynamic scene changes such as illumination and weather changes, with shadows appearing. (d) is an Illuminated image. (e) is the result of the background model based on Mixture Gauss Model. (f) is the result of foreground area detected after improvement. Through comparison, we can see that the algorithm has better target effect and smaller noise.

| (a) Thirty-second frames | (b) Thirty-three frames | (c) Background difference foreground area |
| (d) Light image | (e) Background model | (f) Foreground area under Gauss model |

**Fig. 2.** Target extraction in light changing environment

### 3.3 Motion Detection Parameters

Step 1: Set the resolution of motion detection, that is, according to the format of video (PAL, NTSC) and image resolution (CIF, 2CIF, etc.) as shown in Fig. 3.

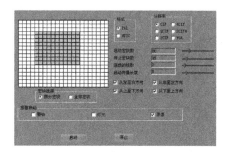

**Fig. 3.** Configuration of alarm linkage

Step 2: Set threshold values of start and stop motion detection. It is required that the threshold value of start is greater than or equal to the threshold value of stop.
Step 3: Set the number of continuous motion frames to start the alarm.
Step 4: Set the macro block size for motion detection.
Step 5: Set the direction of movement of macroblocks.
Step 6: Set the boot mask parameter and set the mask value.
Step 7: Start/Stop motion detection.
Step 8: Display the range of moving objects on the display screen.

### 3.4 Algorithmic Process

First, two consecutive frames are extracted from video. Then, an improved adaptive on-line Gauss mixture model is used to acquire the background model, and the background subtraction method is used to match the moving objects. Finally, the motion detection function is realized in a specific region. The algorithm process is shown in Table 1.

### 3.5 Operation Results

Figure 4 is the result of the video surveillance system when it starts motion detection. It shows that the yellow rectangular block is the moving part. Using the detection interval set in Fig. 3 and the improved background subtraction method, the moving regions in two or three adjacent inter-frame images are extracted. When the moving area is detected, the alarm program can be started, and the alarm information can be forwarded to each client by the server.

**Table 1.** Algorithmic process

| Step | Algorithm |
| --- | --- |
| 1 | Import video |
| 2 | Extract two consecutive frames; |
| 3 | Record the historical data of I $\{X_1, X_2, \cdots X_{t-1}\}$ |
| 4 | Estimate probability distribution of t time observations |
| 5 | Queue up the model |
| 6 | Get background model |
| 7 | Match the brightness values of the pixels in this position |
| 8 | Update model according to the maximum matching degree |
| 9 | Use background subtraction method to match the moving objects |
| 10 | Set motion detection parameters |
| 11 | Activate alarm linkage |

**Fig. 4.** Test of alarm linkage

# 4  Conclusion

The experimental results show that if the original background model is unchanged, the detected target will have errors. In this paper, motion detection technology based on improved adaptive online Gauss mixture model is applied in video surveillance system. This algorithm can effectively reduce the error probability of target recognition caused by environmental changes, and provide strong technical support for real-time monitoring of traffic abnormalities. The monitoring system has the advantages of wide monitoring range, adaptive moving target detection, good flexibility and high quality, so it is suited for using in the urban traffic system.

**Acknowledgements.** This work is partly supported by the Natural Science Foundation of Jiangsu Province of China (No. BK20161165), the Key Laboratory of Intelligent Industrial Control Technology of Jiangsu Province Research Project (JSKLIIC201705), Xuzhou Science and Technology Plan Projects (KC18011, KC16SH010, KC17072), Ministry of Housing and Urban-Rural Development Science and Technology Planning Project (2016-R2-060).

# References

1. Wei, W., Wu, Q.: Moving target detection based on three frame difference combined with improved gaussian modeling. Comput. Eng. Des. **2105**(8), 203–208 (2014)
2. Chen, L., et al.: A lightweight end-side user experience data collection system for quality evaluation of multimedia communications. IEEE Access **6**(1), 15408–15419 (2018)
3. Jiang, D., Zhang, P., Lv, Z., Song, H.: Energy-efficient multi-constraint routing algorithm with load balancing for smart city applications. IEEE Internet Things J. **3**(6), 1437–1447 (2018)
4. Jiang, D., Huo, L., Lv, Z., Song, H., Qin, W.: A joint multi-criteria utility-based network selection approach for vehicle-to-infrastructure networking. IEEE Trans. Intell. Transp. Syst. **19**(10), 3305–3319 (2018)
5. Chen, L., Jiang, D., Bao, R., Xiong, J., Liu, F., Bei, L.: MIMO scheduling effectiveness analysis for bursty data service from view of QoE. Chin. J. Electron. **26**(5), 1079–1085 (2017)
6. Jiang, D., Wang, Y., Han, Y., Lv, H.: Maximum connectivity-based channel allocation algorithm in cognitive wireless networks for medical applications. Neurocomputing **220** (2017), 41–51 (2017)
7. Jiang, D., Li, W., Lv, H.: An energy-efficient cooperative multicast routing in multi-hop wireless networks for smart medical applications. Neurocomputing **220**(2017), 160–169 (2017)

# A Test System for Vehicular Voice Cloud Service

Li Yu, Kailiang Zhang, Jiang Man, Hao Yu, Yuqing Yao,
and Lei Chen[✉]

Jiangsu Province Key Laboratory of Intelligent Industry Control Technology,
Xuzhou University of Technology, Xuzhou 221018, China
chenlei@xzit.edu.cn

**Abstract.** Some test systems for voice cloud services have been developed in recent years. However, the automobile manufacturers, communications equipment merchants and network operator still lacks methods and tools to evaluate the vehicular voice cloud services from the perspective of the end user experience. Considering the user behavior and user experience, a light weight vehicular voice cloud evaluation system is designed in this paper. The system is able to send voice information to voice cloud server according to user habit, and record the user experience indicators, such as accurate, voice quality, service delay, server computation capacity, and so on. The study shows that the vehicle voice cloud evaluation system can avoid complex communication and language processing, evaluate the performance of the service from view of end user.

**Keywords:** Voice cloud · Vehicular unit · Performance evaluation · Quality of experience

## 1 Introduction

Some new approaches are proposed to predict the network traffic in the end-to-end network [1–3] and analyze the end user experience [4]. This will help to construct the test case and evaluate the user experience. On the premise of guaranteeing user experience, new routing schemes are proposed to increase the energy efficiency [5, 6]. However, it is difficult to measure the performance of these approaches for the emerging service of vehicle voice cloud because of the fast changing network topology and complex communication process. And the exits simulation tools and evaluation methods cannot evaluate the key quality indicators of vehicle voice cloud service.

Since 2000, BMW and Acura, the Apple Corp and Ferrari, Mercedes Benz and Volvo jointly developed the vehicular voice assistant system. BAIDU and IFLYTEK, have published their vehicular speech service based on cloud platform.

Vehicular voice cloud service, as an emerging multimedia service, has attracted more and more users. The vehicle environment is characterized by frequent handover,

© ICST Institute for Computer Sciences, Social Informatics and Telecommunications Engineering 2019
Published by Springer Nature Switzerland AG 2019. All Rights Reserved
H. Song et al. (Eds.): SIMUtools 2019, LNICST 295, pp. 346–352, 2019.
https://doi.org/10.1007/978-3-030-32216-8_33

network topology change, background noise and Doppler Effect, and the user behavior and the traffic flow also greatly affect the user experience [7]. This is difficult during the test. In past decades, many traditional speech quality assessment models have been proposed to evaluate the speech quality in limited communication bandwidth [8]. Because most of voice cloud service transmit voice data through TCP protocol, the low transmit rate only leads to high latency. The high noise affects the recognition precision. By adopting these models, some new approaches are proposed to evaluate the speech quality in high noise environment [9, 10]. However, the evaluation score can not reflect the recognition precision of machine.

From the mentioned above, it can be seen that the vehicular voice cloud will become a common configuration of the car. However, there is no mature testing tool in the market for the user experience evaluation of vehicular voice cloud service.

A test approach, which can be deployed in a car, is proposed in this paper to test the user experience in real scenario. By adopting typical user behavior, our proposed approach is also can simulate the complicated scenarios in the lab environment.

## 2   Design of the Evaluation System

The impacts of protocol and jitter have been evaluated in laboratory environment [11]. However, there are much more factors that can affect the end user experience. Therefore, the test system should be able to evaluate the appreciable indicators in real vehicular environment or in complicated simulated environment.

According to the general architecture of voice cloud service, we proposed a system structure for simulating the user behavior and evaluate the performance indicators of user experience.

In the real vehicular environment, the terminal sends selected typical pre-recorded voice data to cloud. The controller is responsible for issuing test instructions and test scripts to multiple service initiation units and simulation servers. The packets are captured in terminal. The controller indentifies these packets and computes appreciable indicators of the end user.

### 2.1   Recognition Precision Test

For evaluating recognition precision, the terminal calls the API of voice cloud service. First, the test system imports test case of voice. The vehicular terminal preprocesses the voice and sends voice data to cloud. Then the returned data is compared with expected text. This processing is shown in Fig. 1.

### 2.2   Latency Test

All the network packets between terminal and cloud are captured and saved as PCAP file by the test software. The evaluation program opens PCAP file and takes key fields. Through checking the key fields, the first request packet and the last response packet are indentified. This processing is shown in Fig. 2. The latency can be obtained by the timestamps of these packets. However, because different voice cloud services have different protocol, it is impossible to build a common packet inspection program for all voice cloud services. An approach is to build three-level packet inspection templates [12]. The algorithm process is shown in Table 1.

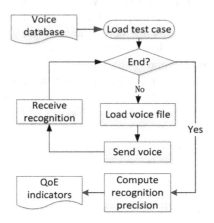

**Fig. 1.** Diagram of recognition precision evaluation.

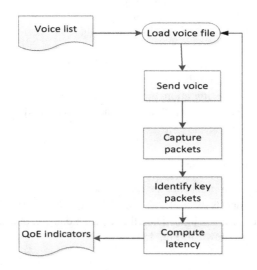

**Fig. 2.** Diagram of latency evaluation.

**Table 1.** Latency computation

| step | Algorithm |
|------|-----------|
| 1 | Capture network data, get pcap_file; |
| 2 | Split the pcap_file into frames; |
| 3 | WHILE the set of frames is not empty |
| 4 | IF (find DNS datagram) and (find target domain name) |
| 5 | Record time_stamp; |
| 6 | Flag=open; |
| 7 | ELSEIF (find a follow TCP server FIN) and (flag ==open) |
| 8 | Compute latency; |
| 9 | Flag=close; |
| 10 | ENDIF |
| 11 | ENDIF |
| 12 | ENDWHILE |

## 3   System Test

The authors test the proposed system in vehicular environment. By analyzing the usage ratio of common sentences, six common sentences in vehicular environment are selected to evaluate the recognition precision and latency of voice cloud service. The most common requests in vehicle voice cloud service are shown in Table 2.

**Table 2.** Statement usage ratio

| Test case | Weather | Scenic spot | Gas | Music | Hotel | Introduce | Other |
|-----------|---------|-------------|------|-------|-------|-----------|-------|
| Proportion | 29.1% | 20.2% | 10.4% | 23.3% | 13.55% | 7.41% | 9.27% |

The sentences include request for forecast, navigation to scenic spot, navigation to gas station, navigation to cafe, music and introduction.

The authors select 10 road spots with various level of background noise to send the voice recognition request. From the first spot to the last one, the background noise of each spot rose by 5%–10%. The precision of each group is shown in Table 3.

**Table 3.** Recognition precision of test cases under each background noise.

| Test case | 1st | 2nd | 3rd | 4th | 5th | 6th | 7th | 8th | 9th | 10th |
|-----------|-----|-----|-----|-----|-----|-----|-----|-----|-----|------|
| Recognition precision | 100% | 80% | 60% | 60% | 60% | 40% | 60% | 10% | 0% | 0% |

The system automatically transmits the voice to cloud and receive the recognition results. The recognition precision is showed in Fig. 3. The background noise gradually increases from spot 1 to spot 10. As the noise increasing, the voice recognition precision experiences an obvious decline.

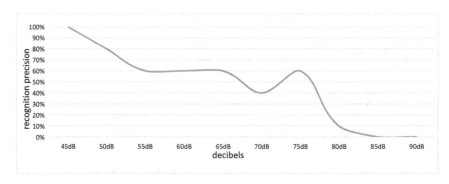

**Fig. 3.** Recognition precision with various level of noise.

The authors select 7 sites which near restaurant, cyber cafe, street, residential area, urban area, park, and shopping mall to evaluate the latency of voice cloud service. These locations have obvious differences in signal-to-noise ratio, channel interference and network congestion. The average delay of test cases at each test point is shown in Table 4.

**Table 4.** Recognition time delay of test cases at each test point.

| Test case | 1st | 2nd | 3rd | 4th | 5th | 6th | 7th |
|---|---|---|---|---|---|---|---|
| Weather | 0.617 | 0.787 | 0.486 | 0.682 | 0.763 | 0.986 | 0.687 |
| Scenic spot | 0.518 | 0.637 | 0.556 | 0.543 | 0.816 | 1.124 | 0.567 |
| Gas station | 0.588 | 0.697 | 0.781 | 0.764 | 0.832 | 1.564 | 0.772 |
| Music | 0.724 | 0.651 | 0.634 | 0.831 | 0.912 | 1.245 | 0.762 |
| Hotel | 0.689 | 0.812 | 0.682 | 0.654 | 0.811 | 0.965 | 0.731 |
| Introduce | 0.867 | 0.821 | 0.614 | 0.627 | 0.849 | 1.265 | 0.639 |

As showed in Fig. 4, the experiment results demonstrate that the scenario strongly affects the latency of voice cloud service, which affects the end user experience.

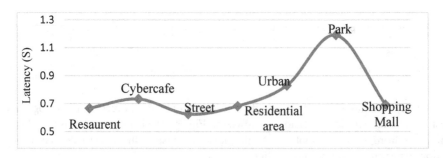

**Fig. 4.** Latency of voice cloud service.

# 4 Conclusions

In this paper, the authors analyze the key factors affecting the user experience of vehicular voice cloud service, and propose a light weight test system framework to evaluate the key indicators from view of end user. The results show that the light weight test system can be deployed in the common terminal of commercial network. And an approach to build complicated test scenarios in laboratory environment is also proposed.

For further, it is essential to collect typical user habit and analyzes the distribution characteristics of user behavior. To simulate the road communication link state, we can build the simulation test scenarios in laboratory environment.

**Acknowledgements.** This work is partly supported by the Natural Science Foundation of Jiangsu Province of China (No. BK20161165), the applied fundamental research Foundation of Xuzhou of China (No. KC17072), Ministry of Housing and Urban-Rural Development Science and Technology Planning Project (2016-R2-060), and the Open Fund of the Jiangsu Province Key Laboratory of Intelligent Industry Control Technology, Xuzhou University of Technology.

# References

1. Jiang, D., Wang, W., Shi, L., Song, H.: A compressive sensing-based approach to end-to-end network traffic reconstruction. IEEE Trans. Netw. Sci. Eng. (2018) https://doi.org/10.1109/tnse.2018.2877597
2. Jiang, D., Huo, L., Song, H.: Rethinking behaviors and activities of base stations in mobile cellular networks based on big data analysis. IEEE Trans. Netw. Sci. Eng. 1(2), 1–12 (2018)
3. Jiang, D., Huo, L., Li, Y.: Fine-granularity inference and estimations to network traffic for SDN. PLoS ONE 13(5), 1–23 (2018)
4. Chen, L., Jiang, D., Bao, R., Xiong, J., Liu, F., Bei, L.: MIMO scheduling effectiveness analysis for bursty data service from view of QoE. Chin. J. Electron. 26(5), 1079–1085 (2017)
5. Jiang, D., Li, W., Lv, H.: An energy-efficient cooperative multicast routing in multi-hop wireless networks for smart medical applications. Neurocomputing 220(2017), 160–169 (2017)
6. Jiang, D., Zhang, P., Lv, Z., Song, H.: Energy-efficient multi-constraint routing algorithm with load balancing for smart city applications. IEEE Internet Things J. 3(6), 1437–1447 (2018)
7. Vegni, A.M., Loscrí, V.: A Survey on Vehicular Social Networks. IEEE Commun. Surv. Tutorials 17(4), 2397–2419 (2015). Fourthquarter
8. Dubey, R.K., Kumar, A.: Non-intrusive speech quality assessment using multi-resolution auditory model features for degraded narrowband speech. IET Signal Proc. 9(9), 638–646 (2015)
9. Zhou, W., He, Q.: Non-intrusive speech quality objective evaluation in high-noise environments. In: 2015 IEEE China Summit and International Conference on Signal and Information Processing (ChinaSIP), pp. 50–54. Chengdu (2015)
10. Islam, M.R., et al.: Non-intrusive objective evaluation of speech quality in noisy condition. In: 2016 9th International Conference on Electrical and Computer Engineering (ICECE), pp. 586–589. Dhaka (2016)

11. Assefi, M., Wittie, M., Knight, A.: Impact of network performance on cloud speech recognition. In: International Conference on Computer Communication and Networks, pp. 1–6. IEEE (2015)
12. Chen, L., et al.: A lightweight end-side user experience data collection system for quality evaluation of multimedia communications. IEEE Access **6**, 15408–15419 (2018)

# Security Analysis on Gait-Based Biometric Fuzzy Commitment Scheme Using Smartphone

Zhang Min$^{(\boxtimes)}$

JiMei University, Xiamen 361021, Fujian, China
`flyinskyzhang@126.com`

**Abstract.** Gait-based biometric systems using smart phones have been developed to replace traditional authentication. It is significantly important to improve the security of the gait-based biometric systems. Systems include both fields of cryptography which provides high security levels of data and gait- based biometrics without need to remember passwords. Fuzzy Commitment Scheme (FCS) is considered as a famous approach to protect the user's data. However, these gait-based biometric systems are hampered by the lack of formal security analysis to prove the security strength and effectiveness. Therefore, this paper gives a comprehensive analysis evaluation on security of fuzzy commitment and proposes a framework of gait-based biometric fuzzy commitment scheme using smart phones. The evaluation results show that a significant security strength resistant to different attacks.

**Keywords:** Gait-based biometric cryptosystem · Fuzzy commit scheme · Security analysis

## 1 Introduction

Traditional security techniques for identification and authentication generally require passwords, PIN, or tokens which are easily attacked. In recent years, biometric has been widely studied in order to address the weakness of traditional authentic mechanisms. These biometric systems refer to behavioral or physical characteristics [1]. With increasingly application of mobile Internet, smart phones have become the media of human and machine interaction. Therefore, the identity authentication of smart phones and various mobile terminals has played an important role in guaranteeing for the security and reliability.

The user identity authentication method based on an inertial mobile sensor named accelerometer has become a hot topic in the research, and the sensor has been widely used in the smart phones for its high cost performance. Therefore, the comprehensive utilization of the information collected by these sensors for identity authentication will become important in the field of identity authentication in the future.

From 2010, the sensor-based gait recognition technology is applied to support existing authentication mechanisms, which are not very convenient in mobile phones [2], and have achieved significant results [3–6]. A first approach of inertial sensor-based gait authentication on mobile phones is proposed by Thang Hoang [7]. Instead of

© ICST Institute for Computer Sciences, Social Informatics and Telecommunications Engineering 2019
Published by Springer Nature Switzerland AG 2019. All Rights Reserved
H. Song et al. (Eds.): SIMUtools 2019, LNICST 295, pp. 353–362, 2019.
https://doi.org/10.1007/978-3-030-32216-8_34

storing original gait templates for user identification, the user was verified via a stored key which was encrypted by gait templates collected from a mobile accelerometer.

The Fuzzy Commitment Scheme (FCS) is developed by Ari and Wattenberg [8] and is considered as one of the template protection which method is based on Error Correcting Code (ECC). A major challenge of biometric cryptosystem is the security analysis that allows comparing different systems. Adamovic [9] presents a method based on information-theoretic analysis of iris biometric that aims to extract homogeneous regions of high entropy and uses FCS to reduce the overall complexity of this kind of systems. Chauhan [10] explores the efficiency of executing fuzzy commitment scheme in conjunction with Reed Solomon code as a novel better alternative to the conventional commitment scheme. Lafkih [11] have discussed the critical elements of the security in the key binding biometric cryptosystems and he [12] proposed a security analysis framework for biometric cryptosystems based on the fuzzy vault system and in paper [13] proposed a framework to evaluate the security of biometric cryptosystems based on the FCS. In paper [14] presented an approach to secure fuzzy commitment scheme against cross-matching-based decodability attack. However, behavioral traits such as gait are rarely studied. A novel lightweight symmetric key generation scheme based on the timing information of gait is proposed in paper [15].

Gait-based biometric authentication system offers more benefits to users than traditional authentication system. However, gait-based biometric features seem to be very vulnerable which are easily affected by different attacks. A rigorous security and privacy evaluation is still missing, especially for the evaluation of real systems using smart phones. In this paper, we propose a security analysis framework of gait-based biometric cryptosystems using smart phones based on the FCS. Firstly, we comprehensively summarize the security evaluation criteria and different metrics. Secondly, we introduce the security analysis framework of gait-based biometric cryptosystems based on the FCS. Thirdly, we evaluate the proposed criteria in the fuzzy commitment scheme for gait authentication.

The rest of the paper is organized as follows: In Sect. 2, an overview of security analysis of FCS is briefly presented. Section 3 will propose scenarios of attacks and different metrics to evaluate the performance and security of gait authentication on smart phones based on the FCS. Section 4 shows the results of the proposed framework. Conclusion and future work are mentioned in Sect. 5.

## 2   An Overview of Security Analysis of the FCS

The main idea of the FCS is to assign a random key to a subject to replace the biometric data itself. In the enrollment phase, we generate the key with gait-based biometric data by using an XOR-ed function which results in a new data called helper data. In the authentication stage, if the query features are close enough to enrolled features which is generated by key and helper data. The gait-biometric cryptosystem based FCS is shown in Fig. 1 as follows.

The enrollment and authentication phases of fuzzy commitment share the helper data (HD for short) and two correlated gait signal feature templates $w$ and $w'$. They try to extract exactly the same hash code of the key $m$.

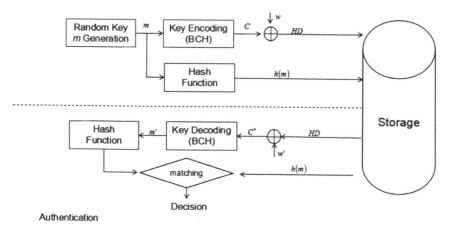

**Fig. 1.** Gait-based biometric cryptosystem based FCS.

The binary BCH code C as the error correcting code corresponds to the key $m$. The stored secure template consists of the hash of the key $h(m)$ and HD. The helper data $HD$ is obtained by codeword $C$ XOR with gait signal template $w$.

$$HD = C \oplus w \tag{1}$$

In the authentication phase, the gait signal template binarized and extracted from the queried biometric sample is XOR-ed with the stored helper data $HD$ to obtain codeword $C^*$:

$$C^* = HD \oplus w' = (C \oplus w) \oplus w' = C \oplus (w \oplus w') \tag{2}$$

Then the codeword $C^*$ can be rewritten as

$$C^* = C \oplus er \tag{3}$$

The matching module compares the hash value of $m'$ which is decoded by BCH with stored hash value $h(m)$. The same hash values of $m$ and $m'$ results into a match. If the hamming distance $D(w, w') = \|w \oplus w'\| = \|er\| \leq \varepsilon$, then there is a match where $\varepsilon$ is the error correction capability of the code.

The security and privacy performance of fuzzy commitment is well analyzed theoretically. In literature, many papers discussed the security analysis of the FCS [9, 12–16]. Rathgeb and Uhl [16] discussed the key elements of the security in biometric cryptosystems. Zhou *et al.* [17] studied the security in biometric security of the FCS. Their work focused on measuring the security and the privacy using the entropy to evaluate the independence and distribution of biometric features.

Lafkih [9, 12, 13] studied the security of key binding biometric cryptosystems based on fuzzy vault and fuzzy commitment respectively. Lafkih [13] proposed a security analysis framework based on several kinds of attacks that could affect biometric cryptosystems and applied on FCS. Different settings would be studied and other metrics would be proposed to analyze the security level of different biometric cryptosystems.

Hong [7] investigated the security of the gait authentication on mobile phones using biometric cryptosystems and fuzzy commitment scheme. But the paper didn't give a detailed framework for security analysis. Sapkal [18] presented a biometric cryptosystem with both fuzzy vault and fuzzy commitment techniques for fingerprint system. In [19], a novel template protection scheme based on fuzzy commitment and chaotic system, and the security analysis approach for unimodal biometric leakage were proposed.

## 3    Proposed Security Analysis Framework of Gait-Based Biometric Cryptosystems Using Fuzzy Commitment

Previous studies on security analysis are mostly based on information-theoretical measurements (such as entropy and leakage rate) which are difficult to estimate in the case of unknown biometric features distribution. There are few security analysis on gait-based biometric cryptosystems using smart phones. Therefore, our contribution is to offer simple, yet theoretically and practically detailed security analysis framework on gait-based biometric cryptosystem using smart phones.

In this paper we propose a security analysis framework for gait-based biometric cryptosystems using fuzzy commitment scheme against different attacks.

### 3.1    Evaluation Criteria and Metrics

For a fuzzy commitment scheme, we take consideration on security, privacy protection ability and unlinkability as security measures referred to [17]. In order to evaluate the performance of gait-based biometric cryptosystems, we use the False Acceptance Rate (FAR) and False Rejection Rate (FRR) which reflect the security and friendless of the system. The security is so important that we would like to achieve the FAR of 0% and the FRR as low as possible.

In order to measure the evaluation criteria, we need to define evaluation metrics against several threats including intrusion, correlation, combination and injection as referred to [13]. The evaluation metrics are used to quantify the different criteria.

### 3.2    Intrusion Threat

The adversary tries to access a system $S_2$ based on the information of another system $S_1$ (helper data $HD_1$ and the key $m_1$), on the assumption that both systems use the same gait-based biometric feature templates ($w$ and $w'$). The adversary can generate gait-based biometric feature template of $S_1$ and use them to access to the second system $S_2$. We calculate the probability using the distance between the helper data $HD_2$ of the system $S_2$ XOR-ed with the gait-based biometric feature template $w$ and the enrolled

BCH codeword $C_2$ is inferior to a threshold ε as the Intrusion Rate in Different System (IRDS).

$$IRDS(\varepsilon) = P(D(HD_2 \oplus w, C_2) < \varepsilon) \qquad (4)$$

In order to measure the evaluation criteria, we need to define evaluation metrics against several threats including intrusion, correlation, combination and injection.

### 3.3   Correlation Threat

Nagar et al. [20] proposed cross matching attack in order to determine whether two 'helper data' are generated from the same user. The error pattern with the smallest hamming distance is considered as the cross-matching distance score.

$$HD_{XOR} = HD_1 \oplus HD_2 = (w_1 \oplus C_1) \oplus (w_2 \oplus C_2) = (w_1 \oplus w_2) \oplus (C_1 \oplus C_2)$$
$$= er \oplus C_3 \qquad (5)$$

If the adversary knows both 'helper data' of both systems S1 and S2, the adversary can estimate the distance between both gait features of the user in both systems.

$$CM_s = min_{C \in X} \|HD_{XOR} \oplus C\| \qquad (6)$$

The cross-matching distance score $CM_s = \|er^*\| \leq \varepsilon$ only if the error pattern can be written as $er = er^* \oplus C_i$.

We can evaluate the vulnerability of the system to this attack by the probability that the distance between different helper data ($HD_{XOR}$) and codeword $C_i$ is lower than a threshold ε:

$$CR_{FC}(\varepsilon) = P(D(HD_1 \oplus HD_2, C_i) < \varepsilon) \qquad (7)$$

### 3.4   Combination Threat

The adversary knows part of the user gait-based biometric features in this attack, and extracts part of his/her own features to complete the biometric template ($w_A = w + w_F$) in which $w_F$ is part of his/her own features) used in the authentication system. We define the probability that the distance between the helper data XOR-ed with the combined template and the enrolled codeword is lower than a threshold ε as follows:

$$CA_{FC}(\varepsilon) = P(D(HD \oplus w_A, C) < \varepsilon) \qquad (8)$$

### 3.5   Injection Threat

The adversary can also inject his/her own gait-based biometric features in the database in order to be accepted by the system. For example, the adversary replaces the stored 'helper data' by a false 'helper data' ($HD_f = replace(HD)$). We measure this criterion via the probability that the distance between the 'helper data' which is forfeited by the adversary and the enrolled codeword C is lower to a threshold ε.

$$IA_{FC}(\varepsilon) = P(D(HD_f \oplus w, C) < \varepsilon) \tag{9}$$

## 4  Simulation and Experimental Results

We used the system on the dataset [4] collected from a built in accelerometer in smart phone for evaluating the security analysis framework. The original dataset consists of gait signals of 30 users carrying a waist-mounted smart phone with embedded inertial sensors. At first, we classify the dataset referred to [4] and extract the walking data as the original dataset. In this study, we consider the gait-based biometric authentication system based on different features extraction approaches. The SFS and SFFS algorithm are used in the first system [21] and BCS system is used in the second system [7]. The performance measurement and security analysis are based on the results achieved from the following part.

### 4.1  Performance Measurement

Receiver Operating Characteristic (ROC) [17] curves are obtained by computing the performance of systems in multiple operating points based on variation of FAR and FRR with tolerance. The overall error rates of our system is also represented by a receiver operating characteristic (ROC) curve which illustrates the relationship between the FAR and the FRR as shown in Fig. 2.

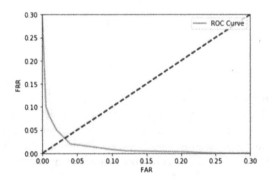

**Fig. 2.** ROC curves of gait authentication system

The Equal Error Rate (EER) is 3.48%, corresponding to an acceptable threshold of ε = 15.289. The ERR indicates the rate at which both FAR and FRR are equal.

## 4.2    Security Analysis Framework of the FCS

Figure 3 shows the IRDS curve. The adversary uses the first system's data and tries to access to the second system. The IRDS rate is increased in accordance with the value of threshold. If the error correction capability is minimal then the adversary is rejected by the system. As shown in Fig. 3, the ability to prevent this attack from being successful is affected by the intra-class variability.

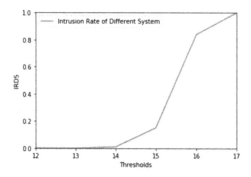

**Fig. 3.**  IRDS curve

In cross-matching attack, the adversary links two different systems' helper data using the same gait-based biometrics of the same user. The adversary can easily access to both systems as the system can correct the distance between both helper data (Fig. 4).

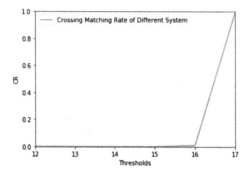

**Fig. 4.**  CR curve

In combination threat, the adversary can randomly combine both gait-biometric features. The adversary tried to use part of the forfeit of the user data instead of the real user data. Figure 5 shows that even if the threshold is minimal, the adversary can have access to the system using combined features with a high probability.

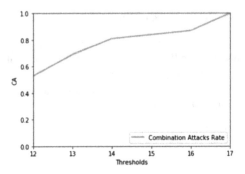

**Fig. 5.** CA curve

In injection attack, the adversary submits fake gait-based biometric features in order to be accepted by the system. As described in Fig. 6, the adversary can have access to the system with a high probability despite of the minimal threshold and random injection.

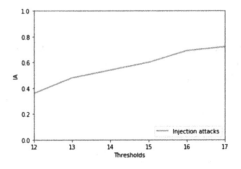

**Fig. 6.** IA curve

If the adversary knows both 'helper data' of both systems S1 and S2, the adversary can estimate the distance between both gait-based biometric features of the user in both systems. As a result, the system can easily refuse the trusted user with the thought of that the stored *HD* is modified in comparison to the enrollment process and contained the fake gait-based biometric templates injected by the adversary.

## 5  Conclusions and Future Work

In this paper, we proposed a security evaluation framework of gait-based biometrics against several attacks that could affect biometric cryptosystems and applied this analysis on gait authentication system on mobile phone by employing fuzzy commitment scheme. The investigation confirms theoretically and practically that cryptosystems based on FCS using smart phones can achieve promising performance in terms of FAR and FRR, and ensure the security level and protection of privacy.

On the field of gait biometric in general there is still a lot of work to do. The performance of gait authentication systems is not competitive to other biometrics. So the future work will focus on the studies of different settings and other metrics proposed to analyze the security level of different biometric cryptosystems.

**Acknowledgment.** This research project was supported by grant no. JAT170325 from Fujian Provincial Education Department Project of China and grant no. 2018J01537 from Fujian natural foundation project.

The author wants to thank the UCI Machine Language Repository and especially the researchers who kept the records and developed the Human Activity Recognition Using Smart Phones Data Set.

# References

1. Jain, A.K., Flynn, P.J., Ross, A.A. (eds.): Handbook of Biometrics. Springer, Berlin (2008). https://doi.org/10.1007/978-0-387-71041-9
2. Tam, L., Glassman, M., Vandenwauver, M.: The psychology of password management: a tradeoff between security and convenience. Behav. Inf. Technol. **29**(3)
3. Frank, J., Mannor, S., Precup, D.: Activity and gait recognition with time-delay embeddings. In: AAAI, pp. 1581–1586 (2010)
4. Hoang, T., Choi, D., Vo, V., Nguyen, A., Nguyen, T.: A lightweight gait authentication on mobile phone regardless of installation error. In: Janczewski, L.J., Wolfe, H.B., Shenoi, S. (eds.) SEC 2013. IAICT, vol. 405, pp. 83–101. Springer, Heidelberg (2013). https://doi.org/10.1007/978-3-642-39218-4_7
5. Derawi, M., Bours, P.: Gait and activity recognition using commercial phones. Comput. Secur. **39**, 137–144 (2013)
6. Lu, H., Huang, J., Saha, T., Nachman, L.: Unobtrusive gait verification for mobile phones. In: Proceedings of the 2014 ACM International Symposium on Wearable Computers, pp. 91–98. ACM (2014)
7. Hoang, T., Nguyen, T., Nguyen, T.: Gait authentication on mobile phone using biometric cryptosystem and fuzzy commitment scheme. Int. J. Inf. Secur. **14**(6), 549–560 (2015)
8. Ari, J., Wattenberg, M.: A fuzzy commitment scheme (1999). http://www.arijuels.com/wp-content/uploads/2013/09/JW99.pdf
9. Adamovic, S., Milosavljevic, M., Veinovic, M., et al.: Fuzzy commitment scheme for generation of cryptographic keys based on iris biometrics. IET Biometrics **6**(2), 89–96 (2017)
10. Chauhan, S., Sharma, A.: Fuzzy commitment scheme based on reed solomon codes. In: International Conference on Security of Information & Networks, pp. 96–99. ACM (2016)
11. Lafkih, M., Mikram, M., Ghouzali, S., and El Haziti, M.: Security analysis of key binding biometric cryptosystems. In: Proceedings of the 5th International Conference on Image and Signal Processing, pp. 269–281 (2012)
12. Lafkih, M., Mikram, M., Ghouzali, S., El Haziti, M., Aboutajdine, D.: Biometric cryptosystems based fuzzy vault approach: security analysis. In: Proceedings of the 2nd International Conference on Innovative Computing Technology, pp. 27–32, Casabkabca (2012)

13. Lafkih, M., Mikram, M., Ghouzali, S., EI Haziti, M., Aboutajdine, D.: Biometric cryptosystems based fuzzy commitment scheme: a security evaluation. Int. Arab J. Inf. Technol. **13**(4), 443–449 (2016)
14. Chauhan, S., Sharma, A.: Securing fuzzy commitment scheme against decodability attack-based cross-matching. In: Woungang, I., Dhurandher, S.K. (eds.) WIDECOM 2018. LNDECT, vol. 18, pp. 39–50. Springer, Cham (2018). https://doi.org/10.1007/978-3-319-75626-4_4
15. Sun, Y., Wong, C., Yang, G. Z., et al.: Secure key generation using gait features for Body Sensor Networks. In: IEEE, International Conference on Wearable and Implantable Body Sensor Networks, pp. 206–210. IEEE (2017)
16. Rathgeb, C., Uhl, A.: A survey on biometric cryptosystems and cancelable biometrics. EURASIA J. Inf. Secur. **2**, 1–25 (2011)
17. Zhou, X., Kuijper, A., Veldhuis, R., et al.: Quantifying privacy and security of biometric fuzzy commitment. In: International Joint Conference on Biometrics, vol. 207, pp. 1–8. IEEE Computer Society (2011)
18. Sapkal, S., Deshmukh, RR.: Biometric template protection with fuzzy vault and fuzzy commitment. In: International Conference on Information and Communication Technology for Competitive Strategies, pp. 1–6. ACM (2016)
19. Wang, N., Li, Q., et al.: A novel template protection scheme for multi biometrics based on fuzzy commitment and chaotic system. Signal Image Video Process. **9**(1), 99–109 (2015)
20. Nagar, A., Nandakumar, K., Jain, A.: Biometric template transformation: a security analysis. In: Proceedings of SPIE Workshop on Electronic Imaging, Media Forensics and Security, San Jose (2010)
21. Anguita, D., Ghio, A., Oneto, L., Parra, X., Reyes-Ortiz, J.L.: A public domain dataset for human activity recognition using smartphones. In: 21th European Symposium on Artificial Neural Networks, Computational Intelligence and Machine Learning, ESANN 2013. Bruges, Belgium, pp. 24–26 (2013)

# Particle Swarm Optimization Algorithm Based on Natural Selection and Simulated Annealing for PID Controller Parameters

Minlan Jiang[(⊠)], Ying Wu, Lan Jiang, and Fei Li

College of Mathematics, Physics and Information Engineering,
Zhejiang Normal University, Jinhua 321004, China
xx99@zjnu.cn

**Abstract.** The values of a PID controller's parameters determine the controller's effect. The particle swarm optimization (PSO) algorithm is often used to optimize the controller's parameters. However, PSO has some inherent defects, such as premature convergence and easily turning into a local optimization. In this paper, an improved particle swarm optimization algorithm based on a natural selection strategy and a simulated annealing mechanism is proposed to optimize the PID controller's parameters. In the improved PSO algorithm, the natural selection strategy is used to accelerate the rate of convergence, and the simulated annealing mechanism is employed to ensure the accuracy of the search and increase its ability to avoid local optima. The improved algorithm not only guarantees the convergence speed but also has a better ability to jump out of the local optimum trap. To verify the performance of the improved algorithm, four types of algorithms are selected to optimize the PID controller parameters of the Second-order Time-delayed System and the Permanent Magnet Synchronous Motor (PMSM) Servo System. They are the PSO algorithm, the optimization algorithm proposed in this paper (NAPSO), the seeker optimization algorithm (SOA), and the genetic algorithm (GA). The results show that the improved algorithm has a better optimal solution.

**Keywords:** PID · PSO · PMSM · GA

## 1 Introduction

In industrial control, proportion integration differentiation (PID) controllers have been widely used. The parameter optimization of PID controller has great influence on PID control system. In recent years, Zhou et al. [1] used particle swarm optimization to find an optimal set of PID control parameters in the target space, and an air-conditioning temperature control system was designed as an example. Wei et al. [2] use a GA algorithm to optimize the PID controller parameters, and they designed a PID controller parameter optimization system that consists of a microcontroller module. The host computer processes the real-time voltage and uses ITAE to evaluate the effectiveness of the optimized PID controller parameters. Zhong et al. [3] proposed a multi-agent simulated annealing algorithm based on a particle swarm optimization algorithm to address continuous function optimization problems. Lin et al. [4] used the multi-agent

H. Song et al. (Eds.): SIMUtools 2019, LNICST 295, pp. 363–373, 2019.
https://doi.org/10.1007/978-3-030-32216-8_35

simulated annealing algorithm to predict protein structure. However, there is no single improved PSO algorithm that is based on the methods of natural selection and simulated annealing. This paper adds two methods into the basic PSO algorithm simultaneously; then, a new PSO algorithm based on natural selection and simulated annealing (NAPSO) is produced. The simulation results show that using the improved algorithm to optimize the PID controller parameters can achieve better control performance.

This paper is organized as follows: Sect. 2 gives a brief description of the PSO algorithm and optimization algorithm. Section 3 introduces the PID Control and discusses the process of NAPSO-PID optimization. Section 4 reports the Second-order Time-delayed System, PMSM servo System and simulation results. Finally, Sect. 5 gives the conclusions of this paper.

## 2 PSO Algorithm and NAPSO Optimization Algorithm

### 2.1 Particle Swarm Optimization (PSO)

Particle Swarm Optimization (PSO) was proposed in 1995 by Dr. Eberhart and Dr. Kennedy and was derived from research on bird flocks' preying behavior. In PSO, every single solution is a "bird" in the search space. We call it a "particle". All of the particles have fitness values that are evaluated by the fitness function to be optimized, and each particle has a velocity to determine the direction and distance of its flight.

At the beginning of the algorithm, the particle swarm is initialized to a set of random values in the solution space. Then, the particles are "flown" through the problem space by following the current optimum particles. In each iteration, every particle is updated by tracking the two best positions: the first position is the best position that it has achieved so far, and this position is called the personal best position ($P_{best}$). The other position that is tracked by the particle swarm optimizer is the best position that is obtained so far by all particles in the population. This position is the global best and is called the global best position ($g_{best}$).

The update equation of the velocity and position is shown by the following expression:

$$v_{i.d}(t+1) = \omega v_{i.d}(t) \\ + c_1 r_1 [p_{best} - x_{i.d}(t)] + c_2 r_2 [g_{best} - x_{i.d}(t)] \tag{1}$$

$$x_{i.d}(t+1) = x_{i.d}(t) + v_{i.d}(t+1) \tag{2}$$

In the D dimension space, $t$ is the iteration number, $v_{i,d}(t)$ is the velocity of particle $i$ at iteration $t$, $x_{i.d}(t)$ is the position of particle $i$ at iteration $t$, and $\omega$ is the inertia weight to be used to control the impact of the previous history of velocities. Here, $c_1$ is the cognition learning factor, $c_2$ is the social learning factor, $\gamma_1$ and $\gamma_2$ are random numbers that are uniformly distributed in [0, 1], $P_{best}$ is the particle best value for the individual variable of particle $i$, and $g_{best}$ is the global best position variable of the particle swarm.

## 2.2   NAPSO Algorithm

When a particle's speed, position $\ell$ and fitness value have been updated, the particle moves to a random position $\ell_1'$ in its neighborhood and computes its new fitness value. The general procedure of NAPSO is illustrated in the flow chart in Fig. 1.

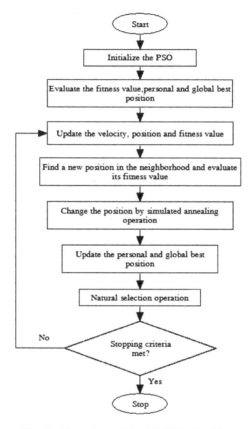

**Fig. 1.** Flow chart of the NAPSO algorithm

$$\ell_1' = \ell + [v_{max} - v_{min}] * \gamma_1 \tag{3}$$

Where $\gamma_1$ is the normally distribution random numbers of D-dimension that are distributed in [0, 1].determines whether to accept the new position and then updates the particle's $P_{best}$ and $g_{best}$. The simulated annealing operation can significantly increase the ability of the algorithm to jump out of the local optimum trap. The system uses the simulated annealing algorithm to determine whether to stay in the new position and thereby improve the rapid convergence effect of the birds. In the improved algorithm, at the end of each iteration, all particles have been ranked by their fitness values, from best to worst, using the better half to replace the other half. In this way, the stronger adaptability particles are saved.

However, both operations have their own disadvantages. The simulated annealing operation will slow the speed of convergence, thus increasing the convergence time. The natural selection operation will reduce the diversity of the samples. These two operations can compensate for each other. The simulated annealing operation can increase the sample diversity, and the natural selection operation can speed up the convergence. The two operations complement each other in the improved algorithm to both ensure the convergence speed of the algorithm and guarantee that the ability of the algorithm to jump out of the local optimal trap will be strengthened.

## 3   PID Controller Parameter Optimization by NAPSO

### 3.1   The PID Control System Based on NAPSO

The proportional-integral-derivative (PID) controller is widely used in industrial control systems. The "textbook" version of the PID algorithm is described by [5]:

$$u(t) = k_p e(t) + k_i \int_0^t e(t)dt + k_d \frac{de(t)}{dt} \tag{4}$$

Where $k_p$ is the proportional gain, $k_i$ is the integral gain, and $k_d$ is the derivative gain.

The core of the PID controller parameters optimization is to use an algorithm to optimize the PID controller's parameters: $k_p$, $k_i$ and $k_d$. When using the NAPSO algorithm to optimize the PID controller's three parameters, Block diagram of the NAPSO-PID control system is shown in Fig. 2.

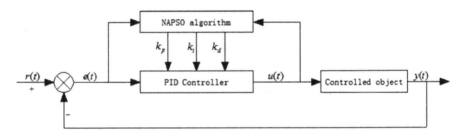

**Fig. 2.** Block diagram of the NAPSO-PID control system

In each iteration, the NAPSO algorithm will optimize the values of the three parameters and deliver the results to the PID controller. The PID controller calculates the control volume $u(t)$ according to formula (4) and delivers it to the controlled object, which gradually reduces the deviation [6].

## 3.2 PID Parameter Optimization Based on NAPSO

The essence of the PID controller parameters optimization is a parameter optimization problem based on an objective function. The objective function is the fitness function. In this paper, the fitness function is defined as an ITAE (Integral Time Absolute Error) index, which is often used to reflect the system's quality in a control system. ITAE represents the integral of the time multiplied by the absolute value of the error, which can be expressed as follows:

$$J = \int_0^\infty t|e(t)|dt \tag{5}$$

The NAPSO algorithm is applied to optimize the PID controller parameters as follows:

*Step 1:* Initialize $\omega$, $c_1$, $c_2$, and calculate the fitness value of each particle. Define the initial $p_{best}$ and initial $g_{best}$. Set T to be the simulated temperature; the initial T is 5000 °C, and the lower limit of $T$ is 1 °C.

*Step 2:* Update the position $l$ and velocity of each particle.

*Step 3:* Evaluate the fitness value $f'$, randomly find a new position $l_1'$ in the neighborhood of the particle, and calculate the new fitness value $(f_1')$ of the new position.

*Step 4:* Compare the fitness value with the new fitness, and evaluate the difference, $\Delta f = f_1' - f'$. If $\Delta f < 0$ and $f_1' < g_{best}$, then replace the original position with the new position.

*Step 5:* If $f_1' > g_{best}$, then keep the original position. If $\Delta f > 0$ and $f_1' < g_{best}$, then generate a random number $(rand(1))$ as a probability. But not $p = \exp((-1)*(f_1' - f')/T) > r4$, $r_4$ is a random number that is uniformly distributed in [0, 1]. Then accept the new position. According to the position of the particle, update the personal best position and global best position.

*Step 6:* When all of the updates of the particles are finished, then rank all of the particles according to the fitness value. Replace the information of half of the particles (position and velocity) with the information of the other half (the better) particles, and update the temperature $T = T * 0.9$.

*Step 7:* Stop searching when the maximum iteration limit or the fitness value limit is reached, and then output the three variables of the particles and their corresponding fitness value; otherwise, return to step 2.

To verify the validity of the algorithm, two different systems (Second-order Time-delayed System and PMSM Servo System) have been considered to illustrate the effectiveness of the proposed method. At the same time, the particle swarm optimization (PSO), seeker optimization algorithm (SOA) [7, 8] and genetic algorithm (GA) were also applied to show the performance of the proposed algorithm.

## 4  Experiments

### 4.1  PMSM Servo System PID Controller Parameters Optimization and Simulation Results

As an important part of Computer numerical control(CNC) machine tools, the servo system directly determines the quality of the machining performance. Currently, the permanent magnet synchronous motor (PMSM) servo system is a high performance servo system that is commonly used in CNC machine tools [9]. The state equation of the PMSM servo system in d-q coordinates is expressed as follows [10]:

$$
\begin{bmatrix} \dot{i}_d \\ \dot{i}_q \\ \dot{\omega}_r \end{bmatrix} = \begin{bmatrix} -R/L & p_n\omega_r & 0 \\ -p_n\omega_r & -R/L & -p_n\varphi_f/L \\ 0 & 3p_n\varphi_f/2J & 0 \end{bmatrix} \begin{bmatrix} i_d \\ i_q \\ \omega_r \end{bmatrix} + \begin{bmatrix} u_d/L \\ u_q/L \\ -T_L/J \end{bmatrix} \tag{6}
$$

To simplify the controller design of the PMSM servo system, $i_d = 0$ is often used in vector control. The PMSM servo system is shown in Fig. 3.

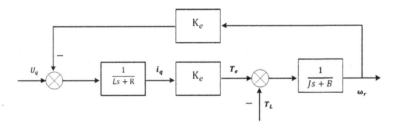

**Fig. 3.** Block diagram of the PMSM servo system

Here, $K_c = \frac{3}{2}p_n\varphi_f$ is the torque coefficient, $K_e = p_n\varphi_f$ is the back EMF constant, and $B$ is the viscosity damping coefficient.

According to Eq. (6) and Fig. 3, the CNC machine feeding servo system in the field orientation (controlled under) can be expressed as follows:

$$
G_2(S) = \frac{K_c}{LJS^2 + (RJ + LB)S + BR + K_cK_e} \tag{7}
$$

The parameters of the PMSM servo system are designed as follows:

$$
L = 8.5e - 3(\mathrm{H}), R = 2.875(\Omega),
$$

$$
J = 0.8e - 3(\mathrm{km \cdot m^2}), B = 0.02(\mathrm{N \cdot m/(rad/s)}), p_n = 4, \varphi_f = 0.175(\mathrm{Wb}),
$$

Equation (7) can be rewritten as follows:

$$G_2(S) = \frac{1.05}{6.8 \cdot 10^{-6}S^2 + 2.47 \cdot 10^{-3}S + 0.7925} \tag{8}$$

In the experiment, the system expressed by Eq. (8) is used as the second controlled object. The system PID controller parameters are optimized by NAPSO, PSO, SOA and GA. The comparisons of the step responses based on the four algorithms are displayed in Fig. 4.

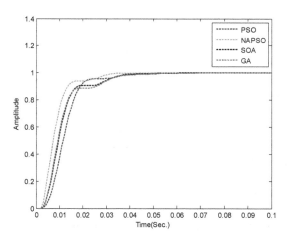

**Fig. 4.** Step responses of the PMSM servo system

Figure 4 shows that the NAPSO optimization step response curve is clearly superior and the convergence speed of the NAPSO is faster than the others. At 0.035 s, the curve of the NAPSO algorithm is closest to the curve of the idea output. The simulation results of the PMSM feed system are presented in Table 1.

**Table 1.** Simulation results of the PMSM servo system

| Tuning method | $k_p$ | $k_i$ | $k_d$ | Settling time (sec) | Overshoot (%) | ITAE value |
|---|---|---|---|---|---|---|
| PSO | 0.1094 | 61.6899 | 0 | 0.03741 | 0 | 12.3795 |
| NAPSO | 0.2058 | 92.2902 | 3.7148e − 004 | 0.02914 | 0 | 8.3796 |
| GA | 0.1363 | 68.0213 | 0 | 0.03615 | 0 | 11.8784 |
| SOA | 0.1116 | 68.3148 | 0 | 0.03562 | 0 | 11.3453 |

As Table 1 shows, the settling time is approximately 0.029 s for NAPSO compared with approximately 0.037, 0.36 and 0.035 for PSO, GA and SOA, respectively. In addition, NAPSO has the best ITAE value of the four algorithms, acquiring an ITAE value of 8.3796, and the ITAE values of PSO, GA and SOA are 12.3795, 11.8784 and

11.3453, respectively. It is clear that NAPSO has the best ITAE value, settling time and overshoot among the four algorithms in the second experiment.

## 4.2    Second-Order Time-Delayed System PID Controller Parameters Optimization and Simulation Results

In modern industrial process control, many systems can similarly be seen as a first- or second-order typical system. In this paper, select the Second-order Time-delayed System as the first controlled object. The mathematical expression of the first controlled object is the following:

$$G_1(s) = \frac{0.05}{s^2 + 0.2s + 0.05} e^{-3s} \qquad (9)$$

Next, with the particle swarm optimization (PSO), seeker optimization algorithm (SOA) and genetic algorithm (GA) to optimize the PID controller's parameters. For the first experiment, to make a fair comparison, the maximum generation, population size, minimum fitness value, range of gains, dimension of search space and initial positions are identical for all of the algorithms. The maximum number of generations is 100, the minimum fitness value is 0.1, the size of the population is 100, and the dimension of the search space is 3. The parameters for the PSO were set as follows: the acceleration constants $c_1$ and $c_2$ are 2, the dimension is 3, and the inertia weight $w = 0.9$. The parameters of the SOA are designed as follows: the minimum membership degree $U_{min} = 0.0111$, the maximum membership degree $U_{max} = 0.95$, the maximum weight $w_{max} = 0.9$, and the minimum weight $w_{min} = 0.1$. In the GA algorithm, the crossover probability is 0.9, and the mutation probability updates in a self-adaptive manner.

The optimize results of the four types of algorithm are shown in Fig. 5, and the step responses are presented in Fig. 6

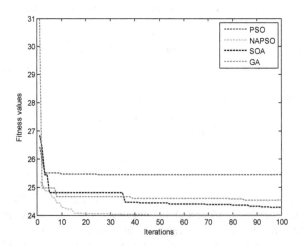

**Fig. 5.** Response curve of the second-order time-delayed system

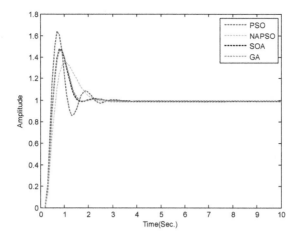

**Fig. 6.** ITAE curves of the second-order time-delayed system

In Fig. 5, at the 15th iteration, the ITAE value of the NAPSO algorithm is approximately 24.08, and the PSO, GA, and SOA are approximately 25.4, 24.6, and 24.8, respectively. It can clearly be seen that the NAPSO algorithm has the best optimized result among the four types of algorithms, and when the four types of algorithms obtain the same fitness value, the NAPSO algorithm requires a much smaller number of iterations than the other algorithms.

In Fig. 6, compared with PSO, the NAPSO has a smaller overshoot and shorter oscillation cycle, and the system can achieve stability more quickly. The accurate simulation results of the Second-order Time-delayed System are given in Table 2.

**Table 2.** Simulation results of the Second-order Time-delayed System

| Tuning method | $k_p$ | $k_i$ | $k_d$ | Settling time (sec) | Overshoot (%) | ITAE value |
|---|---|---|---|---|---|---|
| PSO | 100 | 0 | 80.8380 | 2.6408 | 63.79 | 25.3166 |
| NAPSO | 55.8028 | 0.6136 | 47.2314 | 2.1245 | 36.72 | 24.0218 |
| GA | 75.9074 | 0.6447 | 60.7940 | 1.5371 | 48.80 | 24.7880 |
| SOA | 77.3687 | 68.3148 | 62.7102 | 1.4745 | 47.42 | 24.3978 |

In Table 2, the ITAE value is approximately 24.0218 for NAPSO compared with approximately 25.3166, 24.7880 and 24.3978 for the PSO, GA and SOA, respectively. Furthermore, the system overshoot is 36.72% in the case of NAPSO. Compared with NAPSO, the overshoots of the PSO, GA and SOA are 63.79%, 48.80% and 47.42%, respectively. Overall, the NAPSO has the smaller ITAE value and overshoot among the four algorithms in the first experiment.

From the two experiments, it can be seen that when the initial positions and range of gains are identical for all of the algorithms, the different algorithms produce different values, and the NAPSO algorithm has the better ITAE values in the two experiments. This finding indicates that the NAPSO algorithm has a better capability for a global search than the other two algorithms. It is also clearly obvious that in the NAPSO algorithm, the rapid convergence has improved because the update of the velocity and positions of the particles no longer depend too much on the current best particle.

## 5  Conclusions

The optimization of the PID controller parameters is a hotspot in modem manufacturing technology. In this study, an improved PSO algorithm (NAPSO) based on simulated annealing and natural selection is proposed and used in PID controller parameters optimization. The simulation experiments show that the proposed algorithm performs well in the Second-order Time-delayed System and the PMSM Servo System. The results of the NAPSO were compared with PSO, SOA and GA, with the result that the NAPSO has higher accuracy and faster convergence than the other three algorithms. The proposed algorithm can provide a new method for addressing PID controller parameter optimization and has definite value for applications in modem manufacturing technology. However, the NAPSO has the disadvantage of strong randomicity. In the future, we plan to study which is the more effective method for improving the prediction results.

**Acknowledgment.** This work was supported in part by the National Natural Science Foundation of China (Nos. 51305407, 61571104).

## References

1. Zhou, Y., Nie, J., Han, N., Chen, C., Yue, Z.: Study on PID parameters tuning based on particle swarm optimization. In: Advanced Materials Research, vol. 823, pp. 432–438 (2013)
2. Wei, C., Liu, Z., Li, P., Chen, J., Zhang, S.: The PID parameters optimization method based on GA for NC power supply. In: Huang, B., Yao, Y. (eds.) Proceedings of the 5th International Conference on Electrical Engineering and Automatic Control. LNEE, vol. 367, pp. 97–104. Springer, Heidelberg (2016). https://doi.org/10.1007/978-3-662-48768-6_12
3. Zhong, Y., Ning, J., Zhang, H.: Multi-agent simulated annealing algorithm based on particle swarm optimisation algorithm. Int. J. Comput. Appl. Technol. **43**(4), 335–342 (2012)
4. Lin, J., Ning, J., Du, Q., Zhong, Y.: Multi-agent simulated annealing algorithm based on particle swarm optimization algorithm for protein structure prediction. J. Bionanoscience Sci. **7**(1), 84–91 (2013)
5. Laskawski, M., Wcislik, M.: Sampling rate impact on the tuning of PID controller parameters. Int. J. Electron. Telecommun. **62**(1), 43–48 (2016)
6. Modares, H., Alfi, A., Naghibi, S., Sistani, M.B.N.: Parameter estimation of bilinear systems based on an adaptive particle swarm optimization. Eng. Appl. Artif. Intell. **23**(7), 1105–1111 (2010)
7. Zhu, Y., Dai, C., Chen, W.: Seeker optimization algorithm for several practical applications. Int. J. Comput. Intell. Syst. **7**(2), 353–359 (2014)
8. Chen, C., Li, J., Luo, J., Xie, S., Li, H.: Seeker optimization algorithm for optimal control of manipulator. Ind. Robot **43**(6), 677–686 (2016)

9. Premkumara, K., Manikandan, B.V.: Speed control of brushless DC motor using bat algorithm optimized adaptive neuro-fuzzy inference system. Appl. Soft Comput. **32**, 403–419 (2015)
10. Ouledali, O., Meroufel, A., Wira, P., Bentouba, S.: Direct torque fuzzy control of PMSM based on SVM. Energy Proc. **74**, 1314–1322 (2015)

# HSS-Iteration-Based Iterative Interpolation of Curves and Surfaces with NTP Bases

Liangchen Hu, Huahao Shou$^{(\boxtimes)}$, and Zhenlei Dai

College of Science, Zhejiang University of Technology, Hangzhou 310023, China
shh@zjut.edu.cn

**Abstract.** Based on the Hermitian and skew-Hermitian splitting (HSS) iteration technique [14], a new iterative interpolation technique called HPIA for curves and surfaces with NTP bases and its weighted version WHPIA are proposed. We take the previous iteration and the current iteration into account simultaneously, and establish a function based on NTP bases as a perturbation term in the iteration process. Convergence analyses and the approximate optimal weight of WHPIA are given. Theoretical and experimental results show that HPIA and WHPIA are effective.

**Keywords:** HSS iteration · NTP bases · PIA · Interpolation · Convergence

## 1 Introduction

Essentially, as a popular data fitting technique in recent years, geometric iteration is an iterative method for solving linear equations in linear algebra. Since the geometric iteration method was proposed, it has been widely used in the academic research and engineering practices in the geometric design and related fields [1–5]. By using the technique of geometric iteration, not only achieved better results by addressing traditional problems of geometric design, such as offset curves, degree reduction, and polynomial approximation to rational curves and surfaces and etc., but also has been successfully applied to adaptive data fitting, large scale data fitting, symmetric surface fitting, generation of curves interpolating given positions, tangent, and curvature vectors, generation of quality guaranteed quadrilateral and hexahedral meshes, generation of trivariate B-spline solids.

The technique of geometric iteration in geometric design was originated and developed by Lin et al. [6–13]. In 2004, Lin proved the property of profit-and-loss for non-uniform cubic B-spline curves and surfaces [6], and for blending curves and tensor product blending patches with normalized totally positive(NTP)

Supported by the National Science Foundation of China (No. 61572430).

H. Song et al. (Eds.): SIMUtools 2019, LNICST 295, pp. 374–384, 2019.
https://doi.org/10.1007/978-3-030-32216-8_36

bases in 2005 [7]. The approach of geometric iteration is called progressive iterative approximation(PIA) in [7], which addresses both interpolation and approximation (including EPIA [8] and LSPIA [5,9]). Lin has given the PIA iterative
formats with NTP bases in [6,7] as follows,
the case of curve:

$$
\begin{aligned}
&[\boldsymbol{A}_2^{k+1}, \boldsymbol{A}_3^{k+1}, \cdots, \boldsymbol{A}_{n-1}^{k+1}] \\
&=(\boldsymbol{I} - \boldsymbol{N})[\boldsymbol{A}_2^k, \boldsymbol{A}_3^k, \cdots, \boldsymbol{A}_{n-1}^k], k = 0, 1, \cdots
\end{aligned}
\tag{1}
$$

the case of surface:

$$
\begin{aligned}
&[\boldsymbol{A}_{11}^{k+1}, \boldsymbol{A}_{12}^{k+1}, \cdots, \boldsymbol{A}_{1n}^{k+1}, \cdots, \boldsymbol{A}_{m1}^{k+1}, \boldsymbol{A}_{m2}^{k+1}, \cdots, \boldsymbol{A}_{mn}^{k+1}] \\
&=(\boldsymbol{I} - \boldsymbol{N})[\boldsymbol{A}_{11}^k, \boldsymbol{A}_{12}^k, \cdots, \boldsymbol{A}_{1n}^k, \cdots, \boldsymbol{A}_{m1}^k, \boldsymbol{A}_{m2}^k, \cdots, \boldsymbol{A}_{mn}^k] \\
&, k = 0, 1, \cdots, \boldsymbol{N} = \boldsymbol{N}_1 \otimes \boldsymbol{N}_2
\end{aligned}
\tag{2}
$$

where the difference vector $\boldsymbol{A}_i^k$ or $\boldsymbol{A}_{ij}^k$ is calculated as

$$
\begin{cases}
\boldsymbol{A}_i^k = (\boldsymbol{Q}_i - \boldsymbol{C}^k(u_i)) \\
\boldsymbol{A}_{ij}^k = (\boldsymbol{Q}_{ij} - \boldsymbol{C}^k(u_i, v_j))
\end{cases}
$$

On the other hand, (1) and (2) can be written in matrix form as $\boldsymbol{P}^k = (\boldsymbol{I} - \boldsymbol{N})\boldsymbol{P}^{k-1} + \boldsymbol{Q}$, where $\boldsymbol{P}^k$ is a column vector of control vertexes, $\boldsymbol{I}$ is identity
matrix, $\boldsymbol{N}$ is totally positive(TP) collocation matrix and $\boldsymbol{Q}$ is a column vector
of data points. In [10], Lu present a new and efficient method for weighted PIA
of data points by using NTP bases. The progress can be written in matrix form
as $\boldsymbol{P}^k = (\boldsymbol{I} - \omega\boldsymbol{N})\boldsymbol{P}^{k-1} + \boldsymbol{Q}$. And he proved that the weighted PIA based on
an NTP basis of the space has the fastest convergence rate when

$$
\omega = \frac{2}{1 + \lambda_n(\boldsymbol{N})},
$$

where $\lambda_n(\boldsymbol{N})$ is the smallest eigenvalue of $\boldsymbol{N}$.

Bai et al. proposed the use of the Hermitian/skew-Hermitian splitting(HSS)
iteration method [14]. Theoretical analysis has shown that this HSS-iteration
converges unconditionally to the exact solution of the system of linear equations
$\boldsymbol{Ax} = \boldsymbol{b}$. Based on the HSS-iteration technique, we present a new iteration
method and its weighted version for progressive iteration approximation of data
points by using NTP bases and prove their convergence. The iterative process of
these two methods consists of two steps, and the iterative difference vectors in
the two steps are different from each other. For convenience, we call them HPIA
and WHPIA, respectively.

## 2    Iterative Format of HPIA

### 2.1    The Case of Curves

Given an NTP basis $\{N_i(u)\}_{i=0}^n$ and a control vertexes set $\{P_i^0\}_{i=0}^n$ in $\mathbb{R}^2$ or $\mathbb{R}^3$, we can generate the initial curve

$$C^0(u) = \sum_{i=0}^n P_i^0 N_i(u),$$

We assign control vertexes set $\{P_i^0\}_{i=0}^n$ with a real increasing parameters set $\{u_i\}_{i=0}^n$, i.e. $u_0 < u_1 < \cdots < u_n$.

Then, the remaining curves of the sequence, $C^k(u)$ for $k \geq 1$, can be calculated as follows

$$C^k(u) = \sum_{i=0}^k P_i^k N_i(u),$$

where

$$\begin{cases} P_i^k = P_i^{k-1/2} + \Delta_{1i}^k \\ \Delta_{1i}^k = P_i^0 - [\frac{1}{2}(C^k(u_i) + C^{k-1/2}(u_i)) \\ \qquad + \frac{1}{2}(C^{k-1/2}(N_i) - C^k(N_i))] \\ P_i^{k-1/2} = P_i^{k-1} + \Delta_{2i}^k \\ \Delta_{2i}^k = P_i^0 - [\frac{1}{2}(C^{k-1}(u_i) + C^{k-1/2}(u_i)) \\ \qquad + \frac{1}{2}(C^{k-1/2}(N_i) - C^{k-1}(N_i))] \end{cases} \tag{3}$$

In (3), $C^k(N_i)$ is defined as follows

$$C^k(N_i) = \sum_{j=0}^n P_j^k N_i(u_j), i = 0, \cdots, n, k = 0, \frac{1}{2}, 1, \cdots,$$

which is a function that takes bases as variables. Since $\lim_{k \to \infty} \{P_i^{k-1/2}\}_{i=0}^n = \lim_{k \to \infty} \{P_i^k\}_{i=0}^n$, we have $\lim_{k \to \infty} (C^{k-1/2}(N_i) - C^k(N_i)) = 0$. Here, we consider $C^k(N_i)$ as a perturbation term in the iteration process.

We call (3) as HPIA format of curves, which consists of two steps and replaces the iterative step length of each control vertex in PIA.

### 2.2    The Case of Surfaces

Given two NTP bases $\{N_i(u)\}_{i=0}^n$, $\{S_j(v)\}_{j=0}^m$ and a control vertexes set $\{P_{ij}^0\}_{i=0,j=0}^{n,m}$ in $\mathbb{R}^3$, we can generate the initial surface

$$C^0(u,v) = \sum_{i=0}^n \sum_{j=0}^m P_{ij}^0 N_i(u) S_j(v).$$

We assign control vertexes set $\{P_{ij}^0\}_{i=0,j=0}^{n,m}$ with two real increasing parameters set $\{u_i\}_{i=0}^n$ ,i.e., $u_0 < u_1 < \cdots < u_n$ and $\{v_j\}_{j=0}^m$ ,i.e., $v_0 < v_1 < \cdots < v_m$.

Like the case of curves, we can take $C^k(N,S) = \sum_{i=0}^n \sum_{j=0}^m P_{ij}^k N(u_i)$ $S(v_j), k = 0, 1, \cdots$ as a perturbation term. Then, the remaining surfaces of the sequence, $C^k(u,v)$ for $k \geq 1$, can be calculated as follows

$$C^k(u,v) = \sum_{i=0}^n \sum_{j=0}^m P_{ij}^k N_i(u) S_j(v).$$

where

$$\begin{cases} P_{ij}^k = P_{ij}^{k-1/2} + \Delta_{1ij}^k \\ \Delta_{1ij}^k = P_{ij}^0 - [\frac{1}{2}(C^k(u_i,v_j) + C^{k-1/2}(u_i,v_j)) \\ \qquad + \frac{1}{2}(C^{k-1/2}(N_i,S_j) - C^k(N_i,S_j))] \\ P_{ij}^{k-1/2} = P_{ij}^{k-1} + \Delta_{2ij}^k \\ \Delta_{2ij}^k = P_{ij}^0 - [\frac{1}{2}(C^{k-1}(u_i,v_j) + C^{k-1/2}(u_i,v_j)) \\ \qquad + \frac{1}{2}(C^{k-1/2}(N_i,S_j) - C^{k-1}(N_i,S_j))] \end{cases} \qquad (4)$$

We call (4) as HPIA format of surfaces, which, like the case of curves, also consists of two steps and replaces the iterative step length of each control vertex in PIA.

*Remark 1.* From (3) and (4), we will get $\lim_{k\to\infty} C^k(u_i) = P_i^0$ or $\lim_{k\to\infty} C^k(u_i,v_j) = P_{ij}^0$, If for any $\varepsilon > 0$, there is a natural number $T$, when $k, s > T$ ,$\|P_i^k - P_i^{k-1}\| < \varepsilon$ or $\|P_{ij}^k - P_{ij}^{k-1}\| < \varepsilon$.

## 3   Convergence Analysis

**Lemma 1.** *Given any two non-singular collocation matrices* $N_1 = (N_j(u_i))_{i,j=0}^{n,n}$, $N_2 = (S_j(v_i))_{i,j=0}^{m,m}$, *which is defined on two NTP bases* $\{N_j(u)\}_{j=0}^n$, $\{S_j(v)\}_{j=0}^m$. *And assuming that* $\lambda_i(N_1), i = 0, 1, \cdots, n, \lambda_i(N_2), i = 0, 1, \cdots, m$ *are their eigenvalues respectively. Then,*

*(1)* $0 < \lambda_i(N_1) \leq 1, 0 < \lambda_i(N_2) \leq 1$,
*(2)* $0 < \lambda_i(N_1 \otimes N_2) \leq 1$, *here* $\otimes$ *is Kronecker product.*

The proof of this Lemma 1 can be found in Theorems 2.1 and 2.2 of [2].
The two iterative processes of (3) and (4) can be written in matrix form

$$\begin{cases} \left(I + \frac{1}{2}N_-\right) P^k = \left(I - \frac{1}{2}N_+\right) P^{k-1/2} + P^0 \\ \left(I + \frac{1}{2}N_+\right) P^{k-1/2} = \left(I - \frac{1}{2}N_-\right) P^{k-1} + P^0 \end{cases} \qquad (5)$$

where $I$ is the identity matrix, $N_+ = N + N^T$, $N_- = N - N^T$, and $N = N_1$ or $N = N_1 \otimes N_2$, $(\cdot)^T$ is the transpose of matrix $(\cdot)$. Then, we get iterative matrix of (5) as follows

$$M = \left(I + \frac{1}{2}N_-\right)^{-1}\left(I - \frac{1}{2}N_+\right)\left(I + \frac{1}{2}N_+\right)^{-1}\left(I - \frac{1}{2}N_-\right).$$

Now what we need to prove is that the iterative sequence $\{P^k\}$ of control vertexes converges to the unique solution $P^*$, i.e., $\rho(M) < 1$.

**Theorem 1.** *The two iterative processes of (3) and (4) are convergent, if the bases $\{N_j(u)\}_{j=0}^n$ and $\{S_j(v)\}_{j=0}^m$ are totally positive and their collection matrices $N_1$ and $N_2$ are non-singular.*

*Proof.* Based on the similarity in-variance of spectral radius, the symmetric matrix $N_+$, and the anti-symmetric matrix $N_-$, we have

$$\rho(M) = \rho\left(\left(I - \frac{1}{2}N_+\right)\left(I + \frac{1}{2}N_+\right)^{-1}\left(I - \frac{1}{2}N_-\right)\left(I + \frac{1}{2}N_-\right)^{-1}\right)$$

$$\leq \left\|\left(I - \frac{1}{2}N_+\right)\left(I + \frac{1}{2}N_+\right)^{-1}\left(I - \frac{1}{2}N_-\right)\left(I + \frac{1}{2}N_-\right)^{-1}\right\|_2$$

$$\leq \left\|\left(I - \frac{1}{2}N_+\right)\left(I + \frac{1}{2}N_+\right)^{-1}\right\|_2 \left\|\left(I - \frac{1}{2}N_-\right)\left(I + \frac{1}{2}N_-\right)^{-1}\right\|_2.$$

$$\because N_-^T = -N_-$$

$$\therefore \left(\left(I - \frac{N_-}{2}\right)\left(I + \frac{N_-}{2}\right)^{-1}\right)^T\left(I - \frac{N_-}{2}\right)\left(I + \frac{N_-}{2}\right)^{-1}$$

$$= \left(I - \frac{N_-}{2}\right)^{-1}\left(I + \frac{N_-}{2}\right)\left(I - \frac{N_-}{2}\right)\left(I + \frac{N_-}{2}\right)^{-1}$$

$$= \left(I - \frac{N_-}{2}\right)^{-1}\left(I - \frac{N_-}{2}\right)\left(I + \frac{N_-}{2}\right)\left(I + \frac{N_-}{2}\right)^{-1}$$

$$= I$$

$\therefore \left(I - \frac{N_-}{2}\right)\left(I + \frac{N_-}{2}\right)^{-1}$ is a unitary matrix, i.e., $\left\|\left(I - \frac{N_-}{2}\right)\left(I + \frac{N_-}{2}\right)^{-1}\right\|_2 = 1.$

Thus, $\rho(M) \leq \left\|\left(I - \frac{1}{2}N_+\right)\left(I + \frac{1}{2}N_+\right)^{-1}\right\|_2 = \max_{\lambda_i \in \lambda(N_+/2)}\left|\frac{1-\lambda_i}{1+\lambda_i}\right|$. From Lemma 1, we know $\lambda_i > 0, i = 0, 1, \cdots, n$, so $\rho(M) < 1$. This completes the proof. $\square$

## 4    Iterative Format of WHPIA

Similar to weighted PIA, we can accelerate the iterative process of the HPIA in a weighted approach. Thus, (3) and (4) can be written in two weighted forms respectively as follows

$$
\begin{cases}
\boldsymbol{P}_i^k = \boldsymbol{P}_i^{k-1/2} + \omega_1 \boldsymbol{\Delta}_{1i}^k, \, \boldsymbol{P}_i^{k-1/2} = \boldsymbol{P}_i^{k-1} + \omega_1 \boldsymbol{\Delta}_{2i}^k \\
\boldsymbol{P}_{ij}^k = \boldsymbol{P}_{ij}^{k-1/2} + \omega_2 \boldsymbol{\Delta}_{1ij}^k, \, \boldsymbol{P}_{ij}^{k-1/2} = \boldsymbol{P}_{ij}^{k-1} + \omega_2 \boldsymbol{\Delta}_{2ij}^k
\end{cases}.
$$

And their matrix forms can be obtained from (5)

$$
\begin{cases}
\left( \boldsymbol{I} + \frac{1}{2}\omega \boldsymbol{N}_- \right) \boldsymbol{P}^k = \left( \boldsymbol{I} - \frac{1}{2}\omega \boldsymbol{N}_+ \right) \boldsymbol{P}^{k-1/2} + \omega \boldsymbol{P}^0 \\
\left( \boldsymbol{I} + \frac{1}{2}\omega \boldsymbol{N}_+ \right) \boldsymbol{P}^{k-1/2} = \left( \boldsymbol{I} - \frac{1}{2}\omega \boldsymbol{N}_- \right) \boldsymbol{P}^{k-1} + \omega \boldsymbol{P}^0.
\end{cases}
\tag{6}
$$

The iterative matrix of (6) is as follows

$$
\boldsymbol{M} = \left( \boldsymbol{I} + \frac{1}{2}\omega \boldsymbol{N}_- \right)^{-1} \left( \boldsymbol{I} - \frac{1}{2}\omega \boldsymbol{N}_+ \right) \left( \boldsymbol{I} + \frac{1}{2}\omega \boldsymbol{N}_+ \right)^{-1} \left( \boldsymbol{I} - \frac{1}{2}\omega \boldsymbol{N}_- \right).
$$

From Theorem 1, we know $\rho(\boldsymbol{M}) \le \max\limits_{\lambda_i \in \lambda(\boldsymbol{N}_+/2)} \left| \frac{1-\omega\lambda_i}{1+\omega\lambda_i} \right|, \lambda_i > 0, i = 0, 1, \cdots,$ $n, \omega > 0$ i.e., $\rho(\boldsymbol{M}) < 1$ . Thus, the iterative process (6) is convergent.

**Theorem 2.** *Given two non-singular collocation matrices, $\boldsymbol{N}_1 = (N_j(u_i))_{i,j=0}^{n,n}$, $\boldsymbol{N}_2 = (S_j(V_i))_{i,j=0}^{m,m}$ , which are defined on two NTP bases $\{N_j(u)\}_{j=0}^n$, $\{S_j(v)\}_{j=0}^m$. The HPIA with weight has the approximate fastest convergence rate when*

$$
\omega^* = \frac{2}{\sqrt{\lambda_{max}(\boldsymbol{N} + \boldsymbol{N}^T)\lambda_{min}(\boldsymbol{N} + \boldsymbol{N}^T)}},
$$

*where $\boldsymbol{N} = \boldsymbol{N}_1$ or $\boldsymbol{N} = \boldsymbol{N}_1 \otimes \boldsymbol{N}_2$.*

*Proof.* It is proved in [14] that the optimal spectral radius is

$$
\frac{1}{\omega^*} = \sqrt{\lambda_{max}\left( \frac{\boldsymbol{N} + \boldsymbol{N}^T}{2} \right) \lambda_{min} \left( \frac{\boldsymbol{N} + \boldsymbol{N}^T}{2} \right)},
$$

thus,

$$
\omega^* = \frac{2}{\sqrt{\lambda_{max}(\boldsymbol{N} + \boldsymbol{N}^T)\lambda_{min}(\boldsymbol{N} + \boldsymbol{N}^T)}}.
$$

$\square$

## 5   Simulation

In this section, two examples are used for simulation to demonstrate the effectiveness of the proposed methods HPIA and WHPIA, and to make a simple comparison with PIA [6, 7] and WPIA [10]. First, we give two test examples as follows, those are, an example of iterative curve interpolation and an example of iterative surface interpolation.

*Example 1.* 12 data points are taken in plane to constitute a $1 \times 12$ sequence:
((165, 150) (75, 150) (75, 225) (170, 265) (150, 165) (90, 165) (90, 210) (120, 220) (135, 180) (105, 180) (105, 195) (120, 195))

*Example 2.* 48 data points are taken in space to constitute a $7 \times 9$ matrix:

$$
\begin{pmatrix}
(0,0,0) & (0,0,0) & (0,0,0) & (0,0,0) & (0,0,0) & (0,0,0) & (0,0,0) & (0,0,0) & (0,0,0) \\
(0,-8,-10) & (8,-8,-10) & (8,0,-10) & (8,8,-10) & (0,8,-10) & (-8,8,-10) & (-8,0,-10) & (-8,-8,-10) & (0,-8,-10) \\
(0,-10,0) & (10,-10,0) & (10,0,0) & (10,10,0) & (0,10,0) & (-10,10,0) & (-10,0,0) & (-10,-10,0) & (0,-10,0) \\
(0,-15,10) & (15,-15,10) & (15,0,10) & (15,15,10) & (0,15,10) & (-15,15,10) & (-15,0,10) & (-15,-15,10) & (0,-15,10) \\
(0,-6,30) & (6,-6,30) & (6,0,30) & (6,6,30) & (0,6,30) & (-6,6,30) & (-6,0,30) & (-6,-6,30) & (0,-6,30) \\
(0,-6,50) & (6,-6,50) & (6,0,50) & (6,6,50) & (0,6,50) & (-6,6,50) & (-6,0,50) & (-6,-6,50) & (0,-6,50) \\
(0,-8,-55) & (8,-8,-55) & (8,0,-55) & (8,8,-55) & (0,8,-55) & (-8,8,-55) & (-8,0,-55) & (-8,-8,-55) & (0,-8,-55)
\end{pmatrix}
$$

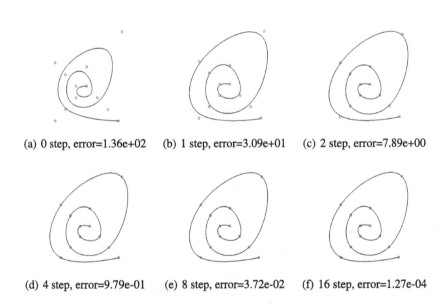

(a) 0 step, error=1.36e+02    (b) 1 step, error=3.09e+01    (c) 2 step, error=7.89e+00

(d) 4 step, error=9.79e-01    (e) 8 step, error=3.72e-02    (f) 16 step, error=1.27e-04

**Fig. 1.** HPIA iterative interpolation of curve example

Here, we choose B-spline to verify the effectiveness of HPIA and WHPIA, there are two reasons: on the one hand, B-spline has many excellent properties in expressing shapes; on the other hand, B-spline bases are NTP bases. We adopt cubic non-uniform B-spline and use centripetal parameterization method to calculate parameters of data points. The internal knots are determined by parameters of data points. The fitting error at each iteration level is taken as the total Euclidean norms of the adjusting vectors.

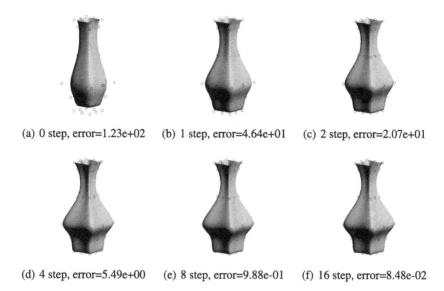

(a) 0 step, error=1.23e+02          (b) 1 step, error=4.64e+01          (c) 2 step, error=2.07e+01

(d) 4 step, error=5.49e+00          (e) 8 step, error=9.88e-01          (f) 16 step, error=8.48e-02

**Fig. 2.** HPIA iterative interpolation of surface example

$$
\begin{cases}
\varepsilon\_curve_k = \sum_{i=0}^{n} \|\mathbf{\Delta}_i^k\| \\
\varepsilon\_surface_k = \sum_{i=0}^{n} \sum_{j=0}^{m} \|\mathbf{\Delta}_{ij}^k\|.
\end{cases}
$$

The experimental results of the method proposed in this paper are shown in Figs. 1, 2, 3 and 4, where subfigure (a) represents the initial state of iteration, and (b)–(f) respectively illustrate the results after 1, 2, 4, 8 and 16 iterations, and the corresponding iteration error is attached to below the corresponding subfigure. It can be seen that the error of the weighted HPIA at the same iteration level is much smaller than that of the unweighted HPIA, which exemplifies the validity of the weighted version WHPIA.

In addition, Figs. 5 and 6 illustrate the results of 16 iterations obtained by interpolating the data points in example 1 and example 2 using four methods, HPIA, WHPIA, PIA and WPIA. Due to the fact that the error of the later iteration is smaller, so to get a better look at the iterative effects, there are two parts of each figure, namely the first eight iterations and the next eight iterations. It can be seen that WHPIA performs best in Figs. 5 and 6, followed by HPIA. The examples used in this section are only intended to demonstrate the effectiveness of the methods presented by us. For other examples, we cannot guarantee that our approaches converge faster than PIA and WPIA because the spectral radius will vary with the NTP bases.

382    L. Hu et al.

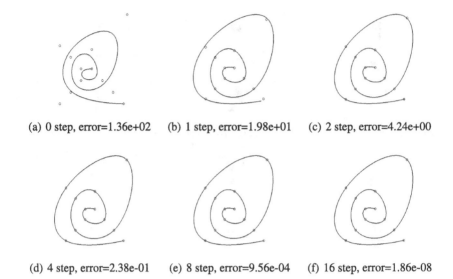

(a) 0 step, error=1.36e+02    (b) 1 step, error=1.98e+01    (c) 2 step, error=4.24e+00

(d) 4 step, error=2.38e-01    (e) 8 step, error=9.56e-04    (f) 16 step, error=1.86e-08

**Fig. 3.** WHPIA iterative interpolation of curve example

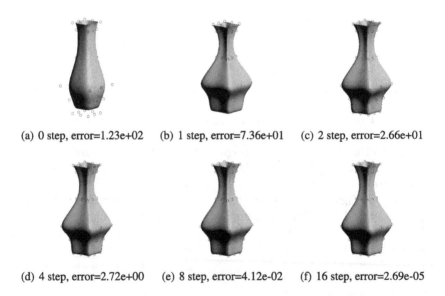

(a) 0 step, error=1.23e+02    (b) 1 step, error=7.36e+01    (c) 2 step, error=2.66e+01

(d) 4 step, error=2.72e+00    (e) 8 step, error=4.12e-02    (f) 16 step, error=2.69e-05

**Fig. 4.** WHPIA iterative interpolation of surface example

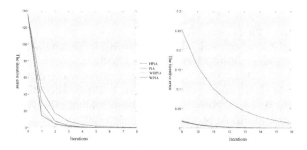

**Fig. 5.** Error comparison of iterative curve interpolation using four methods

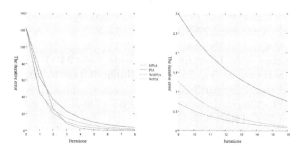

**Fig. 6.** Error comparison of iterative surface interpolation using four methods

# 6   Conclusion

In this paper, based on the HSS iterative method for solving linear equations, a new PIA approach called HPIA was proposed to solve the problems of curves and surfaces interpolation with normalized totally positive bases. And then, we weighted it to speed up the convergence rate of the iterative process, namely WHPIA, and gave the approximate value of the fastest convergence weight. Experimental results show that HPIA and WHPIA are effective in progressive iterative approximation of curves and surfaces. However, due to various NTP bases, it is not clear which method in WPIA and WHPIA has a smaller spectral radius, so it is impossible to prove theoretically which method has the fastest convergence speed.

# References

1. Lin, H., Jin, S., Liao, H., et al.: Quality guaranteed all-hex mesh generation by a constrained volume iterative fitting algorithm. Comput.-Aided Des. **67–68**(C), 107–117 (2015)
2. Lu, L.: Sample-based polynomial approximation of rational Bzier curves. J. Comput. Appl. Math. **235**(6), 1557–1563 (2011)
3. Hu, Q.: An iterative algorithm for polynomial of rational triangular Bézier surfaces. Appl. Math. Comput. **219**(17), 9308–9316 (2013)

4. Lin, H.: Adaptive fitting by the progressive-iterative approximation. Comput. Aided Geom. Des. **29**(7), 463–473 (2012)
5. Lin, H., Zhang, Z.: An efficient method for fitting large data sets using T-splines. SIAM J. Sci. Comput. **35**(6), A3052–A3068 (2013)
6. Lin, H., Wang, G., Dong, C.: Constructing iterative non-uniform B-spline curve and surface to fit data points. Sci. China: Ser. F **47**(3), 315–331 (2004)
7. Lin, H., Bao, H., Wang, G.: Totally positive bases and progressive iteration approximation. Comput. Math. Appl. **50**(3/4), 575–586 (2005)
8. Lin, H., Zhang, Z.: An extended iterative format for the progressive-iteration approximation. Comput. Graph. **35**(5), 967–975 (2011)
9. Deng, C., Lin, H.: Progressive and iterative approximation for least squares B-spline curve and surface fitting. Comput.-Aided Des. **47**(1), 32–44 (2014)
10. Lu, L.: Weighted progressive iteration approximation and convergence analysis. Comput. Aided Geom. Des. **27**(2), 129–137 (2010)
11. Delgadoa, J., Peña, J.: Progressive iterative approximation and bases with the fastest convergence rates. Comput. Aided Geom. Des. **24**(1), 10–18 (2007)
12. Maekawa, T., Matsumoto, Y., Namiki, K.: Interpolation by geometric algorithm. Comput.-Aided Des. **39**(4), 313–323 (2007)
13. Deng, C., Ma, W.: Weighted progressive interpolation of Loop subdivision surfaces. Comput.-Aided Des. **44**(5), 424–431 (2012)
14. Bai, Z., Golub, G., Ng, M.: Hermitian and skew-Hermitian splitting methods for non-Hermitian positive definite linear systems. SIAM J. Matrix Anal. Appl. **24**(3), 603–626 (2003)

# Attention-Based Hybrid Model for Automatic Short Answer Scoring

Hui Qi[1,2], Yue Wang[1,2], Jinyu Dai[1,2], Jinqing Li[1,2], and Xiaoqiang Di[1,2(✉)]

[1] School of Computer Science and Technology,
Changchun University of Science and Technology, Changchun, China
`dixiaoqiang@cust.edu.cn`
[2] Jilin Province Key Laboratory of Network and Information Security,
Changchun, China

**Abstract.** Neural network models have played an important role in text applications, such as document summaries and automatic short answer questions. In previous existing works, questions and answers are together used as input in recurrent neural networks (RNN) and convolutional neural networks (CNN), then output corresponding scores. This paper presents a method for measuring the score for short answer questions and answers. This paper makes scoring by establishing a hierarchical word-sentence model to represent questions and answers and using the attention mechanism to automatically determine the relative weight of questions and answers. Firstly, the model combines CNN and Bidirectional Long Short-Term Memory Networks (BLSTM) to extract the semantic features of questions and answers. Secondly, it captures the representation vector of relevant questions and answers from the sentence-level features. Finally, all feature vectors are concatenated and input to the output layer to obtain the corresponding score. Experiment results show that the model in this paper is better than multiple baselines.

**Keywords:** Attention-based hybrid model · Automatic short answer scoring · BLSTM · CNN

## 1 Introduction

Automatic Short Answer Scoring (ASAS) refers to the scoring of answers to short answers without human intervention. The process is mainly to judge the similarity between the answer and the standard answer in terms of words and semantics. In most cases, the answer and the standard answer are not necessarily identical. Answers with similar meanings are acceptable. In addition to the need to have strong professionalism, the reviewer needs to be patiently thinking, and the number of short answer questions is significantly higher than objective questions. Therefore, there are two disadvantages of the manual scoring methods for short answer questions in the scoring process, such as the difficulty of ensuring fairness, the speed and lower efficiency of scoring. As for the automatic scoring

H. Song et al. (Eds.): SIMUtools 2019, LNICST 295, pp. 385–394, 2019.
https://doi.org/10.1007/978-3-030-32216-8_37

of short answer questions, it's the key issue to effectively utilize the information in the answer and the reference answer. It also serves as a research point in natural language processing, and has a significance for automatic evaluation of short answer scoring.

Therefore, the establishment of a complete automatic scoring model is the key point to the automatic evaluation of short-answer questions. Traditional scoring models use sparse features, such as word bags, part-of-speech tags, grammatical complexity metrics, and essay lengths, but these features may be affected by time consumption and sparse data features. Recently, it has been proved that the results of using neural network models are better, compared to traditional manual feature statistical models. Specifically, the distributed word representation is used to input, and the neural network model is used to combine the word information to obtain a single dense vector form in the entire answer. A score is given based on the non-linear neural layer on the representation. It has been demonstrated that neural network models are more effective than statistical models in different fields without manual features.

Deep learning gradually evolves from the distribution representation of the initial computational words to the calculation of distributed representations of phrases, sentences, and texts that contain more semantic information. The most basic application of word vectors is calculating the semantic similarity of two words. Correspondingly, when obtaining the sentence vector from the model trained by the complete corpus, we can also give the semantic similarity of the two sentences. Therefore, we can use the neural network method of deep learning to represent the answer and the standard answer as a sentence vector contains rich semantic information, then scoring the similarity among vectors as the semantic similarity between the answer and the standard answer. Currently, Convolutional Neural Networks (CNN) and Recurrent Neural Networks (RNN) are two mainstream architectures of Deep Neural Networks (DNN), which have been widely used to handle automatic test scoring tasks. The CNN can obtain features by stacking multiple layers including a convolutional layer and a merged layer. The RNN can handle the sequential problem of propagating historical information through the chained neural network architecture, and deal with sequence problems [5, 14], such as bidirectional long short-term memory networks (BLSTM) model [16]. Combining the advantages of both RNN and CNN, this paper proposes a score based on hybrid RNN and CNN to calculate the answers of the short answer questions and applies a hierarchical attention mechanism at the word and sentence level [21].

In this study, the model uses the mixed attention network of BLSTM and CNN to capture the most important semantic information in the short answer questions. BLSTM and CNN have been proven to be very effective for simulating answer sequences and useful for learning long-term dependent data. For traditional BLSTM and CNN networks, it is important to enter each word in the sentence, which is reasonable for traditional automatic short answer scoring tasks. The main contribution of our work can be summarized as follows: (1) we explore the attention-based hybrid model to measure automatic short answer scoring; (2) we apply an attention mechanism, which can enhance the mutual relation between the aspect term and its corresponding sentences, and prevent the irrelevant words from getting more attention; (3) we carry out the experiment on the dataset by utilizing multiple methods.

The rest of this paper is organized as follows: Sect. 2 briefly introduces the work related to this study. Section 3 describes the model in detail. Experimental results are reported in Sect. 4. Section 5 concludes this paper.

## 2    Related Work

In the past, scholars have proposed many automatic short answer scoring methods. Project Essay Grade [13] is one of the earliest automated scoring systems that use linear regression to predict scores. Developed by the Educational Testing Service, E-Rater [2] was one of the first systems to use operational scoring in high-stakes assessments. The model utilizes many different features in scoring, the model building approach, and the final score assignment algorithm. Chen et al. [4] used a voting algorithm based on the initial scores and similarities between essays to iteratively train the system and score the essays. McNamara et al. [12] attempted to translate what we might observe in human raters within a computational algorithm by using hierarchical classification with different variables allowed to enter at each level. Fala et al. [7] developed systems that predict holistic essay scores based on features extracted from opinion expressions, topical elements, and their combinations. They also attempted to incorporate more different features into the text scoring model. Klebanov and Flor [11] showed that the higher scoring essays tend to have higher percentages of both highly associated and dis-associated pairs, and lower percentages of mildly associated pairs of words. Somasundaran et al. [15] used lexical chains, and interactions between lexical chains and explicit discourse elements, which can be harnessed for representing coherence to assess paper score.

Recently, Alikaniotis et al. [1] used the long short-term memory model (LSTM) to automatically learn paper scoring tasks, thus eliminating the need for any predefined feature templates. It uses score-specific word embeddings (SSWEs) to word representation. The last hidden state of the bidirectional LSTM is used for these representations. Taghipour and Ng [17] used the automated essay scoring LSTM model, which utilizes common word embedding and uses the average combined value of all hidden states of the LSTM layer as a paper representation. Dong and Zhang [6] obtained the final text representation by processing the text into sentences and using two layers of CNN at the sentence and text levels. Bahdanau [3] proposed a mechanism for attention in machine translation. Bahdanau applied the base concern model to machine translation, which allows the decoder to observe different parts of the source statement at each step of the output generation, rather than encoding all source statements into fixed-length vectors and explicitly finding the soft alignment of the current position and between input sources. Since then, the attention mechanism has been further used. Zhang [10] proposed a CNN based on attention pool representation sentence that uses the intermediate sentence representation generated by BLSTM as a reference to the local representation produced by the convolutional layer to obtain attention weight. Yang [18] designed Hierarchical Attention Networks (HANs) for document classification, and this document classification was applied to two levels of attention mechanisms at the word and sentence level. Yujun [20,21] proposed Hybrid Attention Networks (HANs), which combined selective attention to the vocabulary and character level. The model first applied RNN and CNN to extract the semantic features of the text. Among them, the model of this paper is most closely related to the HANs model, and the HANs model represents a sentence with a hierarchical attention mechanism.

The work of this paper is to systematically investigate the sentence-level and text-level modeling of CNN and LSTM, and notes the effectiveness of the network to automatically select more relevant n-grams and sentences for the task. Compared to the existing researches, this paper proposes to study the sentence representation based on the hybrid network HANs model of hybrid RNN and CNN. Model combined semantics and captured long-distance dependencies among words has significant advantages. In addition, this paper proposes a hierarchical attention mechanism to capture the semantic concerns in each sentence and the model helps to filter out noise that is unrelated to the overall sentiment [19].

## 3    An Attention-Based Hybrid Model

As shown in Fig. 1, we propose an attention-based hybrid model combining BLSTM and CNN which contains four components:

(1) Input layer: input two diverse sentences of questions and answers to this model;
(2) Embedding layer: map each word of a sentence of questions and answers into a low-dimension vector;
(3) Hybrid attention layer: produce a weight vector, and concatenate word-level features into a sentence of questions and answers feature vector by multiplying the weight vector;
(4) Output layer: calculate score by concatenating sentences of questions and answers feature vector.

Later in this section, these components will be presented in detail.

### 3.1    Word Embeddings

Given a sentence of questions and answers composed of N words $S = \{w_1, w_2, ..., w_N\}$, every word $w_i$ is converted into an embedding vector $e_i$. A word $w_i$ is transformed into its word embedding $e_i$ by using the matrix-vector product:

$$e_i = W^w v^i \qquad (1)$$

The embedding matrix $W^w$ is the parameter to be learned, $W^w \in \mathbb{R}^{d^w|V|}$, where $V$ is a fixed-sized vocabulary, and $d^w$ is the size of word embeddings. It is a

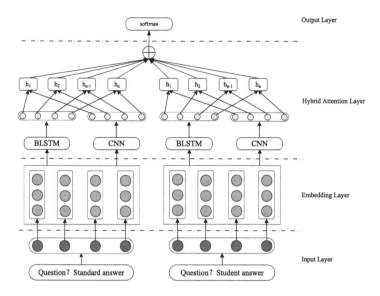

**Fig. 1.** The architecture of the Attention-based Hybrid model.

hyper-parameter to be set by user. The word vector $v^i$ is a vector of size $|V|$ which has value 1 at index $e_i$ and 0 at all other positions. Then a sentence of questions and answers is fed into the next layer as a vector $E_S = \{e_1, e_2, ..., e_n\}$.

The goal of embedding layer is to represent each word in sentences with a d-dimensional vector. The whole embedding space is used, in which the embedding is updated after each batch.

## 3.2 Hybrid Attention

The motivation of attention is inspired by the observation that different words should have different contributions to the final semantic representation of a sentence of questions and answers. When reading a sentence, people often pay attention to a word or several words, and these words can reflect meaning of the answer. So, we use attention mechanism focused on word-level to implement this motivation.

We only pay attention to these words whose semantic relationship have a great impact on sentence of questions and answers meaning through word-level attention mechanisms. BLSTM and CNN can extract the feature representations in word-level attention architecture. On the attention layer, the output is the concatenated representations.

In Fig. 2(a), the BLSTM produces the output vectors $[h_1, h_2, ..., h_n]$. As Eq. (2) shows, we can use an attention-weighted sum of output vectors to generate the representation $S_\alpha$ of a sentence of questions and answers. The attention-weight $\alpha_i$ is shown in Eq. (4), where $W_\alpha$ is a word of weight. And Eq. (3) represents the output of hidden layer.

$$S_\alpha = \sum_{i=1}^{l}(\alpha_i h_i) \tag{2}$$

$$u_i = tanh(W_h h_i + b_h) \tag{3}$$

$$\alpha_i = softmax(W_\alpha u_i) \tag{4}$$

The attention mechanism gets the representation $S_\alpha$ for the output of forward and backward LSTM from the formulas described above. The BLSTM network proposed in [8,9] can be utilized. Past features (via forward states) and future features (via backward states) for a specific time can be used. Except for the need to unfold the hidden states efficiently, the forward and backward passes over the unfolded network through time are performed in a similar way to the forward and backward passes of conventional networks.

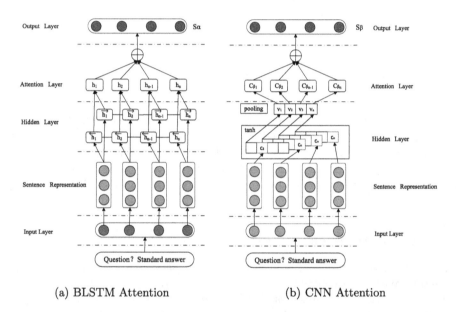

(a) BLSTM Attention          (b) CNN Attention

**Fig. 2.** The architectures of BLSTM and CNN attention networks. $S_\alpha$ indicates the attentive sentence representation of forward and backward LSTM, $S_\beta$ indicates the attentive sentence representation of CNN.

In Fig. 2(b), the convolutional layer output vectors is $[c_1, c_2, ..., c_n]$. Each element of the vector $v_i$ is calculated by a tanh function using each convolution feature $c_i$ in the hidden layer. And the attention weight $\beta_i$ decides the information of convolution features by a softmax function. Afterwards, the pooling vector $C_\beta$ is computed by a weighted sum of the convolutional layer output. We can compute attentive representation whose output vectors is $C_\beta$ as follows:

$$v_i = tanh(W_c c_i + b_c) \qquad (5)$$

$$\beta_i = softmax(W_\beta v_i) \qquad (6)$$

$$C_\beta = \sum_{i=1}^{l} (\beta_i c_i) \qquad (7)$$

Multiple local representations can be learned by using CNN. The attentive representations are produced by various CNNs through a max function, and are then fed into the model to obtain the final pooling feature vector. And Eq. (8) shows that the representation $S_\beta$ of a sentence of questions and answers, where k is the length of the convolution window.

$$S_\beta = argmax(C_\beta k) \qquad (8)$$

## 4    Experiments

Our experiments are performed on Windows platform with the memory of 16 GB and the program is written in Python. This paper evaluates the performance of our model for dataset identification. Since the dataset contains a lot of Chinese, we use Jieba to segment the data and train the word vector. The configuration, results and analysis details of the experiments are as follows.

### 4.1    Datasets

The exam question dataset contains 1669 pairs of short answer questions and answers. Each short answer question corresponds to the standard answer and the student answer, and there is a corresponding score. In the experiment, the dataset is subjected to word segmentation and the spaces and punctuation were removed. The data is randomly divided into 1335 training examples and 334 verification samples. The data in Fig. 3 is a part of the dataset.

### 4.2    Baselines

This article compares our model with several traditional methods for calculating answer scores as follows. This paper selected four machine learning baselines, including SVMs, CNNs, BLSTMs, and Attention-BLSTMs [9,19].

### 4.3    Experimental Settings

For all the experiments, we use Jieba to preprocess the dataset, including word segmentation, stop words, word vector matrix, and initialize word representation in the word embedding layer with the 300-dimensional word vectors pre-trained from the dataset. Embeddings for word that are not presented in the model are randomly initialized. In our dataset, the full score of the standard answer is 2 points. So we classify the candidate according to the possible score of the

| Question | Standard Answer | Student's Answer | Standard score | Student's score |
|---|---|---|---|---|
| 叙述中断机制在操作系统中的地位和作用。 | 中断是操作系统实现多个程序并行的基础。在操作系统中处于枢纽的地位。操作系统任何程序的运行都离不开中断系统的响应机制。在这个意义上，可以说中断才会引起进程的调度切换。同时，任何运行中的错误，计算机都通过发送中断来报告错误，据能处理。完全可以说，没有中断，就没有现代意义下的操作系统。 | 中断系统是计算机的重要组成部分。实施控制、故障自动处理、计算机与外围设备间的数据传递往往采用中断系统。中断系统的应用大大提高了计算机效率。计算机的中断系统能够实现cpu和多任务事件的处理能力。中断机制的现代计算机系统中的基础设施之一。它在系统中起着连接信司操作作用，以协调系统的各种外部事件的响应处理。中断是实现多道程序设计的必要条件，中断对cpu对系统运生的某个事件作出的一种反应。引起中断的事件称为中断源。中断源向cpu提出处理的请求称为中断请求。发生中断时被打断程序的暂停点称为断点。cpu暂停现行程序所转为相应中断程序称为中断处理。而返回断点的过程称为中断返回。中断的实现流程软件和硬件综合完成，硬件部分以继续件装置，软件部分为软件处理程序。 | 2 | 2 |
| 举例说明什么是虚拟设备技术。提示：以打印机为例，说明如何对其进行虚拟化。 | 利用存储设备（主要是磁盘）来代替I/O设备，如输出应把输出设备的信息存入磁盘，在适当的时候，再通过相应的输出设备把信息从磁盘中复制出来。通常把用来代替独占设备的那部分磁盘空间称为虚拟设备。 | 虚拟设备是指通过虚拟技术将一台独立设备变换为若干台逻辑设备，供若干个用户进程同时使用，这种经过虚拟技术处理的设备称为虚拟设备。以打印机为例，当用户进程要求打印输出时，操作系统同意打印输出，但并不真正把打印机分配给该用户进程，而是为进程在磁盘上的输出井中分配一个空间区域，并将要打印的数据送入其中，同时还为用户进程申请一张打印请求表，将用户的打印要求填入其中，再将该请求打印表挂在打印机的I/O请求队列上。如果还有进程要求打印输出，系统的可以接受该请求，为进程完成上述操作。 | 2 | 2 |
| 叙述中断机制在操作系统中的地位和作用。 | 中断是操作系统实现多个程序并行的基础。在操作系统中处于枢纽的地位。操作系统任何程序的运行都离不开中断系统的响应机制，在这个意义上，可以说中断才会引起进程的切换。同时，任何运行中的错误，计算机都通过发送中断来报告错误，据能处理。完全可以说，没有中断，就没有现代意义下的操作系统。 | 中断系统是计算机的重要组成部分。实施控制、故障自动处理。计算机与外围设备间的数据传递往往采用中断系统。中断系统的应用大大提高了计算机效率。中断系统可以加强CPU对于多任务事件的处理能力。中断机制在系统的枢纽连接网络作用，以协调系统对各种外部事件的响应成和处理。中断是CPU对于系统发生的某个事件做出的反应。 | 2 | 2 |
| SGA主要有那些部分，主要作用是什么 | （1）数据高速缓冲区：存放着Oracle系统最近使用过的数据库数据块。<br>（2）共享池：相当于程序高速缓冲区，所有的用户程序都存放在共享SQL池中。<br>（3）重做日志缓冲区：用于被I/O区在对数据进行修改的操作过程中生成的重做记录。 | 数据块高速缓存区：保存了从数据文件中检索到的数据块的镜像拷贝使得获取和修改数据时候大大的提高可了性能 | 2 | 1 |
| 举例说明什么是虚拟设备技术。提示：以打印机为例，说明如何对其进行虚拟化。 | 利用存储设备（主要是磁盘）来代替I/O设备，如输出应把输出设备的信息存入磁盘，在适当的时候，再通过相应的输出设备把信息从磁盘中复制出来。通常把用来代替独占设备的那部分磁盘空间称为虚拟设备。 | 虚拟设备是将I/O占的 | 2 | 0 |

**Fig. 3.** Examples of questions and answers from the dataset.

student answer, then we will divide the possible score into 3 categories: 0, 1, 2. Parameter details are listed in Table 1. During the process of training, we do not update the pre-trained word embeddings. We choose the model which works best on the train set, and then evaluate it on the validation set. This paper uses adaptive estimation for optimization. The backpropagation algorithm is used to calculate the gradient of all parameters during training.

**Table 1.** The experimental parameter settings.

| Hidden layer size | Learning rate | Decay rate | Dropout rate | Kernel size | Batch size | Epochs |
|---|---|---|---|---|---|---|
| 200 | 0.01 | 0.8 | 0.3 | 3 | 64 | 100 |

## 4.4 Results and Analysis

For the HANs model, the questions are entered into the model in chronological order and their parameters are the same. Table 2 compares HANs in this paper with other state-of-the-art answer score methods.

Accuracy, Precision, Recall, and F1 are used to evaluate the performance of the proposed model. Four metrics are used to evaluate the quality of each model. Our model performs very well and training takes about 30 min at a time, which indicates that the model in this paper is very effective in improving learning ability. This is because we uses a word-level mixed attention mechanism to increase the weight of meaningful words in the answer to take into account local information and summary information.

Table 2. Comparison of experimental results.

| Method | Accuracy | Precision | Recall | F1 |
|--------|----------|-----------|--------|-----|
| SVMs | 0.7377 | 0.3623 | 0.1276 | 0.2332 |
| CNNs | 0.8978 | 0.9023 | 0.8892 | 0.8965 |
| BLSTMs | 0.9074 | 0.9215 | 0.9024 | 0.9081 |
| Att-BLSTMs | 0.9086 | 0.9190 | 0.9056 | 0.9067 |
| **This work** | **0.9697** | 0.9703 | 0.9687 | 0.9694 |

As can be seen from Table 2, we use the model to learn different classifiers based on training data, and the proposed model performs better than the other four models. Figure 4 shows the accuracy and loss of the test set and validation set for 100 periods in the HANs model. We can see that the HANs model achieves the highest prediction accuracy and the lowest loss.

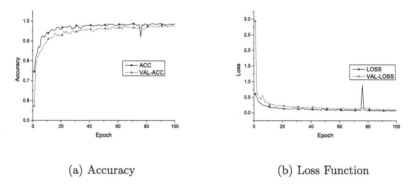

(a) Accuracy                                   (b) Loss Function

**Fig. 4.** Accuracy and Loss Function of Train Set and Validation Set for 100 epoch times. Acc and Loss indicate train set accuracy and loss function, Val-Acc and Val-Loss indicate validation set accuracy and loss function.

# 5 Conclusion

This paper proposes a new neural network model called HANs for Automatic Short Answer Scoring. CNN is used to obtain better local information and BLSTM to focus the model on the information related to the answer, which is encouraged by the attention-based neural network model to pay attention to the words surrounding its similarity. Then, the output of CNN and BLSTM get better results. This paper tests our model HANs on the dataset and obtains an accuracy of 0.9697, which reveals that HANs is efficient and has competitive performance compared to other models.

# References

1. Alikaniotis, D., Yannakoudakis, H., Rei, M.: Automatic text scoring using neural networks, pp. 715–725 (2016)
2. Attali, Y., Burstein, J.: Automated essay scoring with e-rater®; vol 2.0. J. Technol. Learn. Assess. 4(2), i–21 (2006)
3. Bahdanau, D., Cho, K., Bengio, Y.: Neural machine translation by jointly learning to align and translate. Comput. Sci. (2014)
4. Chen, Y.Y., Liu, C.L., Chang, T.H., Lee, C.H.: An unsupervised automated essay scoring system. IEEE Intell. Syst. **25**(5), 61–67 (2010)
5. Chorowski, J., Bahdanau, D., Serdyuk, D., Cho, K., Bengio, Y.: Attention-based models for speech recognition. Comput. Sci. **10**(4), 429–439 (2015)
6. Dong, F., Zhang, Y.: Automatic features for essay scoring - an empirical study. In: Conference on Empirical Methods in Natural Language Processing (2016)
7. Farra, N., Somasundaran, S., Burstein, J.: Scoring persuasive essays using opinions and their targets. In: NAACL 2015 Workshop on Innovative Use of NLP for Building Educational Applications (2015)
8. Graves, A.: Generating sequences with recurrent neural networks. Comput. Sci. (2013)
9. Graves, A., Mohamed, A.R., Hinton, G.: Speech recognition with deep recurrent neural networks **38**(2003), 6645–6649 (2013)
10. Johnson, R., Zhang, T.: Effective use of word order for text categorization with convolutional neural networks. Eprint Arxiv (2014)
11. Klebanov, B.B., Flor, M.: Word association profiles and their use for automated scoring of essays. In: Proceedings of Annual Meeting of the Association for Computational Linguistics ACL, pp. 1148–1158 (2013)
12. Mcnamara, D.S., Crossley, S.A., Roscoe, R.D., Allen, L.K., Dai, J.: A hierarchical classification approach to automated essay scoring. Assessing Writ. **23**, 35–59 (2015)
13. Project Essay Grade: Project essay grade, peg (2003)
14. Pang, L., Lan, Y., Guo, J., Xu, J., Wan, S., Cheng, X.: Text matching as image recognition (2016)
15. Somasundaran, S., Burstein, J., Chodorow, M.: Lexical chaining for measuring discourse coherence quality in test-taker essays, Martin (2014)
16. Sutskever, I., Vinyals, O., Le, Q.V.: Sequence to sequence learning with neural networks **4**, 3104–3112 (2014)
17. Taghipour, K., Ng, H.T.: A neural approach to automated essay scoring. In: Conference on Empirical Methods in Natural Language Processing (2016)
18. Yang, Z., Yang, D., Dyer, C., He, X., Smola, A., Hovy, E.: Hierarchical attention networks for document classification. In: Conference of the North American Chapter of the Association for Computational Linguistics: Human Language Technologies, pp. 1480–1489 (2017)
19. Zhou, X., Wan, X., Xiao, J.: Attention-based LSTM network for cross-lingual sentiment classification. In: Conference on Empirical Methods in Natural Language Processing, pp. 247–256 (2016)
20. Zhou, Y., Li, C., Xu, B., Xu, J., Cao, J.: Hierarchical Hybrid Attention Networks for Chinese Conversation Topic Classification (2017)
21. Zhou, Y., Xu, J., Cao, J., Xu, B., Li, C.: Hybrid attention networks for chinese short text classication. Computacion Y Sistemas **21**(4), 759–769 (2017)

# Performance Evaluation of a Unified IEEE 802.11 DCF Model in NS-3

Yachao Yin, Yayu Gao$^{(\boxtimes)}$, and Xiaojun Hei

Huazhong University of Science and Technology, Wuhan 430074, China
{yinyachao,yayugao,heixj}@hust.edu.cn

**Abstract.** The IEEE 802.11 Distributed Coordination Function (DCF) is a basic component in the medium access control (MAC) protocol of Wireless Local Area Networks (WLANS). Recently, a unified analytical framework has been proposed [1] to capture the fundamental features of IEEE 802.11 DCF networks, which provides various accurate performance predication in NS-2 simulations. In the past a few years, NS-3 is widely considered an emerging and promising network simulator for researchers and engineers to validate their analytical models based on simulation experiments. Similar to NS-2, NS-3 provides a thorough 802.11 PHY and MAC protocol stack, the accuracy of which is, nevertheless, not yet been fully investigated. In this paper, we conduct a performance evaluation study of the unified IEEE 802.11 DCF analytical model in [1] with NS-3. Various network scenarios (distinct conditions, varying system parameters, different access modes and network topologies.) are conducted. The performance evaluation study shows that the theoretical predication closely matches with NS-3 simulation results. This case study implies that not only the theoretical model is a credible model for homogeneous IEEE 802.11 DCF networks but also NS-3 WiFi module can provide 802.11 network simulations as well as NS-2.

**Keywords:** Performance evaluation · NS-3 · IEEE 802.11 DCF

## 1 Introduction

Recently, a unified analytical framework has been proposed for IEEE 802.11 DCF networks in [1]. Different from the classic Bianchi's model in [2], the behavior of each Head-of-Line (HOL) packet, including backoff collision, successful transmission, has been captured based on a discrete-time Markov renewal process. This analytical framework has been evaluated using NS-2 simulation experiments, which demonstrates that it is a simple yet accurate model for IEEE 802.11 DCF networks.

Network simulation is a commonly-used methodology for properly producing the behavior of a real system, which plays an indispensable role in communication systems and computer networks owing to its scalability, stability and repeatability. Recently, NS-3 is recognized as an emerging and promising discrete-event

H. Song et al. (Eds.): SIMUtools 2019, LNICST 295, pp. 395–406, 2019.
https://doi.org/10.1007/978-3-030-32216-8_38

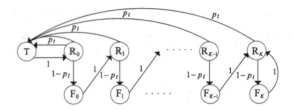

**Fig. 1.** An embedded Markov chain $\{X_j\}$ of the state transition process of an individual HOL packet in IEEE 802.11 DCF networks [1].

network simulator for students, researchers and developers. Different from the antiquated simulator NS-2, NS-3 has a modular core written in C++, and a Python scripting interface (similar to OTcl in NS-2), which better mimics real systems and supports software integration and updatable models [3]. Based on these excellent features, NS-3 has been achieving momentum in research and education.

NS-3 is instrumented with a detailed model of the MAC layer for the WiFi module, however, there exist very few studies to validate the NS-3 MAC layer model due to its complexity. A number of studies have been conducted to validate of the physical layer and the channel model in NS-3 [4–8]. Patidar et al. reported a preliminary validation study of the MAC layer of NS-3 by varying the number of nodes [9]. Baldo et al. [10] validated the NS-3 MAC model using a testbed. In this paper, we provide a performance evaluation study of the aforementioned unified IEEE 802.11 DCF analytical model proposed in [1] with NS-3. This work can also serve as a validation of the NS-3 MAC implementation for IEEE 802.11 DCF networks from an analytical perspective.

The remainder of this paper is organized as follows. Section 2 describes the major analytical results of the unified framework. Simulation setup is outlined in Sect. 3. Section 4 presents the simulation results including how to tune the NS-3 simulator and discusses the validation between simulation and theoretical analysis. Finally, we conclude the paper in Sect. 5.

## 2 Validation Setup

In this section, we present the unified analytical framework for IEEE 802.11 DCF networks [1] and outline the expressions of the network sum rate $\hat{D}$ for both unsaturated and saturated network, both the basic access and RTS/CTS modes. We aim to evaluate the accuracy of the NS-3 MAC layer model based on the analytical results obtained based on this model, which has been validated by the well-known NS-2 in [1].

### 2.1 Analytical Framework for IEEE 802.11 DCF Networks

A unified analytical framework for IEEE 802.11 DCF networks is established to model the behavior of each HOL packet as a discrete-time Markov renewal process in [1]. Figure 1 shows the embedded Markov chain $X_i$, which denotes the state of a HOL packet at the $i$th transition including the state of successful transmission $T$, the state of waiting for request $R_i$ and the state of collision $F_i$.

In an IEEE 802.11 DCF network, we consider there are $n$ nodes with packet transmissions over a noiseless channel, where each node has an infinite buffer and each head-of-line (HOL) packet has an infinite maximum number of retransmission attempts. Suppose that each node has identical backoff parameters, including the initial backoff window size $W$ and the cutoff phase $K$. Assume that each node is equipped with a traffic arrival rate of $\lambda$. For an unsaturated network in [1], the normalized throughput $\hat{\lambda}_{out}$, which is defined as the percentage of time for successful transmissions, is given by

$$\hat{\lambda}_{out} = n\lambda. \tag{1}$$

In a saturated network, each node always has a packet ready for transmission. As shown in [1], the normalized throughput $\hat{\lambda}_{out}$ is derived as

$$\hat{\lambda}_{out} = \frac{-\tau_T p_A \ln p_A}{1 + \tau_F - \tau_F p_A - (\tau_T - \tau_F)p_A \ln p_A}, \tag{2}$$

where $\tau_T$ and $\tau_F$ denote the holding times of HOL packets in successful transmission and collision states (in unit of time slots), respectively, and $p_A$ is the non-zero root of the fixed-point equation of the steady-state probability of successful transmission of HOL packets given that the channel is idle, $p$:

$$p = \exp\left\{ -\frac{2n}{W \cdot \left(\frac{p}{2p-1} + \left(1 - \frac{p}{2p-1}\right)(2(1-p))^K\right)} \right\}. \tag{3}$$

where $n$ is the number of nodes, $W$ is the initial backoff window size, $K$ is the cutoff phase ($K = \log_2(\frac{CW_{\max}}{CW_{\min}})$).

Note that the normalized throughput $\hat{\lambda}_{out}$ evaluates how efficient the time is used for successful transmissions. It, however, does not reflect how much information can be transmitted in terms of bits per second. Therefore, in this paper, we focus on the network sum rates, which is defined as the number of information bits that are successfully transmitted per second. Thus, in an unsaturated network, the network sum rate $\hat{D}$ can be written as

$$\hat{D} = \hat{\lambda}_{out} \cdot \frac{\frac{8PL}{R_D \sigma}}{\tau_T} \cdot R_D = \frac{8PL \cdot n\lambda}{\sigma \tau_T}. \tag{4}$$

from (1), where $PL$ denotes the packet payload length (in the unit of bytes).

For a saturated network, its network sum rate $\hat{D}$ is determined by (1) the normalized throughput $\hat{\lambda}_{out}$, (2) the fraction of time that is used for packet payload transmission in each successful transmission, and (3) the transmission rate $R_D$. It can then be written from (2)

$$\hat{D} = \hat{\lambda}_{out} \cdot \frac{\frac{8PL}{R_D \sigma}}{\tau_T} \cdot R_D = \frac{-8PL \cdot p_A \ln p_A}{\sigma\left(1 + \tau_F - \tau_F p_A - (\tau_T - \tau_F)p_A \ln p_A\right)}. \tag{5}$$

In the parameter settings of NS-3, when a node encounters a collision, the node will go through a period of ACK time-out or CTS time-out. Therefore, the holding times of successful transmission and collision states of basic access mechanism can be written as

$$\tau_T^{ba} = \frac{\left(\frac{8PL}{R_D} + \frac{8MH}{R_D} + 2PH + \frac{8ACK}{R_B} + SIFS + DIFS\right)}{\sigma} \tag{6}$$

and

$$\tau_F^{ba} = \frac{\frac{8PL}{R_D} + \frac{8MH}{R_D} + PH + ACKTimeout + DIFS}{\sigma} \tag{7}$$

respectively. $R_B$ denotes the basic rate (in the unit of Mbps). MAC header (MH) and ACK frames are in the unit of bytes. PHY header (PH), DCF interframe space (DIFS) and short interframe space (SIFS) are in the unit of $\mu$s.

With the RTS/CTS mode, the holding times in successful transmission and collision states can be written as

$$\tau_T^{rts} = \frac{\frac{8PL}{R_D} + \frac{8MH}{R_D} + 4PH + \frac{8(RTS + CTS + ACK)}{R_B} + 3SIFS + DIFS}{\sigma} \tag{8}$$

and

$$\tau_F^{rts} = \frac{\frac{8RTS}{R_B} + PH + CTSTimeout + DIFS}{\sigma} \tag{9}$$

respectively, where RTS and CTS are in the unit of bytes.

## 2.2  Comparison Between Dai's Unified Model and the Classic Bianchi's Model

A widely adopted model of IEEE 802.11 DCF networks was proposed by Bianchi in [2], where a classic two-dimensional Markov chain established for the backoff process of each saturated node. The differences between Bianchi's classic model and Dai's unified models are:

(1) In Bianchi's model, it only considers the case where the network is saturated. However, in Dai's model, the performance of both unsaturated and saturated network conditions are studied.
(2) In Bianchi's model, it only focuses on throughput, while a unified analysis of stability, throughput, and delay performance are fully studied in Dai's model. The results of both models are shown to be consistent in the saturated throughput.
(3) Performance analysis of Bianchi' model and a series of its follow-up studies is based on numerical calculation, which, nevertheless, renders difficulties for performance optimization. However, due to the explicit nature of Dai's model, explicit expressions of maximum network throughput and the optimal backoff parameters are derived in both homogeneous and heterogeneous IEEE 802.11 DCF networks in [1,11–14].

(4) Dai's model for homogeneous IEEE 802.11 DCF networks is further extended to various heterogeneous IEEE 802.11 DCF networks in [12–15].

As Bianchi's model is limited to the analysis of saturated network throughput, we introduce Dai's model to fully validate the NS-3 WiFi module. In turn, with the accuracy of Dai's model has been verified in NS-2, we further increase the credibility of Dai's model by the simulations with the NS-3 WiFi module.

## 3    NS-3 Simulation Setup

In this section, we will first describe the overall architecture of NS-3 WiFi module, and then we will introduce the details of simulation setup.

### 3.1    NS-3 WiFi Module

An overview of NS-3 WiFi module architecture is shown in Fig. 2. In NS-3 WiFi networks, nodes contain a WifiNetDevice object to hold together WifiChannel, WifiPhy, WifiMac, and WifiRemoteStationManager. When an application initiates transmission, the WifiNetDevice interface sends the packet to WifiMac class which handles high MAC level functions such as different MAC types, beacon, association, and so forth. DcaTxop handles the request access to the channel from DcfManager. When access is granted, DcaTxop pushes the packet to MacLow for initiating data transmission. WifiPhy class is mainly designed to receive packet and tracking energy consumption. WifiChannel is designed to interconnect with the WifiPhy so that packets can be received through the channel.

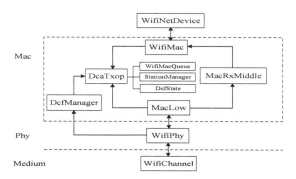

**Fig. 2.** WiFi module architecture of NS-3 simulator

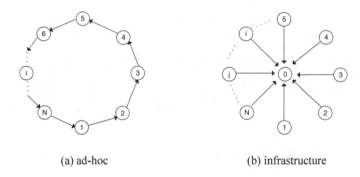

(a) ad-hoc                    (b) infrastructure

**Fig. 3.** Network topology

## 3.2   Simulation Setup

We consider both the ad-hoc mode and the infrastructure mode with varying system parameters to implement detailed comparisons between simulation results and the mathematical model of IEEE 802.11 DCF networks shown in Fig. 3, it is well known that in the infrastructure networks, the access point (AP) needs to continuously transmit a beacon frame to inform the node of the fundamental information in the network and the association between nodes and AP is also necessary. In an ad-hoc network, on the other hand, the additional channel activity due to association (beacon transmission, active scanning etc.) are avoided. Note that we focus only on packet payload transmissions and ignore the association effect in the mathematical model. Therefore, it can be expected that we can obtain simulation results closer to our mathematical analysis in the ad-hoc node.

In the ad-hoc network, the number of nodes is set to increase by 5 each time in the range of 5 to 50. Each node sends a packet to an adjacent node with date rate of 54 Mbps. Each node serves as both a transmitter and a receiver. Therefore, the aggregated network sum rate is the sum of the date rate of each node.

**Table 1.** System parameter settings [17].

| PHY header (PH) | 20 μs | ACKTimeout | 69 μs |
|---|---|---|---|
| MAC header (MH) | 36 bytes | CTSTimeout | 69 μs |
| ACK | 14 bytes | DIFS | 34 μs |
| RTS | 20 bytes | SIFS | 16 μs |
| CTS | 14 bytes | Slot Time $\sigma$ | 9 μs |
| $CW_{min}$ | 15 | $CW_{max}$ | 1023 |

In the simulation experiments, we utilize the default WiFi channel and the physical layer from the YANS model [16], and choose the AdhocWifiMac as

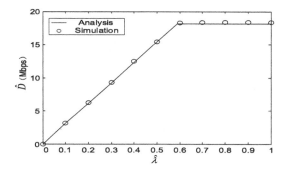

**Fig. 4.** Network sum rate $\hat{D}$ versus aggregate input rate $\hat{\lambda}$ in IEEE 802.11 DCF network with basic access mechanism. $PL = 1023$ bytes. $n = 50$. $W = 16$. $K = 6$. $R_D = 54$ Mbps. $R_B = 6$ Mbps.

the type of the MAC layer. Currently, NS-3 has supported several IEEE 802.11 standards, and we select the 802.11a standard as the WiFi standard with date rate and basic rate from 6, 9, 12, 18, 24, 36, 48 to 54 Mbps. The value of system parameters are summarized in Table 1.

## 4    Performance Evaluation

In this section, we will present a series of designed DCF simulations in NS-3, and demonstrate the comparison between analytical results with Dai's model and simulation results with NS-3 WiFi module. In particular, to evaluate the performance of Dai's model in the NS-3 WiFi module, we first increase the traffic arrival rate to load the network from unsaturated to saturated modes, and then set varying number of nodes $n$, the initial backoff window size $W$ and the cutoff phase $K$ to obtain the simulation results.

### 4.1    Network Performance versus Traffic: Unsaturated to Saturated

In NS-3, we increase the aggregate input rate $\hat{\lambda} = n\lambda$ to load the network states from unsaturated to saturated, and $\lambda$ is the probability to generate a new packet every $\tau_T$ time slots. By steadily increasing $\hat{\lambda}$, the network transits from the unsaturated to saturated states.

Figure 4 shows that network sum rate $\hat{D}$ increases and eventually saturates as the aggregate input rate $\hat{\lambda}$ grows. In fact, the network is unsaturated when each node has a low $\hat{\lambda}$, where $\hat{D}$ linely increases with $\hat{\lambda}$, each HOL packet can be successfully transmitted. As $\hat{\lambda}$ increases, each node always has a packet to transmit and the network becomes saturated. In this case, the network sum rate $\hat{D}$ not longer increases with $\hat{\lambda}$, and is determined by the system backoff parameters.

## 4.2  Saturated Throughput versus Key System Parameters

For a saturated IEEE 802.11 DCF network, it can be seen that network sum rate $\hat{D}$ depends on the number of nodes, the initial backoff window size and the cutoff phase from Eqs. (3) and (5). In this section, we compare the network sum rate of the simulation and theoretical results by tuning distinct system parameters.

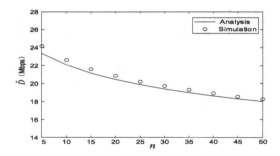

**Fig. 5.** Network sum rate $\hat{D}$ versus the number of nodes $n$ in a saturated IEEE 802.11 DCF network with basic access mechanism. $PL = 1023$ bytes. $W = 16$. $K = 6$. $R_D = 54$ Mbps. $R_B = 6$ Mbps

Figure 5 compares network sum rate $\hat{D}$ obtained in NS-3 with the theoretical results by varying the number of nodes $n$. As shown in Fig. 5, the NS-3 simulation results are close to the theoretical curve except when $n$ takes a small value such as $n = 5$. The reason is that $\hat{D}$ is determined by the limiting probability of the successful transmission of HOL packets $p$ in the mathematical model and $p$ is obtained under an implicit assumption that $n$ is sufficiently large. Therefore, when $n < 5$, the theoretical network sum rate may slightly deviate from the simulation results.

In Fig. 6a, it can be observed that network sum rate $\hat{D}$ obtained in NS-3 and theoretical analysis are well matched by tuning the initial backoff window size $W$. The network sum rate $\hat{D}$ increases first and then decreases as $W$ increments. When $W$ increases, each node achieves a larger backoff window size to avoid collision and thus the network achieves higher network sum rate due to fewer collisions. However, when $W$ continues to increase, each node may have a longer backoff duration so that the channel can be idle for a long time. In this case, the utilization of channel will be reduced, leading to a decreased network sum rate.

As shown in Fig. 6b, network sum rate $\hat{D}$ of theoretical model is close to the NS-3 simulation results. When the cutoff phase $K$ increases, $\hat{D}$ is monotonically increasing. With a larger $K$, the maximum backoff window size will increase. In this case, each node has a higher probability of choosing a different backoff window size to avoid collisions and thus the network has higher network sum rate due to fewer collisions.

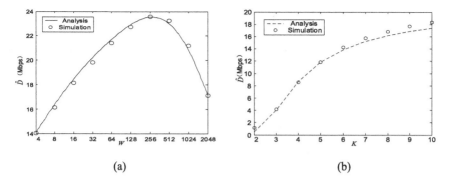

**Fig. 6.** Network sum rate $\hat{D}$ versus backoff parameters in a saturated IEEE 802.11 DCF network with basic access mechanism. (a) $\hat{D}$ versus the initial backoff window size $W$. (b) $\hat{D}$ versus the cutoff phase $K$. With $PL = 1023$ bytes. $n = 50$. $R_D = 54$ Mbps. $R_B = 6$ Mbps.

### 4.3   Basic vs. RTS/CTS Access Modes

In the IEEE 802.11 standard, the DCF protocol is equipped with two access modes, including the default basic access mechanism and the optional RTS/CTS mechanism. With the basic access, the node first sends a packet after the DIFS duration if it senses the channel idle. Otherwise, the node chooses a backoff window size for the backoff process. If the node receives the ACK frame, it confirms that its packet is successfully received by the destination. Otherwise, if the node does not receive the ACK frame after the ACK time-out period, the node restarts the backoff process.

Different from the basic access, the node first sends a short RTS frame to reserve the channel in RTS/CTS access. If the RTS frame is successfully received by the destination, and the destination sends the CTS frame to all nodes so that other nodes will not contend for the channel and the node can successfully reserve the channel to send the packet. Then, the packet transmission starts and is confirmed to be successful by the ACK frame or starts the backoff process after the CTS time-out period.

Figure 7 demonstrates how the network sum rate $\hat{D}$ varies with the packet payload $PL$ in both modes. In the simulation experiments, we set the date rate to 54 Mpbs and 24 Mbps, respectively with the same settings of $n = 50$, $W = 16$ and $K = 6$. As shown in Fig. 7, a good match can be observed between the theoretical analysis and simulation results, which provides a good indication that Dai's model can be served as a considerably credible model to validate the WiFi MAC layer in both NS-2 and NS-3.

### 4.4   Ad-Hoc vs. Infrastructure

A wireless ad-hoc network is a decentralised type of wireless network. Each node is both a sender and a receiver. It can transmit packets to other nodes and receive a packet from a sending node. However, an infrastructure network is generally centralized based on pre-defined network facilities, where a station must communicate with an access point (AP) first to access the network. The additional channel activity due to association (beacon transmission, active scanning etc.) is added compared to an ad-hoc network.

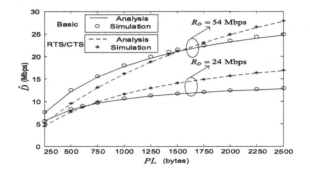

**Fig. 7.** Network sum rate $\hat{D}$ versus the packet payload $PL$ in a saturated IEEE 802.11 DCF network with basic access and RTS/CTS. $n = 50$. $W = 16$. $K = 6$. $R_B = 6$ Mbps.

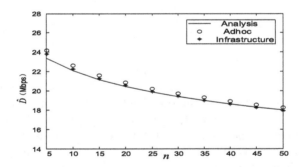

**Fig. 8.** Network sum rate $\hat{D}$ versus the number of nodes $n$ in a saturated IEEE 802.11 DCF network with basic access in ad-hoc and infrastructure mode. $PL = 1023$ bytes. $n = 50$. $W = 16$. $K = 6$. $R_D = 54$ Mbps.

Figure 8 depicts the effect of the association activity in the infrastructure network on network sum rate performance. By comparing the relation between network sum rate $\hat{D}$ and the number of nodes $n$ in the ad-hoc and infrastructure networks, the network sum rate $\hat{D}$ in the ad-hoc network is slightly higher than that in infrastructure network due to the extra time overhead of the association activities in the infrastructure mode.

# 5   Conclusion

In this paper, we conduct a performance evaluation study of the unified IEEE 802.11 DCF analytical model [1] against the IEEE 802.11 MAC simulation model in NS-3. We have instrumented the simulator with different scenarios including traffic conditions varying from unsaturated to saturated, system parameters including the number of nodes $n$, the initial backoff window size $W$ and the cutoff phase $K$, and varying the packet payload $PL$ in the basic access and RTS/CTS modes. Our study shows that the unified analytical framework proposed for homogeneous IEEE 802.11 DCF networks matches closely with the NS-3 MAC model. The work demonstrates that (1) NS-3 WiFi module can work accurately for 802.11 model validations; (2) the unified analytical framework proposed in [1] is a simple yet solid theoretical tool for performance evaluation of homogeneous IEEE 802.11 networks.

**Acknowledgments.** The authors thank Rohan Patidar for his help in our NS-3 experiments. This work was supported in part by the National Natural Science Foundation of China (No. 61402186, No. 61370231).

# References

1. Dai, L., Sun, X.: A unified analysis of IEEE 802.11 DCF networks: stability, throughput and delay. IEEE Trans. Mob. Comput. **12**(8), 1558–1572 (2013)
2. Bianchi, G.: Performance analysis of the IEEE 802.11 distributed coordination function. IEEE J. Sel. Areas Commun. **18**(3), 535–547 (2000)
3. Gupta, S.G., Ghonge, M.M., Thakare, P.D., Jawandhiya, P.M.: Open-source network simulation tools: an overview. Proc. IJARCET **2**(4), 1629–1635 (2013)
4. Pei, G., Henderson, T.: Validation of ns-3 802.11 b PHY model, May 2009. http://www.nsnam.org/~pei/80211b.pdf
5. Barsocchi, P., Oligeri, G., Potorti, F.: Validation for 802.11 b wireless channel measurements, ISTI-CNR, via Moruzzi, l, Technical report, ISTI-2006-TR-29, June 2006
6. Di Stefano, A., Scaglione, A., Terrazzino, G., et al.: On the fidelity of IEEE 802.11 commercial cards. In: Proceedings of IEEE WICON, pp. 10–17, July 2005
7. Liu, J., Yuan, Y., Nicol, D.M., et al.: Empirical validation of wireless models in simulations of ad hoc routing protocols. Simulation **81**(4), 307–323 (2005)
8. Fuxjager, P., Ricciato, F.: Collecting broken frames: error statistics in IEEE 802.11 b/g links. In: Proceedings of IEEE ICST WiOPT, pp. 30–35, April 2008
9. Patidar, R., Roy, S., Henderson, T.R., et al.: Validation of Wi-Fi network simulation on NS-3 (2017)
10. Baldo, N., Requena-Esteso, M., Núñez-Martínez, J., et al.: Validation of the IEEE 802.11 MAC model in the NS3 simulator using the EXTREME testbed. In: Proceedings of SIMUTools, March 2010
11. Gao, Y., Dai, L.: Optimal downlink/uplink throughput allocation for IEEE 802.11 DCF networks. IEEE Wirel. Commun. Lett. **2**(6), 627–630 (2013)
12. Gao, Y., Sun, X., Dai, L.: Throughput optimization of heterogeneous IEEE 802.11 DCF networks. IEEE Trans. Wireless Commun. **12**(1), 398–411 (2013)

13. Gao, Y., Sun, X., Dai, L.: IEEE 802.11e EDCA networks: modeling, differentiation and optimization. IEEE Trans. Wirel. Commun. **13**(7), 3863–3879 (2014)
14. Gao, Y., Sun, X., Dai, L.: Achieving optimum network throughput and service differentiation for IEEE 802.11 e EDCA networks. IEEE WCNC **13**(7), 362–367 (2013)
15. Gao, Y., Dai, L., Hei, X.: Throughput optimization of multi-BSS IEEE 802.11 networks with universal frequency reuse. IEEE Trans. Wirel. Commun. **65**(8), 3399–3414 (2017)
16. Lacage, M., Henderson, T.R.: Yet another network simulator. In: Proceedings of WNS2, October 2006
17. IEEE Std. 802.11-2007 Part 11: Wireless LAN Medium Access Control (MAC) and Physical Layer (PHY) Specifications. IEEE, June 2007

# An Improved Ant Colony-Based Alternate Path Selection Method for Wide-Area Protection System in Optical Communication Network of Power Grid

Hailin Gu[✉], Xing Huang, Li Li, Ruowei Li, and Jinghua Yao

State Grid Liaoning Electric Power Company, Shenyang, China
18741895598@139.com

**Abstract.** Wide-area protection system has a strict requirement on real-time and reliability of communication network. Currently, the path selection algorithm that meets the requirements of wide-area protection system communication can calculates an optimal master path while meeting the requirements on real-time and reliability. After some link or node in the master path fails, the router in the communication network can detects the fault of the link or node and needs to re-calculate a transmission path and re-release the path information. Unfortunately, the sum of the fault detection time, the new path calculation time and the update time of new path has exceeded the tolerance delay of wide-area protection system. For solving this problem, 1 + 1 protection scheme is proposed in this paper. We employs an improved ant colony algorithm to calculate the master path and the alternate path, which meet the real-time and reliability requirement of wide-area protection system. As soon as the master path fails, it will immediately launch the alternate path, so that it can save the delay spent in detecting the fault of link or node and re-release the path information. Finally, a case study is carried out and it is proved that the improved ant colony can find the optimal master and alternate paths.

**Keywords:** Wide-area protection system · Path selection · Alternate path · Ant colony

## 1 Introduction

Relay protection system is an important part in power system. Most of conventional protection systems only collect local or limited fault information, which bring negative effect on the selectivity and fastness of protection for complex power system. The Wide-Area Protection System (WAPS) can obtain global information from the power system. At the same time, from the global perspective of the entire system, the stability, selectivity, accuracy and reliability of the protection system are improved. Furthermore, WAPS has potential to take coordinated measures to avoid the cascade trip-off or black out of power system [1, 2]. Initially it was proposed to avoid the long-term voltage collapse [3]. In recent years, with the rapid development of power system communication networks, WAPS has received extensive attention from many scholars.

© ICST Institute for Computer Sciences, Social Informatics and Telecommunications Engineering 2019
Published by Springer Nature Switzerland AG 2019. All Rights Reserved
H. Song et al. (Eds.): SIMUtools 2019, LNICST 295, pp. 407–415, 2019.
https://doi.org/10.1007/978-3-030-32216-8_39

Wide-area protection systems are one of the key factors in wide area protection. Therefore, the real-time, reliability, security and self-healing of the communication system are strictly required. Especially when the smart grid communication fails, it is also important to select the appropriate path to transmit information to the destination quickly and reliably in the wide area protection system [4].

Currently path selection algorithm mostly adopts the concentrated methods based on graph theory such as Dijkstra or Bellman-Ford algorithm to find the shortest path, which has been extensively used in communication network, such as OSPF in the Internet. Wide-area Protection System has a strict requirement on real-time, reliability and self-healing of communication system. Therefore, many scholars calculates a path selection with QoS parameters such as bandwidth, delay and reliability. The literature [5] propose a robust routing algorithm to reach the higher network energy efficiency, which is based on optimization problem. In [6], it describes how to employ Dijkstra algorithm to acquire the path with the minimum hop count. The literature [7, 8] studies the reliability of power communication network and self-healing after network failure. In [9], an optimization model that maximizes path reliability under constraints of communication delay is established. This literature [10, 11] is to minimize the network's bit energy consumption parameter, and then we propose the energy-efficient minimum criticality routing algorithm, which includes energy efficiency routing and load balancing. For the requirements of wide-area protection communication system, a path selection model based on MPLS to meet the QoS requirements of wide-area protection system is established in [12].

Wide-area protection system has strict requirements on real-time, reliability, self-healing of the communication network. Especially after the master path fails, the communication system still can reliably transmit the data via the alternate path. Above algorithms mainly acquire an optimal master path and several nodes-disjoint or link-disjoint alternate paths, but QoS parameters are not taken into account to meet the requirements of wide-area protection system. The optimal primary path is calculated to meet the real-time and reliability requirements of the path selection algorithm that satisfies the wide-area protection system communication requirements. After some link or node in the master path fails, the router in the network detects the fault of the link or node and needs to re-calculate a transmission path and re-release the path information. Unfortunately, the sum of the fault detection time, the new path calculation time and the update time of new path has exceeded the tolerance delay of wide-area protection system. For solving this problem, 1 + 1 protection scheme is proposed in this paper. We employs an improved ant colony algorithm to calculate the master path and the alternate path, which meet the real-time and reliability requirement of wide-area protection system. As soon as the master path fails, the alternate path will be started immediately, so that it can save the delay spent in detecting the fault of link or node and re-release the path information.

The rest of this paper is organized as follows: multi-path selection model is introduced in Sect. 2; the solution based on improved ant colony for the model is proposed in Sect. 3; the case study and result analysis are carried out in Sect. 4; finally, we conclude in Sect. 5.

## 2 Multi-path Selection Model

### 2.1 Path Reliability

In the network topology, each path can be treated as a set of links and nodes. The reliability of the path is affected by the availability of links and nodes. Given there are $n$ paths $path_1\ path_2\ path_3.\ \cdots path_k \cdots path_n$ between source node and destination node, the collection of nodes passed by $path_k$ is $C_{path_k} = \{c_1, c_2, \cdots, c_m\}$, the collection of links is $E_{path_k} = \{e_1, e_2, \cdots, e_{m-1}\}$. Path is made up by nodes and links in the way of series connection, whose reliability is the product of availability rate of each link between nodes times the availability rate of each node. The expression of path reliability is as follows:

$$P_{path_k} = \prod_{i=1}^{m-1} A_{e_i} A_{c_i} \tag{1}$$

$P_{path_k}$ is reliability of $path_k$, $n$ means total number of nodes passed by the path, $A_{e_i}$ means availability rate of the $i$-th link on $path_k$. $A_{c_i}$ means availability rate of the $i$-th node on $path_k$.

### 2.2 Delay

Information transmission delay is mainly determined by factors such as communication media, transmission distance and number of network equipment passed. Total delay of information and data passed along the $path_k$ equals to the sum of transmission delay, treatment delay and queuing delay and the expression for information transmission delay of the path is as follows:

$$T_{path_k} = \sum_{i=1}^{n-1} \frac{d_{e_i}}{\frac{2}{3}v} + t + \Delta t \tag{2}$$

$$t = \frac{1}{\gamma} \sum_{(i,j)} \frac{\lambda_{ij}}{\mu_{ij} - \lambda_{ij}} \tag{3}$$

In the formula, $T_{path_k}$ is the information transmission delay of $path_k$, $d_{e_i}$ is length of link $e_i$, the transmission velocity of information in optical fiber is 2/3 of velocity of light, namely, 2/3 $v$, $\Delta t$ is treatment delay of node, $t$ is the queuing delay of node, $\lambda_{ij}$ means the birth rate of data package in the queue of link $(i, j)$, namely, the speed of service data package joining the queue, $\mu$ means death rate, namely, the speed of service being finished and leaving the queue, and $\gamma$ is total arrival rate of the system.

## 2.3   Optimization Model for Path Selection

To meet the requirements of wide-area protection communication, and enhance its reliability by studying the master path and alternate path, an optimization model is established as follows:

$$\left\{ \begin{array}{l} \min T(T_{path_1}, T_{path2}, \cdots, T_{path_k}) \\ s.t \quad P(P_{path_1}, P_{path2}, \cdots, P_{path_k}) > P_0 \end{array} \right. \tag{4}$$

In the above formula, $T(.)$ is the network transmission delay of selected path, $P(.)$ is the reliability of a path selected from candidate paths. The reliability of power communication network is one of the decisive factors on whether wide range protection can realize its preset function. $P_0$ is the minimal reliability permitted for transmission of wide range protection information in the power communication network, and if the reliability of the path is larger than $P_0$, it will be reserved as a candidate path. In the paper, the value of $P_0$ is set as 0.950. Based on the routine selection mathematical model put forward, several paths with a high reliability and instantaneity are found between designated source node and destination node.

Very high transients are required in wide area protection communication systems. For provincial medium-sized power grids, the central dispatch master station needs to obtain measurement information for all substations within 20 ms. In other words, the time for each substation to issue a master station control command should also be controlled within 20 ms. However, when the host path for information transmission fails, the delay in detecting the path failure and the waiting delay of the reconstructed path often exceed the delay allowed by the wide range of protection on the communication system. Therefore, a channel should be selected to transmit the minimum total delay without crossing any node of the host path to ensure that the standby path is initiated once the host path fails, resulting in reduced fault detection latency and latency. The final delay path reconstruction, the information transmission delay is less than 20 ms.

## 3   Solution Based on Ant Colony

Based on the basic algorithm of ant colony, modify the expecting factor to establish a model of optimal path. Multiple transmission paths of different quality from source node to destination node are found by improved ant colony algorithm, and select secondary alternate path from them which does not cross with any node of host path. Once the host path for transmission protection and control fails, it can quickly switch to the alternate path, thereby improving the immediacy and reliability of the WRPS. The specific steps of improved algorithm are as follows:

(1)  Initialized parameters

Set the initial parameters: number of nodes $n$ and number of ants $k$, transition probability of ants $P_{ij}^k$, intensity of pheromone on the edge $(i, j)$ $\tau_{ij}$, motivation degree for node $i$ to transit to node $j$ is $\eta_{ij}$, pheromone volatile parameter $\alpha$, maximum iterations $N_{C_{\max}}$, delay for ant when passing edge $(i, j)$ $T_{ij}$, maximum link availability rate on the edge $(i, j)$ is $E_{ij}$, $\rho$ and $\varepsilon$ are parameters introduced by the algorithm.

(2) Put ant $k$ at the source node $S$.
(3) The ant selects path based on formulas (5), (6) and (7).

$$P_{ij}^k(t) = \begin{cases} \frac{\tau_{ij}^k(t)\eta_{ij}^k(t)}{\sum_{s \in allowed_k} \tau_{is}^\alpha(t)\eta_{is}^\beta(t)}, & j \in allowed_k \\ 0 & otherwise \end{cases} \tag{5}$$

$$\eta_{ij} = \frac{1}{T_{ij}} \tag{6}$$

$$\tau_{ij}(t+n) = \rho_1 \cdot \Delta\tau_{ij}(t) + \Delta\tau_{ij}(t, t+n) \tag{7}$$

$allowed_k$ means the collection of nodes that can be selected by ant $k$ in the next step, the transition probability $P_{ij}^k(t)$ is in direct proportion to $\tau_{ij}^\alpha \, \eta_{ij}^\beta$. $\eta_{ij}$ reflects the motivation degree for node $i$ to transition to node $j$, $T_{ij}$ means the delay for ant when passing edge $(i, j)$, $\tau_{ij}$ means pheromone track intensity on the edge $(i, j)$, $\Delta\tau_{ij}$ means the track pheromone per unit length left by ant on the edge $(i, j)$, $\alpha$ and $\beta$ are two important parameters.

(4) Each path generated by ant will undergo a partial renewal based on formula (8).

$$\tau(r, s) \leftarrow (1 - \rho) \cdot \tau(r, s) + \rho \cdot \Delta\tau(r, s) \tag{8}$$

(5) Before each ant generates a path, it will repeat steps (3) and (4) in cycle.
(6) A whole renewal will be conducted based on formula (9).

$$\tau(r, s) \leftarrow (1 - \alpha) \cdot \tau(r, s) + \alpha \cdot \Delta\tau(r, s) \tag{9}$$

(7) Repeat steps (3)–(6) in cycle until the iterations reach the designated number or there is no better solution after several iterations.
    By improving the ant colony algorithm, the performance of the algorithm is improved, the ant's ability to search is also enhanced, and the stagnation of the algorithm is effectively avoided.

## 4   Case Simulation and Result Analysis

### 4.1   Case Study

As shown in Fig. 1, the paper takes the network topology of some architecture of Shandong's power grid as an example. The topology comprises 12 nodes and 21 links. In the bracket of node 1 (0.1, 0.998), 0.1 ms means queuing delay of node 1, 0.998 means availability rate of node 1. In the bracket (0.234, 0.997) on the link between node 2 and 3, 0.234 ms means transmission delay of link between node 2 and 3, 0.997 means availability rate of link between node 2 and node 3. Transmission velocity of information in the channel $v = 2 \times 10^8$ m/s, and given the treatment delay of nodes at $\Delta t = 0.1$ ms.

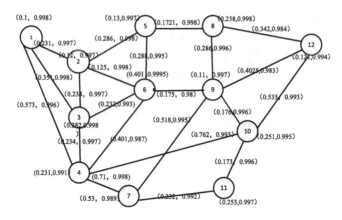

**Fig. 1.** Network topology

## 4.2  Simulation Result Analysis

With the parameters of Table 1 and multi-path routine algorithm suggested by the paper, a simulation is conducted in MATLAB. The actual state of link in network topology model is compared with the simulation result of improved ant colony algorithm, which indicates that the path selected by routine algorithm keeps consistent with the actual optimal path. The simulation experiment takes solving host and alternate paths between node 1 (source node) and node 12 (destination node) in Fig. 1, and the Figs. 2, 3, and 4 are optimal path and several secondary paths obtained from the routine algorithm introduced by the paper.

**Table 1.** Average normalized values of the pheromone of paths.

| Path  | Nodes | Max delay/ms |
|-------|-------|--------------|
| Path1 | 1 → 2 → 5 → 8 → 12 | 1.5191 |
| Path2 | 1 → 2 → 6 → 9 → 12 | 1.5645 |
| Path3 | 1 → 3 → 6 → 9 → 12 | 1.9075 |
| Path4 | 1 → 2 → 3 → 6 → 9 → 12 | 2.2876 |
| Path5 | 1 → 4 → 10 → 12 | 2.3520 |
| Path6 | 1 → 4 → 10 → 9 → 12 | 2.5055 |

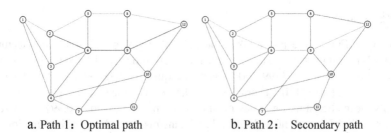

a. Path 1: Optimal path               b. Path 2:  Secondary path

**Fig. 2.** The path according to the algorithm of this paper

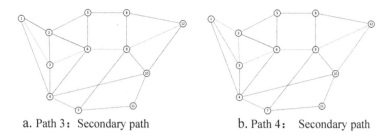

a. Path 3: Secondary path                    b. Path 4:    Secondary path

**Fig. 3.** The path by the algorithm of this paper

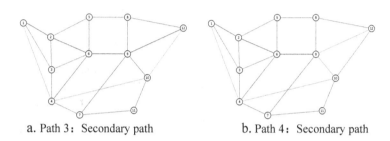

a. Path 3: Secondary path                    b. Path 4: Secondary path

**Fig. 4.** Path algorithm obtained

According to the above three figures, we find the main path and several alternate paths using the algorithm of this paper. According to the picture, several alternate paths are different. The delay results are calculated and analyzed as shown in the following Tables 1 and 2.

**Table 2.** Parameters of paths in the network.

| Path | Reliability | Quality | Path selection |
|------|-------------|---------|----------------|
| Path1 | 0.986 | 1 | Host path |
| Path2 | 0.989 | 2 | |
| Path3 | 0.985 | 3 | Optimal alternate path |
| Path4 | 0.990 | 4 | |
| Path5 | 0.992 | 5 | Secondary path |
| Path6 | 0.898 | 6 | |

According to data of Tables 1 and 2, the routine algorithm computes several multi-path routines with different quality from source node to destination node. Path 1 meets the reliability constraint and its path transmission delay is the minimal. Therefore path 1 is taken as optimal path obtained by the routine algorithm, which is the host path for transmission protection and control. The selection of alternate paths will be based on quality sequence, and follow the principle of not crossing with any node of host path, with an attempt to cut the delay for detecting host path fault and delay for reissuing routine list when the host path fails. Path 2 and 4 do not meet the requirement of not crossing with any node of host path 1; Path 6 does not meet the reliability constraint; Path 3 is the secondary path that meets double conditions of not crossing with node of Path 1 and reliability constraint, while with the minimal total transmission delay, so Path 3 is taken as the optimal alternate path for transmission protection and control and path 5 taken as secondary path for the purpose.

## 5 Conclusion

In this paper, in the network topology model of wide-area protection communication system, an improved ant colony algorithm is used to search several path routines of different quality between source node and destination node, and select the optimal alternate path. The multipathing procedure obtained in this paper enhances the reliability of a wide range of protection communication systems. Once the optimal path routine used by the wide-range protection communication system fails, it will quickly start the secondary standby routine, which can reduce the delay of detecting host path failures and delay the list of re-release routines to meet the requirements of the communication network, and protect reliability and immediacy of the power supply.

## References

1. Cai, J.Y., et al.: Current status and prospect of wide-area protection (dynamic stability control) technologies. Power Syst. Technol. **28**(8), 20–25 (2004)
2. Jiang, D., Huo, L., Song, H.: Rethinking behaviors and activities of base stations in mobile cellular networks based on big data analysis. IEEE Trans. Netw. Sci. Eng. **1**(1), 1–12 (2018)
3. Jiang, D., et al.: A joint multi-criteria utility-based network selection approach for vehicle-to-infrastructure networking. IEEE Trans. Intell. Transp. Syst. **19**(10), 3305–3319 (2018)
4. Han, X.-J., et al.: Study on relaying protection based on the multi-agent system. Relay **36**, 1–5 (2008)
5. Jiang, D., et al.: An optimization-based robust routing algorithm to energy-efficient networks for cloud computing. Telecommun. Syst. **63**(1), 89–98 (2016)
6. Nafarieh, A., Raza, M., Robertson, W.: A comprehensive analysis of QoS-based routing mechanisms over shared mesh protected optical infrastructures. J. Ambient Intell. Hum. Comput. **6**(4), 463–472 (2015)
7. Liao, H.: Study of communications in wide area protection systems. Southwest Jiaotong University (2008)
8. Xiong, X.-F., et al.: Reliability model research of electric power communication system. Relay **35**, 28–32 (2007)
9. Xiong, X., Wu, L., Chen, X.: Routing selection for wide-area protection based on communication reliability and time-delay requirement. Autom. Electr. Power Syst. **35**(3), 44–48 (2011)

10. Jiang, D., et al.: Energy-efficient multi-constraint routing algorithm with load balancing for smart city applications. IEEE Internet Things J. **3**, 1437–1447 (2016)
11. Jiang, D., et al.: Topology control-based collaborative multicast routing algorithm with minimum energy consumption. Int. J. Commun Syst **30**(1), e2905 (2017)
12. Xiong, X., Tan, J., Lin, X.: Routing algorithm for communication system in wide-area protection based on MPLS. J. Electr. Technol. **28**(6), 257–263 (2013)

# Parameter Optimization Strategy of Fuzzy Petri Net Utilizing Hybrid GA-SFLA Algorithm

Wei Jiang, Kai-Qing Zhou[✉], and Li-Ping Mo

College of Information Science and Engineering, Jishou University,
Jishou 416000, Hunan, China
kqzhou@jsu.edu.cn

**Abstract.** Fuzzy Petri net (FPN) is a powerful tool to model and analyze the knowledge-based systems (KBSs) or expert systems (ESs). The accuracy of the reasoning result is a bottleneck to hinder the further development of FPN because of lacking self-learning capability. To overcome this issue, a hybrid GA-SFLA algorithm is proposed in this paper to improve the precision of each parameter of a given FPN model. The proposed algorithm combines the advantages both of GA and SFLA and includes three phases, which are generating chromosome by encoding the multi-dimensional solution which reflects all initial frogs, gaining a better individual as well as seeking the optimal solution by executing the local search and global search operations of SFLA. Finally, an FPN model is used to test the feasibility of the proposed algorithm. Simulation results reveal that all parameters of the given FPN model have the higher precision by implementing the GA-SFLA than that of implementing GA and SFLA, respectively.

**Keywords:** Parameter optimization · Fuzzy Petri net · Genetic Algorithm (GA) · Shuffled Frog-Leaping Algorithm (SFLA)

## 1 Introduction

Knowledge-based systems (KBSs) or expert systems (ESs), are a form of computerized artificial intelligence programming to capture and employ knowledge for settling complex problems, such as fault diagnosis or inference [1–3]. However, the uncertainties of objective rooted in people's information and knowledge are widely existed in the real world. Hence, it is required that the ESs need to reflect these uncertainties and fuzzy information in the knowledge representation and modeling processing [4–6]. The last few decades have witnessed a series of new methods for representing knowledge and automatic reasoning implementation, such as fuzzy production rule (FPR) [7], fuzzy Petri net (FPN) [8], Semantic Web [9] and frame-based representation [10], etc.

FPN is kind of high-level Petri nets (HLPNs) based on the backward extension principle [11]. Due to the graphical description capability and the systemic mathematical analysis mechanism, FPN can accurately depict the uncertainty and is commonly used in the modeling, analyzing, and reasoning for KBSs and ESs [7, 12, 13].

© ICST Institute for Computer Sciences, Social Informatics and Telecommunications Engineering 2019
Published by Springer Nature Switzerland AG 2019. All Rights Reserved
H. Song et al. (Eds.): SIMUtools 2019, LNICST 295, pp. 416–426, 2019.
https://doi.org/10.1007/978-3-030-32216-8_40

Nowadays, fruitful reasoning algorithms using FPN were borne and employed into different industrial areas for specific functions, such as fault diagnosis, path recognized, traffic schedule, process monitor, and so on [14, 15].

There are various successful FPN and its industrial applications. However, another bottleneck of FPN-how to obtain the more accurate final reasoning result of the goal output place-is still in the initial phase because the existing FPN formalism lacks of self-learning ability to improve the accuracy of relevant parameters value. Shen et al. developed two kinds of machine learning PN (MLPN) models to enhance the self-learning of the Petri net (PN) by supervised and unsupervised learning algorithms based on artificial neural network (ANN) [16]. Similarly, Tsang et al. proposed a learning strategy of a kind of 14-tuple FPN by using ANN. However, in the training process, training of thresholds of the FPN was neglected because the authors assumed all transitions of FPN can be enabled and fired [17]. Wang et al. employed an efficient genetic particle swarm optimization (GPSO) learning algorithm to execute self-learning function for the parameters of FPN. But the proposed GPSO learning algorithm is not suitable for some more complex and large-scale FPN models [18]. Above three literatures, it reveals that it is a feasible thinking to enhance the self-learning of FPN model and to practice the accuracy of each kind of parameters by using soft computing techniques.

Based on the similar thinking, a hybrid algorithm, namely GA-SFLA approach, is presented in this manuscript at first by combining the advantages of GA and SFLA. Then, the proposed hybrid algorithm is used to execute the training process for improving the accuracy of each type of parameters of FPN. The simulation results indicate that the FPN parameters which are optimized by GA-SFLA own better precision than that of which are optimized by SFLA and GA, respectively.

Remain parts are organized as follows. Section 2 gives the related concepts of FPN and FPR. Section 3 illustrates the framework and implementation steps of the GA-SFLA algorithm in details after analyzing GA and SFLA briefly. Section 4 shows the experimental results of parameters' optimization by performing GA-SFLA, GA and SFLA algorithms one-by-one on the same FPN case. Section 5 recalls and summarizes the entire manuscript.

## 2  Fuzzy Petri Net and Fuzzy Production Rule

FPN and FPR are two major formalisms which have been applied to fulfil the KBS requirements. This section introduces the basic concepts both of FPN and FPR. Then, the corresponding FPN model of different types of FPR is generated, respectively.

### 2.1  Fuzzy Petri Net

FPN generally defined as the following 8-tuple formalism.

$$FPN \quad \sum = (P, T, I, O, M, \mu, W, CF), \quad \text{where}$$

- $P = \{p_1, p_2, \cdots, p_n\}$ represents a finite set of places, where $n$ represents the number of places in the rule;
- $T = \{t_1, t_2, \cdots, t_m\}$ represents a finite set of transitions, where $m$ represents the number of transitions in the rule;
- $I(O)$ is the input (output) function, i.e., the mapping relation between places and transitions;
- $M = (m_1, m_2, \cdots, m_n)^T$ indicates the identity of places;
- $w_i$ indicates the weight of places $p_i$, i.e., the support degree for the rule establishment by preconditions $p_i$;
- $CF_j$ indicates the credibility, i.e., the true extent of the conclusion after transitions $t_j$ fired;
- $\mu : \mu \rightarrow (0, 1]$, $\mu_i$ is the threshold of transitions $t_j$.

## 2.2 Fuzzy Production Rule

FPR is a commonly used to represent the uncertainties in expert systems [19–21]. General FPRs are formalized and described as follows.

$$if \quad D(\lambda) \quad then \quad Q \quad (CF, \mu, w), \quad where$$

- $D$ is a limited set of preconditions, $D = \{D_1, D_2, \cdots D_n\}$;
- $Q$ is a limited set of conclusions, $Q = \{Q_1, Q_2, \cdots Q_m\}$;
- $\lambda$ is the true extent of each precondition, $\lambda \in [0, 1]$;
- $CF$ is the credibility of the rule; $CF \in (0, 1]$ is the credibility of the conclusion obtained after the rule is executed;
- $\mu$ is the threshold of the rule, $\mu \in (0, 1]$;
- $w$ is the weight of each precondition, $w \in (0, 1]$.

## 2.3 Correspondence Between FPN and FPR

After comparing with these formalisms, the correspondence between an FPR and FPN could be listed in Table 1

**Table 1.** The corresponding relationship between an FPR and FPN

| FPR | FPN |
|---|---|
| FPRs | FPN model |
| FPR | Transition |
| Precondition and Conclusion | Place |
| Range of application of rule | Extension of transition |
| Weight of rule ($w$) | Input weight from place to transition ($w$) |
| True extent of each precondition ($\lambda$) | Value of Token ($M(p_i)$) |
| Threshold of rule ($\mu$) | Threshold of transition ($\mu$) |
| Credibility of the rule ($CF$) | Credibility from transition to place ($CF$) |

FPRs can be divided into three main types, which are 'simple', 'or', and 'and' rules according to different relationship among conditions.

**Type 1: Simple Rule**

*if   $D(\lambda)$   then   $Q$   $(w = 1, \mu, CF)$*

**Type 2: And Rule**

*if   $D_1(\lambda_1)$   and   $D_2(\lambda_2)$   and   $\cdots$   and $D_n(\lambda_n)$   then   $Q$   $(\sum_{i=1}^{n} w_i = 1, \mu, CF)$*

**Type 3: Or Rule**

*if   $D_1(\lambda_1)$   or   $D_2(\lambda_2)$   or   $\cdots$   or   $D_n(\lambda_n)$   then   $Q(w_i = 1, \mu_i, CF_i)$*
The corresponding FPN models of three types of FPR are illustrated in Fig. 1.

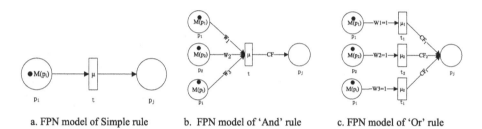

a. FPN model of Simple rule          b. FPN model of 'And' rule          c. FPN model of 'Or' rule

**Fig. 1.** The corresponding FPN model for each type of FPR

# 3   Hybrid GA-SFLA Algorithm

GA and SFLP are two common powerful evolutionary optimization algorithms to handle various complex engineering problems. In this section, brief introductions of GA and SFLP algorithms are given at first. Next, a hybrid algorithm based on the advantages both GA and SFLA is demonstrated in details.

## 3.1   Genetic Algorithm (GA)

GA is one of the most popular optimization algorithms based on stochastic search mechanism. Three basic operators-selection, crossover and mutation-are used to present a population of solutions in the implementation process of GA. In the initial phase, an initial population is created by a set of random solutions. A new population will be generated from the previous population by using three basic operators repeatedly till the termination criteria is reached [22]. The main advantages of GA could be summarized into three points. First, fit solutions could be found in a very less time. Next, a wide range of solutions could be evaluated based on the random mutation operator. Finally, it is easy to realize the coding operation for each solution [23–25].

## 3.2  Shuffled Frog-Leaping Algorithm (SFLA)

SFLA is a kind of optimization algorithms which is inspired by analyzing the behavior of frogs located in swamps to seek optimum location of food [26]. SFLA owns two different search abilities, local search as well as global search, to ensure obtain the optimum solution for complex problems [27]. Compared with other intelligent computing techniques, SFLA can gain optimal solution by the better performance of the global search because SFLA integrates the advantages both genetic from memetic algorithm (MA) and social behavior from particle swarm optimization (PSO) [28, 29].

## 3.3  Hybrid GA-SFLP Algorithm

In this manuscript, a hybrid GA-SFLP algorithm is proposed in this article to improve the self-learning capability of FPN by combining the advantages of GA and SFLA.

The GA-SLFP algorithm could be classified into three phases.

Function of the first phase is to generate each chromosome in the initial population by encoding the multi-dimensional solution which reflects all initial frogs.

The second phase is to gain a better individual by implementing the main algorithm frame of GA based on the obtained in the population under a give a fixed number.

The third phase is to the global optimal solution by implementing the local search and global search operations of SFLA for the better individuals got from phase 2.

The entire flowchart of the proposed GA-SFLA algorithm as shown in Fig. 2.

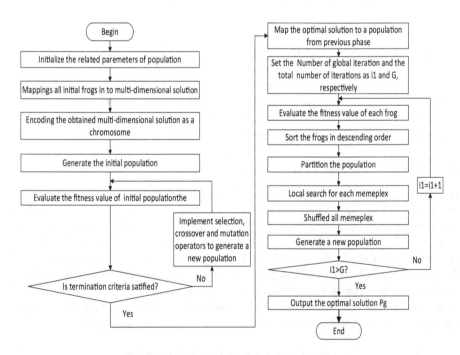

**Fig. 2.** Flowchart of the GA-SFLA algorithm

## 4 Experiment and Analysis

In this section, an FPN model is selected to reveal the feasible of the proposed GA-SFLA algorithm. Meanwhile, GA, SFLA and GA-SFLA algorithms are executed to optimize the different types parameters of the same FPN model.

### 4.1 Experiment Design

In general, FPN model, there are only three types of parameters. Hence, GA, SFLA and GA-SFLA algorithms are employed to optimize the three types of parameters (weight, threshold, credibility) one-by-one based on following principles (Take the credibility optimization as a case) in this experiment. In the initialization phase, the individual solutions are generated based on the range $CF_i \in (0, 1](i = 1, \cdots, 5)$ randomly. The maximum and the minimum value of the individual could be set as $[1, 1, 1, 1, 1]$ and $[CF_1, CF_2, CF_3, CF_4, CF_5]$ (listed in Table 2).

- Calculate the fitness of each solution and implement the corresponding algorithm.
- Output the gained optimal individual solution.

**FPN Model Selection Criteria**
In this experiment, a simple KBS with 4 FPRs is selected to generate the corresponding FPN model. These four FPRs include three types of FPRs, which are simple rule, 'or' rule, and 'and' rule. Meanwhile, the meaning of each place is neglected because the goal of this experiment is to discuss the parameter optimization issue of the FPN model. The fours FPRs are listed below.

$$
\begin{array}{llllllll}
R1 & if & d_1 & or & d_2 & then & d_3 & (\mu_1, CF_1, \mu_3, CF_3) \\
R2 & if & d_1 & then & d_2 & (\mu_2, CF_2) \\
R3 & if & d_3 & and & d_4 & and & d_5 & then \quad d_6 \quad (w_1, w_2, w_3, \mu_4, CF_5) \\
R4 & if & d_3 & then & d_7 & (w_4, w_5, \mu_5, CF_5)
\end{array}
$$

The corresponding FPN model of above FPRs is generated as shown in Fig. 3.

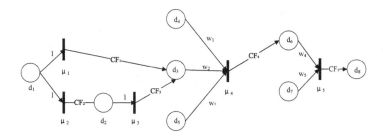

**Fig. 3.** The corresponding FPN model of 4-FPR KBS

**Experiment Parameters' Setting**

In this experiment, the expected values of three types of parameter, which are given by expert, are shown in Table 2.

Table 2. The expected values of three types of parameters

| Parameter | | | | | | | | | | | | | | |
|---|---|---|---|---|---|---|---|---|---|---|---|---|---|---|
| Weight ($w$) | | | | | Threshold ($\mu$) | | | | | Credibility ($CF$) | | | | |
| $w_1$ | $w_2$ | $w_3$ | $w_4$ | $w_5$ | $\mu_1$ | $\mu_2$ | $\mu_3$ | $\mu_4$ | $\mu_5$ | $CF_1$ | $CF_2$ | $CF_3$ | $CF_4$ | $CF_5$ |
| 0.2 | 0.3 | 0.4 | 0.5 | 0.6 | 0.7 | 0.9 | 0.6 | 0.8 | 0.7 | 0.3 | 0.4 | 0.2 | 0.5 | 0.4 |

- For the entire GA-SFLA algorithm, the population size = 50 and the max number of iterations G = 300
- Other parameters are assigned based on the classical GA and SFLA algorithms.

## 4.2    Experimental Results and Analysis

Each algorithm is implemented five times. The final experimental results of each algorithm are listed in Tables 3, 4 and 5, respectively.

Table 3. Five times' experimental results by implementing GA

| Parameter | | $1^{st}$ result | $2^{nd}$ result | $3^{rd}$ result | $4^{th}$ result | $5^{th}$ result | Means |
|---|---|---|---|---|---|---|---|
| Weight | $w_1$ | 0.2548 | 0.2256 | 0.2323 | 0.2907 | 0.2656 | 0.25380 |
| | $w_2$ | 0.3240 | 0.3219 | 0.3362 | 0.3205 | 0.3170 | 0.32392 |
| | $w_3$ | 0.4511 | 0.4158 | 0.4146 | 0.4022 | 0.4386 | 0.42446 |
| | $w_4$ | 0.5067 | 0.5133 | 0.5119 | 0.5033 | 0.5028 | 0.50760 |
| | $w_5$ | 0.6106 | 0.6245 | 0.6100 | 0.6176 | 0.6040 | 0.61334 |
| Threshold | $\mu_1$ | 0.7404 | 0.7238 | 0.7148 | 0.7200 | 0.7149 | 0.72278 |
| | $\mu_2$ | 0.9216 | 0.9025 | 0.9230 | 0.9182 | 0.9115 | 0.91428 |
| | $\mu_3$ | 0.6123 | 0.6248 | 0.6172 | 0.6088 | 0.6031 | 0.61324 |
| | $\mu_4$ | 0.8085 | 0.8124 | 0.8344 | 0.8115 | 0.8191 | 0.81718 |
| | $\mu_5$ | 0.7240 | 0.7206 | 0.7057 | 0.7237 | 0.7201 | 0.71882 |
| Credibility | $CF_1$ | 0.3049 | 0.3198 | 0.3246 | 0.3214 | 0.3343 | 0.32100 |
| | $CF_2$ | 0.4196 | 0.4104 | 0.4216 | 0.4140 | 0.4092 | 0.41496 |
| | $CF_3$ | 0.2010 | 0.2059 | 0.2079 | 0.2262 | 0.2220 | 0.21260 |
| | $CF_4$ | 0.5344 | 0.5037 | 0.5205 | 0.5044 | 0.5207 | 0.51674 |
| | $CF_5$ | 0.4481 | 0.4812 | 0.4124 | 0.4443 | 0.4176 | 0.44066 |

**Table 4.** Five times' experimental result by implementing SFLA

| Parameter | | 1st result | 2nd result | 3rd result | 4th result | 5th result | Means |
|---|---|---|---|---|---|---|---|
| Weight | $w_1$ | 0.4450 | 0.3352 | 0.5907 | 0.3804 | 0.3521 | 0.42068 |
| | $w_2$ | 0.4275 | 0.3451 | 0.4698 | 0.4881 | 0.5611 | 0.45832 |
| | $w_3$ | 0.4899 | 0.5374 | 0.4750 | 0.6868 | 0.5384 | 0.54550 |
| | $w_4$ | 0.6052 | 0.5488 | 0.5514 | 0.6200 | 0.6226 | 0.58960 |
| | $w_5$ | 0.8161 | 0.7158 | 0.6641 | 0.6750 | 0.6579 | 0.70578 |
| Threshold | $\mu_1$ | 0.7188 | 0.8276 | 0.7296 | 0.7335 | 0.8319 | 0.76828 |
| | $\mu_2$ | 0.9044 | 0.9999 | 0.9388 | 0.9550 | 0.9488 | 0.94938 |
| | $\mu_3$ | 0.7188 | 0.6019 | 0.7004 | 0.6886 | 0.6399 | 0.66992 |
| | $\mu_4$ | 0.8826 | 0.8693 | 0.8225 | 0.8659 | 0.8881 | 0.86568 |
| | $\mu_5$ | 0.7752 | 0.7270 | 0.7493 | 0.7415 | 0.7536 | 0.74932 |
| Credibility | $CF_1$ | 0.4707 | 0.3001 | 0.5079 | 0.5033 | 0.3567 | 0.42774 |
| | $CF_2$ | 0.6056 | 0.4885 | 0.4183 | 0.5583 | 0.7120 | 0.55654 |
| | $CF_3$ | 0.3525 | 0.2019 | 0.4060 | 0.3753 | 0.3105 | 0.32924 |
| | $CF_4$ | 0.6617 | 0.5920 | 0.5505 | 0.6853 | 0.5058 | 0.59906 |
| | $CF_5$ | 0.5748 | 0.6260 | 0.5055 | 0.5408 | 0.5572 | 0.56086 |

**Table 5.** Five times' experimental result by implementing GA-SFLA

| Parameter | | 1st result | 2nd result | 3rd result | 4th result | 5th result | Means |
|---|---|---|---|---|---|---|---|
| Weight | $w_1$ | 0.2297 | 0.2203 | 0.2145 | 0.2177 | 0.2221 | 0.22086 |
| | $w_2$ | 0.3218 | 0.3017 | 0.3062 | 0.3245 | 0.3089 | 0.31262 |
| | $w_3$ | 0.4043 | 0.4156 | 0.4192 | 0.4114 | 0.4232 | 0.41474 |
| | $w_4$ | 0.5003 | 0.5062 | 0.5033 | 0.5158 | 0.5052 | 0.50616 |
| | $w_5$ | 0.6056 | 0.6114 | 0.6047 | 0.6005 | 0.6035 | 0.60414 |
| Threshold | $\mu_1$ | 0.7025 | 0.7029 | 0.7038 | 0.7134 | 0.7022 | 0.70496 |
| | $\mu_2$ | 0.9033 | 0.9123 | 0.9083 | 0.9040 | 0.9199 | 0.90956 |
| | $\mu_3$ | 0.6056 | 0.6135 | 0.6140 | 0.6083 | 0.6157 | 0.61142 |
| | $\mu_4$ | 0.8030 | 0.8053 | 0.8078 | 0.8033 | 0.8033 | 0.80454 |
| | $\mu_5$ | 0.7023 | 0.7049 | 0.7060 | 0.7020 | 0.7078 | 0.70460 |
| Credibility | $CF_1$ | 0.3097 | 0.3021 | 0.3007 | 0.3002 | 0.3196 | 0.30646 |
| | $CF_2$ | 0.4042 | 0.4074 | 0.4219 | 0.4007 | 0.4017 | 0.40764 |
| | $CF_3$ | 0.2100 | 0.2290 | 0.2159 | 0.2068 | 0.2042 | 0.21318 |
| | $CF_4$ | 0.5124 | 0.5086 | 0.5025 | 0.5071 | 0.5020 | 0.50652 |
| | $CF_5$ | 0.4137 | 0.4089 | 0.4003 | 0.4025 | 0.4150 | 0.40826 |

Table 6 lists the expected value of the parameters and the related means of simulation results by implementing GA, SFLA and GA-SFLA algorithms, respectively.

**Table 6.** Five times' experimental result by implementing SFLA

| Parameter | | Expected value | Means of each parameter of simulation results | | |
|---|---|---|---|---|---|
| | | 1st result | GA | SFLA | GA-SFLA |
| Weight | $w_1$ | 0.2 | 0.25380 | 0.42068 | 0.22086 |
| | $w_2$ | 0.3 | 0.32392 | 0.45832 | 0.31262 |
| | $w_3$ | 0.4 | 0.42446 | 0.54550 | 0.41474 |
| | $w_4$ | 0.5 | 0.50760 | 0.58960 | 0.50616 |
| | $w_5$ | 0.6 | 0.61334 | 0.70578 | 0.60414 |
| Threshold | $\mu_1$ | 0.7 | 0.72278 | 0.76828 | 0.70496 |
| | $\mu_2$ | 0.9 | 0.91428 | 0.94938 | 0.90956 |
| | $\mu_3$ | 0.6 | 0.61324 | 0.66992 | 0.61142 |
| | $\mu_4$ | 0.8 | 0.81718 | 0.86568 | 0.80454 |
| | $\mu_5$ | 0.7 | 0.71882 | 0.74932 | 0.70460 |
| Credibility | $CF_1$ | 0.3 | 0.32100 | 0.42774 | 0.30646 |
| | $CF_2$ | 0.4 | 0.41496 | 0.55654 | 0.40764 |
| | $CF_3$ | 0.2 | 0.21260 | 0.32924 | 0.21318 |
| | $CF_4$ | 0.5 | 0.51674 | 0.59906 | 0.50652 |
| | $CF_5$ | 0.4 | 0.44066 | 0.56086 | 0.40826 |

According to Table 6, the obtained means of each parameter of the FPN by executing GA-SFLA algorithm are much better than that of GA and SFLA. Take a case as CF5, the expected value given by expert is 0.4, gained value by executing GA, SFLA and GA-SFLA is 0.44066, 0.56086 and 0.40826 based on 300 iterations. Hence, compared with GA and SFLA, the simulation results own higher precision by implementing GA-SFLA. It is further indicated that the FPN owns a stronger self-learning capability by using the GA-SFLA algorithm.

## 5  Conclusion

Focusing on the self-learning issue of FPN, a hybrid GA-SFLA algorithm has been presented in this paper to improve the precision of each parameter of the given FPN model. The proposed algorithm includes three steps: each chromosome in the initial population is generated by encoding the multi-dimensional solution which reflects all initial frogs at first. Then, the classical GA is used to gain a better individual. Finally, the local search and global search operations of SFLA are executed to obtain the optimal solution. A case study was used to illustrate advantages of the proposed algorithm by comparing the simulation results based on different algorithms. The results show that the FPN owns a stronger self-learning capability by using the GA-SFLA algorithm.

**Acknowledgement.** This work is supported by the National Natural Science Foundation of China (Nos. 61741205, 61462029).

# References

1. Paredes-Frigolett, H., Gomes, L.F.A.M.: A novel method for rule extraction in a knowledge-based innovation tutoring system. Knowl.-Based Syst. **92**, 183–199 (2016)
2. Nasiri, S., Zenkert, J., Fathi, M.: Improving CBR adaptation for recommendation of associated references in a knowledge-based learning assistant system. Neurocomputing **250**, 5–17 (2017)
3. Merone, M., Soda, P., Sansone, M., Sansone, C.: ECG databases for biometric systems: a systematic review. Expert Syst. Appl. **67**, 189–202 (2017)
4. Yusup, N., Zain, A.M., Hashim, S.Z.M.: Evolutionary techniques in optimizing machining parameters: review and recent applications (2007–2011). Expert Syst. Appl. **39**(10), 9909–9927 (2012)
5. Zain, A.M., Haron, H., Sharif, S.: Application of GA to optimize cutting conditions for minimizing surface roughness in end milling machining process. Expert Syst. Appl. **37**(6), 4650–4659 (2010)
6. Adnan, M.M., Sarkheyli, A., Zain, A.M., Haron, H.: Fuzzy logic for modeling machining process: a review. Artif. Intell. Rev. **43**(3), 345–379 (2013)
7. Zhou, K.Q., Mo, L.P., Jin, J., Zain, A.M.: An equivalent generating algorithm to model fuzzy Petri net for knowledge-based system. J. Intell. Manuf. **30**, 1831–1842 (2017)
8. Yeung, D.S., Wang, X.Z., Tsang, E.C.: Handling interaction in fuzzy production rule reasoning. IEEE Trans. Syst. Man Cybern. Part B (Cybern.) **34**(5), 1979–1987 (2004)
9. Spätgens, T., Schoonen, R.: The semantic network, lexical access, and reading comprehension in monolingual and bilingual children: an individual differences study. Appl. Psycholinguist. **39**(1), 225–256 (2018)
10. Ghimire, D., Jeong, S., Lee, J., Park, S.H.: Facial expression recognition based on local region specific features and support vector machines. Multimed. Tools Appl. **76**(6), 7803–7821 (2017)
11. Zhou, K.Q., Zain, A.M., Mo, L.P.: Dynamic properties of fuzzy Petri net model and related analysis. J. Central South Univ. **22**(12), 4717–4723 (2015)
12. Zhou, K.Q., Zain, A.M., Mo, L.P.: A decomposition algorithm of fuzzy Petri net using an index function and incidence matrix. Expert Syst. Appl. **42**(8), 3980–3990 (2015)
13. Zhou, K.Q., Gui, W.H., Mo, L.P., Zain, A.M.: A bidirectional diagnosis algorithm of fuzzy Petri net using inner-reasoning-path. Symmetry **10**, 192 (2018)
14. Zhou, K.Q., Zain, A.M.: Fuzzy Petri nets and industrial applications: a review. Artif. Intell. Rev. **45**(4), 405–446 (2016)
15. Liu, H.C., You, J.X., Li, Z., Tian, G.: Fuzzy Petri nets for knowledge representation and reasoning: a literature review. Eng. Appl. Artif. Intell. **60**, 45–56 (2017)
16. Shen, V.R., Chang, Y.S., Juang, T.T.Y.: Supervised and unsupervised learning by using Petri nets. IEEE Trans. Syst. Man Cybern.-Part A: Syst. Hum. **40**(2), 363–375 (2010)
17. Tsang, E.C., Yeung, D.S., Lee, J.W.: Learning capability in fuzzy Petri nets. In: IEEE SMC 1999 Conference Proceedings, vol. 3, pp. 355–360. IEEE (1999)
18. Wang, W.M., Peng, X., Zhu, G.N., Hu, J., Peng, Y.H.: Dynamic representation of fuzzy knowledge based on fuzzy petri net and genetic-particle swarm optimization. Expert Syst. Appl. **41**(4), 1369–1376 (2014)
19. Yeung, D.S., Tsang, E.C.: Weighted fuzzy production rules. Fuzzy Sets Syst. **88**(3), 299–313 (1997)
20. Tsang, E.C., Yeung, D.S., Lee, J.W., Huang, D.M., Wang, X.Z.: Refinement of generated fuzzy production rules by using a fuzzy neural network. IEEE Trans. Syst. Man Cybern. Part B (Cybern.) **34**(1), 409–418 (2004)

21. Ding, Z., Zhou, Y., Zhou, M.: Modeling self-adaptive software systems by fuzzy rules and Petri nets. IEEE Trans. Fuzzy Syst. **26**(2), 967–984 (2018)
22. Nabaei, A., et al.: Topologies and performance of intelligent algorithms: a comprehensive review. Artif. Intell. Rev. **49**(1), 79–103 (2018)
23. İnkaya, T., Akansel, M.: Coordinated scheduling of the transfer lots in an assembly-type supply chain: a genetic algorithm approach. J. Intell. Manuf. **28**(4), 1005–1015 (2017)
24. Morini, M., Pellegrino, S.: Personal income tax reforms: a genetic algorithm approach. Eur. J. Oper. Res. **264**(3), 994–1004 (2018)
25. Hou, Y., Wu, N., Zhou, M., Li, Z.: Pareto-optimization for scheduling of crude oil operations in refinery via genetic algorithm. IEEE Trans. Syst. Man Cybern.: Syst. **47**(3), 517–530 (2017)
26. Sarkheyli, A., Zain, A.M., Sharif, S.: The role of basic, modified and hybrid shuffled frog leaping algorithm on optimization problems: a review. Soft. Comput. **19**(7), 2011–2038 (2015)
27. Hasanien, H.M.: Shuffled frog leaping algorithm for photovoltaic model identification. IEEE Trans. Sustain. Energy **6**(2), 509–515 (2015)
28. Kawaria, N., Patidar, R., George, N.V.: Parameter estimation of MIMO bilinear systems using a Levy shuffled frog leaping algorithm. Soft. Comput. **21**(14), 3849–3858 (2017)
29. Dash, R.: Performance analysis of a higher order neural network with an improved shuffled frog leaping algorithm for currency exchange rate prediction. Appl. Soft Comput. **67**, 215–231 (2018)

# Joint Transmit Power Allocation and Power Splitting for SWIPT System with Time Reversal

Zuoliang Liu[1,2]([✉]) [iD] and Shanxue Chen[1,2]

[1] School of Communication and Information Engineering, Chongqing University of Posts and Telecommunications, Chongqing 400065, China
472741757@qq.com
[2] Chongqing Key Lab of Mobile Communications Technology, Chongqing 400065, China

**Abstract.** In the simultaneous wireless information and power transfer (SWIPT) system, time reversal (TR) is a special signal processing technology used to enhance the signal strength at the receiving end and improve the signal-to-noise ratio. In this paper, we study the joint transmit power allocation and power splitting algorithm for SWIPT system with TR. Considering a multi-input and single-output (MISO) SWIPT communication system, TR is introduced to construct a novel channel model, and the closed-form expression of energy efficiency (EE) is analyzed. An important problem is to maximize the energy efficiency by jointly transmit power allocation and power splitting, which is a two-element fractional non-convex problem. To solve it, we transform this problem to a convex optimization problem by a parametric method, and then solve it by one-dimensional search and CVX. Numerical results are provided to validate our proposed algorithm.

**Keywords:** Time reversal · Simultaneous wireless information and power transfer · Energy efficiency optimization

## 1 Introduction

With the development of energy revolution, the focus of people is no longer limited to oil, heat and so on, but for the renewable energy explored by advanced science and technology. The radio-frequency signals is a new renewable energy, which can be used to charge the device and send information synchronously, and thus it becomes one of the research hotspots in information transmission and security communication [1–3].

Simultaneous wireless information and power transfer (SWIPT) makes full use of these two characteristics of radio-frequency signals and attracts scholars' attention. The concept of SWIPT was first proposed by Varshney [4], who had made great progress in the entire communication industry. As data traffic grows and energy consumption increases, future wireless networks will pursue a communication method with higher energy efficiency [5–8]. However, most of the existing SWIPT literatures focus on the study of maximizing throughput, maximizing sum rate, and maximizing spectral efficiency [9–13], the maximization of energy efficiency (EE) got little attention. In the

H. Song et al. (Eds.): SIMUtools 2019, LNICST 295, pp. 427–436, 2019.
https://doi.org/10.1007/978-3-030-32216-8_41

case of satisfying the corresponding constraints, the maximization EE algorithm of SWIPT was studied only in broadcast channel, multiple access, relay network and wireless sensor network respectively [14–17]. Although these optimization algorithms improve the EE, it is limited by the signal strength of power splitter (PS) to some extent. The principle of time reversal (TR) is to use the spatio-temporal focusing effect generated by multipath propagation to enhance the signal strength at the receiving end, and simplify the receiver structure [18–20]. In [21], some researchers introduced TR into the SWIPT eavesdropping system, and proposed a new physical layer security transmission scheme, which greatly improved the transmission security of the system.

For the problem of maximizing EE in TR-SWIPT system, we consider to use TR to improve the achievable information rate and energy harvested firstly, and then propose an EE problem with transmit power allocation and power splitting. The objective function of the problem is a two-dimensional non-linear non-convex programming problem, which can be transformed into a linear convex optimization problem by the transformation of the objective function, and then the optimal solution is obtained by one-dimensional search and CVX. By means of numerical simulations, the effects of the signal-to-noise ratio (SNR), the number of antenna, the number of multipath, and the search accuracy on energy efficiency are analyzed, and the comparison of EE with other systems [1, 21] will be also discussed in the later.

The remainder of this paper is organized as following

- Section 2 to describe the system model and communication process of TR-SWIPT.
- Section 3 to present the problem planning and algorithm design.
- Section 4 to show numerical results, and Sect. 5 shows conclusion.

## 2   System Model

This section describes the specific communication process of the TR-SWIPT system, and analyzes the corresponding transmission signals and EE expressions.

Consider a point-to-point TR-SWIPT system with only one transmitter and one receiver, where the transmitter is equipped with M transmits antennas and the receiver is equipped with one antenna. For convenience, the PS adopts a separate structure and a dynamic power splitting mode, and the channel state information (CSI) of the system remains unchanged during the complete communication process. In addition, perfect CSI has been known to the system.

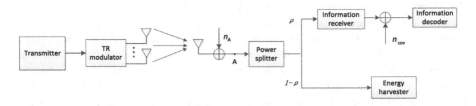

**Fig. 1.** TR-SWIPT system model

The system model of TR-SWIPT is shown in Fig. 1, and the communication process on the frequency selective fading channel can be divided into three steps, as shown below.

- Step 1. The information receiver or energy receiver in the PS transmits the sounding signal, and then the transmitter receives the sounding signal and analyzes the CSI.
- Step 2. The TR modulator modulates the signal according to the CSI, and then the transmitter transmits the modulated signal to the PS via multiple antennas.
- Step 3. The PS receives the transmitted signal, and then splits the received signal into two parts, one for the information decoder (ID), and the other for the energy harvester (EH). At this point, a completed communication process is implemented.

Based on the above communication process, we will first analyze the signal received at point A. Let $P$ represent the average transmit power of the antenna, and let $s$ $(E[|s|^2] = 1)$ denote the data symbol to be transmitted. Modeling a frequency selective fading channel into a linear tap delay model, $\boldsymbol{h}_m \in \mathbb{C}^L$ $(E[|h_m[l]|] = 0,$ $E[|h_m[l]|^2] = \sigma_{m,l}^2, l = 1, 2, \cdots, L$ is the number of multi-paths) denotes channel vector between the $m$th $(m = 1, 2, \cdots, M)$ transmission antenna and receiver, and antennas are independent of each other. Moreover, $\boldsymbol{n}_A$ is the additive white Gaussian noise introduced by the antenna with zero mean and variance $\sigma_A^2$, Thus the signal at point A is

$$y_A = \sqrt{P}s \sum_{m=1}^{M} \boldsymbol{h}_m * \boldsymbol{g}_m + \boldsymbol{n}_A \tag{1}$$

where $\boldsymbol{g}_m \in \mathbb{C}^L$ represents TR pre-modulated vector for the signal, and can be written as

$$g_m[l] = h_m^*[L+1-l] \left/ \sqrt{\sum_{m=1}^{M} \|\boldsymbol{h}_m\|^2} \right. \tag{2}$$

where $h_m^*[L+1-l]$ denotes the complex conjugation of $h_m[l]$, and $g_m[l]$ has been normalized.

As the signal is transmitted to point a, we can see from the literature [22] that for the signal transmitted after time-reversed modulation, the signal power is less lost during transmission, and most of the power is concentrated in the center tap. So, we only need to take the value of $L$ th tap to get the ideal signal power. Let $p_A$, $p_{ID}$ and $p_{EH}$ represent the power of received signal, the power of ID and the power of EH, respectively, as indicated in (3)–(5).

$$p_A = p_{\text{sig}} + \sigma_A^2 \tag{3}$$

$$p_{ID} = \rho p_A + \sigma_{cov}^2 = \rho \left( P \left| \sum_{m=1}^{M} g_m[L] * h_m[L] \right|^2 + \sigma_A^2 \right) + \sigma_{cov}^2 \tag{4}$$

$$p_{EH} = (1-\rho)p_A = (1-\rho) \left( P \left| \sum_{m=1}^{M} g_m[L] * h_m[L] \right|^2 + \sigma_A^2 \right) \tag{5}$$

where $p_{sig}$ denotes ideal signal power, and $\rho \in [0,1]$ represents power splitting. Moreover, conversion noise $n_{cov}$ ($E[|n_{cov}|] = 0$, $E[|n_{cov}|^2] = \sigma_{cov}^2$) is the additive noise introduced by the wireless signal to baseband signal conversion.

## 3   Problem Planning and Algorithm Design

In this section, we propose a two-element fractional non-convex problem with joint transmit power allocation and power splitting, and find optimal solution by a parametric method, one-dimensional search and CVX.

### 3.1   Problem Planning

Based on the TR-SWIPT system, we define SNR$(P, \rho)$, $R(P, \rho)$ and $Q(P, \rho)$, i.e. (6)–(8), as SNR, achievable information rate and harvested energy, respectively.

$$\text{SNR}(P, \rho) = \frac{\rho P_{sig}}{\rho \sigma_A^2 + \sigma_{cov}^2} = \frac{\rho P \left| \sum_{m=1}^{M} g_m[L] * h_m[L] \right|^2}{\rho \sigma_A^2 + \sigma_{cov}^2} \tag{6}$$

$$R(P, \rho) = B\log_2 \left( 1 + \left( \rho P \left| \sum_{m=1}^{M} g_m[L] * h_m[L] \right|^2 \right) \middle/ \left( \rho \sigma_A^2 + \sigma_{cov}^2 \right) \right) \tag{7}$$

$$Q(P, \rho) = \zeta(1 - \rho)(p_{sig} + \sigma_A^2) = \zeta(1 - \rho) \left( P \left| \sum_{m=1}^{M} g_m[L] * h_m[L] \right|^2 + \sigma_A^2 \right) \tag{8}$$

where $\zeta$ represents the conversion efficiency of energy which is not the focus of this article, and for the convenience of simulation we set $\zeta = 0.8$, namely linear energy conversion. B denotes the system bandwidth. Note that the above performance indicators are all within the unit time.

Then, assume the circuit power consumption of TR-SWIPT system is $P_C$. As we use the harvested energy as compensation for $P_C$, the total energy expense of entire system $Q_{total}(P, \rho)$ is derived as Eq. (9), and EE $\eta_e$ as Eq. (10).

$$Q_{total}(P, \rho) = P_C + P - Q(P, \rho) \tag{9}$$

$$\eta_e = \frac{R(P, \rho)}{Q_{total}(P, \rho)} \tag{10}$$

In Eq. (10), whether it is increasing $R(P, \rho)$ or reducing $Q_{total}(P, \rho)$ by the system, the EE can be increased. However, for practical reasons, the system can obtain a maximum EE only when constraint is satisfied. So, this problem P1 of EE can be formulated as

$$\max_{\rho, P} \eta_e = R(\rho, P)/Q_{total}(\rho, P) \tag{11}$$

$$\text{s.t. } R(\rho, P) \geq R_{min} \tag{11a}$$

$$Q(\rho, P) \geq Q_{min} \tag{11b}$$

$$0 \leq P \leq P_{max} \tag{11c}$$

$$0 \leq \rho \leq 1 \tag{11d}$$

where $R_{min}$ is the minimum achievable information rate requested data rate for the QoS, $P_{max}$ denotes the maximum transmit power for antenna, and $Q_{min}$ represents the minimum harvested energy.

## 3.2 Algorithm Design

After some mathematical analysis with Hessian matrix of Eq. (11), we can know that the P1 is a two-element fractional problem with joint transmit power allocation and power splitting, and a non-convex problem at the same time [23]. It is difficult to solve a non-convex problem, so we consider a parametric method as Eq. (12), as $F(\eta_e)$ is equal to zero, the optimal solution of Eq. (12) is also the optimal solution of problem P1, which is specifically proved in [23].

$$F(\eta_e) = \max_{\rho, P} \{R(\rho, P) - \eta_e^* Q_{total}(\rho, P)\} \tag{12}$$

where $\eta_e^*$ is the global optimal solution to the problem.

So, the problem P1 can be converted into the problem P2 through above analysis, as shown in the formula (13).

$$\max_{\rho, P} R(\rho, P) - \eta_e Q_{total}(\rho, P) \tag{13}$$

$$\text{s.t. } R(\rho, P) \geq R_{min} \tag{13a}$$

$$Q(\rho, P) \geq Q_{min} \tag{13b}$$

$$0 \leq P \leq P_{\max} \qquad (13c)$$

$$0 \leq \rho \leq 1 \qquad (13d)$$

Continue to analyze the problem P2, we find that the Hessian matrix of Eq. (13) is always less than or equal to 0 as Eq. (14). In other words, it means that the objective function of P2 is concavity, and the in-Eq. (13a) also is a concavity constraint by the same way. Moreover, Eqs. (13b), (13c) and (13d) are linear, that's to say, the problem P2 can be seen as a convex problem, and can be solved by any convex optimization methods. Based on the above analysis, the key point of solving the problem P2 is that the value of $\eta_e^*$ is not known, and fortunately the literature [24] proposes a method of solving the optimal value by iteratively updating $\eta_e$.

$$\partial^2 [R(\rho, P) - \eta_e Q_{\text{total}}(\rho, P)] / \partial P^2 \leq 0 \qquad (14)$$

CVX is a modeling system for constructing and solving convex optimization, so we build an optimization algorithm based on CVX and iteratively updating algorithm [24], the specific algorithm is shown in Table 1, where k is the search precision, and n represents the number of iterations.

**Table 1.**  EE algorithm

---

Optimization algorithm for EE

---

(1) System initialization, set $\eta_e = 0$ and $n = 1$, assume $\delta$ is a small enough positive number, and $S \in \mathbb{C}^{(1/k) \times 3}$ is a zero matrix.

(2) Loop $\rho = 0 : k : 1$

    If  The constraints of P2 are satisfied

        (a) Use CVX to find the optimal solution of $F(\eta_e)^{\#}$, $\rho^{\#}$ and $P^{\#}$,

        (b) Store the optimal solution of $F(\eta_e)^{\#}$, $\rho^{\#}$ and $P^{\#}$ in the $n$ th line of S.

    End if.    End loop.

(3) Search for the largest $F(\eta_e)$ in the first column of S, and get the corresponding $\rho_L$ and $P_L$.

(4) If $R(\rho_L, P_L) - \eta_e Q_{\text{total}}(\rho_L, P_L) \succ \delta$

    (a) Get $\eta_e = R(\rho_L, P_L) / Q_{\text{total}}(\rho_L, P_L)$,

    (b) Set $n = n+1$, and reset S to zero matrix. Then go back to step (2).

    Else

        Get the optimal solution and end algorithm.    End if.

---

# 4  Numerical Results

In this section, we numerically evaluate the performance of optimization algorithm for EE in link level simulation platform. The general simulation parameters are shown in Table 2.

**Table 2.** Simulation parameters

| Simulation parameters | Values |
|---|---|
| Channel bandwidth B | 10 MHz |
| Threshold of end $\delta$ | 0.001 |
| Circuit power consumption $P_C$ | 25 W |
| Minimum harvested energy $Q_{min}$ | 20 dBm |
| Delay spread | 14 μs |

In Fig. 2, we can observe that the performance of EE can achieve improvement at high SNR region for k = 0.01 compared to k = 0.1, k = 0.2 and k = 0.02, this is because the optimal solution may be hidden in the unsearched value of $\rho$. Therefore, the more comprehensive the search value k, the larger the value of EE. However, when the SNR is small, the search accuracy has little effect on EE. In addition, with the increase of SNR, $R(\rho, P)$ is more dominant than $Q_{total}(\rho, P)$, thus improving the EE of system.

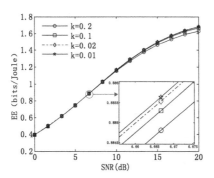

**Fig. 2.** Effect of SNR and search accuracy on EE when $R_{min}$ = 100 kbps, $P_{max}$ = 30 dBm, and $P_{cov}$ = −10 dBm

In Fig. 3, we change the antennas number M and multi-paths number L, and then calculate the value of EE correspondingly. As M and L increase, EE of the system increases also. From the formula analysis, when M and L increase, the ideal signal power $\sum_{m=1}^{M} g_m[L] * h_m[L]$ to be split is increasing, thereby further increasing the factor of system energy efficiency.

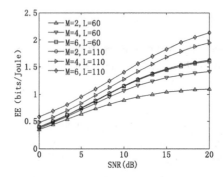

**Fig. 3.** Effect of antennas number and multi-paths number on EE when $R_{min}$ = 120 kbps, $k$ = 0.1, $P_{max}$ = 30 dBm, and $P_{cov}$ = −20 dBm

In Fig. 4, we compare the EE performance with three systems, namely conventional SWIPT system [1], non-optimized TR-SWIPT system [21] and optimized TR-SWIPT system. In more detail, as in the lower SNR, the ideal signal power is equal to the noise power, so the constraint of problem P2 is not satisfied, resulting the energy efficiency is zero. Furthermore, when problem P2 is feasible, the EE performance is better than the other two systems. It is worth noting that no matter how the SNR changes, the non-optimized TR-SWIPT system is always superior to conventional SWIPT, which indicating that the TR itself has good optimization performance.

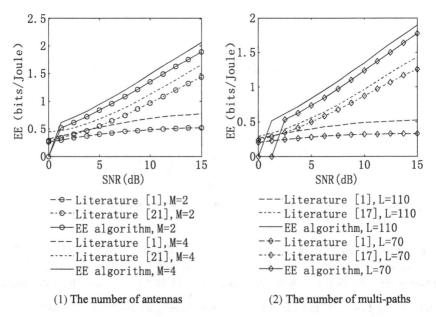

(1) The number of antennas        (2) The number of multi-paths

**Fig. 4.** Comparison of EE of different transmission schemes when $R_{min}$ = 120 kbps, k = 0.1, $P_{max}$ = 30 dBm, and $P_{cov}$ = −20 dBm

# 5    Conclusion

This paper considers a point-to-point transmission communication system of broadband TR-SWIPT. Firstly, the specific communication process is analyzed in frequency selective fading channel, then, the mathematical model of TR-SWIPT system is established and the EE expression is also derived, finally, a non-convex fraction of maximize EE is converted into convex by function transformation and an EE optimization algorithm by jointly transmit power allocation and power splitting is proposed. From the simulation results, some conclusions can be drawn as below

(1)    The value of EE will increase as the SNR, number of antennas, and number of multi-paths increase.
(2)    In the higher SNR area, the search accuracy has a greater impact on energy efficiency.
(3)    TR can improve the EE of SWIPT, therefore, the optimization algorithm proposed in this paper performs better than conventional SWIPT.

# References

1. Zhou, X., Zhang, R., Ho, C.K.: Wireless information and power transfer: architecture design and rate-energy tradeoff. IEEE Trans. Commun. **61**(11), 4754–4767 (2013)
2. Khandaker, M.R.A., Wong, K.K.: SWIPT in MISO multicasting systems. IEEE Wirel. Commun. Lett. **3**(3), 277–280 (2014)
3. Wu, D., Si, S., Wu, S., Wang, R.: Dynamic trust relationships aware data privacy protection in mobile crowd-sensing. IEEE Internet Things J. **5**, 2958–2970 (2017)
4. Arshney, L.R.: Transporting information and energy simultaneously. In: IEEE International Symposium on Information Theory, Toronto, ON, Canada, pp. 1612–1616. IEEE, July 2008
5. Sun, Q., Li, L., Mao, J.: Simultaneous information and power transfer scheme for energy efficient MIMO systems. IEEE Commun. Lett. **18**(4), 600–603 (2014)
6. Jiang, D., Zhang, P., Lv, Z., et al.: Energy-efficient multi-constraint routing algorithm with load balancing for smart city applications. IEEE Internet Things J. **3**(6), 1437–1447 (2016)
7. Jiang, D., Xu, Z., Li, W., et al.: An energy-efficient multicast algorithm with maximum network throughput in multi-hop wireless networks. J. Commun. Netw. **18**(5), 713–724 (2016)
8. Jiang, D., Li, W., Lv, H.: An energy-efficient cooperative multicast routing in multi-hop wireless networks for smart medical applications. Neurocomputing **220**(2017), 160–169 (2017)
9. Claessens, S., Rajabi, M., Pan, N., Pollin, S., Schreurs, D.: Measurement-based analysis of the throughput-power level trade-off with modulated multisine signals in a SWIPT system. In: 89th ARFTG Microwave Measurement Conference, Honolulu, HI, USA, pp. 1–4. IEEE, June 2017
10. Ma, L., Wang, Y., Xu, Y.: Sum rate optimization for SWIPT system based on zero-forcing beamforming and time switching. In: 13th International Wireless Communications and Mobile Computing Conference, Valencia, Spain, pp. 351–356. IEEE, June 2017
11. Sun, J., Zhang, W., Sun, J., Wang, C., Chen, Y.: Energy-spectral efficiency in simultaneous wireless information and power transfer. In: IEEE/CIC International Conference on Communications, Chengdu, China, pp. 1–6. IEEE, July 2016

12. Jiang, D., Xu, Z., Liu, J., et al.: An optimization-based robust routing algorithm to energy-efficient networks for cloud computing. Telecommun. Syst. **63**(1), 89–98 (2016)
13. Jiang, D., Wang, Y., Han, Y., et al.: Maximum connectivity-based channel allocation algorithm in cognitive wireless networks for medical applications. Neurocomputing **220**, 41–51 (2017)
14. Tang, J., So, D.K.C., Zhao, N., Shojaeifard, A., Wong, K.: Energy efficiency optimization with SWIPT in MIMO broadcast channels for internet of things. IEEE Internet Things J. **5**(4), 2605–2619 (2018)
15. Zewde, T.A., Gursoy, M.C.: Energy-efficient resource allocation for SWIPT in multiple access channels. In: Annual Conference on Information Science and Systems, Princeton, NJ, USA, pp. 246–251. IEEE, March 2016
16. Zhou, X., Li, Q.: Energy efficiency optimisation for SWIPT AF two-way relay networks. Electron. Lett. **53**(6), 436–438 (2017)
17. Guo, S., Shi, Y., Yang, Y., Xiao, B.: Energy efficiency maximization in mobile wireless energy harvesting sensor networks. IEEE Trans. Mob. Comput. **17**(7), 1524–1537 (2017)
18. Wang, B., Wu, Y., Han, F., Yang, Y., Ray Liu, K.J.: Green wireless communications: a time-reversal paradigm. IEEE J. Sel. Areas Commun. **29**(8), 1698–1710 (2011)
19. Bouzigues, M.A., Siaud, I., Helard, M.: Turn back the clock: time reversal for green radio communications. IEEE Veh. Technol. Mag. **8**(1), 49–56 (2013)
20. Chen, Y., et al.: Time-reversal wireless paradigm for green internet of things: an overview. IEEE Internet Things J. **1**(1), 81–98 (2014)
21. Chen, Y., et al.: Time reversal SWIPT networks with an active eavesdropper: SER-energy region analysis. In: IEEE 84th Vehicular Technology Conference, Montreal, QC, Canada, pp. 1–5. IEEE, February 2016
22. Han, F., Yang, Y.H., Wang, B., Wu, Y., Ray Liu, K.J.: Time-reversal division multiple access in multi-path channels. In: Global Tele Communications Conference, Kathmandu, Nepal, pp. 1–5. IEEE, December 2011
23. Dinekebach, W.: On nonlinear fractional programming. Manag. Sci. **13**(7), 492–498 (1967)
24. Zhang, C., Zhao, H., Li, W., Zheng, K., Yang, J.: Energy efficiency optimization of simultaneous wireless information and power transfer system with power splitting receiver. In: Personal, Indoor, and Mobile Radio Communication, Washington, DC, USA, pp. 2135–2139. IEEE, June 2014

# Development of an Effective Method of Tariff Formation for Rural Areas: The Case of Russian Federation

João Paulo Pereira[1]([⊠]) [iD], Daria Zamotajlova[2] [iD], and Elena Popova[2] [iD]

[1] Polytechnic Institute of Bragança, Campus de Santa Apolónia, 5300-302 Bragança, Portugal
jprp@ipb.pt
[2] Kuban State Agrarian University, 13 Kalinina Street, 350044 Krasnodar, Russian Federation
idalia@mail.ru, elena-popov@yandex.ru

**Abstract.** The conducted researches have shown that the features of the housing and communal sector do not allow talking about the possibility of calculating the "optimal" tariff rate. Also in the current conditions in Russia, tariff methods that are successfully used abroad (for example, the method of reinvested capital) cannot be used. The correct approach to housing and communal tariff formation is the calculation of compromise tariffs, the size of which takes into account the interests of consumers of services, resource-supply organizations, public authorities and investors. Development of an effective method of tariff formation for rural areas is particularly acute. The correct approach to housing and communal tariff formation is the calculation of compromise tariffs, the size of which takes into account the interests of services' consumers, resource-supply organizations, public authorities and investors. Compromise approach for tariffs' formation can also become an effective instrument not only in Russia: it can be applied in countries where it is sufficient to calculate housing and communal services' social demand and its budget coverage (e.g. because of the increasing number of migrants).

**Keywords:** Housing and communal complex · Method of tariff formation · Compromise prices and tariffs · Social demand · Rural areas

## 1 Introduction

The issue of developing an effective methodology for tariff formation becomes important for rural areas, whose housing and communal complex is currently in the worst condition, according to experts, compared to the national average [1–3]. Due to the fact that ensuring the effective functioning of the agro-industrial complex is one of the highest priorities, methodological support of its activities (including the creation and maintenance of a sustainable housing and communal system) is of particular importance. It is also necessary to develop an effective algorithm that can be used to provide subsidies to the population and agro-industrial enterprises.

© ICST Institute for Computer Sciences, Social Informatics and Telecommunications Engineering 2019
Published by Springer Nature Switzerland AG 2019. All Rights Reserved
H. Song et al. (Eds.): SIMUtools 2019, LNICST 295, pp. 437–447, 2019.
https://doi.org/10.1007/978-3-030-32216-8_42

The use of the proposed methodology in the process of reorganization of the housing and communal complex of rural areas will form a basis for its further development. It must be noted that the housing and communal complex of rural areas is not only life-supporting for the population, but also is the basis for the functioning of agro-industrial enterprises.

The authors expect a further study on this topic, the main direction of which will be the finalization of the methodology, taking into account the emerging requirements for resource conservation.

## 2  Socio-Market Compromises

The compromise price modeling is very effective in different spheres [4–6]. Let us consider the mathematical model of the social and market compromise in the market of housing and communal services of Russian Federation.

Let $N$ be the number of final consumers of the goods (for example, social groups of the population) that can be ranked by the amount of money $d$ that they can allocate for the purchase of a certain product (service):

$$d_1 > d_2 > \ldots > d_k > \ldots > d_N. \tag{1}$$

$Y_{Hk}$ is the minimum necessary rate of consumption of goods by one $k$-th consumer. In the case of a complex of goods, $Y_{Hk} = 1$.

At the price of the goods in the market $P^Y = P$, can delineate all final consumers of the goods (services) to solvent and insolvent. Those consumers for whom the minimum necessary amount of consumption of the goods (services) will be less than or equal to the amount of money that they are able to allocate for their acquisition ($Y_{Hk}P \le d_k$), will be solvent. The number of both types of consumers is determined by the level of a fixed price.

Consumers can be considered as solvent if:

$$d_k \ge PY_{Hk}, k = 1, 2, \ldots, N_1(P). \tag{2}$$

Insolvent are customers for whom:

$$d_k \le PY_{Hk}, k = N_1(P) + 1, \ldots N. \tag{3}$$

The total amount of the regulatory requirement of all insolvent consumers of the goods is determined:

$$\widehat{Y}(P) = \sum_{k=N_1(P)+1}^{N} Y_{Hk}, \tag{4}$$

as well as the total amount of payment means available to consumers on the market of the goods:

$$D_2(P) = \sum_{k=N_1(P)+1}^{N} d_k \tag{5}$$

With a fixed price $P$, it is possible to determine solvent consumers as a set $N_1$; consumers are ready to present their bankroll in the volume of $D_1(P) = \sum_{k=1}^{N_1} d_k$ on the services market. Insolvent consumers enter into the aggregate $(N - N_1)$ and are ready to present their bankroll in the market of services in the amount of $D_2(P)$ Solvent and insolvent consumers will present their bankroll in the following amount:

$$D' = \sum_{k=1}^{N} d_k. \tag{6}$$

Payment means and fixed compromise prices of the consumer market uniquely determine the means of payment and the prices of the general commodity market: $P^{\hat{X}} = P^{\hat{X}}(P)$.

In the commodity sector of the product (service) there are $m$ enterprises that produce and sell goods (provide services) under various conditions and determine their production and economic parameters.

At a fixed price of goods (services) in the market $P^{\hat{X}}$, we can determine the values of $I_l$:

$$I_l = \left(P^{\hat{X}} - c_l\right)\bar{X}_l - D_{Hl}, \tag{7}$$

where $D_{Hl} = (3_{0l} + \mu J_l)(1 + \rho)$,

where $\rho$ – the part of payments to budgets of all levels; $3_{0l} + \mu J_l$ – normative marginal income of the enterprise.

Then $I_l$ is the excess income of the enterprise. Thus, the enterprises present in this economic sector and selling a specific product (providing a specific service) can be ranked in descending order $I_l$:

$$I_1 > I_2 > \ldots > I_l > \ldots I_m. \tag{8}$$

At a price $P$, those enterprises whose excess income will be different from zero $(I_l \geq 0)$ can be considered as competitive.

The fixed price $P$ also delineates all the enterprises present in the industry to competitive and uncompetitive. The quantity of both of them is regulated by the price level.

The enterprises can be considered as competitive if:

$$(P^{\hat{X}} - c_l)\hat{X}_l - D_{Hl} = I_l \geq 0, l = 1, 2, \ldots, m_l(P). \tag{9}$$

Uncompetitive are those enterprises for which:

$$(P^{\hat{X}} - c_l)\hat{X}_l - D_{Hl} = I_l < 0, l = m_l(P) + 1, \ldots, m. \tag{10}$$

The aggregate competitive producer at a fixed price $P$ is defined as the set $m_1$ that has the following parameters:

$$c^1 = \sum_{l=1}^{m_1(P)} \frac{c_l}{m_l(P)}; \ 3_0^l = \sum_{l=1}^{m_1(P)} 3_{0l};$$

$$J^l = \sum_{l=1}^{m_1(P)} J_l; \bar{X}^l = \sum_{l=1}^{m_1(P)} \bar{X}_l;$$

$$D_H^l = (3_0^l + \mu J^l)(1 + \rho). \tag{11}$$

A set of uncompetitive producers at a price $P$ can be defined as a cumulative uncompetitive producer with the following production and economic parameters:

$$c^2 = \sum_{l=m_l+1}^{m} \frac{c_l}{m_2}; \ 3_0^2 = \sum_{l=m_l+1}^{m} 3_{0l};$$

$$J^2 = \sum_{l=m_l+1}^{m} J_l; \bar{X}^2 = \sum_{l=m_l+1}^{m} \bar{X}_l;$$

$$D_H^2 = (3_0^2 + \mu J^2)(1 + \rho). \tag{12}$$

The market, generally "recognizes" only a solvent buyer and a competitive seller. At the same time, insolvent consumers are partially solvent and will bring their money $D_2(P)$ to the market. So the total amount of payment means will be equal to $D' = \sum_{k=1}^{N} d_k.$

Therefore, the model of a market-based trade-off between aggregate demand and aggregate supply in the consumer market will be as follows:

$$P^{XY} = P^*(P) = max\left\{ \arg max_P \left( \frac{D'}{P} - \frac{D_H(P)}{P - c(P)}; \frac{D'}{\bar{Y}^1(P)} \right) \right\}. \tag{13}$$

Here $D_H(P)$ is the minimum margin income of the aggregate competitive seller at the price $P$ of the consumer market; $c(P) = P^{\hat{X}}(P) + 3$ – the average cost of sold goods per unit; $\bar{Y}^l(P) = (E - \hat{A})\hat{X}^l(P); \hat{A}(P)$ is the matrix of average coefficients of labor costs for competitive enterprises.

If it turns out that $N_1(P^*) < N$, then this will mean that $D_2(P^*) > 0$ and $\hat{Y}(P^*) - \frac{D_2(P^*)}{P^*} = Y_S > 0$, where $Y_S$ is the social demand for the goods of insolvent consumers, which is also called non-marketable. The total volume of market and non-market demand will be:

$$Y_F(P^*) = Y^*(P^*) + Y_S(P^*) = \frac{D_1(P^*)}{P^*} + \widehat{Y}(P^*). \tag{14}$$

Coverage of social demand is possible only due to state regulation. The necessary budgetary allocations used to cover this demand can be defined as follows.

From the formula (15) it is possible to receive the sum of necessary payment means in the consumer market in that situation when the compromise volume of purchase and sale will make $Y^0 = Y_F(P^*)$:

$$D = D_H \frac{\left(1 + \sqrt{1 + 4\frac{Y^0 c}{D_H}}\right)^2}{4}; \tag{15}$$

$$D(P^*) = D_H^1 \frac{1}{4} \left(1 + \sqrt{1 + 4\frac{Y_{all}(P^*)c(P^*)}{D_H^1}}\right)^2. \tag{16}$$

In this case, the amount needed to finance from the budget to cover social demand for services will be:

$$\Delta D = D(P^*) - D'. \tag{17}$$

It is obvious that state subsidies allocated to consumers from budgets of different levels to cover social demand can violate the compromise equilibrium that has developed in the market. In case when consumers present $D(P^*)$ payment means on the market, that is, they will provide demand in the amount of $Y_F(P^*)$ at the price of $P^*$, it may exceed the supply of the product due to limitations in the production capacities of enterprises which are competitive, and also because of the unfavorable fixed $P^*$ for uncompetitive enterprises.

In case of occurrence of similar situations, the government should restore the broken balance by introducing in action various levers of state regulation (for example, budgetary and tax).

Let us consider possible situations.

If $Y_F(P^*) \leq \bar{Y}^1(P^*)$, then competitive enterprises at a fixed price $P^*$ can cover social demand by using production facilities more fully. In this situation, enterprises can increase their marginal revenue by increasing the total number of provided services, which is beneficial to them. The government in this case will not conduct any additional procedures for regulation in the housing and communal sector.

If $Y_F(P^*) > \bar{Y}^1(P^*)$, the government should involve in the production-market process the capacities of uncompetitive enterprises at the price of $P^*$.

In this situation, two scenarios are possible.

1. $Y_F(P^*) - \bar{Y}^1(P^*) \leq \bar{Y}^2(P^*)$.

   In this case, in order to cover the consumers' need for services, the government will be sufficient to attract uncompetitive enterprises with fixed price $P^*$ into the industry. With the help of direct subsidies, the government will be able to increase the attractiveness of the industry for previously uncompetitive enterprises, covering their current costs or providing tax incentives. The volume of additional production in this case will be:

$$Y_F(P^*) - \bar{Y}^1(P^*) = \Delta Y(P^*). \tag{18}$$

Let us denote the amount of direct government subsidies through $\Delta 3$, and the amount of tax benefits through $\Delta \rho$ ($0 < \Delta \rho < \rho$); in this case it is possible to obtain a condition under which uncompetitive enterprises can make a profit in the production of goods and services in the amount of $\Delta Y$:

$$(P^{*\hat{x}} - c^2)\Delta Y + \Delta 3 = (1 + \rho - \Delta \rho)(3_0^2 + \mu J^2). \tag{19}$$

$$\Delta Y(P^*) = \frac{(1+\rho-\Delta\rho)(3_0^2+\mu J^2)-\Delta 3}{P^{*\hat{x}}-c^2}. \tag{20}$$

Equating (18) and (20), taking into account (14) we obtain:

$$Y_F - \bar{Y}_1 = \frac{D_1(P^*)}{P^*} + \hat{Y}P^* - \bar{Y}_1 = \frac{(1+\rho-\Delta\rho)(3_0^2+\mu J^2)-\Delta 3}{P^{*\hat{x}}-c^2}. \tag{21}$$

$$\Delta 3 + \Delta\rho 302 + \mu J 2 = 1 + \rho 302 P^* + \mu J 2 P^* - P^* X - c2 P^* D 1 P^* P^* X + Y P^* - Y 1(P^*). \tag{22}$$

Expression (22) allows to determine the amount of budgetary funds necessary to equalize the trade-offs of supply and demand at a fixed price $P^*$. The total amount of public funds needed to establish a social and market compromise will be:

$$\Delta D + \Delta 3 + \Delta\rho(3_0^2 + \mu J^2) = \left( D(P^*) - D' + +(1 + \rho)(3_0^2(P^*) + +\mu J^2(P^*)) \right) - (P^{*\hat{x}} - c^2(P^*)) \left[ \frac{D_1(P^*)}{P^{*\hat{x}}} + \hat{Y}(P^*) - \bar{Y}^1(P^*) \right]. \tag{23}$$

2. $\Delta Y_F(P^*) - \bar{Y}^1(P^*) > \bar{Y}^2(P^*)$.

In this situation, it is required to create new production capacities that will help to satisfy demand in the following volume:

$$\Delta \tilde{Y} = Y_F - \bar{Y}^1 - \bar{Y}^2. \tag{24}$$

Then, in addition to the amount of funds calculated with the help of formula (23), governmental appropriations or (and) preferential credits are needed to create these capacities in a particular sphere.

From formula (13) it is obvious that finding the parameters of the social-market compromise by determining the compromise price $P^*$ requires an iterative procedure of calculations with the replacement of $D'$ by $D(P^*)$ from formula (16). In addition, different procedures are needed in order to harmonize the compromise parameters of the commodity and consumer markets.

In this case the following calculation scheme can be proposed:

1. The decision process begins with a price of the consumer market $P_0$ for $D = D'$. At step $k$, using market matching procedures and solving the problem (4), we obtain the prices $P_k^*$ and $P_k^{*\bar{X}}$;
2. Using formulas (9–11) with the price $P_k^{*\bar{X}}$, we determine the parameters of aggregate competitive and uncompetitive producers;
3. By the formula (14) we define $Y_F\left(P_k^*\right)$.
4. By the formula (16) we find $D\left(P_k^*\right)$.
5. By the model (13), we determine $P_{k+1}^*\left(P_k^*\right)$ for $D' = D\left(P_k^*\right)$ and the parameters from step 2.
6. If $P_{k+1}^* \neq P_k^*$, then go back to step 2. If $P_{k+1}^* = P_k^* = P^*$, then go to step 7.
7. By formulas (17), (22) and (23), the amounts of budgetary funds necessary for social and market regulation of the final consumer of the goods are calculated. Proceed to step 8.
8. End of calculations; results' analysis.

It is obvious that the government is limited in means of socio-economic regulation [7, 8]. In this regard, the general task of regulating final consumption should be formulated as the task of achieving maximum social effect with limited means.

If the government has a total amount of funds $\Delta D_G$ to ensure the social (non-market) demand in accordance with established consumption norms, the criterion for optimality of funds' distribution $\Delta D_G$ can be the minimum of the sum of squares of deviations in purchases of goods by insolvent consumers at compromise prices of the consumer market $\left\{P_j^*\right\}_{j=1}^n$ from the volume of needs according to the established norms of consumption, taking into account the relative weights of consumer's goods values.

If in all commodity sectors can be obtained data for determining the parameters of aggregate solvent and insolvent consumers and parameters of aggregate competitive and uncompetitive producers at each price level $P_j$, $j = 1, 2, ..., n$, then the compromise price of the consumer market $P_j^*$ and the sum of state subsidies to consumers $\Delta D_j$ can uniquely determine the amount of initially insolvent consumers' purchases:

$$Y_{2j}\left(P_j^*, \Delta D_j\right) = \frac{D_{2j}\left(P_j^*\right) + \Delta D_j}{P_j^*} = \frac{\left(D_{2j} + \Delta D_j\right)\left(D_j - D_{Hj}\right)}{c_j\left(D_j + \sqrt{D_j D_{Hj}}\right)}, \tag{25}$$

where $D_j = D_{1j}\left(P_j^*\right) + D_{2j}\left(P_j^*\right) + \Delta D_j$ is the amount of money from buyers on the market of the $j$-th product, taking into account state subsidies; $Y_{2j}$ for fixed $P_j^*$ is defined as a function of $\Delta D_j$; $\hat{Y}_j\left(P_j^*\right)$ is determined for a fixed price $P_j^*$ in the form of constants.

The necessary subsidies for producers in all product segments are determined according to (18, 20, 22) as follows.

In those commodity segments for which there are not enough reserve capacities of competitive producers, the following condition will be fulfilled:

$$Y_j^*\left(P_j^*\right) > \bar{Y}_j^1 \text{ or } \Delta Y_j = Y_j^*\left(P_j^*\right) - \bar{Y}_j^1\left(P_j^*\right) > 0. \tag{26}$$

In this case, in order to involve capacities in the turnover through governmental regulation, the following condition must be fulfilled:

$$\left(P^{*\hat{X}} - c_j^2\right)\Delta Y_j + \Delta 3_j = (1 + \rho + \Delta\rho)D_{jH}^2. \tag{27}$$

Or:

$$\Delta Y_j = \frac{(1+\rho+\Delta\rho)D_{jH}^2 - \Delta 3_j}{\left(P^{*\hat{X}} - c_j^2\right)}. \tag{28}$$

Equating (26) and (28) and solving the equation for the necessary sums of state financing of competitive enterprises, we get:

$$\Delta 3_j + \Delta\rho D_{jH}^2(P_j^*) = (1 + \rho)D_{jH}^2 - \left(P^{*\hat{X}} - c_j^2(P_j^*) - \bar{Y}_j^1(P_j^*)\right). \tag{29}$$

Then we can define the general problem of final production market's regulation:

$$\begin{aligned}
&\min_{\{\Delta D_j\}} \sum_{j=1}^{n} b_j^2 \left[Y_{2j}\left(P_j^*, \Delta D_j\right) - \hat{Y}P_j^*\right]^2 \\
&= \min_{\{\Delta D_j\}} \sum_{j=1}^{n} b_j^2 \left[\frac{\left(D_{2j}(P_j^*) + \Delta D_j\right)\left(D_j(P_j^*) - D_{Hj}^1(P_j^*)\right)}{c_j^2(P_j^*)\left(D_j(P_j^*) + \sqrt{D_j(P_j^*)D_{Hj}^1(D_{Hj}^1)}\right)} - \hat{Y}\left(P_j^*\right)\right]^2
\end{aligned} \tag{30}$$

under conditions:

$$\sum_{j=1}^{n}\left[(1-\rho)D_{jH}^2\left(P_j^*\right) - \left[P^{*\hat{X}} - c_j^2\left(P_j^*\right)\left(Y_j^*\left(P_j^*\right)\right)\right] + \Delta D_j\right] = D_{gov}; \tag{31}$$

$$\Delta D_j \geq 0, j = 1, 2, \ldots, n.$$

The problem (31) is similar in structure to the following problem:

$$\sum_{i=1}^{n} b_i^2 \left( \frac{D_i(D_i - D_{iH})}{c_j \left( D_i + \sqrt{D_{iH} D_i} \right)} - Y_i^0 \right)^2 = min \tag{32}$$

under conditions:

$$\sum_{i=1}^{b} D_i = \bar{D},$$

$$D_i \geq D_{iH}, i = 1, 2, \ldots, n.$$

However, its specific character lies in the dependence of its parameters on the compromise prices $\left\{ P_j^* \right\}$.

## 3 Modeling of Compromise Tariffs for Housing and Communal Services

The authors developed a methodology for compromise tariff formation in the housing and communal sector [9], which is based on the principles of social and market compromise (Fig. 1).

Based on this methodology, it is planned to develop a decision support system, which will be used both at housing and communal enterprises. At housing enterprises, the proposed decision support system is designed to automate the following functions: ranking of consumers of services; ranking of service providers; searching for the most suitable to each other consumer and service provider; calculation of the trade-off tariff for the service; analysis of the received tariff.

In connection with the fact that the legislation in Russia establishes the right of homeowners to independently set the rates for housing services (taking into account the proposals of housing organizations), the developed methodology can be fully used by housing enterprises, in homeowners' associations and managing organizations.

The size of communal services' tariffs is set at the regional level; that's why it is impossible to fully use the proposed methodology at communal enterprises. However the decision support system can automate the following functions: ranking of services' consumers; ranking of services' providers; searching of the most suitable to each other consumer and service provider.

Also the decision support system, based on the developed methodology of compromise tariff formation can be used by government. At this level it is expedient to automate all the stages of the methodology within the framework of the subsystem; in this case the stages of determining social demand and calculating the amount of subsidies for each group of consumers should be given special attention.

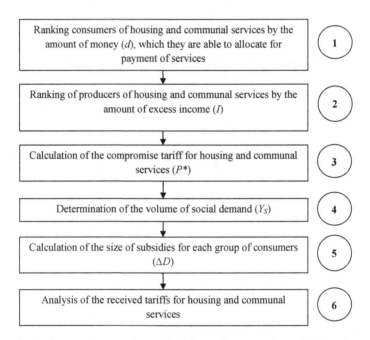

**Fig. 1.** Stages of a complex methodology of compromise tariff formation

The results of compromise tariffs' intermediate calculations are given in Table 1.

**Table 1.** Results of tariff's recalculation

| Type of service | Cost price, rub. | Current rate, rub. | Rate of return, rub. | Buyer's max bankroll, rub. | Compromise tariff, rub. |
|---|---|---|---|---|---|
| Cold water | 13,6 | 21,14 | 2,2 | 21,0 | 20,11 |
| Sewerage | 7,44 | 12,47 | 1,5 | 12,0 | 11,51 |
| Hot water | 92,36 | 132,2 | 10,5 | 130,0 | 129,03 |
| Heating | 1296,34 | 1507,04 | 28,5 | 1505,0 | 1503,2 |
| Garbage removal | 0,4 | 1,71 | 0,7 | 1,5 | 1,26 |

## 4   Conclusion

The implementation of the developed methodology and the proposed decision support system into the work of the housing and communal services industry as well as the application of the developed methodological recommendations, will help to achieve the following results: release of additional funds for the modernization of the housing and communal services; improving the quality of provided housing and communal services;

increasing the investment attractiveness of the sector; general improvement of the social and economic situation in Russia.

The developed methodology of compromise tariff formation can be successfully applied not only in Russia, but also in countries where the calculation of the social demand and the size of the budgetary subsidies necessary for its coverage is needed.

Necessity in such technique can arise, for example, in countries with a large number of migrants, who are using various subsidies. The application of the methods and tools proposed by the authors will allow to substantially rationalize the calculation process of both tariffs for housing and communal services and the size of subsidies.

The developed methodology if necessary can be adapted for use in industries where social demand for goods and services should be taken into account and here it is also necessary to determine the amount of possible subsidies.

# References

1. Jukic, B., Jukic, N., Parameswaran, M.: Data models for information sharing in e-partnerships: analysis, improvements, and relevance. J. Organ. Comput. Electron. Commer. **12**, 175–195 (2002)
2. Lummi, K., Rautiainen, A.: Development options and impacts of distribution tariff structures. Tampere University of Technology, Filand, p. 65 (2017)
3. Zamotajlova, D., Kurnosova, N., Reznikov, V.: Methodological approaches to estimation of management organizations' efficiency of activity in housing and communal sphere. Kuban State Agrarian University (2017)
4. Chan, H.K., Chan, F.T.S.: Effect of information sharing in supply chains with flexibility. Int. J. Prod. Res. **47**, 213–232 (2009)
5. Davcik, N.S., Piyush, S.: Impact of product differentiation, marketing investments and brand equity on pricing strategies: a brand level investigation. Eur. J. Mark. **49**, 760–781 (2015)
6. Alcalde, J., Peris, J.E.: Sharing costs and the compromise solution. University of Alicante, D. Quantitative Methods and Economic Theory (2017)
7. Ryahovskaya, A.: Government regulation of the economy in crisis. Scientific works of the Free Economic Society of Russia (2016)
8. Kardash, V.A.: Conflicts and Trade-Offs in a Market Economy. Nauka, Moscow (2006)
9. Zamotajlova, D., Popova, E., Gorkavoy, P., Nedogonova, T.: Compromise tariff formation as one of the bases of development of the housing and communal complex of rural areas. Kuban State Agrarian University (2018)

# Study the Preprocessing Effect on RNN Based Online Uyghur Handwriting Word Recognition

Wujiahemaiti Simayi, Mayire Ibrayim, and Askar Hamdulla[✉]

Institute of Information Science and Engineering,
Xinjiang University, Urumqi, China
askar@xju.edu.cn

**Abstract.** There is little work done on unconstrained handwritten Uyghur word recognition by implementing deep neural networks. This paper carries out a comparative study to see the preprocessing effect on training a neural network based online handwriting Uyghur word recognition system. Bidirectional recurrent neural network with connectionist temporal classification is implemented for unconstrained handwriting word recognition experiments on a dataset of 23400 Uyghur word samples. The results are directly obtained from model output without any lexicon or language model. Experiments showed that proper preprocessing can improve the training speed very effectively. The comparative study conducted in this paper can be good reference for later studies.

**Keywords:** Online handwriting recognition · Preprocessing · Input representation · Recurrent neural networks · Connectionist temporal classification · Uyghur words

## 1 Introduction

Online handwriting recognition is conducted on the traced pen-tip movement trajectory information [1]. The first-hand online handwritten samples are usually coarse trajectories that need proper preprocessing. Although, deep neural networks have been showing their strength to learn from raw input [2], good preprocessing can alleviate the need for very large number training data and improve model generalization [3]. Shortening the handwritten trajectory is helpful to speed up network training at least. This paper conducts comparative experiments to see the effect of preprocessing on model training process on Uyghur online handwritten word samples, based on recurrent neural network and connectionist temporal classification-CTC [7].

Uyghur is a typical alphabetic script which of 32 basic character/letter types. Each character type has several specific character forms which are selectively used based on the character position within a word. There are 128 character forms in Uyghur alphabet. Most handwriting word recognition studies so far have been being conducted using a holistic approach or with help of certain lexicon [4]. The applied model in this paper

H. Song et al. (Eds.): SIMUtools 2019, LNICST 295, pp. 448–458, 2019.
https://doi.org/10.1007/978-3-030-32216-8_43

maps handwritten word trajectory into string of characters in Uyghur alphabet directly without external lexicon help.

Study on Artificial intelligent systems has been gaining more and more attention in many fields [11, 12]. The handwriting word recognition experiments in this paper will be a reference for later study and development of intelligent systems in this field, too. The remainder of this paper is organized as follows. Section 2 introduces the performed preprocessing methods in detail. Section 3 describes the applied model for online handwriting word recognition. Preprocessing effects and experiment results are given in Sect. 4 a brief conclusion is drawn in Sect. 5.

## 2 Preprocessing

Figure 1 illustrates some online handwritten Uyghur word samples where temporal neighbor strokes are drawn using different colors and annotated at the beginning of each stroke. We can see that randomness and invasion to writing regulation in all handwritten samples.

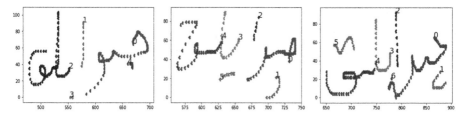

**Fig. 1.** Different handwritten word samples for a word

Preprocessing is hoped to decrease the disturbing content in raw trajectory and improve the input representation thus can alleviate the need for large volume of data [3]. The preprocessing techniques applied in this paper includes redundant removing, point insertion, sampling, and turn-point selection. Figure 2 shows the workflow of preprocessing operations implemented in our experiments.

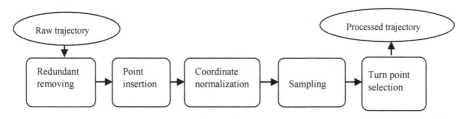

**Fig. 2.** Preprocessing workflow on handwritten trajectory

## 2.1    Remove Redundant Points

A handy threshold based redundant removing technique is implemented on each stroke of handwritten word trajectory. The removing thresholds are set based on average neighbor point distance in the stroke trajectory. Each neighbor point couples are visited and treated according to removing conditions. The distance between neighbor points are calculated using Eq. (1).

$$D = |P_i - P_{i-1}| = \sqrt{(x_i - x_{i-1})^2 + (y_i - y_{i-1})^2} \tag{1}$$

where $P_i(x_i, y_i)$ and $P_{i-1}(x_{i-1}, y_{i-1})$ are point coordinates of a point and its previous neighbor, D refers the distance between the neighbor points.

If the distance from a point to its previous neighbor is greater than 3 times of average neighbor-point distance, this point is treated as noise and removed. 1/2 of the average neighbor point distance is used as duplication removing threshold. If the distance from a point to its previous neighbor is smaller than the duplication removing threshold, this point is removed from the trajectory.

## 2.2    Point Insertion

Point insertion is made between the neighbor points which have larger distance than threshold value. For avoiding generated extra points between strokes, point insertion to sample trajectory is applied on stroke level only. The insertion threshold is set by 0.01 times of the larger criteria of width or height of sample shape, so it is varied sample to sample.

$$N = \frac{|P_1 - P_2|}{thr\_d} \tag{2}$$

$$x_i = x1 + \frac{\Delta x}{N} * i \tag{3}$$

$$y_i = y1 + \frac{\Delta y}{N} * i \tag{4}$$

In Fig. 3, $P_1(x_1, y_1)$ and $P_2(x_2, y_2)$ are the neighbor points that need point insertion between them. $\Delta x$ and $\Delta y$ are the horizontal and vertical distances calculated by their coordinates. Euclidian distance between them is obtained using Eq. (1). $N$ is The number of points to be inserted and $thr\_d$ is the distance threshold for point insertion, see Eq. (2). The coordinates of each insertion point is set according to Eqs. (3) and (4) where $(x_i, y_i)$ are the coordinate values of the $i^{th}$ inserted point.

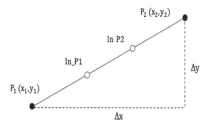

**Fig. 3.** Inserting points

### 2.3   Coordinate Normalization

The recorded point coordinates are normalized to be within certain interval by simple min-max normalization using Eqs. (5)–(8). Points in trajectory are moved to be zero started and within (0, 1) values both horizontal and vertical coordinates.

$$W = max(X) - min(X) \tag{5}$$

$$H = max(Y) - min(Y) \tag{6}$$

$$x_i = \frac{X_i - min X}{max(W, H)} \tag{7}$$

$$y_i = \frac{Y_i - min(Y)}{max(W, H)} \tag{8}$$

where $(X_i, Y_i)$ and $(x_i, y_i)$ are point coordinate values before and after normalization; $X$ and $Y$ represents the sets of horizontal and vertical coordinates of a sample trajectory, respectively. The normalizing factor (denominator) uses the maximum criteria of shape width $W$ and height $H$, thus the aspect ratio of the sample shape is kept.

### 2.4   Sampling

In order to make even handwritten trajectory, an equal distance based sampling is implemented. Stroke based sampling with distance threshold is applied on each stroke to avoid missing delayed strokes which are crucial to distinguish characters and words. Specifically, if the distance between a point and its previous neighbor is smaller than threshold distance, this point is discarded; otherwise, it is selected and kept as sampled point.

### 2.5   Turn Point Selection

Turn-points are very much informative that they express substantial direction change of pen-tip movement during handwriting. Using only turn-points greatly decreases the trajectory length than using all trajectory points. Again, selecting turn points is performed on stroke level in order to avoid losing character distinguishing marks.

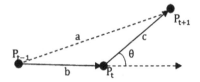

**Fig. 4.** Pen-tip direction change

Direction change $\theta$ at a point in trajectory is obtained by its previous and next neighbor points using Eq. (9), where $P_{t-1}$ and $P_{t+1}$ are the previous and next neighbor points of point $P_t$; And the Euclidian distances between them are noted as $a, b, c$ as illustrated in Fig. 4. A point in trajectory is detected as critical turn point if direction change $\theta$ exceeds threshold of $\pi/12$.

$$\theta = \pi - arccos\left(\frac{b^2 + c^2 + a^2}{2bc}\right) \qquad (9)$$

Figure 5 compares the visual effect of the handwritten word samples before and after preprocessing. The original trajectory has very large values and a great number of points, as shown in Fig. 5(a). After preprocessing, the coordinate values are squeezed to be within (0,1). And the trajectory length has got reduced significantly while still keeping readability, as in Fig. 5(b).

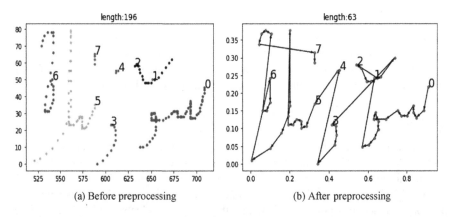

(a) Before preprocessing                    (b) After preprocessing

**Fig. 5.** Visual effect of preprocessing on handwritten trajectory

## 3   Unconstrained Handwriting Word Recognition System

### 3.1   Input Representation

Two input representation are used in the comparative training experiments in this paper. First one simply uses two dimensional [x,y] values. The second representation uses six dimensions which include point coordinates (x,y), pen-tip movement direction $(\Delta x, \Delta y)$, two dimensional pen-tip state of up or down [6]. Pen-tip movement direction $(\Delta x, \Delta y)$ is easily got by calculating the differences of neighbor point positions by Eqs. (10) and (11). Then pen-state is known as pen-down if a point stays in the same stroke with his previous neighbor and marks as [1, 0], otherwise marked as [0,1] which notes pen-up state.

$$\Delta x = x_t - x_{t-1} \tag{10}$$

$$\Delta y = y_t - y_{t-1} \tag{11}$$

where $(x_t, y_t)$ and $(x_{t-1}, y_{t-1})$ are the coordinates of current and adjacent previous points within trajectory.

### 3.2  System Architecture

A recurrent neural network based unconstrained handwriting word recognition system with LSTM cells in recurrent layers, as shown in Fig. 6(a), is applied to recognize online handwritten word trajectories in this paper.

The bidirectional recurrent layer in the system has two sub-layers (forward and backward) which read the input sequence in opposite directions, either right-left of left-right [6]. Each cell in a recurrent layer controls input, output and state values to the next state with gate mechanism. The outputs of sub-layers, noted $Y_{forward}$ and $Y_{backward}$, are concatenated get overall output of the bidirectional recurrent layers as in Eqs. (12)–(14) and Fig. 6(b).

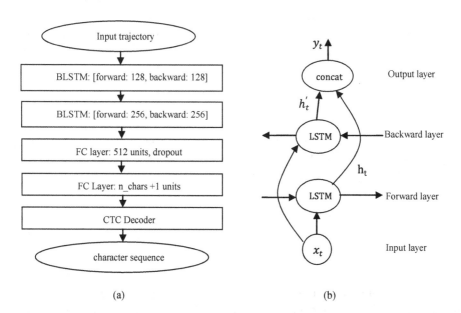

(a)                                      (b)

**Fig. 6.** Architecture of unconstrained handwritten word recognition system (a) Model Architecture (b) Bidirectional LSTM layer

$$Y_{forward} = h_t = [y_{l1}, y_{l2}, \ldots y_{lN}] \tag{12}$$

$$Y_{backword} = h_t' = [y_{r1}, y_{r2}, \ldots y_{rN}] \tag{13}$$

$$Y = concat(Y_{forward}, Y_{backward}) \tag{14}$$

Where $y_{rN}$ and $y_{lN}$ represents the output of the $N^{th}$ node of in right-left and left-right sub-recurrent layers. $Y_{forward}$ and $Y_{backward}$ are the outputs of the two inverse sub-layers and $Y$ is the of the bi-directional recurrent layer. The fully connection layers learn the further generalized features from recurrent layers.

This paper uses connectionist temporal classification to make character string outputs directly from the handwriting trajectory input to realize unconstrained handwriting word recognition system [7]. Since the ground truth word transcriptions are based on specific character shapes, the last fully connection layer is equipped with 128+1 units. Then CTC calculates the most possible character sequence as output.

## 4    Dataset and Configuration

### 4.1    Dataset

A total of 23400 online handwritten Uyghur word samples have been collected from 26 writers for 900 word classes. Each writer is asked to write all word classes continuously on handwriting tablet in order to make the collected samples more natural and challenging. Each handwritten word sample in the established dataset contains the recorded pen-tip coordinates on handwriting tablet, associated Unicode based ground-truth word transcription and some general information such as trajectory length, total number of strokes etc. The samples from 22 writers are arranged to be in train set, while the ones of remained 4 writers are used to be the test set. The train set has 19800 samples and test set contains 3600 samples for 900 word classes, respectively.

### 4.2    Configurations

Training experiments are performed on TitanX GPU with 12G RAM. During training, a small portion of train samples (10 batches) is used as validation set and not participated in model parameter adaptation. Character error rate CER and character accurate rate CAR [8] are used as main evaluation metrics by Eqs. (15) and (16).

$$CER = \frac{D_e + S_e + l_e}{N_t} \tag{15}$$

$$CAR = 1 - \frac{D_e + S_e + l_e}{N_t} \tag{16}$$

where $N_t$ is number of total characters in reference text; $D_e, S_e, I_e$ denote the substitution, deletion and insertion errors, respectively.

All variables of the network are initialized by variance scaling initialize [9]. Stochastic gradient descent with Adam optimizer is applied for all experiments [10]. Initial learning rate is set 0.001 and decreased by half when no improvement seen in continues 3 epochs. No regularization except dropout is implemented with drop-rate of 0.5. Training is stopped after 10 epochs failed to make any progress on validation set. In order to save the training time, only 10 batches of the train and validation sets are used to navigate the model performance during training with CER metric.

## 5  Experiments and Discussion

### 5.1  Experiments

In order to see the effect of preprocessing on training process, the same training configurations are implemented for all comparative experiments. In the first group of experiments, two dimensional input representations respectively by raw, normalized and preprocessed trajectory values are used as input. The second group of experiments uses six dimensional input representations respectively based on raw, normalized and preprocessed trajectories, again. In the context of these experiments1, the raw, coordinate normalized and preprocessed trajectories are noted by Raw-[x,y], Norm-[x,y] and Prep-[x,y], respectively. The six dimensional inputs are also noted by Raw-dim6, Norm-dim6 and Prep-dim6 accordingly in Table 1 and Fig. 7.

### 5.2  Discussion on Results

**Speed.** The speed improvement in RNN training is very much preferred, because RNNs are usually slow for their recurrent connections. In training, the shortened trajectories such as Prep-[x,y] and Prep-dim6 representations have benefited almost 3 times speed-up over the ones with original trajectory lengths. As given in Table 1, the shortened representations only take around 5 min per training epoch while representations with original lengths need longer than 15 min. Recognition on short input trajectories is also faster than long sequences, too. The Prep-[x,y] and Prep-dim6 representations needed around 0.028 s to recognize a sample by average. Recognition time for a sample from the raw or the normalized only (Norm) representations took averagely around 0.09 s.

**Performance in Training.** In both group of comparative experiments, the training on raw trajectories experienced very unpleasant journey and ended up with severe divergence. In the following discussion, we only give figures of training process on the normalized and preprocessed trajectories.

**Table 1.** Comparison handwriting recognition systems

| Input | Mean Seq_len | Model Size(M) | No.ep | T/ep (min) | Tr_CER (%) | Te_CER (%) | Te_CAR (%) | Av-recT (s) |
|-------|--------------|---------------|-------|------------|------------|------------|------------|-------------|
| Raw-[x,y] | 221 | 16.2M | 73 | ~15.6 | 35.73 | 40.54 | 59.46 | 0.092 |
| Norm-[x,y] | 211 | 16.2M | 105 | ~15.6 | 11.81 | 21.94 | 79.06 | 0.092 |
| Prep-[x,y] | 67 | 16.2M | 66 | ~5.1 | 15.99 | 23.59 | 76.41 | 0.025 |
| Raw-dim6 | 221 | 16.25M | 80 | ~16 | – | – | – | 0.095 |
| Norm-dim6 | 211 | 16.2M | 72 | ~16 | **6.92** | **19.32** | **93.06** | 0.095 |
| Prep-dim6 | 58 | 16.25M | 100 | ~5.3 | 11.61 | 23.48 | 76.52 | 0.028 |

Where Tr_CER and Te_CER are the character error rates on train and test sets, respectively, Te_CAR means character accurate rate on test set; No.ep and T/ep the number of epochs that training stopped and average time spent per epoch. Av-recT means average recognition time per sample

*Two Dimensional Representation.* Since raw coordinate values of points are very large, training on Raw-[x,y] representation was hard and suffered by incredibly big fluctuation. In contrast, Normalized coordinate values experienced very good training performance despite some zig-zags on error curve in Fig. 7(a). Prep-[x,y] based Training performed a very fast improvement of model performance at the beginning 30 epochs for, see Fig. 7(b). There is no obvious overfitting found during training but some degree of fluctuation accompanied from the beginning to the end. However, it is very obvious that the shorted trajectory loses much information from the original handwritten trajectory. Therefore, Norm-[x,y] inputs which kept all information from the original trajectory produced better performance than Prep-[x,y] representation.

*Six Dimensional Representation.* Raw-dim6 representation couldn't make pleasing performance both on train and validation sets, again. The normalized coordinate values from Norm-dim6 produced almost steady decline of error during training as plotted in Fig. 7(c). The training and validation curves of the six dimensional representation indicate better model generality than of two dimensional ones. The difference of training and validation errors is small until the training prepared to stop. Norm-dim6 representation obtained the highest recognition performance on whole train and test sets comparing with other comparative experiments in this paper, see Table 1. Comparing with Norm-[x,y] representation, more information in Norm-dim6 made faster convergence, too. Prep-dim6 showed the fastest convergence on train set among the experiments that 40 epochs reached train error rate of 5% (CER). After 30 epochs of training, see Fig. 7(d), training saw some degree of overfitting although model showed almost steady performance in later epochs. This may indicate that smaller models will be preferred for Prep-dim6 representation. Among all experiments, The Norm-dim6 representation found itself best fit for the model capacity and reached a good generalization of 19.32% CER on test set which is best recognition result among the compared training experiments in this paper and can be further improved with proper training configurations.

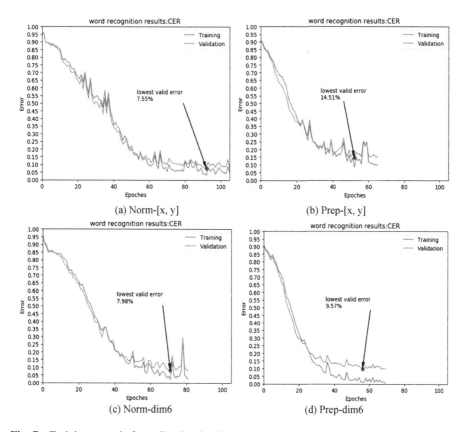

**Fig. 7.** Training records for online handwritten word recognition (The results are based on 10 batches from train and validation sets)

## 6  Conclusion

In both groups of comparative training experiments using two and six dimensional input representations, the pre-processed inputs are found much faster to complete an epoch of training than using raw trajectory. Experiments showed that raw trajectories with large range of coordinate values are hard to be trained. Excessive preprocessing will lose trajectory information and may cause harm for model training. More informative input representation shows better training behavior than just using trajectory coordinates. The normalized trajectory coordinates with more features produced the best performance for training and generalization. Investigating the different deep neural network structures is the main content of our next work.

**Acknowledgment.** This work is supported by National Science Foundation of China (NSFC) under grant number 61462081 and 61263038. The first author is very much grateful to the National Laboratory of Pattern Recognition of CASIA for providing the experimental environment.

# References

1. Liu, C.L., Yin, F., Wang, D.H., Wang, Q.F.: Online and offline handwritten Chinese character recognition: benchmarking on new databases. Pattern Recogn. **46**(1), 155–162 (2013)
2. Graves, A., Liwicki, M., Bunke, H., Schmidhuber, J., Fernández, S.: Unconstrained on-line handwriting recognition with recurrent neural networks. In: Conference on Neural Information Processing Systems, pp. 458–464. DBLP, Vancouver (2007)
3. Liu, C.L.: Handwritten Chinese character recognition: effects of shape normalization and feature extraction. In: Doermann, D., Jaeger, S. (eds.) SACH 2006. LNCS, vol. 4768, pp. 104–128. Springer, Heidelberg (2008). https://doi.org/10.1007/978-3-540-78199-8_7
4. Simayi, W., Ibrayim, M., Tursun, D., Hamdulla, A.: A survey on the classifiers in on-line handwritten Uyghur character recognition system. Int. J. Hybrid Inf. Technol. **9**(3), 189–198 (2016)
5. Chammas, E., Mokbel, C., Likforman-Sulem, L.: Handwriting recognition of historical documents with few labeled data. In: 2018 13th IAPR International Workshop on Document Analysis Systems (DAS), 43–48. IEEE (2018)
6. Zhang, X.Y., Yin, F., Zhang, Y.M., Liu, C.L., Bengio, Y.: Drawing and recognizing Chinese characters with recurrent neural network. IEEE Trans. Pattern Anal. Mach. Intell. **40**(4), 849–862 (2018)
7. Graves, A., Fernández, S., Gomez, F, Schmidhuber, J.: Connectionist temporal classification: labeling unsegmented sequence data with recurrent neural networks. In: Proceedings of the 23rd International Conference on Machine Learning, Pittsburgh, Pennsylvania, USA, pp. 369–376. ACM, New York (2006)
8. Su, T.H., Zhang, T.W., Guan, D.J., Huang, H.J.: Off-line recognition of realistic Chinese handwriting using segmentation-free strategy. Pattern Recogn. **42**(1), 167–182 (2009)
9. He, K., Zhang, X., Ren, S., Sun, J.: Delving deep into rectifiers: surpassing human-level performance on imagenet classification. In: Proceedings of the IEEE International Conference on Computer Vision, pp. 1026–1034. IEEE, Santiago (2015)
10. Kingma, D.P., Ba, J.: Adam: a method for stochastic optimization. In: The 3rd International Conference for Learning Representations. http://arxiv.org/abs/1412.6980, San Diego (2015)
11. Jiang, D., Huo, L., Lv, Z., et al.: A joint multi-criteria utility-based network selection approach for vehicle-to-infrastructure networking. IEEE Trans. Intell. Transp. Syst. **19**(10), 3305–3319 (2018)
12. Jiang, D., Li, W., Lv, H.: An energy-efficient cooperative multicast routing in multi-hop wireless networks for smart medical applications. Neurocomputing **2017**(220), 160–169 (2017)

# Point Target Detection Based on Quantum Genetic Algorithm with Morphological Contrast Operation

Guofeng Zhang[1,2] and Askar Hamdulla[1(✉)]

[1] Institute of Information Science and Engineering, Xinjiang University,
Urumqi 830046, China
askar@xju.edu.cn
[2] Changji Institute of Technology College, Changji 831100, China

**Abstract.** Robust small target detection of infrared clutter background has drawn great interest of scholars. Recently, morphological filter is playing a significant role in detecting infrared point target. Generally, the background clutter and targets are diverse in the case of each image. Traditional fixed structural elements cannot acquire to successful point target detection in complex background. Therefore, a new method is introduced based on quantum genetic algorithm to optimize and obtain structural element which is used as morphological filter for point target detection in original Infrared images. Then, morphological contrast operation is proposed to enhance areas of point targets after the filtered image is obtained. Thus, an enormous background clutter and noise are suppressed and the contrast between target and background are observably increased. Finally, by setting proper threshold, the point targets can be detected perfectly. Experimental evaluation results show that the proposed method is effective and robust with respect to detection accuracy.

**Keywords:** Structural elements · Quantum genetic algorithm · Morphological contrast operation · Background suppression

## 1 Introduction

Detection technology of weak point target has become the focus of scientists in recent decades, especially in the field of military monitoring and the application. When the target is far away from the infrared detection system, it is considered as a point target, and the area in the image only occupies 1–3 pixels and lacks obvious information of size, shape and texture. The gray value is low. Therefore, it is easy to be submerged in complicated background. In order to detect point target accurately, various algorithms of point target detection have been proposed in the past few decades. Some approaches, such as Max-mean filter and Max-median filter [1, 3], are proposed by Deshpande et al. in 1999, which are simple and easy to accomplish. However, it cannot remove edges of the clouds and structural backgrounds. In 1988, Hadhoud and Thomas proposed two dimensional least mean square filter (TDLMS) [1, 4, 9] to predict the background based on iteration. This is a typical adaptive filter that is estimated by the weighted average of neighboring pixels. Objectively, TDLMS filter is very effective as the background

H. Song et al. (Eds.): SIMUtools 2019, LNICST 295, pp. 459–468, 2019.
https://doi.org/10.1007/978-3-030-32216-8_44

condition is relatively homogeneous or self-correlated. Unfortunately, there is a high false alarm rate to the strong fluctuation of background clutters and low Signal-to-Clutter-Ratio (SCR) [1–3, 6, 8]. In addition, the operation procedure of TDLMS is complex. Mathematical morphology was founded by French mathematicians Matheron G and Serra J in 1964. Mathematical morphology filter is an excellent method used that has obtained satisfactory effects in infrared point target detection. The choices of structural element size and shape will seriously affect the processing of digital images. In the traditional morphological filter, a fixed size and shape of the structural elements are chosen entirely by the designer's experience, so it is difficult to guarantee different targets detection from diverse infrared images and help to detect the targets precisely.

As this issue, the paper proposed a new and adaptive improved combination based on Top-hat [1, 2, 6, 7, 9, 10] and Bottom-hat transformations after using quantum genetic algorithm (QGA) [5, 10] to optimize the size and shape of structural elements from learning and training the samples. Therefore, different images use optimized structural elements to eliminate effects from complex background and certain noises. QGA is suitable for finding global optimal solution in searching spaces. If the binary mode is the structural elements of $4 \times 4$ size, the searching spaces will have $2^{16} = 65,536$ search in each image, the structural elements must be adapted with the background features and targets so that the targets can be detected by lower false alarm rate. Due to the huge searching space, the QGA is used for designing adaptive structural elements to match the desired features in the infrared images.

The filtered effect of the optimized structural elements is significantly better than that of the unoptimized ones. Morphological contrast operation (MCO) is proposed in this paper, which exploits the original infrared image to add the Top-hat and then subtract the Bottom-hat to augment sensitive areas of the targets. Finally, binary images are obtained by threshold segmentation method. This also verifies the correctness of combination Top-hat and Bottom-hat transformations to enhance the target ideas proposed in this paper. The point target detection algorithm based on QGA with MCO is evidently effective and robust for complex background and noise clutter.

## 2  Feature Analysis for Point Target Image

The image of point target under complex conditions can be described as three parts [6, 9]:

$$I(x,y,t) = B(x,y,t) + T(x,y,t) + N(x,y,t) \tag{1}$$

where $I(x,y,t)$ represents infrared image contained point target, $B(x,y,t)$ represents the background, $T(x,y,t)$ represents dim point targets, $N(x,y,t)$ represents random noise clutter, (x, y) represents the pixel location, t denotes different intervals of frames. For infrared weak point target detection, signal-to-clutter ratio (SCR) [1–4, 6, 8, 10] is a key factor affecting the quality of detection, it is defined as follow:

$$SCR = \frac{\mu_t - \mu_b}{\sigma_b} \tag{2}$$

Where $\mu_t$ is the average gray value of target region, $\mu_b$ is the local area pixels' average intensity, $\sigma_b$ is standard deviation of neighboring area pixels. Increasing of SCR value leads to high contrast of target area which is easier to detect. Moreover, raising of large background suppression factor (BSF) value can lightly eliminate background clutter and reduce false alarms. The SCR gain (SCRG) [1–4, 6, 8, 10] and BSF [1, 2, 8, 10] are defined as Eqs. (3) and (4) respectively.

$$SCRG = \frac{SCR_{out}}{SCR_{in}} \tag{3}$$

$$BSF = \frac{\sigma_{in}}{\sigma_{out}} \tag{4}$$

$\sigma_{iin}$ and $\sigma_{out}$ are the clutter standard deviations of the infrared image before and after filter respectively. SCRG represents the enlargement of target signal relative to background in the detection image. BSF represents the suppression level of background. The bigger values of SCRG and BSF are, the better the results of performance are.

## 3   Morphological Contrast Operation (MCO)

Recently, mathematical morphology filter for image enhancement and segmentation has been applied quickly and is playing a great potential role in weak point target detection. Mathematical morphology has four basic operations: dilation, erosion, opening and closing operations. The opening and closing operations are able to respectively remove off the bright and dark regions which are smaller than the size of structural elements. The opening and closing operators of morphology are described as:

$$(I \circ b)(x, y) = [I(x, y) \ominus b(s, t)] \oplus b(s, t) \tag{5}$$

$$(I \bullet b)(x, y) = [I(x, y) \oplus b(s, t)] \ominus b(s, t) \tag{6}$$

where $\oplus$ and $\ominus$ are defined as dilation and erosion operations, $b(s, t)$ is structural elements, $I(x, y)$ is original infrared image. Top-hat and Bottom-hat are defined as follows:

$$TH(x, y) = [I(x, y) - (I \circ b)(x, y)] \tag{7}$$

$$BH(x, y) = [(I \bullet b)(x, y) - I(x, y)] \tag{8}$$

For $TH$ is the sensitive area of bright target, $BH$ is the sensitive area of dark target, generally, small targets are brighter than local background areas. The Top-hat transform can be used for bright targets on dark background, while Bottom-hat transformation is applied for the opposite case.

Contrast enhancement mainly refers to enhancing or sharpening the characteristics of an image. This paper proposes a MCO to enhance point target regions. It can be achieved by assembling the filtered image from Top-hat and Bottom-hat in parallel. The original image added Top-hat to enhance the bright target, and Bottom-hat is subtracted from the resulting image to enhance the dark target. In other words, MCO is that original image plus $TH$ minus $BH$, which is defined as Eq. (9).

$$
\begin{aligned}
MCO(x,y) &= I(x,y) + TH(x,y) - BH(x,y) \\
&= I(x,y) + I(x,y) - (I \circ b)(x,y) - ((I \bullet b)(x,y) - I(x,y)) \\
&= 3I(x,y) - (I \circ b)(x,y) - (I \bullet b)(x,y)
\end{aligned}
\tag{9}
$$

Some potential point targets are enhanced through the above operations. Experiment shows that MCO can effectively enhance weak point target by suppressing background clutter and random noise to lower level to achieve success.

The key of point target detection relies on choice of structural elements. Traditional fixed structural elements are unsuitable for different targets detection from diverse infrared images. Based on this reason, the choice of structural elements should be adaptive as the background and small targets change in order to gain accurate detection. In this paper, a method of point target contrast enhancement based on MCO is proposed after having been employed by adaptive structural element filter, in which QGA below is proposed to optimize the structural elements, which attributes to its ability on searching global optimal solution.

# 4 Structure Element of Optimization by QGA

Narayanan first proposed QGA. Han et al. introduced quantum bits and quantum revolving gates into genetic algorithms. Quantum bits are defined as a vector existed on the unit circle which is depicted on two-dimensional plane composed of a pair of orthogonal basis of the two quantum states $\{|0\rangle, |1\rangle\}$. Quantum bits can be expressed as $|\varphi\rangle = \alpha|0\rangle + \beta|1\rangle$, $|\varphi\rangle$ is a representation of a quantum state, $\alpha, \beta$ is a pair of plural defined probability amplitude. For example, a chromosome length [2] of m, it can be defined as binary encoding string $Q(t) = \left( \left| \begin{matrix} \alpha_1 \\ \beta_1 \end{matrix} \right| \begin{matrix} \alpha_2 \\ \beta_2 \end{matrix} \left| \begin{matrix} \alpha_3 \\ \beta_3 \end{matrix} \right| \begin{matrix} \cdots \\ \cdots \end{matrix} \left| \begin{matrix} \alpha_m \\ \beta_m \end{matrix} \right| \right)$ and $\alpha_i^2 + \beta_i^2 = 1 (i = 1, 2, \ldots, m)$.

An encoding with m-bit quantum bits can be expressed as $2^m$ different states, and the number of genes in chromosome [2] is the length of the chromosome. In this method, each binary bit in the structure element is modelled with a gene in the chromosome. The figure below shows that the $4 \times 4$ structure element is modelled with a chromosome length of 16 bits. For example, a chromosome equals [0,1,0,0;0, 1,1,0;0,1,1,0;0,0,0,0], structural elements are shown as follow in the Fig. 1.

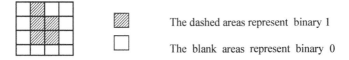

The dashed areas represent binary 1

The blank areas represent binary 0

**Fig. 1.** A structure element is modeled with the chromosome.

After quantum bits of chromosome have been encoded by a matrix of probability amplitude pair, quantum rotation gate will be implemented. It is a main adjustment strategy for updating population in QGA, which is defined as common matrix U.

$$U = \begin{bmatrix} \cos\theta & -\sin\theta \\ \sin\theta & \cos\theta \end{bmatrix}$$

Quantum rotation operation is shown as follow:

$$\begin{bmatrix} \alpha_i^{t+1} \\ \beta_i^{t+1} \end{bmatrix} = \begin{bmatrix} \cos\theta_i & -\sin\theta_i \\ \sin\theta_i & \cos\theta_i \end{bmatrix} \bullet \begin{bmatrix} \alpha_i^t \\ \beta_i^t \end{bmatrix}$$

Where $\left(\alpha_{i}^t, \beta_{i}^t\right)$ is quantum coding at the ith quantum bits from the tth generation in the structure of chromosome and $\theta_i$ is the rotation angle. The size and direction are executed based on a pre-designed adjustment strategy. The purpose of the rotation operation is to achieve the transition between states and speed up convergence rate to realize an optimal solution of point target detection. Compared with traditional genetic algorithms, QGA can quickly converge to global optimal solutions at a smaller population.

## 5  The Fitness Function [10]

Since the fitness function is the only certain indicator of the choice of individual survival opportunity in the population, it directly determines the evolutionary behavior of the population. The fitness function plays a decisive role in describing quantum bit, it offers an optimizing criterion such as convergence criterion and termination criterion of QGA. In other words, the fitness function not only plays the evolutionary behavior of the population, but also acts a decisive part in describing quantum bits.

In this paper, the fitness function is established based on the Minimum Mean Squared Error (MMSE), under criterion of MMSE, the objective adaptive function is defined as $E = \frac{1}{MN} \sum_{t=1}^{L} (Y_t - d_t)^2$, where MN is the number of training samples, $Y_t$ is the expectation of output signal, and $d_t$ is the expectation of output corresponding to the tth value of input, t is the maximal value of tth output matrix after each morphological filter. The flow chart of algorithm [5] using MCO with the structural elements optimized by QGA to detect point target is shown as follow in the Fig. 2.

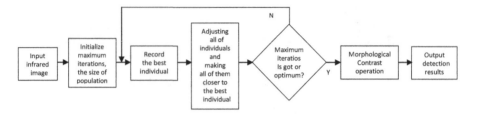

**Fig. 2.** The flow chart of using QGA with MCO to detect point target.

## 6   Compare to Several Methods

### 6.1   Experiment 1

To compare the results of the proposed methods with other approaches based on TDLMS filter, Max-median filter, Top-hat transformation, and Fixed structural elements filter, four different backgrounds are given in different clutter and noisy background respectively. The point targets are marked with red circles. The results of 3D maps in the Fig. 3 are shown as following after background clutter are suppressed.

Comparisons of experiment result between the classical methods and the proposed method are shown in the Fig. 3. It can be inferred that the TDLMS, Max-median filter, Top-hat transformation, and Fixed structural elements cannot well enhance the target areas and still there is a lot of background clutter around the target areas. While the QGA with CMO has better performance compared with the previous methods by improving the contrast between target and background. It is shown three-dimensional (3D) graphs in the seventh row in the Fig. 3.

### 6.2   Experiment 2 (BSF and SCRG Comparisons)

The results of SCRG and BSF evaluation parameters for the TDLMS, Max-median filter, Top-hat transformation, Fixed structural elements filter and Proposed methods are shown respectively as Tables 1 and 2.

As shown in Tables 1 and 2, it can be seen that Top-Hat transformation and Fixed structure element filter achieve bigger values of BSF and SCRG than other traditional methods. However two metrics are not stable and consistent. TDLMS and Max-median filter have poor ability to suppress complex background and the effects are relatively insignificant for point target enhancement. Compared to TDLMS, Max-median filter, Top-hat transformation, and Fixed structural elements filter, it is indicated clearly that the proposed algorithm achieves the best performance on two metrics for different clutter and noisy backgrounds. In which the values in boldface indicate the higher quality. From the Table 1, it is also exhibited clearly that the proposed method not only has better effect in terms of improving image-contrast enhancement, but also has stronger clutter suppression ability, especially for lower SCR images.

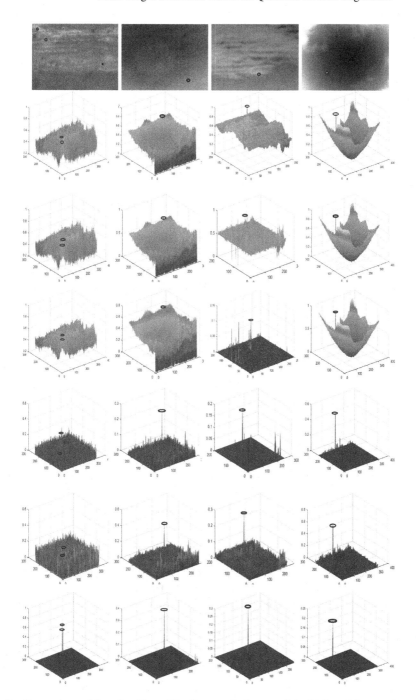

**Fig. 3.** Comparison of five algorithms. The first row indicates original infrared figures shown as image a1, a2, a3 and a4 in different clutter and noisy background respectively; The second row (b1–b4) indicates the 3D gray distribution of original infrared figures; The third row (c1–c4) to the seventh row (g1–g4) indicates filtered results of the 3D feature graphs of TDLMS, Max-median filter, Fixed structure element filter, Top-Hat transformation and Proposed method respectively.

**Table 1.** SCRG values in different algorithms for diverse infrared images.

| SCRG | Image a1 | Image a2 | Image a3 | Image a4 |
| --- | --- | --- | --- | --- |
| TDLMS | 1.4394 | 2.4061 | 1.5816 | 1.9034 |
| Max-median filter | 1.0632 | 1.6491 | 1.2827 | 1.9098 |
| Top-Hat transformation | 1.7652 | 2.9174 | 5.3710 | 2.0417 |
| Fixed structure element filter | 5.7556 | 8.4635 | 9.3173 | 1.9143 |
| Proposed method (QGA with MCO) | **36.7845** | **12.0662** | **10.004** | **3.2693** |

**Table 2.** BSF values in different algorithms for diverse infrared images.

| BSF | Image a1 | Image a2 | Image a3 | Image a4 |
| --- | --- | --- | --- | --- |
| TDLMS | 1.0130 | 1.005 | 1.1125 | 1.0016 |
| Max-median filter | 1.1184 | 1.0148 | 1.0052 | 1.0001 |
| Top-Hat transformation | 6.4431 | 12.6274 | 12.9605 | 7.5506 |
| Fixed structural elements filter | 1.8336 | 4.4161 | 6.5789 | 19.8621 |
| Proposed method (QGA with MCO) | **18.1753** | **56.6755** | **43.5512** | **146.8314** |

## 7  Threshold Segmentation Method

After MCO, final input infrared image is obtained, in order to extract the point target, a segmentation method is used in the result image, which is defined as Eq. (10).

$$T = \mu + k \times \sigma \tag{10}$$

Where $\mu$ is the average value of the image, $\sigma$ is the standard variance of the image, k is a constant determined experientially. The results of 3D maps below are shown in Fig. 4 after threshold segmentation. Red circles marked represent point target in every image of segmentation.

Above experiments with different background show the results of the threshold segmentation. Top-hat transformation seems to be more effective for figure k3 and k4 in the Fig. 4, but for figure k1 and k2 in the Fig. 4, it does not filter out residual clutters successfully. Fixed structural elements filter can detect point target successfully for figure j3 in the Fig. 4, but for figure j1 and j4 in the Fig. 4, the background with high brightness cannot be suppressed effectively. TDLMS and Max-median filter have a large number of false targets in the Fig. 4, it fails to filter out the messy clutter. Compared with TDLMS, Max-median filter, Top-hat transformation, Fixed structural elements filter. The results of the threshold segmentation can be seen obviously that our method have the superiority on clutter suppress and point target enhancement. Finally it can successfully extract point target in different clutter backgrounds respectively.

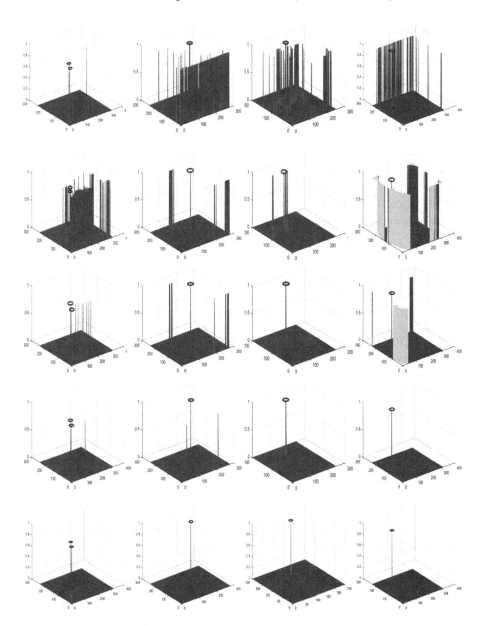

**Fig. 4.** The results of threshold segmentation. The first row to fifth row indicate 3D maps corresponding to threshold segmentation of TDLMS method (h1–h4), Max-mean filter (i1–i4), Fixed structural elements' filtering method (j1–j4), Top-hat transformation (k1–k4) and Proposed method (l1–l4) respectively. (Color figure online)

# 8  Conclusion

Qualitative and quantitative experimental results have shown the superiority of the MCO with the structural elements optimized by QGA. In this paper, Structural elements are modeled by genes in chromosome, individual survival is determined by fitness function, quantum revolving gate implements the population updating. The preferred structural elements can be used for morphological filtering to adapt to the target and background characteristics preferably in different images. The contrast enhancement algorithm was used to enhance sensitivity of the target areas. Finally, threshold segmentation method was employed to extract the point target successfully. Compared with several classical detection methods, the proposed method based on QGA with MCO have high reliability and good robustness under different clutter backgrounds for size of target tend to point in support domain.

# References

1. Li, J., Li, S., Zhao, Y., Jing-nan, M.A., Huang, H.: Background suppression for infrared dim and small target detection using local gradient weighted filtering. In: International Conference on Electrical Engineering and Automation (2016)
2. Marvasti, F.S., Mosavi, M.R., Nasiri, M.: Flying small target detection in IR images based on adaptive toggle operator. IET Comput. Vis. **12**(4), 527–534 (2018)
3. Zhang, H., Zhang, L., Yuan, D., Chen, H.: Infrared small target detection based on local intensity and gradient properties. Infrared Phys. Technol. **89**, 88–96 (2018)
4. Bai, K., Wang, Y., Song, Q.: Patch similarity based edge-preserving background estimation for single frame infrared small target detection. In: IEEE International Conference on Image Processing, pp. 181–185 (2016)
5. Zhang, L.Y., Du, Y.X., Li, B.: Research on threshold segmentation algorithm and its application on infrared small target detection algorithm. In: International Conference on Signal Processing, pp. 678–682 (2015)
6. Wei, H., Tan, Y., Lin, J.: Robust infrared small target detection via temporal low-rank and sparse representation. In: International Conference on Information Science, pp. 583–587 (2016)
7. Yao, Y., Hao, Y.: Small Infrared target detection based on spatio-temporal fusion saliency. In: 17th IEEE International Conference on Communication Technology (2017)
8. Zhang, H., Niu, Y., Zhang, H.: Small target detection based on difference accumulation and Gaussian curvature under complex conditions. Infrared Phys. Technol. **87**, 55–64 (2017)
9. Xie, K., Fu, K., Zhou, T., Yang, J., Wu, Q., He, X.: Small target detection using an optimization-based filter. In: International Conference on Acoustic, pp. 1583–1587 (2015)
10. Deng, L., Zhu, H., Zhou, Q., Li, Y.: Adaptive top-hat filter based on quantum genetic algorithm for infrared small target detection. Multimed. Tools Appl. **77**, 10539–10551 (2018)

# Analysis of Phonemes and Tones Confusion Rules Obtained by ASR

Gulnur Arkin and Askar Hamdulla[(✉)]

Institute of Information Science and Engineering, Xinjiang University,
Urumqi 830046, China
askar@xju.edu.cn

**Abstract.** This paper is based on the exploration of the effective method of erroneous phoneme pronunciation of Chinese mandarin learners whose mother tongue is Uyghur and the solution of major problems of language education, concerning the learner's pronunciation, it uses a different method, namely data-driven approach, and the Automatic Speech Recognition (ASR) is also used to recognize phonemes of the pronunciation of Chinese mandarin learners whose native language is Uyghur. The phoneme sequence is identified and then the standard pronunciation phonemes corresponding to the recognized phonemes are used as the target phonemes to obtain the mapping relation of each target phoneme and recognition phoneme, thus the possible phoneme error categories and possible erroneous rules in Uyghur learners' pronunciation can be obtained, which may give some help to the Uyghur learners to learn the Chinese auxiliary language system and the corresponding pronunciation evaluation model.

**Keywords:** Non-native speakers of Chinese · Speech recognition · Confusion rules · Pronunciation evaluation

## 1 Introduction

With the continuous development of the global economy, exchanges and cooperation in political, economic, cultural and educational fields among various countries have become more and more frequent (Jiang and Wang et al. 2018a; Jiang et al. 2016). Travelling and learning abroad is also increasingly common. Therefore, in addition to the mother tongue, many people choose another language as the second language. In ethnic minority areas of China, the Mandarin Chinese, as a national language, has been very crucial from primary school, junior high school, high school to college. Efficient spoken language learning requires one-on-one, face-to-face interaction between teachers and students. However, this approach is constrained by space, time and economic conditions (Ito et al. 2007; Stanley and Hacioglu 2012; Wang and Lee 2012). In recent years, with the development of science and technology, online education has become more and more popular. The Cloud-centric powerful computing resources, highly popularized mobile smart devices and rapidly developed voice processing technologies have enabled computer-assisted language learning System (CALL) to become more and more popular (Witt 1999; Ye and Young 2005; Qian et al. 2011).

H. Song et al. (Eds.): SIMUtools 2019, LNICST 295, pp. 469–476, 2019.
https://doi.org/10.1007/978-3-030-32216-8_45

However, the detection and diagnosis of pronunciation errors at the phonemic level, as a core module of the CALL system, still need to be further improved in accuracy.

Each language has its own vowel phonemic system. There are thirty-two phonemes in the phonological system of the modern Uyghur standard language. Eight of which are vowel phonemes but no diphthong. In contrast, Chinese has not only single vowels but also diphthongs and four triphthongs. In fact, it does not have any practical significance in terms of the phoneme itself, however, its function is very huge, the main difference lies in distinguishing the meaning and specifically distinguishing the different languages speed and different words (Ladefoged and Johnson 2015) Mandarin Chinese and Uyghur belong to the Sino-Tibetan language and Altaic languages respectively, and there are great differences in phonetics between these two languages, Chinese belongs to the isolated language (Thurgood and LaPolla 2003), and the Altaic language belongs to the agglutinative language (Zhao and Zhu 1985). There exists hierarchical relationship among phonemes, syllables, words, sentences, specifically, how the phonemes to form syllables, how syllables to form a specific single word, and how the word to form a sentence to express a certain meaning, these are the horizontal combination of phonetics, belonging to the scope of horizontal combination (Shifeng 2009). When learners learn another language, the old phonetic perception and production systems play an auxiliary or interference role (Lo et al. 2010). Certain types of phonetic errors are the product of interference effect, they are predictable, interpretable and understandable, and many research institutes have begun to pay attention to this issue, and they started to explore the system. For non-native speakers of languages, they attach particular importance to computer-aided Chinese language learning systems, which are especially suitable for ethnic minority areas. Now, relevant literature on the comparison of two languages almost can't be found, while this literature is to record the confusion rules, in order to improve the quality of pronunciation, and strive for accuracy.

The methodologies involved in this study are mainly aimed at Uyghur learners (L1) whose native language belongs to the Altai language family, and they have some Mandarin learning experience. Uyghur pronunciation is different from Mandarin pronunciation, some of its pronunciation cannot be found in Mandarin Chinese pronunciation, based on this, learners habitually use Uyghur pronunciation as a benchmark to learn Chinese Mandarin, focusing on pronunciation perception and aspects of producing, pronouncing ways and parts, finding the native phonemes that are similar but slightly different with Mandarin Chinese to replace the pronunciation, thus the difference caused by the substitution may cause confusion of pronunciation or certain pronunciation errors (Troung 2004). To sum up, through the collection of learners' pronunciations, we can get a comparative analysis of Uyghur cross-linguistic phonological contrast in linguistic and phonemic when they say Mandarin Chinese and wrong pronunciation characteristics with the data-driven method, so as to draw a reasonable phoneme confusion rule. At the same time, we will devote ourselves to exploring how to summarize the phonemic confusion between L1 and L2, establishing an experimental database based on the phoneme analysis, and how to combine the speech recognition technology and phonemic confusion to evaluate the accuracy of phoneme pronunciations, so as to establish an automatic detection method for phonetic erroneous pronunciation specifically designed for Uyghur who studies Chinese. Therefore, this study has actual theoretical research value.

## 2 Experimental Data and Preparation

### 2.1 Experimental Subjects

50 Uyghur speakers' sound recordings have been collected, all of them are students of Xinjiang University, aged from 20–26 years (Means 23), and their native language is Uyghur, Mandarin Chinese is their second language, they do not have language listening problems, and their parents are Uyghur, who use Uyghur as a communicative language in daily communication. 50 speakers were born in Xinjiang, fluent in Uyghur (the Native-tongue-using Minority Nationality Students), and their learning time on Chinese mandarin is more than ten years, their Chinese MHK oral test scores are above 45.

### 2.2 Experimental Process

Each speaker was sitting in a sound booth during the experiment, and the microphone was five centimeters from the speaker. The voice used in the experiment was collected in a dedicated recording studio, using equipment like a laptop, external sound card, microphone and some interconnecting data lines. The use of external sound card can adjust the volume of sound, reduce the noise, and monitor the situation of the plosive sound, etc. Recordings were under computer control by a program in Matlab, each data sampling point is digitized into bits, and the sampling rate is 16 Hz. Participants' read materials are Chinese sentences, each participant needs to record 300 Mandarin sentences (50 * 300 = 15000) and each sentence contains 5 to 11 words. The recognition results are obtained through Chinese speech recognition system of Tsinghua University.

## 3 Data-Driven Approaches

### 3.1 Processes and Methods

It is well-known that people habitually form a system of relative perception production when acquiring language (e.g., mother tongue). When people learn another language (for example, ethnic minority areas mainly learn Chinese, bilingual learning), the original system might produce auxiliary or interference effect, it promotes learners to learn another language when playing an auxiliary role, and the pronunciation errors are often specific when interfering. Fortunately, they are predictable, interpretable and understandable, the burden of recognition system will be reduced due to the integration of these prior knowledge (Dong and Zhao 2006; Wang et al. 2011), giving full play to the role of recognition.

The comparative analysis of cross-linguistic phonology, as a linguistic transfer theory, mainly focuses on the comparison of L1 and L2 (Gass and Selinker 1992). The misunderstanding of non-knowledge among learners (Uyghur) can cause confusion. We focus on learners' phonetic aspect, using a different method, namely data-driven, to carry on a relevant test to it, namely the automatic phoneme recognition, to analyze the recognition result emphatically, specially to mainly dissect some wrong pronunciation that produced among them, emphatically to discuss around wrong pronunciation and standard pronunciation, studying the related mapping relation between them, with this particular mapping relation (Jiang et al. 2018b) it automatically generate the relevant rules, and this rule is mainly for additional phoneme confusion. The data-driven approach is mainly used here to get the rules of phoneme confusion, and the flow chart is as follows (Fig. 1).

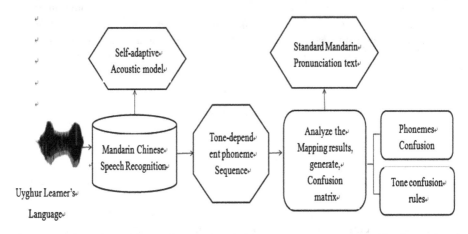

**Fig. 1.** The flow chart of the confusion rules of phonemes and tones generated by the results of ASR recognition is analyzed

The main method is, firstly to identify the phonemes of Chinese mandarin learners whose mother tongue is Uyghur based on the phoneme, and each Uyghur speaker is transformed automatically in the recognition to obtain the recognition sequence. Secondly, the standard phonetic phoneme is used as the target phoneme to obtain the mapping relation of the target phoneme x (i) and the recognition phoneme y (j). The relationship can be replaced, deleted, inserted and misread. Meanwhile, to count the mapping and calculate frequency) P x(i)| y(j):

$$P x(i)|y(j) = (Times\ of\ recognition\ phoneme\ y(j)/Times\ of\ target\ phoneme\ x\,(i)) * 100\% \quad (1)$$

Finally, the recognition accuracy is obtained by confusing the rules and calculating the frequency.

## 3.2  Phoneme Confusion Matrices and Rules

**Vowel Confusion Matrices and Rules**
We found out phoneme list with possible pronunciation mistakes by the way of automatic speech recognition to generate confusion matrix, and filtered each vowel, diphthong and consonant table map by threshold value to generate their own confusion rules (Table 1).

**Table 1.** The 1st–12th columns of vowel confusion matrix obtained from data driven experiment

|      | a   | o  | e   | i    | u   | v   | er  | ie  | ai  | ei  | ao  | ou  |
|------|-----|----|-----|------|-----|-----|-----|-----|-----|-----|-----|-----|
| a    | 341 | 0  | 4   | 4    | 0   | 0   | 0   | 0   | 6   | 0   | 6   | 0   |
| o    | 0   | 80 | 0   | 0    | 4   | 0   | 0   | 0   | 0   | 0   | 0   | 0   |
| e    | 1   | 2  | 695 | 9    | 5   | 0   | 0   | 2   | 0   | 0   | 3   | 8   |
| i    | 5   | 0  | 26  | 1148 | 12  | 0   | 0   | 3   | 21  | 5   | 0   | 0   |
| u    | 0   | 3  | 7   | 11   | 508 | 0   | 0   | 0   | 0   | 0   | 5   | 1   |
| v    | 0   | 0  | 0   | 0    | 1   | 150 | 0   | 0   | 0   | 0   | 0   | 0   |
| er   | 1   | 0  | 0   | 0    | 0   | 0   | 185 | 1   | 0   | 0   | 0   | 0   |
| ie   | 0   | 0  | 0   | 4    | 0   | 0   | 0   | 167 | 0   | 0   | 0   | 0   |
| ai   | 4   | 0  | 1   | 15   | 2   | 0   | 0   | 0   | 478 | 2   | 2   | 4   |
| ei   | 0   | 0  | 1   | 5    | 0   | 0   | 0   | 0   | 0   | 133 | 0   | 0   |
| ao   | 1   | 2  | 14  | 0    | 4   | 0   | 0   | 1   | 0   | 0   | 256 | 7   |
| ou   | 0   | 3  | 4   | 1    | 4   | 0   | 0   | 0   | 3   | 0   | 1   | 232 |
| ia   | 1   | 5  | 0   | 0    | 1   | 0   | 0   | 1   | 0   | 0   | 0   | 2   |
| ua   | 0   | 0  | 0   | 0    | 0   | 0   | 0   | 0   | 0   | 0   | 0   | 0   |
| uo   | 0   | 0  | 17  | 0    | 6   | 0   | 1   | 0   | 2   | 0   | 0   | 2   |
| ve   | 0   | 0  | 0   | 0    | 0   | 1   | 0   | 0   | 0   | 0   | 0   | 0   |
| iao  | 0   | 0  | 15  | 1    | 1   | 2   | 0   | 0   | 0   | 0   | 1   | 1   |
| iou  | 0   | 0  | 0   | 0    | 0   | 0   | 0   | 0   | 0   | 0   | 0   | 0   |
| uai  | 0   | 0  | 0   | 0    | 0   | 0   | 0   | 0   | 0   | 0   | 0   | 3   |
| uei  | 0   | 0  | 0   | 0    | 0   | 0   | 0   | 0   | 0   | 0   | 0   | 0   |
| an   | 2   | 0  | 0   | 5    | 0   | 0   | 0   | 0   | 0   | 1   | 4   | 0   |
| en   | 4   | 0  | 2   | 16   | 0   | 0   | 0   | 0   | 0   | 0   | 0   | 0   |
| in   | 0   | 0  | 8   | 7    | 0   | 0   | 0   | 1   | 0   | 0   | 0   | 0   |
| vn   | 0   | 0  | 0   | 0    | 0   | 0   | 0   | 0   | 0   | 0   | 0   | 0   |
| ian  | 0   | 0  | 0   | 5    | 0   | 4   | 0   | 2   | 1   | 0   | 0   | 0   |
| uan  | 0   | 0  | 0   | 1    | 0   | 0   | 0   | 0   | 2   | 0   | 0   | 0   |
| van  | 0   | 0  | 0   | 0    | 0   | 0   | 0   | 0   | 0   | 0   | 0   | 0   |
| uen  | 0   | 0  | 0   | 0    | 0   | 0   | 0   | 0   | 0   | 0   | 0   | 0   |
| ang  | 0   | 0  | 3   | 0    | 0   | 0   | 0   | 0   | 0   | 0   | 3   | 0   |
| eng  | 0   | 0  | 0   | 0    | 4   | 4   | 0   | 0   | 0   | 0   | 1   | 0   |
| ing  | 0   | 0  | 0   | 2    | 0   | 0   | 0   | 0   | 0   | 0   | 0   | 0   |
| ong  | 4   | 0  | 1   | 4    | 1   | 0   | 0   | 0   | 8   | 4   | 0   | 1   |
| iang | 0   | 0  | 0   | 0    | 2   | 0   | 0   | 0   | 0   | 0   | 0   | 0   |
| uang | 0   | 0  | 0   | 0    | 0   | 0   | 0   | 0   | 0   | 0   | 0   | 0   |
| ueng | 0   | 0  | 0   | 0    | 0   | 0   | 0   | 0   | 0   | 0   | 0   | 0   |
| iong | 0   | 0  | 0   | 0    | 0   | 0   | 0   | 0   | 0   | 0   | 0   | 0   |

**Table 2.** The confusion rules list of monophthong, diphthong that obtained from data driven experiment

| Target phoneme | Replace | Delete | Insert | Misreading | ASR correct recognition probability |
|---|---|---|---|---|---|
| a | e | | i | e, i, ia | 52.14% |
| o | u | | u | u, ou | 58.39% |
| e | a, i | | | a, i, ie, o | 51.63% |
| i | e, ie, ai | | e, a | e, a, ai, ei | 49.54% |
| u | o, ou | | o | ou, o, ao, e | 45.51% |
| v | u | | | | 45.45% |
| er | | | | a, ie | 46.95% |
| ie(ě) | i | | | i | 60.72% |
| ai | a, i | i | | a, ie, ei | 52.58% |
| ei | e | | | e, i | 44.48% |
| ao | a | a | u | o, ou, u, ie | 45.96% |
| ou | u | o | | u, ao, ai, a | 52.37% |
| ia | ie | i, a | | ie, ou | 49.72% |
| ie | | | | | 0.00% |
| ua | | | | | 49.18% |
| uo | u, ou | u, o | | u, o, ou, | 46.45% |
| ve | | | | v | 60.00% |
| iao | ao | i | | ao, e, ou | 55.33% |
| iou | | | | | 0.00% |
| uai | | | | ou | 54.62% |
| uei | | | | | 0.00% |
| an | en, in | | | en, in, ang | 50.69% |
| en | in | | | an, in, eng | 45.64% |
| in | en | | | an, en, vn | 42.29% |
| vn | | | | | 42.85% |
| ian | iao | | ng | uo, iao, iang, ing | 43.16% |
| uan | van | n | i, ng | ing, uai, ua | 49.43% |
| van | uan | | | ian, uan, | 42.59% |
| uen | | | | | 0.00% |
| ang | an | | n | an, en, eng, ong | 50.72% |
| eng | ang | | o, a | ang, ong, iang | 41.94% |
| ing | ang | i | a, u | ian, uan, ang, iang | 42.34% |
| ong | | | | uan, uang | 51.60% |
| iang | | i | | ing, ang | 47.88% |
| uang | | u | | ang | 71.66% |
| ueng | uang | | | uang, uo | 33.33% |
| iong | | | | eng | 40.00% |

From Table above, the confusion matrices and confusion rules of vowels and diphthongs can be seen. If the target phoneme is a consonant, but it is recognized as a vowel in the specific recognition, we neglect this recognition error, and the reverse is equally true. Vowel phoneme mapping, statistical frequency and recognition accuracy, all of which have presented in the tables, the first column is the target phoneme, the recognition phoneme that the behavior matches the target phoneme, without listing the mapping of phoneme that not to be considered (Table 2).

# 4 Conclusions

In this paper, we mainly analyze the results of 50 Uyghur learners through Chinese speech recognition. The samples are collected and the sample information is obtained through recognition on them, and based on this, the error analysis is carried out, and then the relevant rules and laws are obtained. It has introduced two cases of learners' possible pronunciation erroneous phonemes in detail; first, according to the reasons leading to erroneous pronunciation of learners, the cross-linguistic phonological comparison method is used to predict phonemic confusion, for Uyghur learners, their personal factors will also lead to confusion. With the help of data-driven, the extra phoneme confusion is summarized and the related situation of the two methods is clarified precisely, hoping that the phoneme confusion rules can provide linguistic priori knowledge for speech recognition. In the meantime, the next step is to establish a pronunciation evaluation system specifically targeting Uyghur Chinese learners by using the pronunciation rules obtained from this study in combination with speech recognition.

**Acknowledgments.** This work was supported by the National Natural Science Foundation of China (NSFC; grant 61462085, 61662078, and 61633013).

# References

Ito, A., Lim, Y.-L., Suzuki, M.: Pronunciation error detection for computer-assisted language learning system based on error rule clustering using a decision tree. Acoust. Sci. Technol. **28** (2), 131–133 (2007)

Stanley, T., Hacioglu, K.: Improving L1-specific phonological error diagnosis in computer assisted pronunciation training. In: INTERSPEECH 2012 [S.l.]: ISCA, pp. 827– 830 (2012)

Jiang, D., Wang, W., Shi, L., Song, H.: A compressive sensing-based approach to end-to-end network traffic reconstruction. IEEE Trans. Netw. Sci. Eng. (2018a). https://doi.org/10.1109/tnse.20182877-597

Wang, Y.B., Lee, L. S.: Improved approaches of modeling and detecting error patterns with empirical analysis for computer-aided pronunciation training. In: ICASSP 2012 [S.l.], pp. 5049 –5052. IEEE (2012)

Jiang, D., Zhang, P., Lv, Z.: Energy-efficient multi-constraint routing algorithm with load balancing for smart city applications. IEEE Internet Things J. **3**(6), 1437–1447 (2016)

Witt, S.M.: Use of Speech Recognition in Computer-Assisted Language Learning. [S.l.], Cambridge University (1999)

Ye, H., Young, S.J.: Improving the speech recognition performance of beginners in spoken conversational interaction for language learning. In: INTERSPEECH 2005. [S.l.]: ISCA, pp. 289 –292 (2005)

Jiang, D., Huo, L., Song, H.: Rethinking behaviors and activities of base stations in mobile cellular networks based on big data analysis. IEEE Trans. Netw. Sci. Eng. 1(1), 1–12 (2018b)

Qian, X.J., Meng, H., Soong, F.K.: On mispronunciation Lexicon generation using joint sequence multigrams in computer-aided pronunciation training (CAPT). In: INTERSPEECH 2011. [S.l.]: ISCA, PP. 865 –868 (2011)

Ladefoged, P., Johnson, K.: A Course in phonetics, 7th edn. Peking University Press, Peking (2015)

Thurgood, G., LaPolla, R.J.: The Sino-Tibetan Languages. London Routledge, China (2003)

Zhao, X., Zhu, Z.: Uyghur Language. National press, China (1985)

Shifeng, F.: Experimental Phonology Exploration. Peking University Press, China (2009)

Lo, W.K., Zhang, S., Meng, H.M.: Automatic derivation of phonological rules for mispronunciation detection in a computer-assisted pronunciation training system. In: INTERSPEECH 2010, pp. 765– 768 (2010)

Troung, K.: Automatic Pronunciation Error Detection in Dutch as a Second Language: an Acoustic-Phonetic Approach, Utrecht University (2004)

Dong, B., Zhao, Q.W.: Automatic scoring of flat tongue and raised tongue in computer-assisted Mandarin learning. In: ISCSLP2006. [S.l.]: IEEE, pp. 2–7 (2006)

Wang, S., Li, H.: Research on the evaluation of spoken language scale intelligence for second language learning. Chin. J. Inf. Sci. 25(6), 142–148 (2011)

Gass, S., Selinker, L.: Language Transfer in Language Learning, pp. 22–113. John Benjamins Publishing Company, Amsterdam (1992)

Zhang, R.: Research on automatic evaluation method of Mandarin Chinese pronunciation. Harbin Institute of Technology, pp. 72–101 (2013)

# Network Recovery for Large-Scale Failures in Smart Grid by Simulation

Huibin Jia[(✉)], Hongda Zheng, Yonghe Gai, and Dongfang Xu

School of Electrical and Electronic Engineering,
North China Electric Power University, Baoding, China
huibin.jia@foxmail.com

**Abstract.** Large-scale natural disaster or malicious attacks could cause serious damage to the power communication network in smart grid. If the damaged network cannot be repaired timely, great threat will be brought to the secure and stable operation of power grid. Therefore, an importance-based recovery method for large-scale failure has been proposed in smart grid by simulation. Firstly, the link importance for the whole network is calculated according to the solution of the link importance for the services type and the importance of services type for the power communication network. Secondly, a fault recovery model with the sum of the importance of each fault link has been established to recover more important communication services under the condition of limited resources. Finally, we propose a heuristic algorithm to reduce the expenditure of time, and then compare the results of the model with the 0–1 integer programming method to verify the feasibility of the method. The experimental results show that the links which carry high-priority can get priority to be repaired in the paper, thus it ensures the safe and stable operation of power communication network.

**Keywords:** Network recovery · Smart grid · Large-scale failures · Simulation

## 1 Introduction

Communication network is the basis for guaranteeing the safe and stable operation of the smart grid. It is heavily depended to support the services of urgent protection and control in smart, especially in times of emergency. When the large-scale failure are caused by nature disaster, blackout, and malicious, huge economic losses and serious social impact will be brought, if the failure of network cannot be restored timely [1–3]. For example, in 2005, the serious accident of large-scale communication optical cable interruption in Central China Power Grid has caused the central China Network to be basically in a state of paralysis, which poses a great threat to the safety of the power grid. In the south of China, a large number of interconnected optical cables have been disrupted due to snow disaster, which has led to the split operation of the communication network and seriously affected the stable operation of the power system. After the large-scale failures of communication network in smart grid, it takes a large number of manpower, material, financial and other resources to restore the power, which results in the recovery of the power communication network after a large-scale failure cannot be fully expanded at the

H. Song et al. (Eds.): SIMUtools 2019, LNICST 295, pp. 477–485, 2019.
https://doi.org/10.1007/978-3-030-32216-8_46

same time. Therefore, it is essential that repairing the damaged infrastructures of smart grid, at least to the point where mission-critical services can be supported [4].

There have been a lot of research on large-scale network failure recovery in telecommunication network. An iterative segmentation and deletion method has been proposed, which decomposes the problem of large-scale network recovery into sub problems and the set of network component has been obtained [5]. The importance assessment method for damaged network components has been proposed in [6], the network component is repaired according to their importance. In [7], a GSR heuristic algorithm for maximizing network traffic has been proposed, it combines multiple fault components randomly, and decreases the computation time by reducing the number of fault components. In [8], a fault probability detection method based on wave energy has been proposed, which can prevent and protect large-scale networks, improve the efficiency of uninterrupted transmission of data, and reduce the interruption time on a large-scale of network. A forward and backward-based heuristic algorithm has been proposed to solve the multi-stage network recovery after large-scale network failures [9]. In [10], superposition network technology has been used to calculate multiple routing configurations in advance to prevent simultaneous network failures, thereby improving the network tolerance performance of disaster.

However, the communication network is different from the telecommunication network [11]. There are multiple services. Each service has different delay and reliability requirement, and importance of each service is also different smart grid. Therefore, after the large-scale failures of communication network, how to repair the important service quickly and ensure the reliable operation of power system is particularly important. In the paper, an importance-based recovery method for large-scale failure has been proposed in smart grid by simulation. In the method, the link importance is calculate by K shortest path algorithm [12], the heuristic algorithm, considering the characteristics of power communication network, has been proposed to solve the problem. In the algorithm, we consider the link importance and the priority of communication network. Thus, the critical services in power communication network is firstly and quickly repaired.

## 2    The Characteristics of Communication Network in Smart Grid

According to the relevant regulations of the security protection management system in smart grid,the services can be divided into four major categories and safety zones, such as operation control services(Safe Area I), operation information services(Safe Area II), management information services(Safe Area III), and management Office services(Safe Area IV). The detailed information about the relative importance of each service is introducing in [13].

A method for calculating the importance of service is also given in [13]. Firstly, the relative importance values of each service is calculated, and it is represented by $a_i^{Sum}$, as shown in Eq. (1). Secondly, $a_i^{Sum}$ is normalized according to the Eq. (2). After the normalization, the minimum value of $\left(a_i^{Sum}\right)'$ may be 0, which means that the importance of the service is 0 and the service can be discarded. Obviously, it is unreasonable. Therefore, it needs to be mapped to the interval [X, 1] according to the Eq. (3). When the value of X is 0.1, the distance between the maximum and minimum of the importance for each service is 10. Finally, the values of the importance for each service are shown in Table 1.

$$a_i^{Sum} a_i^{Sum} = \sum_{j=1}^{6} a_{ij} \tag{1}$$

$$\left(a_i^{Sum}\right)' = \frac{a_i^{Sum} - \left(a_i^{Sum}\right)_{\min}}{\left(a_i^{Sum}\right)_{\max} - \left(a_i^{Sum}\right)_{\min}} \tag{2}$$

$$Q_i = \left(a_i^{Sum}\right)'(1-X) + X \tag{3}$$

**Table 1.** The importance of power services in smart grid

| Services | Importance | Services | Importance |
|---|---|---|---|
| 550 kV Protective Relay | 1.00 | Video Conferencing | 0.38 |
| 220 kV Protective Relay | 0.95 | Video Monitoring in Substation | 0.34 |
| Safety and Stability System | 0.91 | Protection Information Management | 0.29 |
| Wide-Area Measurement | 0.86 | Lightning Location Detection | 0.29 |
| Dispatching Automation | 0.72 | Administrative Telephone | 0.19 |
| Dispatching Telephone | 0.57 | Office Automation | 0.10 |
| Electric Energy Telemetering | 0.53 | | |

In order to simplify the analysis, 13 kinds of services can be divided into 5 types according to the approximation of importance and the characters of services. The importance of each type is the average of all services in this type, as shown in Table 2.

**Table 2.** The division of service types and related parameters

| Type | Services | Importance of type/$w^m$ | Transmission bandwidth/$b_m$ |
|---|---|---|---|
| I | 550 kV Protective Relay<br>220 kV Protective Relay | 0.98 | 2 |
| II | Safety and Stability System | 0.91 | 2 |
| III | Wide-Area Measurement<br>Dispatching Automation;<br>Dispatching Telephone;<br>Electric Energy Measurement Telemetry | 0.67 | 2 |

(*continued*)

**Table 2.** (*continued*)

| Type | Services | Importance of type/$w^m$ | Transmission bandwidth/$b_m$ |
|------|----------|-------------------------|------------------------------|
| IV | Video Conferencing | 0.33 | 2 |
|    | Video Monitoring in Substation | | |
|    | Protection Information Management | | |
|    | Lightning Location Detection | | |
| V  | Administrative Telephone | 0.15 | 1 |
|    | Office Automation | | |

## 3 Recovery Strategy and Algorithm

### 3.1 Problem Description

Link importance is a standard to evaluate the performance of links to the network, and it is also the reference to allocate limited recovery resources for the damaged links. The damaged links with high importance has the priority to use the recovery resources and can be repaired firstly.

There are many services in the communication network of smart grid. The services can be divided into different types which represent by $M$ according their characteristics. If we calculate the paths for each service of one type with the $K$ shortest paths algorithm, the ratio which the frequency of the $K$ shortest paths traverses link (i, j) and the frequency of the $K$ shortest paths traverses all kinks reflects the importance of link (i, j) for this type. We define it as Eq. (4).

$$\pi_{ij}^m = \frac{F_{(i,j)}^m}{F^m} \tag{4}$$

As shown in Eq. (1), if we calculate the $K$ shortest paths for each service in the $m$-th type, $F_{(i,j)}^m$ can represent the frequency that $K$ shortest paths traverse the link (i, j) and $F^m$ can represent the number of all links that $K$ shortest paths traverses. However, different types of service have different weight for the network which represent by $w^m$. The importance of the same link may different from different types. So, we use $q_{ij}^m$ to describe the importance of the link (i, j) in the $m$-$th$ type for the network, as shown in Eq. (5).

$$q_{ij}^m = w^m \pi_{ij}^m \tag{5}$$

Considering the characteristics of the services in the communication network of smart grid, the recovery result is evaluated by $f(Q)$, which is the sum of the link importance values of the repaired links. We define it as the objective function in Eq. (6).

The flow balance constraint is given by Eq. (7), where $x^p_{ij}$ represents if the service $p$ traverses link (i, j), going from node $i$ to node $j$. If the service $p$ traverses link (i, j), $x^p_{ij} = 1$; otherwise, $x^p_{ij} = 0$. The capacity constraint of each link is shown in Eq. (8), where $B_{ij}$ represents the bandwidth of the link (i, j) before the large-scale failure and $b_{ij}$ represents the bandwidth of the link (i, j) after large-scale failure in the network.

We assume that 1 unit of recovery resources is consumed in the link per kilometer, so the recovery resources which the damaged link (i, j) is to be consumed is introduced in Eq. (9), where $d_{ij}$ represents the length of link (i, j).

Recovery resources are limited throughout the total recovery stages, so the constraint in Eq. (10) is to limit the resource, which is represented by $R$. If the damaged link (i, j) is repaired, $x_{ij} = 1$; otherwise, $x_{ij} = 0$. $r_{ij}$ represents the resource of repairing the damaged link (i, j). Finally, Eq. (8) represent that a damaged link can be repaired only once throughout the recovery stages.

The network recovery problem can be formulated as follows:

Objective function:

$$\max f(Q) = \sum_{m=1}^{M} \sum_{(i,j) \in \Lambda} x_{ij} q^m_{ij} \tag{6}$$

Subject to:

$$\sum_{(i,j) \in E} x^p_{ij} - \sum_{(j,i) \in E} x^p_{ji} = \begin{cases} 1 & i = p(\theta) \\ -1 & i = p(\theta) \\ 0 & others \end{cases} \tag{7}$$

$$\sum_{m=1}^{M} \sum_{p=1}^{P_m} b_m x^p_{ij} \leq b_{ij} + (B_{ij} - b_{ij}) x_{ij} \tag{8}$$

$$r_{ij} = (B_{ij} - b_{ij}) d_{ij} \tag{9}$$

$$\sum_{m=1}^{M} \sum_{(i,j) \in \Lambda} x_{ij} r_{ij} \leq R \tag{10}$$

$$\sum_{m=1}^{M} x_{ij} \leq 1 \tag{11}$$

## 3.2   The Proposed Algorithm

The mathematical model described above is 0–1 programming, which is NP-hard. When the model is solved by searching, its computation time will increase exponentially as the number of damaged links increases [14]. Especially when the extent of failure is larger, it is extremely difficult to determine an appropriate recovery order within a practical time. Therefore, we propose a link importance-based heuristic algorithm as follows:

Firstly, the importance of each damaged link in different types is obtained according to the Eq. (4)–(5), and they are sorted in the descending order. Secondly, we repair the damaged links from the high priority type to the low priority type. Note that the damaged link which has been repaired in high priority of type, will not be repaired again in low priority of type. Finally, the objective value can be calculated according to the damaged links which has been selected to repair.

---
**Algorithm:**

Input: The damaged links set of different types $L_m$, repaired links set $L$,

1 Divide all services into $M$ types and each type of services have the priority $m$, which 0 represent the highest priority.

2 Calculate $q_{ij}^m$ for all damaged links in different types of services, and sort them in descending order;

3 while $m \leq M$ and $R \geq 0$ do

4    while $L_m \neq \phi$ and $R \geq 0$ do

5      Find the damaged links (i,j) with the maximum of $q_{ij}^m$;

6      if $x_{ij} = 0$ then

6        $R = R - r_{ij}$ and $x_{ij} = 1$;

       └Move the link (i,j) from $L_m$ to L;

7 └m=m+1;

8 Calculate the objective function value according $L$;

---

## 4  Computational Experiments

In this experiment, we use the network topology of the backbone transmission network of Guangdong province as Fig. 1, which consist of 14 nodes and 16 links. The number between nodes represent the distance of them (*KM*). Meanwhile, we assume that all links is partial damaged or damaged completely besides the link of (7, 8) and (6, 7). The capacity of links before failure and after failure are shown in Table 3, and the transmission rate in this experiment is $2 \times 10^8$ m/s. The distribution of different types services (s, d) in the network is shown in Table 4, where s represent the source and d represent the destination of the services.

In the experiment, we verify the performance of the proposed algorithm for the target values under the different resources. The resource for recovering the damaged network is {100, 200, 300, 400, 500, 600, 700, 800}, respectively. The results is shown

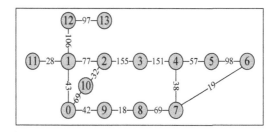

**Fig. 1.** The backbone transmission network topology of Guangdong Province

**Table 3.** The bandwidth of links before and after failure in network

| Links | The bandwidth before/after failure | Links | The bandwidth before/after failure |
|---|---|---|---|
| (0, 1) | 10240/0 | (2, 10) | 10240/8000 |
| (0, 9) | 10240/0 | (4, 5) | 10240/10000 |
| (0, 10) | 10240/1000 | (4, 7) | 10240/8000 |
| (1, 2) | 10240/1000 | (5, 6) | 10240/10000 |
| (1, 11) | 10240/2000 | (6, 7) | 10240/10240 |
| (1, 12) | 10240/2000 | (7, 8) | 10240/10240 |
| (2, 3) | 10240/4000 | (8, 9) | 10240/0 |
| (3, 4) | 10240/4000 | (12, 13) | 10240/0 |

**Table 4.** The distribution of different services in network

| Services (s, d) | Type × number | Services (s, d) | Type × number |
|---|---|---|---|
| (0, 1) | II × 5 + III × 20 + IV × 5 + V × 10 | (1, 2) | I × 1 + II × 2 |
| (0, 2) | II × 3 + III × 12 + IV × 3 + V × 6 | (1, 11) | I × 1 + II × 2 |
| (0, 3) | II × 2 + III × 8 + IV × 2 + V × 4 | (2, 3) | I × 1 + II × 2 |
| (0, 4) | II × 5 + III × 20 + IV × 5 + V × 10 | (3, 4) | I × 1 + II × 2 |
| (0, 5) | II × 2 + III × 8 + IV × 2 + V × 4 | (3, 10) | I × 1 + II × 2 |
| (0, 6) | II × 6 + III × 24 + IV × 6 + V × 12 | (4, 5) | I × 1 + II × 2 |
| (0, 7) | II × 3 + III × 12 + IV × 3 + V × 6 | (4, 7) | I × 1 + II × 2 |
| (0, 8) | II × 2 + III × 8 + IV × 2 + V × 4 | (5, 6) | I × 1 + II × 2 |
| (0, 9) | II × 2 + III × 8 + IV × 2 + V × 4 | (6, 7) | I × 1 + II × 2 |
| (0,10) | II × 2 + III × 8 + IV × 2 + V × 4 | (7, 8) | I × 1 + II × 2 |
| (0, 11) | II × 3 + III × 4 + IV × 1 + V × 2 | (8, 9) | I × 1 + II × 2 |
| (0, 12) | II × 4 + III × 8 + IV × 6 + V × 5 | (13, 14) | II × 3 + III × 12 + IV × 3 + V × 6 |

in Fig. 2, where (a) is the comparison of target values with 0–1 programing and heuristic algorithm and (b) is the recovery result of different types of services.

It can be seen from the Fig. 2(a) that the gap between the optimal value and the value of the proposed algorithm is getting smaller with the increasing of resources. The

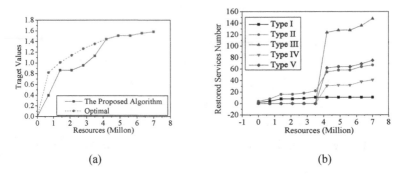

(a)                              (b)

**Fig. 2.** The result of network recovery under different resources

more the resources is, the better the performance of the proposed algorithm. Moreover, the target values of proposed algorithm is the same as the optimum when the resource is more than 4 million.

We can see from the Fig. 2(b) that the types of services which have high priority has been restored firstly when the resource is little. Meanwhile, the types of services which have low priority is restored gradually with the increasing of resource.

As discussed above, it can show that as the resources increase, the proposed algorithm can acquire the good recovery performance when the network have a large-scale failure. The gap between the proposed algorithm and the optimal value is much lower with the increasing of resource. Meanwhile, the types of services which have high priority can be restored firstly to ensure the safe operation of smart grid. Therefore, we can conclude that the proposed algorithm in this paper is suitable for the recovery of large-scale network failure.

## 5   Conclusion

When the smart grid has been destroyed by the large-scale failures, the objective of network recovery in smart grid is to restore the types of services which have high priority firstly. So, a subset of the damaged components is selected to repair after a large-scale failure with the limited recovery resources. We have formulated the problem as 0–1 programming model, which is NP-hard. A Link Importance-based heuristic algorithm has been proposed to solve the problem. Simulation experiments have shown that the heuristic algorithm provides a good solution. However, according to the experimental results, we can find that there is a gap between the heuristic algorithm and the optimal value. In the future work, a better combination optimization method should be found, so that the best recovery effect can be reached as soon as possible after the large-scale failure.

**Acknowledgement.** This work was supported by the Natural Science Foundation of China grant No. 61472037; the Fundamental Research Funds for the Central Universities 2017 MS113.

# References

1. Cleveland, F.: Enhancing the reliability and security of the information infrastructure used to manage the power system. In: Power Engineering Society General Meeting. IEEE (2007)
2. Kamrul, I.M., Oki, E.: Optimization of OSPF link weight to minimize worst-case network congestion against single-link failure. In: IEEE International Conference on Communications. IEEE (2011)
3. Jiang, D., Wang, W., Shi, L., Song, H.: A compressive sensing-based approach to end-to-end network traffic reconstruction. IEEE Trans. Netw. Sci. Eng. (2018). https://doi.org/10.1109/tnse.2018.2877597
4. Yu, H., Yang, C.: Partial network recovery to maximize traffic demand. IEEE Commun. Lett. **15**, 1388–1390 (2011)
5. Bartolini, N., et al.: Network recovery after massive failures. In: IEEE/IFIP International Conference on Dependable Systems and Networks, pp. 97–108. IEEE (2016)
6. Bartolini, N., et al.: On critical service recovery after massive network failures. IEEE/ACM Trans. Netw. **25**, 2235–2249 (2017)
7. Genda, K., Kamamura, S.: Multi-stage network recovery considering traffic demand after a large-scale failure. In: IEEE International Conference on Communications. IEEE (2016)
8. Izaddoost, A., Heydari, S.S.: Enhancing network service survivability in large-scale failure scenarios. J. Commun. Netw. **16**, 534–547 (2014)
9. Wang, J., Qiao, C., Yu, H.: On progressive network recovery after a major disruption. In: 2011 Proceedings IEEE INFOCOM, pp. 1925–1933 IEEE (2011)
10. Horie, T., et al.: A new method of proactive recovery mechanism for large-scale network failures In: International Conference on Advanced Information NETWORKING and Applications, pp. 951–958. IEEE (2009)
11. Jiang, D., Huo, L., Lv, Z., et al.: A joint multi-criteria utility-based network selection approach for vehicle-to-infrastructure networking. IEEE Trans. Intell. Transp. Syst. **19**(10), 3305–3319 (2018)
12. Berclaz, J., et al.: Multiple object tracking using k-shortest paths optimization. IEEE Trans. Pattern Anal. Mach. Intell. **33**, 1806–1819 (2011)
13. Fan, B., Tang, L.: Vulnerability analysis of power communication network. Proc. CSEE **34**, 1191–1197 (2014)
14. Jiang, D., Wang, Y., Han, Y., et al.: Maximum connectivity-based channel allocation algorithm in cognitive wireless networks for medical applications. Neurocomputing **220**, 41–51 (2017)

# Matrix-Variate Restricted Boltzmann Machine Classification Model

Jinghua Li[1]([✉]), Pengyu Tian[1], Dehui Kong[1], Lichun Wang[1],
Shaofan Wang[1], and Baocai Yin[2]

[1] Beijing Key Laboratory of Multimedia and Intelligent Software Technology,
Faculty of Information Technology, Beijing University of Technology,
Beijing 100124, China
lijinghua@bjut.edu.cn
[2] College of Computer Science and Technology, Faculty of Electronic
Information and Electrical Engineering, Dalian University of Technology,
Dalian 116620, China

**Abstract.** Recently, Restricted Boltzmann Machine (RBM) has demonstrated excellent capacity of modelling vector variable. A variant of RBM, Matrix-variate Restricted Boltzmann Machine (MVRBM), extends the ability of RBM and is able to model matrix-variate data directly without vectorized process. However, MVRBM is still an unsupervised generative model, and is usually used to feature extraction or initialization of deep neural network. When MVRBM is used to classify, additional classifiers are necessary. This paper proposes a Matrix-variate Restricted Boltzmann Machine Classification Model (ClassMVRBM) to classify 2D data directly. In the novel ClassMVRBM, classification constraint is introduced to MVRBM. On one hand, the features extracted by MVRBM are more discriminative, on the other hand, the proposed model can be directly used to classify. Experiments on some publicly available databases demonstrate that the classification performance of ClassMVRBM has been largely improved, resulting in higher image classification accuracy than conventional unsupervised RBM, its variants and Restricted Boltzmann Machine Classification Model (ClassRBM).

**Keywords:** ClassMVRBM · MVRBM · RBM

## 1 Introduction

Currently, more and more multiple array data are widely acquired in modern computer vision research, such as 2D images, 3D videos and 4D light fields etc. [19]. It is well known that vectorizing multiway data is a common used method, however, such vectorization process inevitably leads to possible data structure break and dimension curse. How to model the multiway data more appropriately so as to process and analyze it effectively is the key problem. Many methods have been proposed during the past years. Take 2D images (matrix-style) for example, such as 2D Principle Component Analysis (2DPCA) [1, 2], and 2D Linear Discriminant Analysis (2DLDA) [3].

H. Song et al. (Eds.): SIMUtools 2019, LNICST 295, pp. 486–497, 2019.
https://doi.org/10.1007/978-3-030-32216-8_47

Unfortunately, 2DPCA and 2DLDA are still linear methods, which both aim to find an optimal linear projection matrix to reduce dimension or classify.

RBM is an effective model for nonlinear modeling [4], it is becoming one of the most popular methods, which is widely used in speech/image feature extraction, feature representation [5] and the initialization of deep neural network, typical RBM variants include Gaussian-Bernoulli RBM (GBRBM) [6], Improved Gaussian-Bernoulli RBM (IGBRBM) [7] and Tensor-variate Restricted Boltzmann Machines [8] etc. Especially, Larochelle et al. [9] proposed ClassRBM to implement the classification task, which extended the ability of RBM. After that, Peng et al. [10] integrates infinite RBM and the classification RBM for Radar high resolution range profile recognition. However, when RBM and ClassRBM are used to process image signals, the 2D image matrices must be transformed into 1D image vectors in advance, such process leads to possible high dimensional vector and spatial structural damage of image. Qi et al. [11] proposed MVRBM model, which has been successfully applied to represent 2D signal. Furthermore, Liu et al. [12] proposed improved MVRBM named MVGRBM, which assumes the matrix data entries follow Gaussian distributions. However, MVRBM and MVGRBM are still unsupervised generative models. When the goal is to classify the image data, an additional classifier must be introduced, such as nearest neighbor classifier or neural network. Inspired by Hugo, this paper adds the label constraint to the existing MVRBM model, i.e., we propose a Matrix-variate Restricted Boltzmann Machine Classification Model (ClassMVRBM), which is capable of classifying the images directly.

## 2   Definition of ClassMVRBM Model

In this section, we propose a ClassMVRBM model for image classification. Firstly, we introduce the definition of the fundamental MVRBM, and then the definition of the proposed model is detailed.

### 2.1   Definition of MVRBM

The MVRBM [11] is a bipartite undirected probabilistic graphical model connecting stochastic matrix-style visible units and matrix-style hidden units by tensor-style weights. To formulate the model, we define the follow variables: $X = [x_{ij}] \in \mathbb{R}^{I \times J}$ is a matrix variable of the visual layer, and corresponds to the input observation. $H = [h_{kl}] \in \mathbb{R}^{K \times L}$ is a matrix variable of the hidden layer, and represents the features extracted from the input. $\mathcal{W} = [w_{ijkl}] \in \mathbb{R}^{I \times J \times K \times L}$ denotes the connecting relationship of $X$ and $H$, which is a fourth-order tensor. $B = [b_{ij}] \in \mathbb{R}^{I \times J}$ and $C = [c_{kl}] \in \mathbb{R}^{K \times L}$ are the matrix-style biases in the visual units and the hidden ones. Therefore, $\Theta' = \{\mathcal{W}, B, C\}$ defines all the model parameters of MVRBM. The MVRBM defines an energy function for joint configuration $(X, H)$ as shown in formula (1):

$$E(X, H; \Theta') = -\sum_{i=1}^{I}\sum_{j=1}^{J}\sum_{k=1}^{K}\sum_{l=1}^{L} x_{ij}h_{kl}w_{ijkl} - \sum_{i=1}^{I}\sum_{j=1}^{J} x_{ij}b_{ij} - \sum_{k=1}^{K}\sum_{l=1}^{L} h_{kl}c_{kl}. \quad (1)$$

Based on the aforementioned energy function (1), MVRBM defines the joint probability distribution of the visual variates and hidden ones as formula (2):

$$p(X, H; \Theta') = \frac{1}{Z(\Theta')} \exp\{-E(X, H; \Theta')\}, \tag{2}$$

where $Z(\Theta')$ is the normalization constant. Maximum likelihood estimation is generally introduced to solve the model parameter $\Theta'$, and the log likelihood of $X$ is defined by formula (3).

$$\underset{\Theta'}{\mathrm{Max}}\ell = \frac{1}{N} \sum_{n=1}^{N} \log(\sum_{H \in \mathbb{H}} \exp\{-E(\mathbf{X}^{(n)}, H; \Theta')\}) - \log Z(\Theta'), \tag{3}$$

here, $N$ represents the number of the samples and $\mathbf{X}^{(n)}$ means the $n^{th}$ input sample.

## 2.2    Definition of ClassMVRBM

MVRBM has been successfully used to represent 2D signal, however, MVRBM is still an unsupervised generative model. This paper aims to design an improved MVRBM with the performance of classification, to this end, the classification constraint is added to the existing MVRBM. Specially, as depicted in Fig. 1, we connect an additional label layer to the previous hidden layer. Therefore, in the novel model there are two branches, and the left is the original MVRBM, while the right one is the newly added classification one.

To introduce our model, we define additional variables as follows: $\mathbf{y} = [y_t] \in \mathbb{R}^T$ is a label vector, and indicates the classification of the input data by one-hot coding. $\mathcal{P} = [p_{tkl}] \in \mathbb{R}^{T \times K \times L}$ is the connecting weight of $\mathbf{y}$ and $H$, indicating the relationship between the label variable and the hidden features. $\mathbf{d} = [d_t] \in \mathbb{R}^T$ is the bias vector of the label layer. Refer to (1), we define the novel joint energy function formulated as below.

$$E(X, \mathbf{y}, H; \Theta) = - \sum_{i=1}^{I} \sum_{j=1}^{J} \sum_{k=1}^{K} \sum_{l=1}^{L} x_{ij} h_{kl} w_{ijkl} - \sum_{i=1}^{I} \sum_{j=1}^{J} x_{ij} b_{ij} - \sum_{t=1}^{T} \sum_{k=1}^{K} \sum_{l=1}^{L} y_t h_{kl} p_{tkl}$$
$$- \sum_{t=1}^{T} y_t d_t - \sum_{k=1}^{K} \sum_{l=1}^{L} h_{kl} c_{kl}, \tag{4}$$

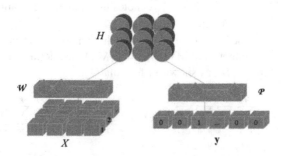

**Fig. 1.** Graphical illustration of ClassMVRBM

In view of $\mathcal{W}$ is a four-order tensor, which enables the model parameters to increase greatly. To reduce the model parameters, this paper assumes $w_{ijkl} = u_{ki}v_{lj}$ by tensor analysis and decomposition [13], therefore, the revised energy function is in the following:

$$
E(X, \mathbf{y}, H; \Theta) = -\sum_{i=1}^{I}\sum_{j=1}^{J}\sum_{k=1}^{K}\sum_{l=1}^{L} x_{ij}h_{kl}u_{ki}v_{lj} - \sum_{i=1}^{I}\sum_{j=1}^{J} x_{ij}b_{ij} - \sum_{t=1}^{T}\sum_{k=1}^{K}\sum_{l=1}^{L} y_{t}h_{kl}p_{tkl}
$$
$$
- \sum_{t=1}^{T} y_{t}d_{t} - \sum_{k=1}^{K}\sum_{l=1}^{L} h_{kl}c_{kl}.
$$

(5)

Defining matrix-style variables $U = [u_{ki}] \in \mathbb{R}^{K \times I}$ and $V = [v_{lj}] \in \mathbb{R}^{L \times J}$, therefore, $\Theta = \{U, V, \mathcal{P}, B, C, \mathbf{d}\}$ indicates all model parameters of ClassMVRBM, here, the definition of $\mathcal{W}, B, C$ is same to that of MVRBM. Based on the formula (5), the joint distribution of $X, \mathbf{y}, H$ is defined as follows:

$$
p(X, \mathbf{y}, H; \Theta) = \frac{\exp(-E(X, \mathbf{y}, H))}{Z(\Theta)},
$$

(6)

$Z(\Theta)$ is the normalized constant and written as:

$$
Z(\Theta) = \sum_{X, \mathbf{y}, H} \exp(\{-E(X, \mathbf{y}, H; \Theta)\}).
$$

(7)

## 3   Optimization of ClassMVRBM Model

Given the training data pairs $D_{\text{train}} = \{(\mathbf{X}^{(1)}, \mathbf{y}^{(1)}), \cdots, (\mathbf{X}^{(n)}, \mathbf{y}^{(n)}), \cdots (\mathbf{X}^{(N)}, \mathbf{y}^{(N)})\}$, the most popular training objective for RBMs and its variants is generative, that is, maximizing the joint probability is the training objective. Therefore, the equivalent minimized negative log likelihood objective function can be written as:

$$
\min L_{gen}(D_{\text{train}}) = -\sum_{n=1}^{N} (\log p(X^{(n)}, \mathbf{y}^{(n)})) = -\sum_{n=1}^{N} (\log p(\mathbf{y}^{(n)}|X^{(n)}) + \log p(X^{(n)}))
$$
$$
= -\sum_{n=1}^{N} \log p(\mathbf{y}^{(n)}|X^{(n)}) - \sum_{n=1}^{N} \log p(X^{(n)}).
$$

(8)

According to (8), our proposed ClassMVRBM includes two parts, one is the conditional probability part, and the other is the marginal distribution of the input samples. Since our training data are labeled and for the test sample, a good prediction of the target classification is the only interesting point, therefore, this paper only focuses on the supervised part in (8), that is, the condition probability is the only objective function as follows.

$$\min_{\Theta} L(\Theta) = -\sum_{n=1}^{N} \log(p(\mathbf{y}^{(n)} \mid X^{(n)}; \Theta)). \tag{9}$$

For a single sample pair $(\mathbf{X}^{(n)}, \mathbf{y}^{(n)})$, we derive:

$$\begin{aligned}
\log p(\mathbf{y}^{(n)}|X^{(n)}) &= \log \frac{p(X^{(n)}, \mathbf{y}^{(n)})}{p(X^{(n)})} \\
&= \log \sum_{H} \exp(-E(X^{(n)}, \mathbf{y}^{(n)}, H)) - \log \sum_{\mathbf{y}, H} \exp(-E(X^{(n)}, \mathbf{y}, H)).
\end{aligned} \tag{10}$$

With respect to any parameter $\theta$ of $\Theta$ in ClassMVRBM, the gradient of $\log p(\mathbf{y}^{(n)}|X^{(n)})$ is:

$$\begin{aligned}
& \frac{\partial \log p(\mathbf{y}^{(n)}|X^{(n)})}{\partial \theta} \\
&= \frac{\sum_{H} \exp(-E(X^{(n)}, \mathbf{y}^{(n)}, H)) \frac{\partial(-E(X^{(n)}, \mathbf{y}^{(n)}, H))}{\partial \theta}}{\sum_{H} \exp(-E(X^{(n)}, \mathbf{y}^{(n)}, H))} - \frac{\sum_{\mathbf{y}, H} \exp(-E(X^{(n)}, \mathbf{y}, H)) \frac{\partial(-E(X^{(n)}, \mathbf{y}, H))}{\partial \theta}}{\sum_{\mathbf{y}, H} \exp(-E(X^{(n)}, \mathbf{y}, H))} \\
&= \sum_{H} p(H|X^{(n)}, \mathbf{y}^{(n)}) \frac{\partial}{\partial \theta}(-E(X^{(n)}, \mathbf{y}^{(n)}, H)) - \sum_{\mathbf{y}, H} p(\mathbf{y}, H|X^{(n)}) \frac{\partial}{\partial \theta}(-E(X^{(n)}, \mathbf{y}, H)).
\end{aligned} \tag{11}$$

According to (11), the two terms around the minus sign needed to be solved, respectively. Analyze the parameters $\Theta = \{U, V, \mathcal{P}, B, C, \mathbf{d}\}$ to be optimized, since the optimization process does not include the reconstruction of the input $X$, and the input biases are not involved in the computation of $p(\mathbf{y}|X)$, the gradient with respect to $B$ is 0. The bias vector $\mathbf{d}$ in the label layer is special and only the label position is updated. In this paper, we assume the position of classification label is $t$, the gradient of the bias component $d_t$ is as follows:

$$\frac{\partial \log p(y_t^{(n)}|X^{(n)})}{\partial d_t} = 1 - p(y_t^{(n)}|X^{(n)}), \quad y_t^{(n)} \in \{1, \cdots, M\}. \tag{12}$$

Here, $M$ is the number of categories. For the other parameters $\theta \in \{U, V, \mathcal{P}, C\}$, the derivative of the log likelihood function with respect to every parameter is computed below. Firstly $\frac{\partial E}{\partial \theta}$ is calculated, and then $\sum_{H} p(H|X^{(n)}, \mathbf{y}^{(n)}) \frac{\partial}{\partial \theta}(-E(X^{(n)}, \mathbf{y}^{(n)}, H))$ and $\sum_{\mathbf{y}, H} p(\mathbf{y}, H|X^{(n)}) \frac{\partial}{\partial \theta}(-E(X^{(n)}, \mathbf{y}, H))$ in the objective function (11) are calculated, respectively. To calculate the gradient $\frac{\partial E}{\partial \theta}$, we first take calculating $\frac{\partial E}{\partial U}$ as an example. According to (5), we have

$$\frac{\partial E(X^{(n)}, \mathbf{y}^{(n)}, H; \Theta)}{\partial u_{ki}} = -\sum_{j,l} x_{ij}^{(n)} v_{lj} h_{kl}. \tag{13}$$

The corresponding matrix-style representation is:

$$\frac{\partial E(X^{(n)}, \mathbf{y}^{(n)}, H; \Theta)}{\partial U} = -HVX^{(n)T}. \tag{14}$$

Similarly, the derivatives with respect to other parameters can be calculated, and we discover that the gradients $\frac{\partial E}{\partial \theta} (\theta \in \{U, V, \mathcal{P}, C\})$ all include $h_{kl}$ or $H$, furthermore, for any binary hidden variable unit $h_{kl}$ in the hidden layer $H$,

$$\sum_{h_{kl} \in \{0,1\}} p(h_{kl}|X^{(n)}, \mathbf{y}^{(n)}) \times h_{kl} = p(h_{kl} = 1|X^{(n)}, \mathbf{y}^{(n)}). \tag{15}$$

The activation probability of one single unit in the hidden layer is defined by the following,

$$p(h_{kl} = 1|X, \mathbf{y}; \Theta) = \sigma(c_{kl} + \sum_{i=1}^{I} \sum_{j=1}^{J} x_{ij} u_{ki} v_{lj} + \sum_{t=1}^{T} y_t p_{klt}), \tag{16}$$

where $\sigma$ is the sigmoid function, $\sigma(a) = 1/(1 + \exp(-a))$. It is easy to see that the hidden unit is influenced by not only the visual layer but also the labeled one. In terms of matrix representation, the aforementioned conditional probability can be written as:

$$p(H = 1 | X^{(n)}, \mathbf{y}^{(n)}; \Theta) = \sigma(C + UX^{(n)}V^T + \mathcal{P}_{t\bullet\bullet}) . \tag{17}$$

Here, $\sigma$ applies on the entries of the corresponding matrices. $\mathcal{P}_{t\bullet\bullet}$ denotes all the weights between the $t^{th}$ label component in the label vector and the units in the hidden layer.

With regard to the second term in (11),

$$\sum_{\mathbf{y}, H \in \{0,1\}} p(\mathbf{y}, H|X^{(n)})H = p(\mathbf{y}|X^{(n)}) = \frac{\sum_H \exp(-E(X^{(n)}, \mathbf{y}, H))}{\sum_{\mathbf{y}^*, H} \exp(-E(X^{(n)}, \mathbf{y}^*, H))}, \tag{18}$$

Of which, $\mathbf{y}$ in the numerator represents a special category, while $\mathbf{y}^*$ in the denominator represents all possible categories. Where,

$$\begin{aligned}
&\sum_H \exp(-E(X^{(n)}, \mathbf{y}, H)) \\
&= \exp(d_t) \sum_{h_{11}} \exp(h_{11}(c_{11} + \sum_t \mathcal{P}\mathbf{y} + \sum_{i,j} UX^{(n)}V^T)) \cdots \sum_{h_{kl}} \exp(h_{kl}(c_{kl} + \sum_t \mathcal{P}\mathbf{y} + \sum_{i,j} UX^{(n)}V^T)) \\
&= \exp(d_t)(1 + \exp(c_{11} + \sum_t \mathcal{P}\mathbf{y} + \sum_{i,j} UX^{(n)}V^T)) \cdots \exp(1 + (c_{kl} + \sum_t \mathcal{P}\mathbf{y} + \sum_{i,j} UX^{(n)}V^T)) \\
&= \exp(d_t + \sum_{k,l} \log(1 + \exp(c_{kl} + \sum_t \mathcal{P}\mathbf{y} + \sum_{i,j} UX^{(n)}V^T)))
\end{aligned} \tag{19}$$

In summary, we have:

$$\frac{\partial L(\Theta)}{\partial U} = \sum_{n=1}^{N} \sigma(C+UX^{(n)}V^T+\mathcal{P}_{t\cdots})VX^{(n)^T} - \sum_{n=1}^{N}\sum_{y^*} p(y^* \mid X^{(n)})\sigma(C+UX^{(n)}V^T+\mathcal{P}_{t^*\cdots})VX^{(n)^T}$$

$$\frac{\partial L(\Theta)}{\partial V} = \sum_{n=1}^{N} \sigma(C+UX^{(n)}V^T+\mathcal{P}_{t\cdots})^T UX^{(n)} - \sum_{n=1}^{N}\sum_{y^*} p(y^* \mid X^{(n)})\sigma(C+UX^{(n)}V^T+\mathcal{P}_{t^*\cdots})^T UX^{(n)}$$

$$\frac{\partial L(\Theta)}{\partial \mathcal{P}_{y^*\cdots}} = \sum_{n=1}^{N} \sigma(C+UX^{(n)}V^T+\mathcal{P}_{t\cdots})\mathbf{y}^{(n)} - \sum_{n=1}^{N}\sum_{y^*} p(y^* \mid X^{(n)})\sigma(C+UX^{(n)}V^T+\mathcal{P}_{t\cdots})$$

$$\frac{\partial L(\Theta)}{\partial C} = \sum_{n=1}^{N} \sigma(C+UX^{(n)}V^T+\mathcal{P}_{t\cdots}) - \sum_{n=1}^{N}\sum_{y^*} p(y^* \mid X^{(n)})\sigma(C+UX^{(n)}V^T+\mathcal{P}_{t^*\cdots})$$

(20)

The gradient values used to update the parameters of the model are as follows:

$$\Delta U^{(t)} = \alpha \Delta U^{(t-1)} + \lambda(\frac{\partial L(\Theta)}{\partial U} - \xi_1 U^{(t-1)})$$

$$\Delta V^{(t)} = \alpha \Delta V^{(t-1)} + \lambda(\frac{\partial L(\Theta)}{\partial V} - \xi_1 V^{(t-1)})$$

(21)

$$\Delta \mathcal{P}^{(t)} = \alpha \Delta \mathcal{P}^{(t-1)} + \lambda(\frac{\partial L(\Theta)}{\partial \mathcal{P}} - \xi_2 \mathcal{P}^{(t-1)})$$

$$\Delta C^{(t)} = \alpha \Delta C^{(t-1)} + \lambda \frac{\partial L(\Theta)}{\partial C}$$

$$\Delta \mathbf{d}^{(t)} = \alpha \Delta \mathbf{d}^{(t-1)} + \lambda \frac{\partial L(\Theta)}{\partial \mathbf{d}}$$

Of which, $\lambda$ is the learning rate, $\alpha$ is the momentum, and $\xi_1$ and $\xi_2$ is the weight regularizer. The training algorithm of ClassMVRBM is presented as follows.

---

**Algorithm 1**: Training of ClassMVRBM
___
**Input:** Training pairs set $D = \{(\mathbf{X}^{(1)},\mathbf{y}^{(1)}),\cdots,(\mathbf{X}^{(n)},\mathbf{y}^{(n)}),\cdots,(\mathbf{X}^{(N)},\mathbf{y}^{(N)})\}$ , learning rate $\lambda$
(0.01), momentum $\alpha$ (0.5), weight regularizer $\xi_1$ (0.001), weight regularizer $\xi_2$ (0.00001), the
maximum iteration number Z (100 ), batch size $s$ ( $s$ =2M, that is, there two sample pairs for each
category in each batch) .
**Output:** Model parameters   $\Theta = \{U,V,\mathcal{P},B,C,\mathbf{d}\}$
**Initialization:** Initialize $U,V$ and $\mathcal{P}$ randomly, set the bias $C = B = 0, \mathbf{d} = 0$ and the gradient
increments $\Delta U = \Delta V = \Delta \mathcal{P} = \Delta C = \Delta B = \Delta \mathbf{d} = 0$.
**for** iteration step $z = 1 \rightarrow Z$ **do**
    Divide $D$ into $N/2M$ batches $D_1,\cdots,D_m,\cdots,D_{N/2M}$ of size $s$

    **for** batch $m = 1 \rightarrow N/2M$ **do**
        **for** the sample pairs $(\mathbf{X}^{(n)},\mathbf{y}^{(n)}) \in D_m$ **do**

        $y^0 \leftarrow \mathbf{y}^{(n)}, X^0 \leftarrow \mathbf{X}^{(n)}, \overline{H^0} \leftarrow sigmoid(C+UX^0V^T+\mathcal{P}_{y^0\cdots})$

        #Notation: $a \leftarrow b$ means $a$ is set to $b$, $y^0$ corresponds to the label component.
        **for** $\theta \in \Theta$ **do**        # Update $\theta \in \Theta$ :
        Compute the derivatives of the objective function with respect to all the parameters refer
        to Eq. (20), here, $N$ in the Eq. (20) is equal to batchsize $s$ .
        Update the gradient with Eq. (21)
        Update $\Theta$ with a gradient-based solver $\theta = \theta - \Delta\theta$
        **end for**
        **end for**
    **end for**
**end for**

---

# 4    Experimental Results

To evaluate the performance of our method, we conduct two types of experiments on four publicly available image databases. The first type of experiment aims to evaluate the classification performance of ClassMVRBM relative to RBM, MVRBM and other unsupervised methods, and the second type of experiment aims to compare the classification performance of ClassMVRBM with ClassRBM, respectively for 2D signal and the general vectorized 1D signal. In addition, we also conduct the sensitivity test for some parameters.

## 4.1    The Experimental Datasets

This paper conducts experiments on image databases MNIST, Ballet, ETH80 and Coil_20. All programs are coded by MATLAB and implemented on an Intel Core i7, 3.60 GHz CPU machine with 12 GB RAM. The datasets are listed as follows:

**MNIST Database** [14]: MNIST is a dataset of handwritten digits images database including 60,000 training samples and 10,000 testing samples. Each image is one digit among 0–9, and each one is a gray image with the size of $28 \times 28$.

**Ballet Database** [15]: This dataset includes 8 kinds of complex ballet actions, totally 44 videos clips are cut from the Ballet DVD video, and each clip has 107–506 frames. The paper randomly selects 200 frames from each kind of action for training, while the remaining images are used for testing. Similarly, all images are down-sampled to $32 \times 32$ and transformed to gray scale.

**ETH80 Database** [16]: ETH80 dataset includes 8 categories (apples, cars, cows, cups, dogs, horses, pears and tomatoes). Each category consists of 10 different objects, and each object is collected from 41 different views. Therefore, there are totally $8 \times 10 \times 41 = 3280$ images. We randomly select the images of 21 views ($8 \times 10 \times 21 = 1680$) for training while the others from the additional 20 views ($8 \times 10 \times 20 = 1600$) for testing. All images are down-sampled to $32 \times 32$ and transformed to gray scale.

**Coil_20 Database** [18]: There are 20 kinds of different objects in this database, and each object includes 72 images taken under different views, and all images are down-sampled to $32 \times 32$, and transformed to gray scale. We randomly select 36 images for training while the rest 36 images for testing.

## 4.2    Experimental Results

### Experiment 1: The Classification Performance Evaluation of ClassMVRBM and Other Unsupervised RBMs and Variants

This section aims to compare the classification accuracy of our proposed ClassMVRBM with other unsupervised methods such as RBM, IGBRBM, MVRBM and MVIGRBM. Note that RBM, IGBRBM, MVRBM and MVIGRBM are unsupervised and mainly used to extract features of the input, we use the nearest neighbor classifier for classification. The comparative experiments are conducted on image datasets MNIST, Ballet and ETH80. Table 1 shows the classification accuracy of five algorithms: RBM, IGBRBM, MVRBM, MVGRBM and ClassMVRBM on three datasets. Of which, the classification accuracy of unsupervised RBM, IGBRBM, MVRBM and MVGRBM are reported in [11] when the iteration times and all parameters are adjusted to the best. In the same way, the classification accuracy of our proposed ClassMVRBM is obtained when the iteration times are 100 and all the other parameters are adjusted to the most optimal by grid search. In the Table 1, the bold figures are the best results in the comparison.

According to Table 1, the classification accuracy of ClassMVRBM is much higher than other four unsupervised methods on the MNIST, Ballet and ETH80 datasets. It can be concluded when adding the classification constraint to MVRBM, on one side, the extracted feature representations are discriminative, on the other side, when the conditional probability is directly used to classify, our proposed discriminative model pays more attention to the difference between categories, which enables the proposed method be obviously more robust for modeling relative less and more complicated input data such as Ballet and ETH80 datasets. Therefore, our proposed model demonstrates the significant superiority.

**Table 1.** Classification accuracy of ClassMVRBM and other unsupervised methods

|        | RBM    | IGBRBM | MVRBM  | MVGRBM | ClassMVRBM |
|--------|--------|--------|--------|--------|------------|
| MNIST  | 0.9515 | 0.9398 | 0.9670 | 0.9700 | **0.9725** |
| Ballet | 0.3779 | 0.9216 | 0.3505 | 0.9357 | **0.9509** |
| ETH80  | 0.5281 | 0.8750 | 0.3969 | 0.8894 | **0.9053** |

**Experiment 2: The Classification Accuracy Comparison of ClassMVRBM with ClassRBM**

In this experiment, we will compare the classification accuracy of ClassRBM and ClassMVRBM on three databases: Ballet, ETH80 and Coil_20. ClassMVRBM and ClassRBM are both classification models, the difference lies in when ClassRBM is used to classify 2D images, the images need to be vectorized firstly. To make the comparison fair, the number of neurons in the hidden layer of ClassRBM and ClassMVRBM is set consistent. That is, when the hidden dimension of ClassMVRBM is $20 \times 20$, then the hidden dimension of ClassRBM is 400. Table 2 demonstrates the classification accuracy of ClassRBM and ClassMVRBM when all parameters are adjusted to the most optimal by grid search. According to Table 2, it is easy to see that the classification performance of ClassMVRBM is better than that of ClassRBM. It's not difficult to conclude that to model 2D signal, ClassMVRBM performs better than ClassRBM, which is due to that ClassMVRBM does not vectorize the images and keeps the spatial structure better.

**Table 2.** Classification accuracy comparison of ClassMVRBM and ClassRBM

| Methods | ClassRBM | ClassMVRBM |
|---------|----------|------------|
| Ballet  | 0.9114   | **0.9509** |
| ETH80   | 0.5078   | **0.9053** |
| Coil_20 | 0.9779   | **0.9896** |

ClassMVRBM is sensitive to the hidden size and iteration times. In the following experiments, we discuss the classification accuracy of ClassMVRBM under different hidden sizes and iteration times. As regards to the hidden size, the grid search method [17] is introduced to find the optimal hidden size so as to attain the highest classification accuracy. According to the preceding description of the datasets, the input size of Ballet, Coil_20 and ETH80 are all $32 \times 32$, for the sake of dimensionality reduction, we conduct experiments successively assuming the hidden size is $15 \times 15$, $18 \times 18$, $20 \times 20$, $25 \times 25$, $28 \times 28$ and $32 \times 32$. As shown in Table 3, the larger the hidden size, the higher the classification accuracy, however, when the hidden size increases to $32 \times 32$, the classification accuracy decreases instead. Especially, $28 \times 28$ is the optimal hidden size and with the highest classification performance. It is not difficult to conclude when the hidden size is small, the extracted feature dimension is limited, and the less model parameters generally leads to the under fitting, thus the smaller hidden size brings the lower classification accuracy. But when the hidden size is more than $28 \times 28$, the classification accuracy decreases, which probably results from the overfitting caused by the excessive model parameters.

The influence of the iteration times for classification performance is reported in Table 4. Note that as the iteration times increased, the classification accuracy increased. However, when the iteration times are more than 200, the accuracy decreased. According to Table 4, the best optimal iteration times are about 100 and we can conclude that the increased iteration times over 100 probably lead to the over fitting. This implies that our proposed classification model converges rapidly.

**Table 3.** Classification accuracy comparison under different hidden layer sizes on various datasets

| Hidden size | $15 \times 15$ | $18 \times 18$ | $20 \times 20$ | $25 \times 25$ | $28 \times 28$ | $32 \times 32$ |
|---|---|---|---|---|---|---|
| Ballet | 0.8165 | 0.8432 | 0.8875 | 0.9165 | **0.9509** | 0.9053 |
| Coil_20 | 0.3999 | 0.3999 | 0.5139 | 0.9229 | **0.9896** | 0.8653 |
| ETH80 | 0.7888 | 0.7975 | 0.8388 | 0.8546 | **0.9053** | 0.8632 |

**Table 4.** Classification accuracy comparison under different iteration times on various datasets

| Iteration times | 10 | 30 | 50 | 100 | 200 | 500 |
|---|---|---|---|---|---|---|
| Ballet | 0.3838 | 0.6657 | 0.8547 | **0.9365** | 0.9309 | 0.9073 |
| Coil_20 | 0.6753 | 0.8289 | 0.9264 | **0.9719** | 0.9597 | 0.9253 |
| ETH80 | 0.6516 | 0.7713 | 0.8782 | **0.8946** | 0.8830 | 0.8632 |

# 5   Conclusions

In this paper, we introduce a novel classification model called Matrix-variate Restricted Boltzmann Machine Classification Model (ClassMVRBM). Inspired by ClassRBM, ClassMVRBM integrates classification constraints to MVRBM and presents the optimized objective function of conditional probability to solve the model parameters.

Since the proposed ClassMVRBM directly models the images without the vectorized process, which keeps the spatial structure of the images better. Furthermore, the classification constraint and the conditional probability objective function ensure the discriminability of the learnt features. The experiments are carried out on four benchmark datasets, MNIST, Ballet, Coil_20 and ETH80. The corresponding results demonstrate the superiority of ClassMVRBM. However, the hidden features extracted based on our proposed model still lack the discriminative analysis like the within-class and between-class scatter constraints, we shall extent our work for tackling the task in future.

**Acknowledgments.** This research is supported by NSFC (No.61772049, 61602486), BJNSF (No.4162009), Beijing Educational Committee (No. KM201710005022) and Beijing Key Laboratory of Computational Intelligence and Intelligent System.

# References

1. Wang, H., Wang, J.: 2DPCA with L1-norm for simultaneously robust and sparse modelling. Neural Netw. **46**(10), 190–198 (2013)
2. Ju, F., Sun, Y., Gao, J., Hu, Y., Yin, B.: Image outlier detection and feature extraction via L1-norm-based 2D probabilistic PCA. IEEE Trans. Image Process. **24**(12), 4834–4846 (2015)
3. Li, M., Yuan, B.: 2D-LDA: a statistical linear discriminant analysis for image matrix. Pattern Recogn. Lett. **26**(5), 527–532 (2005)
4. Wang, J., Wang, W., Wang, R., Gao, W.: Image classification using RBM to encode local descriptors with group sparse learning. In: Proceedings of International Conference on Image Processing, pp. 912–916. IEEE, Canada (2015)
5. Dahl, G.E., Dong, Y., Li, D., Acero, A.: Context-dependent pre-trained deep neural networks for large-vocabulary speech recognition. IEEE Trans. Audio Speech Lang. Process. **20**(1), 30–42 (2011)
6. Nair, V., Hinton, G.E.: Rectified linear units improve restricted Boltzmann machines. In: Proceedings of the 27th International Conference on Machine Learning, Israel, pp. 807–814 (2010)
7. Cho, K., Ilin, A., Raiko, T.: Improved learning of Gaussian-Bernoulli restricted Boltzmann machines. In: Honkela, T., Duch, W., Girolami, M., Kaski, S. (eds.) ICANN 2011. LNCS, vol. 6791, pp. 10–17. Springer, Heidelberg (2011). https://doi.org/10.1007/978-3-642-21735-7_2
8. Nguyen, T., Tran, T., Phung, D., Venkatesh, S.: Tensor-variate restricted Boltzmann machines. In: Proceedings of the Twenty-Ninth National Conference on Artificial Intelligence, pp. 2887–2893. AAAI, USA (2015)
9. Larochelle, H., Mandel, M., Pascanu, R., et al.: Learning algorithms for the classification restricted Boltzmann machine. J. Mach. Learn. Res. **13**(1), 643–669 (2012)
10. Peng, X., Gao, X., Li, X.: An infinite classification RBM model for radar HRRP recognition. In: International Joint Conference on Neural Networks, pp. 1442–1448, IEEE, USA (2017)
11. Qi, G., Sun, Y., Gao, J., Hu, Y., Li, J.: Matrix variate restricted Boltzmann machine. In: The proceeding of 2016 International Joint Conference on Neural Networks, pp. 389–395. IEEE, Canada (2016)

12. Liu, S., Sun, Y., Hu, Y., Gao, J., Ju, F., Yin, B.: Matrix variate RBM model with Gaussian distributions. In: The proceeding of 2017 International Joint Conference on Neural Networks, pp. 808–815. IEEE, USA (2017)
13. Gao, J., Guo, Y., Wang, Z.: Matrix neural networks. In: Cong, F., Leung, A., Wei, Q. (eds.) ISNN 2017. LNCS, vol. 10261, pp. 313–320. Springer, Cham (2017). https://doi.org/10. 1007/978-3-319-59072-1_37
14. LeCun, Y., Bottou, L., Bengio, Y., Haffner, P.: Gradient-based learning applied to document recognition. Proc. IEEE **86**(11), 2278–2324 (1998)
15. Wang, Y., Mori, G.: Human action recognition by semilatent topic models. IEEE Trans. Pattern Anal. Mach. Intell. **31**(10), 1762 (2009)
16. Leibe, B., Schiele, B.: Analyzing appearance and contour based methods for object categorization. In: Proceedings of IEEE Computer Society Conference on Computer Vision and Pattern Recognition, pp. 1–7. IEEE, USA (2003)
17. Tenenbaum, J., Silva, V., Langford, J.: A global geometric framework for nonlinear dimensionality reduction. Science **290**(5500), 2319–2323 (2000)
18. Nene, S., Nayar, S., Murase, H.: Columbia object image library (COIL-20). Technical report CUCS-005-96, USA (1996)
19. Qi, N., Shi, Y., Sun, X., Wang, J., Yin, B., Gao, J.: Multi-dimensional sparse models. IEEE Trans. Pattern Anal. Mach. Intell. **40**(1), 163–178 (2018)

# The Adaptive PID Controlling Algorithm Using Asynchronous Advantage Actor-Critic Learning Method

Qifeng Sun$^{(\boxtimes)}$, Hui Ren, Youxiang Duan, and Yanan Yan

University of Petroleum, Qingdao 266580, China
sunqf@upc.edu.cn

**Abstract.** To address the problems of the slow convergence and inefficiency in the existing adaptive PID controllers, we proposed a new adaptive PID controller using the Asynchronous Advantage Actor-Critic (A3C) algorithm. Firstly, the controller can parallel train the multiple agents of the Actor-Critic (AC) structures exploiting the multi-thread asynchronous learning characteristics of the A3C structure. Secondly, in order to achieve the best control effect, each agent uses a multilayer neural network to approach the strategy function and value function to search the best parameter-tuning strategy in continuous action space. The simulation results indicated that our proposed controller can achieve the fast convergence and strong adaptability compared with conventional controllers.

**Keywords:** Deep Reinforcement Learning · Asynchronous Advantage Actor-Critic · Adaptive PID control

## 1 Introduction

The PID controller is a control mechanism of loop feedback, which is widely used in industrial control system [1]. Based on the investigation of conventional PID controller, the adaptive PID controller adjusts parameters online according to the state of the system. Therefore, it has better system adaptability. At present, the majority of the adaptive PID controllers are as follows: The fuzzy PID controller [2], which adopts the ideology of matrix estimations like [3, 4]. It takes the error and the error rate as the input and adjusts the parameters by querying fuzzy matrix table in order to satisfy the requirement of the self-tuning PID parameters. The limitation of this method is that it needs much more prior knowledge. Moreover, this method has a large number of parameters, so that it needed to be optimized [5].

The adaptive PID controller [6, 7] can achieve effective control without identifying the complex nonlinear controlled object using the good approximation ability of the neural network to nonlinear structure. It is difficult to obtain the teacher signals in the supervised learning process. The evolutionary adaptive PID controller [8] has difficulty in achieving real-time control because it requires less prior knowledge [9]. The adaptive PID controller based on reinforcement learning [10] solves the problem that the teacher's signal is difficult to obtain by unsupervised learning process. What is

H. Song et al. (Eds.): SIMUtools 2019, LNICST 295, pp. 498–507, 2019.
https://doi.org/10.1007/978-3-030-32216-8_48

more, the optimization of the control parameters is simple. The Actor-Critic (AC) adaptive PID [11, 12] is the most widely used in the reinforcement-learning controller. However, the convergence speed of the controller is affected by the correlation of the learning data in the AC algorithm [13].

Google's DeepMind team proposed the Asynchronous Advantage Actor-Critic (A3C) learning algorithm [14]. This algorithm adopts multi strategies such as [15] to train multiple agents in parallel, each agent will experience different learning state, so the correlation of the learning sample is broken while improving the computational efficiency [16]. This algorithm has been applied in many domain [17, 18].

Under the several problems in view of discovery, the contributions of this paper are as follows:

1. To address the problem of data relevance and the teacher signal, we draw lessons from the A3C algorithm that enhancing the learning rate with an aim to train agent in the parallel threads.
2. In order to improve the precision and adaptive ability of the controller, we use two BP neural network to approach policy function and value function separately.
3. Extensive simulation results and discussions demonstrated that our proposed adaptive PID controlling algorithm outperforms the conventional PID controlling algorithms.

In Sect. 2, we present the related work about the adaptive controller. In Sect. 3, we present our design of A3C-PID controller. Section 4 describes the result that we apply A3C-PID to the position control of stepper motor. Section 5 discusses the results achieved so far and presents some directions for further work.

## 2  Related Work

The conventional PID controlling algorithms can be roughly classified into two categories including the neural network PID controllers and reinforcement learning PID controllers.

### 2.1  Related Works with Adaptive Controller Based on Neural Network

The paper [19] proposed a method utilizing the neural network to reinforce the performance of PID controller for the nonlinear system. Although the initial parameters of neural network can be determined by artificial test, it is not enough to ensure the reliability of the manual result. Based on this, the author of [20] adopt the genetic algorithm to obtain the optimal initial parameters of the network. However, the genetic algorithm is easily to fall into local optimum. In order to solve the problem, author of [21] appended the immigration mechanism, 10% of the elite population and the inferior population were selected as the variant population, to the neural network adaptive PID controller.

## 2.2    Related Works with Reinforcement Learning Adaptive Controller

The authors of [10] proposed a PID controller that combining the ASN reinforcement learning network with fuzzy math. Despite this method does not need too much accurate training samples compared the neural network PID, its structure is too complex to guarantee the real-time performance for itself. In view of this point, literature [22] designed an adaptive PID controller based on Actor-Critic algorithm. The controller has simple structure that formed just one RBF network. However, it convergences slowly owing to the learning sample of Actor-Critic algorithm is relevance.

# 3    A3C Adaptive PID Control

## 3.1    Structure of A3C-PID Controller

The design of A3C adaptive PID controller is to combine the asynchronous learning structure of A3C with the incremental PID controller. Its structure is as shown in Fig. 1. The whole process is as follow: for each thread, the initial error $e_m(t) = y'(t) - y(t)$ enters the state converter to calculate $\Delta e_m(t) = e_m(t) - e_m(t-1)$ $\Delta^2 e_m(t) = e_m(t) - 2 * e_m(t-1) + e_m(t-2)$ and output the state vector $S_m(t) = [e_m(t), \Delta e_m(t), \Delta^2 e_m(t)]^T$. Then the Actor (m) maps the state vector $S_m(t)$ to three parameters, $K_p$ $K_i$ and $K_d$, of PID controller. The updated controller acts on the environment to receive the reward $r_m(t)$. After n times, Critic (m) receives $S_m(t+n)$ which is the state vector of the system. Finally it produces the value function estimation $V(S_{t+n}, W'_v)$ and n-step TD error $\delta_{TD}$, which are viewed as the important basis for updating parameters. The formula of the reward function is shown as Formula (1)

$$r_m(t) = \alpha_1 r_1(t) + \alpha_2 r_2(t) \tag{1}$$

$$r_1(t) = \begin{cases} 0, & |e_m(t)| < \varepsilon \\ \varepsilon - e_m(t), & other \end{cases} \quad r_2(t) = \begin{cases} 0, & |e_m(t)| \le |e_m(t-1)| \\ |e_m(t)| - |e_m(t-1)|, & other \end{cases}$$

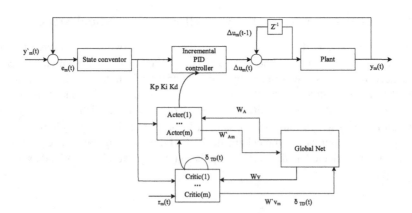

**Fig. 1.** Adaptive PID control diagram based on A3C learning

In the next step, the Actor (m) and the Critic (m) send their own parameters $W'_{am}$, $W'_{vm}$ and the generated $\delta_{TD}$ into the Global Net to update $W_a$ and $W_v$ with the policy gradient and the descend gradient. Accordingly, the Global Net passes their $W_a$ and $W_v$ to Actor (m) and Critic (m), making them continue to learn new parameters.

## 3.2  A3C Learning with Neural Networks

Multilayer feed-forward neural network [23], also known as BP neural network, is a back-propagation algorithm for multilayer feed-forward networks. It has strong ability for nonlinear mapping and is suitable for solving problems with complex internal mechanism. Therefore, the method uses two BP neural networks respectively to realize the learning of policy function and value function. The network structure is as follows:

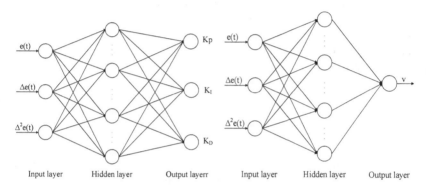

**Fig. 2.** Network structure of Actor-Critic

As shown in Fig. 2, the Actor network has 3 layers:

The first level is the input layer. The input vector $S = \left[ e_m(t), \Delta e_m(t), \Delta^2 e_m(t) \right]^T$ represents the state vector. The second layer is the hidden layer. The input of the hidden layer as follows:

$$hi_k(t) = \sum_{i=1}^{n} w_{ik}x_i(t) - b_k \quad k = 1, 2, 3 \ldots 20 \tag{2}$$

Where, k represents the number of neurons in the hidden layer, $w_{ik}$ is the weights connected the input layer and the hidden layer, $b_k$ is the bias of the k neuron. The output of the hidden layer as follows:

$$ho_k(t) = \min(\max(hi_k(t), 0), 6) \quad k = 1, 2, 3 \ldots 20 \tag{3}$$

The third layer is the output layer. The input of the output layer as follows:

$$yi_o(t) = \sum_{j=1}^{k} w_{ho}ho_j - b_o \quad o = 1, 2, 3 \tag{4}$$

Where, $o$ represents the number of neurons in the output layer, $w_{ho}$ is the weights connected the hidden layer and the output layer, $b_o$ is the bias of the k neuron.

The output of the output layer as follows:

$$yo_o(t) = \log\left(1 + e^{yi_o(t)}\right) \quad o = 1, 2, 3 \tag{5}$$

Actor network does not output the value of $K_p$ $K_i$ and $K_d$ directly, but output the mean and variance of the three parameters. Finally, the actual value of $K_p$, $K_i$ and $K_d$ is estimated by the Gauss distribution. The Critic network structure is similar to the Actor network structure. As shown in Fig. 3, the Critic network also uses BP neural networks with three layers' structure. The first two layers are the same as the layers in the Actor network. Obviously, the difference lies in the output layer of the Critic network which has only one node to output the value function $V(S_t, W'_v)$ of the state.

In the A3C structure, Actor and Critic networks use n-step TD error method [24] to learn action probability function and value function. In the learning method of this algorithm, the calculation of the n-step TD error $\delta_{TD}$ is realized by the difference between the state estimation value $V(S_t, W'_v)$ of the initial state and the estimation value after n-step, as followed:

$$\delta_{TD} = q_t - V\left(S_t, W'_v\right) \tag{6}$$

$$q_t = r_{t+1} + \gamma r_{t+2} + \cdots + \gamma^{n-1} r_{t+n} + \gamma^n V\left(S_{t+n}, W'_v\right)$$

The $0 < \gamma < 1$, represents the discount factor, is used to determine the ratio of the delayed returns and the immediate returns. $W'_v$ is the weight of the Critic network. The TD error $\delta_{TD}$ reflects the quality of the selected actions in the Actor network. The performance of the system learning is:

$$E(t) = \frac{1}{2}\delta_{TD}^2(t) \tag{7}$$

After calculating the TD error, each Actor-Critic network in the A3C structure does not update its network weight directly, but updates the Actor-Critic network parameters of the central network (Global-Net) with its own gradient. The update formulas are as follows:

$$W_a = W_a + \alpha_a\left(dW_a + \nabla_{w'a} \log \pi\left(a|s; W'_a\right)\delta_{TD}\right) \tag{8}$$

$$W_v = W_v + \alpha_c\left(dW_v + \partial\delta_{TD}^2/W'_v\right) \tag{9}$$

Where $W_a$, which is stored by the central network, is the weight of Actor network, $W'_a$ represents the weights of Actor network in AC structure, $W_v$ is the weight of Critic network in the central network, $W'_v$ represents the Critic network weights for each AC structure, $\alpha_a$ is the learning rate of Actor and $\alpha_c$ is the learning rate of Critic.

# 4  Position Control of Two Phase Hybrid Stepping Motor

## 4.1  Modeling and Simulation of Two Phase Hybrid Stepping Motor

In this paper, a two phase hybrid stepping motor is used to control in the simulation experiment. Firstly, we need to establish a mathematical model, however the two phase hybrid stepping motor is a highly nonlinear mechanical and electrical device, so that it is difficult to accurately describe it. Therefore, the mathematical model of a two phase hybrid stepping motor is studied in this paper. It is simplified and assumed to be as follows: The magnetic chain in the phase winding of the permanent magnet varies with the rotor position according to the sinusoidal law. The magnetic hysteresis and the eddy current effect are not considered while the mean and fundamental components of the air gap magnetic conductance are considered. The mutual inductance between the two phase windings is ignored. On the basis of the above limit, the mathematical model of the two phase hybrid stepping motor can be described by the Eqs. 10–14.

$$u_a = L\frac{di_a}{dt} + Ri_a - k_e\omega\,\sin(N_r\theta) \tag{10}$$

$$u_b = L\frac{di_b}{dt} + Ri_b - k_e\omega\,\sin(N_r\theta) \tag{11}$$

$$T_e = -k_e i_a \sin(N_r\theta) + k_e i_e \cos(N_r\theta) \tag{12}$$

$$J\frac{d\omega}{dt} + B\omega + T_L = T_e \tag{13}$$

$$\frac{d\theta}{dt} = \omega \tag{14}$$

In above formulas, $u_a$ and $u_b$ are two-phase voltage and current respectively of A and B, $R$ is winding resistance, $L$ is winding inductance, $k_e$ is torque coefficient, $\theta$ and $\omega$ are rotation angle and angular velocity of motor respectively, $N_r$ is the number of rotor teeth, $T_e$ is electromagnetic torque of hybrid stepping motor, $T_L$ is Load torque, $J$ and $B$ are the load moment of inertia and the viscous friction coefficient respectively. It can be seen from the mathematical model of a two phase hybrid stepping motor that the two phase hybrid stepping motor is still a highly nonlinear and coupled system under a series of simplified conditions.

The simulation model of two phase hybrid stepping motor servo control system is built by Simulink in Matlab. The simulation is shown in Fig. 3.

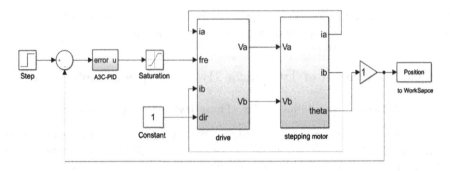

**Fig. 3.** The simulation of servo system

The parameters of the motor are as follows: $L = 0.5\,\mathrm{H}$, $N_r = 50$, $R = 8\,\Omega$, $J = 2\,\mathrm{g.cm^2}$, $B = 0\,\mathrm{Nms/rad}$, $N = 100$, $T_L = 0$, $k_e = 17.5\,\mathrm{Nm/A}$. The N is the reduction ratio of the harmonic reducer. The A3C-PID controller parameters are set as follows: $m = 4$, $\alpha_a = 0.001$, $ts = 0.001\,\mathrm{s}$, $\alpha_c = 0.01$, $\varepsilon = 0.001$, $\gamma = 0.9$, $n = 30$, $K = 3000$. The simulation results are shown in Figs. 4, 5 and Table 1.

**Table 1.** The comparison of controller performance

| Controller | Overshoot (%) | Rise time (ms) | Steady state error | Adjustment time (ms) |
|---|---|---|---|---|
| A3C-PID | 0.1571 | 18 | 0 | 33 |
| AC-PID | 0.1021 | 21 | 0 | 48 |
| BP-PID | 2.1705 | 12 | 0 | 32 |

Dynamic performance of the A3C, BP, and AC adaptive PID controller are shown on Fig. 4. In the time of early simulation (20 cycles), the BP-PID controller has a faster response speed and a shorter rise time (12 ms), but it has a higher overshoot of 2.1705%. On the contrary, both the AC-PID and the A3C-PID controller have smaller overshoot as 0.1571% and 0.1021%. But the adjustment time of AC-PID is long (48 ms), and the rise time is 21 ms. In contrast, A3C-PID controller has better stability and rapidity.

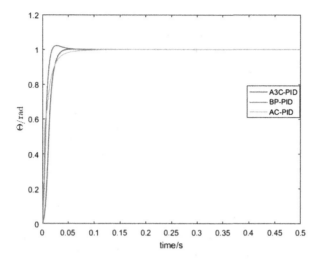

**Fig. 4.** Position tracking

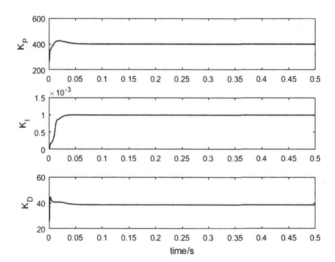

**Fig. 5.** The result of controller parameter turning

Figure 5 shows the process of adaptive transformation of A3C-PID controller parameters. As be seen from Fig. 5, the A3C-PID controller is able to adjust the PID parameters based on errors in different periods. At the beginning of the simulation, the tracking error of system is large. In order to ensure a fast response speed of the system, $K_P$ is continuously increasing while $K_d$ is reducing. Then the system is in order to prevent from having a high overshoot, which limits the increasing of $K_i$. With the error decreasing, $K_P$ begins to decrease. Meanwhile, the value of $K_i$ is gradually increased to eliminate the cumulative error. However, a small amount of overshoot is caused. $K_d$ tends to be stable at this stage because it has a large influence on the system. When the final tracking error comes to 0, $K_P$, $K_i$ and $K_d$ reach a steady state. Simulation results show that the A3C-PID controller has an excellent adaptive capability.

## 5 Conclusions

In this paper, a new PID controller is proposed with asynchronous advantage actor-critic algorithm. The controller uses the BP neural network to approach the policy function and the value function. BP neural network have the strong ability in nonlinear mapping which can enhance the adaptive ability of the controller. The learning speed of A3C PID controller is accelerated with the parallel training in CPU multithreading. The method of asynchronous multi-thread training reduces the correlation of the training data and makes the controller more stable. In the simulation of nonlinear signal and inverted pendulum, the control accuracy of A3C-PID controller is higher than others PID controllers.

Current work includes that we use the controller to control the position of two phase hybrid stepping motor and analyze the performance of controller such as: overshoot, rise time, steady state error and adjustment time. According to these work, it confirmed the effectiveness and application significance of the algorithm. Finally, our aim is to make the controller apply to the multi-axis motion control and the actual industrial production.

## References

1. Adel, T., Abdelkader, C.: A particle swarm optimization approach for optimum design of PID controller for nonlinear systems. In: International Conference on Electrical Engineering and Software Applications, pp. 1–4. IEEE (2013)
2. Savran, A.: A multivariable predictive fuzzy PID control system. Appl. Soft Comput. 13(5), 2658–2667 (2013)
3. Jiang, D., Wang, W., Shi, L., Song, H.: A compressive sensing-based approach to end-to-end network traffic reconstruction. IEEE Trans. Netw. Sci. Eng. (2018). https://doi.org/10.1109/tnse.2018.2877597
4. Jiang, D., Huo, L., Li, Y.: Fine-granularity inference and estimations to network traffic for SDN. PLoS One 13(5), 1–23 (2018)
5. Zhang, X., Bao, H., Du, J., et al.: Application of a new membership function in nonlinear fuzzy PID controllers with variable gains. Inf. Control 2014(5), 1–7 (2014)
6. Cao-Cang, L.I., Zhang, C.F.: Adaptive neuron PID control based on minimum resource allocation network. Appl. Res. Comput. 32(1), 167–169 (2015)
7. Patel, R., Kumar, V.: Multilayer neuro PID controller based on back propagation algorithm. Procedia Comput. Sci. 54, 207–214 (2015)
8. Wang, X.S., Cheng, Y.H., Wei, S.: A proposal of adaptive PID controller based on reinforcement learning. J. China Univ. Min. Technol. 17(1), 40–44 (2007)

9. Su, Y., Chen, L., Tang, C., et al.: Evolutionary multi-objective optimization of PID parameters for output voltage regulation in ECPT system based on NSGA-II. Trans. China Electrotech. Soc. **31**(19), 106–114 (2016)
10. Akbarimajd, A.: Reinforcement learning adaptive PID controller for an under-actuated robot arm. Int. J. Integr. Eng. **7**(2), 20–27 (2015)
11. Chen, X.S., Yang, Y.M.: A novel adaptive PID controller based on actor-critic learning. Control Theory Appl. **28**(8), 1187–1192 (2011)
12. Bahdanau, D., Brakel, P., Xu, K., et al.: An actor-critic algorithm for sequence prediction. arXiv preprint arXiv:1607.07086 (2016)
13. Wang, Z., Bapst, V., Heess, N., et al.: Sample efficient actor-critic with experience replay. arXiv preprint arXiv:1611.01224 (2016)
14. Mnih, V., Badia, A.P., Mirza, M., et al.: Asynchronous methods for deep reinforcement learning. In: International Conference on Machine Learning, pp. 1928–1937 (2016)
15. Jiang, D., Huo, L., Lv, Z., et al.: A joint multi-criteria utility-based network selection approach for vehicle-to-infrastructure networking. IEEE Trans. Intell. Transp. Syst. **19**, 3305–3319 (2018)
16. Liu, Q., et al.: A survey on deep reinforcement learning. Chin. J. Comput. **41**(01), 1–27 (2018)
17. Qin, R., Zeng, S., Li, J.J., et al.: Parallel enterprises resource planning based on deep reinforcement learning. Zidonghua Xuebao/Acta Autom. Sin. **43**(9), 1588–1596 (2015)
18. Liao, F.F., Xiao, J.: Research on self-tuning of PID parameters based on BP neural networks. Acta Simulata Syst. Sin. **07**, 1711–1713 (2005)
19. Guo-Yong, L.I., Chen, X.L.: Neural network self-learning PID controller based on real-coded genetic algorithm. Micromotors Servo Tech. **1**, 43–45 (2008)
20. Sheng, X., Jiang, T., Wang, J., et al.: Speed-feed-forward PID controller design based on BP neural network. J. Comput. Appl. **35**(S2), 134–137 (2015)
21. Ma, L., Cai, Z.X.: Fuzzy adaptive controller based on reinforcement learning. Cent. South Univ. Technol. **29**(2), 172–176 (1998)
22. Liu, Z., Zeng, X., Liu, H., et al.: A heuristic two-layer reinforcement learning algorithm based on BP neural networks. J. Comput. Res. Dev. **52**(3), 579–587 (2015)
23. Xu, X., Zuo, L., Huang, Z.: Reinforcement learning algorithms with function approximation: recent advances and applications. Inf. Sci. **261**, 1–31 (2014)
24. Yang, S.Y., Xu, L.P., Wang, P.J.: Study on PID control of a single inverted pendulum system. Control Eng. China **S1**, 1711–1713 (2007)

# Network Emulation as a Service (NEaaS): Towards a Cloud-Based Network Emulation Platform

Junyu Lai[1,2(✉)] ⓘ, Jiaqi Tian[1] ⓘ, Dingde Jiang[1] ⓘ, Jiaming Sun[1] ⓘ,
and Ke Zhang[1] ⓘ

[1] School of Aeronautics and Astronautics, University of Electronic Science
and Technologies of China, Xiyuan Ave no. 2006, Chengdu, China
{laijy,tianjq,jiangdd,sunjm,zhangk}@uestc.edu.cn
[2] Science and Technology on Communication Networks Laboratory,
Shijiazhuang, China

**Abstract.** Network emulation is an essential method to test network architecture, protocol and application software during a network's entire life-cycle. Compared with simulation and test-bed methods, network emulation possesses the advantages of accuracy and cost-efficiency. However, legacy network emulators are typically restricted in scalability, agility, and extensibility, which builds barriers to prevent them from being widely used. In this paper, we introduce the currently prevalent cloud computing and related technologies including resource virtualization, NFV (network functional virtualization), SDN (software-defined networking), traffic control and flow steering to the network emulation domain. We design and implement an innovative cloud-based network emulation platform, aiming at providing users Network Emulation as a Service (NEaaS), which can be conveniently deployed on both public and private clouds. We carried out performance evaluation and discussion on this platform. It turns out, the platform can significantly outperform most legacy network emulators regarding to the scalability, agility, and extensibility, with much lower emulation costs.

**Keywords:** Network emulation · Cloud computing · NFV (network functional virtualization) · SDN (software-defined networking) · Flow steering

## 1 Introduction

Modern networking systems are getting far more complicated than before. It is already difficult to rely on theoretical methods to analyze network performance. Therefore, network testing technologies are of great importance to the design and implementation of network architecture, protocols and upper layer applications. There are mainly three network testing methods.

Firstly, computer simulation is a technique whereby a software program models the behavior of a network by calculating the interaction between the different network entities (nodes, links, etc.). Most simulators use discrete event simulation, and the simulation method cannot be very precise due to inaccurate models, although its

H. Song et al. (Eds.): SIMUtools 2019, LNICST 295, pp. 508–517, 2019.
https://doi.org/10.1007/978-3-030-32216-8_49

running speed is usually fast and the cost is pretty low. Secondly, a live test-bed is a platform for conducting rigorous and transparent testing of network protocols and applications. It is a prototype of the target network, and is the most accurate method with the highest cost. Thirdly, network emulation is a technique for the performance testing of original protocols and applications over a virtual network, which is different from computer simulation where purely mathematical models are applied. A network emulator appears to be a real network, and is with medium cost and high accuracy.

This paper focuses on network emulation, which has been researched for more than half century. However, due to technology constraints, traditional network emulators have been restricted in scalability, agility, and extensibility for a long time, which significantly influenced their applications in a larger scale. This research introduces the currently prevalent cloud computing and related ICT technologies including resource virtualization, NFV, SDN, traffic control and flow steering to the network emulation domain, aiming at eliminating the above restrictions. More preciously, the major contribution of this paper is to design and implement an innovative cloud-based network emulation platform, to provide users Network Emulation as a Service (NEaaS). The NEaaS can be deployed either public or private cloud to satisfy diverse user needs.

The remaining part of this paper goes as follows. The related work in industry and academia are briefly reviewed in Sect. 2, followed by the innovative design of the cloud-based network emulation platform in Sect. 3, and its implementation details in Sect. 4. Performance evaluation of the proposed emulation platform is presented in Sect. 5. Finally, Sect. 6 concludes the paper and provides the outlook.

## 2   Related Work

In industry, in 2003, Wellington and Kubischta [1] from General Dynamics presented an approach for integrating and testing wireless systems in the laboratory with real-time emulation of ad hoc radio networks. In 2006, Yousefi'zadeh et al. [2] from Boeing Company collaborated with University of California reported the addition of emulation functionality to the NEWS testbed capturing fading wireless link effects. In 2007, Bonney et al. [3] from Architecture Technology Corporation, developed a hardware-in-the-loop emulator known as ABSNE that creates a controllable, repeatable, virtual network environment. Also in 2007, Beuran et al. [4] from NICT of Japan, had presented the design of QOMET, a wireless LAN emulator, with a versatile two-stage scenario-driven design. The details of the improved model and additional functionality were given in 2008 [5], and in 2015 [6], the authors again presented a framework for evaluating wireless network performance through emulation, using a hybrid design. In 2008, Ahrenholz et al. [7] from Boeing Phantom Works, presents CORE (Common Open Research Emulator), a real-time network emulator that allows rapid instantiation of hybrid topologies composed of both real hardware and virtual network nodes. Also in 2008, Nickelsen et al. [8] from Aalborg University and FTW described how to create reproducible test conditions by emulating the wireless links. In 2015, Soles et al. [9] from University of West Florida, collaborated with Northrop Grumman Aerospace Systems, researched on the need to provide an emulation method for studying the interaction among diverse hardware and software components.

In academia, Giovanardi et al. [10–12] from University of Ferrara described the emulation facility in the Simple Ad hoc simulator (SAM), which is able to emulate many unicast routing protocols with a real exchange of signaling and data packets. In 2007, Maier et al. [13] from University of Stuttgart focused on scalable network emulation problems, and present a comparison of different virtual machine (VM) implementations (Xen, UML) and their virtual routing approach (NET). In 2009, Mehta et al. [14], described a new emulation architecture that is scalable, modular, and responds to real time changes in topology and link characteristics. In 2014, Balasubramanian et al. [15] from Vanderbilt University, described a rapid development and testing framework for a distributed satellite system. In 2015, To et al. [16] from Universidad Galileo, presented the Dockemu tool for emulation of wired and wireless networks.

Although there have already been a plenty of emulators as introduced above, most of them are serving for dedicated purposes, and are to some extent, restricted in scalability, agility, and extensibility. In the last decade, cloud computing and its related ICT technologies have developed rapidly, which motivates the researchers to leverage these promising technologies to be applied in developing network emulators in an innovative manner.

# 3   Innovative Cloud-Based Network Emulation Platform

## 3.1   Vital Feature Requirements on Modern Network Emulator

Current networking systems appear to be with a large number of nodes, wired or wireless links, and dynamic topologies, which introduces new requirements on modern network emulators. Firstly, scalability. Emulator should support the number of emulated nodes from several to tens of thousands, without changing the hardware and software architecture. Secondly, agility. Building of a target emulation scenario should be fast enough to satisfy the user QoE. Thirdly, extensibility. Emulator should be extensible to hold newly appeared nodes and links in a convenient manner. Fourthly, low-cost. Without sacrificing emulation accuracy, emulator can emulate larger scale networks.

## 3.2   Network Node Emulation Scheme

The principle of network node emulation is to utilize the VMs created and allocated by the cloud platform to imitate the nodes in target networks. More precisely, to emulate a router node, the cloud platform calls the underlying hypervisor to create a VM instance, and then allocates this VM to the emulator. Considering the fact that the targeted router itself is a computer, it would be straight forward to adopt the allocated VM to emulate that router.

### 3.3   Network Link Emulation Scheme

Emulating target network links relies on using the virtual network links of the cloud platform. The cloud virtual network consists of virtual links which connect multiple VMs. Therefore, to emulate a specific link between two nodes in the target network, the emulator sets a virtual link between the two corresponding VMs. The physical and mac layer characteristics of the target link shall be accurately mapped to the network layer attributes of the virtual network link.

### 3.4   Network Topology Emulation Scheme

Both wired and wireless network topology will change as time goes. For wired network, the reason could be the failures happened on some certain links or nodes. While for wireless network, it may be the consequence of link break caused by node mobility, nodes failure, etc. To emulate network topology is to dynamically control and adjust the virtual network links between the VMs in a fast enough manner to satisfy the emulation needs.

### 3.5   Architecture of the Cloud-Based Network Emulation Platform

An architecture of the cloud-based network emulation platform is designed and presented in Fig. 1, which is divided into four layers: resource virtualization layers, cloud computing layers, emulation core layers, and emulation interface layers.

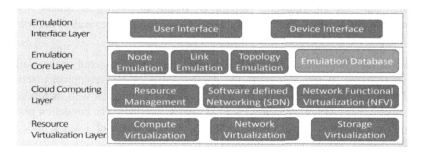

**Fig. 1.** Architecture of the cloud-based emulation platform.

**Resource Virtualization Layer.** Its functionality is to abstract, virtualize and pool all sorts of underlying hardware resources. The major modules are included: (1) Compute virtualization. This module creates VMs that acts like a real computer with an operating system; (2) Network virtualization. The module combines hardware network resources and network functionality into a single, software-based administrative entity; (3) Storage virtualization. This module presents a logical view of all the physical storage resources, treating all storage media in the system as a single pool of storage.

**Cloud Computing Layer.** It is a cloud Operating System, responsible for providing resources in different forms according to the upper layer's requirements in real-time. Primarily, this layer consists of three modules: (1) Resource management. The module allocates and frees compute, network, and storage resources to satisfy the emulation needs; (2) SDN. This module contains two type of entities, i.e., SDN controller and virtual switch located in physical machine. Together with the network virtualization module of the lowest layer, this module can provide traffic control and flow steering functionalities, which are the key features to implement link and topology emulations; (3) NFV. The module embodies the principle of node emulation. Each node in the target network can be emulated by a generic VM with NFV enhancement, which includes dedicated functionality implementations of the target node by means of software.

**Emulation Core Layer.** It contains three modules covering node, link and topology emulations, respectively, plus with one emulation database storing emulation status and parameter values: (1) Node emulation. By calling the lower layer's resource management and NFV module, this layer can accomplish the tasks of node emulation; (2) Link emulation. The resource management and SDN modules were utilized to control the accessibility among arbitrary nodes, together with network ports settings on the emulated nodes to define the characteristics of the corresponding links; (3) Topology emulation. This module still relies on the lower layer's resource management and SDN modules, and considers all the nodes and links, which form the emulated network topology to be consistent with the target network; (4) Emulation database. The database to record and store the parameter values of the emulated nodes, links and topologies. The users can store an emulation scenario by means of writing the status of all its elements into the database, and later on, the scenario can again be recalled according to the database.

**Emulation Interface Layer.** Two types of interfaces are considered in the platform: (1) User Interface. It provides users the graphic interface to accomplish a series of typical emulation operations, such as creation of nodes, links, as well as topologies, management of emulation scenarios, etc.; (2) Device Interface. The emulation platform supports the connections to real network nodes. It could be either a single node or an external network consisting of an amount of real nodes.

# 4    Implementation Details

The hardware components of the cloud based emulation platform is illustrated in Fig. 2. It consists of a number of COTS computers and switches. More precisely, all the computers are X86 based (i.e., AMD 1700X, 64G RAM, 500G SSD), five of which are emulation nodes, the rest two are emulation and SDN controller, respectively.

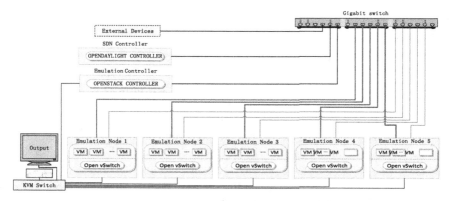

**Fig. 2.** Hardware components of the cloud-based emulation platform.

### 4.1 Implementation of Resource Virtualization Layer

Considering the balance among efficiency, generality, and cost, Linux Kernel based Virtual Machine (KVM) is adopted as the hypervisor. KVM requires a CPU with hardware virtualization extensions. A wide variety of guest operating systems work with KVM, including many flavors and versions of Linux, BSD, Solaris, Windows, OS X, Android, Solaris 10, etc. which support the emulation nodes installed with diverse operating systems. KVM is installed and configured in each emulation node to virtualize and pool all the compute, storage, and network resources. In particular, VMs with diverse profiles are created on top of host machines by KVM, according to emulation needs.

### 4.2 Implementation of Cloud Computing Layer

OpenStack, OpenDaylight (ODL), and Open vSwitch (OVS) are employed to implement the three modules in this layer. OpenStack is a free and open-source software for cloud computing, mostly deployed as IaaS, whereby virtual servers and other resources are made available to users. OpenStack consists of interrelated components that control diverse hardware pools of compute, storage, and networking resources. Users either manage it through a web-based dashboard, through command-line tools, or through RESTful web services. OpenStack has a modular architecture with various project names for its components. The goal of the ODL project is to promote SDN and NFV, with a clear focus on network programmability. ODL is a modular open platform for customizing and automating networks of any size and scale. In the emulation platform, Openstack and OVS are deployed on the emulation and the emulation controller nodes. ODL is installed on the SDN controller node. By using ODL plug-in to replace OpenStack Neutron's original ones, the designed functionalities can be achieved.

### 4.3    Implementation of Emulation Core Layer

The emulation platform is B/S model based. The primary functions, such as node, link and topology emulations, are implemented in the web server side, together with the database record the emulation status. Both of the web server and the database are deployed on the emulation controller. Users can utilize any browser to access that web server, and to accomplish their emulation tasks.

The web server includes node, link and topology emulation module. The node emulation module is responsible for the creation, configuration, and deletion of the emulated nodes. It mainly calls the OPENSTACK dashboard API to accomplish these tasks. The link emulation module can then configure the emulated node's network ports to imitate the ports of the target nodes. Linux Traffic Control is the major tool adopted to set the bitrate, delay and packet loss attributes of the network ports. The SDN controller is also commanded by the link emulation module via ODL Controller API to creation the virtual links connecting the emulated nodes. On the basis of node and link emulation, the topology module supports the emulation for both the static topology which keeps unchanged during the emulation, and the dynamic topology which changes according to user settings or predefined trace files. All the above modules programmed in Java at the server side, follows the MVC (Model, View and Controller) design pattern.

As afore mentioned, a database module is designed to store emulation status. MySQL is chosen to be the DBMS. Hieratical tables are built to record the emulation parameter values and the relations.

### 4.4    Implementation of Emulation Interface Layer

This layer contains user interface and device interface modules, serving for different purposes. The user interface is the front-end of the web server. Technologies, such as HTML5, jQuery, Ajax, jTopo, etc. are employed to construct the web-based user interface. Users can conveniently create and configure emulation scenarios. The web pages designed for emulation tasks and their logical relations are given in Fig. 3. To realize the united emulation between the emulation platform and a part of the real network, the device interface module is developed. A real network device can be directly attached to the emulation platform, and an inner agent, corresponding to the external device will be created automatically, and will be connected to the external device via a virtual L2 link. Figure 4 illustrates the implementation principles.

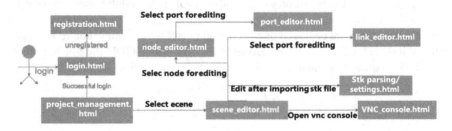

**Fig. 3.** Web pages designed for emulation tasks and their logical relations.

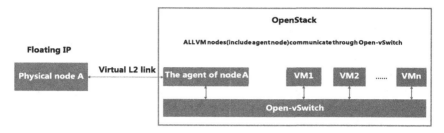

**Fig. 4.** Implementation principles for device interface module.

# 5 Performance Evaluation

## 5.1 Performance Metrics Introduction

The proposed emulation platform can conquer most legacy emulator's defects in scalability, agility and extensibility. Therefore, the number of emulated nodes supported by the platform is chosen as the metric for scalability, while the creation time of an emulation scenario is selected as the measure of agility. The platform can create different types of emulated nodes and links only restricted by the VM and channel templates, and thus has a very good extensibility.

## 5.2 Evaluation and Discussion

For the scalability evaluation, the number of emulated nodes a single emulation node can support has been tested; the quantity of the emulated nodes supported by the platform shall be the summation of the nodes all the physical nodes can emulate. Experiments show that around 50 emulated nodes can simultaneously run on each single emulation node, and for 5 emulation nodes of the same profile, 250 emulated nodes shall be supported. The number can be linearly scaled up by simply increasing the number of physical emulation nodes.

For the agility evaluation, a scenario with 100 emulation nodes is investigated. The experiments of creating 10 emulated nodes on a single machine is carried out, and it turns out 27 s is consumed, which means around 2.7 s are needed for creating one emulation node. Since the platform has 5 physical emulation nodes, and each nodes can create VMs independently, the time spent on building the scenario is around 5.4 s, excluding the detailed configuration time for each node.

To summarize, the proposed platform's performances on scalability, agility and extensibility are much better than most legacy emulators.

# 6 Conclusion

Network emulation is regarded as the most promising network testing method due to its balance on cost and accuracy. This paper focused on solving network emulation's inherent shortcomings in scalability, agility and extensibility. In particular, the paper designed and implemented an innovative cloud-based network emulation platform aiming at providing users NEaaS. Performance evaluation and discussion illustrated that the proposed platform can effectively outperform legacy network emulators regarding to scalability, agility, and extensibility.

The potential research work we have planned for the next step includes the following two points: Firstly, the cost of VM-based emulation is still high, light- weighted virtualization technologies, i.e., Docker, will be investigated to replace VMs. Secondly, the target network's heterogeneous nodes of diverse hardware architectures, such as ARM, Sparc, and Power PC, are currently emulated by X86 architected VMs, which is inaccurate to some extent. Emulation for heterogeneous nodes will be further studied.

**Acknowledgement.** This work is partially supported by the Science and Technology on Communication Networks Laboratory(Grant No. XX17641X011-03), the 54th Research Institute of China Electronics Technology Group Corporation, and the National Natural Science Foundation of China (Grant No. 61402085 and 61872051).

# References

1. Wellington, R.J., Kubischta, M.D.: Wireless network emulation for distributed processing systems. In: IEEE Military Communications Conference, 2003. MILCOM 2003, Boston, MA, USA, vol. 1, pp. 475–480 (2003). https://doi.org/10.1109/MILCOM.2003.1290149
2. Yousefi'zadeh, H., Li, X., Furmanski, W., Lofquist, D.B.: Emulation of fading wireless link effects in NEWS wired testbed. In: MILCOM 2007 - IEEE Military Communications Conference, Orlando, FL, USA, pp. 1–7 (2007). https://doi.org/10.1109/MILCOM.2007. 4455162
3. Bonney, J., Bowering, G., Marotz, R., Swanson, K.: Hardware-in-the-loop emulation of mobile wireless communication environments. In: 2008 IEEE Aerospace Conference, Big Sky, MT, USA, pp. 1–9 (2008). https://doi.org/10.1109/AERO.2008.4526345
4. Beuran, R., Nguyen, L.T., Latt, K.T., Nakata, J., Shinoda, Y.: QOMET: a versatile WLAN emulator. In: 21st International Conference on Advanced Information Networking and Applications (AINA 2007), Niagara Falls, ON, Canada, pp. 348–353 (2007). https://doi.org/ 10.1109/AINA.2007.116
5. Nickelsen, A., Jensen, M.N., Matthiesen, E.V., Schwefel, H.: Scalable emulation of dynamic multi-hop topologies. In: 2008 The Fourth International Conference on Wireless and Mobile Communications, pp. 268–273 (2008). https://doi.org/10.1109/ICWMC.2008.44
6. Beuran, R., Tariq, M.I., Miwa, S., Shinoda, Y.: Wireless network performance evaluation through emulation: WiMAX case study. In: 2015 International Conference on Information Networking (ICOIN),Cambodia, pp. 265–270 (2015). https://doi.org/10.1109/ICOIN.2015. 7057894
7. Ahrenholz, J., Danilov, C., Henderson, T.R., Kim, J.H.: CORE: a real-time network emulator. In: MILCOM 2008 - 2008 IEEE Military Communications Conference, San Diego, CA, USA, pp. 1–7 (2008). https://doi.org/10.1109/MILCOM.2008.4753614
8. Ramneek, Choi, W., Seok, W.: Wireless network mobility emulation over wired testbeds: areview. In: 2015 17th International Conference on Advanced Communication Technology (ICACT), Seoul, South Korea pp. 431–435 (2015). https://doi.org/10.1109/ICACT.2015. 7224832

9. Soles, L.R., Reichherzer, T., Snider, D.H.: Creating a cost-effective air-to- ground network simulation environment. In: Southeast Conference 2015, Fort Lauderdale, FL, USA, pp. 1–5 (2015). https://doi.org/10.1109/SECON.2015.7132897
10. Giovanardi, A., mazzini, G.: Emulation architecture implementation and design. In: 2006 3rd Annual IEEE Communications Society on Sensor and Ad Hoc Communications and Networks, Reston, VA, USA, pp. 723–728 (2006). https://doi.org/10.1109/SAHCN.2006.288537
11. Giovanardi, A., Mazzini, G.: Ad hoc routing protocols: emulation vs simulation. In: 2005 2nd International Symposium on Wireless Communication Systems, Siena, Italy, pp. 140–144 (2005). https://doi.org/10.1109/ISWCS.2005.1547673
12. Giovanardi, G., Mazzini, G., Veronesi, R.: Network emulation in the SAM simulator. In: 2005 IEEE 16th International Symposium on Personal, Indoor and Mobile Radio Communications, Berlin, Germany, pp. 1302–1306 (2005). https://doi.org/10.1109/PIMRC.2005.1651651
13. Maier, S., Grau, A., Weinschrott, H., Rothermel, K.: Scalable network emulation: a comparison of virtual routing and virtual machines. In: 2007 12th IEEE Symposium on Computers and Communications, Las Vegas, NV, USA, pp. 395–402 (2007). https://doi.org/10.1109/ISCC.2007.4381529
14. Mehta, D., Jaeger, J., Faden, A., Hebert, K., Yazdani, N., Yao, H.: A scalable architecture for emulating dynamic resource allocation in wireless networks. In: MILCOM 2009 - 2009 IEEE Military Communications Conference, Boston, MA, USA, pp. 1–7 (2009). https://doi.org/10.1109/MILCOM.2009.5379801
15. Balasubramanian, D., Dubey, A., Otte, W.R., Emfinger, W., Kumar, P.S., Karsai, G.: A rapid testing framework for a mobile cloud. In: 2014 25th IEEE International Symposium on Rapid System Prototyping, New Delhi, India, pp. 128–134 (2014). https://doi.org/10.1109/RSP.2014.6966903
16. To, M.A., Cano, M.: DOCKEMU – a network emulation tool. In: 2015 IEEE 29th International Conference on Advanced Information Networking and Applications Workshops, pp. 593–598. https://doi.org/10.1109/WAINA.2015.107

# A Study of RNN Based Online Handwritten Uyghur Word Recognition Using Different Word Transcriptions

Wujiahemaiti Simayi, Mayire Ibrayim, and Askar Hamdulla[✉]

Institute of Information Science and Engineering,
Xinjiang University, Urumqi, China
askar@xju.edu.cn

**Abstract.** Recurrent neural networks-RNN based online handwriting Uyghur word recognition experiments are conducted applying connectionist temporal classification in this paper. Handwritten trajectory is fed to the network without explicit or implicit character segmentation. The network is trained to transcribe the input word trajectory to a string of characters directly. According to the writing characteristics of Uyghur, experiments are designed using two Unicode word transcriptions respectively based on 32+2 basic character types and 128 specific character forms to represent a word. The training process and recognition results based on same network architecture show that both transcription methods are applicable. The word transcription system using basic 34 character types showed better performance than the one using 128 specific character forms in our experiments. 13.96%, 14.73% character error rates (CER) have been observed respectively for char34 system and char128 system.

**Keywords:** Online handwriting recognition · Recurrent neural networks · Connectionist temporal classification · Uyghur word transcription

## 1 Introduction

Handwriting recognition technology based on recorded trajectory with temporal information is called online handwriting recognition, while offline handwriting recognition works on the handwritten shape images which only provide spatial information [1]. Achievements on both online and offline handwriting recognition has been witnessed on well-investigated script kinds [2, 3]. Several competitions were held to improve the handwriting recognition technology on the popular scripts [4, 5]. General pattern recognition systems including recurrent neural networks with connectionist temporal classification-CTC are proving themselves robust for the variety of the script kinds, especially for alphabetic scripts, both in isolated and cursive writing styles [11].

Uyghur is an alphabetic script which is one of the important languages in northwest China and Central Asia. Previous studies on Uyghur handwriting recognition mainly uses classic pattern recognition framework which requires tremendous human observation and expert design to extract features for later classification [6, 7]. A first successful end-to-end unconstrained handwriting recognition system by Li et al. [8]

H. Song et al. (Eds.): SIMUtools 2019, LNICST 295, pp. 518–527, 2019.
https://doi.org/10.1007/978-3-030-32216-8_50

achieved good results on printed text images. It is fact that recognition of handwritten shapes is more difficult than printed ones.

According to the written characteristic of Uyghur, a word has two kinds of Unicode based representations that either based on character types or specific character forms. In order to compare the effect of the two word transcription methods, this paper conducts comparative handwritten word recognition experiments using recurrent neural networks with connectionist temporal classification-CTC. The experiments are designed in unconstrained recognition manner that the applied model can map handwritten trajectory into sequence of characters directly without prior segmentation and lexicon help.

Research on the application of intelligent systems has been gaining more and more attention in recent years [13, 14]. The handwriting word recognition experiments in this paper will be a reference for later study and development of intelligent systems. The remaining content is arranged in several sections where Sect. 2 introduces Uyghur alphabet and word transcription methods; Sect. 3 details the implemented model structure; Experiment design and results on the collected dataset are described in Sect. 4. At last, Sect. 5 draws a brief conclusion.

## 2  Alphabet and Word Transcription

Uyghur is one of the typical alphabetic scripts. Like other alphabetic scripts, a word is composed of several characters/letters arranged by language rules. There is an interesting word formation characteristic in Uyghur that a word can be transcribed in two different ways. As given in Table 1, an Uyghur word can be split to two kinds of character sequences, which are respectively based on character forms and character types.

**Table 1.** Different Unicode representations of a word

| Unicodes | Character in the word | Word |
|---|---|---|
| by character forms | ق + ﻫ + ﻝ + ﻱ + ﺍ + ﺭ + ﻪ + ﭺ = | چىرايلىق |
| by character types | ق + ى + ل + ي + ا + ر + ى + چ = | چىرايلىق |

There are 32 basic Uyghur characters that each of them has several different character shapes according to position within a word. In addition, there are one special component character (char-33) and a compound character (34). The component character is very commonly used in typewriting and the compound character always occurs in handwriting for its ligature shape. According to the alphabet in Table 2, there are 32 +2 basic character types and total 128 character forms.

An Uyghur word can be recorded and represented by two Unicode strings either by using unicodes of specific 128 character forms or by 32+2 character representative forms. The perfect morphological rules made it possible to arrange corresponding character forms according to the ordered character types of the word. This word coding property is similar to other Arabic based scripts. Although not all character forms are frequently used, this paper takes all 128 character forms and 34 character types into consideration, for the character labels are suppressed with low confidence if they are not present in the word transcription.

**Table 2.** Uyghur alphabet

| End | Mid | Begin | Single | Rep | No. | End | Mid | Begin | Single | Rep | No. |
|---|---|---|---|---|---|---|---|---|---|---|---|
| ـﻚ | ـكـ | كـ | ك | ك | 20 | ﺎئ | | | ئ | | |
| ـل | ـلـ | لـ | ل | ل | 21 | ـا | | | ا | ا | 1 |
| ـم | ـمـ | مـ | م | م | 22 | ـئە | | | ئە | | |
| ـن | ـنـ | نـ | ن | ن | 23 | ـە | | | ە | ه | 2 |
| ـھ | ـھـ | ھـ | ھ | ھ | 24 | ـب | ـبـ | بـ | ب | ب | 3 |
| ـۇ | | | ۇ | | | ـپ | ـپـ | پـ | پ | پ | 4 |
| ـو | | | و | و | 25 | ـت | ـتـ | تـ | ت | ت | 5 |
| ـۈ | | | ۈ | | | ـج | ـجـ | جـ | ج | ج | 6 |
| ـۆ | | | ۆ | ۆ | 26 | ـچ | ـچـ | چـ | چ | چ | 7 |
| ـۋ | | | ۋ | | | ـخ | ـخـ | خـ | خ | خ | 8 |
| ـۇ | | | ۇ | ۇ | 27 | ـد | | | د | د | 9 |
| ـۈ | | | ۈ | | | ـر | | | ر | ر | 10 |
| ـۇ | | | ۇ | | | ـز | | | ز | ز | 11 |
| ـۆ | | | ۆ | ۆ | 28 | ـژ | | | ژ | ژ | 12 |
| ـۇ | | | ۇ | | | ـس | ـسـ | سـ | س | س | 13 |
| ـۇ | | | ۇ | ۇ | 29 | ـش | ـشـ | شـ | ش | ش | 14 |
| ـېي | ـېيـ | ېيـ | ېي | | | ـغ | ـغـ | غـ | غ | غ | 15 |
| ـي | ـيـ | يـ | ي | ي | 30 | ـف | ـفـ | فـ | ف | ف | 16 |
| ـى | ـىـ | ىـ | ى | | | ـق | ـقـ | قـ | ق | ق | 17 |
| ـى | ـىـ | ىـ | ى | ى | 31 | ـك | ـكـ | كـ | ك | ك | 18 |
| ـيي | ـييـ | ييـ | يي | يي | 32 | ـگ | ـگـ | گـ | گ | گ | 19 |
| | ـؤ | ؤ | ؤ | 33 | | | | | | | |
| ـل | | | ل | لا | 34 | | | | | | |

Rep, Single, Begin, Mid and End means the representative form, isolated form, beginning form, intermediate form and ending form of a character respectively.

# 3   End-to-End Handwriting Recognition System

## 3.1   Input

Raw handwritten trajectory is processed to make short and informative trajectory. The implemented preprocessing techniques include duplication removing and critic point selection. In order to enrich the informative content of the raw input, two dimensional direction vector $(\Delta x, \Delta y)$ and another two dimensional pen-state vector are added to the point coordinates of each point [9]. Thus, each point in input sequence is in shape of $[x, y, \Delta x, \Delta y, PS[0], PS[1]]$ where PS is for pen-state. Pen-state is confirmed conveniently by order of neighbor strokes as in that [0, 1] means pen-up state while [1, 0] is for pen-down state. The temporal direction factor is simply calculated using Eq. (1).

$$\Delta x = x_i - x_{i-1} \tag{1}$$

$$\Delta y = y_i - y_{i-1} \tag{2}$$

### 3.2 Model Architecture

A deep neural network including two bidirectional recurrent layers and two fully connected layers are applied to build online handwriting word recognition system as shown in Fig. 1(a).

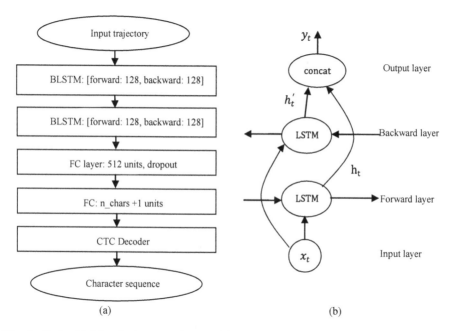

**Fig. 1.** End-to-End handwritten word recognitions system (a) Model architecture (b) Bidirectional recurrent layer

Considering the subtlety to gradient vanishing of recurrent networks, Long Short Term Memory-LSTM is applied for each cell or unit of the recurrent layers in this paper. The output of the first recurrent layers is directly sent to the second recurrent layer to obtain more generalized sequential feature. The fully connected layers are assumed to further generalize the learned features from the recurrent layers. One of the most effective regularization methods for neural networks, Dropout, is applied on the fully connected layers to avoid overfitting, because dense connectivity in fully connection layers makes large number of variables to the network. The number of neurons in the last fully connected layer is set by the number of characters to make word transcription and a Blank label used for CTC decoding. CTC decoder provides the last output string (character sequence) by calculating the most possible character sequence.

### 3.3    Bidirectional LSTM Layer

Handwriting is usually written in either from right to left or from left to right direction. However, many disorders happen in actual handwriting even in small handwriting case such as words. Observing handwritten trajectory from both right-left and left-right directions is more helpful and fit for the nature of online handwritten trajectory [10]. A bidirectional recurrent layer consists two sub recurrent layers. Input sequence is fed to one recurrent layer in original order while another one receives the input sequence in reverse order. Each LSTM cell in a recurrent layer controls input, output and state values to the next state with gate mechanism, as given in Eqs. (2)–(6).

$$i_t = sigm(W_i x_t + U_i h_{t-1} + b_i) \tag{2}$$

$$f_t = sigm(W_f x_t + U_f h_{t-1} + b_f) \tag{3}$$

$$o_t = sigm(W_o x_t + U_o h_{t-1} + b_o) \tag{4}$$

$$c_t = f_t \odot c_{t-1} + tanh(W_o x_t + U_o h_{t-1} + b_o) \tag{5}$$

$$h_t = o_t \odot tanh(c_t) \tag{6}$$

Where $W_i$, $W_f$, $W_o$ are the input-hidden weight matrix, $U_i$, $U_f$, $U_o$ are the state-state weight matrix and $b_i$, $b_f$, $b_o$ are bias vectors, respectively. $I_t$, $f_t$, $o_t$ are the activation values at the input, forget and output gates, while $c_t$ and $h_t$ are the state and output values of the cell.

The output of the two sub-recurrent layers are concatenated into longer sequence, see Fig. 1(b) and Eqs. (7)–(9).

$$Y_{forward} = h_t = [y_{r1}, y_{r2}, \ldots y_{rN}] \tag{7}$$

$$Y_{backward} = h'_t = [y_{r1}, y_{r2}, \ldots y_{rN}] \tag{8}$$

$$Y = concat(Y_{forward}, Y_{backward}) \tag{9}$$

Where $y_{rN}$ and $y_{lN}$ represents the output of the $N^{th}$ node of in right-left and left-right sub-recurrent layers. $Y_{forward}$ and $Y_{backward}$ are the outputs of the two inverse sub-layers and $Y$ is last output of a bi-directional recurrent layer.

### 3.4    Output

The output is the sequence of alphabet characters that are assumed to be in the handwritten trajectory input [11]. The number of nodes in the last fully connection layer which its output is decoded into character string is set by the number of the alphabetic characters that the word transcription based on, either by 32+2 overall character types or by 128 specific character shapes, with adding the Blank label especially designed for CTC decoding. Therefore, this paper proposes two systems based on 32+2 basic character types or 128 specific character forms to compare their performances. In this way, an input trajectory is transcribed into two different sequences of Unicode characters by the two systems.

# 4  Experiments

## 4.1  Dataset

A dataset has been established by collecting online handwritten word samples from 26 different writers. The dataset contains 900 word classes and each word is recorded in two different character unicode strings, respectively using character type unicodes and character form unicodes. Each writer is asked to write all word classes continuously. The recorded handwritten word trajectories of each writer are saved in separate binary files, with POTEX extension. Each handwritten word sample contains sequentially recorded pen-tip (x, y) coordinates. A stroke is separated from its neighbor by a special stroke-end mark and complete word trajectory is ended by another word-end mark. A handwritten word sample in binary files is put together with its two word transcriptions mentioned above and overall trajectory information including trajectory length, number of strokes etc. The collected 23400 handwritten word samples are divided into training and test sets with respect to the writers to conduct writer independent word recognition experiments. 19800 samples from 22 writers are put in training set while the remained 3600 samples from other 4 writer are used as test set. Statistics on the collected datasets found that words which have 4–10 characters are the most common ones. The longest word is recorded to have 22 characters in the dataset used in this paper. The calculated average numbers of characters is 7.8. The longest and average handwritten word trajectory lengths are found to hold 1023 and 221 points, respectively.

## 4.2  Design and Configuration

In preprocessing, a point is removed if its distance to previous neighbor is less than half of the average neighbor distance in the stroke. For critical point selection, threshold of $\Pi/6$ is found appropriate in our case. By preprocessing, the average trajectory length is shorted to 67.

According to unicode representations of a word, either by character types or character forms, two unconstrained handwriting word recognition systems are compared in this paper. The two systems are differed only in the width of the last fully connection (FC)-output layer. The system which transcribes input trajectory to a sequence of basic character types is set with 32+2+1 units in the last FC-output layer and noted char34 system in this paper. The another system uses 128+1 units at the last FC layer to generate output sequence of specific character shapes and named char128 system in this context. The transcribed model output is used as word recognition result directly without help of any lexicon search and external language models.

The model performance is evaluated using character error rate-CER and character accurate rate- CAR metric [12] and calculated using Eqs. (10) and (11).

$$CER = \frac{De + Se + Ie}{Nt} \qquad (10)$$

$$CAR = 1 - \frac{De + Se + Ie}{Nt} \qquad (11)$$

where $(Nt)$ is the total characters in the reference text. $(Se)$, $(De)$, $(Ie)$ denote substitution errors, deletion errors and insertion errors, respectively. Sum of these three errors are just the minimum edit distance to align the output sequence to ground truth and calculated by dynamic programming.

The experiments are conducted using one GTCx980 GPU with 4G RAM for acceleration of training. One of most favored self adaptive optimizers-Adam is implemented in all experiments. Samples from one writer in training set are temporarily used for performance validation during training and remained samples from 21 writers are used to update network parameters. Train samples are rearranged randomly in each epoch and put 64 samples in a minibatch. Global learning rate is lowered by decreasing factor of 0.5 when no improvement seen in successive 3 epochs on validation set.

Training is performed for two sessions in succession. In the first session, initial learning rate and drop-rate is set as 0.001 and 0.5, while the values are set as 0.00001 and 0.75 in the second session of training. Both training sessions use the same early stopping mechanism that training is stopped when 10 successive epochs cannot see any progress on validation set. The generalization ability of the trained model is evaluated on the test set which contains 3600 samples from new 4 writers.

### 4.3   Results and Discussion

To compare the performances of the two systems, the training procedure is recorded using evaluation results on 10 batches of train and validation set against per epoch of training, as in Fig. 2. Thanks to the short and rich informative input representation obtained by preprocessing, the applied model has got very fast error decline both on train and validation sets. Word transcription using 34 character types has shown better performance than using 128 character forms. Using character type based transcription had steadier decline in training error than using character forms based transcription method.

Table 3 gives word recognition results and some other details from the experiments using 34 character type based and 128 character forms based word transcription methods. Since both models are same or very similar in architecture, they are observed to have similar number of variables that each one has almost 1.9M variables and comparable model sizes, see Table 3. Comparing with char34 system, char128 system takes little bit longer time to complete an epoch of training. The char34 system completes an epoch of training for about 4.2 min, while the char128 system uses an average of 5.7 min. In order to save training time, only 10 batches train and validation subsets are used to navigate the model performance during training. It is also found that char34 system is faster than char128 system on recognition performance, too. The average recognition time per sample for char34 is 0.019 s while char128 system takes about two times longer time to recognize a sample, 0.039 s.

**Table 3.** Comparison of char34 and char128 systems

| Model | No. vars | Model size | No. ep | T/ep | Av-recT | Tr_CER | Te_CER | Te_CAR |
|---|---|---|---|---|---|---|---|---|
| Char128 | 1994117 | 7.79M | 112 | ~5.7 min | 0.039 s | 1.78% | 14.73% | 85.27% |
| Char34 | 1849451 | 7.22M | 105 | ~4.2 min | 0.019 s | 0.93% | **13.96%** | **86.04%** |

Tr_CER and Te_CER: CER on train and test sets, No. ep number of epochs the training stopped, T/ep: average training time per epoch, Av-recT average recognition time per sample, Te_CAR: average character accurate rate on test set.

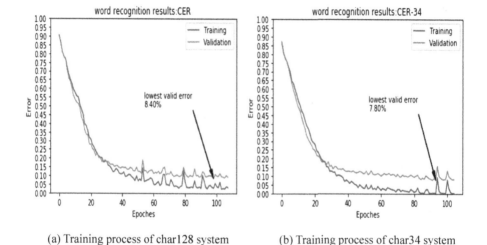

(a) Training process of char128 system    (b) Training process of char34 system

**Fig. 2.** Training process of char34 and char128 system (results are based on 10 epochs)

Both char34 and char128 systems reached substantial low CER on train set, which are 0.93% and 1.78%, respectively. Also, it can be seen that char34 got better training than char128 system. Evaluation on test set which contains 3600 samples for 900 word classes also showed encouraging results for both systems. 14.73% and 13.96% CER, or 85.27% and 86.04% CAR, results are given for char128 and char34 systems, respectively. The recognition results indicate the superiority of char34 system than char128 system.

According to the training procedure and word recognition results, the experiments in this paper provided good results both systems and showed that char34 system had better performance than char128 system in almost all criteria listed n Table 3. This can be analyzed that char128 system wants to find each specific character form in handwritten trajectory. However, a handwritten word, especially in cursive natured scripts, always misses some character forms because joining with neighbor characters or casual continues handwriting. The handwritten word sample in Fig. 3(a) has missed some character shapes, and Fig. 3(b) shows a handwritten word trajectory with false written character forms.

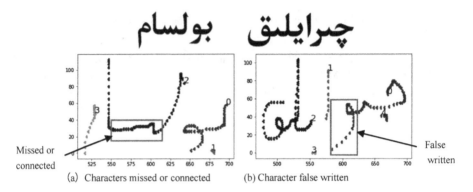

Fig. 3.  Some handwritten word samples with printed shapes

Nevertheless, both samples in Fig. 3 are readable and the character forms can be identified within the word context. RNN's capability of using long context information make the labeling by 34 character types more applicable to the casual nature of handwritten word samples. By comparison, labels by 34 character types are more general to detect characters from handwritten word trajectory. Perhaps, using 128 char labels are more suitable for recognizing printed texts instead of handwritten ones.

## 5  Conclusion

This paper conducts unconstrained online handwriting word recognition experiments using recurrent neural networks on online Uyghur handwritten words. The connectionist temporal classification maps the input handwritten trajectory to a sequence of characters directly and without any lexicon help. According to the writing characteristics of Uyghur, two word transcription methods based on 34 character types and 128 character forms are used as ground-truth labels respectively. Experiment results demonstrate that both word transcription methods are applicable and effective. In experiments, char34-character type based system has better performance in training and evaluation process than char128-character form based system. Char34 and char128 systems obtained 13.96% and 14.73% character error rates on the test set respectively. Different model architectures are to be investigated to further improve the recognition results in later study.

**Acknowledgment.** This work is supported by National Science Foundation of China (NSFC) under grant number 61462081 and 61263038. The first author is grateful to the National

Laboratory of Pattern Recognition of CASIA (Institute of Automation, Chinese Academy of Sciences) for providing excellent study and experiment environment.

# References

1. Liu, C.L., Yin, F., Wang, D.H., Wang, Q.F.: Online and offline handwritten Chinese character recognition: benchmarking on new databases. Pattern Recogn. **46**(1), 155–162 (2013)
2. Graves, A., Liwicki, M., Bunke, H., Schmidhuber, J., Fernández, S.: Unconstrained on-line handwriting recognition with recurrent neural networks. In: Conference on Neural Information Processing Systems, pp. 458–464. DBLP, Vancouver (2007)
3. Wu, Y.C., Yin, F., Liu, C.L.: Improving handwritten Chinese text recognition using neural network language models and convolutional neural network shape models. Pattern Recogn. **65**(C), 251–264 (2016)
4. Yin, F., Wang, Q.-F., Zhang, X.-Y., Liu, C.-L.: ICDAR 2013 Chinese handwriting recognition competition. In: 2013 12th International Conference on Document Analysis and Recognition (ICDAR), pp. 1464–1470. IEEE, Washington, DC (2013)
5. El Abed, H., Märgner, V.: ICDAR 2009-Arabic handwriting recognition competition. Int. J. Doc. Anal. Recogn. (IJDAR) **14**(1), 3–13 (2011)
6. Ibrahim, M.: Key technologies for recognition of online handwritten Uyghur characters and word. Ph.D. thesis, Wuhan University, China (2013)
7. Simayi, W., Ibrayim, M., Tursun, D., Hamdulla, A.: Survey on the features for recognition of on-line handwritten Uyghur characters. Int. J. Sig. Process. Image Process. Pattern Recogn. **9**(3), 45–58 (2015)
8. Li, P., Zhu, J., Peng, L., Guo, Y.: RNN based Uyghur text line recognition and its training strategy. In: 2016 12th IAPR Workshop on Document Analysis Systems (DAS), pp. 19–24. IEEE, Santorini (2016)
9. Zhang, X.Y., Yin, F., Zhang, Y.M., Liu, C.L., Bengio, Y.: Drawing and recognizing Chinese characters with recurrent neural network. IEEE Trans. Pattern Anal. Mach. Intell. **40**(4), 849–862 (2018)
10. Liwicki, M., Graves, A., Fernàndez, S., Bunke, H., Schmidhuber, J.: A novel approach to on-line handwriting recognition based on bidirectional long short-term memory networks. In: Proceedings of the 9th International Conference on Document Analysis and Recognition, ICDAR (2007)
11. Graves, A.: Connectionist temporal classification. In: Graves, A. (ed.) Supervised Sequence Labelling with Recurrent Neural Networks. SCI, vol. 385, pp. 61–93. Springer, Heidelberg (2012). https://doi.org/10.1007/978-3-642-24797-2_7
12. Su, T.H., Zhang, T.W., Guan, D.J., Huang, H.J.: Off-line recognition of realistic Chinese handwriting using segmentation-free strategy. Pattern Recogn. **42**(1), 167–182 (2009)
13. Jiang, D., Huo, L., Li, Y.: Fine-granularity inference and estimations to network traffic for SDN. PLoS One **13**(5), 1–23 (2018)
14. Jiang, D., Huo, L., Lv, Z., et al.: A joint multi-criteria utility-based network selection approach for vehicle-to-infrastructure networking. IEEE Trans. Intell. Transp. Syst. **19**(10), 3305–3319 (2018)

# Computer Generated Hologram-Based Image Cryptosystem with Multiple Chaotic Systems

Chuying Yu and Jianzhong Li[✉]

Hanshan Normal University, Chaozhou 521041, China
henry_stu@163.com

**Abstract.** Based on computer generated hologram (CGH) and multiple chaotic systems, a novel image encryption scheme is presented, in which shuffling the positions and changing the values of image pixels are combined to confuse the relationship between the ciphertext and the original image. In the encryption process, the complex distribution is permuted by use of the designed scrambling algorithm which is based on Chen's chaotic system and logistic maps firstly. Subsequently, the Burch's coding method is used to fabricate the CGH as the encrypted image. Finally, the pixel values of the encrypted CGH are changed by sine map to withstand statistical analysis attacks. Simulation results demonstrate that the proposed method has high security level and certain robustness against statistical analysis attacks, data loss and noise disturbance.

**Keywords:** Computer generated hologram · Chaos · Security and encryption

## 1 Introduction

With the rapid development of computational technology and modern optical technology, digital computer is widely used to simulate, calculate and deal with all kinds of optical processes [1, 2]. In recent years, the optical information processing technique has been applied in information security [1–8] because of its excellent characteristics, such as high-speed parallel processing of information with multiple degrees of freedom. Since the double random phase encryption (DRPE) technique has been developed [3], a number of improved optical image encryption methods have been proposed [1, 2, 4]. However, it is difficult to transmit the encrypted complex data, which is obtained by the traditional optical encryption techniques, through the network. Computer generated hologram (CGH), which is often employed to implement optical encryption schemes [2, 5, 6], is an effective method of the digitization of encrypted data. In comparison with conventional optical holography, CGHs have the advantage of being easily and effectively generated by computer.

In this paper, a novel image encryption scheme with off-axis Fourier transform CGH and multiple chaotic maps is proposed. In this method, shuffling the positions and changing the pixel values are performed simultaneously. In the encryption process, the complex distribution is permuted by use of the designed scrambling algorithm which is based on Chen's chaotic system and logistic maps first. Then the Burch's coding method is used to fabricate the CGH as the ciphertext. To resist statistical analysis

H. Song et al. (Eds.): SIMUtools 2019, LNICST 295, pp. 528–538, 2019.
https://doi.org/10.1007/978-3-030-32216-8_51

attacks, the pixel values of the obtained CGH are changed by sine map. The simulations demonstrate the validity and performance of the proposed method.

## 2 Related Background

### 2.1 Fourier Transform Computer Generated Hologram Based on Burch's Method

Let $O(x, y) = A(x, y)\exp[j\varphi(x, y)]$ and $R(x, y) = A_r\exp[j2\pi\rho\varphi_r(x, y)]$ be the object wave and the parallel reference wave, respectively. And let $|A(x, y)|_{max} = 1$ and $A_r = 1$, then the transmittance of the off-axis Fourier transform CGH based on Burch's coding method can be expressed as follows [8]:

$$
\begin{aligned}
h(x, y) &= |O(x, y) + R(x, y)|^2 \\
&= |A(x, y)|^2 + A_r^2 + 2A_rA(x, y)\cos[2\pi\rho\varphi_r(x, y) - \varphi(x, y)] \\
&= 0.5\{1 + A(x, y)\cos[2\pi\rho\varphi_r(x, y) - \varphi(x, y)]\}.
\end{aligned}
\tag{1}
$$

where $\rho$ is the carrier frequency. With the conjugate reference wave, the hologram can be reconstructed by inverse discrete Fourier transform. For further details the reader is referred to [8].

### 2.2 Chen's Chaotic System

The three-dimensional Chen's chaotic system is described as following [9]

$$
\begin{aligned}
\dot{x} &= a(y - x), \\
\dot{y} &= (c - a)x - xz + cy, \\
\dot{z} &= xy - bz,
\end{aligned}
\tag{2}
$$

where $a$, $b$ and $c$ are parameters. The system has chaotic behavior when $a = 35$, $b = 3$, $c \in [20, 28.4]$.

### 2.3 Logistic Map

The logistic map, which is a 1D nonlinear chaos function, is expressed as [7]

$$
x_{n+1} = \mu x_n(1 - x_n),
\tag{3}
$$

where $\mu$ is the logistic map parameter, and $\mu \in [0, 4], x_n \in (0, 1)$. When $3.5699456 < \mu \leq 4$, the dynamical system is in chaotic state.

### 2.4 Sine Map

The sine map is also a 1D chaos function and defined as [10].

$$x_{n+1} = [\gamma \sin(\pi x_n)]/4, \tag{4}$$

where $\gamma$ is sine map parameter. when $0 < \gamma \le 4$, sine mapping works in a chaotic state.

## 3  The Chaos-Based Image Scrambling Method

In the proposed scrambling technique, the chaotic sequences generated by Chen's system and logistic map are used to permute the plaintext image. Suppose the size of the input data $I(x, y)$ is $M \times N$, the scrambling method is described as follows

(1) Initialize $XC(1)$, $YC(1)$ and $ZC(1)$ randomly and choose an arbitrary natural number $L$ first, then iteratively generate the chaotic sequences $XC(i)$, $YC(i)$ and $ZC$ $(i)$ whose lengths are all $L$ by using Eq. (2). Here, $i = 1, 2, ..., L$.

(2) Generate three integers $p1, p2$ and $p3$ which are between 1 and $L$ randomly first. In other words, $1 \le p1 \le L$, $1 \le p2 \le L$ and $1 \le p3 \le L$. Then calculate the initial value $XL(1)$ of logistic map according to the following Eqs. (5) and (6)

$$X(1) = [XC(p1) + YC(p2) + ZC(p3)]/3, \tag{5}$$

where $XC(p1)$, $YC(p2)$ and $ZC(p3)$ are the $p1^{th}$ element in XC, the $p2^{th}$ element in YC and the $p3^{th}$ element in ZC, respectively.

$$XL(1) = 10^5 \times abs(X(1)) - fix(10^5 \times abs(X(1))), \tag{6}$$

where $fix(x)$ is the operation that rounds the elements of x toward zero.

(3) Using $XL(1)$ and Eq. (3), generate the chaotic sequences $XL(i)$ whose length is $MN$ $+T$ iteratively. Here, $i = 1, 2, ..., MN+T$, $T$ is an arbitrary natural number.

(4) Truncate $NM$ elements of $XL(i)$ from the p4th element to obtain a chaotic sequence $S = \{XL(i), i = p4, p4 + 1,..., p4 + MN-1\}$. Here, $p4$ is a random integer which is between 1 and $T$.

(5) Sort the sequences $S$ in ascending order to obtain a new sequence $SN$ and its corresponding permutation indices $ISN$. There are $MN$ elements in $ISN$. The relations between $S$ and $SN$ is $SN = S(ISN)$. For example, the $m^{th}$ element in $SN$ corresponds to the $ISN(m)^{th}$ element in $S$.

(6) With the zigzag algorithm [11], map $I(x, y)$ into an 1D array $I1$. The length of $I1$ is $MN$.

(7) Then the permutation indices $ISN$ is employed to permute $I1$ and the scrambled vector $I2$ can be achieved as follows

$$I2 = I1(ISN). \tag{7}$$

(8) Finally, apply the inverse zigzag scan process [11] to $I2$, the permuted image $SI$ can be obtained.

The inverse image scrambling process is similar to the image scrambling process. In inverse scrambling process, obtain the permutation indices $ISN$ as described in steps (1)–(5) with the same initial values and control parameters of the chaotic functions first. Then the scrambled image $SI$ is mapped into an 1D vector $SI1$ by use of the zigzag algorithm. Subsequently, permute $SI1$ back to their original position according to the following equation

$$SI2(ISN) = SI1. \tag{8}$$

After applying the inverse zigzag algorithm to $SI2$, the decrypted image can be retrieved.

## 4   The Encrypted Computer Generated Hologram

The presented algorithm is divided into three parts. First the complex distribution is permuted by the proposed scrambling scheme. Then the CGH is generated by employed Burch's method. Lastly, sine map is applied to change the pixel values of the shuffled-CGH. Supposing $f(x_0, y_0)$ denotes the input image with size $M \times N$, the proposed method is described as follows.

(1) To reduce the dynamic range of the hologram, $f(x_0, y_0)$ should be multiplied by a random phase, which can be expressed as

$$f_1(x_0, y_0) = f(x_0, y_0)\exp[j2\pi\phi(x_0, y_0)], \tag{9}$$

where $\phi(x_0, y_0)$ is a random function distributed uniformly in the interval $[0, 1]$.

(2) By use of the Fourier transform, the object wave $O(x, y)$ can be obtained.

$$O(x, y) = DFT[f_1(x_0, y_0)] = A(x, y)\exp[j\varphi(x, y)], \tag{10}$$

where DFT() represents discrete Fourier transform operator.

(3) Permute the object wave $O(x, y)$ and the reference wave $R(x, y)$ to obtain $O_p(x, y)$ and $R_p(x, y)$ by the proposed chaos-based scrambling method shown in sub-Sect. 2.3 with the parameters $XC(1)$, $YC(1)$, $ZC(1)$, $c$, $\mu$, $p1$, $p2$, $p3$, and $p4$.

(4) With $O_p(x, y)$ and $R_p(x, y)$, the shuffled hologram transmittance $h(x, y)$ can be achieved by using Eq. (1). When $h(x, y)$ is 8-bit (256 levels) quantized, the gray-level computer generated hologram $HG$ can be obtained.

(5) To resist statistical analysis attacks, sine map is adopted to change the pixel values of the shuffled hologram $h(x, y)$. Initialize $XS(1)$ randomly and choose an arbitrary natural number $v$ first, then iteratively generate the chaotic sequences $XS(i)$ whose length is $MN+V$ by use of Eq. (4). Here, $i = 1, 2, \ldots, MN+V$. Then truncate $NM$ elements of $XS(i)$ from the $s1^{\text{th}}$ element to get a chaotic sequence $XS1 = \{X(i), i = s1, s1 + 1, \ldots, s1 + MN-1\}$.

(6) Compute the chaotic sequence $XS1$ using the following equation

$$XS2 = \text{mod}(round((abs(XS1) - floor(abs(XS1)))10^{14}, 256), \qquad (11)$$

where round(x) rounds the elements of x to the nearest integers, floors(x) rounds the element of x to the nearest integers less than or equal to x, abs(x) is returns the absolute value of x, and mod(x, y) returns the remainder after division, respectively. Then apply the inverse zigzag scan process to the 1D vector XS2 to obtain the two-dimensional integer matrix XS3.

(7) Finally, change the pixel values of the permuted CGH to achieve the encrypted CGH according to the following Eq. (12)

$$HGP = HG \oplus XS3, \qquad (12)$$

where the symbol $\oplus$ represents the exclusive OR operation bit-by-bit.

The parameters $XC(1)$, $YC(1)$, $ZC(1)$, $XS(1)$, c, $\mu$, $\gamma$, $p1$, $p2$, $p3$, $p4$ and $s1$ are used as private keys and form a large key space in the encryption and decryption processes. The decryption process is described as follows:

(1) Use the same parameters $XS(1)$, $\gamma$ and $s1$ to obtain XS3 as described in steps (5)–(6) first.
(2) Perform the exclusive OR operation between HGP and XS3 to obtain the permuted hologram HG using Eq. (13)

$$HG = HGP \oplus XS3, \qquad (13)$$

(3) With the parameters $XC(1)$, $YC(1)$, $ZC(1)$, c, $\mu$, $p1$, $p2$, $p3$ and $p4$, HG is permuted by the proposed inverse scrambling process mentioned in Subsect. 2.3 to obtain HG1.
(4) With the conjugate reference wave, the reconstruction RG of the CGH can be obtained by using inverse DFT. Thus, the decrypted image is achieved.

## 5  Simulation Results

The presented method is carried out to verify the feasibility of the cryptosystem with the image "Lena" shown in Fig. 1(a), which size is 256 × 256. The experiments were performed using MATLAB. Since the CGH is under-sampled, the input image is expanded to 560× 560 pixels to deal with the under-sampling problem and obtain spatial separation of the reconstructed terms, as shown in Fig. 1(b). The parameters of the cryptosystem are $XC(1) = -10.058$, $YC(1) = 0.368$, $ZC(1) = 37.368$, $c = 28$, $\mu = 3.8$, $\gamma = 3.92$, $L = 10^5$, $T = 10^5$, $V = 10^5$, $p1 = 35762$, $p2 = 29637$, $p3 = 88365$, $p4 = 15759$ and $s1 = 51123$, respectively. To measure the quality of the decrypted image, the peak signal-to-noise ratio (PSNR) [12] was used to calculate the similarity between the original plaintext image and the decrypted image. If the PSNR value is larger than 40 dB, the decrypted image almost has no difference from the original one in visual quality.

## 5.1   Performance of the Encryption System

Using the proposed encryption scheme, the plaintext image is encrypted, and the ciphertext shown in Fig. 1(c) is acquired. To evaluate the performance of the proposed scheme, the ciphertext is decrypted using both correct and incorrect keys. Figures 1(d)–(e) exhibit the well reconstructed image and decrypted image with the correct keys respectively. As shown in Fig. 1(e), the PSNR of the decrypted image is above over 45 dB when all the keys are correct.

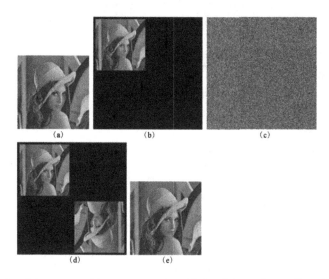

**Fig. 1.** Results of the proposed image encryption: (a) the plaintext image 'Lena' ($256 \times 256$); (b) the expansion image ($560 \times 560$); (c) the ciphertext ($560 \times 560$); (d) the reconstruction of (c) ($560 \times 560$); (e) the decrypted image with correct keys ($256 \times 256$) (PSNR = 45.05).

Now we explore the sensitivity of recovered image to slight change of the cipher keys. The decrypted images with the wrong decryption keys $XC(1) = XC(1) + 10^{-15}$, $YC(1) = YC(1) + 10^{-14}$, $ZC(1) = ZC(1) + 10^{-14}$, $XS(1) = XS(1) + 10^{-14}$, $c = c + 10^{-14}$, $\mu = \mu + 10^{-14}$, $\gamma = \gamma + 10^{-15}$, $p1 = p1 + 1$, $p2 = p2-1$, $p3 = p3 + 1$, $p4 = p4 + 1$ and $S1 = S1 + 1$ are illustrated in Fig. 2(a)–(l), respectively. It can be observed from Fig. 2(a)–(g) that any valid information cannot be obtained from the decrypted images when the absolute values of the deviations of $XC(1)$ and $\gamma$ are up to $10^{-15}$ and those of $YC(1)$, $ZC(1)$, $XS(1)$, $c$ and $\mu$ are up to $10^{-14}$, respectively. Additionally, as can be seen from Fig. 2(h)–(l), all the decrypted images are unrecognizable if the parameters $p1, p2$, $p3, p4$ and $S1$ are less 1 or more 1 than the correct value. All the PSNR values of the decrypted images in Fig. 2 are less than 10 dB. Please note that the other keys remain correct while a key is changed in the mentioned above experiments. Because the key space of the cryptosystem consists of the parameters $XC(1)$, $YC(1)$, $ZC(1)$, $XS(1)$, c, $\mu$, $\gamma$, $p1, p2$, $p3, p4$ and $s1$, the entire key space of the encryption scheme is $10^{15} \times 10^{14} \times 10^{14}$ $10^{14} \times 10^{14} \times 10^{14} \times 10^{15} \times 10^{5} \times 10^{5} \times 10^{5} \times 10^{5} \times 10^{5} = 10^{125} \approx 2^{415}$.

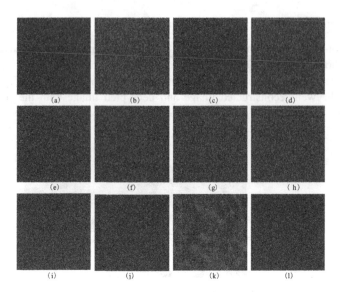

**Fig. 2.** The decrypted images with incorrect keys: (a) the decrypted images with $XC(1) = XC(1) + 10^{-15}$ (PSNR = 8.57); (b) the decrypted images with $YC(1) = YC(1) + 10^{-14}$ (PSNR = 9.15); (c) the decrypted images with $ZC(1) = ZC(1) + 10^{-14}$ (PSNR = 8.73); (d) the decrypted images with $XS(1) = XS(1) + 10^{-14}$ (PSNR = 8.82); (e) the decrypted images with $c = c + 10^{-14}$ (PSNR = 8.98); (f) the decrypted images with $\mu = \mu + 10^{-14}$ (PSNR = 9.01); (g) the decrypted images with $\gamma = \gamma + 10^{-15}$ (PSNR = 9.13); (h) the decrypted images with $p1 = p1 + 1$ (PSNR = 9.18); (i) the decrypted images with $p2 = p2 - 1$ (PSNR = 8.97); (j) the decrypted images with $p3 = p3 + 1$ (PSNR = 8.72); (k) the decrypted images with $p4 = p4 + 1$ (PSNR = 9.46); (l) the decrypted images with $S1 = S1 + 1$ (PSNR = 8.75).

## 5.2   Robustness of the Proposed Scheme Against Attacks

Except for having a large key space, a desirable encryption technique should also well withstand various attacks such as statistical attack and occlusion attack.

Several types of statistical analysis including histogram analysis, entropy analysis, and correlation analysis are performed in the experiments. Figure 3(a) and (b) show histograms of the original image and the encrypted image, respectively. As shown in Fig. 3(b), the experiment result is nearly uniform. So, the histograms of ciphertext cannot provide any useful information for the attacker to carry out this kind of statistical analysis attack.

The entropy is the most outstanding feature of the randomness [13]. The information entropy of an image f can be computed according to the following Eq. (14).

$$H(f) = \sum_{i=1}^{255} P(f_i) \log_2 \frac{1}{P(f_i)}, \tag{14}$$

where $P(f_i)$ represents the probability of symbol $f_i$. For a purely random source emitting $2^N$ symbols, the entropy is $H(f) = N$. For example, the theoretical entropy of the image with 256 gray levels is 8.

Using Eq. (14), the entropy of the original image and ciphered image can be calculated. They are 7.4363 and 7.9994, respectively. The entropy of the encrypted image is very close to the theoretical value of 8. It means that the proposed encryption method is secure upon entropy attack.

Because each pixel is highly correlated with its adjacent pixels either in horizontal, vertical or diagonal direction in an image, the cryptanalysis can be carried out by employing this characteristic. The 3000 pairs of adjacent pixels in vertical, horizontal and diagonal directions are randomly selected from the plain images and the ciphertext to probe the corrections of the adjacent pixels by calculating their corresponding correlation coefficient $r_{xy}$ [13]. The bigger absolute value of $r_{xy}$ is, the stronger correlation is. The correlation coefficients of the plain image and the ciphertext are shown in Table 1 and the distributions are shown in Figs. 4 and 5. From Table 1 and Fig. 5, it is evident that a random relation exists in the ciphered image. Not only correlation coefficient but also the figures illustrate that neighboring pixels of the ciphered image have no correlation. The encryption method improves the image's security.

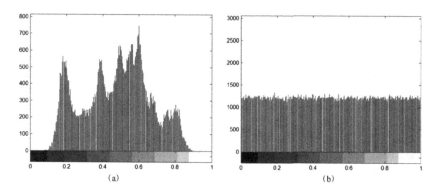

**Fig. 3.** (a) Histogram of plain image 'Lena', (b) histogram of ciphered image.

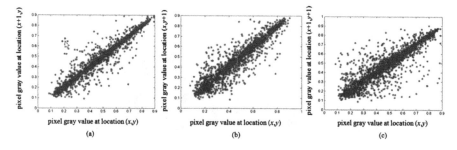

**Fig. 4.** Correlation between two adjacent pixels in 'Lena': (a) horizontal correlation; (b) vertical correlation; (c) diagonal correlation.

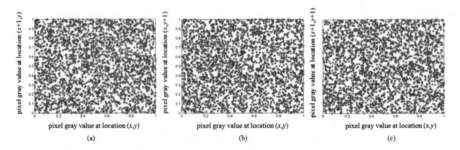

Fig. 5. Correlation between two adjacent pixels in the encrypted image: (a) horizontal correlation; (b) vertical correlation; (c) diagonal correlation.

Table 1. Results of correlation coefficients.

| Direction | Lena | Encrypted image |
|---|---|---|
| Horizontal | 0.9680 | −0.0079 |
| Vertical | 0.9424 | 0.0024 |
| Diagonal | 0.9175 | 0.0272 |

In the noise attack experiments, the ciphertext is added with the Gaussian random noise with mean value 0 and standard deviation 15. Figure 6(a) is the encrypted image distorted by Gaussian noise with mean value 0 and standard deviation 15. The reconstruction is displayed in Fig. 6(b). The recovered image which PSNR is 11.03 dB is shown in Fig. 6(c). Though the decrypted image depicted in Fig. 6(c) is interfered seriously and the corresponding PSNR is small, it can still be recognized among the noise.

During data transmission, information loss also often occurs. The robustness of the proposed method against occlusion attack which is regarded as data loss is tested. Figure 7(a) shows the ciphertext occluded by 10%. Figures 7(b)–(c) exhibit the corresponding reconstructed image and decrypted image obtained by use of all correct keys. Though the PSNR of the decrypted image is less than 13 dB, it can still be distinguished.

Fig. 6. Robustness against noise. (a) the encrypted image undergone noise attack; (b) the reconstruction of (a) with all correct keys; (c) the decrypted image (PSNR = 11.03).

**Fig. 7.** Robustness against occlusion. (a) the encrypted image with 10% occlusion; (b) the reconstruction of (a) with all correct keys; (c) the decrypted "Lena" (PSNR = 12.52)

# 6 Conclusion

In this paper, based on CGH technique and chaotic theory, a new image encryption method is proposed. Permuting the positions and changing the values of image pixels are combined simultaneously to enhance the security of our scheme. The proposed approach has the following merits: (1) the method is highly sensitive to the secret keys and it has a large enough key space to resist all kinds of brute-force attacks; (2) the encrypted image has a good statistical property; (3) the encrypted holograms which are generated by computer are real-value data, so they are convenient for storage and transmission.

**Acknowledgment.** This work is partly supported by the Natural Science Foundation of Guangdong Province (No.2018A0303070009, No. 2014A030310038), the Educational and Commission of Guangdong Province (No. 2015KTSCX089).

# References

1. Liu, Z.J., Xu, L., Lin, C., et al.: Image encryption scheme by using iterative random phase encoding in gyrator transform domains. Opt. Lasers Eng. **49**(4), 542–546 (2011)
2. Xi, S., Wang, X., Song, L., et al.: Experimental study on optical image encryption with asymmetric double random phase and computer-generated hologram. Opt. Express **25**, 8212–8222 (2017)
3. Refregier, P., Javidi, B.: Optical image encryption based on input plane and fourier plane random encoding. Opt. Lett. **20**, 767–769 (1995)
4. Nischal, N.K., Joseph, J., Singh, K.: Securing information using fractional fourier transform in digital holography. Opt. Commun. **235**, 253–259 (2004)
5. Pan, W., Wun, W.W., Zhang, X.L.: Encryption algorithm of virtual optical based on computer-generated hologram and double random phase. Chin. J. Lasers **36**(s2), 312–317 (2009)
6. Wang, Y.Y., Wang, Y.R., Wang, Y., et al.: Optical image encryption based on binary fourier transform computer-generated hologram and pixel scrambling technology. Opt. Lasers Eng. **45**(7), 761–765 (2007)
7. Singh, N., Sinha, A.: Optical image encryption using Hartley transform and logistic map. Opt. Commun. **282**, 1104–1109 (2009)

8. Tricoles, G.: Computer generated holograms: an historical review. Appl. Opt. **26**, 4351–4357 (1987)

9. Guan, Z.H., Huang, F.J., Guan, W.J., et al.: Chaos-based image encryption algorithm. Phys. Lett. A **346**(1), 153–157 (2005)

10. Belazi, A., Ellatif, A.A.: A simple yet efficient S-box method based on chaotic sine map. Optik **130**, 1438–1444 (2017)

11. Smila, M., Sankar, S.: Novel algorithms for finding an optimal scanning path for JPEG image compression. IJETCSE **8**, 230–236 (2014)

12. Shen, J.J., Ren, J.M.: A robust associative watermarking technique based on vector quantization. Digital Signal Process. **20**, 1408–1423 (2010)

13. Akhshani, A., Behnia, S., Akhavan, A., et al.: A novel scheme for image encryption based on 2D piecewise chaotic maps. Opt. Commun. **283**(17), 3259–3266 (2010)

# Study and Hardware-in-the-Loop Simulation of Flight Mach Control System Based on Fuzzy Control Theory

Gan Cui[1,2]([✉]) and Huiqiang Zhang[1]

[1] School of Aerospace Engineering, Tsinghua University,
Beijing 100084, China
cuigan@aliyun.com
[2] Beijing Electro-Mechanical Engineering Institute of CASIC,
Beijing 100074, China

**Abstract.** An efficient and reliable flight Mach controller is specially needed for an Aircraft. A Flight Mach Fuzzy Controller (FMFC) based on modern Fuzzy control theory is designed for an Unmanned Aerial Vehicle (UAV) using a turbojet engine. The theory and process of designing control law is introduced and its control performance is optimized by changing the scaling factor. In order to evaluate the control performance, the mathematical simulation and hardware-in-the-loop simulation are carried out respectively, and the simulation results are compared. The evaluation shows good control performance to stabilize the UAV flight Mach number to the target Mach number quickly by controlling the engine work condition.

**Keywords:** Unmanned Aerial Vehicle · Flight Mach number · Fuzzy control · Hardware-in-the-loop simulation

## 1 Introduction

The Flight Mach Control System (FMCS), which controls the engine work condition to ensure that the aircraft flight according to the desired Mach number, plays an important role in the flight performance of an Unmanned Aerial Vehicle (UAV) [1]. However, because the models of aircraft trajectory and engine are incredibly complicated and strongly nonlinearized, an efficient and reliable control methodology is required [2]. Intelligent fuzzy control laws do not presuppose the strict mathematical model of the control object, different from classical model-based control approaches, and is expected to be able to flexibly handle the change of the characteristics of the control object [3]. A number of studies have already demonstrated that the fuzzy control is a feasible and flexible approach to flight control and can provide adequate control performance across the flight envelope [4–6]. In these approaches, however, the evaluation of control performance usually stays at the level of mathematical simulation without considering the factors of real products, which affects the control quality.

Hardware-in-the-loop (HIL) simulation is a technique that is used in the development and test of complex real-time embedded systems [7]. In order to be close to the

H. Song et al. (Eds.): SIMUtools 2019, LNICST 295, pp. 539–548, 2019.
https://doi.org/10.1007/978-3-030-32216-8_52

natural processes, an effective simulation platform is built by adding some real hardware products, such as engine Electronic Control Unit (ECU), and fuel supply mechanism. These products are apparently smaller and cheaper, as compared to the complicated products which are replaced by the mathematical simulation models to avoid high costs and high risks.

In this paper, a Flight Mach Fuzzy Controller (FMFC) based on modern fuzzy control theory is designed for an UAV using a turbojet engine, considering the interconnection factor of Aircraft Flight Control System and Propulsion System. The error and error rate of flight Mach number are used as the input variables of controller, and the engine rotation speed difference is used as the output variable. The theory and process of designing control law is introduced. And the control performance is optimized by changing the scaling factor. To evaluate the control performance, a hardware-in-the-loop simulation system is built, and the result is discussed by comparing with the mathematical simulation result. The evaluation showed good control performance to stabilize the UAV flight Mach number to the target Mach number quickly.

## 2   Flight Mach Control System

The FMCS which uses the control algorithm to change engine condition by calculating the supply fuel, is the significant constituent part of an UAV, and its function is ensuring that the aircraft flight according to the desired Mach number from the Airborne Control Compute (ACC). The operating principle of FMCS is shown in Fig. 1.

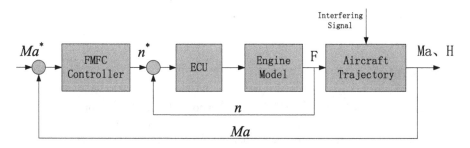

**Fig. 1.** Sketch map of FMCS principle

When the UAV is cruising, the ACC will calculate a target Mach number in real time and sends it to FMFC, according to the current flight condition and the subsequent flight requirements. The FMFC compares the actual flight Mach number $Ma$ and the target Mach number $Ma^*$. If $Ma$ is larger than $Ma^*$, the engine rotation speed $n^*$ should be smaller to decrease the engine thrust for decelerating the UAV. On the contrary, if $Ma$ is smaller than $Ma^*$, the engine rotation speed $n^*$ should be larger to increase the engine thrust for speeding the aircraft. If $Ma$ is the same with $Ma^*$, the engine rotation speed will stay its position to keep the balance of thrust and drag. When the flight Mach number drift off the scheduled variable, the FMCS will change the engine condition in good time to keep the flight Mach number to the set point needed.

## 3 Flight Mach Fuzzy Controller

The static and dynamic characteristics performance of the FMCS depends largely on the performance of the FMFC. The fuzzy control system is a digital and intelligent control system, with a kind of feedback closed loop structure, the composition heart of which is an intelligent fuzzy controller [7]. The design major components of the FMFC include the pretreatment, the fuzzification, the rules, the inference engine and the defuzzification, as shown in Fig. 2.

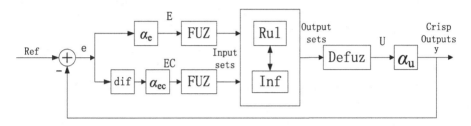

**Fig. 2.** FMFC structure

### 3.1 Pretreatment and Fuzzification

The pretreatment means deciding the input and output variables to the inference part, and quantifying these variables to form the fuzzy space [8]. The FMFC consists of double inputs and single output. The Mach number error $e = Ma - Ma^*$ and error rate $\Delta e = (Ma - Ma^*)/T$ are chosen as the input variables, where $T$ is the control cycle time. The output of the fuzzy inference part is used as an engine rotation speed difference $\Delta n = n - n^*$. For simplicity, the same quantization domains are used for all control variables: $\{-6, -5, -4, -3, -2, -1, 0, 1, 2, 3, 4, 5, 6\}$.

This fuzzification determines the corresponding degree of each variable within the associated membership function [8]. Seven fuzzy subsets same for all control variables are chosen: (NB, NM, NS, Z0, PS, PM, PB},

where

NB = negative big,
NM = negative middle,
NS = negative small,
Z0 = zero,
PS = positive small,
PM = positive middle,
PB = positive big.

Two triangular fuzzy membership functions are used to determine the membership of fuzzy linguistic values decided by the input (Fig. 3) and output (Fig. 4). In Fig. 3, the initial values of indexes {a, b, c, d, e, f} are set as {−0.06, −0.04, −0.02, 0.02, 0.04, 0.06} according to the experience. In fact, these values play an important part in the performance of FMFC and need to be optimized. More details about the optimization will be discussed in Sect. 4.2.

### 3.2  Fuzzy Rules and Inference

The inference manages all the operations specified by the fuzzy rules with their logical operators, and aggregates the outputs of these fuzzy rules as the fuzzified output [8]. Two types of usual methods to determine the fuzzy control rules exist in the literature: the synthetic reasoning and the experience induction [9]. In this paper, the experience induction method is adopted to obtain a total of 49 if-then rules that cover the complete input/output space as Table 1. The experience is extracted from the Mach number control process described in Sect. 2, utilizing a strategy resembles to that of a classic PD controller since the rules are predicated on errors and error rates. Examples of the rules in Table 1 are:

R1: if $e$ is NB and $\Delta e$ is NB, then $\Delta n$ is PB;
R2: if $e$ is NM and $\Delta e$ is NM, then $\Delta n$ is PB.

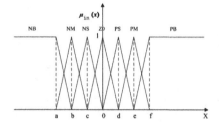    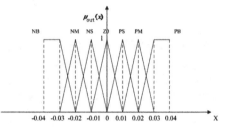

**Fig. 3.** Input membership function          **Fig. 4.** Output membership function

**Table 1.** The fuzzy rules

| $\Delta n$ / $e$ | NB | NM | NS | Z0 | PS | PM | PB |
|---|---|---|---|---|---|---|---|
| NB | PB | PB | PB | PB | PM | PS | Z0 |
| NM | PB | PB | PM | PM | PS | Z0 | Z0 |
| NS | PB | PM | PM | PS | Z0 | Z0 | NS |
| Z0 | PM | PS | PS | Z0 | NS | NS | NM |
| PS | PS | Z0 | Z0 | NS | NM | NM | NB |
| PM | Z0 | Z0 | NS | NM | NM | NB | NB |
| PB | Z0 | NS | NM | NB | NB | NB | NB |

For implication functions and the compositional rules of inference, Mamdani's minimum-operation is utilized. Then, the expression of the new membership function is obtained as follows:

$$\mu_c(\Delta n) = [w_1 \wedge \mu_{PB}(\Delta n)] \vee [w_2 \wedge \mu_{PB}(\Delta n)] \tag{1}$$

where

$$w_1 = \mu_{NB}(e) \wedge \mu_{NB}(\Delta e) \tag{2}$$

$$w_2 = \mu_{NM}(e) \wedge \mu_{NM}(\Delta e) \tag{3}$$

### 3.3  Defuzzification

The resulting fuzzy set is defuzzified to yield a crisp value. The popular defuzzification method used within the Mamdani defuzzification block is weighted average method [9], which can be calculated for a discrete membership function as follows:

$$\Delta n = \frac{\sum_{j=1}^{k} \mu_{C_j}(w_j) w_j}{\sum_{j=1}^{k} \mu_{C_j}(w_j)} \tag{4}$$

At last, the target engine rotation speed $n^*$ of the next $T + 1$ can be obtained according to Eq. (5).

$$n^* = n + \alpha_u \Delta n \tag{5}$$

Where, $n$ is the engine rotation speed of the present $T$, $\alpha_u$ is the scaling factor of the output.

## 4  Simulations

In this part, the FMFC control performance is examined for the flight Mach number control process in a complex system that is built according to Fig. 1. The mathematical simulation and hardware-in-the-loop simulation are carried out respectively. The goal is to test the ability of the control system to stabilize the UAV flight Mach number.

### 4.1  Mathematical Simulation

Validation of the FMFC is done on the test platform built according to Fig. 1, consisting of the FMFC, the ECU model, the engine model and the aircraft trajectory model. The function of ECU model is calculating the supply fuel flow to the engine according to the target engine rotation speed $n^*$ from FMFC. The engine model and the aircraft trajectory model that is built to simulate the steady state operation of the UAV are complex, and can calculate accurately the parameters that consist of flight Mach number, flight altitude, engine rotation speed and thrust. The platform and all the models are written in *C#* language.

The simulation is assumed to take place at a typical flight condition of Mach 0.72 at 5 km altitude that the engine rotation speed is 85% of the maximum speed as shown in Table 2 Example A. The UAV needs to be accelerated to Mach 0.8. Whereafter, the FMFC activates and assumes the control authority.

**Table 2.** Simulation conditions

| Parameter | Symbol | Example A | Example B |
|---|---|---|---|
| Altitude (km) | $H$ | 5 | 8 |
| Mach number | $Ma$ | 0.72 | 0.716 |
| Engine rotation speed | $n/n_{\max}$ | 85% | 85% |
| Target mach number | $Ma^*$ | 0.8 | 0.65 |
| Control cycle time (s) | $T$ | 5 | 5 |

The simulation result is shown in Fig. 5. The maximum overshoot is 0.1 for Mach number. It can be clearly learned that the controller has performed a good work for controlling the Mach number to achieve and stabilize the target. Although a long period of oscillations are observed before reaching the stable target because the initial values of the variables membership is not reasonable that is needed to be optimized.

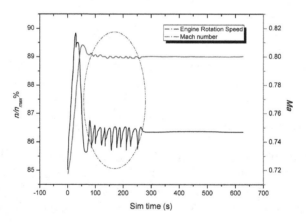

**Fig. 5.** Result of mathematical simulation

## 4.2 Optimization

In order to improve the controller performance, the control variable scale factors ($\alpha_e, \alpha_{ec}$ and $\alpha_u$) are adjusted as the optimization parameters to modify the membership function of the all variables. Figure 6 shows the effect of the scale factors to the control performance. The smaller $\alpha_e$ or the bigger $\alpha_u$ gives rise to the oscillation and overshoot, while the bigger $\alpha_{ec}$ leads to overshoot only.

The objective function of the optimization is defined in Eq. (6).

$$J = \min \left( \int_0^{t_z} |e(t)|dt \right) \tag{6}$$

Where, $t$ is the simulation time, and $e(t)$ is the error of Mach number to the target Mach number. According to the optimization results, it is probable to achieve good control performance when the scales are chosen as $\alpha_e = 1.29$, $\alpha_{ec} = 0.31$, and $\alpha_u = 0.9$. The results contrast before and after the optimization is shown in Fig. 7. The contrast shows that the time response is quick and overshoots are tiny.

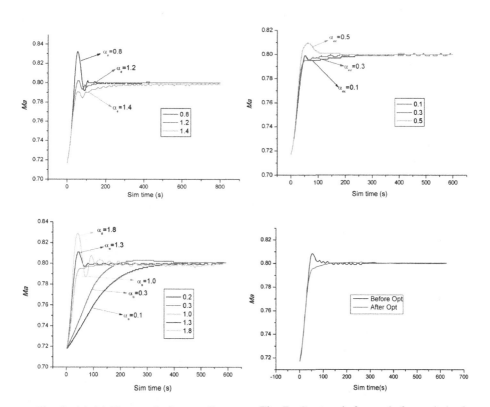

**Fig. 6.**  (a)–(c) Three scale factors effect          **Fig. 7.**  Contrast before and after optimization

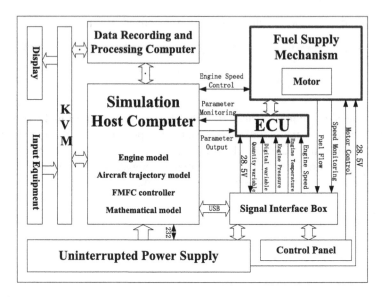

**Fig. 8.** HIL system architecture diagram (the bold solid frames are real products)

### 4.3    Hardware-in-the-Loop Simulation

The Hardware-in-the-loop simulation system is built on the basis of mathematical simulation by replacing partial mathematical models with real products [10, 11]. The system consists of Electronic Control Unit (ECU), Fuel Supply Mechanism (FSM), Simulation Host Computer (SHC), Data Recording and Processing Computer (DRPC), Signal Interface Box (SIB), and Uninterrupted Power Supply (UPS), as shown in Fig. 8. The FSM is one of a series of actuators that the ECU controls on an internal combustion engine to ensure optimal engine performance. These two real products work together to achieve the fuel supply function of the engine, by reading values from a multitude of parameters within the engine model, interpreting the data using the complex control algorithms, and adjusting the engine actuators. The Engine model, aircraft trajectory model, FMFC controller and the other related mathematical models run on the SHC computer.

Two Simulation Examples (A and B) are carried out to test the performance of the FCFC controller. The condition of example A is the same with that in Sect. 4.1. The simulation of example B is assumed to take place at a flight condition of Mach 0.716 at 8 km as shown in Table 2.

The comparison results of mathematical simulation and the hardware-in-the-loop simulation in the same condition are shown in Fig. 9. It can be clearly learned that the controller has performed an excellent work for the tracking task, and the results of mathematical simulation and the hardware-in-the-loop simulation are almost the same. The relative error of the stabilized final Mach number defined as $\theta$ in Eq. (7) is less than 2%, while the engine rotation speed are quite different that is especially for example B, as represent in Fig. 9(b). The result of hardware-in-the-loop simulation is more hysteretic and stable, which is because the system has delayed effect benefit from

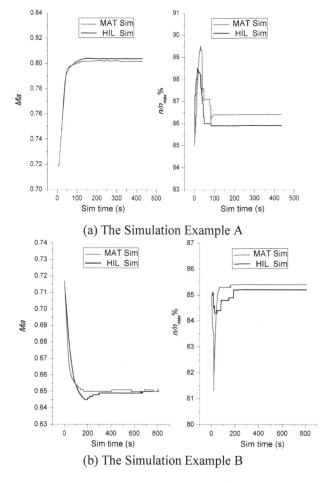

(a) The Simulation Example A

(b) The Simulation Example B

**Fig. 9.** Comparison of mathematical simulation and hardware-in-the-loop simulation

adding the real products, and the ECU has more detailed algorithm to calculate the fuel flow than mathematical simulation model.

$$\theta = \frac{\max(|e(t)|)}{Ma^*} \times 100\% \tag{7}$$

## 5   Conclusions

Flight Mach Fuzzy Controller (FMFC) based on modern fuzzy control theory is designed for an UAV using a turbojet engine, and the control performance is optimized by changing scaling factor. A hardware-in-the-loop simulation system is built to evaluate the control performance, and the relative error of the stabilized final Mach number is less than 2%, meaning that the controller has performed an excellent work for the tracking task.

This study indicates that, although the flight condition for the UAV is complicated and changeable, the FMFC controls the flight Mach to the target Mach number quickly. This conclusion is proved by the test including the mathematical simulation and hardware-in-the-loop simulation.

In the future, the work is expected to integrate the FMFC with the roll, Angle of attack and Angle of sight controller using fuzzy logic concept, and create more realistic hardware-in-the-loop simulation environment.

# References

1. Purnachander, D.: Aircraft dutch roll control by fuzzy logic controller. Int. J. Latest Trends Eng. Technol. 3(5), 38–46 (2015)
2. Ross, I.M., Fahroo, F.A.: Perspective on methods for trajectory optimization. In: AIAA Paper 2002, p. 4727 (2002)
3. Suratia, P., Patel, J., Rajpal, R.: FPGA based fuzzy logic controller for plasma position control in ADITYA Tokamak. Fusion Eng. Des. 87(11), 1866–1871 (2012)
4. Erginer, B., Altug, E.: Design and implementation of a hybrid fuzzy logic controller for a quadrotor VTOL vehicle. Int. J. Control Autom. Syst. 10(1), 61–70 (2012)
5. Hector, G., Qian, G., Jiang, C.S.: Fuzzy terminal sliding-mode control for hypersonic vehicles. J. Intell. Fuzzy Syst. 33(3), 1831–1839 (2017)
6. Jan, B., Frantisek, D., Pavol, F., Daniela, P.: Autonomous flying with quadrocopter using fuzzy control and ArUco markers. Intell. Serv. Robot. 10(3), 185–194 (2017)
7. Lijun, Z., Yingyue, X.: Application of normalized LCF method in flight/propulsion controller design. Acta Aeronaut. et Astronaut. Sin. 21(3), 267–269 (2000)
8. Kevin, M.P., Yurkovich, S.: Fuzzy Control. Tsinghua University Press, Beijing (2001)
9. Jantzen, J.: Foundations of Fuzzy Control: A Practical Approach, 2nd edn. Wiley, Hoboken (2013)
10. Kai-long, C., Shou-sheng, X., Jin-hai, H.: Semi-physical simulation experiment system of fuel integration control system for turbofan engine. J. Propul. Technol. 28(4), 422–427 (2007)
11. Zheng, W., Wu, G., Xu, G.: Adaptive fuzzy sliding-mode control of uncertain nonlinear system. In: 3rd International Conference on Management, Education, Information and Control, pp. 707–711 (2015)

# Spatial Propagation Measurement and Analysis of Millimeter-Wave Channels at 28 GHz

Ruonan Zhang[1], Yang Wang[1(✉)], Changyou Li[2], Yi Jiang[1], and Bin Li[1]

[1] Department of Communication Engineering,
Northwestern Polytechnical University, Xi'an 710072, Shaanxi, China
540164982@qq.com
[2] Department of Electronics Engineering, Northwestern Polytechnical University,
Xi'an 710072, Shaanxi, China

**Abstract.** The millimeter-wave (mmWave) band will play an important role in the fifth generation (5G) cellular system. The analysis of the propagation characteristics based on measurements in the mmWave spectrum is crucial for the system design and network deployment. In this paper, we present a channel measurement campaign at 28 GHz in the urban microcell (UMi) scenario by utilizing a 3-dimensional (3D) channel sounder. The transmitter was placed on the top of a three-storey building to emulate a base station, and the receiver was moved to several positions on the ground to emulate mobile stations in the line-of-sight (LOS) and not-line-of-sight (NLOS) scenarios. We utilized four steering high-gain horn antennas to capture the multipath components (MPCs) incoming from all directions and thus measured the power delay profiles (PDPs) as well as the angular power spectra (APSs) of the channels. We have analyzed the impact of the surrounding buildings and trees on the mmWave propagation based on the measurement results. It is shown that the signal power can be enhanced in the NLOS scenarios by building reflections and foliage introduces significant attenuation for the mmWave signals.

**Keywords:** Millimeter-wave · 28 GHz · Channel measurement · Propagation

## 1 Introduction

The shortage of bandwidth resources has become a challenge for the mobile communication systems globally [1]. The frequency bands in the current cellular systems and wireless local area networks (WLANs) have been crowded already due to the rapid increase of electronic devices. These have motivated the exploitation of the millimeter-wave (mmWave) frequency spectrum, especially for densely populated areas such as downtowns, shopping malls, and airports [2]. Therefore, it is necessary to investigate the propagation characteristics

© ICST Institute for Computer Sciences, Social Informatics and Telecommunications Engineering 2019
Published by Springer Nature Switzerland AG 2019. All Rights Reserved
H. Song et al. (Eds.): SIMUtools 2019, LNICST 295, pp. 549–558, 2019.
https://doi.org/10.1007/978-3-030-32216-8_53

of the mmWave bands to provide the guidance for the theoretical analysis, simulation, and deployment of future mmWave networks.

Many channel measurement campaigns in the mmWave band, including indoor and outdoor scenarios, have been done [5]. The authors in [4] studied the propagation characteristics of the indoor scenario at 28 GHz. The second-order fading statistics are shown. The authors in [3] carried out channel measurements at 28 GHz in an indoor environment. The multipath components (MPCs) and some parameters such as APS were obtained. The measurements in [6] were done for the outdoor scenario, and the authors analyzed the small-scale fading model. However, most of the existing literatures focus on the large-scale fading (path loss and shadowing) of the mmWave channels, and the range of distance is usually more than 200 m. Few literatures have studied the temporal and angular distributions of received signal energy in an urban microcell (UMi) scenario. In addition, the influence of buildings and trees on the mmWave signal propagation in the cellular network scenarios has not been fully explored. Therefore, field measurement to observe the multipath propagation and obtain the small-scale parameters of mmWave propagation paths is still lack.

In this paper, a measurement campaign on the 28 GHz mmWave channels using a spatial-temporal multipath channel sounder is presented. The campaign was performed in a typical UMi scenario. The transmitter (TX) was placed on the top of a three-storey canteen to emulate a base station (BS), and the receiver (RX) was moved to several positions on the ground to emulate mobile stations (MSs) in both the line-of-sight (LOS) and not-line-of-sight (NLOS) scenarios. In the NLOS case, the direct propagation paths were blocked by dense foliage. We utilized four high-gain horn antennas that rotated horizontally on the RX to capture the MPCs incoming from all directions and measured the small-scale parameters of propagation paths, including power, excess delay, and angle of arrival (AoA). Then we obtained the power delay profiles (PDPs) and angular power spectra (APSs) of the mmWave channels.

Furthermore, based on the measurement results, we have analyzed the scattering effect of the surrounding buildings on the mmWave signal propagation in the LOS scenario and the obstructing effect of the blocking trees in the NLOS scenario. It is found that the scattering and reflection by objects have different effects on the channel characteristics. Reflection from buildings has positive influence in some cases, while the scattering and obstructing by trees and foliage cause significant attenuation. The results show that the received signals can be enhanced in some specific NLOS environments.

The rest of the paper is organized as follows. Section 2 describes the channel sounder used in the measurement campaign. Section 3 presents the measurement scenario and process. The measurement results and analysis of the PDPs and APSs are discussed in Sect. 4. Section 5 concludes the paper and points out future research issues.

## 2    Channel Measurement System

### 2.1    28 GHz Channel Sounder

In this work, a spatial-temporal multipath channel sounder was utilized to perform the measurement on the 28 GHz mmWave channels. The TX and RX systems are shown in Fig. 1 and the architectures are shown in Fig. 2. The TX system consists of an arbitrary waveform generator (AWG), a vector signal generator, a power amplifier, and a sector antenna with a beam width of 120°. The baseband signal used in this measurement campaign is the repeat of a pseudo-noise sequence (PN-sequence), with the bandwidth of 160 MHz. On the TX side, the IQ signals are generated by an arbitrary waveform generator, and then modulated by BPSK on the 28 GHz carrier. The radio frequency (RF) signal is amplified by a power amplifier before being transmitted through the sector horn antenna.

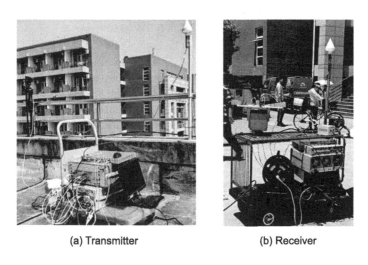

(a) Transmitter                    (b) Receiver

**Fig. 1.** Photos of the channel sounder.

The RX consists of a down converter and a vector signal transceiver (VST). Four high-gain horn antennas are placed on a horizontal tablet on a rotator. The four antennas are facing different directions and perpendicular to each other. The rotator is controlled by a computer and rotates horizontally by the step of ten degree. All the equipments on the RX side are put on a cart. The height of the four horn antennas is 1.3 m. The RF signals received by the four antennas are sent to a down converter. Then the intermediate-frequency (IF) signals are captured by a VST with four input ports. Finally, the demodulated I/Q signals are sampled and stored in a harddisk array for off-line processing.

Meanwhile, GPS-triggered rubidium clocks are used on the TX and RX to ensure the synchronization in transmitting and receiving the probing signals.

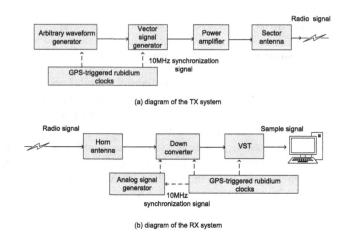

(a) diagram of the TX system

(b) diagram of the RX system

**Fig. 2.** Measurement system diagram.

## 2.2   Calibrations of System

Before field measurement, we need to conduct a the system calibration of the TX and RX systems to ensure the accuracy of the measurement data. The signal phase offsets are introduced by the equipments at each step. We need to ensure that the phases of the received signals are only determined by the channel propagation. Through the calibration experiment, we can acquire the phase effect of the system and removed it from the measurement data. The steps of the system calibration are as follows.

We remove one antenna on the RX and then connect the receiving port directly to the transmitting port on the TX. The power of the transmitted signal is −30 dBm. Then we can obtain the channel impulse response (CIR) of the radio chain without the antenna. Similarly, the same operation is repeated for the other three receiving ports. The CIRs (i.e., the gains and phase shifts) of the radio chains will be used to remove the effect of the measurement system when we analyze the captured probing signals. As an illustrative example, the calibration result of one antenna is presented in Fig. 3.

Meanwhile, to eliminate the gains and phase offsets introduced by the transmitting and receiving antennas, we have measured the antenna patterns in a microwave chamber and then de-embed them from the received signals. Thus, the antenna responses are removed in the captured propagation parameters.

## 3   Channel Measurement Scenario

The measurement campaign was conducted in a street canyon environment on the campus of Northwestern Polytechnical University. It is a typical UMi scenario.

The TX was located on the top of a 10-meter-high building. Both the LOS and NLOS scenarios were included, depending on if the direct propagation paths

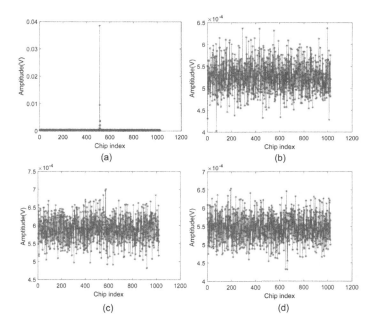

**Fig. 3.** The receiving port of one antenna is connected directly to the transmitting port. (a) The CIR of the connected radio chain. (b), (c), and (d) The CIRs of the other three antennas.

**Fig. 4.** The environment of measurement campaign. (a) The LOS scenario with direct propagation path. (b) The NLOS scenario where the direct path was blocked by dense foliage.

were blocked by the dense foliage. The range of the measurement distance is from 24 to 40 m.

When conducting the measurement, the RX was moved to four positions on the ground to emulate MSs. For example, two RX locations are shown in the photos in Fig. 4. At each position, as described in Sect. 2.1, the four horn antennas rotated with a step size of ten degrees, completing a sweep of 360° in the horizontal plane. The VST collected the received probing signals on the four horn antennas simultaneously. Note that the sector antenna of the TX was adjusted to always point to the RX.

## 4    Measurement Results and Analysis

### 4.1    APS

The results of APS are shown in Fig. 5, together with the environment diagram. The results and analysis are discussed in two aspects as follows. The observations in the LOS scenario are analyzed below.

(1) From Fig. 5(a), it can be observed that at RX1 the power in the LOS direction has the highest value, which was −9 dBm at the angle of 180°. The propagation distance of the LOS path was the shortest, with the lowest attenuation.
(2) The power at 0°, which is opposite to the LOS direction, is slightly lower than the power of the LOS path, but higher than other directions. This is due to the apartment buildings A and B behind RX1. The signals propagating to the apartment buildings A and B were reflected back and received by the RX. Therefore the finally received signal power was enhanced.
(3) On the left side of RX1 there standed a billboard. This may explain why the power at 260° was −15 dBm. This is because the signals reflected by the billboard were received at RX1. Meanwhile, this caused the difference between the power arrival on the two sides of RX1, which leaded to the dissymmetry of the APS.

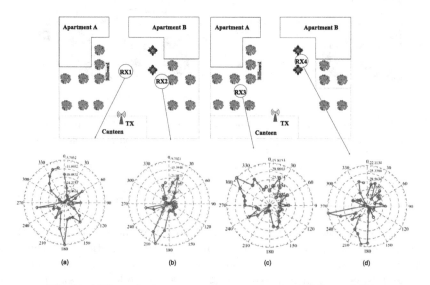

**Fig. 5.** APS at the four measurement spots from RX1 to RX4.

(4) From (b), similarly, we can find the LOS path at 200°, with the maximum power intensity about −10 dBm. About −20 dBm signals were detected on the opposite direction. This is because the wall behind RX2 reflected the signals.

(5) On the right side of the polar plot in (b), the power level is obviously lower than other directions. This is because the two sides of RX2 were surrounded by trees and shrubs. Signals impinging the trees were scattered and absorbed and thus there were no significant reflections.

Comparing the similarities and differences between (a) and (b), we have noticed that the wave beams in both the polar plots were concentrated and narrow. This is due to the significant high-power component of the LOS propagation path. The MPCs by reflection, scattering, and diffraction were much less significant. However, the surrounding environments of position RX1 and RX2 were different. RX1 was in a relatively open space while around RX2 there were trees and buildings nearby. The relevant discussion will be presented at the end of this section.

The observations in the NLOS scenario are analyzed below.

(1) Firstly, the maximum power intensity shown in (c) and (d) is small than that in (a) and (b). There was no direct link between the TX and RX. The signals must be received at RX through at least one reflection or diffraction. Thus, the intensity of the received power was much lower than that of the LOS path.

(2) In (c), the direction of the connection line between the TX and RX3 was at 120° approximately. Because of the obstruction of the thick foliage in this direction, the power intensity was lower than others directions. On the contrast, at the angle of 310°, the power intensity reached the peak at −15 dBm. This is because the tree was shorter than others around RX3. Therefore the signals arrived at the walls of the apartment building and were reflected back to RX3, increasing the received power.

(3) Other wave beams, whose power intensities were between the maximum and the minimum in (c), were caused by reflection and scattering from the foliage. The power of these MPCs was smaller than those caused by the reflection on the external walls of the apartment buildings.

(4) From (d), it is observed that the results have a similar pattern with (c). The direct link at 220° was blocked by the tree severely. As a result, the power was at a low level around −30 dBm. In contrast, at the angle of 260° and 190°, the power intensities were higher than others. This is because that at RX4, the obstructor was a single tree and the surrounding was relatively open. The radio waves may propagate to RX4 from other directions.

(5) At the angle of 300 and 120°, the signal power was quite low. But on the back side of RX4, there were some signals impinging with the power of −28 dBm. This is due to the reflection from the wall of the apartment buildings B.

RX3 and RX4 were both located in the shadow of the trees. But there were more reflections received by RX4. By comparing the APS results in the LOS scenario, it can be seen that the foliage has a significant effect on the 28 GHz propagation characteristics.

The measurement results in this campaign show that in some specific environments, the received signal power can be enhanced. For example, the signals arrived at the back of RX1 were enhanced by the reflection from the wall. Reflection from construction, billboards, vehicles, streetlights, etc. may arrive at the RX from any directions. These MPCs can cause positive influence for the signal reception. However, trees/foliage cannot cause positive signal construction as shown in this measurement campaign. Signals are scattered and absorbed by them, resulting in severe signal power attenuation.

## 4.2    PDP

Figure 6 illustrates the PDPs in the LOS and NLOS scenarios. The $x$-axis represents the excess delay and the $y$-axis represents the index of the PN-sequence chips. The $z$-axis represents the power intensity. The multipath excess delay is

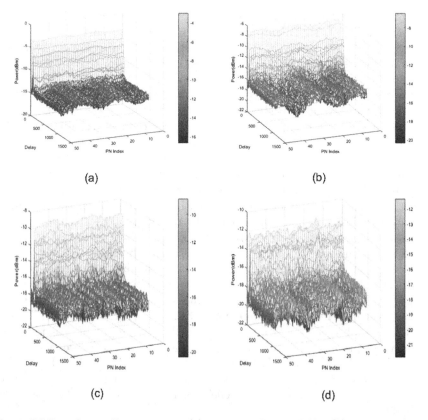

(a)

(b)

(c)

(d)

**Fig. 6.** PDP at four collection spots. (a) corresponding to RX1. (b) corresponding to RX2. (c) corresponding to RX3. (d) corresponding to RX4.

defined with respect to the most significant path, whose time delay was 100 chips approximately. Analysis and comparison for the LOS scenario are presented as follows.

(1) The fluctuation of the received power at RX2 was severer than at RX1. This reflects the difference in actual surrounding environments. The trees around RX2 limited the reception of signals, and thus the received signal power fluctuated within some ranges. This echoes the discussion in the previous subsection.

(2) Excess delay is determined by the distance of propagation. Due to the dense surrounding of trees, RX2 mainly received the MPCs scattered from other objects. As a result, the excess delay in Fig. 6(b) is much more spread.

In the NLOS scenario, the maximum excess delay was longer, which was because of the relatively more spreaded MPCs comparing with the LOS scenario. However, the MPCs with excess delay more than 200 chips detected at RX3 were less than at RX4, which is because the impinging signals at RX3 were blocked by the trees and fewer MPCs could be received. Consequently, in the NLOS case, the presence of trees can reduce the excess delay and delay spread.

It should be noted that this study has focused only on specific environments. More raw data need to be collected in measurements. The results in our work could match the discussions above. Further studies, such as the effect of the pedestrians have been taken into account to perfection this work.

## 5 Conclusion

In this paper, a measurement campaign on the 28 GHz mmWave channels by utilizing a spatial multipath channel sounder was conducted in a typical UMi scenario. We measured the power, time of arrival, and angle of arrival of the propagation paths at four MS positions, including both the LOS and NLOS scenarios. Based on the measurement data, the channel propagation characteristics including the CIR, APS, and PDP are analyzed. The measurement results indicate that the scattering, reflection, and blocking by the surrounding objects have significant effects on the mmWave channel propagation. The trees introduce severe attenuation on the received power due to the scattering. However, in the NLOS environments, the reflection from objects such as the external walls of buildings can enhance the received power level. The observations in this work can provide guidance in the subsequent studies of the channel modelling and simulations for the mmWave frequency spectrum. Further studies on the channel characterization, such as the effect of pedestrians on the mmWave propagation, will be studied in the future works.

**Acknowledgement.** This work was supported in part by the National Natural Science Foundation of China (61571370 and 61601365), in part by the Natural Science Basic Research Plan in Shaanxi Province (2016JQ6017), in part by the Fundamental Research Funds for the Central Universities (3102017O-QD091 and 3102017GX08003), and in part by the China Postdoctoral Science Foundation (BX20180262).

# References

1. Rappaport, T.S., Sun, S., Mayzus, R.: Millimeter wave mobile communications for 5G cellular: it will work!. IEEE Access **1**, 335–349 (2013)
2. Zhang, R., Zhou, Y., Lu, X.: Antenna deembedding for mmWave propagation modeling and field measurement validation at 73 GHz. IEEE Trans. Microwave Theory Tech. **65**(10), 3648–3659 (2017)
3. Huang, J., Feng, R., Sun, J.: Comparison of propagation channel characteristics for multiple millimeter wave bands. In: IEEE 85th Vehicular Technology Conference 2017, VTC Spring, pp. 1–5 (2017)
4. Gulfam, S.M., Nawaz, S.J., Baltzis, K.B.: Characterization of second-order fading statistics of 28 GHz indoor radio propagation channels. In: 7th International Conference on Modern Circuits and Systems Technologies 2018, MOCAST, pp. 1–4 (2018)
5. Kim, J.H., Yoon, Y., Chong, Y.J.: The delay spread characteristics of 28 GHz band at LOS environments. In: URSI Asia-Pacific Radio Science Conference 2016, URSI AP-RASC, pp. 1953–1955 (2016)
6. Samimi, M.K., MacCartney, G.R., Sun, S.: 28 GHz millimeter-wave ultrawideband small-scale fading models in wireless channels. In: IEEE 83rd Vehicular Technology Conference 2016, VTC Spring, pp. 1–6 (2016)

# Study and Implementation of Minority Mobile Application Recommendation Software

Xiaofeng Wang[1,2], Dongming Tang[1,2(✉)], Hui Zheng[1,2], and Ke Zhang[3]

[1] The Key Laboratory for Computer Systems of State Ethnic Affairs Commission, Southwest Minzu University, Chengdu, China
tdm_2010@qq.com
[2] School of Computer Science and Technology, Southwest Minzu University, Chengdu, China
[3] School of Computer Science and Engineering, University of Electronic Science and Technology of China, Chengdu, China

**Abstract.** The development of network technology has greatly enhanced the degree of informationization of life. Although computers and mobile phones in developed regions have spread all over, there are still some minority peoples living in remote areas that have problems such as low mobile penetration rate, scattered national application software, language barriers which is due to information occlusion. In this case, this paper uses the collaborative filtering algorithm and the recommendation algorithm based on content to implement the recommendation system, use the loop neural network to implement the smart translation function, and finally incorporate other techniques to design an ethnic minority applications recommendation App that is suitable for ethnic minorities. This App is convenient for them to learn Chinese, strengthen their communication with the outside world, improve their living standards and expand their horizons. At the same time, this software can speed up the popularization of smartphones and promote the development of information technology in minority areas.

**Keywords:** Ethnic minorities · Collaborative filtering algorithm · App recommendation

## 1 Introduction

China is a multi-ethnic country. The minority people are an indispensable part of the forest of our nations. Ethnic Minority areas are mostly located in mountainous areas with poor natural environment, with backward culture, education, economy and so on. To develop, we need to strengthen exchanges with other countries, so it is necessary for us to improve the communication between minorities and foreign countries. Smart mobile phones, as a means of communication, have been basically popularized in ethnic minority areas, and used as the primary means for most people to obtain information. However, until now, there is no App for promoting the knowledge and culture of ethnic minorities, which undoubtedly hinders the mutual understanding and

© ICST Institute for Computer Sciences, Social Informatics and Telecommunications Engineering 2019
Published by Springer Nature Switzerland AG 2019. All Rights Reserved
H. Song et al. (Eds.): SIMUtools 2019, LNICST 295, pp. 559–566, 2019.
https://doi.org/10.1007/978-3-030-32216-8_54

communication between ethnic minorities and the outside world, and also hinders the spread of ethnic culture.

By investigating the major application store, we find that the supported minority languages in App store are very few, mainly the two languages of Tibetan and Uighur. Most of the applications that support minority languages are the typewriting, dictionary and translation application. Compared with other Chinese Apps, these Apps are relatively weaker in the ability of human-computer interaction. Popular Apps for ethnic minorities, such as Holvoo, Ehshig and Bainu, are only designed for one minority language. The most popular phones only support Chinese. A small part of smart phones can set up ethnic minority languages, but how to find applications suitable for their learning, entertainment and life from the millions of App for minority people who are not familiar with Chinese?

In order to solve the above problems, this paper proposes a software which can be used to search Apps for minority people. This paper designed an application to solve the retrieval and usage problems caused by the language barrier. Based on the language, culture and usage preferences of ethnic minorities, the application recommends users their favorite mobile Apps.

## 2    System Development

### 2.1    Background Analysis

In recent years, products and services related to mobile information are changing the survival and competition mode of traditional industries and further affecting people's lives [1]. However, these changes do not appear to be obvious in minority areas, so we propose the recommended Apps to promote the development of minority areas, help enjoy the convenience and speed brought by the development of modern information technology. At present, minority smartphone users are still in great demand for applications, moreover, learning and entertainment, as the important part of people's lives, are particularly crucial and essential demand module in the applications. Therefore, considering the above factors and the difficulty of resource development, we decided to choose learning and entertainment as the main content of application recommendation.

### 2.2    Platform Configuration

Main configuration of the server: Ubuntu Server 16.04 LTS Linux, PHP Laravel framework [2], Nginx [3], MySQL, PHP, Python. Finally, this paper deploys the mobile terminal software to make it easy for users to use.

## 3 System Functions

The whole system consists of server and mobile client application. The server mainly includes: data crawling; data processing and storage; screening and recommendation. The client is an ordinary mobile phone application. The main function modules are: smart App recommendation; one-stop search App; one-click real-time translation. The overall software architecture diagram is shown in Fig. 1.

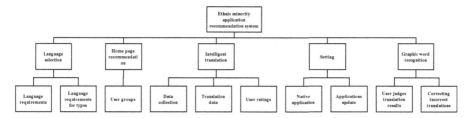

**Fig. 1.** App function modules

Among them, "language selection", "home page recommendation" and "intelligent translation" these three functional modules are the main part of the recommendation platform, mainly providing users with different kinds of demand services. "Language Selection" function module not only enable users of different ethnic groups to use the software, but also enable them to learn and inherit their own language in this fast-paced era. This function module provides convenient ethnic application search and download function for ethnic minority compatriots who are not familiar with Chinese; on the other hand, it also provides them with the opportunity to learn other national languages. When users switch the language to other national languages, bilingual or even multi-lingual learning can also be carried out. "Home recommendation" function module firstly recommends minority applications in the highly download, and then the mainstream App sales list. This allows fewer and more dispersed minority applications to be downloaded centrally. The function module of "screenshot translation" provides users with the translation function outside the application. The popular Apps, such as Meituan, Taobao etc., are all Chinese software. Even if the user switches the language of the mobile phone system, it is still displayed in Chinese, which brings operational difficulties to many minority users. As long as the recommendation App is running in the background, users can click the hover ball screenshot in other applications to point-to-point translation.

According to the criterion of several main minority languages used by Chinese ethnic minorities at present, based on the analysis of the types of language demanded by smartphone users and the number of requirements for each language, the right language should be chosen from the point of view of design and use.

### 3.1  Home Recommendation App

The home recommendation database mainly consists of three sub-databases: user preferences, user groups, and user reports in that these factors can basically reflect the user's demand for software. The formation of user preferences firstly predicts user preferences through users' basic data and behavior, and then secondly mines user historical behavior data to discover users' preferences. User groups are mainly divided by information such as mother tongue, race, gender and geographic location, and aggregate the common preferences of a certain group of users. User reports are formed by user feedback, correction of data, and optimization of the smart recommendation system. Ultimately, this software can group users based on different preferences and recommend applications with similar tastes.

### 3.2  Graphic Word Recognition

The database of picture-text recognition is composed of three sub-databases: collecting graphic text data, identifying graphic text data, and identifying and correcting. It is free open interface for other developers to collect image data. Collect the image wanted to identify and convert it into TIF format to generate the box file. Summarize the image and text data submitted by the client and classify similar images for evaluation.

### 3.3  Intelligent Translation

In recent years, with the "deep learning technology" and other artificial intelligence machine translation added, machine translation is more and more powerful. It is no longer just translating one word into another language but is able to constantly recall complex sentences that have already been understood to understanding the specific meaning of each pronoun. In addition, we have to understand that machine translation is a process of decoding and encoding. For example, when translating Chinese into Tibetan, the original Chinese text should be first decoded into "neural code" and then encoded to generate the Tibetan language.

## 4  Software Functions Implementation

The design and development of recommendation mobile phone App for minority applications is based on the needs of users, the significance and feasibility of development. Drawing on the design concepts of several mainstream application stores in China, this paper establishes the structure according to the requirements of "harmony and different" of various national cultures in China.

In the process of software functions implementation, first of all, this paper uses Java language to design the page controls and display modules. The screen capture of App interface is shown in Fig. 2.

**Fig. 2.** Snapshot of APP

Then, the main function is to apply the external screenshot click translation function. For example, we open Alipay, take a screenshot through the floating ball and then click to translate, as shown in Fig. 3. Users can submit data for translation training through the interface and evaluate the translation quality [4, 5]. Then it feedbacks to the neural machine translation training model to improve the translation quality.

**Fig. 3.** Snapshot of provided translation function for another App by touch point ball

## 4.1   Key Modules Implementation

Recommendation function is the key and emphasis of the whole recommendation App implementation and is also an important part of the whole system. One of the main functions of the recommendation App is to recommend the Apps that conform to local characteristics to ethnic minority compatriots, so the recommendation function plays an important role in the development. It not only has the recommendation function of traditional application store, but also has the characteristics of national characteristic recommendation.

The collaborative filtering algorithm was proposed by Goldberg et al. in 1992. The principle of collaborative filtering algorithm is as follows: firstly, the user's basic data is predicted by the user's preferences; secondly, the person with similar interests is divided into the same group; finally, the user's favorite software is recommended to other users with similar interests. For example, I like Meitu Xiuxiu and the recommendation algorithm will recommend Meitu Xiuxiu to other users in the same group. The algorithm flows chart shown in Fig. 4 [6]. The content-based recommendation algorithm [7], which does not consider human factors, only considers the things with the same keywords and tags. Its implementation principle is as follows: First, it makes recommendations based on the similarity between the collected information resources and user interests; then, by calculating the vector similarity between the user interest model and the applied feature vector, it recommends the application with high similarity to the client of the model; finally, because each customer operates independently, they have their own independent feature vectors, this algorithm ignores the interests of other users. Therefore, there is no problem that the evaluation level is high or low and it is possible to recommend a new application or recommend an unpopular application. These advantages make content-based filtering recommendation systems unaffected by cold-start and sparse issues.

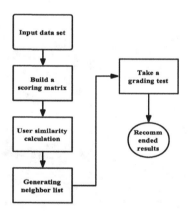

**Fig. 4.** Flow of d User-based CF

The application recommends the software through collaborative filtering algorithm. Based on the evaluation of content recommendation, it can recommend more personalized results to each user so that it is more convenient access to information. This paper uses Python to crawl the minority and Han nationality App in the main application store and then selects the star rating and user rating as input and calculates the correlation between App by using Pearson correlation evaluation. Now that the prediction is completed, this paper presents a recommendation to the user based on a similar App. The flow chart of the whole process is as follows in Fig. 5:

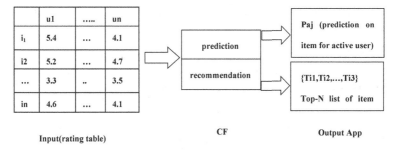

**Fig. 5.** App recommendation process

## 4.2    Database Development

In order to obtain real-time and useful data information, reduce the power consumption of ICT network devices [8], and prevent the loss of information in the process of transmission [9–11], this paper chooses a better network interface [12]. All the data in the minority application recommendation App is reflected in the database. Every function mentioned above has corresponding data in the database and its own attributes, which can facilitate the management of various data [13]. Of course, in addition to database development, the configuration of the App server and other development environments need pay attention. After running the program, the normal use of the recommended App can be guaranteed only if the databases can be connected properly.

## 5    Conclusion

At present, the development of Apps for ethnic minorities in China is increasing year by year. But ethnic applications are scattered, and most ethnic minority users are unaware of their existence. For another, due to the obstacles to the cognition of Chinese, many efficient and convenient Chinese Apps are not popularized in minority areas, which hinders the development of ethnic areas to a certain extent. Therefore, this paper mainly combines the characteristics of ethnic minorities and the needs of users and designs the main function module of ethnic minority application recommendation App. This can help minority users to make reasonable and effective use of network resources, promote economic development and increase cultural inheritance and exchanges.

Now many mainstream application stores such as Huawei, Xiaomi serve basically the Han population from the interface design to App search. The recommendation App has language selection function with mainstream minority languages. This makes it possible for ethnic minority compatriots to overcome language barriers. The recommendation App also gives priority to the recommendation of minority-related App, which solves the problem of scattered application of ethnic minorities. The recommendation software provides mobile phone users with the external click translation function so that minority users can use mobile phones with no language barriers in other App. With this paper' work, it is bound to accelerate the development of information technology in minority areas.

**Acknowledgements.** This research is supported by the Fundamental Research Funds for the Central Universities of Southwest Minzu University under Grant No. 2018NQN39, and the 6th Innovation and Entrepreneurship Leading Talents Project of Dongguan.

# References

1. Turkle, S.: Technology and human vulnerability. A conversation with MIT's Sherry Turkle. Harv. Bus. Rev. **81**(9), 43–50 (2003)
2. Putra, L., Michael, Yudishtira, Kanigoro, B.: Design and implementation of web based home electrical appliance monitoring, diagnosing, and controlling system. Procedia Comput. Sci. **59**, 34–44 (2015)
3. Schwartz, M.J.: Nginx Patches Critical Web Server Software Vulnerability. Information-week – Online (2013)
4. Lee, Y., Park, I., Cho, S., Choi, J.: Smartphone user segmentation based on app usage sequence with neural networks. Telemat. Inform. **35**(2), 329–339 (2018)
5. Wu, P., et al.: Bigdata logs analysis based on Seq2seq networks for cognitive internet of things. Future Gener. Comput. Syst. **90**, 477–488 (2019)
6. Huang, J., Yan, H.: Indoor localization algorithm based on cooperative of state matrix and Kalman filter. J. Netw. **8**(5), 1796–2056 (2013)
7. Brbić, M., Arko, I.P.: Tuning machine learning algorithms for content-based movie recommendation. Intell. Decis. Technol. Int. J. **9**(3), 233–242 (2015)
8. Jiang, D., Zhang, P., Lv, Z., et al.: Energy-efficient multi-constraint routing algorithm with load balancing for smart city applications. IEEE Internet Things J. **3**(6), 1437–1447 (2016)
9. Jiang, D., Wang, W., Shi, L., Song, H.: A compressive sensing-based approach to end-to-end network traffic reconstruction. IEEE Trans. Netw. Sci. Eng. (2018). https://doi.org/10.1109/tnse.2018.2877597
10. Jiang, D., Huo, L., Song, H.: Rethinking behaviors and activities of base stations in mobile cellular networks based on big data analysis. IEEE Trans. Netw. Sci. Eng. (2018). https://doi.org/10.1109/tnse.2018.2861388
11. Jiang, D., Huo, L., Li, Y.: Fine-granularity inference and estimations to network traffic for SDN. PLoS ONE **13**(5), 1–23 (2018)
12. Jiang, D., Huo, L., Lv, Z., et al.: A joint multi-criteria utility-based network selection approach for vehicle-to-infrastructure networking. IEEE Trans. Intell. Transp. Syst. **19**(10), 3305–3319 (2018)
13. Yuan, H., Jun, S., Jinjing, S.: The research of multiparty application modeling supported network architecture description method. Int. J. Distrib. Sens. Netw. **5**(1), 26 (2009)

# DSWIPT Scheme for Cooperative Transmission in Downlink NOMA System

Kai Yang, Xiao Yan$^{(\boxtimes)}$, Qian Wang, Kaiyu Qin, and Dingde Jiang

School of Aeronautics and Astronautics,
University of Electronic Science and Technology of China, Chengdu 611731, China
yanxiao@uestc.edu.cn

**Abstract.** In this paper, we focus on the issue how to reduce the throughput performance gap between the cell-center user and the cell-edge user in a downlink two-user non-orthogonal multiple access (NOMA) system. To this end, we apply the Simultaneous Wireless Information and Power Transfer (SWIPT) protocol to the NOMA scheme and propose a dynamic SWIPT (DSWIPT) cooperative NOMA scheme, in which both the time allocation (TA) ratio and power splitting (PS) ratio can be adjusted dynamically to improve the performance of the cell-edge user in the system. Specifically, we derive two analytical expressions for the outage probability (OP) of the cell-center user and the cell-edge user to study the DSWIPT NOMA scheme's influence on the system. And we also propose an optimization algorithm to find the optimal TA ratio and PS ratio for maximizing the sum-throughput of the system. The numerical results show that the analytical results are in accordance with the Monte-Carlo simulation results exactly and the DSWIPT NOMA scheme has a better performance in both the sum-throughput of the system and the OP of the cell-edge user comparing with the non-cooperative NOMA scheme and the SWIPT NOMA scheme.

**Keywords:** Non-orthogonal multiple access (NOMA) ·
Dynamic simultaneous wireless information and power transfer
(DSWIPT) · Time allocation ratio · Power splitting ratio ·
Outage performance

## 1 Introduction

As one of the latest, most frontier and concerned technologies, the Fifth Generation (5G) is widely recognized as the key to realise the Internet of Everything (IoE). However, only limited number of the users can be served in the conventional multiple access schemes because of the limitation in the number of orthogonal resources blocks [1]. As a promising candidate, the non-orthogonal multiple

This work was supported by the National Natural Science Foundation of China (Grant No. 61601091), and the National Natural Science Foundation of China (Grant No. 61801093).

H. Song et al. (Eds.): SIMUtools 2019, LNICST 295, pp. 567–577, 2019.
https://doi.org/10.1007/978-3-030-32216-8_55

access (NOMA) has been received more and more attention recently [2,3]. The core idea of NOMA is that multiple users are multiplexed in the power-domain on the transmitter side and multi-user signal is seperated with a successive inter-ference canceller (SIC) on the receiver side [2]. And in NOMA, it is an essential issue how to improve the data rate of the cell-edge user without doing harm to the Quality of Service (QoS) of the cell-center and the system. One possi-ble solution to the issue is using cooperative transmission. Cooperative NOMA transmission was first proposed in [4], in which the cell-center user worked as a relay to improve the reception reliability of the cell-edge user. The author in [5] treated the decoding time of the cell-center user as a random variable and proposed a dynamic decode-and-forward based cooperative NOMA scheme with spatially random users, in which the outage performance of the system was improved. An another category of cooperative NOMA is the application of Simultaneous Wireless Information and Power (SWIPT) in NOMA, which was first proposed in [6]. The author in [7] proposed three cooperative transmission schemes utilizing hybrid SWIPT and antenna selection protocols to resolve the fairness issue of data rate between the cell-center user and the cell-edge user. In [8], the author invested a scenario where a user was in a poor channel and had to communicate with the base station with a dedicated relay. The SWIPT cooperative NOMA protocol was used in the relay and the author proposed an algorithm to get the optimal relaying transmission scheme to minimize the outage probability (OP) of the user. The author in [9] considered a downlink two-user NOMA where the SWIPT protocol was applied at the cell-center user. And the gradient decent method was used in the paper to find the optimal value of the PS ratio to maximize the sum-throughput of the system.

In this paper, we study a downlink two-user NOMA system, where one user can work as a relay to improve the OP of another user. Particularly, a dynamic SWIPT protocol is proposed and used at the cell-center user for cooperative transmission. In the DSWIPT NOMA scheme, both the power splitting (PS) and time allocation (TA) ratios can be adjusted dynamically. By this way, the fairness issue of data rate between the cell-center user and the cell-edge user can be solved without jeopardizing the sum-throughput of the system.

The rest of the paper is organized as follows. In Sect. 2, the system model for studying the dynamic SWIPT cooperative NOMA is introduced. In Sect. 3, the OP expressions of the cell-center user and the cell-edge user in the system are derived. And a joint optimization algorithm is proposed to maximize the sum-throughput of the system. In Sect. 4, numerical results are provided. Finally, Sect. 5 is the conclusion.

## 2   System Model

Figure 1 depicts a downlink two-user NOMA system, where a base station S communicates with a cell-center user $U_N$ and a cell-edge user $U_F$ simultaneously. Each node works in half-duplex mode. All wireless channels in the system follow independent and identically distributed (i.i.d) Rayleigh block flat fading. And the channels coefficient $h_{iv}(i \in \{S, U_N\}, v \in \{U_N, U_F\})$ between different nodes are constant during each transmission, where $|h_{iv}|^2$ is an exponential random variable with mean $\lambda_{iv}$. Additionally, the background noise $n_i$ $(i \in \{U_N, U_F\})$ is a complex Gaussian random variable with mean zero and variance $\sigma^2$.

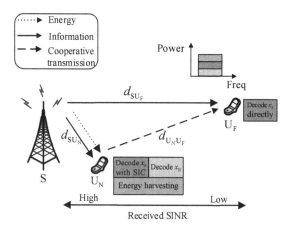

**Fig. 1.** Downlink two-user cooperative NOMA system model, which consists of a base station denoted by S and two paired users denoted by $U_N$ and $U_F$. SIC is performed at $U_N$ to decode $x_N$.

To improve the outage performance of $U_F$, we consider the application of SWIPT protocol at $U_N$. The entire transmission period $T$ can be divided into two phases. In the first phase, $U_N$ harvests energy from received RF signals launched by S within the time $(1 - \alpha)T$, where $\alpha$ $(0 < \alpha < 1)$ denotes the TA ratio. And the energy is simultaneously splitted for storing and information decoding with a ratio $\beta$ and $1 - \beta$, where $\beta$ $(0 < \beta < 1)$ denotes the PS ratio. At the same time, $U_F$ decodes information transmitted from S directly. In the second phase, within the time $\alpha T$, $U_N$ as a relay transmits signals to $U_F$ with the full energy stored in the first phase if $U_N$ has decoded the information successfully. At the meantime, $U_F$ keeps performing information decoding by employing the selection combining (SC) technique [7]. Additionally, S keeps transmitting during the entire transmission period $T$.

According to the principle of NOMA, the message $x_i$ $(i = N, F)$ for $U_i$ is coded in a superposition manner with a different power allocation coefficients $\sqrt{p_i}$ at S, where $E[x_i^2] = 1$. Here we assume $0 < p_N < p_F < 1$ and $p_N + p_F = 1$. At S, the coded message $\sqrt{p_N}x_N + \sqrt{p_F}x_F$ is transmitted with the power $P_s$ during the entire transmission period. Hence, the received signal at $U_i$ from S can be shown as

$$y_i = (\sqrt{p_N P_s}x_N + \sqrt{p_F P_s}x_F)h_{SU_i}d_{SU_i}^{-l} + n_{U_i}, \tag{1}$$

where $h_{SU_i}$ denotes the small-scale Rayleigh fading coefficient between S and $U_i$ with $h_{SU_i} \sim \mathcal{CN}(0,1)$, $n_{U_i}$ denotes the additive white Gaussian noise (AWGN) at $U_i$ with $n_i \sim \mathcal{CN}(0, \sigma^2)$, $d_{SU_i}$ denotes the distance between S and $U_i$, and $l$ denotes the path loss exponent.

The power received by $U_N$ is splitted up into two parts simultaneously. One part is used for information decoding with the ratio $1-\beta$, and the other part is used for energy storing with the ratio $\beta$. Hence, with the help of successive interference cancellation (SIC), the data rate at $U_N$ for decoding $x_i$ can be shown as

$$R_N^{x_F} = (1-\alpha)log_2(1 + \frac{(1-\beta)p_F P_s|h_{SU_N}|^2 d_{SU_N}^{-l}}{(1-\beta)p_N P_{rms}|h_{SU_N}|^2 d_{SU_N}^{-l} + \sigma^2}), \tag{2}$$

$$R_N^{x_N} = (1-\alpha)log_2(1 + \frac{(1-\beta)p_N P_s|h_{SU_N}|^2 d_{SU_N}^{-l}}{\sigma^2}). \tag{3}$$

And the energy stored during the first phase at $U_N$ can be shown as:

$$E_N = (1-\alpha)T\eta\beta P_s|h_{SU_N}|^2 d_{SU_N}^{-l}, \tag{4}$$

where $\eta$ $(0 < \eta < 1)$ denotes the energy conversion efficiency of $U_i$.

During the first phase, the received Signal to Interference plus Noise Ratio (SINR) at $U_F$ for decoding $x_F$ directly can be shown as

$$\gamma_F^{x_F} = \frac{p_F P_{rms}|h_{SU_F}|^2 d_{SU_F}^{-l}}{p_N P_s|h_{SU_F}|^2 d_{SU_F}^{-l} + \sigma^2}. \tag{5}$$

If $U_N$ has decoded $x_F$ in the first phase, S and $U_N$ will transmit message $x_F$ to $U_F$ synchronously during the second phase. If not, $U_N$ keeps silence and S transmits alone. The transmission power of $U_N$ can be shown as

$$P_N = \frac{E_N}{\alpha T} = (\frac{1-\alpha}{\alpha})\eta\beta P_{[s]}|h_{SU_N}|^2 d_{SU_N}^{-l}. \tag{6}$$

At $U_F$, the received signal from $U_N$ can be shown as

$$y_{FN} = \sqrt{P_N}x_F h_{U_N U_F} d_{U_N U_F}^{-l} + n_{U_F}, \tag{7}$$

where $h_{U_N U_F}$ denotes the small-scal Rayleigh fading coefficient between $U_N$ and $U_F$ with $h_{U_N U_F} \sim \mathcal{CN}(0,1)$, $d_{U_N U_F}$ denotes the distance between $U_N$ and $U_F$.

According to (6) and (7), with the help of $U_N$, the received SINR at $U_F$ for decoding $x_F$ can be shown as

$$\gamma_{FN}^{x_F} = \frac{\eta\beta P_s|h_{SU_N}|^2|h_{U_N U_F}|^2 d_{SU_N}^{-l} d_{U_N U_F}^{-l}(\frac{1-\alpha}{\alpha})}{\sigma^2}, \tag{8}$$

Finally, $U_F$ selects signals with high SINR for reception. So the received SINR at $U_F$ during the second phase can be written as

$$\gamma_F^{sc} = \max\{\gamma_F^{x_F}, \gamma_{FN}^{x_F}\}. \tag{9}$$

Based on the signal reception model above, the data rate of $U_F$ at the end of the transmission period can be expressed as

$$R_F^{x_F} = \begin{cases} (1-\alpha)log_2(1+\gamma_F^{x_F}) + \alpha log_2(1+\gamma_F^{sc}) & R_N^{x_F} \geq R_F^{th}, \\ log_2(1+\gamma_F^{x_F}) & R_N^{x_F} < R_F^{th}, \end{cases} \tag{10}$$

where $R_F^{th}$ denote the target data rate of decoding $x_F$.

## 3    Performance Analysis

### 3.1    Outage Performance

$U_N$ will suffer a service outage when its data rate is below the target data rate. According to the principle of SIC, $U_N$ should decode $U_F$ first before decoding $U_N$. So, the OP of $U_N$ can be written as

$$P_{out}^N = Pr(R_N^{x_F} < R_F^{th}) + Pr(R_N^{x_N} < R_N^{th}, R_N^{x_F} \geq R_F^{th}), \tag{11}$$

where $R_F^{th}$ and $R_N^{th}$ denote the target data rates to decode $x_F$ and $x_N$, respectively. And we also define $\gamma_{N,\alpha}^{x_N} \triangleq 2^{\frac{R_N^{th}}{1-\alpha}} - 1$, $\gamma_{N,\alpha}^{x_F} \triangleq 2^{\frac{R_F^{th}}{1-\alpha}} - 1$, $\varepsilon_1 \triangleq \frac{(1-\beta)p_F P_s d_{SU_N}^{-l}}{\sigma^2}$, $\varepsilon_2 \triangleq \frac{(1-\beta)p_N P_{[s]}d_{SU_F}^{-l}}{\sigma^2}$, $\zeta \triangleq \frac{p_F}{p_N}$.

**Theorem 1.** *The closed form expression of the OP at $U_N$ can be show as:*

$$P_{out}^N = \begin{cases} 1 - \min\{e^{-\mu_1}, e^{-\mu_2}\} & \alpha < 1 - \nu, \\ 1 & \alpha \geq 1 - \nu, \end{cases} \tag{12}$$

*where* $\mu_1 = \frac{\gamma_{N,\alpha}^{x_F}}{\varepsilon_1 - \varepsilon_2 \gamma_{N,\alpha}^{x_F}}$, $\mu_2 = \frac{\gamma_{N,\alpha}^{x_F}}{\varepsilon_2}$, $\nu = \frac{R_F^{th}}{log_2(1+\zeta)}$.

*Proof.* Define $X = |h_{SU_N}|^2$. Plugging (2) and (3) into (11), the OP of $U_N$ can be written as

$$P_{out}^N = Pr(\frac{\varepsilon_1 X}{\varepsilon_2 X + 1} < \gamma_{N,\alpha}^{x_F}) + Pr(\varepsilon_2 X < \gamma_{N,\alpha}^{x_N}, \frac{\varepsilon_1 X}{\varepsilon_2 X + 1} \geq \gamma_{N,\alpha}^{x_F}). \tag{13}$$

For the case $\alpha \geq 1 - \nu$, we obtain $(\varepsilon_1 - \varepsilon_2 \gamma_{N,\alpha}^{x_F})X \leq 0$, so that the OP of $U_N$ is always equal to 1. And for the case $\alpha < 1 - \nu$, (11) can be written as

$$P_{out}^N = Pr(X < \mu_1) + Pr(X < \mu_2, X \geq \mu_1). \tag{14}$$

Based on the probability distribution of $X$ and done by some algebraic manipulations, the OP expression of $U_N$ can be shown in (12). And the proof of the Theorem 1 is completed.    □

$U_F$ will suffer a service outage when its data rate is below the target data rate. And the data rate of $U_F$ depends on whether $U_N$ decodes $x_F$ successfully or not in the first phase. Based on (10), the OP of $x_F$ can be written as

$$P_{out}^F = \Pr((1-\alpha)log_2(1+\gamma_F^{x_F}) + \alpha log_2(1+\gamma_F^{sc}) < R_F^{th}, R_N^{x_F} \geq R_F^{th})$$
$$+ \Pr(log_2(1+\gamma_F^{x_F}) < R_F^{th}, R_N^{x_F} < R_F^{th}). \tag{15}$$

In order to use the notations conveniently, we define $\Phi_i \triangleq cos(\frac{2i-1}{2I}\pi)$, $w_i \triangleq \frac{(1-\alpha)R_F^{th}}{2}(\Phi_i + 1)$, $\gamma_{w_i,\alpha} \triangleq 2^{\frac{w_i}{1-\alpha}} - 1$, $\gamma_{w_i,\alpha}^{x_F} \triangleq 2^{\frac{R_F^{th}-w_i}{\alpha}} - 1$, $\theta_1 \triangleq \frac{p_F P sd_{SU_F}^{-l}}{\sigma^2}$, $\theta_2 \triangleq \frac{p_N P sd_{SU_F}^{-l}}{\sigma^2}$, $\theta_3 \triangleq \frac{\eta\beta P sd_{SU_N}^{-l} d_{U_N U_F}^{-l} (\frac{1-\alpha}{\alpha})}{\sigma^2}$, $\kappa_1 \triangleq \frac{2^{R_F^{th}}-1}{\theta_1 - \theta_2(2^{R_F^{th}}-1)}$.

**Theorem 2.** *The approximate expression of OP at $U_F$ can be given as*

$$P_{out}^F \approx \frac{(1-\alpha)R_F^{th}}{2I} \sum_{i=1}^{I} \left( \sqrt{1-\Phi_i^2}(1 - \exp(-Q_3(\alpha, w_i))) \right.$$
$$\times (\exp(-\mu_1)(1 - 2\sqrt{Q_4(\alpha, w_i)})K_1(2\sqrt{Q_4(\alpha, w_i)})) \tag{16}$$
$$\left. \times \exp(-Q_1(\alpha, w_i))Q_2(\alpha, w_i) \right) + (1 - e^{-\kappa_1})(1 - e^{-\mu_1}),$$

*where $K_1(\cdot)$ is the modified Bessel function for the second kind, and*

$$Q_1(\alpha, w_i) = \frac{\gamma_{w_i,\alpha}\sigma^2}{(p_F - \gamma_{w_i,\alpha}p_N)Psd_{SU_F}^{-l}}, \tag{17}$$

$$Q_2(\alpha, w_i) = \frac{2^w p_F \sigma^2 ln2}{(p_F - \gamma_{w_i,\alpha}p_N)^2 Psd_{SU_F}^{-l}}, \tag{18}$$

$$Q_3(\alpha, w_i) = -\frac{\gamma_{w_i,\alpha}^{x_F}}{\theta_1 - \gamma_{w_i,\alpha}^{x_F}\theta_2}, \tag{19}$$

$$Q_4(\alpha, w_i) = \frac{\gamma_{w_i,\alpha}^{x_F}}{\theta_3}. \tag{20}$$

*Proof.* We define $W = (1-\alpha)log_2(1+\gamma_F^{x_F})$, $Y = |h_{SU_F}|^2$, $Z = |h_{U_N U_F}|^2$. And without loss of generality, we consider $W \leq (1-\alpha)R_F^{th}$ [5].

The cumulative distribution function of random variable $W$ can be shown as

$$F_W(w) = 1 - \exp(-\frac{\gamma_{w,\alpha}\sigma^2}{(p_F - \gamma_{w,\alpha}p_N)Psd_{SU_F}^{-l}}). \tag{21}$$

Based on the cumulative distribution function $F_W(w)$, the Probability Density Function (PDF) of $W$ can be shown as

$$f_W(w) = \exp(-\frac{\gamma_{w,\alpha}\sigma^2}{(p_F - \gamma_{w,\alpha}p_N)Psd_{SU_F}^{-l}})\frac{2^w p_F \sigma^2 ln2}{(p_F - \gamma_{w,\alpha}p_N)^2 Psd_{SU_F}^{-l}}. \tag{22}$$

Secondly, we derive the OP of $U_F$. Plugging (5), (9) and the random variable $W$ into (15), the OP of $U_F$ can be written as

$$P_{out}^F = q_{out}^{\Psi_1} + q_{out}^{\Psi_2}$$

$$= E_W(P(\max\{\frac{\theta_1 Y}{\theta_2 Y + 1}, XZ\theta_3\} < 2^{\frac{R_F^{th} - W}{\alpha}} - 1, \frac{\varepsilon_1 X}{\varepsilon_2 X + 1} \geq \gamma_{N,\alpha}^{x_F})) \quad (23)$$

$$+ P(\frac{\theta_1 Y}{\theta_2 Y + 1} < 2^{R_F^{th}} - 1, \frac{\varepsilon_1 X}{\varepsilon_2 X + 1} < \gamma_{N,\alpha}^{x_F}).$$

Done by some algebraic manipulations, $q_{out}^{\Psi_1}$ can be expressed as

$$q_{out}^{\Psi_1} = \int_0^{(1-\alpha)R_F^{th}} (1 - \exp(-\frac{\gamma_{w,\alpha}^{x_F}}{\theta_1 - \gamma_{w,\alpha}^{x_F}\theta_2}))$$

$$\times (\exp(-\mu_1)(1 - 2\sqrt{\frac{\gamma_{w,\alpha}^{x_F}}{\theta_3}}K_1(2\sqrt{\frac{\gamma_{w,\alpha}^{x_F}}{\theta_3}}))f_W(w)dw, \quad (24)$$

where $K_1(\cdot)$ is the modified Bessel function for the second kind.

The direct calculation of (24) will be very complicated. By using Gauss-Chebyshev quadrature, we approximate the expression (24) as

$$q_{out}^{\Psi_1} \approx \frac{(1-\alpha)R_F^{th}}{2I} \sum_{i=1}^{I} \left(\sqrt{1 - \Phi_i^2}(1 - \exp(-Q_3(\alpha, w_i)))\right.$$

$$\times (\exp(-\mu_1)(1 - 2\sqrt{Q_4(\alpha, w_i)})K_1(2\sqrt{Q_4(\alpha, w_i)}))$$

$$\left.\times \exp(-Q_1(\alpha, w_i))Q_2(\alpha, w_i)\right), \quad (25)$$

where $Q_1(\alpha, w_i)$, $Q_2(\alpha, w_i)$, $Q_3(\alpha, w_i)$ and $Q_4(\alpha, w_i)$ are defined as (17–20), respectively. And in (23), $q_{out}^{\Psi_2}$ can be written as

$$q_{out}^{\Psi_2} = (1 - e^{-\kappa_1})(1 - e^{-\mu_1}) \quad (26)$$

Thus, plugging (25) and (26) into (23), $P_{out}^F$ can be written as (16). The proof of the Theorem 2 is completed. □

### 3.2   Throughput Performance

In order to maximize the sum-throughput of the system, a joint optimization algorithm for selecting the TA ratio and the PS ratio is proposed in this subsection. Based on (12) and (16), the problem of maximizing the sum-throughput of the system can be expressed as

$$(P1): \max \quad R_s(\alpha, \beta) = (1 - P_{out}^N)R_N^{th} + (1 - P_{out}^F)R_F^{th}$$

$$\text{s.t.} \quad 0 < \alpha < 1, \quad (27)$$

$$0 < \beta < 1,$$

which is a constrained optimization problem.

To solve this problem, we use the penalty function method to change the constrained optimization problem into the unconstrained optimization problem firstly. The penalty function can be expressed as

$$f(\alpha, \beta, r_k) = -R_s(\alpha, \beta) + r_k(\frac{1}{\alpha} + \frac{1}{1-\alpha} + \frac{1}{\beta} + \frac{1}{1-\beta}), \tag{28}$$

where $r_k$ is a series of penalty factors which have decreasing property. Secondly, we use the pattern search method to solve the unconstrained optimization problem since it is hard to calculate the derivative of (28). The details of the proposed optimization algorithm can be summarized as Algorithm 1.

---

**Algorithm 1.** The algorithm of finding the optimal $(\alpha^\star, \beta^\star)$

---

**Require:** $P_s, p_N, p_F, d_{SU_N}, d_{SU_F}, \eta, \sigma^2$ and $f(\alpha, \beta, r_k)$;

1: **Initialization** stopping threshold: $\varepsilon_1, \varepsilon_2$, interior-point: $(\alpha^0, \beta^0)$, obstacle factor: $r_1$, iteration index: $k$, shrinking coefficient: $\delta$; initial step: $\vartheta_0$, accelerated factor: $\tau$, shrinking coefficient: $\varsigma$, coordinate directions: $e_n$ $(n = 2)$;

2: **repeat**

3:     $r_{k+1} = \delta r_k$; $i = 1, j = 1$, $\vartheta = \vartheta_0$; $\boldsymbol{x}^{(1)} = (\alpha^{(k)}, \beta^{(k)})$, $\boldsymbol{y}^{(1)} = \boldsymbol{x}^{(1)}$;

4:     **repeat**

5:         **for** $j = 1; j <$n$; j + +$ **do**

6:             **if** $f(\boldsymbol{y}^{(j)} + \vartheta e_j) < f(\boldsymbol{y}^{(j)})$ **then**

7:                 $\boldsymbol{y}^{(j+1)} = \boldsymbol{y}^{(j)} + \vartheta e_j$;

8:             **else if** $f(\boldsymbol{y}^{(j)} - \vartheta e_j) < f(\boldsymbol{y}^{(j)})$ **then**

9:                 $\boldsymbol{y}^{(j+1)} = \boldsymbol{y}^{(j)} - \vartheta e_j$;

10:             **else**

11:                 $\boldsymbol{y}^{(j+1)} = \boldsymbol{y}^{(j)}$;

12:             **end if**

13:         **end for**

14:         **if** $f(\boldsymbol{y}^{(n+1)}) < f(\boldsymbol{x}^{(i)})$ **then**

15:             $\boldsymbol{x}^{(i+1)} = \boldsymbol{y}^{(n+1)}$; $\boldsymbol{y}^{(1)} = \boldsymbol{x}^{(i+1)} + \tau(\boldsymbol{x}^{(i+1)} - \boldsymbol{x}^{(i)})$; $i := i + 1, j = 1$;

16:         **else**

17:             $\boldsymbol{y}^{(1)} = \boldsymbol{x}^{(i)}$; $\boldsymbol{x}^{(i+1)} = \boldsymbol{x}^{(i)}$; $\vartheta := \varsigma \vartheta$; $i := i + 1, j = 1$;

18:         **end if**

19:     **until** $\vartheta < \varepsilon_2$. Update: $(\alpha^{(k+1)}, \beta^{(k+1)}) = \boldsymbol{x}^{i+1}$;

20: **until** $r_{k+1}B(\alpha^{(k+1)}, \beta^{(k+1)}) < \varepsilon_1$

---

## 4   Simulation Results

In this section, we compare the DSWIPT NOMA scheme with the NOMA scheme [2] and the SWIPT NOMA scheme [9]. The parameters are set up as: $R_N^{th} = R_F^{th} = 1$ bps/Hz; $p_N = 0.1$, $p_F = 0.9$; $n_N = n_F = -100$ dBm/Hz; bandwith $= 1$ MHz; $l = 3$; $\eta = 0.7$; $d_{SU_N} = 2$ m, $d_{SU_F} = 8$ m; $I = 30$. As can be seen

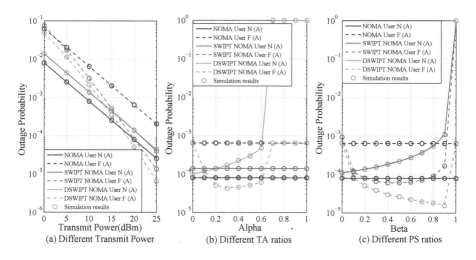

**Fig. 2.** Outage probability versus different transmit power, TA ratios and PS ratios.

from Fig. 2, the analytical results (A) are in exact accordance with Monte-Carlo simulation results, which corroborates our analyses in Sect. 3.

Figure 2 illustrates the OP versus different transmit power, TA ratios and PS ratios of the three schemes. In Fig. 2(a), we can see the OP of $U_F$ in the DSWIPT NOMA scheme has been improved in comparison with that of $U_F$ in [2] and [9]. In Fig. 2(b), we can see that $\alpha$ in the DSWIPT NOMA scheme can be adjusted according to the optimization algorithm proposed in Sect. 3 to maximize the sum-throughput of the system. And $U_N$ will suffer a service outage and the outage performance of $U_F$ will not be improved when $\alpha$ is higher than 0.7, which is because the decoding time of $U_N$ is too short to decode $x_F$ correctly. In Fig. 2(c), we can see $U_F$ in the DSWIPT NOMA scheme has a lower OP comparing with that in [2] and [9]. And the outage performance of $U_F$ in DSWIPT NOMA scheme is getting better as $\beta$ going large.

Figure 3 provides the throughput performance versus the transmit power of the three schemes. In Fig. 3(a), the sum-throughput of the DSWIPT NOMA scheme and the sum-throughput of the NOMA scheme are similar and they are higher than that of the SWIPT NOMA scheme when the SNR is lower than 2.5 dbm. This is because the decoding time in the SWIPT NOMA scheme is short and can't be adjusted flexible, which has a significant influence on the OP of $U_N$. As can be seen in Fig. 3(b), the DSWIPT NOMA scheme has a better performance in the throughput of $U_F$ comparing with the other two schemes, which illustrates the DSWIPT NOMA scheme indeed improves the OP of $U_F$ even though the SNR is low. Thus, the throughput gap between the cell-center user and the cell-edge user can be reduced with the DSWIPT NOMA scheme.

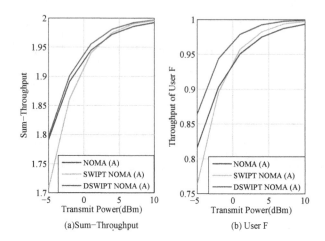

(a)Sum–Throughput                    (b) User F

**Fig. 3.** Throughput of the system and $U_F$ versus the Transmit SNR.

## 5    Conclusion

In this paper, we focus on the issue of throughput fairness between the cell-center user and the cell-edge user in a downlink two-user NOMA system. We have proposed the DSWIPT NOMA scheme and have investigated the outage performance and the throughput performance of the users in the scheme. And we have also proposed an optimization algorithm to get the maximal sum-throughput of the DSWIPT NOMA scheme. The numerical results have illustrated that the throughput performance of the cell-edge user can be enhanced quite a lot without jeopardizing the sum-throughput of the downlink two-users NOMA system when using the DSWIPT NOMA scheme. Consequently, we can say that the DSWIPT NOMA scheme is a significant solution for the issues like fairness in throughput performance between different users.

## References

1. ITU-R M.2083, IMT vision–Framework and overall objectives of the future development of IMT for 2020 and beyond. https://www.itu.int/rec/R-REC-M.2083. Accessed 10 June 2018
2. Saito, Y., Kishiyama, Y., Benjebbour, A., Nakamura, T., Li, A., Higuchi, K.: Non-orthogonal multiple access (NOMA) for future radio access. In: 2013 IEEE 77th Vehicular Technology Conference (VTC Spring), Dresden, Germany, pp. 1–5 (2013)
3. Cai, Y., Qin, Z., Cui, F., Li, G.Y., McCann, J.A.: Modulation and multiple access for 5G networks. IEEE Commun. Surv. Tutorials **20**(1), 629–646 (2018)
4. Ding, Z., Peng, M., Poor, H.V.: Cooperative non-orthogonal multiple access in 5G systems. IEEE Commun. Lett. **19**(8), 1462–1465 (2015)
5. Zhou, Y., Wong, V.W.S., Schober, R.: Dynamic decode-and-forward based cooperative NOMA with spatially random users. IEEE Trans. Wirel. Commun. **17**(5), 3340–3356 (2018)

6. Liu, Y., Ding, Z., Elkashlan, M., Poor, H.V.: Cooperative non-orthogonal multiple access with simultaneous wireless information and power transfer. IEEE J. Sel. Areas Commun. **34**(4), 938–953 (2016)
7. Do, T.N., da Costa, D.B., Duong, T.Q., An, B.: Improving the performance of cell-edge users in MISO-NOMA systems using TAS and SWIPT-based cooperative transmissions. IEEE Trans. Green Commun. Netw. **2**(1), 49–62 (2018)
8. Ye, Y., Li, Y., Wang, D., Zhou, F., Hu, R.Q., Zhang, H.: Optimal transmission schemes for DF relaying networks using SWIPT. IEEE Trans. Veh. Technol. **67**(8), 7062–7072 (2018)
9. Do, T.N., An, B.: Optimal sum-throughput analysis for downlink cooperative SWIPT NOMA systems. In: 2018 2nd International Conference on Recent Advances in Signal Processing, Telecommunications Computing (SigTelCom), pp. 85–90 (2018)

# Large-Scale Fading Measurement and Comparison for O2I Channels at Three Frequencies

Ruonan Zhang, Linyuan Wei[✉], Yi Jiang, Daosen Zhai, and Bin Li

Department of Communication Engineering, Northwestern Polytechnical University,
Xi'an 710072, Shaanxi, China
583310958@qq.com

**Abstract.** Channel measurement and modeling are fundamental and critical for the analysis and simulations of communication systems. For the fifth generation (5G) cellular network, the wireless channel characterization in its application scenarios, such as the *enhanced mobile broadband* (eMBB) and *massive machine type of communication* (mMTC), is critical. In this paper, we investigate the radio propagation at 900 MHz, 2.6 GHz, and 3.5 GHz in *Outdoor-to-Indoor* (O2I) scenario. We performed the channel measurements using a multi-frequency narrow-band sounder to derive the large-scale fading parameters such as the path loss and shadow fading. Then, based on the measurement data, we analyze the differences of the large-scale fading parameters at the three frequencies and the impact of frequency on the channel characteristics. Furthermore, we compare the accuracy of three path loss models specified in the WINNER and 3GPP channel modeling standards according to the measurement results. Finally, we propose the modification on the model coefficients to fit the measurement results better for various carrier frequencies in the O2I scenario. The measurement data and revised channel model can support the signal coverage analysis and subsequent communication system optimization.

**Keywords:** Channel measurement and modeling · O2I · Path loss · Shadow fading

## 1 Introduction

Wireless communication is conducted by radio wave propagation via wireless channels. Because of the presence of scatterers in the environments, radio waves arrive at receivers along different paths (direct, reflection, scattering, diffraction etc.). Therefore, accurate measurement and channel modeling of the large-scale radio propagation characteristics, such as path loss and shadow fading, facilitates the design, deployment, and management of wireless networks. Using channel models to predict the propagation characteristics of radio waves is the basis of performance simulation and evaluation of wireless communication systems.

© ICST Institute for Computer Sciences, Social Informatics and Telecommunications Engineering 2019
Published by Springer Nature Switzerland AG 2019. All Rights Reserved
H. Song et al. (Eds.): SIMUtools 2019, LNICST 295, pp. 578–587, 2019.
https://doi.org/10.1007/978-3-030-32216-8_56

The stochastic channel models based on geometry have been widely used for the link and system-level simulation.

The advent of the fifth generation (5G) mobile systems has extended its application scenarios to a broader sense, including the *enhanced mobile broadband* (eMBB), *massive machine type of communication* (mMTC), and *ultra-reliable and low latency communication* (uLLC) [1]. One of the distinguished features of the 5G networks is all-spectrum access which involves *low-frequency* (LF) bands below 6 GHz and *high-frequency* (HF) bands above 6 GHz such as the mmWave bands, where the former is the core bands used for seamless coverage [2]. As such, the channel modeling of sub6G for coverage in the outdoor-to-indoor (O2I) scenario is worth studying. Due to the vision of 5G about mMTC, Telecommunications agencies and organizations around the world have begun to conduct in-depth studies on the spectrum used in mMTC, such as *China Mobile Communications Corporation* (CMCC) who chooses 900 MHz (Band 8) as the spectrum of module test specification. As for the demand of eMBB, Chinese *Ministry of Industry and Information Technology* (MIIT) has also selected 3.5 GHz as the working spectrum of 5G.

Channel measurements have been conducted widely to prove the feasibility of the above 6 GHz [3]. The O2I scenario has also been studied in this frequency range and the signal power loss due to building penetration is assessed especially in [4] and [5]. However, for O2I scenarios in 5G, the application scenarios for both mMTC and eMMB are requested. At present, there are few studies on the hybrid spectrum coverage analysis and channel modeling for MMTC and eMBB in the O2I scenarios.

In this paper, we perform the multi-frequency O2I channel modeling for the sub6GHz band, including 900 MHz, 2.6 GHz, and 3.5 GHz. According to the coverage analysis at the three frequencies, we can provide guidance for base station selection and network planning. Furthermore, a detailed signal channel modeling and analysis is presented for the radio planning in the 5G. The path loss models defined in WINNER II, WINNER+, and 3GPP technological report are compared based on our measurement data. The results show that the WINNER+ model is closet in this measurement O2I scenario for the three frequencies. Then we further improve the model by revising the model coefficients to fit the measurement data better.

The rest of the paper is organized as follows. Section 2 introduces the channel sounding and presents the measurement environments. Section 3 investigates three standard channel models, select the most suitable channel model, and modifies it with the measurement data. Section 4 concludes the paper with the future research issue.

## 2   Measurement Campaign

### 2.1   Measurement System

This measurement campaign was conducted using a triple-band large-scale channel sounder. Figure 1 shows the measurement equipments. The system uses a *continuous wave* (CW) narrow-band sounding scheme, the transmitter (TX) generates and transmits a single tone at each carrier frequency. In Fig. 1(a), the antennas working at 900 MHz, 2.6 GHz, and 3.5 GHz are installed on the pylons.

As for the receiver (RX), a wide-band antenna, as shown in Fig. 1(b), is adopted to receive all the transmitted signals. In the field measurements on propagation path loss, the three radio frequency (RF) chains in the TX transmit signals simultaneously. The multi-band sounding signals are received on the wideband antenna and input into a *spectrum analyzer* (SA). The SA has been programmed to record the received power at the three marked frequency points for 30 times continuously with the interval of 100 ms. Then it calculates the average power at each frequency and transfer the data to a computer via Ethernet for storage.

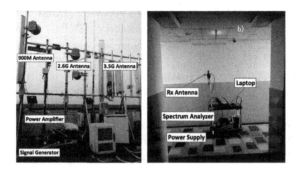

**Fig. 1.** The photos of the multi-band channel sounder. (a) TX System; (b) RX System

### 2.2   Scenario Description

The measurement campaign was conducted in Chengdu, China, in a typical urban microcell (UMi) O2I scenario. The measurement environments and the placement of the RX are shown in Fig. 2.

As shown in Fig. 1(a), the TX was installed on top of a building to emulate a base station (BS). The height of the three antennas was about 26 m. The RX was moved on the floors in a modern apartment building on the opposite side of the TX to emulate a user equipment (UE), as shown in Fig. 1(b) and (2b). The minimum three-dimensional distance between the TX and RX was 50 m.

Figure 2 shows the apartment building layout. Figure 2(a) includes the satellite map of the measurement environment, indicating a typical O2I scenario. In Fig. 2(e), the red number $i$ ($i = 0$, 1, 2, ... 38) represents the RX locations, including three typical indoor scenarios, which are displayed in (b), (c), and (d). Figure 2(b) shows the interior room scenario which is defined as Area One (A1). Figure 2(c) displays the short hall, defined as Area Two (A2). Figure 2(d) is the long hall, namely Area Three (A3). In this campaign, we put the RX on the $10^{th}$, $8^{th}$, $6^{th}$, $4^{th}$ and $3^{rd}$ floors where the positions of the RX in all the A1, A2, and A3 were accurately recorded.

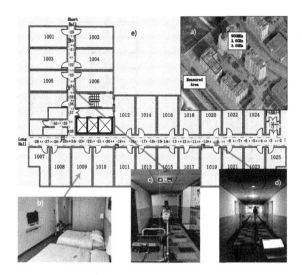

**Fig. 2.** The measurement environment. (a) Satellite map; (b) A1; (c) A2; (d) A3; (e) Measured area layout

## 3   Measurement Results and Modeling

### 3.1   Measurement Results

The diagrams in Fig. 3 demonstrate the distributions of the path loss at the three frequencies on the $10^{th}$ floor. For the room (A1) scenario, the signals can propagate through the windows and achieve good coverage at all the three frequencies. According to the link budget design, the maximum tolerable path loss for the BS-to-UE links is $PL_{th} = 140$ dB. It can be seen that the path loss in the rooms was much smaller than $PL_{th}$ at 900 MHz and 2.6 GHz. Therefore, the BS can cover the room entirely at both the frequencies. It is noticed that the path loss of 3.5 GHz is largest in Room 1016 but Room 1015 and 1019 could be covered very well. It is unexpected and will be discussed in details later.

For the ease of comparison, we defined the *average path loss* (APL) of A1 as the mean path loss of the rooms of 1001, 1002, 1016, and 1020, on each floor in the apartment building. In the short hall (A2) scenario, the path loss at all the three frequencies was obviously larger than that in the rooms of 1001 and 1002, but the path loss at the three frequencies was well below $PL_{th}$, ensuring good coverage in A2. The APL in A2 at 900 MHz, 2.6 GHz, and 3.5 GHz were larger by 12, 18, and 25 dB, respectively, than those in A1.

In the long hall (A3) scenario, it is obvious that the path loss of 900 MHz was almost 110 dB, which was much below $PL_{th}$. However, the path loss of 2.6 and 3.5 GHz was closed to $PL_{th}$, and thus these two bands may not meet the path loss requirement except the locations near the windows. The APLs in A3 at 900 MHz, 2.6 GHz, and 3.5 GHz were larger by 27, 39, and 49 dB, respectively, than that in A1.

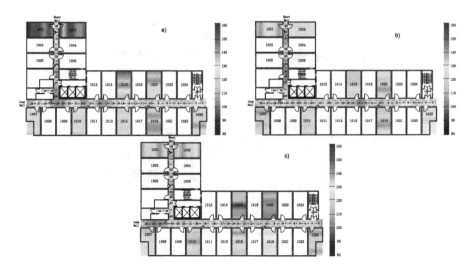

**Fig. 3.** The path loss variation at different locations. (a) 900 MHz; (b) 2.6 GHz; (c) 3.5 GHz.

The unexpected phenomena of 3.5 GHz may be explained with Fig. 4. There was a high-rise building to the west of the measurement apartment building, as shown in Fig. 4. Thus, some signals were reflected into the rooms through the windows, resulting in the decreasing trend of the path loss from the south to the north.

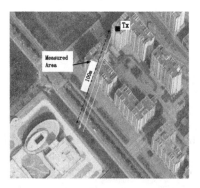

**Fig. 4.** Building reflection

In summary, we can see that the 900 MHz band could provide good coverage for all the areas. Therefore, CMCC has selected 900 MHz as the spectrum band of NB-IoT, which not only can be deployed quickly based on the existing cellular systems, but also can achieve wide area coverage for the terminal devices. As for the 2.6 GHz band adopted in the LTE system, the coverage of the signal basically achieved the coverage requirements. As for the spectrum of 5G, the 3.5 GHz band could provide basic coverage of A2 and the propagation through windows provided the received power and hence determined the O2I coverage for 3.5 GHz in A1. Meanwhile the received power decayed quickly with the depth of the indoor position due to the large path loss. Consequently, the radio signal at 3.5 GHz cannot cover the inner space of buildings without direct propagation through exterior windows. Hence it is necessary to deploy more BSs or increase the transmission power to achieve better coverage.

## 3.2    Channel Model Selection

WINNER II Channel Model [6] has been widely used for link and system-level simulations. The measurement setting of this research is consistent with the definition of the O2I scenario in WINNER II. The model is specified as

$$PL = PL_b + PL_{tw} + PL_{in} + X_{winnerII}, \tag{1}$$

$$\begin{cases} PL_b = 22.7log_{10}(d_{3D}) + 41 + 20log_{10}(f_c), \\ PL_{tw} = 14 + 15(1 - cos\theta)^2, \\ PL_{in} = 0.5d_{in}. \end{cases} \tag{2}$$

In (1) and (2), $f_c$ is the carrier frequency in GHz. $d_{3D}$ is the 3D Tx-to-Rx separation distance in the unit of meters, $\theta$ is the wall-piercing angle of wave, and $d_{in}$ is the distance from the exterior wall to the RX. $X_{winnerII}$ is known as the shadow fading (SF) factor representing the large-scale signal fluctuations resulted from obstructions in propagation environment, $PL_b$ represents the propagation model of signal in free space, while $PL_{tw}$ describes the loss of walls and $PL_{in}$ indicates the additional indoor loss relative to the free space.

WINNER+ Channel Model [7] defines O2I scenario similar as that of Winner II. The model is expressed as (3) and (4) which adds the effect of wall-piercing angle and frequency on path loss of $PL_{tw}$.

$$PL = PL_b + PL_{tw} + PL_{in} + X_{winner+} \tag{3}$$

$$\begin{cases} PL = 22.7log_{10}(d_{3D}) + 27 + 20log_{10}(f_c) \\ PL_{tw} = 31.64 + 15(1 - cos\theta)^2 - 25.2log_{10}(f_c) \\ PL_{in} = 0.5d_{in} \end{cases} \tag{4}$$

3GPP TR38.900 V14.3.1 [8] specifies the O2I path loss model as (5), (6) and (7), which takes path loss through the glass and walls in the propagation link into consideration.

$$PL = PL_b + PL_{tw} + PL_{in} + X_{TR38.900} \tag{5}$$

$$\begin{cases} PL_b = 32.4 + 21log_{10}(d_{3D}) + 20log_{10}(f_c) \\ PL_{tw} = PL_{npi} - 10log_{10}\sum_{i=1}^{N}(P_i \cdot 10^{\frac{l_{material_i}}{-10}}) \\ PL_{in} = 0.5d_{in} \\ l_{material_i} = a_{material_i} + b_{material_i} \cdot f_c \end{cases} \tag{6}$$

$$PL_{tw} = \begin{cases} 5 - 10log_{10}(0.3 \cdot 10^{\frac{-l_{glass}}{10}} + 0.7 \cdot 10^{\frac{-l_{concrete}}{10}}) \\ low - lossmodel \\ 5 - 10log_{10}(0.7 \cdot 10^{\frac{-l_{iirglass}}{10}} + 0.3 \cdot 10^{\frac{-l_{concrete}}{10}}) \\ high - lossmodel \end{cases} \tag{7}$$

In (5), (6) and (7), $PL_{npi}$ is an additional loss and added to the external wall loss to account for non-perpendicular incidence. $l_{material_i}$ represents the loss factor of each materials, and $l_{material_i}$ of windows and walls are $l_{glass} = 2 + 0.2f_c$ and $l_{concrete} = 5 + 4f_c$, respectively. Using the low or high loss model is a simulation parameter that should be determined by the channel models depending on the use of metal-coated glass in buildings and the deployment scenarios. Considering that all the windows of the measurement apartment building did not use the metal-coated glass, we select low-loss model in this work.

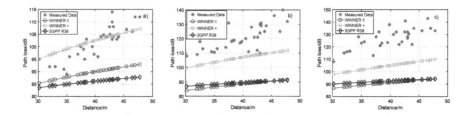

**Fig. 5.** The measurement results and models of the path loss in the A2 scenario. (a) 900 MHz; (b) 2.6 GHz; (c) 3.5 GHz

Because of the large amount of data, the scenario of A2 is selected for modeling and analysis. The results are shown in Fig. 5. According to (1) to (7), the path loss of the three standard models with respect to $d_{3D}$ can be calculated. To observe the difference between the models and the actual measurement data, we conduct the curve fitting. It can observed that the fitting curve according to the WINNER+ model is the closest to the measurement data. At the same time, comparing the mean and variance of the fitting results, WINNER+ has the smallest mean error and variance. Further, the O2I scenario are slightly different in these models, such as base station height, receiver and transmitter distance, which also results in the discrepancies. Based on the observations from Fig. 5, WINNER+ Channel Model is selected for the multi-band large-scale modeling according to our measurement results.

## 3.3   Revesion of Winner+ Channel Model

According to (2), the two main factors, namely, $f_c$ and $d_{3D}$, can be selected to adjust the coefficients of the model. The model is revised according to the Gradient Descent (GD) algorithm, and the appropriate interval is determined to select suitable coefficients of $f_c$ or $d_{3D}$. The *hypothetical function* ($h_\theta(x)$) of the Gradient Descent algorithm is

$$h_\theta(d_{3D}, f_c) = \theta_0 \cdot log_{10}(d_{3D}) + \theta_1 \cdot log_{10}(f_c) + \theta_2. \tag{8}$$

Considering that this measurement campaign mainly involves three spectrum bands, we can set the variable $f_c$ as a constant, and thus we reduce the Binary Gradient Descent into one dimensional Gradient Descent and obtain path loss models depending on $f_c$. Hence $h_\theta(x)$ can be updated as

$$h_\theta(d_{3D}) = \theta_0 \cdot log_{10}(d_{3D}) + \theta_1, \tag{9}$$

and the cost function ($J(\theta)$) is

$$J(\theta_0, \theta_1) = \frac{1}{2m} \sum_{i=1}^{m} (h_\theta(d_{3D}^{(i)}) - PL^{(i)})^2. \tag{10}$$

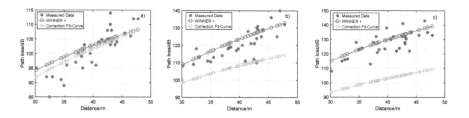

**Fig. 6.** The measurement results and corrected models of the path loss. (a) 900 MHz; (b) 2.6 GHz; (c) 3.5 GHz (Color figure online)

The results are demonstrated in Fig. 6. The blue markers represent the actual measurement data and the red and yellow curves represent the WINNER+ Channel Model ant its correction. It can be observed that the modified model can fit the measurement data better at 900 MHz, and the great deviation between the original model and the measured data is avoided at 2.6 GHz and 3.5 GHz. The revised path loss models at the three measurement frequency points are given as

$$PL = 34.26 \log_{10}(d_{3D}) - 15.98 \log_{10}(f_c) + 15(1 - cos\theta)^2 + 0.5d_{in} + 38.25 \tag{11}$$
$$PL = 39.58 \log_{10}(d_{3D}) - 20.56 \log_{10}(f_c) + 15(1 - cos\theta)^2 + 0.5d_{in} + 59.08 \tag{12}$$
$$PL = 40.21 \log_{10}(d_{3D}) - 17.78 \log_{10}(f_c) + 15(1 - cos\theta)^2 + 0.5d_{in} + 65.10 \tag{13}$$

## 3.4    Shadow Fading

SF is an important large-scale fading parameter. Differences between the measured path loss and path loss model at the RX positions are the SF factor. We use the *Kolmogorov-Smirnov* (K-S) check method to test whether these data are consistent with the lognormal distribution. Theoretically, SF should follow the logarithmic distribution, because SF is due to the power losses caused by barriers such as walls and trees. SF can be counted by multiplying all power losses along a propagation path, which is transformed to the addition of the losses in the logarithmic domain. In accordance with the central limit theory, SF should comply with a normal distribution in the logarithmic domain. Hence, the SF derived from the proposed revised path loss model can also be used to verify the reasonability of the model itself.

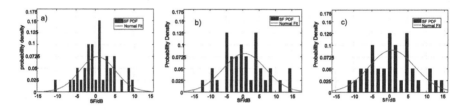

**Fig. 7.** The measurement results and normal distribution of the SF. (a) 900 MHz; (b) 2.6 GHz; (c) 3.5 GHz

As depicted in Fig. 7, the $x$-axis represents the value of the SF in the logarithmic domain, and the $y$-axis represents the probability density of each SF interval. The calculated SF samples at the three frequency points with the modified path loss model basically conforms to the lognormal distribution with the mean value of 0, and the standard deviations, namely $\sigma$, of 900 MHz, 2.6 GHz and 3.5 GHz are 4.5913, 6.6289, and 7.421, respectively.

## 4    Conclusion

In this paper, we select a typical UMi O2I scenario for signal coverage analysis in three spectrum bands, namely 900 MHz, 2.6 GHz, and 3.5 GHz. We conducted extensive field measurement on the signal power attenuation for rooms, short hall, and long hall. We conclude that 900 MHz and 2.6 GHz signals can achieve good coverage for the indoor areas, and by benefitting from the reflection on adjacent buildings, the 3.5 GHz signal guarantees the basic signal coverage in most areas. The observations and analysis can provide guidance for BS deployment and network optimization. At the same time, we compare several standard path loss models by fitting the measurement data. The WINNER+ O2I path loss model is selected and the model coefficients are further adjusted according to the measurement data. Then, the lognormal distributions of the SF samples at the three frequencies are obtained for this O2I channel model. The observation and revised channel models can be used in the analysis and simulation of the cellular systems, and to compare the network performance when working in different frequency bands. The BS deployment and network optimization based on the channel models will be studied in the future works.

**Acknowledgement.** This work was supported in part by the National Natural Science Foundation of China (61571370 and 61601365), in part by the Natural Science Basic Research Plan in Shaanxi Province (2016JQ6017), in part by the Fundamental Research Funds for the Central Universities (3102017O-QD091 and 3102017GX08003), in part by the China Postdoctoral Science Foundation (BX20180262) and sponsored by the seed Foundation of Innovation and Creation for Graduate Students in Northwestern Polytechnical University.

# References

1. Osseiran, A., Federico Boccardi, S.: Scenarios for 5G mobile and wireless communications the vision of the METIS project. IEEE Commun. Mag. **5**(55), 26–35 (2014)
2. IMT-2020(5G)Promotion Group: IMT-2020(5G)PG - White Paper on 5G Concept. Technical report (2015)
3. Kim, M., Iwata, T., Umeki, K., Wangchuk, K., Takada, J.I.: Mm-wave outdoor-to-indoor channel measurement in an open square smallcell scenario. In: 21st International Symposium on Antennas and Propagation 2016, ISAP, pp. 614–615 (2016)
4. Fukudome, H., Akimoto, K., Kameda, S., Suematsu, N., Takagi, T., Tsubouchi, K.: Measurement of 3.5 GHz band small cell indoor-outdoor propagation in multiple environments. In: 22nd European Wireless Conference 2016, EW, pp. 1–6 (2016)
5. Ren, K., Zhang, R., Zhong, Z., Li, C., Li, B.: Extension of 3GPP 3-dimensional channel models for large-scale parameters in the gymnasium scenario. In: International Applied Computational Electromagnetics Society Symposium 2017, ACES, pp. 1–2 (2017)
6. Winner: D1.1.2 V1.2 WINNER II Channel Models. Technical report (2007)
7. Winner: D5.3: WINNER+ Final Channel Models. Technical report (2010)
8. 3GPP RAN: Study on Channel Model for Frequency Spectrum above 6 GHz (Release 14). Technical report (2017)

# Simulated Traffic Sign Classification Using Cross-Connected Convolution Neural Networks Based on Compressive Sensing Domain

Jiping Xiong$^{(\boxtimes)}$, Lingfeng Ye, Fei Wang, and Tong Ye

College of Mathematics, Physics and Information Engineering,
Zhejiang Normal University, Jinhua, Zhejiang, People's Republic of China
xjping@zjnu.cn

**Abstract.** This paper proposes an algorithm of simulated traffic sign recognition based on compressive sensing domain and convolution neural networks for simulated traffic sign recognition. And the algorithm can extract the discriminative non-linear features directly from the compressive sensing domain. The image is transformed into compressive sensing domain by measurements matrix without reconstruction. This paper proposes a cross-connected convolution neural networks (CCNN) with an input layer, 6 six hidden layers (i.e., three convolution layers alternating with three pooling layers), a fully-connected layer and an output layer, where the second pooling layer is allowed to directly connect to the fully-connected layer across two layers. Experimental results show that the algorithm improves the accuracy of simulated traffic sign recognition. The recognition of the algorithm is possible even at low measurement rates.

**Keywords:** Compressive sensing domain · Convolution neural networks ·
CS measurements · Simulated traffic sign recognition

## 1 Introduction

Nowadays, Intelligent Simulation Transportation Systems attract more and more attention in research community and industry [1–4]. Traffic signs classification is one of the foremost important integral parts of simulated driving and advanced driver assistance systems (ADAS) [5–10]. Most of the time driver missed traffic signs due to different obstacles and lack of attentiveness. Automating the process of classification of the traffic signs would significantly help reducing accidents. Classification of traffic signs is not so simple task, images can be affected to adverse variation due to illumination, orientation, and the speed variation of vehicles etc. Normally wide angle camera is mounted on the top of a vehicle to capture traffic signs and other related visual features for ADAS. Such images are distorted due to several external factors including vehicles speed, sunlight, rain etc. Sample images from GTSRB dataset are shown in Fig. 1.

H. Song et al. (Eds.): SIMUtools 2019, LNICST 295, pp. 588–597, 2019.
https://doi.org/10.1007/978-3-030-32216-8_57

**Fig. 1.** Sample images of GTSRB dataset

Traditional computer vision and machine learning based methods were widely used for traffic signs classification [11, 12], but those methods were soon replaced by deep learning based classifiers. In deep learning, convolution neural networks (CNN) is developed in recent years and is a computer pattern recognition method which leads to an extensive attention [13, 14]. CNN is a multilayer preceptor special designed to recognize two-dimensional shapes. The network structure of CNN has highly invariance for translation, scaling, tilting or other forms of deformation. Because CNN does not require pre-processing images and can directly input the original image, it has been successfully applied to simulated traffic sign recognition [15, 16].

At the same time, the research shows that the comprehensive utilization of high level features and low level features are advantageous to improve the recognition performance of the visual system [17–19]. Therefore, based on the traditional convolution neural networks, by introducing the idea of cross-layer connections, the paper refers to a cross-connected convolution neural network model with a nine-layer structure, which is aimed at effectively combining low-level features and high-level features to build a better classifier.

In many computer visualization applications, however, the objective is not perfect recovery of the image, but to determine certain properties of the image. Because most of reconstruction algorithms of compressive sensing computationally expensive and the reconstruction results are poor at low measurement rates. In image recognition, such as simulated traffic sign recognition, we are interested in determining the category to which the object in the image belongs. Following some recent work in this emerging field of compressive sensing domain, we find further the possibility of performing effective high-level inference directly on compressive sensing measurements, without reconstruction. In [20], compressive sensing domain is applied to image recognition, without reconstruction. On the MNIST and ImageNet database, it got good recognition performance.

Therefore, the paper proposed a simulated traffic sign recognition approach using cross-connected convolution neural network based compressive sensing domain. The approach show that convolution neural network can be employed to extract discriminative non-linear features directly from compressive sensing domain. The image is compressed and is converted into the compressive sensing domain as the input of cross-connected convolution neural network, without reconstruction. Cross-connected convolution neural networks is a 9 layers framework with a input layer, 6 six hidden layers (i.e., three convolution layers alternating with three pooling layers), a fully-connected layer and an output layer, where the second pooling layer is allowed to directly connect to the fully-connected layer across two layers. Experimental results show that the algorithm improves the accuracy of simulated traffic sign recognition.

The rest of the paper is organized as follows. Section 2 details the proposed approach to simulated traffic sign recognition. Experimental results are illustrated in Sect. 3. Section 4 concludes the paper.

## 2  Simulated Traffic Sign Recognition Using Cross-Connected Convolution Neural Network Based on Compressive Sensing

This paper proposed a simulated traffic sign recognition approach using cross-connected convolution neural network based compressive sensing domain. First, the image is transformed into compressive sensing domain by measurements matrix without reconstruction. Then, the discriminative non-linear features can be directly extracted by cross-connected convolution neural network. Finally, traffic sign images are recognized by classifier.

### 2.1  Compressive Sensing Domain

**Compressive Sensing**
The compressive sensing (CS), $y \in R^m$, of an image $x \in R^n$ (ordered lexicographically), where $m < n$, are obtained using $y = \Phi x + e$, where $e \in R^m$ is the measurement noise. $\Phi \in R^{m \times n}$, called the measurement matrix with all entries and drawn from certain distributions such as Gaussian, Bernoulli etc. [21]. The problem of recovering x from $y$ is generally ill-posed since the linear system is underdetermined. It has been proven by Candes et al. [22] and Donoho [23] that, by posing additional constraints that $x$ is s-sparse in a basis $\Psi$, $\Phi$ being incoherent with $\Psi$ and $m = O\left(s \log \frac{n}{s}\right)$, the solution to the linear system is unique and $x$ can be recovered perfectly from $y$. This is typically achieved by solving an optimization problem of the form:

$$min_x \quad \|\Psi x\|_1 \quad \text{s.t} \quad \|y - \Phi x\|_2 \leq \epsilon \qquad (1)$$

There exist variants of the optimization problem in (1) which are applicable to compressible signals (since images are not exactly sparse in the wavelet domain).

**Compressive Sensing Domain**
Over the past decade, a great number of algorithms have been designed to solve this problem such as Orthogonal Matching Pursuit [24] and Basis Pursuit [25]. However, these algorithms are computationally expensive in addition to belong ineffective at low

measurement rates. Compressive sensing domain has gained momentum in recent years. Calderbank et al. [26] show that classifiers can be learned directly in the compressive sensing domain. Sankaranarayanan et al. [27] model videos as linear dynamical system (LDS) and use it to acquire and reconstruct CS videos. They also perform classification using the LDS parameters obtained directly from CS measurements. In [28], Matching Pursuit is modified and employed for reconstruction-free signal detection from CS measurements. In [29], a compressive sensing architecture is developed where, instead of perfect reconstruction of the CS images, only relevant parts of the scene i.e., the objects are reconstructed.

In simulated traffic sign recognition, we are interested in determining the category to which the object in the image belongs. Therefore, the paper applies compressive sensing domain to simulated traffic sign recognition. The traffic image is compressed by the measurement matrix. And the image is converted into the compressive sensing domain as the input of cross-connected convolution neural network, without reconstruction.

## 2.2 Cross-Connected Convolution Neural Network

**Convolution Neural Network**
The traditional convolution neural network is a special deep forward neural network model whose structure generally consists of input layer, multiple alternate convolution and pooling layer, full connection layer and output layer. The input layer is usually a matrix, such as an image. From the point of feed-forward network, convolution layer and pooling layer can be regarded as special hidden layers, in addition to output layer, and the full connection layer is the common hidden layer. In the convolution neural network, there are four basic operations which are defined as inner convolution, outer convolution, under-sampling and up-sampling.

Suppose A and B are matrixes, the size are $M \times N$ and $m \times n$, and $M \geq m$, $N \geq n$. Their inner convolution $C = A \ast B$'s elements are defined as below:

$$c_{ij} = \sum_{s=1}^{m} \sum_{t=1}^{n} a_{i+m-s,j+n-t} \cdot b_{st} \qquad (2)$$

Where, $1 \leq i \leq M - m + 1$, $1 \leq j \leq N - n + 1$.
Outer convolution is defined as:

$$A \hat{\ast} B = \widehat{A_B} \ast B \qquad (3)$$

Where, $\widehat{A_B} = \widehat{a_{ij}}$ is a matrix which is got by using 0 for A. The size is $(M + 2m - 2) \times (N + 2n - 2)$, and:

$$\widehat{a_{i,j}} = \begin{cases} a_{i-m+1,j-n+1}, & m \leq i \leq M + m - 1, n \leq j \leq N + n - 1 \\ 0, & \text{else} \end{cases} \qquad (4)$$

If matrix A is divided into blocks without overlapping. Suppose that the size of every block is $\lambda \times \tau$, and use $G_{\lambda,\tau}^A(i,j)$ to represent $ij$th block. The structure is as follows:

$$G_{\lambda,\tau}^A(i,j) = (a_{st})_{\lambda \times \tau} \tag{5}$$

Where, $(i-1) \times \lambda + 1 \leq s \leq i \times \lambda$, $(j-1) \times \tau + 1 \leq t \leq j \times \tau$. $G_{\lambda,\tau}^A(i,j)$' under-sampling is:

$$down\left(G_{\lambda,\tau}^A(i,j)\right) = \frac{1}{\lambda \times \tau} \sum_{s=(i-1) \times \lambda + 1}^{i \times \lambda} \sum_{(j-1) \times \tau + 1}^{j \times \tau} a_{st} \tag{6}$$

The under-sampling of the matrix A by the non-overlapping block with $\lambda \times \tau$ multiple is defined as:

$$down_{\lambda,\tau}(A) = down\left(G_{\lambda,\tau}^A(i,j)\right) \tag{7}$$

The up-sampling of the matrix A by the non-overlapping block with $\lambda \times \tau$ multiple is defined as:

$$up_{\lambda \times \tau}(A) = A \otimes 1_{\lambda \times \tau} \tag{8}$$

Where, $1_{\lambda \times \tau}$ is a matrix with all 1 elements. $\otimes$ represents Kronecker product.

**Cross-Connected Convolution Neural Network**
One drawback of the traditional convolution neural network is that it is difficult to efficiently integrate the lower level features with the higher features to construct a better classifier. Aimed at the problem. The paper introduces a cross-connected convolution neural network for the simulated traffic sign recognition. The network consists of a input layer $x$, three convolution layers $(h_1, h_3, h_5)$, three pooling layers $(h_2, h_4, h_6)$, a full connection layer $(h_7)$ and a output layer $o$, as shown in Fig. 2. The network starts with an image as input. Then, using three interlaced convolution layer and pooling layer extracts the features of the image. Finally, the features extracted from two pooling layers $(h_4$ and $h_6)$ are passed directly to the full connection layer for fusion processing and classification. In the network, the connection from pooling layer $h_4$ to pooling layer $h_7$ strides over two layers and is called cross-connection. At this point, the number of nodes in the full connection layer is the sum of the nodes of the pooling layer $h_4$ and $h_6$. The Table 1 presents the cross-connected convolution neural network, which consists of type, patch size, stride and output size.

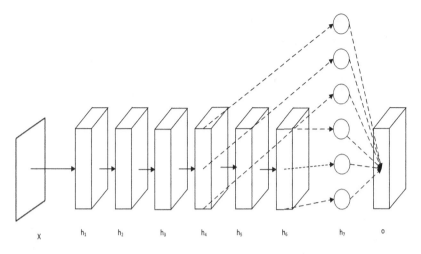

**Fig. 2.** The structure of the cross-connected convolution neural network

**Table 1.** The description of the cross-connected convolution neural network

| Layer | Type | Patch size | Stride | Output size |
|---|---|---|---|---|
| x | Input | | | $32 \times 32$ |
| $h_1$ | Convolution | $5 \times 5$ | 1 | $28 \times 28 \times 6$ |
| $h_2$ | Max pooling | $2 \times 2$ | 2 | $14 \times 14 \times 6$ |
| $h_3$ | Convolution | $5 \times 5$ | 1 | $10 \times 10 \times 12$ |
| $h_4$ | Max pooling | $2 \times 2$ | 2 | $5 \times 5 \times 12$ |
| $h_5$ | Convolution | $2 \times 2$ | 1 | $4 \times 4 \times 16$ |
| $h_6$ | Max pooling | $2 \times 2$ | 2 | $2 \times 2 \times 16$ |
| $h_7$ | Fully-connected | | | 364 |
| o | Output | | | 2 |

# 3 Experimental Results

## 3.1 GTSRB Database

GTSRB (German Traffic Sign Recognition Benchmarks) database is one of the standard database of traffic sign recognition. GTSRB has 43 categories and 51839 images. Each category has 100–1000 images, including prohibitory signs, danger signs and mandatory signs. 39209 images are selected as the training data set, and the rest images is selected as the test data set. There is a distortion in the images, because perspective change, shade, color degradation, weather change and so on. In the database, the size of image is different. After the image converted into compressive sensing domain, the image size is adjusted to $32 \times 32$ as the input of network. Figure 3 is subsets of traffic signs in the GTSRB database.

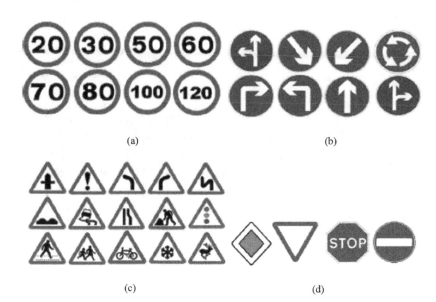

(a)                (b)

(c)                (d)

**Fig. 3.** Subset signs in the GTSRB data set. (a) Speed limit signs. (b) Derestriction signs. (c) Danger signs. (d) Unique signs.

### 3.2 Recognition Rate Comparing

In order to evaluate the effectiveness of the proposed method of simulated traffic sign recognition using cross-connected convolution neural network based on compressive sensing domain, the experiment is done on the GTSRB database. Cross-connected convolution neural network is trained and tested on caffe framework.

**Table 2.** Comparison of recognition of different method

| Method | Speed limit | Prohibitory | Derestriction | Mandatory | Danger | Unique |
|---|---|---|---|---|---|---|
| [30] | 99.47 | 99.93 | 99.72 | 99.89 | 99.07 | 99.22 |
| [31] | 99.86 | **100.00** | **99.95** | 99.89 | 99.89 | 99.87 |
| [30] | 98.61 | 99.87 | 94.44 | 97.18 | 98.30 | 98.63 |
| [12] | 98.82 | 98.27 | 97.93 | 96.86 | 96.95 | **100.00** |
| [32] | 95.95 | 99.13 | 87.50 | 99.27 | 92.08 | 98.73 |
| Proposed method | **99.88** | **100.00** | 99.93 | **99.90** | **99.92** | 99.89 |

From Table 2, compared with other method, the proposed method has some advantages. From the results of the six traffic signs, the proposed method has a higher recognition rate. In speed limit signs, prohibitory signs, mandatory signs and danger signs, the proposed method has obtained the highest recognition rate, and the recognition rate is 99.88%, 100.00%, 99.90% and 99.92%. In derestriction signs and unique signs, compared with the best method, the gap of the proposed method is not big.

**Table 3.** Comparison of the average recognition rate of different method

| Method | Average | Method | Average |
|--------|---------|--------|---------|
| [30] | 99.55 | [12] | 98.14 |
| [31] | 99.88 | [32] | 95.44 |
| [30] | 97.84 | Proposed method | **99.92** |

From Table 3, in the results of the six traffic signs, the proposed method gets highest average recognition rate 99.92%. Compared with the best method, the average recognition rate increased by 0.04%. It shows that the proposed method improves the robustness of the simulated traffic sign recognition.

### 3.3    Comparison of Different Measurement Rates

We train different networks, with the same architecture, at five different measurement rates of MR = 1, 0.25, 0.1, 0.05. If the number of pixels in original traffic sign images is n = 784, these MRs correspond to m = 784, 196, 78, 39 and 8 CS measurement respectively. For the five cross-connected convolution neural networks, the parameters such as learning rate, momentum and weight decay are fixed in order to be compared. The recognition rate on the test set at different measurement rates are shown in Table 4. It shows that the transformation of image to the compressive sensing domain can improve the performance of traffic sign recognition.

**Table 4.** The recognition rate on the test set at different measurement rates

| Measurement rate (MR) | 1 | 0.25 | 0.10 | 0.05 | 0.01 |
|------------------------|------|-------|-------|-------|-------|
| Recognition rate | 99.92 | 98.43 | 97.35 | 94.77 | 60.20 |

## 4    Conclusion

Based on the development of the compressive sensing domain theory and the simulated traffic sign recognition of convolution neural network, the paper proposed a simulated traffic sign recognition using cross-connected convolution neural network based on compressive sensing domain. Using cross-connected convolution neural network directly extracts features from the compressive sensing domain of the image for simulated traffic sign recognition. The image is transformed into compressive sensing main by measurements matrix without reconstruction as the input of cross-connected convolution neural network. The proposed method can extract discriminative non-linear features directly from compressive sensing domain for simulated traffic sign recognition. Experiment on standard traffic sign database GTSRB, it is found that the method improves the recognition accuracy and enhances the robustness of simulated traffic sign recognition.

# References

1. Chhabra, R., Verma, S., Rama Krishna, C.: A survey on driver behavior detection techniques for intelligent transportation systems. In: 2017 7th International Conference on Cloud Computing, Data Science & Engineering-Confluence. IEEE (2017)
2. Jiang, D., Huo, L., Lv, Z., Song, H., Qin, W.: A joint multi-criteria utility-based network selection approach for vehicle-to-infrastructure networking. IEEE Trans. Intell. Transp. Syst. **PP**(99), 1–15 (2018)
3. Jiang, D., Xu, Z., Wang, W., Wang, Y., Han, Y.: A collaborative multi-hop routing algorithm for maximum achievable rate. J. Netw. Comput. Appl. **57**(2015), 182–191 (2015)
4. Jiang, D., Wang, Y., Yao, C., Han, Y.: An effective dynamic spectrum access algorithm for multi-hop cognitive wireless networks. Comput. Netw. **84**(19), 1–16 (2015)
5. Haloi, M., Jayagopi, D.B.: A robust lane detection and departure warning system. In: IEEE Intelligent Vehicles Symposium (IV), pp. 126–131 (2015)
6. Jiang, D., Xu, Z., Li, W., Chen, Z.: Network coding-based energy-efficient multicast routing algorithm for multi-hop wireless networks. J. Syst. Softw. **104**(2015), 152–165 (2015)
7. Jiang, D., Li, W., Lv, H.: An energy-efficient cooperative multicast routing in multi-hop wireless networks for smart medical applications. Neurocomputing **220**(2017), 160–169 (2017)
8. Jiang, D., Wang, Y., Han, Y., et al.: Maximum connectivity-based channel allocation algorithm in cognitive wireless networks for medical applications. Neurocomputing **220** (2017), 41–51 (2017)
9. Jiang, D., Xu, Z., Li, W., et al.: An energy-efficient multicast algorithm with maximum network throughput in multi-hop wireless networks. J. Commun. Netw. **18**(5), 713–724 (2016)
10. Jiang, D., Zhang, P., Lv, Z., et al.: Energy-efficient multi-constraint routing algorithm with load balancing for smart city applications. IEEE Internet of Things J. **3**(6), 1437–1447 (2016)
11. Le, T.T., Tran, S.T., Mita, S., Nguyen, T.D.: Real time traffic sign detection using color and shape-based features. In: Intelligent Information and Database Systems, pp. 268-278. IEEE (2010)
12. Haloi, M.: A novel pLSA based Traffic Signs Classification System. https://arxiv.org/. Accessed 2015
13. Zhao, Z.H., Yang, S.P., Ma, Z.Q.: The study of license character recognition based on the convolution neural network LeNet-5. J. Syst. Simul. **22**(3), 638–641 (2010)
14. Xu, S.S., Liu, Y.A., Xu, S.: Wood defect recognition based on the convolution neural network. J. Shandong Univ.: Eng. Sci. **43**(2), 23–28 (2013)
15. Mrinal, H.: Traffic Sign Classification Using Deep Inception Based Convolutional Networks. https://arxiv.org/. Accessed 2016
16. Yang, Y., Luo, H., Xu, H., Wu, F.: Towards real-time traffic sign detection and classification. IEEE Trans. Intell. Transp. Syst. **17**, 2022–2031 (2016)
17. Zhong, S.H., Liu, Y., Ren, F.F., Zhang, J.H., Ren, T.W.: Video saliency detection via dynamic consistent spatio-temporal attention modelling. In: Proceedings of the 2013 AAAI Conference on Artificial Intelligence, pp. 1063–1069. AAAI, Bellevue (2013)

18. Jiang, D., Nie, L., Lv, Z., et al.: Spatio-temporal Kronecker compressive sensing for traffic matrix recovery. IEEE Access **4**, 3046–3053 (2016)
19. Qi, M.-B., Tan, S.-S., Wang, Y.-X., Liu, H., Jiang, J.-G.: Multi-feature subspace and kernel learning for person reidentication. Acta Automatica Sinica **42**(2), 299–308 (2016)
20. Suhas, L., Kuldeep, K., Pavan, T.: Direct inference on compressive measurements using convolutional neural networks. In: Image Processing (ICIP), pp. 1913–1917 (2016)
21. Sun, Z.J., Xue, L., Xu, Y.M.: Review of deep learning research. Comput. Appl. Res. **29**(8), 2807–2810 (2012)
22. Candès, E.J., Wakin, M.B.: An introduction to compressive sampling. Signal Process. Mag. **25**(2), 21–30 (2008)
23. Candès, E.J., Romberg, J.K., Tao, T.: Stable signal recovery from incomplete and inaccurate measurements. Commun. Pure Appl. Math. **59**(8), 1207–1223 (2006)
24. Donoho, D.L.: Compressed sensing. IEEE Trans. Inf. Theory **52**(4), 1289–1306 (2006)
25. Tropp, J.A., Gilbert, A.C.: Signal recovery from random measurements via orthogonal matching pursuit. IEEE Trans. Inf. Theory **53**(12), 4655–4666 (2007)
26. Chen, S.S., Donoho, D.L., Saunders, M.A.: Atomic decomposition by basis pursuit. SIAM J. Sci. Comput. **20**(1), 33–61 (1998)
27. Sankaranarayanan, A.C., Turaga, P.K., Baraniuk, R.G., Chellappa, R.: Compressive acquisition of dynamic scenes. In: Daniilidis, K., Maragos, P., Paragios, N. (eds.) ECCV 2010. LNCS, vol. 6311, pp. 129–142. Springer, Heidelberg (2010). https://doi.org/10.1007/978-3-642-15549-9_10
28. Duarte, M.F., Davenport, M.A., Wakin, M.B., Baraniuk, R.G.: Sparse signal detection from incoherent projections. In: Acoustics, Speech and Signal Processing, vol. 3, pp. 305–308 (2006)
29. Mahalanobis, A., Muise, R.: Object specific image reconstruction using a compressive sensing architecture for application in surveillance systems. IEEE Trans. Aerosp. Electron. Syst. **45**(3), 1167–1180 (2009)
30. Sermanet, P., LeCun, Y.: Traffic sign recognition with multi-scale convolutional networks. In: Neural Networks (IJCNN), pp. 2809–2813. IEEE (2011)
31. Stallkamp, J., Schlipsing, M., Salmen, J., Igel, C.: The German traffic sign recognition benchmark: a multi-class classification competition. In: Neural Networks (IJCNN), pp. 1453–1458. IEEE (2011)
32. Zaklouta, F., Stanciulescu, B., Hamdoun, O.: Traffic sign classification using KD trees and random forests. In: Neural Networks (IJCNN), pp. 2151–2155. IEEE (2011)

# Comparative Study of Evolutionary Algorithms for Protein-Ligand Docking Problem on the AutoDock

Zhuoran Liu[1], Changsheng Zhang[1], Qidong Zhao[1], Bin Zhang[1]([✉]),
and Wenjuan Sun[2]

[1] Northeastern University, Shenyang 110819, People's Republic of China
zhangchangsheng@mail.neu.edu.cn, paper820@sohu.com
[2] Shenyang Ligong University, Shenyang 110159, People's Republic of China

**Abstract.** AutoDock is a widely used simulation platform for Protein-ligand docking which is a simulator to provide the field of computer-aided drug design (CADD) with conveniences. Protein-ligand docking establishes docking models and study interaction between the receptor and the ligand, as a part of the most important means in drug development. Protein-ligand docking problem is of great significance to design more effective and ideal drugs. The experiments are simulated on AutoDock with six weighted algorithms such as Lamarckian genetic algorithm, a genetic algorithm with crossover elitist preservation, artificial bee colony algorithm, ABC_DE_based hybrid algorithm, fireworks algorithm, and monarch butterfly optimization. The diversity of search function constructed by different evolutionary algorithms for separate receptors and ligands is applied and analyzed. Performances of distinct search functions are given according to convergence speed, energy value, hypothesis test and so on. This can be of great benefit to future protein-ligand docking progress. Based on the work, appearances are found that performances of the same algorithm vary with different problems. No universal algorithms are having the best performance for diverse problems. Therefore, it is important how to choose an appropriate approach according to characteristics of problems.

**Keywords:** Evolutionary computation · Swarm intelligence · Protein-ligand docking · Search function

## 1 Introduction

In developing period of drug design, inefficiency and high cost is becoming increasingly problematic. Computer-aided drug design (CADD) steps up the process and opens up ideas of drug design as a basis. An indispensable part of CADD is protein-ligand docking. Protein-ligand docking is a practical approach for CADD. The simulation process makes use of the characteristics of receptors and the interaction between receptors and molecules to solve the problem [1–3]. To combine small molecules with protein macromolecules, the position of small molecules should be reasonably adjusted, the ideal location and interaction of the combination is detected according to the complementary principle of docking, and finally a stable complex conformation is

H. Song et al. (Eds.): SIMUtools 2019, LNICST 295, pp. 598–607, 2019.
https://doi.org/10.1007/978-3-030-32216-8_58

obtained. The purpose is to find the best binding sites between ligands and receptors [4].

Steps to solve the protein-ligand docking problem on the simulation platform contain the scoring function and the search algorithm. The scoring function evaluates the energy value of different conformations, which is used to evaluate the binding conformation of ligands and receptors computer simulations predicted. In the process of docking, the binding affinity between ligand and receptor is supposed to be obtained accurately. As the basis of optimization, the scoring function can be directly an adaptive value in the optimization algorithm [5–8]. Scoring function is the key to optimization problems and plays an important role in the results of molecular docking and virtual screening.

Evolutionary algorithms construct the search algorithms. Some researchers have improved these methods on efficiency. Morris published in the paper [9–11] introduces genetic algorithm with Lamarck on the platform of AutoDock (Lamarckian genetic algorithm, LGA) to solve the docking problem [12]. Guan B in the paper [13] proposed a genetic algorithm with crossover elitist preservation (CEPGA) to solve the protein-ligand problem. Some researchers released some modified swarm intelligence algorithms to the protein-ligand problem such as the artificial bee colony algorithm (ABC) [14], ABC_DE_based hybrid algorithm (ADHDOCK) [15]. Evolutionary algorithms are widely applied in many fields, such as data analysis and network optimization [16–20]. Some swarm intelligence algorithms also have good performance in the search process such as fireworks algorithm (FWA) [21], monarch butterfly optimization (MBO) [22].

The AutoDock platform simulates algorithms [23] to settle protein-ligand docking problem. Algorithms have their advantages in different test cases. In this paper, six algorithms are carried out on AutoDock to make a fair comparison, such as LGA, CEPGA, ABC, ADHDOCK, FWA and MBO. Results of solving protein-ligand docking problems of algorithms are calculated and analyzed such as convergence speed, energy value, and hypothesis test. According to analysis, search algorithms have respective advantages and disadvantages in settling the protein-ligand docking problem.

## 2   Materials and Methods

### 2.1   Simulation Platform

AutoDock is a universal simulation software for protein-ligand docking. Many researchers study the protein-ligand docking problem on this platform. AutoDock is an open source molecular simulation software developed and maintained by the Olson laboratory at the Scripps Research Institute [23]. The taken version is AutoDock 4.2.

In this study, AutoDock simulates the protein-ligand docking process. The optimal combination location needs to consider the geometric structure matching of the protein and the ligand and the energy value of the combined position. AutoDock evaluates the resulting conformation and searches for a suitable conformation. The platform uses a specific scoring function to make an evaluation. The search algorithm constructed by the evolutionary computation algorithm searches for the optimal solution.

## 2.2  Materials

Six protein-ligand complexes [24] were chosen from the Brookhaven PDB to compare the performance of the docking techniques. Six docking problems are summarized as test cases in the following:

- HIV-1 Protease/XK263 (1hvr): The cyclic urea HIV-protease inhibitor, XK-263, has ten rotatable bonds, excluding the cyclic urea's flexibility.
- Streptavidin/Biotin (1stp): Biotin, also known as vitamin H or coenzyme R, is a water-soluble B vitamin. Streptavidin/biotin is one of the most tightly binding non-covalent complexes.
- McPC-603/Phosphocholine (2mcp): Phosphocholine is an intermediate in the synthesis of phosphatidylcholine in tissues. The recognition of phosphocholine by FabMcPC-603 is mainly because of the influence of ArgH52.
- b-Trypsin/Benzamidine (3ptb): Benzamidine is a reversible competitive inhibitor of trypsin, trypsin-like enzymes and serine proteases. The recognition of benzamidine by b-trypsin is mainly because of the polar amidine moiety and the hydrophobic benzyl ring.
- Dihydrofolate Reductase/Methotrexate (4dfr): Methotrexate is an antimetabolite that attacks proliferating tissue and selectively induces remissions in certain acute leukemias.
- Influenza Hemagglutinin/Sialic Acid (4hmg): The recognition of sialic acid by influenza hemagglutinin is chiefly because of hydrogen bonding.

## 2.3  Algorithm Analysis

This paper implements and runs the algorithms on the AutoDock, namely LGA, CEPGA, ABC and ADHDOCK, FWA, MBO. The test cases are the same. On the same platform, the performances of six different algorithms are equally compared. Six different evolutionary algorithms are listed below to state the principle of algorithms.

- Lamarckian Genetic Algorithm (LGA): Lamarckian genetic algorithm is coupled with the local search for the genetic algorithm. Local search refers to the current solution around an optimal solution until finding the local optimal solution algorithm. If the solution is not a local optimal solution, the local search can find the optimal solution around the solution. In the search for molecular conformation, local search has the advantage of no need for gradient information about district energy patterns, thus promoting torsional space search.
- Genetic Algorithm with Crossover Elitist Preservation (CEPGA): Good genes from parents can no longer produce good individuals through crossover operation, as original genetic algorithms do not retain the parents of the elitist individual. A crossover elitist preservation (CEP) mechanism incorporated into genetic algorithm is applied to solve protein-ligand docking problems. The crossover elitist preservation mechanism can make sure not to discard optimal solution while

speeding the operation up. In this way, the next generation will be more suitable for the competition of elitist parents and their descendants. Besides, an optimal solution in near space of current solutions which included in GA can be selected by a local search.

- Artificial Bee Colony Algorithm (ABC): The basic structure is divided into the employed bees phase, the onlooker bees phase, and the scout bees phase. The employed bees store information about the food source and share it with other bees with a certain probability. The number of employed bees is the number of food sources. An employee bee is only related to a food source. The onlooker bees observe the dance of employed bees in the hive to determine which food source to choose. Scout bees randomly search for new food sources next to the hive.

- ABC_DE_Based Hybrid Algorithm for protein–ligand docking (ADHDOCK): ABC_DE_based hybrid algorithm is an algorithm for protein–ligand docking, while integrating differential evolution algorithm (DE) and artificial bee colony algorithm (ABC). ABC and DE, two typical optimization methods that have been widely used in various fields, execute in parallel and have the same population during the present algorithm. ADHDOCK incorporates an adaptive population partition mechanism to distribute two subpopulations partition automatically to ABC and DE. On account of the reasonable allocation of computing resources, ADHDOCK is uniquely positioned to take the advantages of ABC and DE, and then avoid local optimum.

- Fireworks Algorithm (FWA): FWA presents a new search manner which searches the potential space by a stochastic explosion process within a local space. At first, N fireworks are initialized randomly. The quality is evaluated to determine the explosion amplitude and the number of sparks for each firework. And fireworks explode and generate different types of sparks within their local space. Finally, N candidate fireworks are selected among the set of candidates, which includes the newly generated sparks as well as the N original fireworks. In order to ensure diversity and balance the global and local search, the explosion amplitude and the population of the newly generated explosion sparks differ among fireworks.

- Monarch Butterfly Algorithm (MBO): MBO simulates the migration behavior of the monarch butterflies in nature. In MBO, all the monarch butterfly individuals are only idealized and located in two lands such as Southern Canada and the northern USA (land 1) and Mexico (land 2). Monarch butterflies of two positions are updated in two ways. At first, the offsprings are generated by migration operator which can be adjusted by the migration ratio. Subsequently, the positions of other butterflies are tuned by butterfly adjusting operator. In other words, the search direction of the monarch butterfly individuals in MBO algorithm is mainly determined by the migration operator and butterfly adjusting operator. Also, the migration operator and butterfly adjusting operator can be implemented simultaneously.

# 3   Materials and Methods

## 3.1   Parameters Setting

In the process of performance testing, each algorithm must be reasonably set the parameters. LGA, CEPGA, ABC, ADHDOCK, FWA and MBO are compared at the AutoDock platform. The initial population is set as 50. These algorithms terminate when the energy function evaluations reach $1.5 \times 10^6$ for each run. The AutoDock platform runs every search algorithms 20 times to solve given test cases. The search algorithm is evaluated the docking results by analyzing the convergence, stability and hypothesis testing.

## 3.2   Convergence Analysis

According to set iterations, the energy value obtained by the algorithm is used to determine the convergence of the algorithm. Figure 1 is the convergence diagrams of the six algorithms for each test case.

The slope of ADHDOCK and ABC in Fig. 1(a) is the smallest, which is at the better convergence position and gets lowest energy value. Moreover, LGA converges slowly and finds the energy close to the lowest. In Fig. 1(b), the slope and the energy value of ABC are in good agreement with our expectation. With the increasing of iterations, results of LGA are approaching the lowest. The convergence rate of CEPGA and FWA is moderate, while the result is relatively high. In Fig. 1(c), the energy value of MBO is getting better as the number of iterations increases and MBO gets the best energy finally. The convergence rate of other algorithms is moderate. In Fig. 1(d), the slope of MBO is stable which can prevent from falling into the local optimal solution early, and MBO has the lowest energy. The convergence rate of all the algorithms in Fig. 1(e) is relatively equal. LGA gets better results. In Fig. 1(f), the convergence rate of LGA is the slowest. ABC get the best energy value whose results change distinctly with the number of iterations increasing. The convergence rate and the solution quality of the same algorithm differ in different test cases.

## 3.3   Algorithm Stability Analysis

Figure 2 shows box plots for each test case. The minimum, the first quartile, the median, the third quartile, the maximum and the outliers of the energy values are calculated to mark on the box plot. The range from the minimum to the maximum shows the variation range of data. The interquartile range shows the likely variation range. The outliers are points out of the range. The protein-ligand docking problem is an optimization problem in need of minimum value. When the shown value or the median value is lower, the algorithm has better solving performance. The box plot with smaller range shows that the algorithm has stability.

According to Figures, the median energy value of ADHDOCK is the lowest in Fig. 2(a) and its minimum energy value is lowest. In Fig. 2(b), ABC finds smaller energy value and the range of ABC is also smallest. In Fig. 2(c), the minimum energy of MBO is lowest. The median energy of ADHDOCK is lowest. The range of CEPGA

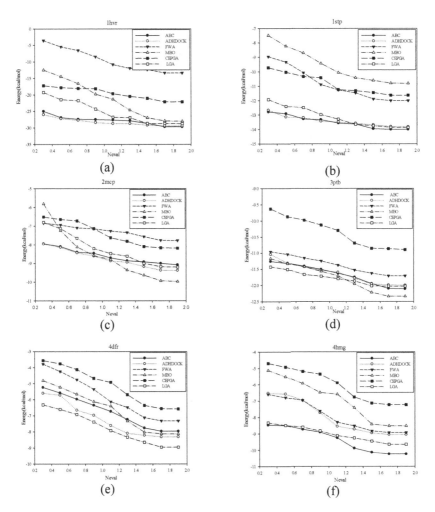

**Fig. 1.** This figure shows the convergence graphs of the six algorithms for each test case. Neval is the number of iterations of the function, and the ordinate is the energy value generated by the docking of the function after iterating specified times.: (a) Convergence diagram of 1hvr; (b) Convergence diagram of 1stp; (c) Convergence diagram of 2mcp; (d) Convergence diagram of 3ptb; (e) Convergence diagram of 4dfr; (f) Convergence diagram of 4hmg.

is the smallest while its results are not good. In Fig. 2(d), MBO gets lowest energy. The range of values of ABC is smallest in Fig. 2(e). And LGA has lowest energy. The median energy of ADHDOCK is lowest. In Fig. 2(f), the median and minimum of the energy of ABC are lowest. The range of FWA is the smallest while its result is not good. It is observed that the distribution of the same algorithm is different for different test cases.

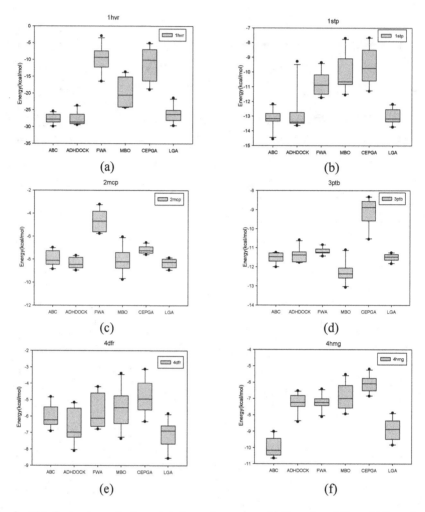

**Fig. 2.** This figure shows the box plots for each test case. (a) Box plot of 1hvr; (b) Box plot of 1stp; (c) Box plot of 2mcp; (d) Box plot of 3ptb; (e) Box plot of 4dfr; (f) Box plot of 4hmg.

### 3.4    Hypothesis Test Results

On six test cases, compared algorithms run for 20 times. Table 1 demonstrates the hypothesis test results. The difference factor p-value determines the quality of the result. In the experiment, $\alpha$ is settled as 0.05. If p-value < 0.05, the current algorithm is superior to the compared algorithm. If p-value > 0.95, the current algorithm is inferior to the compared algorithm. If 0.05 < p-value < 0.95, it shows that the performance of the two algorithms is not very different on this test case.

Some phenomena can be seen through the results of the hypothesis test. For 1hvr, ADHDOCK is better than four compared algorithms. For 1stp, ADHDOCK is better than three compared algorithms. For 4hmg, ABC is better than four compared

**Table 1.** Results of hypothesis tests

| PDB | | ABC | ADHDOCK | FWA | MBO | CEPGA | LGA |
|---|---|---|---|---|---|---|---|
| 1hvr | ABC | – | 0.443 | 0.016 | 0.054 | 0.007 | 0.003 |
| | ADHDOCK | 0.562 | – | 0.019 | 0.009 | 0.009 | 0.005 |
| | FWA | 1 | 1 | – | 1 | 0.702 | 0.998 |
| | MBO | 0.947 | 0.905 | 0.021 | – | 0.012 | 0.020 |
| | CEPGA | 1 | 1 | 0.299 | 1 | – | 0.998 |
| | LGA | 1 | 0.996 | 0.018 | 0.997 | 0.003 | – |
| 1stp | ABC | – | 0.342 | 0.001 | 0.002 | 0.001 | 0.348 |
| | ADHDOCK | 0.665 | – | 0.001 | 0.001 | 0.002 | 0.605 |
| | FWA | 1 | 0.999 | – | 0.475 | 0.142 | 1 |
| | MBO | 0.998 | 0.989 | 0.528 | – | 0.179 | 0.998 |
| | CEPGA | 0.999 | 0.997 | 0.857 | 0.822 | – | 0.996 |
| | LGA | 0.650 | 0.396 | 0.001 | 0.002 | 0.001 | – |
| 2mcp | ABC | – | 0.768 | 0.001 | 0.368 | 0.001 | 0.933 |
| | ADHDOCK | 0.231 | – | 0.001 | 0.170 | 0.001 | 0.881 |
| | FWA | 0.999 | 1 | – | 0.987 | 0.007 | 0.999 |
| | MBO | 0.630 | 0.832 | 0.013 | – | 0.004 | 0.956 |
| | CEPGA | 0.999 | 1 | 1 | 1 | – | 1 |
| | LGA | 0.063 | 0.116 | 0.002 | 0.005 | 0.003 | – |
| 3stp | ABC | – | 0.353 | 0.004 | 0.006 | 0.001 | 0.731 |
| | ADHDOCK | 0.647 | – | 0.067 | 0.194 | 0.001 | 0.787 |
| | FWA | 0.997 | 0.934 | – | 0.732 | 0.190 | 0.999 |
| | MBO | 0.944 | 0.806 | 0.267 | – | 0.007 | 0.986 |
| | CEPGA | 1 | 1 | 1 | 1 | – | 1 |
| | LGA | 0.268 | 0.216 | 0.001 | 0.732 | 0.003 | – |
| 4dfr | ABC | | 0.053 | 0.205 | 0.018 | 0.001 | 0.749 |
| | ADHDOCK | 0.948 | | 0.613 | 0.138 | 0.004 | 0.998 |
| | FWA | 0.796 | 0.388 | | 0.170 | 0.028 | 0.909 |
| | MBO | 0.984 | 0.862 | 0.827 | | 0.095 | 0.999 |
| | CEPGA | 0.999 | 0.996 | 0.971 | 0.138 | | 1 |
| | LGA | 0.250 | 0.002 | 0.009 | 0.170 | 0.001 | |
| 4hmg | ABC | – | 0.014 | 0.036 | 0.014 | 0.005 | 0.490 |
| | ADHDOCK | 0.986 | – | 0.969 | 0.429 | 0.502 | 1 |
| | FWA | 0.962 | 0.030 | – | 0.057 | 0.001 | 1 |
| | MBO | 0.985 | 0.570 | 0.945 | – | 0.523 | 0.999 |
| | CEPGA | 0.995 | 0.495 | 0.999 | 0.470 | – | 1 |
| | LGA | 0.510 | 0.032 | 0.005 | 0.004 | 0.001 | – |

algorithms. ABC is better than three compared algorithms for 1hvr, 1stp, and 3stp. For 1hvr, MBO is better than three compared algorithms. For 1stp, 2mcp, 4df, and 4hmgr, LGA is better than three compared algorithms. Accordingly, from results of the hypothesis test, there is not an algorithm better than others for given six test cases.

# 4   Results Discussion

The primary purpose of this paper is to explore the differences between different evolutionary algorithms in protein-ligand docking. The research shows that search functions constructed by different evolutionary algorithms can achieve satisfactory results respectively under different environments or requirements. In study as mentioned, the results of algorithms are different due to the change of problems. Under parameter setting above, ADHDOCK has highlighted performance for 1hvr, ABC has good performance for 1stp and 4hmg, MBO is best for 2mcp and 3ptb, LGA has good performance for 4dfr. Evaluations of algorithms on six protein-ligand complexes are different.

In general, the experiments show that affected search functions check molecular pairs. Performances of algorithms vary with test cases to be solved.

# 5   Conclusions

Experiments mentioned above demonstrate that different search functions have different effects on respective problems. For every algorithm solving protein-ligand problem, it can perform pretty well in some cases while it has terrible performance in other cases. Consequently, there are no multipurpose algorithms concerning different test cases. Presented algorithms have apparent advantages in specified problems, not in common use. Therefore, it is vital to choose a suited method which is implemented on the same simulation platform to solve protein-ligand problem.

**Acknowledgments.** This study is funded by Shenyang Dongda Emerging Industrial Technology Research Institute.

# References

1. Brooijmans, N., Kuntz, I.D.: Molecular recognition and docking algorithms. Annu. Rev. Biophys. Biomol. Struct. **32**(1), 335–373 (2003)
2. Huang, S.Y., Zou, X.: Advances and challenges in Protein-ligand docking. Int. J. Mol. Sci. **11**(8), 3016–3034 (2010)
3. Jug, G., Anderluh, M., Tomašič, T.: Comparative evaluation of several docking tools for docking small molecule ligands to DC-SIGN. J. Mol. Model. **21**(6), 1–12 (2015)
4. Verlinde, C.L., Hol, W.G.: Structure-based drug design: progress, results and challenges. Structure **2**(7), 577–587 (1994)
5. Huey, R., Morris, G.M., Olson, A.J., Goodsell, D.S.: Software news and update a semiempirical free energy force field with charge-based desolvation. J. Comput. Chem. **10**, 1145–1152 (2007)
6. Jain, A.N.: Scoring functions for protein-ligand docking. Curr. Protein Pept. Sci. **7**(5), 407–420 (2006)
7. Feinstein, W.P., Brylinski, M.: Calculating an optimal box size for ligand docking and virtual screening against experimental and predicted binding pockets. J. Cheminform **7**, 18 (2015)

8. Zeng, X.X., Liao, Y.L., Liu, Y.S., Zou, Q.: Prediction and validation of disease genes using HeteSim Scores. IEEE/ACM Trans. Comput. Biol. Bioinf. **14**(03), 687–695 (2017)
9. Cao, T., Li, T.: A combination of numeric genetic algorithm and tabu search can be applied to molecular docking. Comput. Biol. Chem. **28**(4), 303–312 (2004)
10. Morris, G.M., et al.: Automated docking using a lamarckian genetic algorithm and an empirical binding free energy function. Comput. Chem. J. Comput. Chem **19**(28), 1639–1662 (1998)
11. Guan, B., Zhang, C., Ning, J.: EDGA: a population evolution direction-guided genetic algorithm for protein-ligand docking. J. Comput. Biol. **23**(7), 585–596 (2016)
12. Fuhrmann, J., Rurainsk, A., Lenhof, H.P., Neumann, D.: A new Lamarckian genetic algorithm for flexible ligang-receptor docking. J. Comput. Chem. **31**, 1911–1918 (2010)
13. Guan, B., Zhang, C., Ning, J.: Genetic algorithm with a crossover elitist preservation mechanism for protein–ligand docking. Amb. Express **7**(1), 174 (2017)
14. Uehara, S., Fujimoto, K.J., Tanaka, S.: Protein-ligand docking using fitness learning-based artificial bee colony with proximity stimuli. Phys. Chem. Chem. Phys. **17**(25), 16412–16417 (2015)
15. Guan, B., Zhang, C., Zhao, Y.: An efficient ABC_DE_Based hybrid algorithm for protein-ligand docking. Int. J. Mol. Sci. **19**(4), 1181 (2018)
16. Jiang, D., Huo, L., Song, H.: Rethinking behaviors and activities of base stations in mobile cellular networks based on big data analysis. IEEE Trans. Netw. Sci. Eng. **1**(1), 1–12 (2018)
17. Jiang, D., Huo, L., Lv, Z., et al.: A joint multi-criteria utility-based network selection approach for vehicle-to-infrastructure networking. IEEE Trans. Intell. Transp. Syst. (99), 1–15 (2018)
18. Jiang, D., Zhang, P., Lv, Z., et al.: Energy-efficient multi-constraint routing algorithm with load balancing for smart city applications. IEEE Internet of Things J. **3**(6), 1437–1447 (2016)
19. Jiang, D., Xu, Z., Li, W., et al.: Topology control-based collaborative multicast routing algorithm with minimum energy consumption. Int. J. Commun. Syst. **30**(1), 1–18 (2017)
20. Jiang, D., Xu, Z., Li, W., et al.: An energy-efficient multicast algorithm with maximum network throughput in multi-hop wireless networks. J. Commun. Netw. **18**(5), 713–724 (2016)
21. Tan, Y., Zhu, Y.: Fireworks algorithm for optimization. In: Tan, Y., Shi, Y., Tan, K.C. (eds.) ICSI 2010. LNCS, vol. 6145, pp. 355–364. Springer, Heidelberg (2010). https://doi.org/10.1007/978-3-642-13495-1_44
22. Wang, G.G., Deb, S., Cui, Z.: Monarch butterfly optimization. Neural Comput. Appl. **31**, 1–20 (2015)
23. Morris, G.M., et al.: AutoDock4 and AutoDockTools4: automated docking with selective receptor flexibility. Softw. News Updates **30**(16), 2786–2791 (2009)
24. Hu, X., Balaz, S., Shelver, W.H.: A practical approach to docking of zinc metalloproteinase inhibitors. J. Mol. Graph. Model. **22**(4), 293–307 (2004)

# Image Mosaic Based on Improved Logarithmic Polar Coordinate Transformation and Ransac Algorithm

Dan Li, Lei Chen$^{(\boxtimes)}$, Jun Tian, Dai-hong Jiang, Jin-ping Sun,
and Bin Ding

Key Laboratory of Intelligent Industrial Control Technology of Jiangsu Province,
Xuzhou University of Technology, Xuzhou 221000, Jiangsu, China
lidanonline@163.com, chenlei@xzit.edu.cn

**Abstract.** Complex factors with the electronic noise, X-ray scattering and uneven illumination often disturb the image registration. A new algorithm was proposed in this paper. The improved phase correlation algorithm based on log polar transformation was used to calculate parameters, such as rotation, scaling and translation. Then, the Harris corner matching points were extracted in overlapping positions and purified by the improved Ransac algorithm. Finally, images were processed by NSCT transform algorithm to make the image joint seemed smooth and natural. Experiments confirmed that, the new algorithm is accurate and efficient, and has high robustness to complex environment.

**Keywords:** Image registration · Logarithmic polar coordinates · Mosaic · Ransac algorithm · NSCT transform

## 1 Introduction

In medical images, panoramic image equipment is very expensive and the visual field of most medical imaging devices is limited [1]. Using image stitching technology [2–4] to generate panoramic images has low cost and good effect, but under the influence of complex factors, the result details are blurred. With the development of computer and multimedia technology, the requirement of real-time network transmission of mosaic video images is becoming higher and higher [5–7].

In view of the above problems, a new image registration and stitching algorithm was proposed. First, using the improved phase correlation algorithm of logarithmic polar coordinate transformation to calculate the parameters of scaling, rotation and translation, and estimate the overlapped region. Then, the Harris corner points were extracted and the Ransac algorithm [8, 9] was improved to accurately purify the matching points. Finally, the NSCT transformation algorithm [10] was used and the fusion strategy was formulated to further solve the splicing joint.

© ICST Institute for Computer Sciences, Social Informatics and Telecommunications Engineering 2019
Published by Springer Nature Switzerland AG 2019. All Rights Reserved
H. Song et al. (Eds.): SIMUtools 2019, LNICST 295, pp. 608–614, 2019.
https://doi.org/10.1007/978-3-030-32216-8_59

## 2 Improvement of Logarithmic Polar Coordinate

In order to improve the robustness of different environments, this paper uses the polar coordinate transformation to improve the phase correlation algorithm, which can adapt to the situation of rotation, scaling and displacement.

Step 1: The image $I_1(x, y)$ and $I_2(x, y)$ are converted to $I_1'(u, v)$ after Fourier transform. When $I_1$ and $I_2$ exist translation, rotation, and scaling, the relationship is:

$$I_2(x, y) = I_1(\lambda x \cos\theta_0 + \lambda y \sin\theta_0 - \Delta x, -\lambda x \sin\theta_0 + \lambda y \cos\theta_0 - \Delta y) \quad (1)$$

$\lambda$ is scaling ratio, $\theta_0$ is rotation angle, and $\Delta x$ and $\Delta y$ are translation distances.

$$I_2'(u, v) = \frac{e^{-j2\pi(u\Delta x + v\Delta y)}}{\lambda^2} I_1'((u\cos\theta_0 + v\sin\theta_0)/\lambda, (-u\sin\theta_0 + v\cos\theta_0)/\lambda) \quad (2)$$

Step 2: $\rho = \sqrt{u^2 + v^2}$, $\theta = \arctan(u/v)$, transform the space of the image to the logarithmic polar space:

$$\left| I_2'(\rho\cos\theta, \rho\sin\theta) \right| = \left| I_1'((\rho\cos(\theta - \theta_0)/\lambda, \rho\sin(\theta - \theta_0)/\lambda)) \right| \quad (3)$$

Step 3: $\eta = \log\rho$, $\eta_0 = \log\lambda$, $M_1$ and $M_2$ are the models of $I_1'$ and $I_2'$, $M_2(\eta, \theta) = M_1(\eta - \eta_0, \theta - \theta_0)$. The conjugate power spectrum of $M_2(u, v)$ is $M_2^*(u, v)$. After normalization, the cross power spectrum of the image is expressed as follows:

$$\frac{M_1(u, v)M_2^*(u, v)}{\left| M_1(u, v)M_2^*(u, v) \right|} = e^{-j2\pi(u\eta_0 + v\theta_0)} \quad (4)$$

Step 4: After the inverse Fourier transform, the impulse function is obtained.

$$F^{-1}[e^{-j2\pi(u\eta_0 + v\theta_0)}] = \delta(\eta - \eta_0, \theta - \theta_0) \quad (5)$$

The position of the peak of impulse function means the size of the scaling ratio $\lambda$ and the angle $\theta_0$ of rotation. Inverse transform $I_2$ according to the scaling ratio and the rotation angle, then the translation distance $(\Delta x, \Delta y)$ is calculated with $I_1$ by the phase correlation method.

## 3 Registration and Feature Purification

### 3.1 Corner Extraction

The Harris algorithm detects the corner points by the change of the gray level after moving the local sliding window. Make $I(x, y)$ a gray value at $(x, y)$, $w(x, y)$ is a Gauss filter, and the horizontal vertical position of the window is u and v. $E(u, v)$ is an autocorrelation function in any direction, that is the sum of gray scale error in the window. The expressions of $E(u, v)$ and $w(x, y)$ are as follows:

610    D. Li et al.

$$E(u,v) = \sum_{x,y} w(x,y)[I(x+u,y+v) - I(x,y)]^2 \quad w(x,y) = \frac{1}{2\pi\sigma^2}e^{-\frac{(x^2+y^2)}{2\sigma^2}} \quad (6)$$

The Gauss window function $w(x,y)$ increases the weight of pixels near the center point. $I(x+u,y+v) - I(x,y)$ is the gradient of the image, $\sigma$ is the standard deviation. After the formula (6) is carried out by Taylor's expansion and neglecting the high term, the matrix form of $E(u,v)$ and M are as follows.

$$E(u,v) \cong [u,v]M\begin{bmatrix}u\\v\end{bmatrix} \quad M = \sum_{x,y} w(x,y)\begin{bmatrix}I_x^2 & I_xI_y\\I_xI_y & I_y^2\end{bmatrix} = w(x,y) * \begin{bmatrix}I_x^2 & I_xI_y\\I_xI_y & I_y^2\end{bmatrix} \quad (7)$$

$I_x$ and $I_y$ are the partial derivatives of the $x,y$. $A = I_x^2 * w$, $B = I_y^2 * w$, $C = (I_xI_y) * w$, the corner response function is shown by the following formula.

$$R = \det M - k(\operatorname{tr} M)^2 = (AB - C^2)^2 - k(A+B)^2 \quad (8)$$

The $\sigma_D$ and $s\sigma_D$ are the scale space integral and the differential factor respectively and matrix M is expressed as:

$$M = s\sigma_D^2 w(x,y,\sigma_D) * \begin{bmatrix} I_x^2(x,y,s\sigma_D) & I_x(x,y,s\sigma_D)I_y(x,y,s\sigma_D)\\ I_x(x,y,s\sigma_D)I_y(x,y,s\sigma_D) & I_y^2(x,y,s\sigma_D) \end{bmatrix} \quad (9)$$

## 3.2    Feature Registration

After the corner points are extracted, the feature matching is performed by the normalized cross correlation coefficient. The feature point is centered in a square window $\omega$. The NCC value as a matching principle. $\bar{I}_1$ and $\bar{I}_2$ are the mean value of the gray level of the square window pixels to be matched. When the matching method based on NCC is affected by illumination, scale transformation and noise, the matching accuracy is reduced. Window size is $(2N+1) \times (2N+1)$. $\bar{I}_1$, $\bar{I}_2$ and NCC are expressed as follows:

$$\bar{I}_1 = \frac{1}{(2N+1)^2}\sum_{x,y\in\omega} I_1(x,y)$$

$$\bar{I}_2 = \frac{1}{(2N+1)^2}\sum_{x,y\in\omega} I_2(x,y)$$

$$NCC = \frac{\sum\limits_{x,y\in\omega}[I_1(x,y) - \bar{I}_1][I_2(x,y) - \bar{I}_2]}{\sqrt{\sum\limits_{x,y\in\omega}[I_1(x,y) - \bar{I}_1]^2}\sqrt{\sum\limits_{x,y\in\omega}[I_2(x,y) - \bar{I}_2]^2}} \quad (10)$$

## 3.3   Ransac Algorithm Improvement and Splicing

In order to reduce error matching, an improved Ransac algorithm can eliminate the mismatch feature points. Nine matching points are more convenient to verify the temporary model, it can timely re-select the random sample set.

The maximum and minimum of the coordinates of the matching points are selected from the reference image $I_1$. The matching feature points are divided into M*M blocks. This paple takes $M = 6$. Randomly select 9 different blocks in the $I_1$ and randomly select a matching point from each of the 9 blocks to constitute the sample set with 9 corresponding matching points in image $I_2$. As shown in the following formula, $h_{11}$, ..., $h_{32}$ are degree of freedom.

$$\begin{bmatrix} x \\ y \\ 1 \end{bmatrix} = h \begin{bmatrix} x' \\ y' \\ 1 \end{bmatrix} = \begin{bmatrix} h_{11} & h_{12} & h_{13} \\ h_{21} & h_{22} & h_{23} \\ h_{31} & h_{32} & 1 \end{bmatrix} \begin{bmatrix} x' \\ y' \\ 1 \end{bmatrix} \tag{11}$$

Check whether ninth pairs of matching points are support sets for the basic matrix of the temporary model, if not, 9 pairs of matching points are re-selected. Repeat the Step 2, if it is the support set, the temporary model matrix h is considered as a candidate matrix h. Iteratively calculates the minimum value of the error function $E$ of the matching point pairs, and updates the matrix h, $E = \sum_{i=1}^{P} e_i^2 = \sum_{i=1}^{P} [I_2(x_i', y_i') - I_1(x_i, y_i)]^2$.

## 3.4   Image Fusion

The NSCT algorithm is composed of non sampling Pyramid and non sampling directional filters. While maintaining the translation invariance, it has good direction selectivity, time frequency localization, and multi-resolution characteristics.

Step 1: Suppose $A(x, y)$ and $B(x, y)$ are the overlapped regions. After multiscale decomposition, it can get a series of subband $A_l^k$ and $B_l^k$, $l = 1, 2, 3, ..., L$, L is the largest number of layers of decomposition.

Step 2: For the low frequency subband, the image change is slow, and the direct average fusion method is used, $AB_L^0 = (A_L^0 + B_L^0)/2$.

Step 3: For the high frequency sub-band, it reflects the sensitive edges and details of the human eye. Using high frequency subband weighted fusion method based on regional variance saliency. As shown in formula (12):

$$AB_l^k(x, y) = \begin{cases} \begin{cases} (1 - w)A_l^k + wB_l^k & G(A) \geq G(B) \\ wA_l^k + (1 - w)B_l^k & G(A) < G(B) \end{cases} & M \geq T \\ \begin{cases} A_l^k & G(A) \geq G(B) \\ B_l^k & G(A) < G(B) \end{cases} & M < T \end{cases}$$

$$w = 0.5 - 0.5 \left( \frac{1 - M}{1 - T} \right) \tag{12}$$

Step 4: Reconstructed image and output fused image.

## 4 Experimental Results and Analysis Conclusion

As shown in Fig. 1(f)–(h) are the energy distributions of (a) (b), (a) (c), (a) (d) impulse function respectively. According to the information of large peak parameters, the location of overlapping regions is roughly estimated to reduce the extraction range of feature points in precise registration. Because there is no overlap area in (a) (e), so there is no maximum prominence peak in (i).

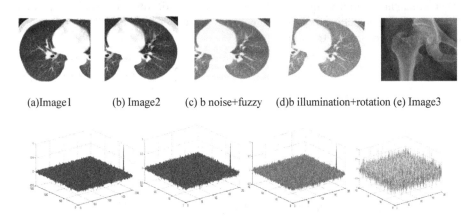

(a)Image1        (b) Image2        (c) b noise+fuzzy    (d)b illumination+rotation (e) Image3

(f)ab impulse function (g)ac impulse function   (h)ad impulse function  (i)ae impulse function

**Fig. 1.** Distribution of impulse function

Figure 2 compares the NCC matching method with the new method. (a) is the result of NCC matching, threshold selection is 0.6. Because of the low resolution, there are a lot of mismatching points. (b) is the result of the improved Ransac algorithm in this paper, the mismatch was removed. (c)–(g) are the matching results under the changes of scaling, noise, rotation, brightness and perspective transformation. (h) is the result of mixing the scaling, rotation and the perspective transformation.

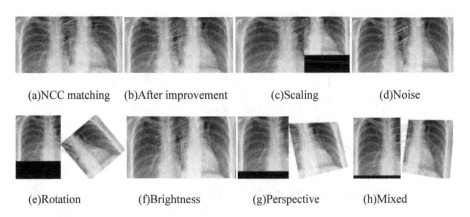

(a)NCC matching    (b)After improvement        (c)Scaling            (d)Noise

(e)Rotation          (f)Brightness          (g)Perspective          (h)Mixed

**Fig. 2.** Image registration

Table 1 is the transformation matrix and corners information of the Fig. 2(c)–(h). The table sets up the parameter values of the degree of freedom for the matrix H between images, and describes the number of points in the image and the number of the matched corners.

**Table 1.** Corner registration and transformation matrix

|  | Scaling | | | Noise | | | Rotation | | |
|---|---|---|---|---|---|---|---|---|---|
| H | 1.4396 | −0.0363 | 75.5787 | 0.9102 | −0.0404 | 75.4524 | 0.8076 | −0.6124 | 34.1210 |
|  | −0.0279 | 1.4439 | 33.8658 | −0.0323 | 0.9288 | 34.2291 | 0.6703 | 0.7795 | −41.4569 |
|  | −0.0004 | −0.0004 | 1.0000 | −0.0005 | −0.0005 | 1.0000 | 0.0001 | 0.0002 | 1.0000 |
| Right image | 64 | | | 117 | | | 168 | | |
| Matching points | 16 | | | 18 | | | 15 | | |
|  | Brightness | | | Perspective | | | Mixed | | |
| H | 0.9666 | 0.0003 | 75.2576 | 0.7379 | −0.1229 | 80.2946 | 1.1633 | 0.3355 | 44.1548 |
|  | −0.0203 | 0.9974 | 33.2290 | −0.0477 | 1.1097 | 6.3354 | −0.0723 | 1.2982 | 21.4007 |
|  | −0.0002 | 0.0000 | 1.0000 | −0.0018 | 0.0009 | 1.0000 | −0.0001 | 0.0013 | 1.0000 |
| Right image | 107 | | | 176 | | | 147 | | |
| Matching points | 22 | | | 16 | | | 15 | | |

Figures 3 and 4 are the comparison of stitching results, (a) is a image of before stitching. (b)–(d) are the results of direct stitching, average gradient stitching and new method stitching. After the fusion and reconstruction of the decomposed low frequency and high frequency subbands, (d) shows the image joint is more smooth and more clear.

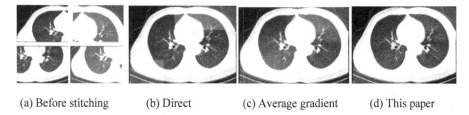

  (a) Before stitching      (b) Direct      (c) Average gradient      (d) This paper

**Fig. 3.** Comparison of lungs stitching results

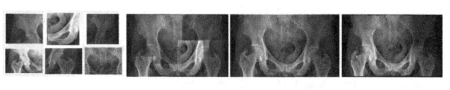

  (a) Before stitching      (b) Direct      (c) Average gradient      (d) This paper

**Fig. 4.** Comparison of hip stitching results

## 5  Conclusion

The new algorithm improves the phase correlation algorithm by using the logarithmic polar coordinate transformation, so that it can adapt to the situation of scaling, rotation and translation between the images adaptively. After using NCC normalized cross-correlation coefficient to extract Harris corners at overlapping positions, the improved Ransac algorithm is used to precisely purify, optimize model parameters. In the mosaic process, we use NSCT transform algorithm to design fusion strategy, which solves the problem of noise accuracy, low resolution and low contrast interference and saves the cost of medical equipment.

**Acknowledgements.** This work is partly supported by the Key Laboratory of Intelligent Industrial Control Technology of Jiangsu Province Research Project(JSKLIIC201705), Xuzhou Science and Technology Plan Projects (KC18011, KC16SH010, KC17078), Major Project of Natural Science Research of the Jiangsu Higher Education Institutions of China (18KJA520012), Ministry of Housing and Urban-Rural Development Science and Technology Planning Project (2016-R2-060).

## References

1. Menon, H.P.: Issues involved in automatic selection and intensity based matching of feature points for MLS registration of medical images. In: International Conference on Advances in Computing, Communications and Informatics, pp. 787–792 (2017)
2. Jia, J., Tang, C.K.: Image stitching using structure deformation. IEEE Trans. Pattern Anal. Mach. Intell. **34**(4), 617–631 (2008)
3. Zhang, F., Liu, F.: Parallax-tolerant image stitching. In: Computer Vision and Pattern Recognition, pp. 3262–3269 (2014)
4. Chia, W.C., Chew, L.W., Ang, L.M., et al.: Low memory image stitching and compression for WMSN using strip-based processing. Int. J. Sens. Netw. **11**(1), 22–32 (2012)
5. Jiang, D., Wang, W., Shi, L., Song, H.: A compressive sensing-based approach to end-to-end network traffic reconstruction. IEEE Trans. Netw. Sci. Eng. (2018). https://doi.org/10.1109/tnse.2018.2877597
6. Jiang, D., Huo, L., Song, H.: Rethinking behaviors and activities of base stations in mobile cellular networks based on big data analysis. IEEE Trans. Netw. Sci. Eng. **1**(1), 1–12 (2018)
7. Jiang, D., Han, Y., Miao, L., et al.: Dynamic access approach to multiple channels in pervasive wireless multimedia communications for technology enhanced learning. J. Intell. Fuzzy Syst. **31**(5), 2497–2509 (2016)
8. El-Melegy, M.T.: RANSAC algorithm with sequential probability ratio test for robust training of feed-forward neural networks. In: International Joint Conference on Neural Networks, vol. 3, no. 14, pp. 3256–3263 (2011)
9. Olofsson, K., Holmgren, J.: Tree stem and height measurements using terrestrial laser scanning and the RANSAC algorithm. Remote Sens. **6**(5), 4323–4344 (2014)
10. Yang, Y., Tong, S., Huang, S., et al.: Multifocus image fusion based on NSCT and focused area detection. IEEE Sens. J. **15**(5), 2824–2838 (2015)

# "Smart Entity" – How to Build DEVS Models from Large Amount of Data and Small Amount of Knowledge?

Thierry Antoine-Santoni, Bastien Poggi, Evelyne Vittori,
Ho Van Hieux$^{(\boxtimes)}$, Marielle Delhom, and Antoine Aiello

University of Corsica, UMR CNRS SPE, Corte, France
`{antoine-santoni_t,ho_vh}@univ-corse.fr`

**Abstract.** University of Corsica and CNRS are working on a scientific program called "Smart Paesi". This project focus on a sustainable rural territories development using advanced artificial intelligence concepts in order to adapt smart city concept (including sustainable development, ICT with by example wireless sensors network, education, e-citizenship, governance) to rural territories and their specificities. In this paper, we introduce a new approach combining discrete event modelling concepts and machine learning methods. This work is a first step towards the conception of a generic and scalable framework allowing model generation from large amount of data.

**Keywords:** Machine learning · DEVS formalism · Model generation · Decision supports · Internet of Thing · Big data

## 1 Introduction

In the recent past, boosted by artificial intelligence (AI) progress, a horde of automation and acceleration technologies in the IT field have been proposed to resolve smart cities problematics with great success [1, 2]. Indeed fewer have been proposed for people who live in rural and isolated territories.

In the same time, we assist to the deployment of low cost Wireless Sensor Network (WSN) over all territories. Due to the success of IoT [3], related technologies have generated an exponential increase of collected data. The challenge today is to explore the potential of this amount of data over artificial intelligence process base and machine learning (ML) in a modeling and simulation context as describe in Fig. 1.

Supported by a "European Fund for Research and Development" (ERDF) and the "Regional Council of Corsica" (RCC), the "Smart Village Scientific Program" (SVSP) [4] proposes newer approaches based on the concept of "real-world people-centric applications" [5]. Built in partnership with two company: EDF (Electricity of France) and SITEC (IT Service Company) the project focuses on four areas of research: environmental data gathering, data visualization, e-democracy and simulation. This paper deals with the last.

H. Song et al. (Eds.): SIMUtools 2019, LNICST 295, pp. 615–626, 2019.
https://doi.org/10.1007/978-3-030-32216-8_60

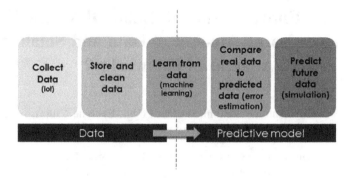

**Fig. 1.** From data to predictive model

Our goal is to provide a robust framework allowing an easy integration of collected data inside a modelling and simulation process by replacing "physical model" with "data model".

## 2 M&S, Data and Machine Learning

Recently, researches in the field of Modeling and Simulation (M&S) have intensively evolved towards hybrid approaches combining M&S background and Artificial Intelligence advances in data mining and machine learning. Nowadays, complementarity of both approaches seems to appear as an evidence. Miller and Buckley [6] argue that they should be used in conjunction through a "modeling continuum" and illustrate their vision upon examples from health care and supply chain management. In [7], the authors provide an extensive comparison of both approaches called respectively "simulation modeling" and "data modeling" and detail their advantages and limitations. They demonstrate their complementarity and suggest a new modeling approach involving both of them. In according to Andreas Tolk [8], the next generation of Modeling & Simulation applications will integrate big data and deep learning tools and methods: "bringing all the three topics together will create synergy that will allow us to significantly improve our services to others science".

An interesting review about ways of combining both approaches in the context of manufacturing and logistics is done in [9]. They focus on the integration of Machine Learning (ML) process from a simulation perspective.

According to literature in the field of M&S, the main benefit of the use of Machine Learning is to improve the efficiency simulation analysis. In other words, it may help to reduce simulation cost. This is particularly useful in the context of complex models requiring extensive resource allocation and leading to very expensive experiments. Recently [10], it has been proposed to use machine learning mechanisms inside a DEVS simulator in order to optimize simulation execution by learning from past simulations.

Wang and Marek-Sadowska [11] suggest a double level learning flow applied to the field of circuit design. ML is first used to reduce input samples by discarding unimportant samples. The selected inputs are then predicted by ML rather than simulated and so simulation cost is reduced.

In the case study of a green-house control system introduced in [4], the global model is a "simulation oriented" one but it internally uses results given by a "data oriented model" ("the controller"). Furthermore, data obtained as outputs from the simulation model enhance the dataset used for the "controller" data oriented model thru another data model called "Optimal Controller Model". Experimental results show that the use of such hybrid model improves significantly control performance and reduce the rate of error.

These hybrid modeling approaches may also be related to "grey-box" modelling in the field of "system (or model) identification" [12]. Grey-box models are defined as combination of "data driven models" (black-box), and "physical based models" (white-box). They combine physics based methods for building the model structure and use data driven to estimate the model parameters. They also benefit from the advantages of both approaches: generalization capabilities from physical models and better accuracy from data driven ones.

On the other hand, M&S models may be used to help in building ML models. Results from simulation may provide data sets allowing to construct data-oriented models. In the field of personalized medicine [13], it shown that the prediction of a cancer treatment efficiency cannot be processed using "pure data" approaches. Authors suggest to integrate simulation as a "pre-processing step in a machine learning pipeline to include detailed expert knowledge".

Similar hybrid approaches are introduced in the domain of "smart manufacturing" [14]. In a case study, simulation results are used to generate data streams that can be used by a diagnostic analytics application ("data oriented model").

In summary, ML may assist M&S in building input samples, estimating unknown input parameters, analyzing output data and validating simulation results. M&S can also assist ML by providing data sets as output results from simulation process.

In the context of smart village, according to the diversity of data and associated processes, it clearly appears that we need to combine both data centered and simulation based approaches. However, we think that defining an integration framework will be a guaranty of the global model coherence.

In order to provide a high level of genericity and interoperability between models and their formalism we choose to build our approach on Discrete Event System Specification (DEVS) formalism. We introduce the concept of "Smart-Entity" (SE) as a specific DEVS model. Background on the formalism is described in next part.

## 3 Back Ground: DEVS Formalism

DEVS is a modelling and simulation formalism proposed by Zeigler [15]. Due to its success since its publication and a large community of users, high number of extension DEVS extensions have been proposed to enrich the classic formalism: dynamic DEVS [16], parallel DEVS [17], Cell-DEVS [18], etc. Due to the number of extensions DEVS is today one of the main used formalism for modeling and simulation in research teams.

This formalism can be considered as a multi-formalism [19] integrating other formalisms such as Petri-Net [20] or differential equations [21].

DEVS allows to represent a wide range of systems. It has been used with success for many applications in various fields such as: agriculture, military, anthropology, engineering, ecology, etc.

The main idea beside this formalism is an explicit separation between modeling description and simulation core. The formalism is based on two mains concepts: "Atomic model" (AM) and "Coupled model" (CM). AM describes the system behavior in a modular way and CM describes the system structure by abstraction levels and model encapsulations. This genericity of model description provides a reusable abstract simulator independent of studied systems.

### 3.1    Atomic DEVS Model

Atomic DEVS model (AM) is the lowest level of abstraction of studied system. It describes the component behavior. This model is defined by the following structure:

$$AM = <XY, S, \delta ext, \delta int, \lambda, ta > \qquad (1)$$

Where:

- X: the set of input ports of the model defined by tuple (port, value)
- Y: the set of output ports of the model defined by tuple (port, value)
- S: the set of model states
- $\delta$ext: the external transition function activated when events are received on model inputs port
- $\delta$int: the internal transition function activated during state change (state time exceed)
- $\lambda$: the ouput function activated when outputs are produced by model
- ta: time advance function defining state duration for each model state

Complex systems are described over several atomic models. Inputs and outputs (IO) of model must be connected to others models IO. This part is insured by coupled DEVS model (CM).

### 3.2    Coupled DEVS Model

CM describe model structure over interconnections and encapsulations. Indeed CM can encapsulate AM and CM models allowing different granularity of system description. This models are described by the following tuple:

CM = <X, Y, D, EIC, IC, EOC, Select>
Where:

- X: the set of input ports of the model defined by tuple (port, value)
- Y: the set of output ports of the model defined by tuple (port, value)
- D: the set of components (AM or CM)
- EIC: External Input Coupling (input to input)

- IC: Internal Coupling (input to output)
- EOC: External Ouput Coupling (output to output)
- Select: selection function used to ordinate model execution when their states expire at the same time.

After this description of DEVS formalism we introduce our approach of Smart Entity".

## 4  Our Approach "Smart Entity"

We choose to build our approach on DEVS formalism in order to maintain a high level of genericity in the decision support framework.

Our framework will allow to define three kinds of DEVS models:

- "white-box" model: atomic or coupled classical DEVS models
- "black-box" model: DEVS atomic wrapper model that encapsulates ML capabilities ("Smart entity Model").
- "grey-box" model: coupled models including at least one Smart entity.

In this part, we focus on "black-box" model by introducing the concept of Smart-Entity Model. We detail structural and behavioral conceptual representations of the Smart Entity Model and we show how these capabilities are embedded into a DEVS atomic model.

### 4.1  SEM Conceptual Structure

The "smart entity model" (SEM) is a generic model based on data approach modeling concepts. As describe on Fig. 2, the model is defined with a fixed number of inputs and outputs ports. This constraint maintains a high level of interoperability between different model on smart entities to represent a global system.

In our approach, two inputs ports are defined: "Environmental Data" (XE) and "Decision data" (XD). XD port can be optional if SE represents an entity on witch no influences can be made. The XE port is connected to outputs of models that represent the unmanageable phenomena of studied system as weather or environmental events (e.g. fire, storm, etc.). The XD port is connected to models that represent the manageable interactions such as decision or users choices.

Two outputs ports are also defined. The outputs ports are: "Interactions" (YI) and "Results" (YR). The YI port is connected to other SEM models in case of interactions between them. The YR port is connected to a "decision model" (DM) in order to estimate efficiency of different decisions scenarios by collecting and observing decisions effects on results. Their outputs values are computed by ML methods provided inside the SEM attributes.

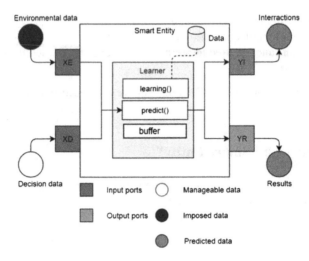

**Fig. 2.** Conceptual structure of SEM

As illustrated in Fig. 2, the SEM also contains a buffer. The goal is to increase the prediction precision by considering previous received data without compromising simulation coherence. Indeed many applications need more than one previous value to predict next value (e.g. past three day rain to predict day rain). In this case SE stores the previous values in a buffer. When prediction function is called, this buffer is passed as an input parameter. At each new event on input port, this buffer is updated with the new value received.

### 4.2 SEM Dynamic Behavior

SEM execution can be decomposed in three parts: "learning", "testing" and "simuling". Transitions between these states are explain on Fig. 3.

At the beginning of process execution, SEM is in the "learning" state. During this state, the model is built from a dataset by using machine learning algorithms. When this step is over, SEM state turns into "testing". Model outputs are collected and analyzed. If their accuracy exceeds a specified threshold SEM state becomes "simuling". Otherwise it goes back to "learning" state and a new machine learning process is performed. At the end of simulations, if some new data has been added to the initial dataset, the size of the added data is quantified. If the increase is significant, a new learning process occurs.

Using of ML methods is based on the principle of "cross-validation". Usually the algorithms use 80% of data to make their learning process and 20% of data to make the validation process. This principle provides an estimation of prediction quality. We reproduce this concept in our architecture and we add the concept of "choosing the best method" for SEM linked dataset.

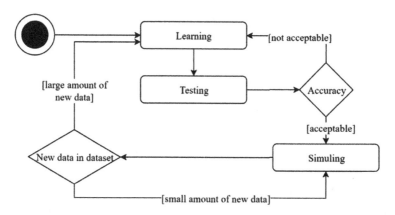

**Fig. 3.** Conceptual representation of SEM states

During "learning" step, the SEM generates several learners based on different machine learning algorithms family. The "learning ()" method is called with database link as parameter. The different algorithms provided by SEM are listed in Table 1.

**Table 1.** Algorithm provided by smart entity

| Category | Method name |
|---|---|
| Linear Regressor | Linear Regression (LR) Huber Regression (HR] Random Sample Concesus Regression (RSCR) |
| Generalized linear model | Stochastic Gradient Descent (SGD) |
| Support vector Regression | SVR with kernel |
| Gaussian Processes Regrettion | Gaussian Process Regression (GPR) |
| Ensemble methods | Kernel Ridge Regression (KRR) Bayesian Ridge Regression (BRR) |
| Decision Tree | Decision Tree Regressor Random Forest Regressor Extra Trees Regressor Gradient Bosting for regression |
| Neural Networks | Neural Network with 2 hidden layers (NN2) Convolutional Neural Network (CNN) Recurrent Neural Network (RNN) Bi-directional Recurrent Neural Network (LSTM) |
| Others | Least Angle Regression (LAR) Automatic Relevance Determination Regression (ARDR) |

During "testing" step, "loss value" (LV) is computed for each instanced learner. Different equations are introduced in literature. In our models, LV is represented by men squared error (MSE) and given by:

$$MSE = \frac{1}{N} \sum_{(x,y) \in D} (y - prediction(x))^2 \tag{2}$$

where

- N is the dataset size
- x is the input of the prediction function
- y is the observed value

The learner with minimum LV is selected to produce model behavior. During simulation when data are received on inputs port, they are combined with buffer values to make predictions. At regular interval the SEM checks the size of its learning database. If number of new records exceed a specified threshold, a new "learning" step occurs. It allows to perform better predictions over simulation time.

### 4.3    SEM as a DEVS Atomic Model

As said before, SEM outputs are generated by a learner object encapsulated inside the SEM. To make an efficient learning, this object needs a large amount a data, pretreated and stored inside a database. Each record is described by

$$<XE, XD, YI, YR> \tag{3}$$

Where:

- XE: {XE1,...,XEn}: the inputs environmental data
- XD: {XD1,...,XDn}: the decision data
- YI = {YI1, ..., YIn}: the results (interactions)
- YR = {YR1, ..., YRn}: the results

This record is enriched by model state variables C added to each record to enhance the learning process with model characteristics. At this end of configuration process, the SEM is ready to learn from the following dataset:

$$<XE, XD, YI, YR, C> \tag{4}$$

This conception allows us to define a SEM as a DEVS atomic model wrapper encapsulating ML capabilities.

The input sets XE and XD are linked to X values of DEVS atomic model (AM). The output sets YI and YR are linked to Y values of DEVS atomic model. C values are linked to DEVS states (S).

Concerning the DEVS functions, they are the same for each SEM independently of modelized system. The δext function stores input values and updates the buffer (function save). The λ function calls the "predict" function of learner and sends value on specified output port. The δint function checks the SEM database and starts a new learning process when needed.

The mapping between DEVS concepts and ML concepts is summarized in Fig. 4.

| DEVS | init | X | | Y | | S | δext() | δint() | λ() | ta() |
|------|------|---|---|---|---|---|--------|--------|-----|------|
| SEM | learning() | XE | XD | YI | YR | C | save() | check_data() | predict() | ta() |

**Fig. 4.** Analogy between DEVS & SEM

## 5  First Results

In order to validate the SE concepts, we build our own machine learning library called "PredictSV". This library is based on several well know Python optimized and scalable libraries: Kereas, Scikit-Learn, Pytorch and Tensorflow. This "PredictSV" library not only merges several ML libraries but also tries to automatize the data pretreatment (e.g. normalization) and the method configuration process in a not fastidious way for the modeler. These aspects are not presented in this paper.

Before applying the SEM on collected data from SVSP, we choose to use robust datasets to compare obtained results with literature. In next step of our development, these datasets will be replaced by SVSP data that we are collecting today.

We choose a dataset relevant to sustainable development as studied in (SVSP): "Weather in Madrid" (WIM). This data has been linked to a SEM integrated in a DEVS architecture as described in Fig. 5.

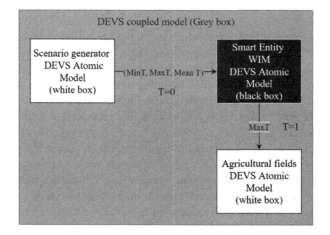

**Fig. 5.** Example of SM utilization for ECE dataset

Smart Entity wrapping has been tested in different ways considering different number of features. For WIM dataset, we try to predict day+1 temperature from minimum, maximum, mean temperature of 8 previous day. An example of best obtained results with double layers neural network is visible on Fig. 6.

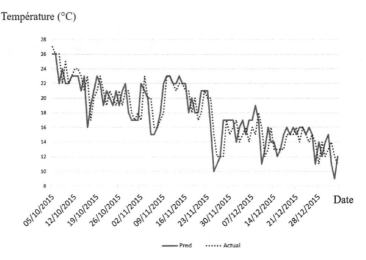

**Fig. 6.** Comparison of SM predict data and real data

First results confirm the interest of our unified approach to approximate physical model behavior.

## 6  Conclusion

Smart Village is a scientific program which combines the collected data using Wireless Sensor Networks, data storage, visualization and prediction.

For the prediction, our goal is to propose a generic model using DEVS formalism whose inputs are produced by Machine Learning methods using large amount of data. This model had to be compatible with classic DEVS models in order to benefit of available models. The "smart entity model" offers a promising solution to this problematic for system on which user dispose of big data but few knowledges.

First results have replaced a model of weather with an acceptable precision level during a DEVS simulation. At this step of our research, we need to perform other tests on different systems and test interactions between different smart entities. Moreover many improvement must be proposed. Indeed, data pretreatment is a central task in machine learning field. We need to propose efficient software solution helping modeler to exploit efficiently provided data. We also need to develop an efficient ML method comparison process in order to provide to the SEM the better predict core.

An important part of our work will be to integrate SEM inside combinational optimization process to provide an intuitive but powerful tool helping rural decision makers to benefit of most recent advances in M&S, ML and optimization fields.

# References

1. Silva, B.N., Khan, M., Han, K.: Towards sustainable smart cities: a review of trends, architectures, components, and open challenges in smart cities. Sustain. Cities Soc. **38**, 697–713 (2018)
2. Kitchin, R.: The real-time city? Big data and smart urbanism. GeoJournal **79**(1), 1–14 (2014)
3. Stankovic, J.A.: Research directions for the internet of things. IEEE Internet Things J. **1**(1), 3–9 (2014)
4. https://smartvillage.universita.corsica/
5. Campbell, A.T., et al.: The rise of people-centric sensing. IEEE Internet Comput. **12**(4), 12–21 (2008)
6. Miller, J.A., Cotterell, M.E., Buckley, S.J.: Supporting a modeling continuum in scalation: from predictive analytics to simulation modeling. In: Proceedings of the 2013 Winter Simulation Conference: Simulation: Making Decisions in a Complex World, pp. 1191–1202 (2013)
7. Kim, B.S., Kang, B.G., Choi, S.H., Kim, T.G.: Data modeling versus simulation modeling in the big data era: case study of a greenhouse control system. Simulation **93**(7), 579–594 (2017)
8. Tolk, A.: The next generation of modeling & simulation: integrating big data and deep learning. In: Proceedings of the Conference on Summer Computer Simulation, pp. 1–8 (2015)
9. Laroque, C., Skoogh, A., Gopalakrishnan, M.: Functional interaction of simulation and data analytics – potentials and existing use-cases. In: Wenzel, S., Peter, T. (eds.) Simulation in Produktion und Logistik 2017, Kassel University Press, Kassel, pp. 403–412 (2017)
10. Saadawi, H., Wainer, G., Pliego, G.: DEVS execution acceleration with machine learning. In: Proceedings of the Symposium on Theory of Modeling & Simulation (TMS-DEVS 2016), Pasadena, California (2016)
11. Wang, L.-C., Marek-Sadowska, M.: Machine Learning in Simulation-Based Analysis, pp. 57–64 (2015)
12. Afram, A., Janabi-Sharifi, F.: Review of modeling methods for HVAC systems. Appl. Thermal Eng. **67**(1–2), 507–519 (2014)
13. Deist, T., Patti, A., Wang, Z., Krane, D., Sorenson, T., Craft, D.: Simulation assisted machine learning. arXiv preprint arXiv:1802.05688 (2018)
14. Shao, G., Shin, S.-J., Jain, S.: Data analytics using simulation for smart manufacturing. In: Proceedings of the 2014 Winter Simulation Conference, pp. 2192–2203 (2014)
15. Zeigler, B.P., Kim, T.G., Praehofer, H.: Theory of Modeling and Simulation, 2nd edn. Academic Press, Inc., Orlando (2000)
16. Barros, F.J.: Modeling formalisms for dynamic structure systems. ACM Trans. Model. Comput. Simul. **7**(4), 501–515 (1997)
17. Chow, A.C.H., Zeigler, B.P.: Parallel DEVS: a parallel, hierarchical, modular, modeling formalism. In: Proceedings of the 26th Conference on Winter Simulation, San Diego, CA, USA, pp. 716–722 (1994)
18. Wainer, G.A.: Cellular modeling with Cell-DEVS: a discrete-event cellular automata formalism. In: Wąs, J., Sirakoulis, G.C., Bandini, S. (eds.) ACRI 2014. LNCS, vol. 8751, pp. 6–15. Springer, Cham (2014). https://doi.org/10.1007/978-3-319-11520-7_2
19. Vangheluwe, H.L.M.: DEVS as a common denominator for multi-formalism hybrid systems modelling. In: CACSD. Conference Proceedings. IEEE International Symposium on Computer-Aided Control System Design (Cat. No.00TH8537), pp. 129–134 (2000)

20. Boukelkoul, S., Redjimi, M.: Mapping between Petri nets and DEVS models. In: 2013 3rd International Conference on Information Technology and e-Services (ICITeS), pp. 1–6 (2013)
21. Kofman, E., Junco, S.: Quantized-state systems: a DEVS approach for continuous system simulation. Trans. Soc. Comput. Simul. Int. **18**(3), 123–132 (2001)

# Optimal Scheduling User Number in Massive MIMO with QoS Requirement

Lei Chen[✉] and Lu Zhang

Jiangsu Province Key Laboratory of Intelligent Industry Control Technology,
Xuzhou University of Technology, Xuzhou 221018, China
chenlei@xzit.edu.cn

**Abstract.** The Massive multiple-input multiple-output (MIMO) system can schedule dozens of end user equipment at each time slot, however, different quality-of-service (QoS) requirements needs different scheduling policy. Some QoS requirements of buffering services are related to the stability of long term transmit rate, and the instantaneous rate depends on the scheduling policy and channel state. Therefore it is difficult to build direct relationship between the QoS requirement and optimal scheduling user number at each time slot in Massive MIMO system. Based on the effective capacity (EC) theory, the relationship among the number of scheduling user, the QoS requirement and the effective transmit rate is built. The simulation result shows that EC can be described by a smooth function of the number of scheduled users and the QoS requirement.

**Keywords:** Massive MIMO · Quality of service · Quality of experience

## 1 Introduction

The huge differentiation among emerging mobile services poses the challenge to guarantee the quality-of-service (QoS). Some new technologies [1–3], such as compressive sensing and big data analysis, are proposed to predict the network traffic and user behavior. Based on network traffic analysis and user behavior analysis, new performance evaluation approaches [4] and routing schemes [5,6] are designed to guarantee the QoS and improve energy-efficiency. According to special QoS requirements, some refined network selection schemes [7] and user selection schemes [8] are designed in access network side. However, the instability of wireless access network is still the bottleneck to improve the end user experience. As two key technologies in the future 5G networks, Massive MIMO

This work is supported in part by the Natural Science Foundation of Jiangsu Province of China (No. BK20161165), the applied fundamental research Foundation of Xuzhou of China (No. KC17072), the Open Fund of the Jiangsu Province Key Laboratory of Intelligent Industry Control Technology, Xuzhou University of Technology. and the Ministry of Housing and Urban-Rural Development Science and Technology Planning Project (2016-R2-060).

H. Song et al. (Eds.): SIMUtools 2019, LNICST 295, pp. 627–632, 2019.
https://doi.org/10.1007/978-3-030-32216-8_61

and small cells are proposed to deal with increasing traffic data and diverse requirements. The base station adopting Massive multiple-input multiple-output (MIMO) technology is usually equipped with a few hundreds of antennas for simultaneously serving a large number of users. The researches have demonstrated that the large number of antennas can increase the spectral efficiency (SE), and effectively improve the end user experience [9]. Because the large number of users are scheduled simultaneously, The scheduling scheme is critical important to guarantee QoS. The first key problem in Massive MIMO scheduling should be the maximum number of user scheduled in a time slot under QoS constraint. In reference [10], a algorithm is proposed to compute the maximum number of user and the power allocation according to the QoS requirements for Massive MIMO. However, the QoS constraint mentioned in [10] is just related to the instantaneous rate. Generally, the QoS is affected by the jitter of a long term rate. Therefore, we analyze the relationship among the number of user, QoS constraint and achievable transmit rate in this paper.

## 2    Effective Capacity of Massive MIMO

We consider a massive MIMO cellular network where the BS of each cell equipped with an array of $M$ antennas communicates with $K$ single-antenna UEs at the time, out of a set of $N$ UEs which have unlimited demand for data. Each cell is assigned an index in the set $\mathcal{L}$. The geographical position of UE $k \in \{1, ..., K\}$ in cell $l \in \mathcal{L}$ is given by $\mathbf{z}_{lk} \in \mathbb{R}^2$. The time-frequency resources are divided into equal frames whose time and bandwidth is smaller or equal to the coherence time and the coherence bandwidth of all UEs respectively. Thus all the channel are static within the frame. Let $\mathbf{h}_{jlk} \in \mathbb{R}^N$ denote the channel response between BS $j$ and UE $k$ in cell $l$, which are drown as realizations from zero-mean circularly symmetric complex Gaussian distributions [11]:

$$h_{jlk} \sim \mathcal{CN}\left(0, d_j\left(\mathbf{z}_{lk}\mathbf{I}_M\right)\right) \tag{1}$$

where $\mathbf{I}_M$ is the $M \times M$ identity matrix. The function $d_j(\mathbf{z})$ gives the variance of the channel attenuation from BS $j$ to any UE position $\mathbf{z}$. Let $S$ be the amount of symbols transmitted in each frame, $B$ out of the $S$ symbols are reserved for pilot signaling. Thus the remaining $S-B$ symbols are allocated for payload data. The symbols have transmit power $p_{lk} = \frac{\rho}{d_{j(\mathbf{z}_{lk})}}$, where $\rho$ is a design parameter for the channel attenuation inversion policy. The policy make the average effective channel gain the same for all UEs:$\mathbb{E}\{p_{lk}\|\mathbf{h}_{llk}\|^2\} = M\rho$. The received download signal at UE $k$ in cell $j$ in a frame is given by:

$$y_{jk} = \sum_{l \in \mathcal{L}} \sum_{m=1}^{K} \mathbf{h}_{ljk}^T \mathbf{w}_{lm} x_{lm} + n_{jk} \tag{2}$$

where $(\cdot)^T$ denotes transpose, $x_{lm}$ is the symbol transmitted to UE $m$ in cell $l$, $w_{lm} \in \mathbb{C}^M$ is the corresponding precoding vector, and $\|w_{lm}\|^2$ is the allocated download transmit power. It can be expressed as

$$w_{lm} = \sqrt{\frac{p_{jk}}{\mathbb{E}_{\mathbf{h}}\{\|\mathbf{g}_{jk}\|^2\}}}\mathbf{g}_{jk} \tag{3}$$

where the average transmit power $p_{jk} \geq 0$ is a function of the UE position, but not the instantaneous channel realizations. The vector $\mathbf{g}_{jk} \in \mathbb{C}^M$ defines the spatial directivity of the transmission and is based on the acquired CSI. The SNIR is given by (see reference [12] for the power control policy):

$$SINR_{jk} = \frac{p_{jk}\frac{\mathbb{E}_{\mathbf{h}}\{\|\mathbf{g}_{jk}\mathbf{h}_{jjk}\|^2\}}{\mathbb{E}_{\mathbf{h}}\{\|\mathbf{g}_{jk}\|^2\}}}{\sum_{l\in\mathcal{L}}\sum_{m=1}^{K} p_{lm}\frac{\mathbb{E}_{\mathbf{h}}\{\|\mathbf{g}_{lm}\mathbf{h}_{ljk}\|^2\}}{\mathbb{E}_{\mathbf{h}}\{\|\mathbf{g}_{lm}\|^2\}} - p_{jk}\frac{\mathbb{E}_{\mathbf{h}}\{\|\mathbf{g}_{jk}\mathbf{h}_{jjk}\|^2\}}{\mathbb{E}_{\mathbf{h}}\{\|\mathbf{g}_{jk}\|^2\}} + \sigma^2}. \tag{4}$$

In reference [12], the achievable Spectral Efficiency in download of cell $j$ can be written by:

$$SE_j = K\left(1 - \frac{B}{S}\right)\log_2\left(1 + \frac{1}{I_j^{scheme}}\right) \tag{5}$$

where

$$I_j^{scheme} = \sum_{l\in\mathcal{L}_j(\beta)\backslash\{j\}}\left(\mu_{jl}^{(2)} + \frac{\mu_{jl}^2 + \left(\mu_{jl}^{(1)}\right)^2}{G^{scheme}}\right) \\ + \frac{\left(\sum_{l\in\mathcal{L}}\mu_{jl}^{(1)}Z_{jl}^{scheme} + \frac{\sigma^2}{\rho}\right)\left(\sum_{\ell\in\mathcal{L}_j(\beta)}\mu_{jl}^{(1)} + \frac{\sigma^2}{B\rho}\right)}{G^{scheme}} \tag{6}$$

where the $G^{scheme}$ and $Z_{jl}^{scheme}$ depends on the different receive combining schemes, $G^{MR} = M$ and $Z_{jl}^{scheme} = K$ with MR combining, while $G^{ZF} = M - k$ and

$$Z_{jl}^{ZF}\begin{cases} K\left(1 - \frac{\mu_{jl}^{(1)}}{\sum_{\ell\in\mathcal{L}_j(\beta)}\mu_{jl}^{(1)} + \frac{\sigma^2}{B\rho}}\right) & \text{if } l \in \mathcal{L}_j(\beta), \\ K & \text{if } l \notin \mathcal{L}_j(\beta). \end{cases} \tag{7}$$

The following notation was used:

$$\mu_{jl}^{(w)} = \mathbb{E}_{\mathbf{z}_{lm}}\left\{\left(\frac{d_j(\mathbf{z}_{lm})}{d_l(\mathbf{z}_{lm})}\right)^w\right\} \text{ for } w = 1, 2. \tag{8}$$

The QoS requirement is often formulated by

$$Pr\left(\max_{1\leq i\leq N} Q_i(0) > B\right) \leq \epsilon. \tag{9}$$

According to reference [13], for some large buffer size $B$, given the QoS constraint $\epsilon$ and by choosing $\theta = -\log(\epsilon)/B$, the QoS requirement can be expressed as an effective capacity (EC) problem:

$$\lambda \leq \min_{1\leq j\leq N} C_k(\theta), \tag{10}$$

where

$$C_k(\theta) = \frac{1}{\theta} \lim_{n \to \infty} \frac{-1}{n} \ln \mathbb{E}\left(e^{-\theta \sum_{t=1}^n r_k(t)}\right), \tag{11}$$

the $r_k(t)$ is the rate allocated to user $k$ in cell $j$ at time $t$. We assume that the scheduling scheme at the base station stochastically picks the $K$ users out of a set of the $N$ active users for transmission, thus the $r_k$ can be written as:

$$r_k(t) = \begin{cases} \frac{N_f}{K}\left(1 - \frac{B}{S}\right)\log_2\left(1 + \frac{1}{I_j^{scheme}}\right), & \text{w.p. } \frac{K}{N}, \\ 0, & \text{w.p. } 1 - \frac{K}{N}. \end{cases} \tag{12}$$

Let $\nu = N_f\left(1 - \frac{B}{S}\right)\log_2\left(1 + \frac{1}{I_j^{scheme}}\right)$, the EC of user $k$ is rewritten as:

$$
\begin{aligned}
C_k(\theta) &= \frac{1}{\theta} \lim_{n \to \infty} \frac{-1}{n} \ln \sum_{\tau=0}^n \left( e^{-\theta \tau \frac{\nu}{K}} P\left\{ \left(\sum_{t=1}^n r_k(t)\right) = \tau \frac{\nu}{K} \right\} \right) \\
&= \frac{1}{\theta} \lim_{n \to \infty} \frac{-1}{n} \ln \sum_{\tau=0}^n \left( e^{-\theta \tau \frac{\nu}{K}} \binom{n}{\tau} \left(\frac{K}{N}\right)^\tau \left(1 - \frac{K}{N}\right)^{(n-\tau)} \right) \\
&= \frac{1}{\theta} \lim_{n \to \infty} \frac{-1}{n} \ln \sum_{\tau=0}^n \left( \binom{n}{\tau} \left(e^{-\theta \frac{\nu}{K}} \frac{K}{N}\right)^\tau \left(1 - \frac{K}{N}\right)^{(n-\tau)} \right) \\
&= \frac{1}{\theta} \lim_{n \to \infty} \frac{-1}{n} \ln \left[1 - \frac{K}{N}\left(1 - e^{-\theta \frac{\nu}{K}}\right)\right]^n \\
&= \frac{-1}{\theta} \ln \left[1 - \frac{K}{N}\left(1 - e^{-\frac{\theta \nu}{K}}\right)\right].
\end{aligned}
\tag{13}
$$

While $\theta \to \infty$ the EC is 0, when $\theta \to 0$ the EC is $\frac{K}{N}\frac{N_f}{K}\left(1 - \frac{B}{S}\right)\log_2\left(1 + \frac{1}{I_j^{scheme}}\right)$. With the assumption that users have same QoS requirements, let $f(K) = C_k(\theta)$ is the function of scheduled user number $K$ at each time slot, with the fixed $\theta$. Therefore, the derivative of this EC function with respect to $K$ is:

$$\nabla f(K) = \frac{K e^{\frac{\theta \nu}{K}} - K - \theta \nu}{(NK\theta)\left(N e^{\frac{\theta \nu}{K}} - K e^{\frac{\theta \nu}{K}} + K\right)}. \tag{14}$$

It is obviously, the value of Eq. (14) is greater than 0, at the point $K = 1$. And the denominator of the Eq. (14) is always greater than 0, the numerator of the Eq. (14) is a oscillatory function. The first inflection point of Eq. (14) is a suboptimal solution. By using binary search, it is easy to find the maximum value of formula (13).

## 3   Simulation Result

In our simulation, two hundred users that are served by one base station equipped one thousand antennas have the same QoS requirement. The pilot reuse factor is 1, and we set the coherence block length to 400, set the SNR to 5 dB, set the pathloss factor to 3.7. The QoS parameter $\theta$ gradually increase from $e^{-10}$ to $e^{10}$, the low value of $\theta$ means non-strict demand for real-time, the high value of $\theta$ means that the service must satisfy high real-time request and high stability. The unit of EC is *bits/S/Hz*. In our simulation algorithm, we first compute the spectral efficiency based on the code in reference [12], and then the EC is obtained according to the formula (13). The simulation result is showed as Fig. 1. The Fig. 2 is a slice of the Fig. 1, as the $\theta = 0.15$. The EC is a smooth function of user number. In the Fig. 1, the QoS requirement is $\log \theta$. With the low value of $\theta$, the point of optimal EC is near to the point of $K = 1$. As the value of $\theta$ increases, the optimal point moves to the point of $K = N$, and the achievable EC descends sharply. Because the higher $\theta$ requires higher stability.

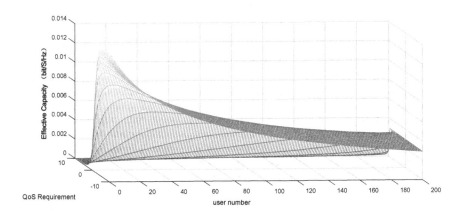

**Fig. 1.** Effective capacity under various QoS requirement.

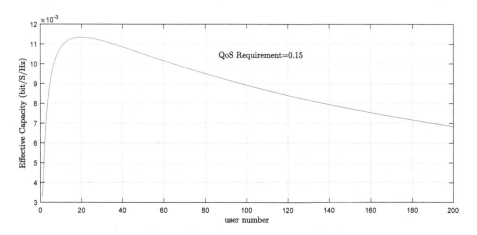

**Fig. 2.** Effective capacity with fixed QoS requirement.

# 4  Conclusion

We deduce the EC function with respective to the number of scheduling users and to the QoS requirement parameter in Massive MIMO system. The EC can be described by a smooth function of the number of scheduled users and the QoS requirement. A simulation is performed under various QoS requirement to survey the characteristics of the function. Designing the fast algorithm to find the optimal scheduling number of users under QoS requirement in Massive MIMO is a practical research work in the future.

# References

1. Jiang, D., Wang, W., Shiand, L., Song, H.: A compressive sensing-based approach to end-to-end network traffic reconstruction. IEEE Trans. Netw. Sci. Eng. (2018). https://doi.org/10.1109/TNSE.2018.2877597
2. Jiang, D., Huo, L., Song, H.: Rethinking behaviors and activities of base stations in mobile cellular networks based on big data analysis. IEEE Trans. Netw. Sci. Eng. **1**(2), 1–12 (2018)
3. Jiang, D., Huo, L., Li, Y.: Fine-granularity inference and estimations to network traffic for SDN. Plos One **13**(5), 1–23 (2018)
4. Chen, L., et al.: A lightweight end-side user experience data collection system for quality evaluation of multimedia communications. IEEE Access **6**(1), 15408–15419 (2018)
5. Jiang, D., Zhang, P., Lv, Z., Song, H.: Energy-efficient multi-constraint routing algorithm with load balancing for smart city applications. IEEE Internet Things J. **3**(6), 1437–1447 (2018)
6. Jiang, D., Li, W., Lv, H.: An energy-efficient cooperative multicast routing in multi-hop wireless networks for smart medical applications. Neurocomputing **220**(2017), 160–169 (2017)
7. Jiang, D., Huo, L., Lv, Z., Song, H., Qin, W.: A joint multi-criteria utility-based network selection approach for vehicle-to-infrastructure networking. IEEE Trans. Intell. Transp. Syst. **19**(10), 3305–3319 (2018)
8. Chen, L., Jiang, D., Bao, R., Xiong, J., Liu, F., Bei, L.: MIMO scheduling effectiveness analysis for bursty data service from view of QoE. Chinese J. Electron. **26**(5), 1079–1085 (2017)
9. Abarghouyi, H., Razavizadeh, S.M., Bjornson, E.: QoE-aware beamforming design for massive MIMO heterogeneous networks. IEEE Trans. Veh. Technol. **67**(9), 8315–8323 (2018)
10. Chaudhari, S., Cabric, D.: QoS aware power allocation and user selection in massive MIMO underlay cognitive radio networks. IEEE Trans. Cogn. **4**(2), 220–231 (2018)
11. Gao, X., Edfors, O., Rusek, F., Tufvesson, F.: Massive MIMO performance evaluation based on measured propagation data. IEEE Trans. Wirel. Commun. **14**(7), 3899–3911 (2015)
12. Björnson, E., Larsson, E.G., Debbah, M.: Massive MIMO for maximal spectral efficiency: how many users and pilots should be allocated? IEEE Trans. Wirel. Commun. **15**(2), 1293–1308 (2016)
13. Wu, D., Negi, R.: Effective capacity: a wireless link model for support of quality of service. IEEE Trans. Wirel. Commun. **2**(4), 630–643 (2003)

# An Improved Exhausted-Food-Sources-Identification Mechanism for the Artificial Bee Colony Algorithm

Jiaxu Ning[1,2]([✉]), Haitong Zhao[2], Peng Sun[3], Yunfei Feng[4],
and Tianyu Zhao[5]

[1] Shenyang Ligong University, Shenyang 110159, People's Republic of China
739250969@qq.com
[2] Northeastern University, Shenyang 110819, People's Republic of China
[3] IOWA State University, Ames, IA 50010, USA
[4] Sam's Club Technology Walmart Inc., Bentonville, AR 72712, USA
[5] College of Electronic Science and Engineering, Jilin University,
Changchun, China

**Abstract.** Artificial bee colony (ABC) algorithm has been widely used to solve the optimization problems. In the existing ABC algorithms, choosing which employed bee giving up its food source only based on its current trial number. It may cause some promising areas are exploited insufficiently and some non-significant areas are searched excessively. Thus, much more searching resources are wasted. To cope with this problem, an improved exhausted food source identification mechanism based on space partitioning (ISP) is designed, which considers the food source states both in the objective space and searching space simultaneously. Then, the proposed mechanism is applied to the basic ABC algorithm and a recently improved ABC algorithm. The experimental results have demonstrated that the ABC algorithms with the designed exhausted food source identification mechanism perform better than the original ABC algorithms in almost all the functions on the CEC2015 test suit.

**Keywords:** Swarm intelligence · Optimization problem · Artificial Bee Colony Algorithm

## 1 Introduction

Swarm intelligence (SI) has become a significant research subfield of artificial intelligence inspired by natural behavior of the swarm individuals [1]. The artificial bee colony (ABC) algorithm is a popular SI-based algorithm by simulating waggle dance and foraging behaviors of real honey bee colonies [2]. Due to the simple concept, easy implementation and fast convergence, ABC has attracted much attention and wide applications in numerical optimization domain and engineering applications [3]–[6].

In the ABC model, when the food sources are abandoned, the employed bee related to it becomes a scout. Then, a food source is produced for this scout, and the scout bee becomes an employed bee again to consume this food source. We can see that the worth of scout lie in that it can make the exhausted food source be abandoned timely to

© ICST Institute for Computer Sciences, Social Informatics and Telecommunications Engineering 2019
Published by Springer Nature Switzerland AG 2019. All Rights Reserved
H. Song et al. (Eds.): SIMUtools 2019, LNICST 295, pp. 633–642, 2019.
https://doi.org/10.1007/978-3-030-32216-8_62

save search effort. In term of simulating the behavior of scout bees, identify the accurate exhausted food source, most of the literatures are the same as the basic ABC algorithm. If there is more than one food source whose trail number exceeds the limit number, literatures [7]–[9] identified the food source with the largest trail number as an exhausted source of food, and [10]–[12] selected only one food source as an exhausted food source. Literature [11] proposed MNIIABC algorithm, where the scout bees also added a judgment mechanism to guarantee that the new generated food source was different from the abandoned exhausted food source. Literature [13] selected a food source according to their probabilities at first. And then judge it whether it is an exhausted food source by comparing its trail number with the limit number.

However, these identification mechanisms perform not well in identifying the exhausted food sources. The larger the area around a food source is not explored, that is, the larger the subspace volume of the food source is, the higher the search frequency of this food source is compared with other food sources, then the trail number will be higher. Therefore, according to the original identification mechanism, it is of great possibility to identify this food source as an exhausted food source, and this recognition is likely to be wrong.

In order to avoid this deficiency, this paper introduces a novel exhausted-food-source-identification mechanism based on space partitioning (ISP) in the scout bees phase, which identifies exhausted food sources more accurately by judging the volume and density of the subspace of every food source. For food sources with the same trail number, the food source with smaller subspace volume and greater subspace density is supposed to be identified as an exhausted food source with great possibility. In addition, the experimental results on the 15 test functions on CEC2015 test suit have demonstrated that ABC algorithms with ISP mechanism perform better than the ABC algorithms with the original identification mechanism.

## 2    The Artificial Bee Colony Optimization Model

Artificial Bee Colony (ABC) is one of the most recently defined algorithms by Karaboga [2], motivated by the intelligent forage behavior of honey bees. In ABC algorithm, the colony of artificial bees consists of three groups of bees: employed bees, onlookers and scouts. A food source represents a possible solution to the problem tobe optimized. The nectar amount of a food source corresponds to the quality of the solution represented by that food source. For every food source, there is only one employed bee. The basic structure of the ABC algorithm can be divided into the initialization stage, employed bee stage, onlooker bee stage and scoutstage.

At the initialization stage, it is supposed that the initial population of the food sources is made up of SN number of n-dimensional real valued vectors, and the $i$th solution of the population can be represented as $\mathbf{x}_i = \{x_{i1}, ..., x_{in}\}$. Then the $SN$ candidate solutions are randomly generated by

$$x_{ij} = l_j + rand(0, 1)(u_j - l_j) \tag{1}$$

where $l_j$ and $u_j$ are the lower and upper bound constraints of the $j$th variable of $x_i$, respectively. At the employed bee stage, each employed bee flies to a food source and explores it by

$$v_{ij} = x_{ij} + \varphi_{ij}(x_{ij} - x_{kj}) \tag{2}$$

where $\varphi_{ij}$ is uniformly distributed random real number in $[-1, 1]$, $k \in \{1, ..., i-1, i+1, ..., SN\}$ is randomly chosen and $j \in \{1, ..., n\}$ is a randomly chosen dimension. After generating the $v_i$ by Eq. (2), there is a greedy selection between $x_i$ and $v_i$ by Eq. (3).

$$x_i = \begin{cases} v_i, & if\ fit(v_i) > fit(x_i), \\ x_i, & otherwise, \end{cases} \tag{3}$$

Where $fit(x_i)$ means the fitness value of $x_i$. For a minimization problem, the fitness value of a solution can be defined as:

$$fit(x_i) = \begin{cases} \frac{1}{1+f(x_i)}, & if\ f(x_i) > 0, \\ 1 + |f(x_i)|, & if\ f(x_i) \le 0, \end{cases} \tag{4}$$

Where $f(x_i)$ is the value of the objective function at $x_i$.

At the onlooker bee stage, every onlooker bee randomly selects a solution from the $SN$ solutions with a probability $p_i$. The probability of a food source chosen by an onlooker bee can be calculated by:

$$p_i = fit(x_i) \Big/ \sum_{i=1}^{SN} fit(x_i) \tag{5}$$

As can be seen from Eq. (5), the solution with a better fitness has a higher probability selected by an onlooker bee. Once the onlooker bee has chosen her food source, an exploitation is made on it by Eq. (2) to generate a new solution, then a greedy selection is made by Eq. (3) between the new solution and the old one to remain a better solution.

After all employed bees and onlooker bees have explored their food sources, there is a check to see whether there is an exhausted food source need tobe abandoned or not at the scout stage. Here the exhausted food means a food source that has not been improved over the last LIMIT cycles. The LIMIT is a predetermined control parameter of the ABC algorithm. If there is an exhausted food source $x_i$, a scout bee discovers a new food source by Eq. (1) to replace it.

## 3   The Exhausted Food Source Identification Mechanism Based on Space Partitioning

As we can see from what have been mentioned in Sect. 2, there is a shortcoming in the ABC algorithm. It is of great possibility to identify an abundant food source as an exhausted food source if we only judge it by comparing the trail number with the Limit number. In the following, we introduced a novel exhausted-food-sources-identification (ISP) mechanism to identify the exhausted food sources, for not giving up a sufficient supply in a sense. That is, for food sources with the same trail number, the food source with smaller subspace volume and greater subspace density is supposed to be identified as an exhausted food source with greater possibility. Therefore, the greater the subspace density is, the greater the probability that this food source will be identified as an exhausted one is. Hence, scout bees utilize this searching space information to make the selection of food source to abandon more accurate.

As is shown in Fig. 1, assuming that the trail numbers in food sources X9 and X10 are both greater than the Limit number and the subspace density of the food source X9 is higher than that of X10, then X9 will be identified as the exhausted food source with a higher probability.

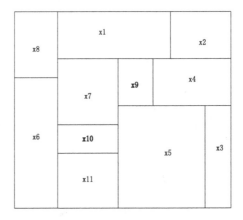

**Fig. 1.** The diagram of sub-regions of the exhausted food sources x9 and x10

Space partitioning in this paper is implemented through a Binary Space Partitioning (BSP) tree [14], which preserves all the historical food sources in the process of iteration. Each leaf node in the tree represents a subspace, the subspaces do not overlap, and the sum of all subspaces is the entire area of all food sources around a hive. While partitioning, the boundary values are determined by using two food sources that belong to the same subspace. The search density for the current subspace is evaluated by the super volume of the subspace.

**Definition 1 (Subspace of x):** Assume x is a food source in the search space A ($x \in$ A), and A is partitioned as the subspace set H by BSP tree, we define the subspace $h \subseteq H$ as the "subspace of x" if $x \in h$ and h is represented by a leaf node of BSP tree.

**Definition 2 (Subspace density of x):** Supposing that there is only one food source x in a subspace h. The subspace density of x can be evaluated by figuring the subspace super volume value of h utilizing Eqs. (6) and (7), where v(x) refers to the subspace size, $u_k$ and $l_k$ are the upper and lower limits for dimension k respectively, and D $(x)$ refers to the subspace density of $x$.

$$v(x) = \prod_{k=1}^{D} (u_k - l_k) \tag{6}$$

$$D(x) = \frac{1}{v(x)} \tag{7}$$

The steps of space partitioning are as follows:

**Step1:** Create an empty BSP tree, where there is only one root node in the tree.
**Step2:** After a new food source $v$ is found, $v$ will be saved in the root node if there is only the root node in the current tree, and the partitioning process will be completed. Otherwise, supposing h is the subspace of v, search the node corresponding to h and the unique solution x stored in it.
**Step3:** Calculate the partition dimension $j$ according to the food sources v and x, and subspace h in the dimension j is divided into two parts.
**Step4:** Create two nodes n1 and n2, save the food sources x and z, the corresponding subspace boundary values. Then insert n1 and n2 as left and right children of node n into the tree.

Based on the above descriptions, the exhausted-food-sources-identification (ISP) mechanism is designed as follows in this paper. In scout bee phase, a scout bee first determines the number N of the candidate food sources whose trail number is greater than the limit number. If N = 0, the scout bees phase ends. If N = 1, identify this food source as an exhausted one and generate a new food source V utilizing Eq. (1) to substitute X meanwhile reset its trail = 0. If N > 1, first find the subspaces of these candidate food sources. Then calculate their subspace density values and the probability values $P_{di}$ utilizing Eqs. (6), (7) and (8) respectively. After that, identify the exhausted food source X utilizing the greedy selection mechanism according to the subspace probability values $P_{di}$. Finally, generate a new food source V utilizing Eq. (1) to substitute X and reset its trail = 0.

$$p_{di} = \frac{D(X_i)}{\sum D(X_i)} \tag{8}$$

In the following, the paper integrates ABC algorithm with ISP to better identify the exhausted food sources, which is called ABC-ISP in the following parts. It is still performed into four steps: initialization phase, employed bees phase, onlooker bees phase and scout bees phase. Except that a BSP tree is created to preserve all the food sources and their subspace boundaries. It is significant to figure out that the ISP mechanism can also be easily integrated with other ABC variants. So, to verify the effectiveness of the ISP mechanism for the sending scout phrase, we also introduce it into the recently proposed improved ABC algorithm called ABCG [15]. And the pseudo-code of ABC algorithm with ISP is presented in Table 1 to better illustrate the integration way of it.

**Table 1.** The pseudo-code description of ABC algorithm with ISP

| AlgorithmABC with ISP |
|---|
| **Begin** |
| 1. Initialize density tree T which only has a root node |
| 2. Initialization phrase |
| 3. Memorize the best food source position |
| 4. Insert food sources into T use algorithm Insert (T, x) |
| 5.**while** not stopping criteria met **do** |
| 6.    Employed bees phrase |
| 7.    Insert food sources founded in the employed bees phrase into T |
| 8.    Onlooker bees phrase |
| 9.    Insert food sources founded in the onlooker bees phrase into T |
| 10.    Memorize the best food source position |
| /* Scout bee phrase*/ |
| 11.    Count the number of candidate exhausted food sources N use trial number |
| 12.    **if** N=1 **then** |
| 13.    Generate a new solution randomly V use Eq.(1) |
| 14.    Replace the exhausted solution with V |
| 15.    Insert ( T,V) |
| 16.    **end if** |
| 17.    **if** N>1 **then** |
| 18.    **for** i=1 to N **do** |
| 19.    Search (T, $X_i$) |
| 20.    Calculate super volume of subspace containing $X_i$ use Eq. (6) |
| 21.    Calculate density probability $P_{di}$ of subspace containing $X_i$ utilizing Eq. (7) |
| 22.    **end for** |
| 25.    Identify the exhausted food source X by a greedy selection mechanism according to $P_{di}$ |
| 26.    Generate a new food source V use Eq. (1) |
| 27    Substitute food source V for X |
| 28.    Insert (T, V) |
| 29.    **end if** |
| 30.**end while** |
| **end** |

## 4  Experimental Results

In this part, the ABC-ISP and the ABCG with ISP mechanism called ABCG-ISP algorithms are tested and computed with the original ABC and ABCG algorithms. All the experiments are tested on 15 test functions of the CEC2015 test suit. The dimension D = 100, the whole search space is set to $[-100, 100]^D$ for all the test functions. All algorithms are terminated when the maximum fitness evaluation number MFE = 10000*D is arrived, and the other parameters of these algorithms are set as the same as in [2] and [15]. All the experiments are done on the same computer (2.93 GHz CPU and 3 GB RAM) with Visual Studio 2008.

The main experiment results are that the algorithms solve the test functions and run 51 times independently to obtain the minimum function values. The achieved maximum, minimum and the mean values by the compared algorithms on each test instance are given in Table 2. The distributions of the obtained results for the compared algorithms are shown as Fig. 2. In this figure, there are five solid lines in every diagram, each solid line from the top to the bottom on behalf of: the maximum point (there may exists abnormal points), quarter-digit, median, three-quarters and the minimum point (there may exists abnormal). For what we care for is to obtain the minimum function optimization, therefore, the smaller the obtained function value is, the quality of the algorithm is better. The performances of all the algorithms can get directly through this box diagrams. And the convergences of the algorithms on the test instances are shown as in Fig. 3.

**Table 2.** Results of compared algorithm based on description statics way

| Function | Result | ABC | ABC-ISP | ABCG | ABCG-ISP |
|----------|--------|---------|---------|---------|----------|
| F1 | Min | 1.40E+07 | 8.98E+06 | 6.84E+06 | 6.50E+06 |
|    | Max | 3.77E+07 | 2.46E+07 | 1.54E+07 | 1.34E+07 |
|    | Mean | 2.76E+07 | 1.51E+07 | 1.11E+07 | 9.32E+06 |
| F5 | Min | 1.03E+04 | 9.75E+03 | 9.64E+03 | 9.05E+03 |
|    | Max | 1.34E+04 | 1.20E+04 | 1.33E+04 | 1.23E+04 |
|    | Mean | 1.19E+04 | 1.11E+04 | 1.16E+04 | 1.12E+04 |
| F8 | Min | 7.07E+06 | 3.06E+06 | 3.48E+06 | 3.13E+06 |
|    | Max | 1.48E+07 | 1.35E+07 | 1.16E+07 | 1.19E+07 |
|    | Mean | 1.09E+07 | 8.33E+06 | 7.40E+06 | 7.24E+06 |
| F10 | Min | 4.59E+05 | 1.04E+06 | 8.67E+04 | 5.12E+04 |
|     | Max | 6.99E+06 | 3.11E+06 | 1.13E+06 | 8.81E+05 |
|     | Mean | 4.06E+06 | 1.86E+06 | 5.30E+05 | 3.49E+05 |
| F14 | Min | 9.79E+04 | 9.74E+04 | 9.82E+04 | 9.73E+04 |
|     | Max | 1.10E+05 | 1.09E+05 | 1.08E+05 | 1.05E+05 |
|     | Mean | 1.04E+05 | 1.01E+05 | 1.02E+05 | 1.00E+05 |

From the Table 2, it can be seen that the ABC-ISP and ABCG-ISP achieved smaller maximum, minimum and the mean fitness values than the ABC and ABCG algorithm respectively, which can be further proved by the Fig. 2. From the convergence curve of these algorithms on the test instances in Fig. 3, we can see that the ABC-ISP and ABCG-ISP not only converge faster than the ABC and ABCG algorithm, but also converge to a better position on each test function. So, we can conclude that the designed ISP mechanism works well.

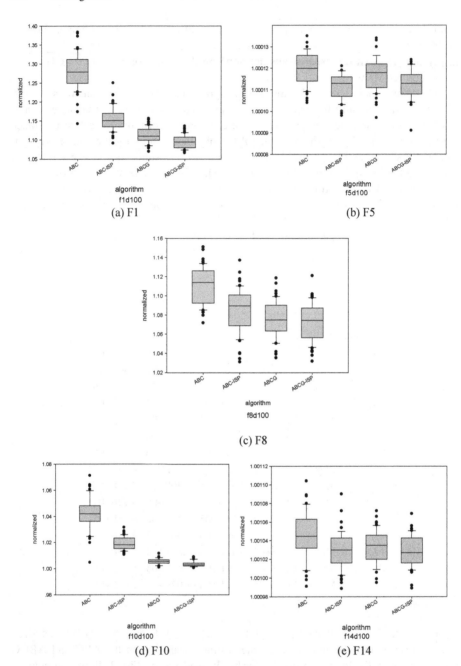

(a) F1

(b) F5

(c) F8

(d) F10

(e) F14

**Fig. 2.** The boxplots of the compared algorithms on CEC2015 test functions

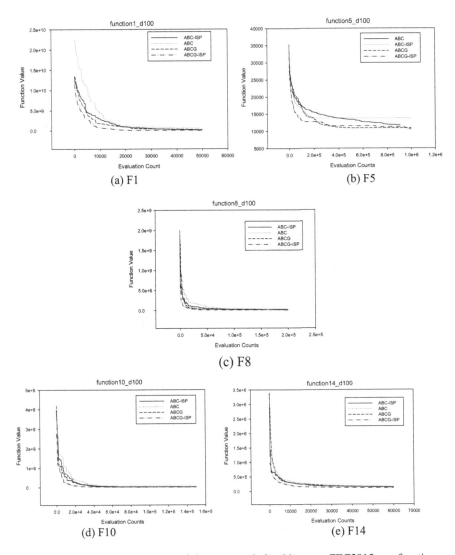

**Fig. 3.** The convergence curves of the compared algorithms on CEC2015 test functions

## 5 Conclusion

In this paper, an improved exhausted food source identification mechanism based on space partitioning (ISP) is designed. Instead of presenting a new hybrid ABC algorithm or integrating an operator of an existing algorithm into ABC, our aim is to model the behavior of foragers in ABC more accurately. By using the new selection mechanism proposed for scoutbees, the ABC algorithms combined with it achieved a better performance than the original versions in terms of solution quality and convergence characteristics. Through this work, we can see that combining the searching space information and objective space information during optimizing process can effectively improve the algorithm performance.

**Acknowledgement.** This work is funded by Shenyang Dongda Emerging Industrial Technology Research Institute.

# References

1. Zhang, S., Lee, C.K.M., Chan, H.K., Choy, K.L., Zhang, W.: Swarm intelligence applied in green logistics: a literature review. Eng. Appl. Artif. Intell. **37**, 154–169 (2015)
2. Karaboga, D., Basturk, B.: A powerful and efficient algorithm for numerical function optimization: artificial bee colony (ABC) algorithm. J. Glob. Opt. **39**(3), 459–471 (2007)
3. Karaboga, D., Beyza, G., Celal, O., Karaboga, N.: A comprehensive survey: artificial bee colony (ABC) algorithm and applications. Artif. Intell. Rev. **42**(1), 21–57 (2014)
4. Jiang, D., Huo, L., Lv, Z., et al.: A joint multi-criteria utility-based network selection approach for vehicle-to-infrastructure networking. IEEE Trans. Intell. Transp. Syst. **pp**(99), 1–15 (2018)
5. Jiang, D., Huo, L., Song, H.: Rethinking behaviors and activities of base stations in mobile cellular networks based on big data analysis. IEEE Trans. Netw. Sci. Eng. **1**(1), 1–12 (2018)
6. Jiang, D., Xu, Z., Li, W., et al.: Topology control-based collaborative multicast routing algorithm with minimum energy consumption. Int. J. Commun Syst **30**(1), 1–18 (2017)
7. Karaboga, D., Gorkemli, B.: A quick artificial bee colony (qABC) algorithm and its performance on optimization problems. Appl. Soft Comput. **23**(5), 227–238 (2014)
8. Gao, W.F., Liu, S.Y.: A modified artificial bee colony algorithm. Comput. Oper. Res. **39**(3), 687–697 (2012)
9. Cui, L., Zhang, K., Li, G., et al.: Modified Gbest-guided artificial bee colony algorithm with new probability model. Soft. Comput. **2017**(2), 1–27 (2017)
10. Yu, W.J., Zhan, Z.H., Zhang, J.: Artificial bee colony algorithm with an adaptive greedy position update strategy. Soft. Comput. **2016**, 1–15 (2016)
11. Zhong, F., Li, H., Zhong, S.: An improved artificial bee colony algorithm with modified-neighborhood-based update operator and independent-inheriting-search strategy for global optimization. Eng. Appl. Artif. Intell. **58**, 134–156 (2017)
12. Bai, W., Eke, I., Lee, K.Y.: An improved artificial bee colony optimization algorithm based on orthogonal learning for optimal power flow problem. Control Eng. Practice **61**, 163–172 (2017)
13. Kishor, A., Chandra, M., Singh, P.K.: An astute artificial bee colony algorithm. In: Deep, K., et al. (eds.) Proceedings of Sixth International Conference on Soft Computing for Problem Solving. AISC, vol. 546, pp. 153–162. Springer, Singapore (2017). https://doi.org/10.1007/978-981-10-3322-3_14
14. Hearn, D., Baker, M.P.: Computer Graphics with OpenGl, 3rd edn. Prentice-Hall, Upper Saddle River (2004)
15. Xiang, W., Meng, X., Li, Y., He, R.: An improved artificial bee colony algorithm based on the gravity model. Inf. Sci. **429**, 49–71 (2018)

# LSTM Network Based Traffic Flow Prediction for Cellular Networks

Shulin Cao[✉] and Wei Liu

State Key Labs of ISN, Xidian University,
Xi'an 710071, Shaanxi, People's Republic of China
slcao_cn@stu.xidian.edu.cn, liuweixd@mail.xidian.edu.cn

**Abstract.** The traffic flow prediction of cellular network requires low complexity and high accuracy, which is difficult to meet using the existing methods. In this paper, we propose an long short-term memory (LSTM) network based traffic flow prediction in which we consider temporal correlations inherently and nonlinear characteristics of cellular network traffic flow data. We use Back Propagation Through Time (BPTT) to train the LSTM network and evaluate the model using mean square error (MSE) and mean absolute error (MAE). Simulation results show that the proposed LSTM network based traffic flow prediction for cellular network is superior to the stacked autoencoder network based algorithm.

**Keywords:** Deep learning · Long short-term memory (LSTM) ·
Traffic flow prediction · Cellular network

## 1 Introduction

With the popularity of smart phones and the upgrading of wireless communication techniques, the demand for data services increases rapidly. Thus, the resource allocation place the critical role for meeting the demand. However, the environment is changed dynamically and the resource allocation based on information at the current moment has a certain time delay, it can not satisfy the demand for resource at the current moment. So traffic flow prediction in cellular network is imperative requirement.

There are many traditional methods for predicting traffic flow in cellular network. For example, In [1], Auto-Regressive Integrated Moving Average (ARIMA), fractional ARIMA, artificial neural network (ANN), and wavelet-based predictors were used for wireless traffic prediction and analyzed computational complexity. The joint Kohonen maps and ARIMA time series models

The financial support of the program of Key Industry Innovation Chain of Shaanxi Province, China (2017ZDCXL-GY-04-02), of the program of Xi'an Science and Technology Plan (201805029YD7CG13(5)), Shaanxi, China, of National S&T Major Project (No. 2016ZX03001022-003), China, and of Key R&D Program - The Industry Project of Shaanxi (Grant No. 2018GY-017) are gratefully acknowledged.

© ICST Institute for Computer Sciences, Social Informatics and Telecommunications Engineering 2019
Published by Springer Nature Switzerland AG 2019. All Rights Reserved
H. Song et al. (Eds.): SIMUtools 2019, LNICST 295, pp. 643–653, 2019.
https://doi.org/10.1007/978-3-030-32216-8_63

method was proposed in [2] which is a short-term traffic prediction. A theory which aims to model the univariate traffic condition data flow as a seasonal autoregressive integrated moving average process was proposed in [3]. In wireless networks, information theory techniques are proposed in [4] for discrete sequence prediction. A multi-resolution finite impulse response neural network learning algorithm based on the maximum overlap discrete wavelet transform was proposed in [5] for network traffic prediction (real world aggregated Ethernet traffic data).

With the development of machine learning techniques, various machine learning methods are used for wireless network traffic flow prediction, the experimental results show that these methods have effectively improved the accuracy of traffic flow prediction. The joint principal component analysis and time series model was proposed in [6] to predict the fluctuation of Internet traffic in the international IP transmission network. An ANN model based on Multilayer Perceptron was proposed in [7] to predict Internet traffic flow in IP networks. Three methods for accurately predicting traffic in TCP/IP-based networks were presented in [8], which included a neural network integration methods and two adaptive time series methods (ARIMA and Holt-Winters) respectively. A short-term network traffic prediction algorithm LSVM-DTW-K based on Chaos Theory and Support Vector Machines was proposed in [9] for wired and wireless campus networks. In [10], the traffic model based on Elman-NN network was used to predict future traffic and the results showed that this method can achieve better performance. In addition, it also includes traffic flow prediction problems when incomplete data exist. There are many other methods of machine learning that have been proposed for traffic prediction, [11–13].

Deep learning has developed rapidly, and prediction methods based on deep learning have also developed, such as in transportation and communication networks. In [14], a stacked autoencoder model (SAE) to learn general traffic flow characteristics, after extracting the traffic characteristics, then this method uses top-level logistic regression to predict traffic flow. Two different artificial neural network methods are proposed in [15], which are multilayer perceptrons and stacked autoencoder for predicting Internet traffic. An underlying deep belief network (DBN) and top-level multitask regression layer deep learning model was proposed in [16], where DBN is used for unsupervised feature learning. The deep learning models that has been used to perform traffic flow prediction that do not fully consider the correlation between time series. Recently, LSTM network has been developed and extensively used on time series prediction, such as, for TCP/IP networks, a model that combines LSTM with deep neural networks was proposed in [17], which utilized autocorrelation features to improve the accuracy of network traffic prediction. So, LSTM network takes full account of the temporal correlation of time series and can remember some of the information entered before so that to exploit the relationship between these time series and improve the prediction accuracy. In this paper, we proposed a LSTM network based traffic flow prediction for cellular network. Time series data were highly related, so we can utilize LSTM that can reserve long-term memory to learn the basic characteristics of cellular network traffic flow data in the cell.

The rest of the paper is organized as follows. We describe the system model in Sect. 2. The LSTM network based traffic flow prediction is described in Sect. 3. The simulation results of the proposed LSTM network based traffic flow prediction for cellular networks are provided in Sect. 4. In Sect. 5, conclusion is offered.

## 2   System Model

The system considered in this paper consists of one micro cell which serves $K$ users as shown in Fig. 1. In this paper, we consider the uplink traffic flow data of the micro cell. The data was collected every time slot and each time slot consists of $n$ minutes. Denote $x^{\langle t \rangle}$ as the traffic flow data at $t$th time slot. In this network, we want to use the collected traffic flow data $\{x^{\langle 1 \rangle}, x^{\langle 2 \rangle}, x^{\langle 3 \rangle}, \cdots, x^{\langle T \rangle}\}$ from $T$ time slots to predict the volume of traffic flow $x^{\langle T+1 \rangle}$ at the $(T+1)$th time slot.

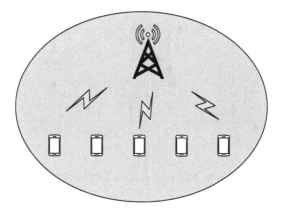

**Fig. 1.** A simple cellular network

## 3   LSTM Network Based Traffic Flow Prediction

### 3.1   LSTM Network

Figure 2 shows the structure of LSTM network used for predicting traffic flow. As shown in Fig. 2, we use $T$ consecutive traffic flow data $\{x^{\langle 1 \rangle}, x^{\langle 2 \rangle}, x^{\langle 3 \rangle}, \cdots, x^{\langle T \rangle}\}$ as the input to the LSTM network to predict cellular traffic flow $x^{\langle T+1 \rangle}$ at the $T+1$ time slot. The traffic flow prediction requires $T$ time steps at a time, and each time step corresponds to an LSTM cell. The LSTM network adopts a self-looping method in which only one data can be entered into the network at a time.

The basic component of LSTM network is the LSTM cell as shown in Fig. 3, the $t$th LSTM cell corresponds to the $t$th time step, which has the ability to

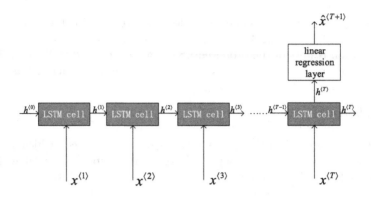

**Fig. 2.** The structure of LSTM network

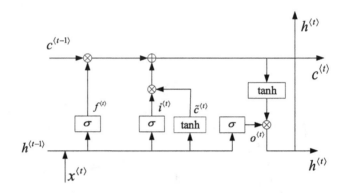

**Fig. 3.** The structure of LSTM cell

remove or add information to a cell's state through a well-designed structure consisting of three different kinds of gates, which are "input gate", "output gate" and "forget gate" [18]. Each gate is a feedforward network layer which consists of one hidden layer, the number of hidden layer neurons denoted as $P$ which is called LSTM cell units. The gate is a way of letting messages pass by and overcoming the vanishing gradient and the exploding gradient. The gate has the ability to choose whether to pass the information by itself and the gate's output value is in the range of (0,1), where 1 means "completely reserved", 0 means "completely discarded". $\sigma(x)$ is the gate function, which is usually chosen as sigmoid function so that the gate function can be expressed as

$$\sigma(x) = \frac{1}{1 + \exp^{-x}} \tag{1}$$

According to Fig. 3, the input of the LSTM cell is $h^{\langle t-1 \rangle}$, $x^{\langle t \rangle}$, $c^{\langle t-1 \rangle}$, where $c^{\langle t-1 \rangle}$ is the cell state at the $t-1$ time step, $h^{\langle t-1 \rangle}$, the output value of cell state at the $t-1$ time step. The output value of the LSTM cell is $\hat{x}^{\langle t+1 \rangle}$ at the $t$ time step.

In LSTM network, $i^{\langle t \rangle}$, $f^{\langle t \rangle}$, and $o^{\langle t \rangle}$ denote the output value of "input gate", "forget gate" and "output gate", which represented by (2), (3) and (4), respectively. The output value of the forget gate decides whether the content of the cell state at $t-1$ time step will add to the update cell state at the $t$ time step. The output value of the input gate decides whether new candidate values $\tilde{c}^{\langle t \rangle}$ could add to cell state, where $\tilde{c}^{\langle t \rangle}$ is expressed as (5). Then, combine $\tilde{c}^{\langle t \rangle}$ and $c^{\langle t-1 \rangle}$ can get the update cell state $c^{\langle t \rangle}$, which indicates the update contents of the cell state stored at the $t$ time step and the cell state is expressed as (6). The output value of the output gate decides whether the updated cell state can influence the output of the LSTM cell, the output value of cell state is expressed as (7) [17].

$$i^{\langle t \rangle} = \sigma(\boldsymbol{W}_i[h^{\langle t-1 \rangle}, x^{\langle t \rangle}] + \boldsymbol{b}_i) \tag{2}$$

$$f^{\langle t \rangle} = \sigma(\boldsymbol{W}_f[h^{\langle t-1 \rangle}, x^{\langle t \rangle}] + \boldsymbol{b}_f) \tag{3}$$

$$o^{\langle t \rangle} = \sigma(\boldsymbol{W}_o[h^{\langle t-1 \rangle}, x^{\langle t \rangle}] + \boldsymbol{b}_o) \tag{4}$$

$$\tilde{c}^{\langle t \rangle} = \tanh(\boldsymbol{W}_c[h^{\langle t-1 \rangle}, x^{\langle t \rangle}] + \boldsymbol{b}_c) \tag{5}$$

$$c^{\langle t \rangle} = i^{\langle t \rangle} * \tilde{c}^{\langle t \rangle} + f^{\langle t \rangle} * c^{\langle t-1 \rangle} \tag{6}$$

$$h^{\langle t \rangle} = o^{\langle t \rangle} * \tanh c^{\langle t \rangle} \tag{7}$$

which the parameters $\boldsymbol{W}_c$, $\boldsymbol{W}_i$, $\boldsymbol{W}_f$ and $\boldsymbol{W}_o$ are weight matrixes corresponding to the network structure of cell state, input gate, forget gate, and output gate, the dimension of them is $P \times (P+1)$, $\boldsymbol{b}_c$, $\boldsymbol{b}_i$, $\boldsymbol{b}_f$, $\boldsymbol{b}_o$ are bias vector corresponding to the network structure of cell state, input gate, forget gate, and output gate, the dimension of them is $P \times 1$ and $\tanh(x)$ is represented as $\frac{\exp^x - \exp^{-x}}{\exp^x + \exp^{-x}}$. The $h^{\langle t \rangle}$ can get the predicted traffic flow value $\hat{x}^{\langle t+1 \rangle}$ through the linear regression layer. Because LSTM network is a self-looping architecture and the parameters it uses for each time step are shared, we continue to train the LSTM network and update these parameters to make predictions more accurate.

For the data of sequence length $T$, the output of the $T$th LSTM cell is also the predict traffic flow data of the LSTM network and the output of the LSTM network needs to consider the input of the previous $T-1$ time step.

## 3.2 Training LSTM Network

When training the LSTM network, we firstly initialize all parameters, usually to a very small number close to 0 and initialize $c^{\langle 0 \rangle}$ and $\hat{x}^{\langle 0 \rangle}$ to 0. Selecting $M$ number of epochs during training, each epoch consists of $N$ batches, the size of each batch is $J$ which means that each batch contains $J$ sequences, each sequence is $\{x^{\langle 1 \rangle}, x^{\langle 2 \rangle}, x^{\langle 3 \rangle}, \cdots, x^{\langle T \rangle}\}$. When we set the parameters we must follow that the batch multiplied by the batch size equals the number of training data set. Initialize $c^{\langle 0 \rangle}$ and $\hat{x}^{\langle 0 \rangle}$ for the end of each batch size training, the epoch indicates that the data of the training set is trained several times, and the batch indicates that the training set is divided into several parts and input into the network for training.

We use Back Propagation Through Time (BPTT) to train the network [19]. Given a set of training samples $\{x^{\langle 1 \rangle}, x^{\langle 2 \rangle}, x^{\langle 3 \rangle}, \cdots, x^{\langle t \rangle}, \cdots, x^{\langle m \rangle}\}$. For the network, we choose the time series of length $T$ as input, and the value of $(T+1)$th time slot as label. For every batch, the loss function is represented by (8) [20]

$$L^{\langle J \rangle}\left(\hat{x}^{\langle t+1 \rangle}, x^{\langle t+1 \rangle}\right) = \frac{1}{J}\sum_{t=1}^{J}\left(x^{\langle t+1 \rangle} - x^{\langle t+1 \rangle}\right)^2 \tag{8}$$

and the whole loss function is showed in (9)

$$L\left(\hat{x}, x\right) = \frac{1}{m}\sum_{t=1}^{m}\left(\hat{x}^{\langle t+1 \rangle} - x^{\langle t+1 \rangle}\right)^2 \tag{9}$$

where $\hat{x}^{\langle t+1 \rangle}$ is the prediction of traffic flow at $t$ time slot, $x^{\langle t+1 \rangle}$ is the actual value at $t+1$ time slot.

$$W_* = \hat{W}_* - \alpha\frac{\partial L\left(\hat{x}, x\right)}{\partial W_*} \tag{10}$$

Where $\alpha$ is learning rate for training LSTM network, $\hat{W}_*$ denotes $W_*$ at previous time step, and $W_*$ can represent $W_c$, $W_i$, $W_f$ and $W_o$. When we adjust the parameters of this network, the objective is to minimize the whole loss function of the network.

## 4    Simulation Results

In this section, we make the evaluation standard to calculate the accuracy of prediction. There are two evaluation standards included in this paper, which are the mean absolute error (MAE) and the Mean Square Error (MSE) [14]. Given a set of training samples $\{x^{\langle 1 \rangle}, x^{\langle 2 \rangle}, x^{\langle 3 \rangle}, \cdots, x^{\langle t \rangle}, \cdots, x^{\langle m \rangle}\}$, the length of training set is $m$. The definitions of them are shown as follows respectively

$$\text{MAE} = \frac{1}{m}\sum_{t=1}^{m}\left|\hat{x}^{\langle t \rangle} - x^{\langle t \rangle}\right| \tag{11}$$

$$\text{MSE} = \frac{1}{m}\sum_{t=1}^{m}\left(\hat{x}^{\langle t \rangle} - x^{\langle t \rangle}\right)^2 \tag{12}$$

The cellular network traffic flow data set is collected from the cell which is collected every 15 min, and finally a total of 3,500 data. 80% of historical data was used for training set to train the network, and the rest of historical data was used for test set to test the performance of the network. In this paper, we use the Keras framework to build the LSTM network module [21], which is a deep learning framework and the underlying library uses theano or tensorflow. When training the LSTM network model, we found that setting the parameters

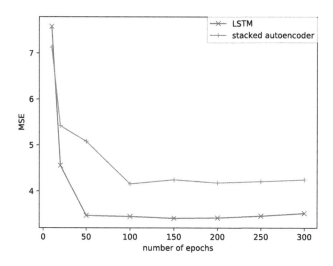

**Fig. 4.** MSE over epochs

$M = 300$, $N = 175$, $J = 20$, $T = 12$ and $P = 4$ to train the LSTM network will get the optimal cellular network traffic flow prediction result.

As shown in Fig. 4, LSTM has a fast convergence rate, which can achieve the best prediction accuracy when the time of epoch is 150 compared to the stacked autoencoder which need epoch 100 times to reach the current optimal prediction, so we choose $M = 150$. From the LSTM curve, it can be seen that the MSE will fluctuate a little during the training process but it will decrease at last. This is because when the new data input to the network, it may not have been trained well to make prediction. When the network is trained well, if you continue to increase the number of training epoch, it will lead to overfit, MSE will always rise.

Figure 5 shows that the variation of MSE with the number of LSTM cell units in the hidden layer in each gate. There is a sharp drop in MSE when the number of LSTM cell units changing from 1 to 4, which indicate that the prediction accuracy is gradually increasing, and the MSE reaches the minimum value when the number of LSTM cell units is 4, where the prediction effect is the best. Then the MSE starts to rise with the number of LSTM cell units increasing, while the prediction accuracy decreases, we choose $P = 4$. Because the LSTM is composed of complex nonlinear functions, the structure is complex to explain. This result can help us to choose the best local value of the cell unit number to make the best prediction for the traffic flow data.

In order to reflect the performance of LSTM in traffic flow prediction, we do a comparative experiment with a stacked autoencoder network. We use the same data set, the same data distribution, and the optimal parameters adjustment. After training network convergence, we get the perform comparison of the LSTM network and stacked autoencoder network, as shown in Table 1. According to

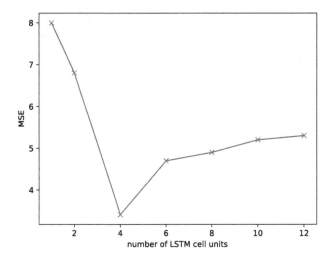

**Fig. 5.** MSE changes with the number of LSTM cell units in the hidden layer in each gate

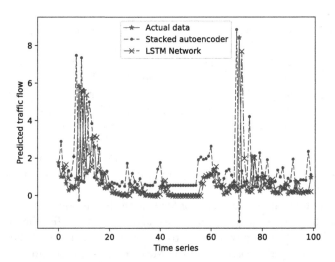

**Fig. 6.** Training data prediction

**Table 1.** Performance comparison of the LSTM network and Stacked autoencoder

| Model | MAE | MSE |
|---|---|---|
| LSTM network | 1.43 | 3.40 |
| Stacked autoencoder | 2.23 | 4.16 |

the results of comparison, we can make the conclusion that the LSTM network improve the accuracy of the cellular network traffic flow prediction.

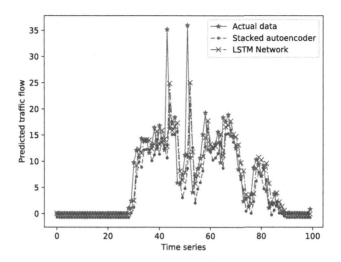

**Fig. 7.** Testing data prediction

Figure 6 shows the prediction of training data. As can be seen from the Fig. 6, the actual data we collected is periodic at most of the time and meets the data requirements of the LSTM network. The traffic flow prediction results of the LSTM network more closely resemble the actual data compared to stacked autoencoder network.

Figure 7 shows the partial prediction data of the testing data. As can be seen from the Fig. 7, our trained LSTM network gains high performance on the test set, indicating that LSTM network has a good generalization capability.

## 5    Conclusion

In this paper we proposed a deep learning based traffic flow prediction model. We extract a time series from the real-time traffic flow of the cellular networks. Then we train a deep learning model called LSTM network using these time series. Since the traffic flow at the current time is highly correlated with the previous time, the LSTM network is quite suitable for the prediction. And our simulation results showed that the proposed LSTM network gain significant performance.

From a practical aspect, with the real-time traffic flow as inputs, the output of the LSTM network will benefit greatly in resource allocation for the service provider. In addition, the high accuracy of the LSTM network traffic flow prediction in the proposed scheme ensures an engaging user experience.

# References

1. Feng, H., Shu, Y.: Study on network traffic prediction techniques. In: International Conference on Wireless Communications, NETWORKING and Mobile Computing, pp. 1041–1044 (2005)
2. Voort, M.V.D., Dougherty, M., Watson, S.: Combining kohonen maps with arima time series models to forecast traffic flow. Transp. Res. Part C Emerg. Technol. **4**(5), 307–318 (1996)
3. Williams, B.M., Hoel, L.A.: Modeling and forecasting vehicular traffic flow as a seasonal ARIMA process: theoretical basis and empirical results. J. Transp. Eng. **129**(6), 664–672 (2003)
4. Katsaros, D., Manolopoulos, Y.: Prediction in wireless networks by Markov chains. Wirel. Commun. IEEE **16**(2), 56–64 (2009)
5. Alarcon-Aquino, V., Barria, J.A.: Multiresolution FIR neural-network-based learning algorithm applied to network traffic prediction. IEEE Trans. Syst. Man Cybern. Part C **36**(2), 208–220 (2006)
6. Babiarz, R., Bedo, J.-S.: Internet traffic mid-term forecasting: a pragmatic approach using statistical analysis tools. In: Boavida, F., Plagemann, T., Stiller, B., Westphal, C., Monteiro, E. (eds.) NETWORKING 2006. LNCS, vol. 3976, pp. 110–122. Springer, Heidelberg (2006). https://doi.org/10.1007/11753810_10
7. Chabaa, S., Zeroual, A., Antari, J.: Identification and prediction of internet traffic using artificial neural networks. J. Intell. Learn. Syst. Appl. **2**(3), 147–155 (2010)
8. Cortez, P., Rio, M., Rocha, M., et al.: Multi-scale Internet traffic forecasting using neural networks and time series methods. Expert Syst. **29**(2), 143–155 (2012)
9. Liu, X., Fang, X., Qin, Z., et al.: A short-term forecasting algorithm for network traffic based on chaos theory and SVM. J. Netw. Syst. Manag. **19**(4), 427–447 (2011)
10. Wang, J., Wang, J., Zeng, M., et al.: Prediction of internet traffic based on Elman neural network. In: Control and Decision Conference, CCDC 2009, Chinese, pp. 1248–1252 (2009)
11. Bengio, Y., Simard, P., Frasconi, P.: Learning long-term dependencies with gradient descent is difficult. IEEE Trans. Neural Netw. **5**(2), 157–166 (2002)
12. Wang, H., Hu, D.: Comparison of SVM and LS-SVM for regression. In: International Conference on Neural Networks and Brain, pp. 279–283 (2005)
13. Chen, Y., Yang, B., Meng, Q.: Small-time scale network traffic prediction based on flexible neural tree. Appl. Soft Comput. **12**(1), 274–279 (2012)
14. Lv, Y., Duan, Y., Kang, W., et al.: Traffic flow prediction with big data: a deep learning approach. IEEE Trans. Intell. Transp. Syst. **16**(2), 865–873 (2015)
15. Oliveira, T.P., Barbar, J.S., Soares, A.S.: Multilayer perceptron and stacked autoencoder for internet traffic prediction. In: Hsu, C.-H., Shi, X., Salapura, V. (eds.) NPC 2014. LNCS, vol. 8707, pp. 61–71. Springer, Heidelberg (2014). https://doi.org/10.1007/978-3-662-44917-2_6
16. Huang, W., Song, G., Hong, H., et al.: Deep architecture for traffic flow prediction: deep belief networks with multitask learning. IEEE Trans. Intell. Transp. Syst. **15**(5), 2191–2201 (2014)
17. Zhuo, Q., Li, Q., Yan, H., Qi, Y.: Long short-term memory neural network for network traffic prediction. In: International Conference on Intelligent Systems and Knowledge Engineering (ISKE), pp. 1–6 (2017)

18. Gers, F.A., Schmidhuber, J.: Recurrent nets that time and count. In: Proceedings of the IEEE-INNS-ENNS International Joint Conference on Neural Networks. IJCNN 2000. Neural Computing: New Challenges and Perspectives for the New Millennium, vol. 3, pp. 189–194 (2000)
19. Hochreiter, S., Schmidhuber, J.: Long short-term memory. Neural Comput. **9**(8), 1735–1780 (1997)
20. Kang, D., Lv, Y., Chen, Y.Y.: Short-term traffic flow prediction with LSTM recurrent neural network. In: 2017 IEEE 20th International Conference on Intelligent Transportation Systems (ITSC), pp. 1–6 (2017)
21. Vidnerova, P., Neruda, R.: Evolving keras architectures for sensor data analysis. In: 2017 Federated Conference on Computer Science and Information Systems (FedCSIS), pp. 109–112 (2017)

# Network Security Situation Prediction Based on Improved WGAN

Jiang Zhu[1,2] and Tingting Wang[1,2(✉)]

[1] School of Communication and Information Engineering,
Chongqing University of Posts and Telecommunications,
Chongqing 400065, China
1325242@qq.com, 1762089088@qq.com
[2] Chongqing Key Lab of Mobile Communications Technology,
Chongqing 400065, China

**Abstract.** The current network attacks on the network have become very complex. As the highest level of network security situational awareness, situation prediction provides effective information for network administrators to develop security protection strategies. The generative adversarial network (GAN) is a popular generation model, which is difficult to train, collapse mode and gradient instability in this network. A Wasserstein distance as a loss function of GAN is proposed. And a difference term is added on the loss function. The improved Wasserstein-GAN (IWGAN) is to improve the classification precision of the situation value. Compared with other forecasting methods, the results show that the method has obvious advantages.

**Keywords:** Situational awareness · Situation prediction · Generative adversarial network · Difference · Wasserstein-GAN

## 1 Introduction

The network security situation prediction is the ultimate goal in the network security situation awareness (NSSA) [1]. NSSA on the premise of extracting and understanding the security element information of real network. Through the observation and analysis of history and current data. Furthermore, the future security trend of the network is speculated.

In the field of network security, situation prediction has become a hot spot. The network security situation prediction is based on the situation value obtained by the network security data in a period of time.

Based on the deepening of machine learning, generative adversarial Network (GAN) [2] is another form based on the micro-generation network, the training of GAN needs to achieve Nash equilibrium, the training of GAN model is unstable. On this basis also made a lot of improvements, such as DCGAN [3] and LSGAN [4]. But in practice this approach does not completely solve the problem. Wasserstein-GAN (WGAN) [5] had a very good effect. In this paper, WGAN is applied to network security, and an improved WGAN situation prediction method is proposed. Taking full account of the dependence of different situation factors, using the correlation of the

H. Song et al. (Eds.): SIMUtools 2019, LNICST 295, pp. 654–664, 2019.
https://doi.org/10.1007/978-3-030-32216-8_64

situation factor time dimension to predict the future network security situation factors, the influence of the historical network security situation on the future situation is more objectively reflected.

## 2 A Method of Situation Prediction Based on Improved WGAN

### 2.1 Generative Adversarial Network

GAN consists of two models, generating model G and discriminant model D, random noise $z$ through G generation as far as possible to follow the real data distribution of the sample G($z$), discriminant model D can determine whether the input sample is real data $x$ or generate data G($z$). Both G and D can be non-linear mapping functions, such as multilayer perceptron. The optimization goal is to achieve Nash equilibrium so that the generator estimates the distribution of data samples. The process of GAN is shown in Fig. 1:

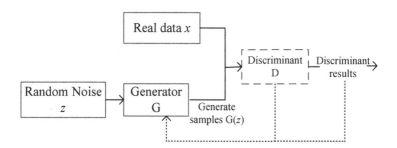

**Fig. 1.** GAN flow chart.

### 2.2 GAN Core Principle Description

The discriminant is a two classification model. The training discriminant is the process of minimizing the cross entropy. The $E(\cdot)$ is the calculation of expected value, $x$ is sampled from the real data distribution $p_{data}(x)$, and $Z$ is sampled in a priori distribution $p_z(z)$. In order to learn the distribution of data $x$, the generator constructs a mapping space $g(z; \theta G)$ by a priori noise distribution $p_z(z)$, and the corresponding discriminant mapping function is $D(x; \theta d)$. The probability of outputting a scalar to represent $x$ as real data is:

$$\min_{G} \max_{D} V(D, G) = E_{x-P_{data(x)}}[\log D(x)]$$
$$+ E_{z-P_{z(z)}}[\log(1 - D(G(z)))] \tag{1}$$

It can obtain the optimal state of the discriminant D when the generator G is fixed by the formula (1). For a specific sample $x$, $P_r(x)$ is the real sample distribution, $P_g(x)$ is the generator produced by the sample distribution, it may come from a real distribution or a generation distribution, and its contribution to the formula (1) Loss function is:

$$-P_r(x)[\log D(x)] - P_g(x)[\log(1 - D(x)]$$  (2)

So that its derivative of D(x) is 0, it concludes:

$$-\frac{P_r(x)}{D(x)} + \frac{P_g(x)}{1 - D(x)} = 0$$  (3)

The best discriminant for simplification is:

$$D^*(x) = \frac{P_r(x)}{P_r(x) + P_g(x)}$$  (4)

This result is intuitively easy to understand, and is to look at the relative proportions of a sample $x$ from the actual distribution and the probability of generating the distribution.

Substituting formula (1), and then a simple transformation can be obtained:

$$E_{x \sim P_{data(x)}} \log \frac{P_r(x)}{\frac{1}{2}[P_r(x) + P_g(x)]} +$$
$$E_{z \sim P_{z(z)}} \log \frac{P_g(x)}{\frac{1}{2}[P_r(x) + P_g(x)]} - 2\log 2$$  (5)

The transformation is to introduce two important similarity metrics for KL divergence [6] and JS divergence [7]:

$$KL(P_1 \| P_2) = E_{x \sim P_1} \log \frac{P_1(x)}{P_2}$$  (6)

$$JS(P_1 \| P_2) = \frac{1}{2} KL \left( P_1 \left\| \frac{P_1 + P_2}{2} \right. \right) + \frac{1}{2} KL \left( P_2 \left\| \frac{P_1 + P_2}{2} \right. \right)$$  (7)

So the formula (5) can be written as:

$$2JS(P_1 \| P_2) - 2\log 2$$  (8)

Under the approximate optimal discriminant, the loss of the minimized generator is equivalent to minimizing the JS divergence. The gradient (approximate) of the generator is 0, and the gradient disappears. Under the condition of KL divergence, the problems such as the gradient imbalance and the penalty imbalance lead to mode collapse [8].

The problem of mode collapse is caused by the gradient disappearance of GAN, the unbalanced gradient and the unbalanced punishment. In GAN, the Wasserstein distance [9] is introduced as the loss function, because of its superior smoothing characteristic relative to KL divergence and JS divergence, the gradient vanishing problem can be solved theoretically.

## 2.3  An IWGAN Algorithm Description

WGAN's biggest contribution is to use Wasserstein distance to replace the JS divergence or KL divergence in GAN, greatly alleviate the problem of GAN difficult to train, Wasserstein distance also called Earth-mover (EM) distance, defined as follows:

$$W(P_r, P_g) = \inf_{\gamma \sim \prod(P_r, P_g)} E_{(x,y \sim \gamma)}[||x - y||] \tag{9}$$

The $\prod(P_r, P_g)$ is a collection of all possible joint distributions of $P_r$ and $P_g$ combined, The lower bound that can be taken to this expectation in all possible joint distributions is defined as Wasserstein distance.

Since the Wasserstein distance definition formula (9) cannot be directly solved, it can be transformed into the following form with an existing theorem:

$$W(P_r, P_g) = \frac{1}{K} \sup_{||f||_L \leq K} E_{x \sim P_r}[f(x)] - E_{x \sim P_g}[f(x)] \tag{10}$$

This process has been proved by the literature [10]. How this distance is solved. First you need to introduce a concept Lipschitz continuous [11]. It's actually an extra restriction on a continuous function f that requires a constant to satisfy any two elements and within the defined domain:

$$|f(x_1) - f(x_2)| \leq K|x_1 - x_2| \tag{11}$$

At this time the Lipschitz constant of the function f is $K$.

In particular, we can define a series of possible function $f_w$ with a set of parameter $w$, at which point the solution formula (9) can be approximated to the following form:

$$KW(P_r, P_g) = \max_{w: ||f_w||_L \leq K} E_{x \sim P_r}[f_w(x)] - E_{x \sim P_g}[f_w(x)] \tag{12}$$

A discriminant network $f_w$ with the parameter $w$ and the last layer is not a Nonlinear activation layer is constructed, and the loss function of the discriminant is given under the condition that the $w$ does not exceed a certain range:

$$L = -E_{x \sim P_r}[f_w(x)] + E_{x \sim P_g}[f_w(x)] \tag{13}$$

The Lipschitz limit is that the gradient of the discriminant does not exceed K (K = 1), and a loss term can be added to the end of the formula to reflect this, which is a difference function, and the loss function is:

$$L = -E_{x \sim P_r}[D_w(x)] + E_{x \sim P_g}[D_w(x)] + \lambda E_{x_1 \sim P_{\hat{x}}, x_2 \sim P_{\hat{x}}} \left[ \frac{|D(x_1) - D(x_2)|}{||x_1 - x_2||} - 1 \right]^2 \tag{14}$$

In other words, they are still sampling randomly on distribution $p_{\hat{x}}$, but two at a time, and then ask them to have a line slope of nearly 1. To limit the distance between the true and false samples, the specific difference can play a role, given the following proof.

**Theorem:** Loss function adding difference term can stabilize gradient value.

Analysis: The discriminant is to try to pull large real sample and the distance between the sample, without the difference limit, usually also want to add a weight Clipping. But it is the overall effect on the sample space, it will inevitably lead to gradient disappear or gradient explosion. The difference is only the true and false sample concentration area, and the gradient is limited to 1 near, controllability is very strong.

Proof: Known $x_r \sim p_{x_r}, x_r \sim p_{x_r}$; supposing $\varepsilon \sim Uniform[0,1]$ is randomly interpolated in the middle of $x_r$ and $x_g$, namely:

$$\hat{x} = \varepsilon x_r + (1 - \varepsilon) x_g \tag{15}$$

At this time $\hat{x}$ satisfied with the distribution of $p_{\widehat{x_r}}$, random sampling on $p_{\widehat{x_r}}$, in which to select two different values, for example $x_1 \sim p_{\hat{x}}, x_2 \sim p_{\hat{x}}$, these two values are real samples and generate samples of the concentration of the selection, control the distance between them, to limit it, can prevent the distance too large or too small distance, to distinguish the discriminant has brought good results. A simple comparison between weight clipping and differential was made, and the advantage of difference was obviously seen.

The Fig. 2 shows that the gradient value changes very little after using the difference term, which gives the discriminant an unexpected effect on the distinction between real and generated samples.    ∎

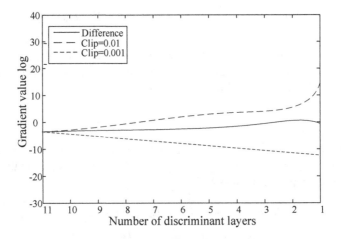

**Fig. 2.** Gradient value comparison

In conclusion, the IWGAN successfully solves the following problems of GAN: Solving the instability problem of GAN training thoroughly, no longer need to be careful about the training degree of balance generator and discriminant; the problem of collapse mode is solved and the diversity of generating samples is ensured; The problem with WGAN is that The discriminant is a multilayer network. The weight clipping is used directly when dealing with Lipschitz constraints, but this method restricts the parameters to the clip range.

In short, a difference is added to the loss function of the difference term, and by judging whether the new loss function is eligible, the generator and the discriminant will be re-trained until the requirement is reached, and the parameters are updated through the Adam algorithm.

The specific algorithm is as follows:

---

**Algorithm 1:** IWGAN algorithm, set in the experiment $\lambda = 10, \alpha = 0.0001, \beta_1 = 0, \beta_2 = 0.9, n = 5, m = 64$ 。

Requirements: $\lambda$ is Penalty factor, $\alpha$ is Learning rate, $n$ is Number of iterations。 $m$ is batch size, Adam algorithm's higher-order parameters $\beta_1, \beta_2$ , $w$ is weight initial value, $\theta$ is generator initial value

  While $\theta$ do

    for $t = 0,...,n$ do

      Sample $\left\{x^{(i)}\right\}_{i=1}^{m} \sim P_r$ is real data

      Sample $\left\{z^{(i)}\right\}_{i=1}^{m} \sim p(z)$ is Generate samples

      $x_r \sim p_{x_r}$ , $x_g \sim p_{x_g}$

      $\varepsilon \sim Uniform[0,1]$

      $\hat{x} = \varepsilon x_r + (1-\varepsilon) x_g$

$$L^i = -E_{x \sim P_r}\left[D_w(x)\right] + E_{x \sim P_g}\left[D_w(x)\right] + \lambda E_{x_1 \sim P_{\hat{x}}, \, x_2 \sim P_{\hat{x}}} \left[\frac{\left|D_w(x_1) - D_w(x_2)\right|}{\|x_1 - x_2\|} - 1\right]^2$$

  end for

$$w \leftarrow Adam\left(\nabla w \frac{1}{m}\sum_{i=1}^{m} L^i, w, \alpha, \beta_1, \beta_2\right)$$

$$\theta \leftarrow Adam\left(\nabla \theta \frac{1}{m}\sum_{i=1}^{m} -D_w\left(G_\theta(z)\right), w, \alpha, \beta_1, \beta_2\right)$$

  end while

---

## 3   Flow Chart of Situation Forecast

In the WGAN prediction model, the convolution neural network (CNN) [12] is used in the generator G and discriminant D, which is also a kind of deep convolution countermeasure generation network, the concrete model is shown in Fig. 3:

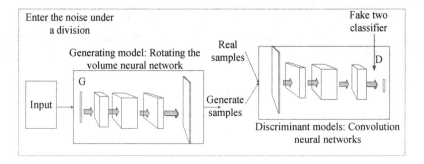

**Fig. 3.** Deep convolution Confrontation Generation network

This article is the before X's days of data as the input of the generator, generate a distribution. The distribution equivalent to $P_g(x)$. After X's days of data as a real data input discriminant. The final distribution equivalent to $P_r(x)$. The discriminant will be judged in the before X's days of data distribution and after X's days of the data to

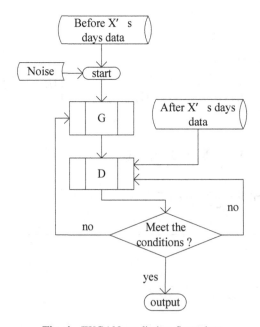

**Fig. 4.** IWGAN prediction flow chart

distinguish. Constantly update the network to reach the probability of approximately 1 of the state. That is to predict the situation before X's days is not going to develop into the situation after X's days.

IWGAN Security situation forecast Flowchart (Fig. 4):

## 3.1 Generative Adversarial Network

Analysis of the attack characteristics of security data, uncertainty and continuity, this paper selects a company from July to September 95 days of firewall, IDs and other historical log information as the original dataset [13]. Make a sample of the daily log information.

Because the security situation value is random, the dimensional difference is big, in order to raise the model the training speed, the situation value carries on the extremum standardization processing, the processing formula is as follows:

$$\hat{X} = \frac{X - X_{\min}}{X_{\max} - X_{\min}} \tag{16}$$

The upper $X_{\min}$ and $X_{\max}$ are the smallest and largest situation values in the sample. $X$ and $\hat{X}$ are the situation values before and after treatment. The network security situation data after the extreme value standardization is shown in Fig. 5.

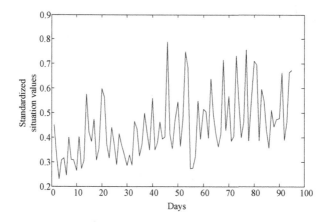

**Fig. 5.** The value of network security situation after extremum

Figure 5 represents a change curve in the situation value in 95 days of log information. In order to deal with the one-dimensional time series samples which are worth to the situation assessment, the topological order dimension is determined to be 5. The refactoring results are shown in Table 1.

**Table 1.** Training data refactoring results

| Input sample | Output sample |
|---|---|
| $X_1, X_2, X_3, X_4, X_5$ | $X_6$ |
| $X_2, X_3, X_4, X_5, X_6$ | $X_7$ |
| ... | ... |
| $X_{74}, X_{75}, X_{76}, X_{77}, X_{78}$ | $X_{79}$ |
| ... | ... |

## 3.2    Analysis and Comparison of Experimental Results

**Convergence Analysis**
After the data is refactored, the specification is tanh [−1, 1]. The batch size in Mini-batch training is 64. All parameter initialization is randomly obtained from the normal distribution of (0 0.02) and the slope of the Leakyrelu is 0.2.

A WGAN loss function with a difference item and no difference is added, as shown in Fig. 6. The former is IWGAN, the later is WGAN. It can be seen clearly that the difference function has brought some effect to WGAN.

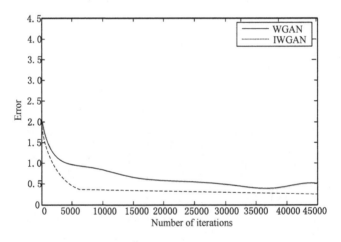

**Fig. 6.** Variation curve of difference with iterative times

**Compared with Other Prediction Methods**
Comparing the IWGAN prediction method with the common GAN improvement methods, such as WGAN, DCGAN and LSGAN, the results are shown in Fig. 7.

We can see from Fig. 7 that the IWGAN prediction method works well. This is because it solves the problem of gradient imbalance and collapse mode.

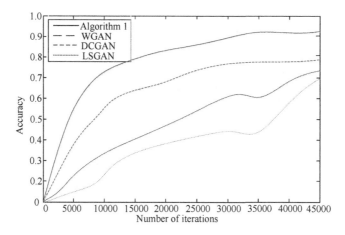

**Fig. 7.** Comparison of accuracy of different forecasting methods

## 4 Conclusion

This paper presents an IWGAN network security situation prediction method, establishes the cyclic neural network model for the real network environment, extracts the network security situation factor training model and forecasts the future network security change trend. Using historical log information, such as firewall and IDs 95 days from July to September, as the original data set, the results show that the method is feasible and of high accuracy.

## References

1. Wu, D., Si, S., Wu, S., et al.: Dynamic trust relationships aware data privacy protection in mobile crowd-sensing. IEEE Internet of Things J. **PP**(99), 1 (2017)
2. Zhang, H., Xu, T., Li, H.: StackGAN: text to photo-realistic image synthesis with stacked generative adversarial networks. 5908–5916 (2016)
3. Yu, Y., Gong, Z., Zhong, P., et al.: Unsupervised representation learning with deep convolutional neural network for remote sensing images (2017)
4. Gulrajani, I., Ahmed, F., Arjovsky, M., et al.: Improved training of Wasserstein GANs (2017)
5. Zhao, Y., Takaki, S., Luong, H.T., et al.: Wasserstein GAN and waveform loss-based acoustic model training for multi-speaker text-to-speech synthesis systems using a WaveNet vocoder (2018)
6. Wu, D., Yan, J., Wang, H., et al.: Social attribute aware incentive mechanism for device-to-device video distribution. IEEE Trans. Multimed. **19**(8), 1908–1920 (2017)
7. Majors, L., Miller, S., Jensen, S.: Oil spill preparedness for polar bears in Alaska. **2014**(1), 299530 (2014)
8. Srivastava, A., Valkov, L., Russell, C., et al.: VEEGAN: reducing mode collapse in GANs using implicit variational learning (2017)
9. Walczak, S.M.: Wasserstein distance (2017)

10. Arjovsky, M., Chintala, S., Bottou, L.: Wasserstein GAN (2017)
11. Jiang, D., Huo, L., Li, Y.: Fine-granularity inference and estimations to network traffic for SDN. PLoS ONE **13**(5), 1–23 (2018)
12. Guo, X., Chen, L., Shen, C.: Hierarchical adaptive deep convolution neural network and its application to bearing fault diagnosis. Measurement **93**, 490–502 (2016)
13. Jiang, D., Huo, L., Song, H.: Rethinking behaviors and activities of base stations in mobile cellular networks based on big data analysis. IEEE Trans. Netw. Sci. Eng. **1**(1), 1–12 (2018)

# Author Index

Printed in the United States
By Bookmasters